Studies in the History of Law and Justice

Volume 3

The purpose of this book series is to publish high quality volumes on the history of law and justice.

Legal history can be a deeply provocative and influential field, as illustrated by the growth of the European universities and the ius commune, the French Revolution, the American Revolution, and indeed all the great movements for national liberation through law. The study of history gives scholars and reformers the models and courage to question entrenched injustices, by demonstrating the contingency of law and other social arrangements.

Yet legal history today finds itself diminished in the universities and legal academy. Too often scholarship betrays no knowledge of what went before, or why legal institutions took the shape that they did. This series seeks to remedy that deficiency.

Studies in the History of Law and Justice will be theoretical and reflective. Volumes will address the history of law and justice from a critical and comparative viewpoint. The studies in this series will be strong bold narratives of the development of law and justice. Some will be suitable for a very broad readership.

Contributions to this series will come from scholars on every continent and in every legal system. Volumes will promote international comparisons and dialogue. The purpose will be to provide the next generation of lawyers with the models and narratives needed to understand and improve the law and justice of their own era.

The series includes monographs focusing on a specific topic, as well as collections of articles covering a theme or collections of article by one author.

More information about this series at http://www.springer.com/series/11794

An Verscuren

The Great Council of Malines in the 18th century

An Aging Court in a Changing World?

Springer

An Verscuren
Department of History
Katholieke Universiteit Leuven
Leuven
Belgium

This study was realized within the framework of the Belgian State Archives with the financial support of the Belgian Science Policy Office.

Additional material to this book can be downloaded from http://extra.springer.com.

ISSN 2198-9842 ISSN 2198-9850 (electronic)
ISBN 978-3-319-09637-7 ISBN 978-3-319-09638-4 (eBook)
DOI 10.1007/978-3-319-09638-4
Springer Cham Heidelberg New York Dordrecht London

Library of Congress Control Number: 2014946442

Printed on acid-free paper

Springer is part of Springer Science+Business Media (www.springer.com)

Preface

When, as a young Master's student in history, I first started researching the Great Council of Malines in preparation for my thesis work, I knew very little about this tribunal and was even less aware of the challenges that were lying ahead of me. In fact, at the time I was mostly interested in the history of crime, and I was looking forward to reading captivating defense pleas by seasoned criminals, gruesome details of torture scenes and harsh court sentences followed by descriptions of public executions. Unsurprisingly, I quickly discovered that many of my initial suppositions about the eighteenth century legal system were ill-founded and that a lot of work was needed to gain an even basic understanding of how to interpret eighteenth century judicial documents. Both the procedure used at the tribunal and the specific jargon employed in the sources were new to me and it was evident that I first needed to thoroughly familiarize myself with them in order to get a grasp on my subject.

Even though my interest in the subject had originally been sparked at least in part by the prospect of uncovering a colorful set of sensational stories—which eventually turned out to be the exception rather than the rule in the eighteenth century criminal case files of the Great Council—I gradually became fascinated by the institution itself and by its people. I even had to admit that I somewhat started to sympathize with the Great Council and its personnel, who during the eighteenth century were constantly fighting for the very survival of their tribunal, being engaged in endless conflicts of jurisdiction with other tribunals and with the government. As a result, the tribunal—and in particular the last century of its existence, as that was seemingly marked by decline and decay—continued to intrigue me even after my Master's thesis on the eighteenth century prosecution office of the Great Council was finished. Enough, in fact, to eventually devote five years of my life to writing its history.

The present book is the result of years of research and was originally written as a dissertation in the context of my Ph.D. work. Although it was at the outset conceived as a more or less purely institutional study of the eighteenth century Great Council of Malines, my budding interest in legal history and my growing understanding of procedure and other legal aspects connected to my subject eventually firmly placed this study at the intersection of law and history. Both of these aspects are present throughout the various chapters of the book.

After a first chapter consisting of a basic introduction to the history of the Great Council and an overview of the relevant historiography, the second chapter focuses on the personnel of the tribunal and analyzes the main prerequisites with which an eighteenth century councilor had to comply. It also discusses how both the incumbent members and the sovereign used their influence to advance their own interests. In addition, a profile of the councilors, their backgrounds and their careers is outlined, which is then compared to that of their predecessors of the late fifteenth, early sixteenth and seventeenth centuries.

In order to get an idea of how the tribunal functioned and how it interacted with other players in the society of the Austrian Netherlands, the third chapter examines the 'framework' in which the eighteenth century Great Council operated. In the first part of this chapter, some background information is provided on the jurisdiction of the tribunal and the procedure used. In addition, the inner workings of the tribunal are examined as well as the dynamics of the relations between the different members of the Great Council. Finally, the councilors' financial sacrifices and rewards are studied. The second part analyzes the position the Great Council held in the eighteenth century Austrian Netherlands by looking at its interactions—and more specifically its conflicts—with other institutions, such as the Magistrate of Malines, the Church, the provincial tribunals and the Privy Council.

The fourth chapter examines the volume and nature of litigation handled by the Council. Literature on other, comparable, tribunals suggests that the eighteenth century was characterized by a 'great litigation decline', in particular at central courts. Was this also true for the Great Council? And if so, how did it manifest itself? Did it demonstrate itself both in appeals and first instance cases? Was there any connection to external, political or other circumstances? What were the possible causes and the consequences for the tribunal as an institution and for the councilors as individuals? And did they in any way attempt to overcome the repercussions—financial and otherwise?

Finally, the last chapter describes what happened to the Great Council in the years 1787–1797. The role of the Councils of Brabant and Hainaut in the resistance to Emperor Joseph II's new judicial organization is notorious, but the literature is completely silent on the Great Council's position in this debate. Moreover, little is known about what happened to the tribunal and its staff during the Brabant Revolution and the first French invasion. In addition, this chapter reconstructs the fate of the tribunal and the councilors in the years after the final take-over of the Austrian Netherlands by the French Republican army in 1794.

Writing this work would not have been possible without the generous financial support of the Belgian Science Policy Office, which fully funded my research. I am also grateful to the Belgian State Archives, which have been my home while writing my dissertation, and to the different members of its staff who introduced me to the wonders of the archives, who were always available to answer my questions and pointed me towards some hidden gems. In particular, I would like to thank Lieve De Mecheleer for her invaluable assistance and guidance. Furthermore, I am indebted to the Archives of the Archdiocese of Malines, to the City Archives of Malines and to the Viennese *Haus-, Hof- und Staatsarchiv* and *Finanz- und Hofkammerarchiv*.

Finally, I would like to express my heartfelt gratitude to my Ph.D. supervisor, Prof. Dr. Eddy Put, who sparked my enthusiasm about an eighteenth century tribunal that turned out to be a richer subject of research than I could ever have imagined and who has been the best guide I could have wished for. The same is true for Dr. Michel Oosterbosch, who showed me the way through the maze of the Great Council's archives. Although it would be difficult to overstate their contributions to this work, any errors that remain are the author's sole responsibility.

As for my wonderful husband, Geert Vermeulen, I hope he will forgive me the endless hours he spent helping me reorder my Excel sheets or as a sounding board for bouncing off ideas on the interpretation of my results. I cannot thank him enough for his support.

Contents

List of Abbreviations

AAM	Aartsbisschoppelijk Archief Mechelen (*Archives of the Archdiocese of Malines*)
ARA	Algemeen Rijksarchief Brussel (*General State Archives, Brussels*)
ARR	Algemene Regeringsraad (*Council of General Government*)
DeptNed	Departement voor de Nederlanden van de Hof -en Staatskanselarij te Wenen (*Department of the Netherlands at the Chancellery of Vienna*)
FHKA	Finanz- und Hofkammerarchiv
GR	Geheime Raad (*Privy Council*)
GRM	Grote Raad van Mechelen (*Great Council of Malines*)
GRMOF	Grote Raad van Mechelen, Officie-Fiscaal (*Great Council of Malines, Office-Fiscal*)
GRMOF BD	Grote Raad van Mechelen, Officie-Fiscaal, Banden en Delen
GRO	Geheime Raad, Oostenrijkse Periode (*Privy Council, Austrian Period*)
HHStA	Haus-, Hof- und Staatsarchiv
INV	Inventarissen van de Derde Afdeling (*Inventories of the third section*)
MD	Handschriftenverzameling (*Collection of Manuscripts*)
PapBout	Papiers des commissaires du gouvernement dits Papiers Bouteville
PRAFT	Provinciaal Archief Frans Tijdvak (*Provincial Archives, French Period*)
RA	Rijksarchief (*State Archives*)
RK	Rekenkamer (*Accounts Chamber*)
ROPB	Recueil des Ordonnances des Pays-Bas
ROPBA	Recueil des Ordonnances des Pays-Bas Autrichiens
RvSt	Raad van State (*Council of State*)

List of Abbreviations

List of Figures

List of Tables

Chapter 1
Introduction

In general, historians writing the annals of an institution are rarely able to resist the temptation to focus on the foundations upon which it was built or on its heyday in terms of power and prestige—with its later years and ultimate vanishing treated as a mere afterthought.[1] Indeed, in institutional history, the 1600s and 1700s are truly the 'forgotten centuries'.[2] While the origins and growth of *Ancien Régime* institutions, their ascent to power and their apex have been extensively examined from multiple perspectives, the final years of their existence have so far been barely touched upon. This observation can certainly be partially attributed to the assumption that an institution in its later years tends to be characterized by *Verfall und Zerfall* (decline and decay).[3] As a consequence, writing its history would amount to nothing more than describing its often slow and steady deterioration.

The Great Council of Malines, officially 'established' in 1474 and abolished in 1797, is no exception to this rule. Even though this tribunal is unmistakably one of the most thoroughly researched institutions of the *Ancien Régime* Netherlands—and in the past, it even boasted its own dedicated research group[4] as well as several

[1] In the editor's preface to a collection of contributions on the history of the *Reichskammergericht*, B. Diestelkamp acknowledged this observation: "Als der Wissenschaftliche Beirat der Gesellschaft für Reichskammergerichtsforschung beschloß, das 5. Wissenschaftliche Kolloquium im Wetzlar unter das Thema 'Das Reichskammergericht am Ende des Alten Reiches und sein Fortwirken im 19. Jahrhundert' zu stellen, war allen Beteiligten bewußt daß es reizvoller sei, sich um die Entstehungsgeschichte einer Institution oder den Höhepunkt ihres Wirkens zu bemühen als um ihr Ende". Diestelkamp, Bernhard, ed. 2002. *Das Reichskammergericht am Ende des alten Reiches und sein Fortwirken im 19.* Jahrhundert. Cologne: Böhlau, VII.

[2] Cochrane, Eric W. 1974. *Florence in the forgotten centuries: 1527–1800: a history of Florence and the Florentines in the Age of the Grand Dukes*. Chicago: University of Chicago Press.

[3] Diestelkamp, Bernhard, ed. 2002. *Das Reichskammergericht am Ende des alten Reiches und sein Fortwirken im 19.* Jahrhundert. Cologne: Böhlau, VII.

[4] Prof. J.Th. de Smidt set up the 'Werkgroep Grote Raad van Mechelen' (Research Center for the Great Council of Malines) in 1969 at the Municipal Archives and University of Amsterdam. (cf. Verkerk, Cornelis L. 1985. De werkgroep 'Grote Raad van Mechelen'. *Holland, Regionaal-historische tijdschrift* 17: 331–340) It was discontinued not long after de Smidt's retirement in 1988.

A. Verscuren, *The Great Council of Malines in the 18th century*,
Studies in the History of Law and Justice 3, DOI 10.1007/978-3-319-09638-4_1

specialized colloquia and expositions[5]—one only needs to consult the contribution of A. Wijffels[6] or an extended bibliography on the Great Council[7] to verify that the majority of the available literature has the sixteenth century as its area of focus. To some extent, the tribunal's own history is an explanatory factor for this pronounced emphasis on the first 100 years of its existence and the scant attention paid to the seventeenth and the eighteenth centuries. Notably, the secession of the Northern provinces in the 1580s and the consequent loss of jurisdiction of the Great Council over the tribunals in these regions—the Council of Holland in particular was a major 'supplier' of appeal cases to the Great Council—constituted a turning point. As might be expected, most Dutch historians display only little interest in what happened afterwards to the Malines tribunal.[8]

The study at hand examines the eighteenth century Great Council of Malines, focusing on the personnel and composition of the tribunal, its functioning and its position within the Austrian Netherlands, the nature and volume of litigation at the Council and its final years in the late eighteenth and early nineteenth centuries. While this work has a strong linkage to legal history, it is in the first place embedded in the domain of institutional history. Indeed, we examined the tribunal as an institution with special attention to its role as instrument of princely policy in the eighteenth century Austrian Netherlands.

The fact that this research project was housed within the Belgian State Archives—providing us with the luxury of working literally in the midst of the Great Council's original records—certainly influenced this study. Primary sources constitute the

---

[5] 1949. *Mechelen, stad. Programma van de historische stoet: 475e verjaring van de vestiging te Mechelen van de Grote Raad.* Malines: Drukkerij de Eendracht; 1973. *500 jaar Grote Raad 1473–1973. Tentoonstelling van Karel de Stoute tot Keizer Karel.* Malines: Cultureel Centrum Spinoy; 1977. *Consilium magnum, 1473–1973: herdenking van de 500e verjaardag van de oprichting van het Parlement en de Grote Raad van Mechelen.* Brussels: Algemeen Rijksarchief.; 1980. *Miscellanea Consilii Magni. Ter gelegenheid van twintig jaar Werkgroep Grote Raad van Mechelen.* Amsterdam: Universiteit van Amsterdam. Faculteit der rechtsgeleerdheid; Cappon, Cornelis, Stuurman, Jan en de Schepper, Hugo. eds. 1984. *Miscellanea Consilii Magni II. Bijdragen over rechtspraak van de Grote Raad van Mechelen.* Amsterdam: Universiteit van Amsterdam Faculteit der rechtsgeleerdheid.

[6] Wijffels, Alain. 1994. Grote Raad voor de Nederlanden te Mechelen (ca.1445–1797). In *De centrale overheidsinstellingen van de Habsburgse Nederlanden*, eds. Erik Aerts e.a., 448–461. Brussels: Algemeen Rijksarchief.

[7] See the bibliography included in this work. Also, for publications until the 1980s: De Schepper, Hugo en Van Answaarden Robert. 1984. Grote Raad van Mechelen. Bibliografie. In *Miscelannea Consilii Magni II.* Eds. Cornelis Capon, Jan Stuurman en de Schepper Hugo, 171–193. Amsterdam: Universiteit van Amsterdam Faculteit der rechtsgeleerdheid.; Snep, M.G.M., Bibliografie van de Grote Raad van Mechelen. In *Miscellanea forensia historica: ter gelegenheid van het afscheid van Prof. mr. J.Th de Smidt* (Verzamelen en bewerken van de jurisprudentie van de Grote Raad, nieuwe reeks, 14), eds. Jacobus de Smidt, Joke M.I. Koster-Van Dijck en Alain Wijffels, 389–398. Amsterdam: Werkgroep Grote Raad van Mechelen.

[8] For example, the chronological scope of the *Chronologische lijsten* of the extended sentences of the Great Council published by the Dutch research group linked to prof. de Smidt is limited to the period between roughly 1470 and 1580. After this date, the Great Council *de facto* no longer had any jurisdiction over the Northern Netherlands.

foundation of our research. Working as an archivist also gave us some idea of how record keeping in the Great Council was done—or not done—and made it possible to look for pieces of the puzzle in sometimes unexpected places. Moreover, it also provided us with some basic insight into the possibilities offered but, even more importantly, into the constraints imposed by the 'surviving archives'. Finally, we observed that (ideas on) record keeping changed significantly throughout the centuries, which inevitably influenced the data available. As a result, both because of their intrinsic importance and because of their significance for our work, the Great Council's archives as well as the influence they have had on our understanding of its eighteenth century history are discussed at several points throughout this work.[9]

1.1 A Short History of the Great Council of Malines[10]

The Early Centuries As Van Rompaey demonstrated, the origins of the Great Council can be traced back to the *curia ducis* of the Burgundy period, a council consisting of both professional jurists and noblemen who advised the dukes on general political, financial and judicial affairs. Under the reign of Philip the Good (1419–1467) the increase in the number of cases the *curia ducis* dealt with induced a specialization of the councilors. While the noblemen were engaged in political matters, legal questions were increasingly assigned to professional jurists. Around 1445, the latter broke away from the *curia ducis* to form a more or less independent institution: the Great Council of Justice. Despite its autonomous status, the Great Council still worked in close cooperation with the ducal council and remained an ambulant tribunal, following the duke wherever he went. Over the next 30 years, the gulf between the Great Council of Justice and the *curia ducis* widened and the former became *de facto* a separate institution. As a consequence, when in 1473 Charles

[9] In general, (the history of) records management is increasingly becoming the subject of historical research. Cf. I-CHORA conferences and publications in *Archival Science*.

[10] With this short summary, we do not aim to provide a comprehensive overview of the history of the Great Council or offer any new insights, but merely wish to draw attention to a few highlights in the history of this tribunal and contextualize it against the broader background of the Burgundy and later Habsburg Netherlands. Moreover, we will focus on how the tribunal's function and position evolved over time and on the way it was made use of by the consecutive rulers of the Netherlands in the implementation of their policies. Unless otherwise indicated, this overview is based on Gilissen, John. 1980. De Grote Raad van Mechelen. Historisch overzicht. In *Miscelannea Consilii Magni. Ter gelegenheid van twintig jaar Werkgroep Grote Raad van Mechelen*, 13–43; Amsterdam: Universiteit van Amsterdam. Faculteit der rechtsgeleerdheid. Maes, Louis Th. 2009. *Het Parlement en de Grote Raad van Mechelen: 1473–1797.* Antwerp: De Vries-Brouwers; Van Rompaey, Jan. 1973. *De Grote Raad van de hertogen van Boergondië en het parlement van Mechelen* (Verhandelingen van de Koninklijke academie voor wetenschappen, letteren en schone kunsten van België. Klasse der Letteren 73). Brussels: Koninklijke Academie voor Wetenschappen, letteren en schone kunsten van België; Wijffels, Alain. 1994. Grote Raad voor de Nederlanden te Mechelen (ca.1445–1797). In *De centrale overheidsinstellingen van de Habsburgse Nederlanden*, eds. Erik Aerts e.a., 448–461. Brussels: Algemeen Rijksarchief.

the Bold 'established' the *Parlement* of Malines with the Ordinance of Thionville, he did not so much create an entirely new institution but rather ratified a situation that had been in existence for several years. For the first time, the tribunal obtained a fixed residence in the city of Malines.

From a mere institutional point of view, the sovereign *Parlement* was merely the 'successor' of the Great Council of Justice: in first and last instance, it dealt with certain *cas réservés* as well as with lawsuits involving privileged persons. Moreover, it also functioned as the court of appeal for a number of Burgundy territories. In theory, the Great Council added an additional instance, but otherwise left the former judicial organization largely in place. However, through the introduction of new techniques such as *évocation*,[11] the princely councils were reinforced at the expense of the local and regional tribunals with the specific goal of arriving at a greater territorial and political unification.[12]

Van Rompaey's study leaves no room for doubt that the establishment of the *Parlement* of Malines had a political significance and responded to a two-fold desire: to complete the Burgundy policy of internal centralization and to underline the dukes' full independence in legal matters, in particular from the King of France and his *Parlement de Paris*. Indeed, while until 1473 the Great Council had functioned as a court of appeal against judgments of some provincial tribunals—the most important ones being Namur, Holland and Luxemburg—the French *Parlement de Paris* was still competent to deal with appeals coming from the larger part of Flanders, allowing the French sovereign to interfere in Burgundy matters.[13] The Ordinance of Thionville eventually deprived the *Parlement de Paris* of its jurisdiction over Flanders: litigants who wished to appeal against a judgment of the Council of Flanders had to turn to the *Parlement* of Malines.

Charles the Bold's death a mere 4 years later signaled the demise of the *Parlement.* Pressured by the Estates-General—which considered the Malines tribunal to be the prime symbol of the Burgundy Dukes' policy of centralization—Charles' daughter Mary granted the Grand Privilege which provided, among others, for the abolition of the *Parlement*. Yet, the Estates-General did not request the complete abolition of the court. Already in 1477, an ambulant Great Council once again functioned as a special tribunal; by the end of the fifteenth century, the workload of the Council was at a level comparable to that of the *Parlement*. The ordinance of Philip

[11] By *évocation* a case could be moved from a lower tribunal where it was introduced to a higher tribunal. Cf. infra, Chap. 3.

[12] De Schepper, Hugo. 2006. Staatsgezag en staatsmacht in de Nederlanden. Verworvenheden en beperkingen van het Bourgondisch-Habsburgse systeem. In *Staatsvorming onder de Bourgondiërs en Habsburgers. Theorie en Praktijk*, eds Hugo de Schepper en Jacques Geurts. Maastricht: Shaker, 25.

[13] However, S. Dauchy demonstrated that the *Parlement de Paris* was far from a diligent instrument of the King's policies. In the bulk of the cases, the judgments of the Council of Flanders were confirmed. Only when the authority of the *Parlement* was at stake did the tribunal explicitly use its power to rebuff the Burgundy Dukes. Dauchy, Serge. 1995. *De processen in beroep uit Vlaanderen bij het Parlement van Parijs (1320–1521) een rechtshistorisch onderzoek naar de wording van de staat en soevereiniteit in de Bourgondisch-Habsburgse periode*. Brussel: Paleis der Academiën, 13.

the Fair of 1504 established the Great Council once and for all in the city of Malines. From that time onwards, the tribunal had its seat in the *Schepenhuis*. In 1619, the councilors moved to the former palace of Margaret of Austria, where they would remain until the very end of the Ancien Régime.

Even though the Great Council quickly recovered from the crisis of 1477, it did not immediately regain jurisdiction over the Council of Flanders. After the abolition of the *Parlement* of Malines, appeals against sentences of the Council of Flanders were again dealt with by the *Parlement* of Paris. In 1521, Charles V forbade the inhabitants of Flanders to appeal to the *Parlement* of Paris against sentences of their provincial tribunal, but it was not until 1526 that the Treaty of Madrid officially recognized the transfer of jurisdiction over Flanders from the Paris tribunal to the Great Council of Malines. In theory, this marked the definite end of French interference in the judicial affairs of the Netherlands, but in practice the *Parlement de Paris* would at several instances in the sixteenth and even early seventeenth centuries attempt to assert an influence over Flanders.[14]

In the meantime, Charles V had tied in with the intermittent attempts of his Burgundy predecessors to unify his possessions in the Netherlands by creating and promoting a more or less hierarchized system of judicial institutions. The central courts corresponded to the litigants' desire for professional competence: compared to the traditional bench of aldermen, the new princely councils guaranteed a much faster administration of justice, coupled with increased objectivity and legal security. In addition, its sentences had a much more broadly accepted legal force. For all these reasons, private persons as well as institutions made an increased use of the sovereign's administration of justice—both on the provincial and the central level—to have their civil disputes settled.[15] The fact that a growing number of people were willing to litigate at a central court was an important step in state formation.[16]

Criminal justice as well was seen as a crucial aspect of state-building, given that it functioned both as a political instrument to affirm 'sovereignty' over a territory and as a social instrument to control violence.[17] The notion of the sovereign's peace

[14] In contrast, the Great Council lost its jurisdiction over the Councils of Brabant and Hainaut in the early sixteenth century. Douxchamps-Lefèvre, Cecile. 1977. Note sur le ressort de la juridiction d'appel du Grand Conseil de Malines au XVe et XVIe siècles. In *Consilium magnum, 1473–1973: herdenking van de 500ᵉ verjaardag van de oprichting van het Parlement en Grote Raad van Mechelen* (Algemeen Rijksarchief en Rijksarchief in de provinciën. Studia 27). Brussels: Algemeen Rijksarchief, 316.

[15] De Schepper, Hugo. 2006. Staatsgezag en staatsmacht in de Nederlanden. Verworvenheden en beperkingen van het Bourgondisch-Habsburgse systeem. In *Staatsvorming onder de Bourgondiërs en Habsburgers. Theorie en Praktijk*, eds. Hugo de Schepper en Jacques Geurts. Maastricht: Shaker, 25.

[16] Sharpe, James Anthony. 1997. The law, law enforcement, state formation and national integration in late medieval and early modern England. In *Le pénal dans tous ses états: justice, états et sociétés en Europe (XII-XXe siècles)* (Publications des Facultés universitaires Saint Louis 74), eds. René Levy and Xavier Rousseaux, 65–80. Brussels: FUSL.

[17] Levy, René and Rousseaux, Xavier. 1992. Etats, justice pénale et histoire: bilan et perspectives. *Droit et Société* 20–21: 53–82.

provided an important centralizing and integrative ideological cement.[18] While sentences in criminal matters were in theory unappealable, the convict could in last instance take recourse to the sovereign: he alone possessed the right to pardon a criminal, which was considered to be his own personal instrument used to express his dominance over the local and provincial tribunals.[19]

At the end of Charles V's reign, the Habsburg sovereigns, in imitation of their Burgundy predecessors, had developed a system of political equilibrium between centralism and autonomy, between monarchal power and particularistic claims. Princely courts and in particular the Great Council as sovereign court of appeal played an important role in uniting the different parts of the Habsburgs' possessions in the Netherlands.

For all sorts of reasons—not in the least because he wished to abandon the model of compromise of his father—Philip II disturbed the existing order. After 1568, resistance turned into civil war, marked by a provincial and particularistic reaction. Eventually, the Netherlands were divided in two parts: while Philip II was able to reconquer the southern provinces, the northern provinces were united in a separate state, the Republic of the United Provinces. In the Southern Netherlands, the revolution constituted a serious step back in the process of state formation and centralization.[20] The war also had grave consequences for the Great Council. First, it had to leave Malines for the city of Namur between 1580 and 1585. But far more importantly: the secession of the Northern Netherlands constituted a serious reduction in jurisdiction for the tribunal; Holland in particular meant a grave loss in quantitative terms.

The 'Forgotten Centuries' The Treaty of Münster of 1648 consolidated the front line between the Northern and the Southern Netherlands as the official border, but this had little or no repercussions for the jurisdiction of the Great Council. The wars of the second half of the seventeenth century, on the other hand, did have consequences for the tribunal and caused another considerable reduction of its authority. For example, in consecutive peace treaties between 1659 and 1713, several territories—among others the Valenciennes region—that had originally taken their appeals to Malines were incorporated into the Kingdom of France.[21] The province

---

[18] Sharpe, James Anthony. 1997. The law, law enforcement, state formation and national integration in late medieval and early modern England. In *Le pénal dans tous ses états: justice, états et sociétés en Europe (XII-XXe siècles)* (Publications des Facultés universitaires Saint Louis 74), eds. René Levy and Xavier Rousseaux, 65–80. Brussels: FUSL.

[19] De Schepper, Hugo. 2006. Staatsgezag en staatsmacht in de Nederlanden. Verworvenheden en beperkingen van het Bourgondisch-Habsburgse systeem. In *Staatsvorming onder de Bourgondiërs en Habsburgers. Theorie en Praktijk*, eds. Hugo de Schepper en Jacques Geurts. Maastricht: Shaker, 25.

[20] De Schepper, Hugo. 2006. Staatsgezag en staatsmacht in de Nederlanden. Verworvenheden en beperkingen van het Bourgondisch-Habsburgse systeem. In *Staatsvorming onder de Bourgondiërs en Habsburgers. Theorie en Praktijk*, eds. Hugo de Schepper en Jacques Geurts. Maastricht: Shaker, 49–50.

[21] Gilissen, John. 1980. De Grote Raad van Mechelen. Historisch overzicht. In *Miscelannea Consilii Magni. Ter gelegenheid van twintig jaar Werkgroep Grote Raad van Mechelen*, 13–43. Amsterdam: Universiteit van Amsterdam. Faculteit der rechtsgeleerdheid; Maes, Louis Th. 2009. *Het*

of Luxemburg as well was temporarily annexed to France: the records of the Great Council do indeed confirm that the inhabitants of Luxemburg were unable to appeal to the Great Council during a certain time in the late seventeenth century.[22]

The War of the Spanish Succession, on the other hand, had only limited influence on the tribunal. During the entire period and through different changes of regime, the Great Council remained in operation, even though the extent of its jurisdiction did vary at times. While between 1700 and 1706 the entirety of the Southern Netherlands had been 'occupied' by French troops, the battle of Ramillies brought Flanders, Brabant and Malines under the rule of the Sea Powers England and the United Provinces. As a consequence, the provinces of Namur and Luxemburg, which were still in French hands, were *de facto* removed from the jurisdiction of the Great Council. The Treaty of Utrecht of 1713 reunited these two provinces with the rest of the Austrian Netherlands, thereby returning them to the sphere of influence of the Great Council.[23]

The reign of Charles VI was a period of calm for the Malines tribunal. It was not until shortly after Maria Theresa's ascension to the throne, that the Great Council lost another part of its jurisdiction when the decision was made to divide the authority over the *Terres de débat* among the Councils of Flanders and Hainaut. The next threat to the Great Council came again from the French, this time in the War of the Austrian Succession. In 1746, French armies conquered Malines. In response, the tribunal moved its residence, first to Namur and eventually to Echternach, where it remained 'in exile' until the end of the war. During this period the Great Council was only competent to deal with appeals from Luxemburg. After its return to Malines in the course of 1749, it more or less resumed its normal activities.

The end of the War of the Spanish Succession also marked the beginning of renewed attempts at unification and centralization. While the efforts of Charles VI to renew the process of centralization were still somewhat timid—his first concern was consolidating the Austrian rule over the Spanish heritage—Maria Theresa managed to get a firmer grip on the Netherlands, without however enforcing radical reforms on her subjects.[24]

Parlement en de Grote Raad van Mechelen: 1473–1797. Antwerp: De Vries-Brouwers. The maps on pages 74, 98, 142 and 152 provide a good overview of the consecutive reductions of the Great Council's jurisdiction; Lenders, Piet. 1995. Ontstaan en ontwikkeling van de moderne staat in de Nederlanden. In *Symposium over de centrale instellingen van de Habsburgse Nederlanden, Brussel 3 december 1994. Tien Bijdragen over de staat, de regering en de ambtenaren van de 16de tot de 18de eeuw* (Standen en Landen Bijzondere Reeks nr. 2), eds. Herman Coppens en Karin Van Honacker, 1–42. Brussels: Standen en Landen.

[22] Cf. Brussels, ARA, GRM 617, 629, 635: distribution records of the late 17th century Great Council.

[23] De Schryver, Reginald. 1987. De Oostenrijkse aanspraken op de Spaans-Habsburgse erfenis. De Zuidelijke Nederlanden tijdens de Spaanse Successieoorlog. 1700–1716. In *Oostenrijks België 1713–1794. De Zuidelijke Nederlanden onder de Oostenrijkse Habsburgers*, ed. Hervé Hasquin, 11–36. Brussels: Gemeentekrediet van België. These episodes also left traces in the distribution records: Brussels, ARA, GRM 617, 618, 629, 630, 635, 636.

[24] Lenders, Piet. 1995. Ontstaan en ontwikkeling van de moderne staat in de Nederlanden. In Symposium over de centrale instellingen van de Habsburgse Nederlanden, Brussel 3 December 1994. Tien Bijdragen over de staat, de regering en de ambtenaren van de 16de tot de 18de eeuw (Standen

Joseph II deliberately abandoned the 'Theresian compromise' and did try to unilaterally impose his ideas in order to arrive at rationalization, unification and centralization of all his possessions. Both directly and indirectly, his policies had repercussions for the Great Council. In 1782, Joseph II granted sovereignty to the Council of Luxemburg and made the sovereign Council of Hainaut the court of appeal for the Council of Tournai, thereby further depriving the Great Council of a part of its jurisdiction. A few years later, in 1787, Joseph II made *tabula rasa* of the entire judicial system, a reform of which the Great Council as well was a victim. However, due to protests and even open rebellion of especially the Estates and Councils of Brabant and Hainaut, the new structure remained in place for just a few days.

In the course of 1789—when the Brabant Revolution was already brewing—the tribunal was awarded additional jurisdiction for the first time in centuries: a large part of the jurisdiction of the abolished Council of Brabant was transferred to the Great Council. Nevertheless, the Malines tribunal could enjoy its increased authority only briefly; the Revolution *de facto* closed down the Great Council. Restoration reinstalled the tribunal but also deprived it from its jurisdiction over Brabant. The first invasion of the French revolutionary armies in November 1792 led to the exile of the tribunal, first to Roermond and then to Düsseldorf. Again the Austrians managed to regain the Southern Netherlands—in March/April 1793—but once again the restoration was only of short duration. The second invasion of the French in June 1794 also marked the end of the Great Council.[25]

1.2 State of the Art: A Short Historiographical Overview

State of Research on the Great Council[26] As mentioned before, the history of the Great Council in the first century of its existence has been amply described from different perspectives. Undoubtedly, J. Th. de Smidt and the Research Center for the Great Council constituted an important impetus for research on the tribunal. Especially their publication of six volumes *Chronologische Lijsten* has been crucial in that regard: these provide a short description of the subject of the extended sentences, issued by the Great Council between 1465 and 1580, together with the names and some identification of the litigants.[27] Unfortunately, their work does not

en Landen Bijzondere Reeks nr. 2), eds. Herman Coppens en Karin Van Honacker, 1–42. Brussels: Standen en Landen.

[25] This is only a short summary of the events of the late 1780s and early 1790s. The fate of the Great Council and its members during this period are discussed more extensively in Chap. 5.

[26] We do not aim to give an exhaustive overview of the historiography of the Great Council. Instead we merely point out the different aspects of the Great Council that have so far been studied. For a more extensive overview, see the bibliography included in this dissertation.

[27] De Smidt, Jacobus e.a. eds. 1966–1988. *Chronologische lijsten van de geëxtenderdeerde sententiën berustende in het archief van de Grote Raad van Mechelen*, 6 volumes. Brussels: Koninklijke Commissie voor de uitgave der oude wetten en verordeningen van België.

reach beyond 1580, the year the Great Council *de facto* lost its jurisdiction over the Northern provinces. J. Monballyu, C. Douxchamps-Lefèvre and Ph. Godding have continued the efforts of the Research Center for the period between 1581 and 1590.[28] In addition, we recently published a list of the late seventeenth and early eighteenth century extended sentences,[29] leaving the last decade of the sixteenth century and a large part of the seventeenth century untouched. The descriptions of the *mémoriaux* by Gaillard[30] is the only other available tool that provides some access to the institutional records of the Great Council—in which the case files or the archives of the office-fiscal are not included—apart from the very general inventory by Van den Bussche.[31]

Other attempts to make the archives more accessible followed in the wake of the initial efforts of J.Th. de Smidt and his collaborators. In different stages during the second half of the 1960s and 1970s, the Research Center published an inventory and description of the case files included in the series 'Appeals from Holland'.[32] In 2006, M. Oosterbosch revised this work and supplemented it with newly discovered materials.[33] He is also responsible for a first inventory of a part of the 'Appeals from Flanders' case files.[34] D. Leyder continued the work on this series, making the cases involving the clergy accessible.[35] Moreover, he published a guide to the archives of the Great Council in order to familiarize future users with the records of the tribunal and their organization.[36]

---

[28] Monballyu, Jos. 1998. Chronologische Lijst van de Nederlandstalige geëxtedeerde sententiën van de Grote Raad van Mechelen (1581–1590). *Handelingen van de Koninklijke Commissie voor de uitgave der Oude Wetten en Verordeningen van België* 39: 79–146. Douxchamps-Lefevre, Cécile. 2003. Les sentences du Grand Conseil de Malines en appel d'instances namuroises (1582–1590). *Handelingen van de Koninklijke Commissie voor de uitgave der Oude Wetten en Verordeningen van België* 44: 59–136; Godding, Philippe and Petit, Roger. 2001. Les sentences du Grand Conseil de Malines relatives au duché de Luxembourg (1582–1590). *Handelingen van de Koninklijke Commissie voor de uitgave der Oude Wetten en Verordeningen van België* 42: 63–201.

[29] Verscuren, An. 2013. *Nadere toegang op de geëxtendeerde sententies van de Grote Raad van Mechelen: 1693–1772.* Brussels: Algemeen Rijksarchief.

[30] Gaillard, Arthur. 1900–1903. *Inventaire des mémoriaux du Grand Conseil de Malines.* Brussels: Weissenbruch.

[31] Van den Bussche, Emile. 1992. Inventaire des registres du Grand Conseil de Malines: avec un supplément pour les Nos 1186 à 1553 (Requêtes et varia en portefeuilles). Brussels: Algemeen Rijksarchief.

[32] Huussen, Arend e.a. 1964–1974. *Inventaris en beschrijving van de processtukken (dossiers) behorende tot de beroepen uit Holland berustende in het archief van de Grote Raad van Mechelen Algemeen Rijksarchief Brussel.* Amsterdam: s.n.

[33] Oosterbosch, Michel. 2006. *Inventaris van het archief van de Grote Raad voor de Nederlanden te Mechelen: procesbundels bereoepen uit Holland 1460–1740.* Brussels: Algemeen Rijksarchief.

[34] Oosterbosch, Michel. 1998. *Grote Raad voor de Nederlanden te Mechelen: procesbundels beroepen uit Vlaanderen: ordinaris processen (nr. 1–1000).* Brussels: Algemeen Rijksarchief.

[35] Leyder, Dirk. 2012. *Inventaire des archives du Grand Conseil des Pays-Bas à Malines: dossiers de procès de Flandre-Clergé 1545*–1792. Brussels: Algemeen Rijksarchief.

[36] Leyder, Dirk. 2010. *Les archives du Grand Conseil des Pays-Bas à Malines (vers 1445–1797).* Brussels: Algemeen Rijksarchief.

Work on first instance case files has been even sketchier and mainly focused on the proceedings from the Northern Netherlands.[37] An alphabetical index, listing the names of the litigants, provides a limited entry into the first instance case files of all regions.[38] Finally, some older inventories—which were presumably compiled during the late eighteenth or nineteenth centuries—have been edited and published, thereby opening up the cases files of the collection of lawsuits concerning 'prominent families' as well as the criminal case files.[39] Many others however, remain as manuscripts or index cards.[40] As a consequence, while in the past half century much effort was invested into enhancing the accessibility of the Great Council's records, there are still several hundreds of meters of case files waiting to be inventoried.

The opening up of the Great Council's archives also led to a stream of publications which illustrate the richness of the Great Council's records and the research opportunities they offer.[41] One of the most important contributions is the already cited study of J. Van Rompaey. In his work on the origins of the Great Council, Van Rompaey demonstrated how the *Parlement* of Malines was used as an instrument of centralization within the Burgundy Netherlands and as a means to express independence in legal matters from the King of France and his *Parlement de Paris*.[42] Within this framework, he examined the composition of the Great Council (and the *Parlement*), its jurisdiction as a first and last instance tribunal and as a court of appeal, and the procedure used. In the present state of research, Van Rompaey's all-encompassing work on the early Great Council as an institution, in which he analyzed both the 'political' significance of the tribunal and its internal organization and workings, is still unique.

[37] Huussen, Arend e.a. 1964–1974. *Inventaris en beschrijving van de processtukken (dossiers) behorende tot de beroepen uit Holland berustende in het archief van de Grote Raad van Mechelen Algemeen Rijksarchief Brussel*. Amsterdam: s.n.The Research Center completed this more or less simultaneously with the work on the *Chronologische Lijsten*.

[38] Lefèvre, Joseph. S.d. *Grand Conseil de Malines. Procès de première instance. Index alphabétique par ordre des défendeurs*. S.l: s.n.

[39] Put, Eddy. 1995. *Grote Raad van Mechelen. Processen van aanzienlijke families (Reeksen A en B)*: werkbeschrijvingen. Brussels: Algemeen Rijksarchief; Put, Eddy. 1995. *Officie-fiscaal van de Grote Raad van Mechelen: werkbeschrijvingen.* Brussels: Algemeen Rijksarchief.

[40] For example Van der Mijnsbrugge, Emile. s.d. *Grand Conseil de Malines. Inventaire des appels de Malines* (Inventaris van de Derde Afdeling 66). S.l.: s.n; Van der Mijnsbrugge, Emile. s.d. *Grand Conseil de Malines. Inventaire des appels des magistrats locaux de la province de Namur* (Inventaris van de Derde Afdeling 85). S.l.: s.n; Van der Mijnsbrugge, E. s.d. *Grand Conseil de Malines. Inventaire des appels de magistrats locaux de Luxembourg* (Inventaris van de Derde Afdeling 75). S.l.: s.n; Etc…

[41] An overview of articles and studies making use of the materials assembled by the Research Center can be found in Snep's bibliography of the Great Council of Malines. Snep, M.G.M. 1988. Bibliografie van de Grote Raad van Mechelen. In *Miscellanea forensia historica: ter gelegenheid van het afscheid van Prof. mr. J.Th. de Smidt* (Verzamelen en bewerken van de jurisprudentie van de Grote Raad, nieuwe reeks, 14), eds. Jacobus de Smidt, Joke M.I. Koster-Van Dijck en Alain Wijffels, 389–398. Amsterdam: Werkgroep Grote Raad van Mechelen.

[42] Van Rompaey, Jan. 1973. *De Grote Raad van de hertogen van Boergondië en het parlement van Mechelen* (Verhandelingen van de Koninklijke Academie voor wetenschappen, letteren en schone kunsten van België. Klasse der Letteren 73). Brussels: Koninklijke Academie voor wetenschappen, letteren en schone kunsten van België.

Studies on specific sub-aspects of the tribunal's early history are much more abundant. The 'legal history' viewpoint is in the first place represented by Van Rhee.[43] Based on the analysis of procedure-ordinances but especially of civil case files, he described in great detail the civil procedure in first instance for the period between 1522 and 1559. The appeal procedure on the other hand has not been investigated quite as thoroughly: while both M. Oosterbosch and J. Van Rompaey have made a few contributions in relation to this theme,[44] no systematic study of the law and practice of appeal proceedings at the Great Council, comparable to Van Rhee's standard work, is available at present. The same is true for the criminal procedure, for which only the somewhat outdated study of Simon is at our disposal.[45] Finally, J.M.I Koster-Van Dijk and A. Wijffels published an article on the procedure in revision at the Great Council between 1473 and 1580.[46]

A. Wijffels is also the author of a study on the reception of Roman and Canon Law in the Netherlands between 1460 and 1580.[47] Based on advocates' uses of references to early and more recent legal authorities in the case files of the Great Council of Malines (and the Court of Holland), Wijffels measured, using a firm quantitative method, to what extent the 'learned law' penetrated into the administration of justice of the early Great Council. Some contributions on the jurisprudence of the Great Council and more specifically on the *arrestographes* are also from his hand.[48]

A prosopographical approach is adopted in the doctoral thesis of A.J.M. Kerckhoffs-de Heij which studies the members of the Great Council who were ac-

[43] Van Rhee, Remco. 1997. *Litigation and legislation: civil procedure at first instance in the Great Council of for the Netherlands in Malines (1522–1559)*. Brussels: Algemeen Rijksarchief.

[44] Van Rompaey, Jan. 1977. *De procedure in beroep bij het Parlement van Mechelen*. In *Consilium magnum, 1473–1973: herdenking van de 500ᵉ verjaardag van de oprichting van het Parlement en de Grote Raad van Mechelen*, 371–381. Brussels: Algemeen Rijksarchief; Introduction to Oosterbosch, Michel. 1998. *Grote Raad voor de Nederlanden te Mechelen: procesbundels beroepen uit Vlaanderen: ordinaris processen (nr. 1–1000)*. Brussels: Algemeen Rijksarchief; Oosterbosch, Michel. 2001. *Appelprocedure, dossierbehandeling en registervoering bij de Grote Raad van Mechelen*. In: *Voortschrijdend procesrecht. Een historische verkenning*, eds. Fred Stevens, Ernest Persoons and Remco Van Rhee, 3–25. Leuven: Universitaire pers Leuven.

[45] Simon, Jules. 1921. La procédure criminelle sous l'ancien régime (Grand Conseil de Malines). *Handelingen van de Koninklijke Commissie voor de uitgave van oude wetten en verordeningen van België* 10: 397–437.

[46] Koster-Van Dijk, Joke M.I. and Wijffels, Alain. 1990. Les procédures en révision au Grand Conseil de Malines (1473–1580). *Publications du Centre Européen d'Etudes Bourguignonnes* 30: 67–97.

[47] Wijffels, Alain. 1985. *Qui millies allegatur: les allegations du droit savant dans les dossiers du Grand Conseil de Lalines (causes septentrionales, ca. 1460–1580)*. Leiden: Brill.

[48] Wijffels, Alain. 1989. Legal Records and Reports in the Great Council of Malines (15th to 18th century). In *Judicial Records, Law Reports and the Growth of Case Law*, ed. John H. Baker, 181–206. Berlin: Duncker und Humblot; Wijffels, Alain. 1997. Grand Conseil de Malines: la rédaction des sentences étendues et le recueil de jurisprudence de Guillaume de Grysperre. In *Case law in the making: the techniques and methods of judicial records and law reports* (*Comparative studies in continental and Anglo-American Legal History* 17) v.1, ed. Alain Wijffels, 299–316. Berlin: Duncker und Humblot.

tive between 1477 and 1531.[49] In the first volume, she described the different positions at the tribunal in the late fifteenth and early sixteenth centuries and concluded with an analysis of the social and cultural backgrounds of the councilors. Unfortunately, she failed to use a rigorous quantitative method, making it difficult to draw comparisons. Her second volume is entirely dedicated to the biographies of the members working at the early Great Council.[50]

An article by C. Thomas discusses the profile of the seventeenth century councilors of the Great Council.[51] As a spin-off of her own doctoral dissertation on the high profile officials in the central government of the Spanish Netherlands, she examined the geographical origin, social background, education and career history of the councilors who worked at the Great Council in the 1600s. Rather than composing detailed biographies for each single one of them, she identified characteristics common to most of the tribunal's seventeenth century members.

Contrary to what might be expected, criminal justice at the Great Council has been only scantily researched. Given that the tribunal had rather limited jurisdiction in criminal affairs, this is perhaps not entirely surprising. Our master's thesis analyzed the functioning of the fiscals in the late eighteenth century, focusing on their 'prosecution policy'—what kind of cases did they deal with?—and on their internal relationships.[52] The scope was limited to the late eighteenth century (1767–1788) and more research on the 'institution' of the office-fiscal, its duties and its relations with the central government is warranted. In addition, a number of case studies are available. A popular presentation of a selection of criminal trials can be found in the catalogue of the exhibition held in Malines in 2004.[53] Other 'famous' criminal cases were published separately and used to illustrate specific legal or general historical issues.[54]

---

[49] Kerckhoffs-De Hey, A.J.M. 1980. *De Grote raad en zijn functionarissen, 1477–1531*. Amsterdam: s.n.

[50] In that regard, her study bears some resemblance to the early twentieth century compilation of—admittedly much shorter—biographies of the presidents, councilors, deputies procurator-general and registrars of the Great Council by Stroobant. He, however, did not apply any chronological limitation. Stroobant, Louis. 1903. *Les magistrats du Grand Conseil de Malines*. Antwerp: s.n.

[51] Thomas, Cathérine. 2013. Hommes d'Etat, hommes de loi. Les conseillers du Grand Conseil de Malines au XVIIe siècle. In *Gouvernance et administration dans les provinces belges (XVIe-XVIIIe siècles)* (Archives et Bibliothèques de Belgique 99), Eds. De Morbeau de Gerbehaye e.a., 399–452. Brussels: Archives et Bibliothèques de Belgique, 155–177. Brussels: Archives et Bibliothèques de Belgique.

[52] Verscuren, An. 2005. *"L'oeil et le bras du Roi?" Het vervolgingsbeleid van het officie-fiscaal van de Grote Raad van Mechelen (1767–1788)*. Unpublished Master's Thesis. Leuven: Katholieke Universiteit Leuven and Verscuren, An. 2006. (S)pionnen van de vorst? De fiscalen van de Grote Raad in de tweede helft van de achttiende eeuw. *Pro Memorie* 8.2: 246–273.

[53] Hüsken, Wim, Installé, Henri and Oosterbosch, Michel (eds). 2004. *De Grote Raad: moord, woordbreuk en andere schandalen*. Brussel: Algemeen Rijksarchief.

[54] E.g. Maes, Louis Th. 1975. Gerechtelijke beslissingen in strafzaken, 16e–18e eeuw. Een vergiftigingszaak 1697–1702. In *De besluitvorming vroeger en nu* (Algemeen rijksarchief en rijksarchief in de provinciën. Educatieve Dienst. Catalogus 49), eds. Hugo de Schepper and John Gilissen, 197–236. Brussels: Algemeen Rijksarchief. The trial, involving a cousin of councilor Frarin who

In addition, case files—both criminal and civil—from the Great Council constitute an important source for thematic studies.[55]Noteworthy are the many case studies examining the litigation coming from a certain geographical territory.[56] As many of these studies are based on the materials assembled by the Research Center and published by its members, it is no surprise that regions and cities of the Northern Netherlands are well represented.[57]

As this short overview demonstrates, historiography on the Great Council is to a large extent concentrated on roughly the first century of the tribunal's existence, with the year 1580 as the end point. The activities of the Research Center for the Great Council of Malines certainly contributed to this: consisting mainly of Dutch historians, their interest in the tribunal remained limited to the period it had jurisdiction over the Northern Netherlands. Their importance for the research on the Great Council is also illustrated by the fact that many studies are based on the archives they made accessible. Moreover, the stream of publications runs dry after the dismantlement of the Center around 1988. Van Rhee's dissertation on the procedure in first instance is the only major volume published after this date.[58]

As a result, the seventeenth and eighteenth century history of the Great Council in its different aspects has been covered only superficially in prior research. 'General' works dealing with the Council tend to barely dedicate a few lines to the 1600s

worked as a secretary at the Great Council, was also used by Simon as a case study to explain the criminal procedure at the Great Council.

[55] It is impossible to enumerate here all the studies which illustrate this point. The bibliography of Van Answaarden and De Schepper—although somewhat outdated—gives an excellent overview of thematic studies based on case files in the Great Council. E.g.: Deelder, C.L. and Huussen, Arend. 1973. Opmerkingen betreffende de kuilvisserij op de voormalige Zuiderzee, voornamelijk in de zestiende eeuw. *Holland, regionaal-historisch tijdschrift* 5: 221–242; Maes, Louis.Th. 1979. Twee arresten van de Grote Raad van Mechelen over de tol van Iersekeroord. In *Recht heeft vele significatie: rechtshistorische opstellen*, ed. Louis Th. Maes, 137–160. Brussels: Ced-Samson; Sicking, Louis. 1998. *Zeemacht en onmacht: maritieme politiek in de Nederlanden 1488–1558*. Amsterdam: Bataafsche Leeuw; Wijffels, Alain. 1997. Höchste Gerichtsbarkeit als Instrument der Friedenserhaltung. In *Friedenssicherung und Rechtsgewährung. Sechs Beiträge zur Geschichte des Reichskammergerichts und der obersten Gerichtsbarkeit im alten Europa*, eds. Bernard Diestelkamp and Ingrid Scheurmann. Bonn: AsKI; Etc.

[56] E.g., De Smidt, Jacobus Th. and Lindijer, Tony. 1999. *Haarlemmers voor de Grote Raad van Mechelen 1458–1578: gebaseerd op Algemeen Rijksarchief Brussel, fonds Grote Raad en Stadsarchief van Haarlem*. Haarlem: Historische Werkgroep/Vereeniging Haerlem; Huijbregts, L.J.J. e.a. 1981. *Leidenaars voor de Grote Raad (1470–1580): processen uit het archief van de Grote Raad (Parlement) van Mechelen met betrekking tot instellingen en bewoners van de stad Leiden*. Leiden: s.n.; Koster-Van Dijck, Joke M.I. 1979. *Gooilanders voor de Grote Raad (1470–1572): Processen uit het archief van de Grote Raad van Mechelen met betrekking tot inwoners en instellingen in en om Gooiland*. Amsterdam: Faculteit der Rechtsgeleerdheid. etc. Fairly recently, A. Wijffels published a comparable study on cities from Zeeland that litigated before the Great Council: Wijffels, Alain. 2002. Zeeuwse steden voor de Grote Raad. *Pro Memorie* 4.2: 266–293.

[57] R. Van Answaarden's study stands out as an exception. Van Answaarden, Robert. 1991. *Les Portugais devant le Grand Conseil des Pays-Bas (1460–1580)*. Paris: Fondation Calouste Gulbenkian.

[58] A study from L. Th. Maes was published posthumously in 2009, but is based on research done by the historian during his lifetime. Maes, Louis Th. 2009. *Het Parlement en de Grote Raad van Mechelen 1473–1797*. Antwerp: De Vries-Brouwers.

and 1700s.[59] Even the disappearance of the tribunal and its misfortunes in the late 1780s did not draw much scholarly attention.[60] Apart from the influence the Research Center had on the chronological scope of the studies on the Great Council, the historians' preference for the earlier centuries is certainly also affected by the fact that the early history of institutions in general and of the Great Council in particular is linked with the process of state formation. For the Southern Netherlands, state-building is in general associated with the Burgundy Dukes and the early Habsburg Sovereigns.[61]

A Comparative Perspective: Early Modern Provincial and Central Courts[62]
The Southern and Northern Netherlands

In the course of the 1990s and early 2000s, several studies were published on provincial councils of the Netherlands. Rather than examining legislation, procedure or reception of Roman law, these publications provide insight into the administration of justice. Several of these studies also analyze the political impact of the provincial tribunals, their influence on the process of state-building and the way the latter is interrelated with their activities as courts. Similar to what we noticed for the Great Council, the bulk of the work in this area focuses on the earlier years of the tribunals.

P. Van Peteghem's dissertation on the Council of Flanders under Charles V is a case in point.[63] Van Peteghem examined how the Council of Flanders' position

---

[59] This is true for, e.g. Gilissen, John. 1977. Oprichting en evolutie van het Parlement/De Grote Raad van Mechelen. In *Consilium magnum, 1473–1973: herdenking van de 500ᵉ verjaardag van de oprichting van het Parlement en de Grote Raad van Mechelen*, 11–24. Brussels: Algemeen Rijksarchief; Leyder, Dirk. 2010. *Les archives du Grand Conseil des Pays-Bas à Malines*. Brussels: Algemeen Rijksarchief.; Maes, Louis Th. 2009. *Het Parlement en de Grote Raad van Mechelen 1473–1797*. Antwerp: De Vries-Brouwers; Wijffels, Alain. 1994. Grote Raad voor de Nederlanden te Mechelen (ca.1445–1797). In *De centrale overheidsinstellingen van de Habsburgse Nederlanden*, ed. Erik Aerts e.a., 448–461. Brussels: Algemeen Rijksarchief.

[60] An article from the late nineteenth century by P. Verhaegen is virtually the only study available dealing with the later years of the Great Council and mainly consists of the publication of a primary source. Verhaegen, P. 1894. Le Grand Conseil de Malines en 1795. *Handelingen van de Koninklijke Kring voor Oudheidkunde, Letteren en Kunst in Mechelen* 5:209–217. In addition, an unpublished master's thesis has the 'later years and disappearance' of the Great Council as its subject. However, it would appear that this work is of uneven quality. Vervondel, Eva. 2004. *De Grote Raad van Mechelen van 1780 tot 1797. De laatste Jaren en de verdwijning*. Unpublished Master's Thesis. Leuven: Katholieke Universiteit Leuven.

[61] For the Netherlands, de Schepper edited and wrote several publications on this theme. E.g., De Schepper, Hugo and Geurts, Jacques eds. 2006. *Staatsvorming onder de Bourgondiërs en Habsburgers. Theorie en Praktijk*. Maastricht: Shaker; Cauchies, Jean-Marie and De Schepper, Hugo eds. 1994. *Justice, grâce et legislation. Genèse de l'Etat et moyens juridiques dans les Pays-Bas, 1200–1600* (Centre de recherches en histoire du droit et des institutions. Cahiers 2). Brussels: Faculté Universitaires Saint-Louis.; Cauchies, Jean-Marie and De Schepper, Hugo. 1997. *Legal tools of public power in the Netherlands, 1200–1600*. In *Legislation and justice*, ed. Antonio Padoa-Schioppa, 229–268. Oxford: Clarendon.

[62] This overview is not intended to be exhaustive but merely aims to identify certain broad trends in the historiographical debates on Early Modern provincial and central tribunals.

[63] Van Peteghem, Paul. 1990. *De Raad van Vlaanderen en staatsvorming onder Karel V (1515–1555): een publiekrechtelijk onderzoek naar centralisatiestreven in de XVII Provinciën*. Nijmegen:

changed as a result of the pressure of the sovereign's pursuit to centralize his disparate possessions in the Netherlands. How did the sovereign strengthen his grip on the Council and how was the Council made use of to serve the sovereign's interests in his fight against the resistance of several institutions and pressure groups? Van Peteghem did not limit himself to a discussion of the changes in jurisdiction, procedure and organization of the Council of Flanders, but looked at how it functioned in practice and how it interacted with princely institutions outside of the province.

The previously mentioned study by Dauchy examines the Council of Flanders—and in particular its relationships with the *Parlement* of Paris—in the context of the Burgundy dukes' attempts to unify and centralize their territories and, even more importantly, to acquire independence from the King of France in legal matters.[64] Through an analysis of the number of appeals against sentences of the Council of Flanders at the *Parlement* of Paris as well as of their subject matter, Dauchy investigated to what extent the Paris supreme court had a real influence on the process of state formation in the Netherlands, both directly as an instrument of royal policy and indirectly in terms of the administration of justice and doctrine. The author came to the conclusion that while the *Parlement de Paris* was far from a docile instrument in the hands of the French King, in practice the Burgundy Dukes had no choice but to sideline it if they wished to arrive at complete sovereignty.

Comparable in chronology and scope to Van Rompaey's study on the Great Council is the work of Ph. Godding on the Council of Brabant under Philip the Good's rule.[65] Before the publication of Godding's study, Gaillard's monumental three volumes on the history, organization and procedure of the Council of Brabant was the only reference work on the tribunal.[66] However, Gaillard only superficially touched upon the establishment and early history of the provincial council. In addition, his study lacks references to the source materials used. Godding's work on the other hand, is firmly based on archival research. This made it possible to indicate discrepancies between the theory—as mentioned in normative texts—and practice, for example in relation to the jurisdiction of the Council. Contrary to Van Rompaey's study, however, Godding's overview of the early history of the provincial Council of Brabant—examining its initial establishment, its organization, its jurisdiction and the different procedures—is mainly an analysis of the tribunal as an institution, without much discussion on its political significance.

M.-C. Le Bailly's doctoral dissertation on the Council of Holland, Zeeland and West-Friesland in the mid-fifteenth century bears some resemblance to Godding's

Gerard Noodt Instituut.

[64] Dauchy, Serge. 1995. *De processen in beroep uit Vlaanderen bij het Parlement van Parijs (1320–1521) een rechtshistorisch onderzoek naar de wording van de staat en soevereiniteit in de Bourgondisch-Habsburgse periode*. Brussel: Paleis der Academiën.

[65] Godding, Philippe. 1999. *Le Conseil de Brabant sous le règne de Philippe le Bon 1430–1467*. Brussels: Académie royale de Belgique. Classe des lettres.

[66] Gaillard, Arthur. 1898–1902. *Le Conseil de Brabant: histoire, organisation, procédure*. Brussels: Lebègue.

work.[67] Yet, the differences are equally important: while the timeframe is more or less the same, her analysis is guided by the question how the Council of Holland was able to deal with the increasing scale of litigation in the fifteenth century. Especially the influence of the new instruction of 1462 and the impact of the institutional changes of 1462 and 1463 on the administration of justice are analyzed. The basis of her study is a relational database which includes all lawsuits registered at the Council of Holland between 1457 and 1467. This database made it possible to measure how the theory of the 1462 instruction was effectively put into practice.

Finally, C. Verhas' dissertation relates to the early High Council of Holland, Zeeland and West-Friesland, established as the 'successor' and counterpart of the Great Council of Malines after it *de facto* lost its jurisdiction over Holland.[68] For the period between roughly 1582 and 1587—which corresponds to the revolutionary years and the more or less definitive secession of the Northern territories from the Spanish Empire—she examined the organization, competence, procedure and registration methods at the Council. In her conclusion, she compared the High Council of Holland to the Great Council of Malines, highlighting how the distinctive characteristics of the former were associated with the circumstances of war in which it found its origin.

So far, no major institutional studies have been published on provincial or central courts in the seventeenth or eighteenth centuries.[69] Nevertheless, certain specific sub-aspects have been the subject of research. Given that contributions which focus on a narrowly defined aspect of the institutions researched often have a more longitudinal approach in terms of timeline, these studies do tend to include the later centuries as well. This is for example true for procedural guides, quite a few of which have been published fairly recently.[70] These analyze and explain, based on firm archival research and illustrated with examples, the procedure used at different provincial councils both in first instance and appeal.

[67] Le Bailly, Marie-Charlotte. 2001. *Recht voor de Raad: rechtspraak voor het Hof van Holland, Zeeland en West-Friesland in het midden van de vijftiende eeuw*. Hilversum: Uitgeverij Verloren.

[68] Verhas, Christel. 1997. *De beginjaren van de Hoge Raad van Holland, Zeeland en West-Friesland*. The Hague: Algemeen Rijksarchief.

[69] The very broad and general publications *Centrale overheidsinstellingen van de Habsburgse Nederlanden, De gewestelijke en lokale overheidsinstellingen in Brabant en Mechelen tot 1795* en *Gewestelijke en lokale overheidsinstellingen in Vlaanderen tot 1795* provide some limited information on the evolution of existing institutions in the eighteenth century.

[70] Berkvens, Aloysius M.J.A. 2011. *Soevereine Raad te Roermond, Justiz-Collegium te Geldern en Staats Hof van Gelre te Venlo. Hoofdlijnen van proceduren in civiele zaken in Spaans en nadien Oostenrijks, Pruisisch en Staats (Opper)-Gelre in eerte aanleg en in hoger beroep 1580–1795*. Hilversum: Uitgeverij Verloren; Le Bailly, Marie-Charlotte and Verhas, Christel. 2006. *Hoge Raad van Holland, Zeeland and West-Friesland (1582–1795): De hoofdlijnen van het procederen in civiele zaken voor de Hoge Raad zowel in eerste instantie als in hoger beroep*. Hilversum: Uitgeverij Verloren; Le Bailly, Marie-Charlotte. 2008. *Hof van Holland, Zeeland en West-Friesland: De hoofdlijnen van het procederen in civiele zaken voor het Hof van Holland, Zeeland en West-Friesland zowel in eerste instantie als in hoger beroep*. Hilversum: Uitgeverij Verloren; Le Bailly, Marie-Charlotte. 2007. *Staatse Raad van Vlaanderen te Middelburg (1599–1795): De hoofdlijnen van procederen in civiele zaken voor de Staatse Raad van Vlaanderen zowel in eerste instantie als in hoger beroep*. Hilversum: Uitgeverij Verloren.

Because of their generally broader chronological scope, prosopographical studies as well usually devote some attention to the 1600s and 1700s, as is the case for the volume on the councilors of the Court of Friesland by B. Hempenius-Van Dijk et al.[71] The publications by C. Douxchamps-Lefèvre and L. Poelgeest dealing with respectively the procurators-general of the Council of Namur,[72] and the members of the High Council of Holland[73] even specifically focus on the eighteenth century.

The eighteenth century is particularly well-represented in studies on criminal justice. While some mainly use criminal case files as sources to study crime in the Ancien Régime society,[74] others analyze the prosecution of crimes by provincial tribunals.[75] With regard to our interest in the Great Council, J. Monballyu's articles on the administration of criminal justice at the Council of Flanders in the later years of its existence deserve special mention. In several contributions he examined the procedure used,[76] discussed the position of the Council of Flanders relating to the reform of the criminal law at the end of the eighteenth century[77] and refuted the generally accepted view that the Council of Flanders had always been entirely sovereign in criminal affairs.[78]

International Context The past few years have witnessed a surge in the interest in European Early-Modern superior courts. In April 2013 a volume was published which traces the history of supreme courts throughout the European continent—including Russia and the Ottoman Empire—from the medieval to the modern

[71] Hempenius-Van Dijck, Barendina e.a. 1999. *De Heeren van den Raeden: biografieën en groepsportret van de raadsheren van het Hof van Friesland, 1499–1811*. Hilversum: Uitgeverij Verloren.

[72] Douxchamps-Lefèvre, Cécile. 1961. *Les procureurs généraux du Conseil de Namur sous le régime autrichien: leur action en matière politique: contribution à l'histoire des institutions et à l'histoire sociale du Namurois au XVIIIe siècle*. Louvain: Publications universitaires de Louvain.

[73] Van Poelgeest, L. 1988. De raadsheren van de Hoge Raad van Holland, Zeeland en West-Friesland in de achttiende eeuw. *Bijdragen en mededelingen betreffende de geschiedenis der Nederlanden* 103.1: 20–51.

[74] E.g., Broers, E.J.M.F.C. 1996. *Beledigingszaken voor de Staatse Raad van Brabant 1586–1795*. Assen: Van Gorcum; Van de Pol, Lotte. 1996. *Het Amsterdams hoerdom. Prostitutie in de zeventiende en achttiende eeuw*. Amsterdam: Wereldbibliotheek.

[75] E.g., Berkvens, Aloysius M.J.A. 1999. *À propos van de affaire Laurent Timmermans*. Maastricht: FdR. Metajuridica; Dupont-Bouchat, Marie-Sylvie and Page-Steffens, Marie-Paule. 2006. Des délits et des peines: l'activité pénale du Conseil Provincial de Namur au XVIIIe siècle. In *La Belgique criminelle: droit, justice, société (XIVe–XXe siècles)*, eds. Marie-Sylvie Dupont-Bouchat and Xavier Rousseaux, 273–316. Louvain-la-Neuve: Academia-Bruylant; Huussen, Arend. 1978. Jurisprudentie en bureaucratie: het Hof van Friesland en zijn criminele rechtspraak in de 18de eeuw. *Low Countries Historical Review* 93.2: 529–550.

[76] Monballyu, Jos. 2001. De hoofdlijnen van de criminele strafprocedure in het graafschap Vlaanderen (16de tot 18de eeuw). In *Voortschrijdend procesrecht. Een historische verkenning*, eds. Fred Stevens, Ernest Persoons and Remco Van Rhee, 63–108. Leuven: Universitaire Pers Leuven.

[77] Monballyu, Jos. 1996. De Raad van Vlaanderen en de hervorming van het strafrecht (1756–1787). *Tijdschrift voor Rechtsgeschiedenis* 54: 47–77.

[78] Monballyu, Jos. 1998. De Raad van Vlaanderen, een soevereine justitieraad in strafzaken? In *Handelingen van het tweede Hof van Holland Symposium gehouden op 14 November 1997 in de Treveszaal te Den Haag*, ed. Rob Huijbrecht, 77–90. The Hague: Algemeen Rijksarchief.

period.[79] In 2007, as a result of a conference on the origins of the *Reichshofrat*, a collection was published on the building stones of early-modern high courts—albeit with a marked focus on the *Reichshofrat* and the *Reichskammergericht*—illustrating the desire of legal historians to arrive at a comparative analysis of European supreme justice in the early-modern times.[80] The same ambition stood at the basis of the volume on European superior courts edited by Diestelkamp a decade earlier.[81]

Provincial councils as well continue to figure prominently in the field of interest of legal historians. For example, only fairly recently, an issue of the *Revue du Nord* was entirely dedicated to different studies on The Parlement of Flanders, a court that was to a high degree influenced by the Great Council of Malines.[82] Around the same time, the jurisprudence of the *Parlement de Flandres*, collected by one of its councilors, was edited by S. Dauchy and V. Demars-Sion.[83]

Nevertheless, discussing the state of research on all supreme or provincial councils, even if limited to Europe and to the eighteenth century, would be a vast enterprise that is outside the scope of this general introduction. We have therefore decided to focus our historiographical overview mainly on the eighteenth century French *Parlement de Paris* and on the *Reichskammergericht* of the Holy Roman Empire. The reason for this selection is two-fold: firstly, both of these courts had jurisdiction over parts of the Netherlands during a certain period of time and secondly, the Great Council had certain characteristics in common with each of these tribunals. Indeed, while the *Reichskammergericht* and the Great Council shared a more or less similar chronology—they were 'established' around 1495 and 1473 respectively, and dissolved around 1806 and 1797—the *Parlement de Paris*, which was about a century and a half older, served as a model for the *Parlement* of Malines. Moreover, the Netherlands were situated somewhere in between the French and the 'German' model of unification and state formation: while unification in the Seventeen Provinces and later the Southern Netherlands never reached the degree of the French state under Louis XIV, it did surpass the only very loose cohesion of the German Empire. As a result, although the differences between these three tribunals are probably just as notable as their similarities, it is useful to look at the historiography of the *Parlement de Paris* and the *Reichskammergericht* to contextualize our own research.

R.-P. Fuchs remarked in his overview of the state of research on the *Reichskammergericht* that it took a long time before a thorough study of the tribunal was ac-

[79] Van Rhee, Remco and Wijffels, Alain (eds.). 2003. *European Supreme Courts. A portrait through history*. London: Third Millennium.

[80] Auer, Leopold, Ogris, Werner and Ortlieb, Eva eds. 2007. *Höchstgerichte in Europa. Bausteine frühneuzeitlicher Rechtsordnungen* (Quellen und Forschungen zur höchsten Gerichtsbarkeit im alten Reich 53). Cologne\—Weimar—Vienna: Böhlau Verlag.

[81] Diestelkamp, Bernhard ed. 1996. *Oberste Gerichtsbarkeit und zentrale Gewalt im Europa der frühen Neuzeit* (Quellen und Forschungen zur höchsten Gerichtsbarkeit im alten Reich 29), Cologne—Weimar—Vienna: Böhlau Verlag.

[82] Le parlement de Flandre à travers ses archives. 2009. *Revue du Nord* 382.

[83] Dauchy, Serge and Demars-Sion, Véronique eds. 2008. *Jurisprudence du Parlement de Flandre*. Brussels: Service public fédéral justice.

complished, firstly because the scattering of its archives severely complicated any research efforts and secondly because the negative attitudes towards the court—which had arisen during the eighteenth century—had a disheartening impact on German historians and encouraged them to mainly criticize its weaknesses and deficiencies.[84]

One of the first contributions on the *Reichskammergericht*, which brought the court to scholarly attention, was from the hand of a non-German historian, P. Nève.[85] He examined the tribunal from a historical-geographical angle, using case files to investigate the jurisdiction the *Reichskammergericht* had over the Netherlands, both from a territorial and a chronological perspective. For our study of the Great Council, his short analysis of the status of the German tribunal in the eighteenth century is particularly interesting. According to Nève, the *Reichskammergericht* became obsolete in the last century of its existence because the tribunal was no longer adapted to the changed circumstances. In response, new, 'modern' courts were established in the different territories of the German Empire. Given that the Great Council was even slightly 'older' than the *Reichskammergericht*, this naturally leads to the question if it suffered the same fate.

Around the same time as Nève, B. Diestelkamp started to display interest in the *Reichskammergericht*. As early as 1976, he published a statistical analysis of previously described lawsuits in order to demonstrate the richness of the materials available, which could be used not only for studies on litigation but also for research on the social backgrounds of the litigants or on the objects of dispute.[86] Apart from his own research, Diestelkamp edited several collections on the tribunal, among others the volume dedicated to the eighteenth century *Reichskammergericht* and its lasting impact in the nineteenth century.[87] However, none of the contributions in this work study the tribunal as an institution; they all focus on some narrowly formulated specific questions: whether the French Revolution influenced the administration of justice at the *Reichskammergericht*, how former officials of the tribunal were compensated for their loss of income when the tribunal was abolished or what happened with the cases from Mecklenburg after the dismantlement of the council.[88]

---

[84] Fuchs provides a state of research on the *Reichskammergericht* between roughly 1970 and 2000. Fuchs, Ralf-Peter. 2003. The Supreme Court of the Holy Roman Empire: the state of research and the outlook. *Sixteenth Century Journal* 34.1: 9–27.

[85] Neve, Paul Lucien. 1972. *Het Rijkskamergerecht en de Nederlanden: competentie-territoir-archieven*. Assen: Van Gorcum.

[86] Diestelkamp, Bernhard. 1976. Das Reichskammergericht im Rechtsleben des 16. Jahrhunderts. In *Rechtsgeschikte als Kulturgeschichte: Festschrift für Adalbert Erler zu 70. Geburtstag*, ed. Hans-Jürgen Becker, 353–369. Aalen: Scientia.

[87] Diestelkamp, Bernhard, ed. 2002. *Das Reichskammergericht am Ende des alten Reiches und sein Fortwirken im 19.* Jahrhundert. Cologne: Böhlau Verlag.

[88] Härter, Karl. 2002. Soziale Unruhen und Revolutionsabwehr: Auswirkungen der Fransözischen Revolution auf die Rechtsprechung des Reichskammergerichts. In *Das Reichskammergericht am Ende des alten Reiches und sein Fortwirken im 19. Jahrhundert*, ed. Bernhard Diestelkamp, 43–104. Cologne: Böhlau Verlag; Mader, Eric-Olivier. 2002. 'Heilige Schulden' des aufgelösten Reichs. Das Problem der Entschädigung des Reichskammergerichtspersonals für den Verlust ihrer Stellen. In *Das Reichskammergericht am Ende des alten Reiches und sein Fortwirken im 19. Jahr-*

A social/prosopographical viewpoint is taken by S. Jahns' two volume study on the personnel of the *Reichskammergericht*. Rather than merely assembling the assessors' biographies—which can be found in volume 2—she described the judges' backgrounds, their education, their opportunities for upward mobility etc. and the evolution of these different aspects over time. Moreover, she also examined the interactions between the personnel of the *Reichskammergericht* and the tribunal itself.[89] The article she wrote in the context of her wider research on the councilors of the eighteenth century German Supreme Court is particularly interesting in that regard. In this contribution, she investigated how the obsoleteness of the tribunal and the fact that it was not adapted to the 'modern times' of the eighteenth century affected its personnel policy and, conversely, how the difficulties in recruiting qualified assessors had an influence on the workings of the court and the way it was perceived.[90]

Contrary to the *Reichskammergericht*, the *Parlement de Paris* has attracted historians' attention from very early on. As a result, the number of publications on the French Supreme Court is absolutely massive. Yet, French historiography mostly studied the *Parlement* of Paris as a political actor, concentrating on its right of remonstration, thereby often overlooking its primary role as a court of justice. Especially for the eighteenth century, literature is focused on the opposition of the *Parlement* against Louis XV's policies,[91] an approach which makes only limited use of the institution's archives. Hildesheimer believed that historians deliberately avoid using the records of the *Parlement*, since they are considered to be an inscrutable mass and, for certain periods, even almost unreadable.[92] Moreover, a certain understanding of and familiarity with the judicial practice of the Ancien Régime as well as some archival intelligence are indispensable when researching the tribunal's functioning.

hundert, ed. Bernhard Diestelkamp, 105–142. Cologne: Böhlau Verlag; Stein, Hans Konrad. 2002. Das Schicksal der unerledigten Mecklenburger Reichskammergerichts Prozesse und die Idee einer obersten Berufungs Instanz in Mecklenburg nach Ende der Reichsgerichte 1806. In *Das Reichskammergericht am Ende des alten Reiches und sein Fortwirken im 19. Jahrhundert*, ed. Bernhard Diestelkamp, 217–249. Cologne: Böhlau Verlag.

[89] Jahns, Sigrid. 2011. *Das Reichskammergericht und seine Richter: Verfassug und Sozialstruktur eines höchsten Gerichts im Alten Reich.* Cologne: Böhlau.

[90] Jahns, Sigrid. 1990. Die Personalverfassung des Reichskammergerichts unter Anpassungsdruck. Lösungen im Spannungsfeld zwischen Modernität und Überalterung. In *Das Reichskammergericht in der deutschen Geschichte: Stand der Forschung, Forschungsperspektiven* (Quellen und Forschungen zur höchsten Gerichtsbarkeit im alten Reich 21), ed. Bernhard Diestelkamp, 59–109. Cologne: Böhlau.

[91] Doyle, William. 1970. The Parlements of France and the breakdown of the Old Régime 1771–1788. *French Historical Studies* 6: 415–458; Egret, Jean. 1970. *Louis XV et l'opposition parlementaire, 1715–1774.* Paris: Colin; Rogister, John. 1995. *Louis XV and the Parlement of Paris, 1737–1755.* Cambridge: Cambridge University Press; Swann, Julian. 1995. *Politics and the Parlement of Paris under Louis XV, 1754–1774.* Cambridge: Cambridge University Press.

[92] Hildesheimer, Francoise. 2004. Exemplaire Parlement… Le fonds du Parlement de Paris aux archives nationales. *Revue de synthèse* 125.1: 45–81.

These obstacles explain why historians of the *Parlement*—and of other institutions as well—have often focused on criminal justice: not only is this typically considered a much more attractive subject of study, the records are also less daunting in terms of volume and more accessible in general. At least for the eighteenth century criminal trials at the *Parlement* an inventory is available.[93] As a result, its activity as a criminal court has been well documented, with criminal cases having served as sources to write the history of crime and its prosecution in Early-Modern France, often with special attention to the eighteenth century.[94] In addition, similarly to what we have determined for other councils, prosopographical studies are generally plentiful: historians examined the personnel of the *Parlement* of Paris as an indirect but accessible means to study the tribunal.[95]

Although a study of the eighteenth century *Parlement* as a court of justice is so far entirely lacking due to the reasons listed above, civil archives were in fact made use of to link the Parliament's opposition against Louis XV to the workings of the tribunal as a judicial institution (and not as a political entity). In an article of 1980, C. Kaiser demonstrated that at the end of the Ancien Régime the *Parlement* suffered from a decline in litigation, causing a diminution in the variable income the councilors received for their work as judges. Consequently, Kaiser considered this drop in revenue to be the main cause of the Parliament's oppositional activity.[96]

In recent years, historians have become ever more interested in this phenomenon of the 'great litigation decline', even independent of the political consequences it might possibly have had. For the *Parlement de Paris*, D. Feutry challenged Kaiser's conclusions. He claimed that, rather than a decrease, there was a considerable pick-up in the Parlement's business throughout the eighteenth century.[97] It must be noted that Feutry is somewhat isolated with his opinion that there was a rise rather than a decline in litigation during the eighteenth century.[98]

---

[93] Ibid, 66.

[94] E.g., Andrews, Richard. 2006. *Law, magistracy and crime in Old Regime Paris, 1735–1789*. Cambridge: Cambridge University Press; Bastien, Pascale. 2006. *L'exécution publique à Paris au XVIIIe siècle. Une histoire des rituels judiciaires*. Seyssel: Champ Vallon; Soman, Alfred. 1992. *Sorcellerie et justice criminelle: le Parlement de Paris (16e–18e siècles)*. Hampshire-Brookfield: Variorum; etc.

[95] For the eighteenth century *Parlement de Paris*, see Bluche, Francois. 1986. *Les magistrats du Parlement de Paris au XVIIIe siècle*. Paris: Economica. In this regard, Krynen's book on the ideology of the judiciary is also worth mentioning. Yet, instead of merely focusing on a prosopographical study of the councilors of the *Parlement de Paris*, he analyzes the position of the judges in French courts in general and their influence on the operation of government. See, Krynen, Jacques. 2009. *L'Etat de justice. France (XIIIe-XXe siècle). Vol 1: l'idéologie de la magistrature ancienne*. Paris: Gaillimard.

[96] Kaiser, Colin. 1980. The deflation in the volume of litigation at Paris in the Eighteenth Century and the waning of the old judicial order. *European Studies Review* 10.3: 309–336.

[97] Feutry, David. 2012. The historian's mountain of paper: the Parlement of Pariss and the analysis of civil suits in the eighteenth century. *French History* 26.3: 277–296.

[98] For example: H. Horwitz and P. Polden, and W.A. Champion observed a serious and consistent diminution in civil litigation for respectively the central and the local courts in 18th century England. R. Kagan noticed the same phenomenon for Castile, where litigation boomed during

In summary, while historians have unmistakably demonstrated an increased interest in civil litigation at different provincial and supreme courts throughout Europe and have gradually shifted their interest somewhat from the sixteenth to the eighteenth century, institutional studies of provincial and central councils as courts of justice during the eighteenth century are few and far between.

State Formation in the Composite State:[99] The Role of Superior Courts and the Administration of Justice Historical research on state building has often been marked by more or less narrow teleological assumptions. In fact, it was assumed that the modern, meaning the national, state of the nineteenth and twentieth centuries was the guideline criterion for historical analysis. In addition, taking Weber's rational-bureaucratic state as a reference point, historians have inevitably focused on criteria such as centralization, territorialization and bureaucratization. Yet, before the age of revolutions, the Early-Modern state rarely had a well-defined territory or population and the ruling authority was seldom, if ever, undivided or monopolized in a single hand. As a result, Holenstein argued that in Early-Modern Europe, state-building was not so much a top-down movement, directed by a sovereign, but was rather the unintended outcome of mutually interacting processes and should therefore be looked at from below.[100]

In both bottom-up and top-down traditions of explaining state-building, legislation but even more the administration of justice are considered to be of crucial importance. Indeed, the power of the monarch spread mostly because of his position as supreme judge: the judicial practice of the prince became the main force behind legal unification and the formation of the state.[101] Especially the establishment of royal tribunals is crucial in this regard.[102] The introduction of appeal and the devel-

---

the sixteenth century but started to flag afterwards. M.-C. Le Bailly examined long-term trends in litigation at several courts in the Northern and Southern Netherlands and also discovered a decline in litigation. Horwitz, Henry and Polden, Patrick. 1996. Continuity or change in the Court of Chancery in the seventeenth and eighteenth centuries? *Journal of British Studies* 35.1: 24–57. Champion, William.A. 1997. Recourse to law and the meaning of the Great Litigation Decline, 1650–1750. Some clues from the Shrewsbury Local Courts. In *Communities and Courts in Britain*, eds. Christopher Brooks and Michael Lobban, 179–198. London: Hambledon Press; Kagan, Richard L. 1981. *Lawsuits and litigants in Castile, 1500–1700*. Chapel Hill: University of North Carolina Press; Le Bailly, Marie-Charlotte. 2011. Langetermijntrends in de rechtspraak bij de gewestelijke hoven van justitie in de Noordelijke Nederlanden van ca. 1450 tot ca. 1800. *Pro Memorie* 13: 30–67.

[99] State formation and state building have been intensively researched from different perspectives by both historians and sociologists. We do not provide an overview of all the different traditions but mainly focus on what is relevant for our own research.

[100] Holenstein, André. 2009. Introduction: Empowering interactions: looking at statebuilding from below. In *Empowering interactions. Political cultures and the emergence of the state in Europe 1300–1900*, eds. Wim Blockmans, André Holenstein and Jon Matthieu, 1–33. Farnham: Ashgate.

[101] Cauchies, Jean-Marie and De Schepper, Hugo. 1997. *Legal tools of public power in the Netherlands, 1200–1600*. In *Legislation and justice*, ed. Antonio Padoa-Schioppa, 229–268. Oxford: Clarendon.

[102] Holmes, Clive. 1997. Legal instruments of power and the state in Early Modern England. In *Legislation and justice*, ed. Antonio Padoa-Schioppa, 269–289. Oxford: Clarendon.

opment of new legal techniques—such as *évocation*—made litigants seek what was due to them in all sorts of conflicts by coming as close as possible to the source of justice.[103]

State-building in the Netherlands in particular was a complex phenomenon. Even under Charles V the Seventeen Provinces were never a unified, centralized entity but rather constituted a prime example of a 'composite state'. This term, coined by H.G. Koenigsberger in an inaugural lecture in 1975,[104] refers to a typical form of political organization in sixteenth century Europe which includes "more than one country under the sovereignty of one ruler".[105] The preservation of these often complex 'composite states' was made possible thanks to the application of the *aeque principaliter* principle, which meant that, even after their union with the 'motherland', the composing parts were administrated as separate entities, with their own laws and privileges.[106] This necessarily involved the perpetuation of Estates and representative institutions. In addition, the composing parts had to be ruled as if the sovereign who held them all together were sovereign of each one of them.[107]

Nevertheless, some degree of integration was called for. Given that Early-Modern princes usually did not have the means to assure a permanent military presence and that this, in any case, would have had an undesirable effect in terms of the popular acceptance of their rule and moral authority with their subjects, "the choice came down to the creation of new institutional organs at the highest level of government, and the use of patronage to win and retain the loyalty of the old administrative and political elites."[108] Indeed, "in return for a degree of benign neglect, local élites enjoyed a measure of self-government, which left them without any urgent need to challenge the status quo. In other words, composite monarchies were built on a mutual compact between the crown and the ruling class of their different provinces which gave even the most arbitrary and artificial of unions a certain stability and resilience."[109]

This was exactly the strategy adopted by the Burgundy Dukes and their early Habsburg successors. The seventeen provinces were initially nothing more than a personal union: while all acknowledged the same sovereign, they also retained to

---

103 Cauchies, Jean-Marie and De Schepper, Hugo. 1997. *Legal tools of public power in the Netherlands, 1200–1600.* In *Legislation and justice*, ed. Antonio Padoa-Schioppa, 229–268. Oxford: Clarendon, 264.

104 The lecture was later published in Koenigsberger, Helmut Georg. 1986. 'Dominium Regale' or 'Dominium Politicum et Regale'. In *Politicians and virtuosi: Essays in Early Modern History*, ed. Helmut Georg Koenigsberger, 1–26. London: University of London.

105 Elliott, John H. 1992. A Europe of composite monarchies. *Past and Present* 137.1: 48–71.

106 Van Honacker, Karin. 1995. Het einde van het ancien régime in de Oostenrijkse Nederlanden: zoeken naar het herstel van een modus vivendi. In *Symposium over de centrale overheidsinstellingen van de Habsburgse Nederlanden. Tien Bijdragen over de staat, de regering en de ambtenaren van de 16*[de] *tot de 18*[de] *eeuw* (Standen en Landen, speciale serie 2), eds. Herman Coppens and Karin Van Honacker, 245–266. Brussels: Algemeen Rijksarchief.

107 Elliott, John H. 1992. A Europe of composite monarchies. *Past and Present* 137.1: 53–54.

108 Elliott, John H. 1992. A Europe of composite monarchies. *Past and Present* 137.1: 55.

109 Elliott, John H. 1992. A Europe of composite monarchies. *Past and Present* 137.1: 57.

a large extent their own particularistic traditions, laws, privileges and institutions, which they staunchly defended, not only against the central government but also against other provinces. In order to achieve some degree of unification and centralization, without however too much hurting the sensitivities of their subjects, the dukes created a hierarchy of institutions, populated with mainly professional jurists. The *Parlement* of Malines was one of these. Indeed, once central governmental councils and officials were able to impose their decisions on institutions and private persons, the Netherlands could reach a higher level of integration.

According to de Schepper, the provincial and central courts played a crucial role in this process: they represented the sovereign's authority and pronounced their judgments in his name. From the very beginning of their rule, the Dukes of Burgundy stimulated the introduction of higher appeal and new procedural techniques in order to encourage litigants to bring their proceedings to the princely courts, thereby limiting the authority of the local, feudal and municipal tribunals. Even though appeal was not possible in criminal trials, which therefore were often judged on the local level, the dukes used the instrument of pardon as the ultimate check on these lower tribunals.[110] While the process of state-building was slightly set back after the death of Charles the Bold, the early Habsburg Sovereigns again tied in with this tradition of using their function as *rex iudex* to arrive at a certain degree of unification and centralization. During the sixteenth century, litigation boomed at royal courts, a phenomenon that is often interpreted as a yardstick for state-building.

Nevertheless, the composite state was brittle and over the course of the sixteenth century, wars, economic depression, religious division and the resulting impulse to achieve further centralization formed a threat to the precious balance. This is exactly what happened under Charles V's successor Philip II. Impatient with the system of *aeque principaliter* and "its corollary of unification by slow, pragmatic, methods",[111] Philip's attempts at fully integrating and even absorbing his Netherlands possessions into the Spanish Empire were met by rebellion and eventually set back the process of unification and centralization for more than a century to come.[112] It was not until the eighteenth century that cautious attempts at state-building were once again undertaken, this time by the Austrian Habsburg monarchs.[113]

---

[110] De Schepper, Hugo. 2006. Staatsgezag en staatsmacht in de Nederlanden. Verworvenheden en beperkingen van het Bourgondisch-Habsburgse systeem. In *Staatsvorming onder de Bourgondiërs en Habsburgers. Theorie en Praktijk*, eds. Hugo de Schepper en Jacques Geurts, 13–50. Maastricht: Shaker.

[111] Elliott, John H. 1992. A Europe of composite monarchies. *Past and Present* 137.1: 62.

[112] De Schepper, Hugo. 2006. Staatsgezag en staatsmacht in de Nederlanden. Verworvenheden en beperkingen van het Bourgondisch-Habsburgse systeem. In *Staatsvorming onder de Bourgondiërs en Habsburgers. Theorie en Praktijk*, eds. Hugo de Schepper en Jacques Geurts, 13–50. Maastricht: Shaker, 49–50.

[113] Lenders, Piet. 1995. Ontstaan en ontwikkeling van de moderne staat in de Nederlanden. In Symposium over de centrale overheidsinstellingen van de Habsburgse Nederlanden. Tien Bijdragen over de staat, de regering en de ambtenaren van de 16de tot de 18de eeuw (Standen en Landen, speciale serie 2), eds. Herman Coppens and Karin Van Honacker, 1–42. Brussels: Algemeen Rijksarchief.

1.3 Defining the Problem

So far, historical research on the Great Council has focused on the late fifteenth and early sixteenth centuries, corresponding to the origins and the first few decades of the tribunal's existence. The historiography on the Great Council is no exception in this regard: the early years of other Ancien Régime institutions typically also received much more attention than the later period of their existence and their ultimate disappearance. We can identify two main factors that explain this observation. Firstly, historians apparently assume that an institution in the years leading up to its disappearance or abolition must necessarily have been in decay.[114] Although especially the eighteenth century is regarded as a period of change and 'innovation' due to the advent of Enlightenment and its new ideas, institutions are generally presumed to have remained stagnant since their establishment 300 years before, leading to an expectation that they are poorly adjusted to the late Ancien Régime society. Secondly, institutions in the Netherlands are often examined as instruments of the centralization policies of the Burgundy Dukes and their early Habsburg successors. This, of course, also results in a particular focus on the fifteenth and sixteenth centuries.

New attempts at state-building were made by the Austrian Habsburgs, and even before, during the transitional years between 1700 and 1715.[115] These early attempts at centralizing decision-making were met with resistance, especially in the years 1717–1719. It was not until the mid-twenties that a new *modus vivendi* was reached, which, for the later period, became known as the 'Theresian compromise'. In practice, this meant that the Austrian government would grant a relatively high degree of independence to its Netherlands possessions in exchange for internal peace and a regular income from taxes.[116] Throughout, the Austrian rulers carefully implemented small yet significant changes in the way the Netherlands were administered: the authority of the Minister Plenipotentiary was expanded—he was primarily the executor of the will of the sovereign—thereby eroding the power of the Governor;[117] the High Council for the Netherlands in Vienna was abolished because it was suspected of being too much imbued with a 'national spirit'; instead, a

---

[114] Diestelkamp, Bernhard, ed. 2002. *Das Reichskammergericht am Ende des alten Reiches und sein Fortwirken im 19*, Vol VII. Jahrhundert. Cologne: Böhlau Verlag.

[115] Lenders, Piet. 1988. Trois façons de gouverner dans les Pays-Bas autrichiens. In *Unité et diversité de l'empire de Habsbourg à la fin du XVIIIe siècle* (Etudes sur le XVIIIe siècle 15), eds Hervé Hasquin and Roland Mortier, 41–53. Brussels: Université de Bruxelles.

[116] Van Honacker, Karin. 1995. Het einde van het ancien régime in de Oostenrijkse Nederlanden: zoeken naar het herstel van een modus vivendi. In *Symposium over de centrale overheidsinstellingen van de Habsburgse Nederlanden. Tien Bijdragen over de staat, de regering en de ambtenaren van de 16*[de] *tot de 18*[de] *eeuw* (Standen en Landen, speciale serie 2), eds. Herman Coppens and Karin Van Honacker, 251. Brussels: Algemeen Rijksarchief.

[117] Aerts, Erik. 2013. Economische interventie van de centrale staat in de Spaanse en Oostenrijkse Nederlanden (1555–1795). In *Gouvernance et administration dans les provinces belges (XVIe-XVIIIe siècles)* (Archives et Bibliothèques de Belgique 99), Eds. De Morbeau de Gerbehaye e.a., 399–452. Brussels: Archives et Bibliothèques de Belgique.

'Department of the Netherlands' was established within the Viennese *Hof-und Staatskanzlei* which stood under direct control of chancellor Kaunitz;[118] several *Jointes* were created, etc.

Joseph II discontinued this tendency of slowly yet steadily introducing small changes into the administration of the Southern Netherlands. Instead, he made *tabula rasa* of the entire existing system, with complete disregard for the sensitivities of his subjects, who were unwilling to give up the achievements of the composite state without a fight. Just as Philip II 200 years later, he had to face rebellion and revolution and eventually even the temporary loss of the Netherlands. His brother Leopold II again tied in with the policy of compromise.

While these evolutions are well-known and have been extensively researched, the role played by the existing institutions in this renewed process of state-building is yet to be examined. In fact, while historians agree that central institutions and especially tribunals—such as the Great Council—were used as instruments of centralization during the fifteenth and sixteenth centuries, nothing is mentioned in literature about their possible part in the Austrian Habsburgs' efforts at arriving at a deeper integration of their Netherlands possession.

This study contributes to the existing historiography in two regards. First, we examine the eighteenth century Great Council as an institution, analyzing its personnel policy, its internal organization, its position within the broader society of the Netherlands, the volume and nature of litigation at the tribunal and finally its disappearance in the late 1780s and early 1790s. Throughout the study of each of these aspects, we assess the impact and significance the Great Council had during the eighteenth century and compare, where possible, with the situation of the late fifteenth and early sixteenth century Council. Questions are asked such as: what was the profile of the eighteenth century councilors and was it any different from their predecessors? Were the procedure and inner workings—established in the mid-sixteenth century—ever reformed to adjust the institution to the changing times? What was the position of the Great Council in the eighteenth century vis-à-vis other institutions in the Austrian Netherlands? Was the volume and nature of litigation in the eighteenth century any different from before? And finally, how did the Great Council respond to Joseph II's reforms and the subsequent revolutionary fever?

Secondly, by means of this institutional study, we examine the role played by the Great Council in the process of state-building in the eighteenth century. If the assumption that eighteenth century institutions were characterized by *Verfall* und *Zerfall* is correct, it is unlikely that the government could still use the Great Council as the instrument of centralization it had once been in the late fifteenth and early sixteenth centuries. The volume of litigation is already telling in that regard: if there was a considerable decline in the number of lawsuits introduced by litigants at the Great Council, the government could no longer use it as a tool to dis-

[118] Dhondt, Luc. 1995. De Nederlanden te Wenen in de 18de eeuw. Institutionele aanwezigheid en onderschikkings-en bestuurswijzen. In *Symposium over de centrale instellingen van de Habsburgse Nederlanden, Brussel 3 december 1994. Tien Bijdragen over de staat, de regering en de ambtenaren van de 16de tot de 18de eeuw* (Standen en Landen Bijzondere Reeks nr. 2), eds. Herman Coppens en Karin Van Honacker, 214–244. Brussels: Algemeen Rijksarchief.

seminate its 'ideas' and 'values' through the administration of justice. Moreover, as a result of the restrictions imposed by the 'composite state' and the principle of the '*monarchie limitée*', the central government had to be careful not to hurt the particularistic sensitivities of the different constituent parts when using a central institution such as the Great Council. Therefore: to what extent were the Austrian Habsburg Sovereigns still able and willing to use the Great Council as an instrument of power? And what were the consequences of their attitude for the Great Council as an institution?

Chronologically, this study is focused on the eighteenth century. This limitation is somewhat arbitrary, although it does to some extent correspond to a political reality. The death of the Spanish King Charles II in 1700, the subsequent War of the Spanish Succession and the eventual transfer of the sovereignty over the Netherlands to the Austrian Habsburg dynasty are a natural starting point. The end is necessarily determined by the abolition of the Great Council in the late 1790s. Nevertheless, our research is not rigorously restricted to the eighteenth century: certain evolutions will be tracked back to the late seventeenth century, while we will also follow the traces left behind by the members of the Great Council and its archives in the early nineteenth century. Given that we cover a period of about 100 years, our subject area has been rather wide in scope. On some occasions, this inevitably required us to focus on broad high-level trends rather than on the specific details of any particular period within our time frame.

We mainly made use of a range of primary, predominantly archival, sources, both from the Great Council itself and from other institutions. Rather than merely focusing on normative texts which describe the 'ideal' situation, we investigated the reality of the tribunal's operations 'on the ground' and examined how far this reality was removed from the norm.

Due to the sheer vastness of the Great Council's archives, a certain degree of selectivity was inevitable. Civil case files, for example, were not taken into account, on the one hand because only a few inventories are available, and on the other hand, because they are often, for various reasons, incomplete. Other major series were used for qualitative and/or quantitative analysis. This is the case for the eighteenth century *mémoriaux*, the correspondence, the recommendations and correspondence from the fiscals, the extended sentences, the dicta, and the distribution records. In addition, isolated documents that do not belong to any major series and that are sometimes not even included in Van den Bussche's general inventory of the Great Council[119]—such as the *Listes des gages du Grand Conseil*—also served as sources. The source materials from the Great Council were supplemented with disparate records from the Privy Council (mainly appointment records and *consultes*) and from the *Comité établi provisoirement pour la Liquidation des Affaires Financières Belgiques*. In addition, we have done research in the city archives and the archives of the archdiocese of Malines and in the *Haus-Hof-und Staatsarchiv* and

[119] Van den Bussche, Emile. 1992. *Inventaire des registres du Grand Conseil de Malines: avec un supplément pour les Nos 1186 à 1553 (Requêtes et varia en portefeuilles)*. Brussels: Algemeen Rijksarchief.

the *Finanz-und Hofkammerarchiv* in Vienna. Each chapter starts with an overview and short typology of the sources used.

Attached to this work are two Excel databases: a smaller one, containing some essential information on the councilors of the eighteenth century Great Council and a fairly large one, comprising the data derived from the distribution records and a few analyses based on this data set. The latter in particular formed the basis of our analysis of the volume of litigation at the Great Council and its evolution over time.

So far, there is to our knowledge not a single systematic quantitative study regarding the activity of the tribunal: neither the case files nor the extended sentences reflect all the cases pending before the court during that period. In addition, contrary to what might be expected, neither the registers of the *rôle* nor the dicta are very helpful in that regard.[120] Especially in the eighteenth century, many lawsuits did not follow the *rôle* procedure. In addition, a large number of lawsuits never reached the judgment phase and therefore did not leave a trace in the dicta registers.

However, based on the information in the distribution records, which are complete for the eighteenth century—unlike for the fifteenth or sixteenth centuries—we were able to compile a list of more than 13,000 civil lawsuits distributed over the course of the eighteenth century. Each of these entries contains the date of distribution, the names and a certain characterization of the litigants, the identification of the councilor-reporter, the procedure used and in case of appeals also the previous instance. For a large number of cases, additional information is available, such as the names of the proctors and the outcome of the lawsuit: was it judged? Were the litigants able to reach a settlement? Was the claim simply dropped? Based on these data, it is not only possible to draw up a fairly accurate image of litigation at the eighteenth century Great Council but also to distill other interesting information, for example on the evolution of the number and nature of lawsuits over the course of the eighteenth century, on the workload of individual councilors, on the duration of lawsuits, etc. In addition, the choice to complete these analyses for the eighteenth century in its entirety made it possible to identify broad long-term trends.

References

1949. *Mechelen, stad. Programma van de historische stoet: 475e verjaring van de vestiging te Mechelen van de Grote Raad*. Malines: Drukkerij de Eendracht.

1973. *500 jaar Grote Raad 1473–1973. Tentoonstelling van Karel de Stoute tot Keizer Karel.* Malines: Cultureel Centrum Spinoy.

1977. *Consilium magnum, 1473–1973: herdenking van de 500^e verjaardag van de oprichting van het Parlement en de Grote Raad van Mechelen*. Brussels: Algemeen Rijksarchief.

1980. *Miscellanea Consilii Magni. Ter gelegenheid van twintig jaar Werkgroep Grote Raad van Mechelen*. Amsterdam: Universiteit van Amsterdam. Faculteit der rechtsgeleerdheid.

Aerts, Erik. 2013. Economische interventie van de centrale staat in de Spaanse en Oostenrijkse Nederlanden (1555–1795). In *Gouvernance et administration dans les provinces belges (XVIe-*

[120] Wijffels, Alain. 2009. Dutch litigation before the Great Council of Mechlin. An additional calendar of the 'Appeals from Holland'. *Tijdschrift voor rechtsgeschiedenis* 77: 539–550.

XVIIIe siècles) (Archives et Bibliothèques de Belgique 99), Eds. Claude De Morbeau de Gerbehaye e.a., 399–452. Brussels: Archives et Bibliothèques de Belgique.

Andrews, Richard. 2006. *Law, magistracy and crime in Old Regime Paris*, 1735–1789. Cambridge: Cambridge University Press.

Auer, Leopold, Ogris, Werner and Ortlieb, Eva eds. 2007. *Höchstgerichte in Europa. Bausteine frühneuzeitlicher Rechtsordnungen* (Quellen und Forschungen zur höchsten Gerichtsbarkeit im alten Reich 53). Cologne—Weimar—Vienna: Böhlau Verlag.

Bastien, Pascale. 2006. *L'exécution publique à Paris au XVIIIe siècle. Une histoire des rituels judiciaires*. Seyssel: Champ Vallon.

Berkvens, Aloysius M.J.A. 1999. *À propos van de affaire Laurent Timmermans*. Maastricht: FdR. Metajuridica.

Berkvens, Aloysius M.J.A. 2011. *Soevereine Raad te Roermond, Justiz-Collegium te Geldern en Staats Hof van Gelre te Venlo. Hoofdlijnen van proceduren in civiele zaken in Spaans en nadien Oostenrijks, Pruisisch en Staats (Opper)-Gelre in eerte aanleg en in hoger beroep 1580–1795*. Hilversum: Uitgeverij Verloren.

Bluche, Francois. 1986. *Les magistrats du Parlement de Paris au XVIIIe siècle*. Paris: Economica.

Broers, Erik Jan M.F.C. 1996. *Beledigingszaken voor de Staatse Raad van Brabant 1586–1795*. Assen: Van Gorcum.

Cappon, Cornelis, Stuurman, Jan G en, de Schepper, Hugo. eds. 1984. *Miscellanea Consilii Magni II. Bijdragen over rechtspraak van de Grote Raad van Mechelen*. Amsterdam: Universiteit van Amsterdam. Faculteit der rechtsgeleerdheid.

Cauchies, Jean-Marie and De Schepper, Hugo eds. 1994. *Justice, grâce et legislation. Genèse de l'Etat et moyens juridiques dans les Pays-Bas, 1200–1600* (Centre de recherches en histoire du droit et des institutions. Cahiers 2). Brussels: Facultés Universitaires Saint-Louis.

Cauchies, Jean-Marie and De Schepper, Hugo. 1997. *Legal tools of public power in the Netherlands, 1200–1600*. In *Legislation and justice*, ed. Antonio Padoa-Schioppa, 229–268. Oxford: Clarendon.

Champion, William A. 1997. Recourse to law and the meaning of the Great Litigation Decline, 1650–1750. Some clues from the Shrewsbury Local Courts. In *Communities and Courts in Britain*, eds. Christopher Brooks and Michael Lobban, 179–198. London: Hambledon Press.

Cochrane, Eric W. 1974. *Florence in the forgotten centuries: 1527–1800: a history of Florence and the Florentines in the Age of the Grand Dukes*. Chicago: University of Chicago Press.

Dauchy, Serge. 1995. *De processen in beroep uit Vlaanderen bij het Parlement van Parijs (1320–1521) een rechtshistorisch onderzoek naar de wording van de staat en soevereiniteit in de Bourgondisch-Habsburgse periode*. Brussels: Paleis der Academiën.

Dauchy, Serge, and Demars-Sion, Véronique eds. 2008. *Jurisprudence du Parlement de Flandre*. Brussels: Service public fédéral justice.

Deelder, C.L. and Huussen, Arend. 1973. Opmerkingen betreffende de kuilvisserij op de voormalige Zuiderzee, voornamelijk in de zestiende eeuw. *Holland, regionaal-historisch tijdschrift* 5: 221–242.

De Schepper, Hugo en Van Answaarden Robert. 1984. Grote Raad van Mechelen. Bibliografie. In *Miscelannea Consilii Magni II*. Eds. Cornelis Capon, Jan Stuurman en de Schepper Hugo, 171–193. Amsterdam: Universiteit van Amsterdam Faculteit der rechtsgeleerdheid.

De Schepper, Hugo. 2006. Staatsgezag en staatsmacht in de Nederlanden. Verworvenheden en beperkingen van het Bourgondisch-Habsburgse systeem. In *Staatsvorming onder de Bourgondiërs en Habsburgers. Theorie en Praktijk*, eds. Hugo de Schepper en Jacques Geurts, 13–50. Maastricht: Shaker.

De Schryver, Reginald. 1987. De Oostenrijkse aanspraken op de Spaans-Habsburgse erfenis. De Zuidelijke Nederlanden tijdens de Spaanse Successieoorlog. 1700–1716. In *Oostenrijks België 1713–1794. De Zuidelijke Nederlanden onder de Oostenrijkse Habsburgers*, ed. Hervé Hasquin, 11–36. Brussels: Gemeentekrediet van België.

De Smidt, Jacobus e.a. eds. 1966–1988. *Chronologische lijsten van de geëxtenderdeerde sententiën berustende in het archief van de Grote Raad van Mechelen*, 6 volumes. Brussels: Koninklijke Commissie voor de uitgave der oude wetten en verordeningen van België.

De Smidt, Jacobus Th. and Lindijer, Tony. 1999. *Haarlemmers voor de Grote Raad van Mechelen 1458–1578: gebaseerd op Algemeen Rijksarchief Brussel, fonds Grote Raad en Stadsarchief van Haarlem*. Haarlem: Historische Werkgroep/Vereeniging Haerlem.

Dhondt, Luc. 1995. De Nederlanden te Wenen in de 18de eeuw. Institutionele aanwezigheid en onderschikkings-en bestuurswijzen. In *Symposium over de centrale instellingen van de Habsburgse Nederlanden, Brussel 3 December 1994. Tien Bijdragen over de staat, de regering en de ambtenaren van de 16de tot de 18de eeuw* (Standen en Landen Bijzondere Reeks nr. 2), eds. Herman Coppens en Karin Van Honacker, 214–244. Brussels: Algemeen Rijksarchief.

Diestelkamp, Bernhard. 1976. Das Reichskammergericht im Rechtsleben des 16. Jahrhunderts. In *Rechtsgeschikte als Kulturgeschichte: Festschrift für Adalbert Erler zu 70. Geburtstag*, ed. Hans-Jürgen Becker, 353–369. Aalen: Scientia

Diestelkamp, Bernhard ed. 1996. *Oberste Gerichtsbarkeit und zentrale Gewalt im Europa der frühen Neuzeit (Quellen und Forschungen zur höchsten Gerichtsbarkeit im alten Reich 29)*, Cologne—Weimar—Vienna: Böhlau Verlag.

Diestelkamp, Bernhard, ed. 2002. *Das Reichskammergericht am Ende des alten Reiches und sein Fortwirken im 19. Jahrhundert*. Cologne: Böhlau Verlag.

Douxchamps-Lefèvre, Cécile. 1961. *Les procureurs généraux du Conseil de Namur sous le régime autrichien: leur action en matière politique: contribution à l'histoire des institutions et à l'histoire sociale du Namurois au XVIIIe siècle*. Louvain: Publications universitaires de Louvain.

Douxchamps-Lefèvre, Cécile. 1977. *Note sur le ressort de la juridiction d'appel du Grand Conseil de Malines au XVe et XVIe siècles. In Consilium magnum, 1473–1973: herdenking van de 500e verjaardag van de oprichting van het Parlement en Grote Raad van Mechelen*. Brussels: Algemeen Rijksarchief, 311–317.

Douxchamps-Lefevre, Cécile. 2003. Les sentences du Grand Conseil de Malines en appel d'instances namuroises (1582–1590). *Handelingen van de Koninklijke Commissie voor de uitgave der Oude Wetten en Verordeningen van België* 44: 59–136.

Doyle, William. 1970. The Parlements of France and the breakdown of the Old Régime 1771–1788. *French Historical Studies* 6: 415–458.

Dupont-Bouchat, Marie-Sylvie, and Page-Steffens, Marie-Paule. 2006. Des délits et des peines: l'activité pénale du Conseil Provincial de Namur au XVIIIe siècle. In *La Belgique criminelle: droit, justice, société (XIVe-XXe siècles)*, eds. Marie-Sylvie Dupont-Bouchat and Xavier Rousseaux, 273–316. Louvain-la-Neuve: Academia-Bruylant.

Egret, Jean. 1970. *Louis XV et l'opposition parlementaire, 1715–1774*. Paris: Colin.

Elliott, John H. 1992. A Europe of composite monarchies. *Past and Present* 137.1: 48–71.

Feutry, David. 2012. The historian's mountain of paper: the Parlement of Pariss and the analysis of civil suits in the eighteenth century. *French History* 26.3: 277–296.

Fuchs, Ralf-Peter. 2003. The Supreme Court of the Holy Roman Empire: the state of research and the outlook. *Sixteenth Century Journal* 34.1: 9–27.

Gaillard, Arthur. 1898–1902. *Le Conseil de Brabant: histoire, organisation, procédure*. Brussels: Lebègue.

Gaillard, Arthur. 1900–1903. Inventaire des mémoriaux du Grand Conseil de Malines. Brussels: Weissenbruch.

Gilissen, John. 1977. Oprichting en evolutie van het Parlement/De Grote Raad van Mechelen. In *Consilium magnum, 1473–1973: herdenking van de 500e verjaardag van de oprichting van het Parlement en de Grote Raad van Mechelen*, 11–24. Brussels: Algemeen Rijksarchief.

Gilissen, John. 1980. De Grote Raad van Mechelen. Historisch overzicht. In *Miscelannea Consilii Magni. Ter gelegenheid van twintig jaar Werkgroep Grote Raad van Mechelen*, 13–43. Amsterdam: Universiteit van Amsterdam. Faculteit der rechtsgeleerdheid.

Godding, Philippe. 1999. *Le Conseil de Brabant sous le règne de Philippe le Bon 1430–1467*. Brussels: Académie royale de Belgique. Classe des lettres.

Godding, Philippe, and Petit, Roger. 2001. Les sentences du Grand Conseil de Malines relatives au duché de Luxembourg (1582–1590). *Handelingen van de Koninklijke Commissie voor de uitgave der Oude Wetten en Verordeningen van België* 42: 63–201.

Hempenius-Van Dijck, Barendina e.a. 1999. *De Heeren van den Raeden: biografieën en groepsportret van de raadsheren van het Hof van Friesland, 1499–1811*. Hilversum: Uitgeverij Verloren.

Hildesheimer, Francoise. 2004. Exemplaire Parlement… Le fonds du Parlement de Paris aux archives nationales. *Revue de synthèse* 125.1: 45–81.

Holenstein, André. 2009. Introduction: Empowering interactions: looking at statebuilding from below. In *Empowering interactions. Political cultures and the emergence of the state in Europe 1300–1900*, eds. Wim Blockmans, André Holenstein and Jon Matthieu, 1–33. Farnham: Ashgate.

Holmes, Clive. 1997. Legal instruments of power and the state in Early Modern England. In *Legislation and justice*, ed. Antonio Padoa-Schioppa, 269–289. Oxford: Clarendon.

Huijbregts, L.J.J. e.a. 1981. *Leidenaars voor de Grote Raad (1470–1580): processen uit het archief van de Grote Raad (Parlement) van Mechelen met betrekking tot instellingen en bewoners van de stad Leiden*. Leiden: s.n.

Huussen, Arend e.a. 1964–1974. *Inventaris en beschrijving van de processtukken (dossiers) behorende tot de beroepen uit Holland berustende in het archief van de Grote Raad van Mechelen Algemeen Rijksarchief Brussel*. Amsterdam: s.n.

Huussen, Arend. 1978. Jurisprudentie en bureaucratie: het Hof van Friesland en zijn criminele rechtspraak in de 18de eeuw. *Low Countries Historical Review* 93.2: 529–550.

Hüsken, Wim, Installé, Henri, and Oosterbosch, Michel (eds). 2004. *De Grote Raad: moord, woordbreuk en andere schandalen*. Brussel: Algemeen Rijksarchief.

Jahns, Sigrid. 1990. Die Personalverfassung des Reichskammergerichts unter Anpassungsdruck. Lösungen im Spannungsfeld zwischen Modernität und Überalterung. In *Das Reichskammergericht in der deutschen Geschichte: Stand der Forschung, Forschungsperspektiven (Quellen und Forschungen zur höchsten Gerichtsbarkeit im alten Reich 21)*, ed. Bernhard Diestelkamp, 59–109. Cologne: Böhlau.

Jahns, Sigrid. 2011. *Das Reichskammergericht und seine Richter: Verfassug und Sozialstruktur eines höchsten Gerichts im Alten Reich*. Cologne: Böhlau.

Kagan, Richard L. 1981. *Lawsuits and litigants in Castile, 1500–1700*. Chapel Hill: University of North Carolina Press.

Kaiser, Colin. 1980. The deflation in the volume of litigation at Paris in the Eighteenth Century and the waning of the old judicial order. *European Studies Review* 10.3: 309–336.

Kerckhoffs-De Hey, A.J.M. 1980. *De Grote raad en zijn functionarissen, 1477–1531*. Amsterdam: s.n.

Koenigsberger, Helmut Georg. 1986. 'Dominium Regale' or 'Dominium Politicum et Regale'. In *Politicians and virtuosi: Essays in Early Modern History*, ed. Helmut Georg Koenigsberger, 1–26. London: University of London.

Koster-Van Dijk, Joke M.I. and, Wijffels, Alain. 1990. Les procédures en révision au Grand Conseil de Malines (1473–1580). *Publications du Centre Européen d'Etudes Bourguignonnes* 30: 67–97.

Koster-Van Dijck, Joke M.I. 1979. *Gooilanders voor de Grote Raad (1470–1572): Processen uit het archief van de Grote Raad van Mechelen met betrekking tot inwoners en instellingen in en om Gooiland*. Amsterdam: Faculteit der Rechtsgeleerdheid.

Krynen, Jacques. 2009. *L'Etat de justice. France (XIIIe-XXe siècle). Vol 1: l'idéologie de la magistrature ancienne*. Paris: Gaillimard.

Le Bailly, Marie-Charlotte. 2001. *Recht voor de Raad: rechtspraak voor het Hof van Holland, Zeeland en West-Friesland in het midden van de vijftiende eeuw*. Hilversum: Uitgeverij Verloren.

Le Bailly, Marie-Charlotte. 2007. Staatse Raad van Vlaanderen te Middelburg (1599–1795): De hoofdlijnen van procederen in civiele zaken voor de Staatse Raad van Vlaanderen zowel in eerste instantie als in hoger beroep. Hilversum: Uitgeverij Verloren.

Le Bailly, Marie-Charlotte. 2008. *Hof van Holland, Zeeland en West-Friesland: De hoofdlijnen van het procederen in civiele zaken voor het Hof van Holland, Zeeland en West-Friesland zowel in eerste instantie als in hoger beroep*. Hilversum: Uitgeverij Verloren.

Le Bailly, Marie-Charlotte. 2011. Langetermijntrends in dc rechtspraak bij de gewestelijke hoven van justitie in de Noordelijke Nederlanden van ca. 1450 tot ca. 1800. *Pro Memorie* 13: 30–67.

Le Bailly, Marie-Charlotte, and Verhas, Christel. 2006. *Hoge Raad van Holland, Zeeland and West-Friesland (1582–1795): De hoofdlijnen van het procederen in civiele zaken voor de Hoge Raad zowel in eerste instantie als in hoger beroep*. Hilversum: Uitgeverij Verloren.

Le parlement de Flandre à travers ses archives. 2009. *Revue du Nord* 382.

Lenders, Piet. 1988. Trois façons de gouverner dans les Pays-Bas autrichiens. In *Unité et diversité de l'empire de Habsbourg à la fin du XVIIIe siècle* (Etudes sur le XVIIIe siècle 15), eds Hervé Hasquin and Roland Mortier, 41–53. Brussels: Université de Bruxelles.

Lenders, Piet. 1995. Ontstaan en ontwikkeling van de moderne staat in de Nederlanden. In *Symposium over de centrale instellingen van de Habsburgse Nederlanden, Brussel 3 december 1994. Tien Bijdragen over de staat, de regering en de ambtenaren van de 16de tot de 18de eeuw* (Standen en Landen Bijzondere Reeks nr. 2), eds. Herman Coppens en Karin Van Honacker, 1–42. Brussels: Algemeen Rijksarchief.

Levy, René, and Rousseaux, Xavier. 1992. Etats, justice pénale et histoire: bilan et perspectives. *Droit et Société* 20–21: 53–82.

Leyder, Dirk. 2010. *Les archives du Grand Conseil des Pays-Bas à Malines (vers 1445–1797)*. Brussels: Algemeen Rijksarchief.

Leyder, Dirk. 2012. *Inventaire des archives du Grand Conseil des Pays-Bas à Malines: dossiers de procès de Flandre-Clergé 1545–1792*. Brussels: Algemeen Rijksarchief.

Mader, Eric-Olivier. 2002. 'Heilige Schulden' des aufgelösten Reichs. Das Problem der Entschädigung des Reichskammergerichtspersonals für den Verlust ihrer Stellen. In *Das Reichskammergericht am Ende des alten Reiches und sein Fortwirken im 19. Jahrhundert*, ed. Bernhard Diestelkamp, 105–142. Cologne: Böhlau Verlag.

Maes, Louis Th. 1975. Gerechtelijke beslissingen in strafzaken, 16e–18e eeuw. Een vergiftigingszaak 1697–1702. In *De besluitvorming vroeger en nu* (Algemeen rijksarchief en rijksarchief in de provinciën. Educatieve Dienst. Catalogus 49), eds. Hugo de Schepper and John Gilissen, 197–236. Brussels: Algemeen Rijksarchief.

Maes, Louis Th. 1979. Twee arresten van de Grote Raad van Mechelen over de tol van Iersekeroord. In *Recht heeft vele significatie: rechtshistorische opstellen*, ed. Louis Th. Maes, 137–160. Brussels: Ced-Samson.

Maes, Louis Th. 2009. *Het Parlement en de Grote Raad van Mechelen: 1473–1797*. Antwerp: De Vries-Brouwers.

Monballyu, Jos. 1996. De Raad van Vlaanderen en de hervorming van het strafrecht (1756–1787). *Tijdschrift voor Rechtsgeschiedenis* 54: 47–77.

Monballyu, Jos. 1998. Chronologische Lijst van de Nederlandstalige geëxtedeerde sententiën van de Grote Raad van Mechelen (1581–1590). *Handelingen van de Koninklijke Commissie voor de uitgave der Oude Wetten en Verordeningen van België* 39: 79–146.

Monballyu, Jos. 1998. De Raad van Vlaanderen, een soevereine justitieraad in strafzaken? In *Handelingen van het tweede Hof van Holland Symposium gehouden op 14 November 1997 in de Treveszaal te Den Haag*, ed. Rob Huijbrecht, 77–90. The Hague: Algemeen Rijksarchief.

Monballyu, Jos. 2001. De hoofdlijnen van de criminele strafprocedure in het graafschap Vlaanderen (16de tot 18de eeuw). In *Voortschrijdend procesrecht. Een historische verkenning*, eds. Fred Stevens, Ernest Persoons and Remco Van Rhee, 63–108. Leuven: Universitaire Pers Leuven.

Neve, Paul Lucien. 1972. *Het Rijkskamergerecht en de Nederlanden: competentie-territoir-archieven*. Assen: Van Gorcum.

Oosterbosch, Michel. 1998. *Grote Raad voor de Nederlanden te Mechelen: procesbundels beroepen uit Vlaanderen: ordinaris processen (nr. 1–1000)*. Brussels: Algemeen Rijksarchief.

Oosterbosch, Michel. 2001. *Appelprocedure, dossierbehandeling en registervoering bij de Grote Raad van Mechelen*. In: *Voortschrijdend procesrecht. Een historische verkenning*, eds. Fred Stevens, Ernest Persoons and Remco Van Rhee, 3–25. Leuven: Universitaire Pers Leuven.

Oosterbosch, Michel. 2006. *Inventaris van het archief van de Grote Raad voor de Nederlanden te Mechelen: procesbundels beroepen uit Holland 1460–1740*. Brussels: Algemeen Rijksarchief.

Put, Eddy. 1995. *Grote Raad van Mechelen. Processen van aanzienlijke families (Reeksen A en B): werkbeschrijvingen*. Brussels: Algemeen Rijksarchief.

Put, Eddy. 1995. *Officie-fiscaal van de Grote Raad van Mechelen: werkbeschrijvingen*. Brussels: Algemeen Rijksarchief.

Rogister, John. 1995. *Louis XV and the Parlement of Paris, 1737–1755*. Cambridge: Cambridge University Press.

Sharpe, James Anthony. 1997. The law, law enforcement, state formation and national integration in late medieval and early modern England. In *Le pénal dans tous ses états: justice, états et sociétés en Europe (XII-XXe siècles)* (Publications des Facultés universitaires Saint Louis 74), eds. René Levy and Xavier Rousseaux, 65–80. Brussels: FUSL.

Sicking, Louis. 1998. *Zeemacht en onmacht: maritieme politiek in de Nederlanden 1488–1558*. Amsterdam: Bataafsche Leeuw.

Simon, Jules. 1921. La procédure criminelle sous l'ancien régime (Grand Conseil de Malines). *Handelingen van de Koninklijke Commissie voor de uitgave van oude wetten en verordeningen van België* 10: 397–437.

Snep, M.G.M. 1988. Bibliografie van de Grote Raad van Mechelen. In *Miscellanea forensia historica: ter gelegenheid van het afscheid van Prof. mr. J.Th de Smidt* (Verzamelen en bewerken van de jurisprudentie van de Grote Raad, nieuwe reeks, 14), eds. Jacobus de Smidt, Joke M.I. Koster-Van Dijck en Alain Wijffels, 389–398. Amsterdam: Werkgroep Grote Raad van Mechelen.

Soman, Alfred. 1992. *Sorcellerie et justice criminelle: le Parlement de Paris (16e–18e siècles)*. Hampshire-Brookfield: Variorum.

Stein, Hans Konrad. 2002. Das Schicksal der unerledigten Mecklenburger Reichskammergerichts Prozesse und die Idee einer obersten Berufungs Instanz in Mecklenburg nach Ende der Reichsgerichte 1806. In *Das Reichskammergericht am Ende des alten Reiches und sein Fortwirken im 19. Jahrhundert*, ed. Bernhard Diestelkamp, 217–249. Cologne: Böhlau Verlag.

Stroobant, Louis. 1903. *Les magistrats du Grand Conseil de Malines*. Antwerp: s.n.

Swann, Julian. 1995. *Politics and the Parlement of Paris under Louis XV, 1754–1774*. Cambridge: Cambridge University Press.

Thomas, Cathérine. 2013. Hommes d'Etat, hommes de loi. Les conseillers du Grand Conseil de Malines au XVIIe siècle. In *Gouvernance et administration dans les provinces belges (XVIe-XVIIIe siècles)* (Archives et Bibliothèques de Belgique 99), Eds. Claude De Morbeau de Gerbehaye e.a., 155–177. Brussels: Archives et Bibliothèques de Belgique.

Van Answaarden, Robert. 1991. *Les Portugais devant le Grand Conseil des Pays-Bas (1460–1580)*. Paris: Fondation Calouste Gulbenkian.

Van de Pol, Lotte. 1996. *Het Amsterdams hoerdom. Prostitutie in de zeventiende en achttiende eeuw*. Amsterdam: Wereldbibliotheek.

Van den Bussche, Emile. 1992. *Inventaire des registres du Grand Conseil de Malines: avec un supplément pour les Nos 1186 à 1553 (Requêtes et varia en portefeuilles)*. Brussels: Algemeen Rijksarchief.

Van der Mijnsbrugge, Emile. s.d. *Grand Conseil de Malines. Inventaire des appels de Malines* (Inventaris van de Derde Afdeling 66). S.l.: s.n.

Van der Mijnsbrugge, E. s.d. *Grand Conseil de Malines. Inventaire des appels de magistrats locaux de Luxembourg* (Inventaris van de Derde Afdeling 75). S.l.: s.n.

Van der Mijnsbrugge, Emile. s.d. *Grand Conseil de Malines. Inventaire des appels des magistrats locaux de la province de Namur* (Inventaris van de Derde Afdeling 85). S.l.: s.n.

Van Honacker, Karin. 1995. Het einde van het ancien régime in de Oostenrijkse Nederlanden: zoeken naar het herstel van een modus vivendi. In *Symposium over de centrale overheidsinstellingen van de Habsburgse Nederlanden. Tien Bijdragen over de staat, de regering en de ambtenaren van de 16de tot de 18de eeuw* (Standen en Landen, speciale serie 2), eds. Herman Coppens and Karin Van Honacker, 245–266. Brussels: Algemeen Rijksarchief.

Van Peteghem, Paul. 1990. *De Raad van Vlaanderen en staatsvorming onder Karel V (1515–1555): een publiekrechtelijk onderzoek naar centralisatiestreven in de XVII Provinciën*. Nijmegen: Gerard Noodt Instituut.

Van Poelgeest, L. 1988. De raadsheren van de Hoge Raad van Holland, Zeeland en West-Friesland in de achttiende eeuw. *Bijdragen en mededelingen betreffende de geschiedenis der Nederlanden* 103.1: 20–51.

Van Rhee, Remco. 1997. *Litigation and legislation: civil procedure at first instance in the Great Council of for the Netherlands in Malines (1522–1559)*. Brussels: Algemeen Rijksarchief.

Van Rhee, Remco, and Wijffels, Alain (eds.). 2013. *European Supreme Courts. A portrait through history*. London: Third millennium publications.

Van Rompaey, Jan. 1973. *De Grote Raad van de hertogen van Boergondië en het parlement van Mechelen* (Verhandelingen van de Koninklijke Academie voor wetenschappen, letteren en schone kunsten van België. Klasse der Letteren 73). Brussels: Koninklijke Academie voor wetenschappen, letteren en schone kunsten van België.

Van Rompaey, Jan. 1977. *De procedure in beroep bij het Parlement van Mechelen*. In *Consilium magnum, 1473–1973: herdenking van de 500e verjaardag van de oprichting van het Parlement en de Grote Raad van Mechelen*, 371–381. Brussels: Algemeen Rijksarchief.

Verhaegen, Paul. 1894. Le Grand Conseil de Malines en 1795. *Handelingen van de Koninklijke Kring voor Oudheidkunde, Letteren en Kunst in Mechelen* 5:209–217.

Verhas, Christel. 1997. *De beginjaren van de Hoge Raad van Holland, Zeeland en West-Friesland*. The Hague: Algemeen Rijksarchief.

Verkerk, Cornelis L. 1985. De werkgroep 'Grote Raad van Mechelen'. *Holland, Regionaal-historische tijdschrift* 17: 331–340.

Verscuren, An. 2005. *"L'oeil et le bras du Roi?" Het vervolgingsbeleid van het officie-fiscaal van de Grote Raad van Mechelen (1767–1788)*. Unpublished Master's Thesis. Leuven: Katholieke Universiteit Leuven.

Verscuren, An. 2006. (S)pionnen van de vorst? De fiscalen van de Grote Raad in de tweede helft van de achttiende eeuw. *Pro Memorie* 8.2: 246–273.

Verscuren, An. 2013. *Nadere toegang op de geëxtendeerde sententies van de Grote Raad van Mechelen: 1693–1772*. Brussels: Algemeen Rijksarchief.

Vervondel, Eva. 2004. *De Grote Raad van Mechelen van 1780 tot 1797. De laatste Jaren en de verdwijning*. Unpublished Master's Thesis. Leuven: Katholieke Universiteit Leuven

Wijffels, Alain. 1985. *Qui millies allegatur: les allegations du droit savant dans les dossiers du Grand Conseil de Lalines (causes septentrionales, ca. 1460–1580)*. Leiden: Brill.

Wijffels, Alain. 1989. Legal Records and Reports in the Great Council of Malines (15th to 18th century). In *Judicial Records, Law Reports and the Growth of Case Law*, ed. John H. Baker, 181–206. Berlin: Duncker und Humblot.

Wijffels, Alain. 1994. Grote Raad voor de Nederlanden te Mechelen (ca.1445–1797). In *De centrale overheidsinstellingen van de Habsburgse Nederlanden*, ed. Erik Aerts e.a., 448–461. Brussels: Algemeen Rijksarchief.

Wijffels, Alain. 1997. Grand Conseil de Malines: la rédaction des sentences étendues et le recueil de jurisprudence de Guillaume de Grysperre. In *Case law in the making: the techniques and methods of judicial records and law reports (Comparative studies in continental and Anglo-American Legal History 17)* v.1, ed. Alain Wijffels, 299–316. Berlin: Duncker und Humblot.

Wijffels, Alain. 1997. Höchste Gerichtsbarkeit als Instrument der Friedenserhaltung. In *Friedenssicherung und Rechtsgewährung. Sechs Beiträge zur Geschichte des Reichskammergerichts und der obersten Gerichtsbarkeit im alten Europa*, eds. Bernard Diestelkamp and Ingrid Scheurmann. Bonn: AsKI.

Wijffels, Alain. 2002. Zeeuwse steden voor de Grote Raad. *Pro Memorie* 4.2: 266–293.

Wijffels, Alain. 2009. Dutch litigation before the Great Council of Mechlin. An additional calendar of the 'Appeals from Holland'. *Tijdschrift voor rechtsgeschiedenis* 77: 539–550.

Chapter 2
The Face of Justice: A Career Analysis of the Eighteenth Century Members of the Great Council

2.1 Introduction

"Le souverain établit, réforme ou supprime des institutions. Dans le quotidien, ses 'très obéissants et fidèles serviteurs et sujets' les forgent, les portent par leur action ou les abandonnent à la léthargie."[1] In the introduction to his biographic dictionary of the civil servants in the central institutions of the eighteenth century Austrian Netherlands,[2] C. Bruneel highlighted the importance of the people populating an institution. R. Mousnier argued that it is even possible to wholly identify an institution by its people.[3] Both authors asserted that to gain a better understanding of any institution of the Ancien Régime, a biographic—and social—study of its members is essential. Indeed, while all administrative bodies were established by the sovereign—and almost all without exception, are regulated by fixed decree—it is indisputable that the human factor molds the institution, gives it its own character and is ultimately responsible for its reputation.[4] Or, as Mousnier stated, we can only speak of an institution if its procedures are incorporated in the men who put them into practice, make them compulsory and thereby impose actions on other people.[5]

[1] Bruneel, Claude and Hoyois, Jean-Paul. 2001. *Les grands commis des Pays-Bas autrichiens: dictionnaire biografphique du personnel des institutions centrales*. Brussels: Algemeen Rijksarchief, 5.

[2] Conspicuously, Bruneel does not count the members of the Great Council among the *grands commis*. Only those councilors who continued their career in the Privy Council, the Council of State, the High Council of the Netherlands in Vienna or anything alike figure in his biographic dictionary.

[3] Mousnier, Roland. 1970. *La plume, la faucille et le marteau: institutions et société en France du moyen âge à la Révolution*. Paris: PUF, 8. "Mais le groupe d'hommes est partie intégrante de l'institution. En simplifiant et en forçant les termes, l'on pourrait presque dire qu'une institution, c'est un groupe d'hommes."

[4] Bruneel, Claude and Hoyois, Jean-Paul. 2001. *Les grands commis des Pays-Bas autrichiens: dictionnaire biografphique du personnel des institutions centrales*. Brussels: Algemeen Rijksarchief, 5.

[5] Mousnier, Roland. 1970. La plume, la faucille et le marteau: institutions et société en France du moyen âge à la Révolution. Paris: PUF, 8.

A. Verscuren, *The Great Council of Malines in the 18th century*,
Studies in the History of Law and Justice 3, DOI 10.1007/978-3-319-09638-4_2

Employing Bruneel's and Mousnier's writings, we composed an image of the councilors of the Great Council of the eighteenth century. During the final century of the tribunal's existence, 94 councilors and eight presidents administered justice in Malines. In theory, at any given time in the eighteenth century, the Great Council counted, divided over two chambers, one president, who was responsible for the smooth running of the tribunal, and 16 councilors, 14 laymen and two clergymen.[6] In general, the *procureur-général* (procurator-general) and *avocat-fiscal* (advocate-fiscal) were selected from the lay councilors and made up the 'prosecution', designed to protect and defend the sovereign's interests.[7]

The appointment records—preserved in the archives of the Privy Council, the Council of State, the Royal Council of Philip V and the *Conseil du gouvernement général*[8]—constitute the primary source for this chapter. As these files were 'confidential' documents, not meant to be distributed outside the small circle of government officials, they allow a privileged view into the inner workings of the administration. The members of both the Great Council and the advising Council—*in casu* predominantly the Council of State (before 1725) and the Privy Council—did not shy away from venting their uncompromising opinions about the candidates in their reports. The 'private' character of these comments—which were always meant to influence the decision-making process—makes it possible to reconstruct the motives and decisive arguments which led to the appointment of a certain candidate. At the same time, they lay bare certain issues connected to the appointments, such as the difficulties surrounding the nomination of fiscals or of clerical councilors.[9] In addition to these files, biographical descriptions of the presidents and councilors of the Great Council resting in the *Manuscrits divers* are used.[10] Even though it is not evident why these short biographies were recorded[11] and experience has proved that they are not always entirely reliable, they do provide vital supplementary information.

[6] Wijffels, Alain. 1994. Grote Raad voor de Nederlanden te Mechelen (ca. 1445–1797). In *De centrale overheidsinstellingen van de Habsburgse Nederlanden*, ed. Erik Aerts e.a., 448–461. Brussels: Algemeen Rijksarchief.

[7] Two registrars and about four to six secretaries completed the main body of the Great Council. However, the procedures used for their appointment and their backgrounds are outside the scope of this work.

[8] Brussels, ARA, GRO, Kartons, 442A, 443A, 443B; Brussels, ARA, RvSt, 651, 653, 654, 655 and 656; ARA, Regentschapsraad van State, 286; Brussels, Koninklijke Raad van Filips V, 1702–1711, 19; Brussels, ARA, ARR, 857, 858, 974.

[9] Cf. infra, 2.2.2.2 Personal merits and 2.2.4 Recruiting *l'oeil et le bras du Roi*.

[10] Brussels, ARA, MD, 860/A, 860/B and 432. The last entry in MD 432 is the biographic portrait of Antoine Reniers; he was appointed in 1789. Therefore, this document does not provide any information on Denis Baujoz, Jean Bernard de Guchtenaere, François d'Hoop and Guillaume Van Cutsem.

[11] We are not exactly sure who composed these prosopographic sketches of the councilors of the Great Council or why this was done. Possibly, it was destined to underline the importance of the Council. Since the last four councilors are not included, we can presume that it is an original eighteenth century compilation.

In this chapter, we first look into the appointment process, describing the procedure and discerning which elements may have motivated the decision to prefer one candidate to another. Outside attempts to influence the procedure are also touched upon. Secondly, we sketch a profile of the councilors as a professional group, taking into account their social background, geographical origin, career path, family ties and education. Throughout, we confront our findings with the characteristics of the members of the Great Council in earlier centuries[12] as well as with the social portrait of councilors in other, more or less comparable institutions.[13]

2.2 The Right Man for the Job: The Appointment Procedure[14]

2.2.1 The Process

The procedure for appointing a councilor to the Great Council is touched upon briefly in the general ordinance of 1559.[15] Article 8 established that the Great Council enjoyed the *droit de terne*, the right to suggest three 'capable and honor-

[12] Kerckhoffs-De Hey, A.J.M. 1980. *De Grote raad en zijn functionarissen, 1477–1531*. Amsterdam: s.n; Thomas, Cathérine. 2013. Hommes d'Etat, hommes de loi. Les conseillers du Grand Conseil de Malines au XVIIe siècle. In *Gouvernance et administration dans les provinces belges (XVIe–XVIIIe siècles)* (Archives et Bibliothèques de Belgique 99), Eds. De Morbeau de Gerbehaye e.a., 155–177. Brussels: Archives et Bibliothèques de Belgique.

[13] Alix, Flore. 2009. Les critères de sélection des hauts fonctionnaires des Pays-Bas méridionaux (1700–1725). *Belgisch tijdschrift voor filologie en geschiedenis* 87: 297–348; Hempenius-Van Dijck, Barendina e.a. 1999. *De Heeren van den Raeden: biografieën en groepsportret van de raadsheren van het Hof van Friesland, 1499–1811*. Hilversum: Uitgeverij Verloren; Gaillard, Arthur. 1898–1902. *Le Conseil de Brabant: histoire, organisation, procédure*. Brussels: Lebègue; Van Poelgeest, L. 1888. De raadsheren van de Hoge Raad van Holland, Zeeland en West-Friesland in de achttiende eeuw. *Bijdragen en mededelingen betreffende de geschiedenis der Nederlanden* 103.1: 20–51.

[14] Lefèvre published several documents concerning the recruitment of civil servants in both the Spanish and Austrian Netherlands: Lefèvre, Joseph. 1975. *Documents concernant le recrutement de la haute magistrature dans les Pays-Bas, sous le régime espagnol, 1555–1700*. Brussels: Palais des Académies; Lefèvre, Joseph. 1939. *Documents concernant le recrutement de la haute magistrature dans les Pays-Bas autrichiens au XVIIIe siècle*. Brussels: Palais des Académies. He also wrote an article on the appointment of judicial officers during the French occupation of the mid-1740s: Lefèvre, Joseph. 1934. Les nominations faites dans la magistrature pendant l'occupation française, 1746–1747. *Revue belge de philologie et d'histoire* 13: 697–711.

[15] *ROPB*, 2ième série, t. 7, pp. 461–492. For the Dutch translation, see: Bolsée, Jean. 1969–1970. L'ordonnance du 8 août 1559 réglant le statut, le style et la manière de procéder du Grand Conseil de Malines (texte néerlandais). *Handelingen van de Koninklijke Commissie voor de uitgave der Oude Wetten en Verordeningen van België* 24: 77–152.

able' nominees to fill each vacancy for a councilor, fiscal or registrar position.[16] The sovereign was committed to appointing one out of those three. Furthermore, none of the candidates was allowed to present gifts or promise favors in order to be selected. The information gathered from the appointment records makes it possible to put this theory on trial and describe how the nomination and selection occurred in practice.

2.2.1.1 The Droit de Terne

The appointment records confirm the habit of selecting three nominees. When a councilor died or was promoted—only once during the eighteenth century did a councilor resign without having another position organized[17]—the Great Council announced the vacancy and invited potential candidates to come forward before a pre-determined date. After the term expired, each councilor had to select three applicants during a joint session of both chambers, ranking them in preference. The nominee with the highest total of ballots behind his name—who, coincidence or not, also always assembled the highest number of first-choice votes—figured first in the ranking, followed by his two closest contenders. In 1759, the procedure was slightly modified: instead of merely hierarchically listing the nominees, the sovereign required the Great Council to specifically state the number of votes each had obtained.[18] The appointment record of Diu as deputy procurator-general proves that these regulations needed time to filter through in practice: in 1763, the Privy Council had to remind the Great Council of this regulation.[19]

Possibly, the Great Council was not very eager to apply the rule. The Council of Brabant, at least, had severe reservations and even refused to comply because it would certainly cause trouble: a newly appointed councilor only had to leaf through the recommendations to know who had voted for another candidate. The consequences of this to the collegial harmony would certainly be disastrous. Moreover—the chancellor of Brabant noted—this formality was useless as the government always appointed the nominee it favored most and completely disregarded the number of votes received![20]

---

[16] Other courts of justice were equally granted this privilege. One example is the Council of Brabant. Cf. Gaillard, Arthur. 1898–1902. *Le Conseil de Brabant: histoire, organisation, procédure*. Brussels: Lebègue, p. 232.

[17] This was the case of councilor Robert Happart. His resignation was not exactly entirely voluntary. Cf. infra, 2.2.3 The 'Result' of the nomination procedure.

[18] *ROPBA*, t. 8, p. 339, October 18, 1759.

[19] Brussels, ARA, GRO 442A, 1763: appointment record of Henri Diu as deputy procurator-general.

[20] Gaillard, Arthur. 1898–1902. *Le Conseil de Brabant: histoire, organisation, procédure*. Brussels: Lebègue, 237: "Du reste, ajouta le chancelier, cette formalité est inutile, car le gouvernement général choisit toujours, parmi les candidats présentés, celui qui lui est le plus agréable, sans se préoccuper du nombre de suffrages qu'il a obtenu." In order to remedy at least the first problem,

It is unclear if the members of the Great Council shared the chancellor's concern that the new regulation would cause internal quibbles. At any rate, the appointment records of Melchior Goubau and Jean Louis Pouppez seem to suggest that at least in the late eighteenth century, the candidates for membership in the Great Council, even before their actual appointment, very well knew how they were ranked.[21] However, they were probably not aware of which councilors had not voted for them. While the central government certainly did not completely disregard the Great Council's rankings, the tribunal may have shared some of the Council of Brabant's frustrations. Indeed, the Great Council's preferences were followed as often as not. Somewhat remarkably, especially in the late seventeenth and early eighteenth centuries, the Great Council's ranking was often disregarded, while in the latter part of the eighteenth century, its advice was usually followed.[22]

Regardless, the tribunal attached great importance to the privilege of pre-selecting three candidates. In several instances, the councilors claimed that they considered the *droit de terne* a 'duty' rather than a prerogative, a matter of conscience, thereby unburdening the sovereign's, and assuring the independence of the procedure.[23] However, while there is no denying that the councilors regarded their right of presentation as an important responsibility, their main motives for defending this privilege were of course of an entirely different nature: the *droit de terne* gave them the opportunity to propose candidates they preferred, not necessarily because of their competence, but rather because of personal reasons, networking concerns, because they needed (to return) a favor etc. There should be no doubt that every nomination involved considerable lobbying.

Only once during the eighteenth century was the Great Council not allowed to compose a *terne* and instead was forced to accept a candidate imposed by the central government. In July 1789, after the promotion of Jacques Joseph de Stassart to the presidency of the Council of Namur, the *Conseil du gouvernement général* (Council of General Government) informed the tribunal in Malines that—due to 'special circumstances'—councilor de Stassart would be replaced by the *pensionaire* of the city of Leuven Antoine Reniers.[24] As far as is known, the members of the Great Council did not protest this infraction of their much cherished privilege. Was it because they had been assured that this was exceptional and would not be considered a rule for the future? Indeed, the next nomination went by the book. Or was this exception tolerated because they had only very recently been awarded the jurisdiction of the abolished Council of Brabant?[25]

---

governor Charles of Lorraine decided that the nominations had to be recorded into a separate register to be personally kept by the chancellor.

[21] Brussels, ARA, ARR 857, petition of Jean Louis Pouppez, January 13, 1788: "C'est avec le plus profond respect que le soussigné ose représenter à votre excellence qu'il est nommé le premier dans le terne des sujets que le grand conseil vient de proposer …".

[22] Cf. Excel database: Councilors of the eighteenth century Great Council.

[23] Brussels, ARA, RvSt 653, 1693: Advice of the Council of State on the petition of Ehrmans.

[24] Brussels, ARA, ARR 857, 1789: appointment record of Antoine Reniers.

[25] Cf. infra, Chap. 5.

2.2.1.2 The Advising Council's Opinion

After the Great Council had nominated three, or if there was an equality of votes, four candidates, it sent its list with some accompanying remarks—about the nominees' personal background, their university studies, their former career, etc.—to the governor, who in turn forwarded it to the advising council. The nominees must somehow have been notified that they were shortlisted. Indeed, after the Great Council's selection—and not before—many of them petitioned the governor[26] to publicize their personal accomplishments, and those of their family members, their loyalty to the Austrian government—this was especially so during or right after a revolt or period of foreign rule[27]—their careers, the number of nominations already received etc. As the Council of State and the Privy Council usually indiscriminately copied these requests into a summarized version, without checking the assertions of the petitioners and without mentioning the source of the information, these could be a powerful tool in promoting one's candidacy.

Yet, overstating one's abilities and accomplishments could backfire. For example, Jean Baptiste Van der Fosse did not shy away from exuding self-importance when writing to the governor in 1776. Not only did he mention his brilliant career at the University of Leuven, he also boasted of his further accomplishments, characterizing them as 'essential' to the sovereign. According to him, his ancestors had even sacrificed their liberty, fortune and their lives for the sovereign, both in the army and in the administration, thereby further proving his dedication and worth. Furthermore, he claimed that his personal successes had earned him the praise and esteem of many distinguished families and important people. Finally, he had been nominated twice for a seat on the Council, with distinction and applause, but he acknowledged that there had been external circumstances which had prevented his appointment so far. He was convinced that this was the moment for his promotion.[28] Van der Fosse's self-aggrandizement gave the Privy Council a rather negative impression of him. In the end, he did receive the appointment, but only because he apologized and told the Privy Council that the letter had filled him with aversion

[26] To name only a few which have been preserved: Jacques Stalins (Brussels, ARA, RvSt 653, 1685: appointment record of Jacques Stalins); Auguste de Steenhault (Brussels, ARA, Regentschapsraad van State 285, 1711: appointment record of Jean Alphonse de Coloma; 1712: appointment record of Auguste de Steenhault); Joseph d'Olmen (Brussels, ARA, RvSt 654, 1723: appointment record of Pierre Claude de St Vaast); Charles Thomas Caimo (Brussels, ARA, GRO 443B, 1738: appointment record of Charles Thomas Caimo); Gilles François Streithagen (Brussels, ARA, GRO 443B, 1741: appointment record of Gilles François Streithagen); Jean Jacques Marci, Pierre André du Trieu and Jean Wouters (Brussels, ARA, GRO 443B, 1742: appointment record of Jean Jacques Marci); Jean Baptiste Van der Fosse (Brussels, ARA, GRO 442A, 1776: appointment record of Jean Baptiste Van der Fosse); Martial de le Vielleuze (Brussels, ARA, GRO 442A, 1777: appointment record of Martial de le Vielleuze); Melchior Goubau, Jean Louis Pouppez and François de Steenhault (Brussels, ARA, ARR 857, 1787–1788: appointment record of Melchior Goubau and Jean Louis Pouppez), etc.

[27] This was especially true in the late 1780s. For example: Brussels, ARA, ARR 857, 1787–1788, appointment record of Melchior Goubau and Jean Louis Pouppez.

[28] Brussels, ARA, GRO 442A, 1776: appointment record Jean Baptiste Van der Fosse.

as well. In fact, he claimed that the only reason he had signed it, was 'because his agent[29] had told him that such a request was the norm at the Great Council'.[30]

In at least one case, the personal opinion of the president of the Great Council was requested. When in early 1789 the position of advocate-fiscal was vacated after the nomination of Jacques Joseph de Stassart to the presidency of the Council of Namur, the Great Council advanced three candidates: Jean Louis Pouppez, Melchior Goubau and François Alexandre de Steenhault, not coincidentally, the three most recently nominated councilors.[31] Given the 'special circumstances'—the reforms of Joseph II, most notably those of 1787, had caused a revolutionary mood throughout the Austrian Netherlands[32]—the *Conseil du gouvernement général* considered it important to appoint *un officier que le gouvernement pût employer avec confiance dans les différens commissions qu'il serait dans le cas de lui donner.* [33] Therefore, president de Fierlant's opinion was confidentially requested; he identified Melchior Goubau as the 'most active' man.

After all the necessary information had been gathered, the advising council finally sent its opinion, including a new ranking—not necessarily corresponding to the Great Council's preferences[34]—to the governor, or, in his absence, to the minister plenipotentiary. He was the one who held the final decision. In general, only very little is known about the motives of the governor(s) or of the minister plenipotentiary to appoint one or another candidate. Especially in the first three decades of the eighteenth century, the governor often did not follow the ranking suggested by the Great Council and/or the Council of State. We can assume that loyalty certainly figured high on the list, as well as family relations.[35]

Only in certain particular circumstances, Vienna would be consulted. For example, after the death of councilor Philippe Rogez in 1776, minister plenipotentiary Starhemberg asked Chancellor Kaunitz' opinion—and his blessing—on a special

[29] Agents or 'lobbyists' were very common in the eighteenth century Austrian Netherlands and functioned as an intermediate between rulers and the ruled. When submitting a petition to the central government in the eighteenth century, the petitioning party often had it edited, signed and presented by an agent. See: Vermeesch, Griet. 2012. Professional lobbying in Eighteenth-century Brussels: The Role of Agents in Petitioning the Central Government Institution in the Habsburg Netherlands. *Journal of Early Modern History* 16: 96–97.

[30] Brussels, ARA, GRO 442A, 1776: appointment record of Jean Baptiste Van der Fosse: "Nous proposons en second lieu l'avocat Vanderfosse, … La requete ci-jointe qu'il a presentée a V.A.R. pour demander la preference sur ces concurrents, n'est pas modeste, il y exalte son merite d'une maniere, qui ne pouvait que laisser une impression desavantageuse sur son jugement et sa delicatesse, s'il n'avait prevenu le rapporteur, qu'il ne s'etoit porté a cette demarche et a signer cette requete telle que son agent la lui avoit presenté, qu'avec repugnance, et sur ce que cet agent lui avait assuré que c'était l'usage."

[31] Cf. infra, 2.2.4 Recruiting *l'œil et le bras du roi.*

[32] Cf. infra, Chap. 5.

[33] Brussels, ARA, ARR 857, appointment record of Melchior Goubau as advocate-fiscal, March 1789. Goubau was originally only provisionally appointed in March. In May, he received his permanent patent letters.

[34] Cf. Excel database: eighteenth century councilors of the Great Council.

[35] Cf. infra, 2.2.2.1 Family matters.

arrangement.[36] The Great Council had requested to appoint two councilors for the same position. Not only Rogez' seat was empty, but by 1776 councilor Daniël Servaes had been absent on 'sick leave' for more than 18 months. While the latter could not be officially replaced—he never resigned—the Council suggested to appoint an additional councilor to remedy the inconveniences caused by his absence. Since there was indeed no chance that Servaes would ever return,[37] Starhemberg took on the suggestion of the Great Council and asked Kaunitz if he would agree to have Jacques Joseph de Stassart and Jean Baptiste Van der Fosse share the seat left empty by the death of Rogez. In that case, de Stassart would be the one to actually replace Rogez while Van der Fosse would take Servaes' place until the latter died or another position became available. Because there was no funding for an additional councilor and Servaes continued to enjoy his salary, Van der Fosse and de Stassart had to share the income of one seat between the two of them. As far as the *épices* were concerned, the former would receive half of the amount granted to the latter. Kaunitz approved the arrangement and agreed to compensate both councilors for their temporary 'loss', by demanding only half of the *médianate* usually paid for a councillorship at the Great Council until both could be fully employed.[38]

2.2.1.3 The Patent Letters and the Oath

After the final decision was made and the appointee had paid the *médianate,*[39] *lettres patentes* (patent letters) were awarded in name of the sovereign. These letters named the person who had to be replaced, enumerated the new appointee's virtues—his sharp mind, his cautiousness, his literary qualities, and his experience in judicial questions—and consequently established him as councilor in order to defend and guard the rights, honors and justice of the sovereign. Furthermore, the letter stated that the new appointee had to vow that he had never made any gifts—except for the usual charges—in order to receive his councillorship. Finally, the sovereign ordered the collector of East-Flanders to pay the accustomed salary in name of the appointee.[40] In order for the councilor to be paid, the patent letters also needed to be registered by the Accounts Chamber.

The appointment procedure ended with the councilor-elect pledging an oath administered by the president or, in his absence, by the senior councilor. This ceremony usually took place a few days up to a month after the issuing of the patent letters. Sometimes a councilor was not admitted to the oath because he had not fulfilled all conditions. Lamosnier for example, had troubles reimbursing the family of Charles

[36] Brussels, ARA, collectie microfilms Wenen, II995-II996 (Vienna, HHStA, Berichte 71, August 10, 1776).

[37] Servaes died in fact in April 1777.

[38] Brussels, ARA, GRO 442A, 1776: appointment record of Jean Baptiste Van der Fosse.

[39] Cf. infra, 3.2.2.4 Financial means.

[40] All patent letters went along established lines, only names and dates were changed. For example: Brussels, ARA, GRO 443B: patent letters of Dominique Joseph Vriesen, June 27, 1759.

Philippe de Waepenaert—the councilor whose place he would occupy at the Great Council—for the charges with which the seat was burdened.[41] It was only after he had fully repaid the loan, that he could take his oath and occupy his place on the Council.[42] In general, it was the date of the oath and not of the *lettres patentes* that determined the seniority of a councilor. Exceptions could be made, but needed to be explicitly registered.[43]

At least three councilors—Jean Alphonse de Coloma, Pierre Van Volden, and Philippe de Beeckman—were awarded a dispensation of the 'grand oath'. It is probably no coincidence that all three paid a large sum on top of their *médianate*.[44] Therefore we have reason to assume that the exemption of the oath-taking must be regarded as some kind of reward for their contribution. Alternatively, it could be possible that it was needed to avoid perjury. In fact, those councilors could not vow that they had not made any inappropriate contributions on top of the regular charges without foreswearing themselves.

Alexandre de Burlen and Guillaume Gielis Hujoel—who had both taken their oath in April 1706—apparently had to take it a second time in 1720. The records show that they both received new patent letters on April 30, 1720 and pledged a new oath on June 28 of the same year.[45] While the reasons for this renewal of their appointment are not explicitly stated, they probably have to be looked for in the War of the Spanish Succession. In fact, Alexandre de Burlen, Guillaume Gielis Hujoel and Christophe-Ernest de Baillet are the only three councilors appointed by Philip V.[46] Chances are that the Austrian government, once it was more or less firmly in charge of the Southern Netherlands, refused to acknowledge the legality of Philips' 'French' regime and therefore also of the patent letters he had awarded. Since de Baillet had by 1720 already pledged a new oath to the House of Habsburg—in 1716 as president of the Great Council—de Burlen and Gielis Hujoel were the only re-

[41] Cf. infra, Chap. 3. Every councilor had to take over a 'loan' from his predecessor to the government. As the government never reimbursed the loan, it was constantly transferred from one councilor to another.

[42] Brussels, ARA, GRO 443B, 1738: appointment record of Jean François Lamosnier.

[43] For example, when Pierre Timmermans, due to his absence from town, took his oath ten days after Jacques Ghison and Jacques Douglas—although his patent letters were issued on an earlier date than those of Ghison and Douglas—it needed to be explicitly stated that Timmermans was senior to Ghison and Douglas. Brussels, ARA, GRO 442A, 1783: appointment record of Jacques François Douglas.

[44] Cf. infra, 2.2.2.4 Financial means. This was also the case for de Lindicq, de Steenhault and Keyaerts but since the appointment records do not contain their patent letters, we have no way of knowing if they had been exempted as well.

[45] Brussels, ARA, GRM 4, f.99r–100v: second patent letters of Alexandre de Burlen; f.101r–102v: second patent letters of Guillaume Gielis Hujoel.

[46] Philips V was sovereign of Malines between roughly late 1700 and May 1706, when after the battle of Ramillies he lost the authority over the province of Brabant, the seigniory of Malines and a major part of Flanders. De Schryver, Reginald. 1987. De Oostenrijkse aanspraken op de Spaans-Habsburgse erfenis. De Zuidelijke Nederlanden tijdens de Spaanse Successieoorlog. 1700–1716. In *Oostenrijks België 1713–1794. De Zuidelijke Nederlanden onder de Oostenrijkse Habsburgers*, ed. Hervé Hasquin, 11–36. Brussels: Gemeentekrediet van België, 16.

maining holders of 'invalid' appointment letters. While dismissing them was probably somewhat problematic—and not necessarily desirable—awarding them new patent letters and having them pledge a new oath to the Austrian emperor might have been a relatively easy solution.[47]

In general, a couple of months elapsed between the death or promotion of one councilor and the appointment of his replacement. However, at certain times in the history of the Great Council, a seat rested empty for one to several years. During the 1720s and the middle to late 1730s a lack of candidates continually postponed the nomination of a new councilor. For example, after the death of Alexandre de Burlen in 1721, it took more than a year to appoint a suitable replacement.[48] When Norbert Van Voorspoel died in 1722, the same problem occurred.[49] In 1735, it proved again difficult to find a decent candidate after the death of Charles Philippe de Waepenaert. According to the Great Council, only nine persons applied, several of whom were very young or not well renowned. Considering that it would be impossible to make a list of three suitable candidates, the Great Council requested and received approval to differ the procedure another month.[50] In the end, it took almost two and a half years before Lasmosnier was appointed as a replacement for de Waepenaert.

While we do not know exactly why it was difficult to find suitable councilors in the 1720s and 1730s,[51] we may assume that the postponement of the appointment of new councilors was often attributable to political circumstances. For example, in the 1740s, it took more than two years to find a decent substitute for Claude Joseph Soteau and Ambroise de Smet. This can however be perfectly explained by the invasion of the French and the corresponding exile of the Great Council to Echternach. The year 1781 can be identified as another bottleneck, when more than a year elapsed between the successive deaths of André Kerens, Pierre Deudon and Hyacinthe de Partz and the appointment of new councilors. The latter case can be attrib-

[47] Councilor Jacques Douglas also had to swear his loyalty to the sovereign a second time in January 1791. This however, was due to the fact that he had taken an alternative oath during the Revolution of 1789–1790. Cf. infra Chap. 5. Brussels, ARA, GRM 5.

[48] Alexandre de Burlen died in November 1721. Jean Henri Kahnn took his seat at the Great Council at the very end of January 1723. Cf. Excel database: 18th century councilors of the Great Council.

[49] Gaillard, Arthur. 1900–1903. *Inventaire des mémoriaux du Grand Conseil de Malines*. Brussels: Weissenbruch, t. 2, p. 371, n°255: "Malines le 24 septembre 1722. Consulte du Grand Conseil au sujet de la pénurie des candidats à la place vacante par le décès du conseiller Norbert Voorspoel."

[50] Brussels, ARA, GRO 442: letter of the governess to the Great Council, November 9 1735. Maria-Elisabeth did not attempt to urge the Great Council to rapidly appoint a new councilor; on the contrary, she fully approved of the Council's attitude in the matter.

[51] Financial reasons might have come into play, but the Austrian government was almost always behind on the councilors' salaries and certainly not only in the 1720s and 1730s. Cf. infra: Chap. 3. On the other hand, the councilors might have had their own reasons to postpone the appointment of a new member. First of all, less colleagues meant that the income the councilors received from the *épices* relatively increased as it had to be divided among less people. Secondly, the councilors also undoubtedly let particular considerations come into play: if they were not able to find a suitable applicant within their own network, they might have deemed it necessary to wait somewhat longer until such a candidate presented himself.

uted to the general problems associated with finding a suitable clerical councilor.[52] The other two corresponded with the change of power between Empress Maria Theresa and Emperor Joseph II and the ensuing substitution of governors. In fact, while Van Velde's patent letters (March 1779) were still signed by Maria Theresa, Ghison's carried the signature of Joseph II (February 1783). Therefore, the delay must be attributed to the transfer of power in Austria and not to any tribulations in the Netherlands or at the Great Council.

2.2.2 The Selection Criteria

The procedure ordinance of 1559 does not prescribe any fixed requirements the candidates for a position at the Great Council had to meet, except that they could not be related—by blood or by marriage—to other members of the Council. Nevertheless, in practice, the candidates did have to fulfill certain prerequisites. As Gilissen has identified,[53] aspiring councilors had to be of 'legal' birth; children born out of wedlock were not taken into consideration. Secondly, they had to originate from one of the provinces of the Southern Netherlands. Thirdly, all candidates had to be holder of at least a master's degree in both laws, acquired form a university in the Southern Netherlands. In the eighteenth century, this was *de facto* Leuven. Finally, a certain minimum age was respected; at the Great Council no member younger than 29 was admitted.[54] In general, the formal requirements imposed on the candidates for the Malines tribunal did not much differ from what was demanded from new-councilors-to-be at other higher tribunals.[55]

Once these initial prerequisites had been fulfilled, other factors came into play. While these are never explicitly mentioned, they can to a large extent be derived from the arguments used in the appointment records. For the early eighteenth century, F. Alix identified the selection criteria for high-level functionaries as follows: (1) personal merits (education, experience, seniority); (2) networks (family members, in-laws, acquaintances, patrons, …); (3) geographical origin; and (4) social origin (especially being of noble descent).[56] These four criteria, together with a

---

[52] Cf. infra, 2.2.2.2 Personal merits.

[53] Gilissen, John. 1980. De Grote Raad van Mechelen. Historisch overzicht. In *Miscelannea Consilii Magni. Ter gelegenheid van twintig jaar Werkgroep Grote Raad van Mechelen*, 13–43. Amsterdam: Universiteit van Amsterdam. Faculteit der rechtsgeleerdheid, 36–37.

[54] Jean Baptiste de Decker, Arnold Vermeulen and Jean Jacques Marci all pledged their oath at age 29.

[55] For the Council of Friesland: see, Hempenius-Van Dijck, Barendina e.a. 1999. *De Heeren van den Raeden: biografieën en groepsportret van de raadsheren van het Hof van Friesland, 1499–1811*. Hilversum: Uitgeverij Verloren, 123; For the Council of Brabant: Gaillard, Arthur. 1898–1902. *Le Conseil de Brabant: histoire, organisation, procédure*. Brussels: Lebègue, t. 2, 221.

[56] Alix looked at the members of predominantly the Council of State and the Council of Finance in its different forms between 1700 and 1725. The councilors of the Great Council or of any other tribunal are not taken into account. It is also important to note that she did not rank her criteria according to importance; it is a mere enumeration of those factors which she identified as coming

few others, were also used when selecting candidates for the Great Council in the eighteenth century.

2.2.2.1 Family Matters

Family ties were without a doubt the most important asset for a person who wanted to further his career in the higher echelons of the central administration during the eighteenth century. Having a parent who (had) occupied an important position in the government inspired confidence and was regarded as some sort of guarantee of the quality of services the new official would deliver.[57] Potential candidates for a councillorship at the Great Council were well aware of the crucial importance of family relations, belaboring the many accomplishments of their ancestors in their requests to the sovereign. Eugene d'Olmen, for example, did not mention anything at all about his professional expertise or his capacities, but instead provided the sovereign with an extensive overview of all his family members, as well as those of his wife, who had served in the central government, boasting several members of the Great and the Privy Council, presidents of the Council of Flanders and chancellors of Brabant.[58]

In case of equality of merits, the candidate who could provide the 'right' ancestry always carried the appointment. In 1744, for example, the Great Council nominated, with an equal number of votes, both Jacques de Cock and Charles Henri Goubau for the seat left empty by the death of Jean Ferdinand Keyaerts. In its advice to the governor, the Privy Council listed the 'accomplishments' of both candidates. De Cock was a strong candidate, as he had been ranked first in the general competition of the faculty of philosophy in 1732 and had earned a law degree in a mere four years, arguing cases before the Great Council very soon after.[59] On the other hand, Goubau's most important merit was that he could count several former councilors of the Great Council and a president of the Privy Council among his relatives. Moreover, in case of equality, the sovereign preferred persons with noble blood, their birth endowing them with a distinction non-noblemen did not possess.[60] As de Cock, contrary to Goubau, did not originate from a noble family, it should be no surprise that the latter was appointed.

Being blue-blooded unquestionably was an important asset.[61] For instance, even though in 1741, the Great Council ranked Jean Charles Van Slabbeeck prior to

into play in the recruitment process. Alix, Flore. 2009. Les critères de sélection des hauts fonctionnaires des Pays-Bas méridionaux (1700–1725). *Belgisch tijdschrift voor filologie en geschiedenis* 87: 297–348.

[57] Alix, Flore. 2009. Les critères de sélection des hauts fonctionnaires des Pays-Bas méridionaux (1700–1725). *Belgisch tijdschrift voor filologie en geschiedenis* 87: 297–348, p. 318.

[58] Brussels, ARA, RvSt 654, 1723: appointment record of Pierre Claude de St Vaast.

[59] Brussels, ARA, GRO 443B, 1744: appointment record of Charles Henri Goubau.

[60] Brussels, ARA, GRO 443B, 1744: appointment record of Charles Henri Goubau.

[61] In case of doubt, the Great Council thoroughly checked a councilor's background, as was the case with Jean-Mathias de Vivario who could not give convincing evidence of his noble birth. All candidates had to provide the Council with a copy of their certificate of baptism. The procurator-

Charles Thomas Caimo, it was the latter who received the promotion. While acknowledging Caimo's merits as an advocate at the Council of Brabant, it was first and foremost his family background to which the Privy Council paid special attention. Caimo, according to the Privy Council, had irreproachable manners, worthy of a councilor, but was also born into a noble family, a quality considered very advantageous, placing him at the top of the list.[62] In its financial policy as well, the Austrian government favored candidates of noble birth:[63] in the course of the eighteenth century, the *médianate* for blue-blooded aspirants to positions at the provincial councils and at the Great Council was cut in half.[64]

A position on the Great Council could also serve as a reward for the zeal a father or other relative had demonstrated in service of the Austrian Crown.[65] For example, in the above mentioned request from Starhemberg to Kaunitz about the replacement of councilor Rogez, the minister plenipotentiary suggested to rank de Stassart first—instead of Van der Fosse as the Great Council had done—because in case two candidates were judged to be equal, the merits of their family members had

general found out that de Vivario's copy was a fraud. Brussels, ARA, GRM 140N, 1789: *Nomination des substituts du procureur général*: de Vivario.

[62] Brussels, ARA, GRO 443B, 1741: appointment record of Charles Thomas Caimo.

[63] Candidates of noble descent never belonged to the 'old' nobility. Members of families such as d'Ursel, d'Arenberg, Egmont etc. never figured on a candidate list. Contrary to the situation in the late Spanish period, the high nobility was again allowed to take up important positions—not so much in tribunals as in the central state councils—from the second decade of the eighteenth century on. However, as they were considered to be 'insubordinate', they were 'put away' after 1725 in the Council of State, which, in the new state structure, had a merely ceremonial function. Alix, Flore. 2009. Les critères de sélection des hauts fonctionnaires des Pays-Bas méridionaux (1700–1725). *Belgisch tijdschrift voor filologie en geschiedenis* 87: 326. Galand as well mentions that even the most highly ranked officials in the Austrian administration—such as Patrice de Neny—still could not aspire to belong to the noble entourage of the 'prince'. Galand, Michèle. 2001. Gages, honneurs, mérites: les hauts fonctionnaires dans les Pays-Bas autrichiens. *Revue belge de philologie et d'histoire* 73.2: 580.

[64] Gaillard, Arthur. 1898–1902. *Le Conseil de Brabant: histoire, organisation, procédure*. Brussels: Lebègue, t. 2, p. 235. In 1743, Maria Theresa had the *médianate* for nobles cut in half. *ROPBA*, t. 5, p. 583, 20 December, 1743.

[65] In the Council of Brabant, it was apparently possible—of course with permission of the sovereign—to resign one's position in order to have a relative appointed. Gaillard, Arthur. 1898–1902. *Le Conseil de Brabant: histoire, organisation, procédure*. Brussels: Lebègue, t. 2, p. 251; Alix also mentions the phenomenon of the *expectatives* (a position promised to someone while it was not yet vacant) and of the *survivances* (assuring in advance that a certain position will be passed down to a family member at the death of an official or at his resignation) at the Privy Council and the Council of Finance. In fact she mentions that, according to Delporte, in the course of the eighteenth century the practice of explicit venality diminished, while that of the *survivances* increased. Cf. Delporte, Laurent. 2001. *Problématique de la vénalité des offices dans les Pays-Bas autrichiens: les approches institutionnelle et discrétionnaire*, Université Libre de Bruxelles, Unpublished Master's Thesis; Alix, Flore. 2009. Les critères de sélection des hauts fonctionnaires des Pays-Bas méridionaux (1700–1725). *Belgisch tijdschrift voor filologie en geschiedenis* 87: 300–303. This was apparently not often applied to the Great Council: we have found only one example of an *expectative* (See, infra: 1.2.2.5 The sovereign's whim) and none at all of a *survivance*. Galand as well notices that awarding a son with a position was considered to be a 'special' additional reward for an official. Galand, Michèle. 2001. Gages, honneurs, mérites: les hauts fonctionnaires dans les Pays-Bas autrichiens. *Revue belge de philologie et d'histoire* 73.2: 567.

to be taken into account. Given that de Stassart's father had successively served as procurator-general of the Council of Namur and as councilor responsible for fiscal matters at the Privy Council, while at present he served as president of the Council of Namur, awarded with the honor of councilor of State, the son should be nominated as *il convient même au service de S.M. d'encourager de cette manière ceux qui y consacrent les jours dans des postes distingués*.[66]

Not only blood relatives, but in-laws as well could open doors to a position on the Great Council: councilor Henri de Villers de Fourneau was the husband of Eleonore Van Goethem, a relative of councilor François Van Goethem. Livine Thérèse van Voorspoel, daughter of councilor Norbert van Voorspoel, married councilor Jean-Baptiste de Decker. Councilor Jean O'Donnogue's daughter Cornelie Marie Anne became councilor Joseph de Richterich's wife. Marie Justine Bervoet—daughter of Juste Bervoet—and Marie Thérèse de Potter—daughter of Guillaume de Potter—married respectively councilors Robert Hyacinthe Happart and Jean Jacques Marci. Councilor Guillaume Pycke courted the daughter of councilor Joseph Stalins and councilor Pierre Joseph Deudon's daughter married councilor Martial de le Vielleuze.[67] Goswin de Fierlant is probably the most famous illustration of the importance of nurturing a network and marrying in the right family. When the sovereign appointed de Fierlant as president of the Great Council, his capabilities were mentioned, but as important as his own merits were those of his uncle and father-in-law Patrice de Neny.[68]

In general, the councilors' kinship relations demonstrate the existence of an intricate network of ties between civil servants in the higher administration. Obviously, the civil service world was a closed one: *homines novi* were rather rare. Being part of a well-connected family was of crucial importance. In that regard, the Great Council's *droit de terne* did not advantage the introduction of 'new' people. In fact, the privilege of the Great Council to designate three candidates benefitted those who had already developed an extensive network within the Austrian administration, thereby putting newcomers at a serious disadvantage.

Yet, family relations could also be an impediment for a career at the Great Council. When a new deputy procurator-general had to be appointed after the promotion of Jean Philippe de Waepenaert to a councillorship, the Privy Council advised against Charles George de Fraux, not only because he did not master the Flemish language but also due to the 'past behaviors of his father'.[69] Family relations especially constituted an obstacle when close relatives already occupied a position in the Council. The ordinance of 1559 excluded fathers, sons and brothers—by blood or by marriage—to simultaneously occupy positions in the Great Council.

---

[66] Brussels, ARA, collectie microfilms Wenen, II995–II996 (Vienna, HHStA, Berichte 71, August 10, 1776).

[67] See Excel database: Councilors of the eighteenth century Great Council.

[68] Brussels, ARA, GRO 443B, 1773: appointment record of Goswin de Fierlant as president of the Great Council.

[69] Brussels, ARA, GRO 442A, 1750: appointment record of Gilles de Cock as deputy procurator-general.

This rule was certainly not always strictly observed and dispensations were awarded: Joseph Theodore Richterich, for example, served for 12 years together with his father-in-law Jean O'Donnogue. Martial de le Vielleuze as well was appointed to the Great Council in 1777—in first instance as an 'extraordinary' councilor to replace Daniël Servaes who was on sick leave—while his father-in-law, Pierre Deudon was a member. In this case, the 20-year long service and merits of Deudon were even mentioned as an argument in favor of appointing his son-in-law.[70] In councils composed of two chambers, having relatives serving together was not always problematic as they could be divided over two different chambers. Only in important matters—such as the nomination of a new councilor, a request for advice from the central government or a 'grand' revision—both chambers conferred together. In that case, an arrangement was usually worked out.[71]

Nevertheless, far from all dispensations requested were granted and family ties were a liability for some aspirants to the Great Council. In October 1791, Emmanuel Goubau asked for a dispensation to serve on the Great Council, which was necessary because his brother was at that time advocate-fiscal at the tribunal. In fact, he believed that there were compelling reasons for him to be exempt of article 6 of the Procedure Ordinance. First, there were numerous examples of councilors with 'forbidden' family relations, with Richterich and O'Donnogue, and Deudon and de le Vielleuze coming directly to mind. Secondly, for over eight years, he had distinguished himself as an advocate at the Great Council and he was at present the acting *pensionaire* of Malines. Thirdly, his father had served on the Great Council. Finally, his behavior during the past troubles led him to believe that he might be allowed to apply for a councillorship. The Privy Council was sympathetic to his request, but the governor remained obdurate, despite Emmanuel Goubau's repeated pleas.[72]

Other relationships besides kinships, such as bonds formed during academic studies, certainly also played a role in gaining a position on the Great Council. In 1757, Christophe Innocent de Bartenstein, Henri Herman and Joseph Ambroise de Crumpipen, Goswin de Fierlant, Jacques Antoine Le Clerc and Jacques Joseph Plasschaert all graduated from the Faculty of Law in Leuven.[73] Alix mentions the existence of 'patrons' who used their own networks to advance the career of their 'protégés': Christophe de Baillet, for example, several times relied on his patron Rialp to climb the proverbial ladder in the Austrian central administration.[74] At least one councilor of the Great Council owed most of his career to protection in high

[70] Brussels, ARA, GRO 442A, 1777: appointment record of Martial de le Vielleuze.

[71] Brussels, ARA, GR, Register 419, f. 152–156, 1751. Request of Jean Jacques Marci to arrange the distribution of revision cases between him and his father-in-law Guillaume de Potter. At other instances however, the two relatives were allowed to reside together in the plenary sessions. Cf. infra, Chap. 3.

[72] Brussels, ARA, GRO 442A, 1791: request for dispensation from Emmanuel Goubau.

[73] Bruneel, Claude and Hoyois, Jean-Paul. 2001. *Les grands commis des Pays-Bas autrichiens: dictionnaire biographique du personnel des institutions centrales*. Brussels: Algemeen Rijksarchief, p. 11.

[74] Alix, Flore. 2009. Les critères de sélection des hauts fonctionnaires des Pays-Bas méridionaux (1700–1725). *Belgisch tijdschrift voor filologie en geschiedenis* 87: 324.

places. Augustin de Steenhault, appointed member of the Great Council in 1712, councilor of the Council of State in 1733, president of the Privy Council in 1739 and member of different prestigious *jointes*[75] was said to be an industrious person with some relevant expertise, but he was also believed to speak and write French badly, to have no culture and to be rather stubborn. Moreover, he continued to cumulate several offices, merely for his personal gain.[76] The fact that he had such a brilliant career, despite the less than flattering comments he received from people within the government, should be almost entirely attributed to the fact that he was a protégé of governess Maria-Elisabeth.[77]

Alix's claims that throughout the period of 1700–1725 the importance of these matrimonial and familial networks tended to diminish and that ever more high officials had ancestors in the military or in the local and provincial rather than in the central administration, do not seem to bear on the Great Council. Having the right family connections continued to be the most essential asset up and until the end of the eighteenth century.

2.2.2.2 Personal Merits: Experience and Seniority

While a candidate's experience was not unimportant as a selection criterion—the appointment records usually mention previous careers—and familiarity with the judicial practice was absolutely a requirement, these factors did not figure at the top of the list. Nevertheless, when it suited the Great Council, it did claim to attach a lot of weight to experience in the field. This was especially the case when a clerical councilor had to be replaced.

The presence of two clerical councilors at the Great Council was a relic from the late fifteenth and sixteenth centuries. Supposedly, they functioned as 'guardians' of the interests of the Roman Catholic Church, especially in matters where clergy were involved.[78] By the eighteenth century, these clerical councilors had little real benefit

[75] For example, he was member and later president of the *Jointe suprême pour les monts-de-piété* and was regularly invited to participate in the session of the *Jointe de cabinet*.

[76] Bruneel, Claude and Hoyois, Jean-Paul. 2001. *Les grands commis des Pays-Bas autrichiens: dictionnaire biographique du personnel des institutions centrales*. Brussels: Algemeen Rijksarchief, 576–577: "Vers la même époque, un mémoire concernant le gouvernement général des Pays-Bas autrichiens le décrit ainsi: 'Steenhoult (*sic*) a toujours passé pour un homme fort laborieux, il a du sçavoir et il trouve aisément des expédiens, mais il écrit et prononce mal en François, il n'a pas du monde, il ne hante que ses inférieurs, on le taxe d'entêtement' (...) 'savant jurisconsulte, mais pour ministre trop arrêté dans ses sentimens et tellement aux règles du Barreau et à l'habitude de s'attirer des affaires de justice et d'agir despotiquement, que l'on ne voit pas qu'à son âge avancé cela puisse changer; et le public ne juge pas avantageusement de ce que, contre la décence de son caractère, il a continué de rester dans la jointe militaire, dans celle du mont-de-piété et dans la Chambre suprême, apparement par rapport à l'utilité des épices ou sportules'."

[77] Galand, Michèle. 2001. Gages, honneurs, mérites: les hauts fonctionnaires dans les Pays-Bas autrichiens. *Revue belge de philologie et d'histoire* 73.2: 569.

[78] Literature is very vague when it comes to the reason why the Great Council had clerical councilors in its midst. At the Council of Brabant and the Council of Flanders, for example, none of the councilors were clergymen.

to the tribunal, because they could not judge and certainly not report on criminal cases. Given that criminal trials were the least rewarding financially—if the councilors were ever paid for their work at all—acting as a reporter in such a case was not exactly popular. Two clerical councilors at the Council meant that there were two members less to which these trials could be distributed.

Moreover, clerical councilors also could not handle cases on the *rôle*,[79] probably simply because they lacked expertise. While the majority did have a law degree, they usually did not have much practical experience: clergy rarely had the opportunity to act as judges ever since ecclesiastical tribunals engaged lay assessors to deal with their cases.[80] Therefore, they may have lacked the skills to act and decide independently, a quality that was required from councilors who presided over the *rôle* sessions. Finally, if a civil case needed to be handed over to the procurator-general—for example because there were falsified documents in the file—the clerical councilors were no longer allowed to judge the case.[81] While their number had already been reduced in the sixteenth century from four to two, the Great Council wished to minimize it even further to one or, if possible, keep them out of the Council entirely. Claiming that the candidates for a clerical councillorship did not have the right capabilities or experience was the most popular—and at times certainly successful—tactic to reach that goal.

The first attempt to have a clerical position filled by a layman was about the time the Great Council returned to Malines from its exile in Echternach. Although Ambroise de Smet had died in 1746, no replacement had yet been appointed by 1749—probably because of the insecure situation. In 1750, the Great Council announced that not a single clergyman had presented himself for the empty seat and that therefore a threesome of laymen was proposed. 'For this one time and this one time only', Governor Charles Alexander of Lorraine agreed to nominate a lay councilor in place of a cleric, on the condition that, in case a clergyman presented himself even if there were no positions immediately available, the Great Council should accept him as additional councilor with full pay until an ordinary councillorship opened up.[82] Due to this requirement, the Great Council was obligated to appeal to the clergy to apply for the vacancy when three years later Gilles de Streithagen was promoted to the Privy Council. Nevertheless, several weeks before the April 11 deadline, the Great Council requested the governor again be allowed to select three laymen, in case no clerics came forward. The Council argued that a new nomination was imperative, since there were already two councilors—Jean Henry Kahnn

[79] Cf. infra, Chap. 3.

[80] Brussels, ARA, GRO 442A, 1777: appointment record of Leopold François de Laing, opinion of the Privy Council: "… il n'est pas étonnant que ceux dudit conseil se sont trouvés dans une sorte de perplexité pour proposer des sujets ecclesiastiques pour en former un terne puisque dans les tribunaux ecclesiastiques mêmes on prend toujours des assesseurs laics pour juger les causes s'y presentant …".

[81] Brussels, ARA, GRO 442A, 1792, appointment record of Guillaume Van Cutsem.

[82] Brussels, ARA, GRO 443A, 1750: appointment record of Jean Charles de Waepenaert as councilor.

and Jean Baptiste Hony—who in practice did not occupy their seats anymore due to their infirmities.[83]

The Privy Council suspected other motives than merely the urge to appoint another councilor as soon as possible. Seeing through the Great Council's pretext to silently remove at least one clerical councilor, the Privy Council advised the governor to decline the request, obligating the Great Council to seriously look for a suitable clerical candidate. The Privy Council seemed to think that the Great Council might have lied about the number of eligible clergymen in order to gradually force the government into conferring all future positions on laymen. Governor Charles de Lorraine followed the Privy Council's advice, but to no avail. In May 1753, the Great Council notified the central government that only one candidate had presented himself, but that he was not eligible because he had not fulfilled all necessary requirements. For the second consecutive time, the Council managed to get a layman, i.c. Ignace Joseph Wirix, appointed. It was only in 1758 and three appointments later that the Council finally proposed a threesome of clergymen to replace the late councilor François Van Goethem. The councilors justified the delay and the constant postponement of the nomination by the need to thoroughly inform themselves about the merits and capacities of the clergymen, which could not be taken for granted.[84]

After the death of Jean Baptiste Hony in 1765, the nomination of a clerical councilor proved to be complicated once again. The Great Council argued the delays were due to the fact that it was difficult to find decent and suitable candidates for these positions. According to the tribunal, clergy lacked the knowledge of elementary legal principles, with little to no experience or practical training. At best, they had a vague idea of modern jurisprudence, though absolutely insufficient to be a judge at the superior court of the Netherlands. Since the Great Council's jurisdiction extended over four different provinces, each with its own particular customs and habits, an acquaintance with the law as taught at the University of Leuven was insufficient. For these reasons, the Great Council preferred to appoint advocates or people with some other relevant experience in the administration of justice, who had worked for at least nine or ten years. According to the Great Council, newly appointed clerical councilors needed this all the more, since they were the first to give their opinions right after the reporter, which deprived them of the possibility of cherry-picking from different judgments.[85]

---

[83] Brussels, ARA, GRO 443B, 1753: appointment record of Ignace Joseph Wirix as councilor.

[84] Brussels, ARA, GRO 443B, 1758: appointment record of Guillaume Felix Brenart.

[85] Brussels, ARA, GRO 443A, 1765: appointment record of Jacques de Partz. Until the very end of the Great Council in 1794, the same problem continued to pop up. The promotion of Felix Brenart to the Episcopal See of Bruges in 1777 engendered once again the same discussion. This time, the Privy Council supported the Great Council's objections and a lay councilor was appointed. Brussels, ARA, GRO 442A, 1777: appointment record of Leopold François de Laing. In 1779, after the death of Nicolas Pouppez, the governor demanded that the councilors would compose a threesome exclusively composed of clergymen. The Great Council did proceed to a nomination but invoked conscientious objections to actually send the list to the Privy Council: in fact, five of the fifteen members had withheld their vote, motivating their refusal with article 8 of the 1559

Yet, notwithstanding what the nomination—and the complications connected to it—of clerical councilors might lead one to suspect, appointments to the Great Council were usually not meritocratically justified. The tribunal—for the above mentioned reasons—simply did not want any clergymen in their midst. Consequently, it was somewhat ironic that in 1793—exactly at the time the number of criminal trials was higher than usual[86]—a third clerical councilor was added to the Great Council, despite its protests. Financial motives rather than his capabilities had convinced the government to appoint clergyman Guillaume Van Cutsem, although the vacancy was for a layman's seat. First of all, the salary of clerical councilors was substantially lower than that of lay members. Additionally, due to the reforms of Joseph II, Van Cutsem, a professor, had moved with the university to Brussels but had lost his position after the restoration of 1791. As a result, he was entitled to a pension of 1380 florins, which he would lose if he became a member of the Great Council.[87] Appointing him was, therefore, in different respects a considerable money-saver for the Austrian government.

Connected to the assessment of a candidate's experience, were his age and seniority, two criteria which were sometimes invoked—in general to advise against a candidate—but which in the end were easily brushed aside. For example, both Arnould Vermeulen and Jean Jacques Marci were considered too young the first time they applied—at respectively 29 and 28—and too inexperienced to be eligible as councilor. In 1741, Marci had graduated a mere two and a half years, despite the minimum of ten years of practice purportedly required by the Great Council. Regardless, both were appointed less than a year later during the next application round.

Not only age but also the number of nominations mattered. Many councilors had been selected at least once and often twice before their actual appointment. The Privy Council in its advice to the sovereign often expressly stated the number of times a candidate had been short-listed.[88] Nevertheless, too many fruitless attempts also could create a bad impression, as was the case with Pierre Deudon. In a comment in the margin, crossed out but still legible, the Privy Council suggested in 1741 that the sovereign might not be happy with Deudon as a councilor since he had already been nominated four times before, but had never been seriously considered.[89]

---

ordinance, which stated that the Great Council should select three persons who were well versed in their fields. This time, however, the Privy Council advised the governor to validate the nomination given that 10 out of 15 members had voted which was still a clear majority. And indeed, in 1779, a canon of the cathedral chapter of Saint Rombouts, Van Velde was appointed. Especially in Van Velde's case, the alleged lack of experience of the candidate invoked by the Great Council was completely unfounded. Before being ordinated as a clergyman, he had worked as an advocate at the Great Council. Brussels, ARA, GRO 442A, 1779: appointment record of Jean Baptiste Van Velde.

[86] Cf. infra, Chaps. 3 and 4.

[87] Brussels, ARA, GRO 442A, 1793: appointment record of Guillaume Van Cutsem.

[88] Brussels, ARA, GRO 443B, 1734: appointment record of Guillaume François Snoy.

[89] Brussels, ARA, GRO 442A, 1741: appointment record of Pierre Joseph Deudon: "Observant qu'en quatre differentes fois qu'il a été propose il n'a su meriter l'attention de V.A.R. soubçon-

2.2.2.3 Geographical Distribution

The 'Grand Privilege' of 1477 had imposed a more or less equal geographical spread of the councilors of the Great Council in order to secure a 'fair' representation for every province which was subject to the tribunal's jurisdiction.[90] The procedure ordinance of 1559, however, did not mention any requirements as to the geographical origin of the Council's members. Nevertheless, until the end of the eighteenth century, being a native of the (Southern) Netherlands[91] was a prerequisite. In 1681, a decree from Emperor Charles II made the conditions even more stringent: from that time on, official letters of naturalization would not suffice for foreign-born candidates to be considered eligible for a position at the Great Council.[92] However, exceptions could still be made: unlike the Councils of Brabant and Friesland,[93] the members of the Great Council did accept foreigners in their midst.[94] The central government, on the other hand, at times needed some convincing to allow an exception. In the early 1720s, the Council of State took this matter rather seriously.

Both in 1720, in replacement of Hubert de Tombeur, and in 1723, after the death of Alexandre de Burlen, the Great Council nominated Jean O'Donnogue, a lawyer of Irish origin, for a councillorship. On both occasions, the Council of State acknowledged his merits, but took the view that, in spite of the letters of naturalization he had received from the sovereign, he could not be considered because of his Irish birth. 'Local' candidates should have preference over foreigners.[95] The Great Council, however, persisted and nominated him a third time in 1724 to replace Nor-

nerent [sic] aisement que sa personne ne lui est pas agreable." As far as we know he had only been nominated three times before (in May 1741, in June 1741 and in August 1741 when respectively Charles Thomas Caimo, Jean Charles Van Slabbeeck and Gilles Streithagen were appointed).

[90] Kerckhoffs-De Hey, A.J.M. 1980. *De Grote raad en zijn functionarissen, 1477–1531*. Amsterdam: s.n, 75.

[91] After the secession of the Northern Netherlands from Spanish Authority, candidates had to come from the provinces under Habsburg rule.

[92] Brussels, ARA, RvSt 654, 1724: appointment record of Jean O'Donnogue: "et d'ailleurs parce que le Grand Conseil est le premier corps de justice d'ou on tire ordinairement les personnes les plus dignes pour entrer dans le haut ministere de ce pays etant fort apparent que par ce motif le feu roi Charles second aiant fait attention combien il importoit à son service d'en exclure les étrangers, a ordonné audit conseil, le distinguant quant à ce point des autres conseils de ce pays, par la reforme de l'an 1681, que doresenavant il ne proposeroit aucunes personnes pour les places qui y viendront à vaquer, qui ne fussent nées ses sujets, encore bien qu'elle eussent été naturalisées."

[93] The Council of Brabant never accepted a non-Brabant native, except for the two seats which could be—but did not have to be—occupied by councilors coming from other provinces. Gaillard, Arthur. 1898–1902. *Le Conseil de Brabant: histoire, organisation, procédure*. Brussels: Lebègue, t. 2, p. 111.; For the Council of Friesland, Hempenius-Van Dijck mentions that being of Fries birth was the only prerequisite imposed on the councilors which was strictly observed up until the late eighteenth century. Hempenius-Van Dijck, Barendina e.a. 1999. *De Heeren van den Raeden: biografieën en groepsportret van de raadsheren van het Hof van Friesland, 1499–1811*. Hilversum: Uitgeverij Verloren, 150.

[94] Seven out of 94 councilors were not born in the Austrian Netherlands. Cf. infra, 1.3.2 Geographical origin.

[95] Brussels, ARA, RvSt 654, 1723: appointment record of Jean Henri Kahnn.

bert Van Voorspoel. Again the opinions in the Council of State were divided. While recognizing O'Donnogue's superior qualities, it was still considered a dangerous precedent to open a seat on the Great Council to non-natives, especially since a position in this tribunal constituted a recruitment pool for vacancies in the highest Austrian administration.[96] In spite of the Council of State's reservations, the governor eventually decided to select O'Donnogue.

In the later eighteenth century, this prohibition to appoint 'non-natives' was apparently circumvented without much trouble. In 1763, Godefroid Tackoen was selected on his first nomination even though he was a native of the prince bishopric of Liège. While it was mentioned that he was not a citizen of the Austrian Netherlands, the dispensation from the 1681 prohibition seemed a mere formality.[97] Similarly, André Kerens in 1768 and Jacques François Douglas in 1783—born in respectively the Northern Netherlands and Hungary—did not face any real opposition when applying for a councillorship.[98] All in all, the problem did not present itself very often: the number of non-natives aspiring to a seat at the Great Council was very limited.

While the geographical origin of the candidates—as long as they were born within the Austrian Netherlands—might not have figured high on the criteria list of the central government, several provincial Estates did consider it important to have 'natives' represent them at the Great Council. Regions where the provincial councils were subordinate to the Great Council's jurisdiction—Flanders, Namur and Luxembourg—tended to write letters of recommendation for the candidates from their area to influence the government's decision. For example, when a position on the Great Council opened up after the death of Jean Ferdinand Keyaerts in 1743, the Estates of Flanders implored the Privy Council to appoint the Flemish born advocate Joseph Huwijn,[99] arguing that his familiarity with the customs of their province would be of vital importance for the Great Council as Flanders provided up to two thirds of the appeal cases.[100] Since at that time only two members of the Great Council were born in Flanders, it was essential to appoint an additional Flemish councilor.[101]

96 Brussels, ARA, RvSt 654, 1724: appointment record of Jean O'Donnogue.

97 Brussels, ARA, GRM 5, f. 146v–148r: naturalization and habilitation letters for councilor Godefroid Tackoen. It is interesting to note that his naturalization letters mention the long years of services rendered by his brother Arnold Henri Tackoen as the main argument to exempt him from the 1681 decree.

98 Brussels, ARA, GRO 443A, 1768: appointment record of André Kerens; ARA, GRO 442A, 1783: appointment record of Jacques François Douglas dit Schot.

99 Huwijn is only one example. Flanders also tried to have the councilor of the Council of Flanders De Jonghe appointed in 1692 (Brussels, ARA, RvSt 653, appointment record of Jean Seghers), councilor Sucx in 1694 (Brussels, ARA, RvSt 653, appointment record of Corneille Janssens d'Hujoel), and pensionary of the city of Menen Jean Baptiste De Decker in 1721 (Brussels, ARA, RvSt 654, appointment record of Jean Baptiste de Decker).

100 While Flanders' claim that it provided two thirds of the appeal cases was somewhat exaggerated, the province was responsible for almost 60 % of the total number of appeals at the Great Council during the eighteenth century. Cf. infra, Chap. 3.

101 Brussels, ARA, GRO 443B, 1744: appointment record of Charles Henry Goubau.

To a lesser extent, the Estates of Namur and Luxemburg also attempted to influence decisions in favor of a candidate of their own region. In 1696 and again in 1699, the Estates of Namur urged the governor to appoint Henri Chabotteau, one of the Council of Namur's members. In both cases, the petitioners stressed the importance of being represented at the Great Council by someone who was experienced in dealing with the specific practices and customs of Namur, given the 'considerable amount of lawsuits' coming from their province.[102] The Council of Luxemburg as well invoked the need for someone in Malines who was thoroughly familiar with Luxemburg's specific laws and habits as an argument to promote one of its own. Moreover, since part of the province was German-speaking, the Council argued it was essential to appoint someone to the Great Council who understood the language.[103]

Similar to the personal requests of the candidates for the Great Council, the Estates' petitions were mentioned in the advice the Council of State or the Privy Council formulated to the governor. While the Estates' arguments were often approved of by the advising council, their success was far from guaranteed. As far as we know, during the eighteenth century, only one Flemish councilor was appointed after a recommendation by the Estates of Flanders.[104] Over time, the significance the provincial Estates attached to having a member of their own province at the Great Council seemed to diminish. Indeed, the request of Flanders to appoint Joseph Huwijn in 1744 was the last of its sort that we were able to find in the appointment records.[105] It might have been that the respective provinces' representation gradually became better balanced, but the data suggests that this was not the case.[106] Alternatively, it is possible that the Estates no longer felt it necessary to petition the governor because representation at the Great Council was no longer regarded as essential. It is probably no coincidence that the early 1740s—the time of the last request—more or less corresponds with the steep decline in the number of lawsuits dealt with by the tribunal.[107]

The Great Council benefited from geographic diversity, predominantly because it needed councilors who could speak and write Flemish. From what we have learned from the records, the standard language at the Great Council was French and several

[102] Brussels, ARA, RvSt 653, 1696: appointment record of Honoré Henri Vanderhaeghen. In the eighteenth century, the Council of Namur provided a mere 7.6 % of all cases dealt with at the Great Council. Cf. infra, Chap. 3.

[103] Brussels, ARA, RvSt 653, 1699: appointment record of Hubert de Tombeur; ARA, RvSt 654, 1723: appointment record of Jean Henri Kahnn. This is a somewhat peculiar argument as cases coming from the German speaking part of Luxemburg were apparently usually translated before the appeal was handled. Cf. infra, Chaps. 2 and 4.

[104] Cf. supra: Jean Baptiste De Decker in 1721.

[105] It is of course possible that these later requests were not preserved in the files. However, since the Privy Council does not mention the existence of recommendations by the provinces in its recommendations to the governor, it is rather unlikely that there have been any at all.

[106] Cf. Excel database: councilors of the eighteenth century Great Council.

[107] Cf. infra, Chap. 3.

councilors knew only a smattering of Flemish if any.[108] Not surprisingly, cases from Flanders were often in Flemish and needed to be dealt with by a reporter who was fluent. In 1787, de Fierlant urged the *Conseil du gouvernement général* to quickly replace Gillis de Cock after his death, because with three other members of the Great Council being employed in Brussels,[109] *ce vuide le gène dans la distribution des causes flamandes*.[110]

2.2.2.4 Financial Means

Venality was commonplace in the Ancien Regime, even in the highest spheres of government.[111] In times when the sovereign needed more funds than usual, venality was rife and a lot of offices went to the highest bidder. In particular during the first two decades of the eighteenth century, when the War of the Spanish Succession constituted an ongoing drain on resources, positions on the Great Council were sold as well.[112] As early as 1699, Henri Chabotteau paid 7000 florins to the sovereign, on top of the regular *médianate* of 800 florins, to contribute to the 'present necessities'.[113] Eight years later, Albert de Lindicq paid 16,000 florins, *médianate* excluded. In exchange, his son-in-law Herman Vander Hemm could succeed him as lieutenant of the fiefs in the territory of Malines. It was explicitly stated that the

[108] For example, councilor Philippe Rogez openly admitted that he had no or only very limited knowledge of Flemish. Cf. Brussels, ARA, GRO 443A, 1771: appointment record of Ignace Joseph Wirix as advocate-fiscal. It is also known that Jacques Joseph de Stassart did not understand enough Flemish to examine witnesses. Cf. Verscuren, An. 2005. *"L'oeil et le bras du Roi?" Het vervolgingsbeleid van het officie-fiscaal van de Grote Raad van Mechelen (1767–1788)*. Unpublished Master's Thesis. Leuven: Katholieke Universiteit Leuven, p. 85. The appointment record of Henri Joseph de Villers de Fourneau as advocate-fiscal on the other hand, mentions "… il [de Villers] ecrit tres bien tant en français qu'en flammand, talent rare et néanmoins essentiel dans un officier public." Brussels, ARA, GRO 443A, 1767.

[109] We presume he refers to councilors Jean Baptiste Van Velde, Jean Baptiste Van der Fosse and Leopold de Laing who were all employed in one of the newly created councils of Joseph II. Cf. infra, Chap. 4.

[110] Brussels, ARA, ARR 857, Letter of de Fierlant to the *Conseil du gouvernement général*, November 1787.

[111] See, for example: Vandenbulcke, Anne. 1992. *Le pouvoir et l'argent sous l'Ancien Régime: la vénalité des offices dans les conseils collatéraux des Pays-Bas espagnols (seconde moitié du XVIIe siècle)* (Standen en Landen 94). Kortrijk: UGA. About venality in eighteenth century France: Doyle, William. 1996. *Venality: the sale of offices in eighteenth century France*. Oxford: Clarendon. About venality in the seventeenth century: Swart, Koenraad. 1949. *Sales of offices in the seventeenth century*. Tha Hague: Martinus Nijhoff.

[112] Hasquin, Hervé. 1973. Les difficultés financières du gouvernement des Pays-Bas autrichiens au début du XVIIIe siècle (1717–1740). *Revue internationale de la Banque* 6: 100–133. The same was true for the Council of Brabant. Cf. Gaillard, Arthur. 1898–1902. *Le Conseil de Brabant: histoire, organisation, procédure*. Brussels: Lebègue, 318.

[113] Brussels, ARA, RvSt 653, 1699: appointment record of Henri Chaboteau.

sum would be disbursed to the troops.[114] For the next few vacancies at the Great Council, all candidates offered to pay an additional sum on top of the *médianate*. Jean Alphonse De Coloma originally proposed 6000 florins as a gift, but raised the bid when Augustin de Steenhault offered the same amount.[115] One year later, the latter's promotion cost him 15,000 florins—*médianate* not included.[116] Pierre Van Volden received his appointment in 1712 for 10,000 florins and his office as a registrar, which was interesting because the sovereign could sell it again.[117] In 1716, Jean Ferdinand Keyaerts and Philippe de Beeckman were both ready to pay 6000 florins for a councillorship.[118]

It was not until 1719, when the war had ended and the Southern Netherlands came under Austrian sovereignty, that the practice of selling offices for a price much higher than the mere *médianate* was questioned. Following complaints from certain applicants, the Council of State assured that it was 'of course' absolutely against the will of his Majesty to sell offices to the highest bidder and left no doubt that the sovereign had always condemned venality.[119] Indeed, candidates should only be judged on their merits rather than their ability to offer the highest sum. Therefore, the appointee was only compelled to the payment of the *médianate*—which in 1719 was fixed at 8000 florins or ten times the original amount of 800 florins—and some other necessary charges, but not to any 'gift'.[120]

However, when the government appointed Jean François Courtois one year later, he had to pay 10,000 florins, which was presented as the 'regular' *médianate* for a position at the Great Council, although it was 2000 florins higher than the amount determined in 1719. Since Courtois was responsible for a very large family and had counted on a *médianate* of a mere 800 florins when he applied for the position in 1718, the sovereign made an exception.[121] Instead of the 10,000 florins, Courtois paid 6000. Five years later, a letter from the governor to the Council of State re-

[114] Brussels, ARA, Regentschapsraad van State, 285, 1707: appointment record of Albert Antoine de Lindicq.

[115] Brussels, ARA, Regentschapsraad van State, 285, 1711: appointment record of Jean Alphonse de Coloma as councilor.

[116] Brussels, ARA, Regentschapsraad van State, 285, 1712: appointment record of Augustin de Steenhault.

[117] Brussels, ARA, Regentschapsraad van State, 285, 1712: appointment record of Pierre Van Volden as councilor.

[118] Brussels, ARA, RvSt 654, 1716: appointment record of Philippe Antoine de Beeckman.

[119] Between roughly 1706 and 1715 the Austrian Netherlands had been ruled by the Anglo-Batavian Conference and while this had been done in the name of Emperor Charles VI, he himself had not had any say. Cf. De Schryver, Reginald. 1987. De Oostenrijkse aanspraken op de Spaans-Habsburgse erfenis. De Zuidelijke Nederlanden tijdens de Spaanse Successieoorlog. 1700–1716. In *Oostenrijks België 1713–1794. De Zuidelijke Nederlanden onder de Oostenrijkse Habsburgers*, ed. Hervé Hasquin, 11–36. Brussels: Gemeentekrediet van België.

[120] Brussels, ARA, RvSt 654, 1720: appointment record of Jean François Courtois.

[121] According to his biography in the *manuscrits divers*, Courtois was appointed *malgré lui*. The first in line, councilor at the Council of Flanders Van Vaerendonck, refused the position because of the amount of the *médianate*, and the second in line, Cordonnier, protégé of Prince Eugene de Savoie, died during a mission in The Hague. Brussels, ARA, MD 432, N°298.

vealed that Courtois still owed 2000 florins on the transaction, but the government let him out of the rest.[122] After 1725, the appointment records do not longer make mention of any 'voluntary gifts'. While it is possible that candidates simply stopped talking about their donations,[123] it is more plausible that the *médianate* of 8000 florins became generally accepted and remained unquestioned during the remainder of the eighteenth century. As a result, compared to the *médianate* of 800 florins requested before 1719, each councillorship now yielded an additional 7200 florins.

At the end of the eighteenth century, the habit of selling an office to the highest bidder returned, albeit in a different form. In the years following Joseph II's failed reforms of 1787, many civil servants who had been appointed in the new administrative and judicial structures became unemployed after the restoration. Not only did they believe to be entitled to a position in some council one way or another—especially if they had stayed loyal to the Austrian authorities during the tensions—they were also often paid a 'pension', at least for a certain amount of time.[124] Therefore, appointing a candidate who enjoyed such a pension did not directly provide the treasury with extra money, but certainly constituted an important saving for the government. That is how Guillaume Van Cutsem—though a clergyman—became appointed in a layman's seat.[125] The appointment records of Jean Louis Pouppez and Melchior Goubau specifically mention that by incorporating Pouppez, Goubau and François de Steenhault in its nomination, the Great Council fulfilled the intentions of his Majesty *qui veut qu'on préfère pour les places de judicature ceux qui ont été servi dans les nouveaux tribunaux de justice qu'on avait établis.*[126]

Nevertheless, even though the possibility of saving money by appointing 'victims' of Joseph II's interventions at the Great Council was certainly appealing and undoubtedly figured as an argument in the decisions of the *Conseil du gouvernement général* and, after 1791, of the Privy Council, the opinions of the Great Council were still taken into account, at least to a certain degree. When Jerôme Staquet, former councilor of the Great Council for Brabant,[127] bombarded the government with requests to be 'returned' to his seat at the Great Council of Malines, claim-

---

[122] Apparently, the governor did not want to establish a precedent, because the letter mentioned in the margin that this note should not be included in any copy and that the registrars themselves were responsible if any issues arose. Brussels, ARA, RvSt 654, 1720: appointment record of Jean François Courtois: "Soit enregistré quoi que cette note n'y soit tenu a peine que les greffiers seront responsables de la prejudice qui en peut resulter."

[123] It is highly unlikely that the candidates just stopped talking about their gifts. During the Ancien Regime, venality was a very common phenomenon and buying an office was certainly nothing to be ashamed of or to remain silent about.

[124] Brussels, ARA, ARR 974: compensations asked by those who served in the new courts of justice of 1787.

[125] Cf. supra, 2.2.2.2 Personal merits.

[126] Brussels, ARA, ARR 857, 1788: appointment records of Jean Louis Pouppez and Melchior Goubau. Jean Louis Pouppez, Melchior Goubau as well as François Alexandre de Steenhault all had served as judges in the new tribunal of first instance in Malines. It was also mentioned that all three of them had behaved excellently during the troubled times that broke out afterwards, when Goubau had especially been in danger of becoming victim to an angry mob.

[127] Cf. infra, Chap. 5.

ing that it was his right to be reappointed in the first available vacancy, the Privy Council rebuffed him. Although he received a pension of 3000 florins "for doing nothing", the Privy Council did not even try to appoint him to a councillorship, convinced that the Great Council would never accept him: first of all, Staquet had not been forwarded by the Great Council and secondly, the members of the tribunal certainly did not like him very much.[128]

2.2.2.5 The Sovereign's Whim

Surely, the wishes of the members of the Great Council were not always fulfilled. Twice during the period under consideration, the councilors had no say at all in the appointment of a new colleague. We already discussed the example of the pensionary of the city of Leuven Antoine Reniers, who was appointed to the Great Council in 1789 without being shortlisted.[129] This was an unmistakable contravention of article 8 of the 1559 ordinance decree, but no protest was voiced, as we may assume, partially because of the special circumstances of the late 1780s and partially because Reniers as pensionary would have had some experience in judicial affairs. When in the late seventeenth century, the Spanish emperor Charles II wanted to unilaterally impose a person named Ehrmans,[130] whose only merit was that his mother had been first lady-companion and later *assafate* of the queen,[131] the councilors did not give in easily.[132]

The name of Ehrmans first appears in the appointment records in 1693.[133] In a letter, Ehrmans mentioned that he received a patent letter from the sovereign, appointing him to the Great Council upon the first available vacancy. The councilors, however, judged his demand to be completely unfounded, unseen in the history of the Council and very detrimental to the administration of justice in the Netherlands. They claimed that it was unthinkable that a position on the Great Council—the highest legal institution in the country—could be conferred upon those favored by the sovereign in Spain because of military, political or familial connections. Nevertheless, Ehrmans wrote a request to the sovereign, demanding to be appointed after

[128] Brussels, ARA, GRO 442A, 1793: records concerning Jerôme Staquet: "Le conseil [privé] en observant cependant qu'on ne pourroit accueillir la demande du suppliant sans s'exposer a beaucoup de difficultés avec le Grand Conseil qui s'opposeroit indubitablement à son entrée au conseil, parce qu'il n'a pas été fait conseiller ensuite d'une nomination (…) Le rapporteur croit aussi que le suppliant devroit bien se contenter de la pension de 3000 fl dont il jouit pour ne rien faire, surtout lorsqu'il n'a *que trop sujet de s'apercevoir qu'il n'est pas agreable au corps dans lequel il voudroit entrer* ...".

[129] Cf. supra, 2.2.1.1 The *droit de terne*.

[130] The archives mention the name 'Ehrmans' as well as 'Ohrmans'. We prefer to use the former since it appears most frequently.

[131] Brussels, ARA, RvSt 653, 1693: appointment record of Jean Joseph de Vreven.

[132] The 'story' is set in the late seventeenth century, but had an effect on councilors who served in the eighteenth century, which is why it is included in our overview.

[133] Brussels, ARA, RvSt 653, 1693: appointment record of Jean Thadée de Grouff.

the death of councilor Schoorman. Obviously, Ehrmans could also count on political support in other high places: on several occasions, Columbanus, councilor of the Count Palatine of the Rhine, urged Governor Maximilian Emanuel of Bavaria to ensure that the Great Council appointed Ehrmans, as it would please his master.[134]

The Great Council, supported by the Council of State, took a firm stand, enumerating all the reasons why Ehrmans had neither the right nor capacity to become a councilor. Not all their arguments were equally sound, since the Malines Council handled its own conditions rather flexibly when nominating three candidates of its own choice.[135] Yet, this time the councilors insisted that appointing a foreigner without knowledge of the country or its languages and customs, who had not been included in a *terne* was impossible in the Netherlands.[136] In its advice, the Council of State entirely supported this reasoning and let the sovereign know that Ehrmans was not eligible.

Ehrmans did not leave it at that and apparently used his influence in Spain. At the end of January 1694, the governor forwarded a letter from the sovereign to the Council of State. Charles II of Spain informed the Council of State that the resistance of the Great Council against Ehrman's appointment was unacceptable. Furthermore, the patent letters which he had personally awarded should be followed. Without delay, Ehrmans had to be appointed to the first available vacancy.[137] Ultimately, Ehrmans never occupied a seat at the Great Council choosing instead to accept redemption money. Somehow, the members of the Great Council made an agreement with him, offering him 10,000 florins, paid for by the newly appointed councilor Janssens on top of his *médianate*, to withdraw his claims on a councillorship.[138]

For the Great Council, it might have seemed an elegant way out. At the same time, it was something of a Pyrrhic victory. The only way to defend their *droit de terne* against encroachments of the central government was by bribing the pretender. Although the result was the same—Ehrmans was never appointed—Charles II never reversed his initial decision and never accepted the inviolability of article 8, leaving the door open for similar maneuvers in the future. Although this is the only example we know of in which the central government tried to place one of its protégés in the Great Council against the wishes of its members,[139] it is certain that

[134] Brussels, ARA, GRM 140N: *Nomination des conseillers: expectative ecartée*: Guillaume Ehrmans, Letter of councilor Columbanus, dated December 11, 1692.

[135] Cf. supra, 2.2.2 The selection criteria.

[136] Brussels, ARA, RvSt 653, 1693: appointment record of Jean Joseph de Vreven.

[137] Brussels, ARA, RvSt 653, 1694: appointment record of Corneille Janssens Hujoel.

[138] Brussels, ARA, RvSt 653, 1694: appointment record of Corneille Janssens Hujoel: "Je denomme Janssens et j'ai ordonné au conseil de finances de payer au conseiller Ehrmans dix mille florins du donatif que le dit Janssens a offert en don pour la dite place."

[139] That is to say: in the period that we studied. Catherine Thomas mentioned that in the seventeenth century, Claude-Ignace le Fébure, personal secretary of Charles II, was imposed. Despite vehement protest, the Great Council had no other option but to accept Le Fébure among its members. Fortunately, he only stayed for a few months before he was recalled to Spain. Yet, he continued to enjoy his salary and *émoluments*. Cf. Thomas, Cathérine. 2013. Hommes d'Etat, hommes de loi. Les conseillers du Grand Conseil de Malines au XVIIe siècle. In *Gouvernance et administration*

the councilors often nominated those who were favored and recommended by the governor, or, even the sovereign himself.

Indeed, the Ehrmans case reiterates that strong kinship networks were crucial to acquire desirable positions in the higher administration. This applies to the eighteenth century and previous centuries alike. C. Thomas identified how in the seventeenth century intermarriage created a very tight-knit 'caste' of functionaries, not only within the Great Council but also in other branches of the government.[140] The same situation can be observed at other tribunals: a candidate needed a good network he could rely on to even stand a chance at an appointment. For example, at the High Council of Holland, Zeeland and West-Friesland—the successor of the Great Council in the Northern Netherlands—the nominees of Holland had to rally the support of one or more cities to be eligible for a councillorship. If a candidate had relatives among the cities' magistrates or if he was already working in a city's administration, his odds at success were rather high.[141] At the Council of Friesland as well, the majority of the councilors originated from the circle of Fries 'regents' and had fathers (in-law) who (had) served at the highest levels in Friesland.[142]

2.2.3 The 'Result' of the Nomination Procedure: The Best and the Brightest?

Did the nomination procedure, with its various steps and selection criteria, really provide the Great Council with the most competent judges? The example of councilor Robert Happart certainly leads us to doubt if that was really the case. Most members of the Great Council served for life or were promoted. Happart was the only eighteenth century councilor of the Great Council who did not experience either event. In May 1741, he wrote his letter of resignation to Maria Theresa, asking to be discharged of his duties, but with permission to keep the title of councilor of the Great Council.[143] Unlike those members who stopped attending the Council

dans les provinces belges (XVIe-XVIIIe siècles) (Archives et Bibliothèques de Belgique 99), Eds. Claude De Morbeau de Gerbehaye e.a, 155–177. Brussels: Archives et Bibliothèques de Belgique.

[140] Thomas, Cathérine. 2013. Hommes d'Etat, hommes de loi. Les conseillers du Grand Conseil de Malines au XVIIe siècle. In *Gouvernance et administration dans les provinces belges (XVIe-XVIIIe siècles)* (Archives et Bibliothèques de Belgique 99), Eds. Claude De Morbeau de Gerbehaye e.a., 155–177. Brussels: Archives et Bibliothèques de Belgique.

[141] Van Poelgeest, L. 1988. De raadsheren van de Hoge Raad van Holland, Zeeland en West-Friesland in de achttiende eeuw. *Bijdragen en mededelingen betreffende de geschiedenis der Nederlanden* 103.1: 27–28.

[142] Hempenius-Van Dijck, Barendina e.a. 1999. *De Heeren van den Raeden: biografieën en groepsportret van de raadsheren van het Hof van Friesland, 1499–1811*. Hilversum: Uitgeverij Verloren, 154–159.

[143] We believe that he was allowed to keep his title. In a lawsuit of 1750, he is still designated as 'councilor Happart.' Cf. Excel database: distribution records of the eighteenth century Great Council. Lawsuit distributed September 28, 1750: Jean Baptiste Van Schoor against councilor Happart.

because of health problems,[144] Happart left the Great Council without any pay. In fact, his resignation was not exactly entirely voluntary. Although in the appointment records, the Privy Council characterized him as an honorable man—*il est de bonne vie et moeurs*—and praised his previous work as an alderman of Brussels,[145] he had been working at the Great Council for only a few years when he ran into serious trouble. The debts he had incurred continued to accumulate and he became involved in several lawsuits against his creditors.[146]

Already in 1739, Governess Maria Elisabeth expressed her worries and imposed restrictions on the free use of his income: registrar de Robiano had to collect Happart's salary and withhold 800 florins on his report money to be distributed to his creditors. At the same time, Happart was ordered to limit his expenses: within two weeks, he had to dispose of his carriage and horses and reduce the number of his domestic workers to two.[147] Happart ignored these measures: instead of selling his horses and carriage himself, they were seized by his creditors. Accordingly, he gave the impression of dismissing two of his domestics, but secretly rehired them afterwards, only to end up never paying them.[148] In the meantime, he continued to plunge himself into debt, and committed several misdeeds, unworthy of his status as councilor. He even did not shy away from stealing from his colleagues.[149]

In 1741, the procurator-general of the Great Council summoned Happart before court, starting a criminal investigation against him, asking his dismissal.[150] In fact, his colleagues were appalled by his behavior and were especially concerned about the damages his actions may have on the image of the Council. Not only had he ignored all their attempts to make proper arrangements to appease his creditors, but he had also continued to get hold of money in all sorts of sinister and illicit ways *au*

---

144 Cf. infra, 2.3.4 Further career.

145 Brussels, ARA, GRO 443B, 1734: appointment record of Guillaume François Snoy.

146 Brussels, ARA, GRM 631–632: distribution records. These records mention all lawsuits initiated at the Great Council which were distributed to a councilor who acted as reporter. At several times during the 1730s, Happart became involved in lawsuits against his creditors. Eg. March 7, 1737: le seigneur Smets contre le conseiller Happart; April 1, 1737: la veuve Cuijckens contre le conseiller Happart; November 7, 1737: Paul Provost contre le conseiller Happart; January 9, 1738 le notaire Melaert contre le conseiller Happart; January 14, 1738: Balthazar Joseph Vander Hoeven contre le conseiller Happart; November 18, 1738: Martin Robijns contre le conseiller Happart; December 11, 1738: Marie Françoise du Bois veuve du seigneur Mosselman contre le conseiller Happart; January 16, 1739: Les heritiers de Jacques de Gortter contre le conseiller Happart; etc. Cf. Excel database: distribution records of eighteenth century Great Council.

147 Brussels, ARA, MD 432, n°318: Robert Hyacinthe Joseph Happart. Letter of Governess Maria Elisabeth, 1739.

148 Brussels, ARA, GRMOF, 561, 1741: trial initiated by the procurator-general of the Great Council concerning the excesses committed by councilor Happart of the Great Council.

149 Brussels, ARA, GRMOF 561, 1741: in his testimony, deputy procurator-general Deudon declared that Happart had borrowed two silver spoons and forks from him but that he had never been able to recover them despite several admonitions.

150 Brussels, ARA, GRMOF 561, 1741. The process file only contains the request of the procurator-general and the preliminary investigations. Probably Happart's resignation also brought an end to the criminal proceedings against him.

grand scandal du public, qui ne peut comprendre comment un conseil aussi illustre que respectable puisse souffrir plus longtemps parmi sa compagnie un membre de cette espèce ... Sensing that a disgraceful discharge was looming, Happart took the honorable way out and resigned.

Obviously, the nomination procedure, using family and networks as the main criterion proved to be problematic in some cases. Happart's example illustrates this point: rather than because of his superior qualities, he was selected because of his noble blood.[151] Yet, it did not really have to end as disastrously. Augustin de Steenhault—who was among the most high profile members of the Great Council—also received somewhat uneven appraisals by the central government.[152] Consequently, the question should be asked: was the central government really looking for the most intelligent and capable people to recruit for the Great Council (or, for that matter, in higher administration)? It is very likely that loyalty and obedience were much more valued. The Austrian government wished to recruit officials it could trust to carry out its orders and maintain peace and tranquility in the Netherlands. The appointment procedure was in the first place aimed at recruiting loyal, trustworthy, conscientious and compliant councilors. While this still failed in the case of Happart, councilor de Steenhault certainly fit into that category; the same was true of Goswin de Fierlant, who did combine loyalty and a sharp mind.

2.2.4 Recruiting l'oeil et le bras du Roi: The Appointment of the Fiscals[153]

If the councilors were supposed to be loyal and trustworthy, this was even more crucial for the fiscals of the Great Council. Yet, throughout the eighteenth century, the Great Council experienced considerable difficulties finding replacements when procurator-generals or advocate-fiscals resigned or passed away. Given the general dearth of candidates, the selection criteria used for councilors would usually be worthless. It was evident that the principal reason for the lack of interest was financial: in 1716 when procurator-general Remy du Laury had to be replaced, the Great Council needed nine months to find someone among its members to take up the position.

According to the tribunal, the problem derived from the Council of Finance which was consistently behind in paying the fiscals' salaries, despite their difficult

[151] Brussels, ARA, GRO 443B, 1734: appointment record of Guillaume Snoy.

[152] Cf. supra, 2.2.2.1 Family matters.

[153] For more information on the eighteenth century office-fiscal, see: Verscuren, An. 2005. *"L'oeil et le bras du Roi?" Het vervolgingsbeleid van het officie-fiscaal van de Grote Raad van Mechelen (1767–1788)*. Unpublished Master's Thesis. Leuven: Katholieke Universiteit Leuven and Verscuren, An. 2006. (S)pionnen van de vorst? De fiscalen van de Grote Raad in de tweede helft van de achttiende eeuw. *Pro Memorie* 8.2: 246–273.

and often strenuous work.[154] And even if paid on time, their income was absolutely insufficient. Regular advocates of the Great Council earned much more than a procurator-general or advocate-fiscal and they did not travel outside the city for work. Therefore, the Great Council concluded, it was not surprising that these positions were unpopular. It was argued that if the government was interested in attracting good, hard-working fiscals, it should raise their hourly wages as well as the compensation they drew for making copies and for commissions outside the city.[155] Obviously, not much was done: after the resignation of Jean Ferdinand Keyaerts as procurator-general in 1742, there was again not a single volunteer for the position. A majority finally designated Joseph Richterich, Theodore Snoy, Claude Sotteau and Jean Charles Van Slabbeeck as 'appointed volunteers', ranked according to seniority; the governor selected the penultimate.[156]

The problems worsened after advocate-fiscal Jean Guillaume de Potter stepped down in 1744.[157] Again, there were no volunteers, and this time, none of the first three councilors appointed by majority voting—Joseph Richterich, Theodore Snoy and François de Meuldre—agreed to accept the position. By then, the minister plenipotentiary—Count de Königsegg-Erps—had become rather annoyed with the recurring difficulties associated with the appointment of fiscals and warned the Privy Council that if the Great Council was not able to find three capable candidates to fulfill the position, he would propose 'efficient measures' in order to remedy the problem. Despite his threat, the next three candidates selected—Jean Baptiste Van Slabbeeck, Charles Thomas Caimo and Pierre Deudon—also felt the position insufferable.

In a long letter, Van Slabbeeck requested to be excused, formulating some doubts about his capabilities to fulfill the duties of an advocate-fiscal; an excellent judge was not necessarily an excellent fiscal.[158] The central government did not accept Van Slabbeeck's refusal and pursued the matter further with him and Caimo. The true reason the councilors refused to serve as procurators-general and advocates-fiscal came to the surface. It was more the fear of a loss in income that held Van Slabbeeck back from accepting the position than inability. According to both councilors, the fiscals missed out on 500 florins each year because they were not allowed to report cases. Caimo as well as Van Slabbeeck took the view that there

[154] Brussels, ARA, RvSt 651, 1716: appointment record of Jean Ferdinand Keyaerts as procurator-general.

[155] Brussels, ARA, GRM 140N: succession of Remy du Laury as procurator-general, 1716.

[156] Brussels, ARA, GRO 442A, 1742: appointment record of Claude Sotteau as procurator-general.

[157] De Potter was forced by the governor to resign as advocate-fiscal after his youngest son had—though more or less accidentally—mortally wounded another man in a bar fight. In addition, his other son and daughter had written two rather aggressive letters in defense of their younger brother, attacking the behavior of procurator-general Sotteau and of the Great Council as a *corpus* in the affair. Brussels, ARA, GR, Register 400, 1742, f. 280–305, and Register 401, 1743, f.14–26. The youngest son was in the end awarded mercy, though under certain conditions, while his brother and sister were both severely reprimanded for their indecent and insulting letters.

[158] Brussels, ARA, GRO 443A, 1744: appointment record of Jean Baptiste Van Slabbeeck as advocate-fiscal.

should be no more impediments for a procurator-general or advocate-fiscal to act as a reporter. Only the decree of Count Mansfelt, dating from 1590 when the fiscals were busy dealing with the riots, stood in the way of a decent income. The second reason why these positions were not exactly popular was the same as in 1716: the delay in the payment of their salary and expenses. The Privy Council suggested that the Council of Finance should look into the possibility of raising the income of the fiscals and make sure that in the future their salaries would be paid on time. Moreover, it proposed to seek the Great Council's advice on the possibility of having the procurator-general and advocate-fiscal report cases, without however telling which other remedies—raising their salary—were looked into.[159]

The Great Council flatly opposed the suggestion of allowing fiscals to be reporters, claiming that the public prosecutors were already overburdened with work. Furthermore, their frequent absences would entail the postponement of their cases, causing them to drag on for a long time and thereby creating a serious disadvantage for the parties concerned. In addition, the Great Council argued, Mansfelt's decree had not been issued solely with an eye to the exceptional circumstances of the 1590s but was added to the original instruction of 1559 as a permanent and eternal law. Therefore, the Great Council opposed the revoking of the decree of 1590, all the more so since—unlike what Van Slabbeeck and Caimo claimed—the fiscals earned more rather than less than their fellow councilors, as they were paid for every single one of their tasks. The tribunal maintained that for all these reasons, the aversion to the positions of procurator-general and advocate-fiscal should solely be attributed to the delay in payment, rather than their alleged lower income. Urging the Council of Finance to reimburse the fiscals on time would entirely solve the problem.[160] Eventually, Van Slabbeeck did end up being appointed advocate-fiscal because of his 'superior qualities'. The Privy Council followed the advice of the Great Council, ranking him first, making the subtle remark that it was his modesty that had caused his initial refusal.[161]

The appointment of Jean Philippe de Waepenaert as procurator-general in 1750 after the death of Claude Sotteau was less troublesome.[162] Eleven years later, however, de Waepenaert requested to be relieved of his duties as procurator-general,

---

[159] Brussels, ARA, GRO 443A, 1744: appointment record of Jean Baptiste Van Slabbeeck as advocate-fiscal.

[160] Brussels, ARA, GRO 443A, 1744: appointment record of Jean Baptiste Van Slabbeeck as advocate-fiscal: advice of the Great Council.

[161] Brussels, ARA, GRO 443A, 1744: appointment record of Jean Baptiste Van Slabbeeck as advocate-fiscal: advice of the Privy Council.

[162] Nevertheless, it still took almost three years to appoint a new procurator-general. Again, there were no volunteers for the position, and Jean Philippe de Waepenaert was considered the only viable candidate of the three nominees, Charles Thomas Caimo and Charles Henri Goubau being characterized as 'not very active or resolved'. The only argument against de Waepenaert was his youth and lack of experience, as he had only recently, i.e. one month before, been promoted to a councillorship. Yet, considering that he had been a deputy procurator-general before and therefore had an intimate knowledge of the Great Council and the duties associated with the public prosecution office, the Privy Council deemed him ready for the job. Brussels, ARA, GRO 443A, 1750: appointment record of Jean Philippe de Waepenaert as procurator-general.

while still being allowed to retain his councillorship. He maintained his request was due to deteriorating health, eyesight problems, and the doctors' advice to reduce his workload. Furthermore, the needs of his large family coupled with his failing health and visual deficiencies meant that he could not exercise his duties as a fiscal with the same dedication, so he asked to be relieved of his responsibilities as procurator-general.[163] The sovereign accepted his resignation and ordered the Great Council to proceed to a new nomination, which turned out to be an almost exact repeat of the previous one. Again, no volunteers came forward and again the Great Council selected three councilors by majority of votes, ranking them according to seniority: Henri Theodore Jacobs, Joseph Wiro de Bors and Daniël Servaes. The governor followed the Great Council's opinion and appointed the former.[164] It is somewhat notable that in its advice, the Privy Council remarked that Servaes had already served for 15 years as fiscal in the provincial Council of Flanders and [qu'il] ***paroit mériter de jouir de repos auquel il est parvenu par sa promotion a une place de conseiller du Grand Conseil.*** Apparently, a councillorship in the Great Council was not considered to be burdensome!

The issue escalated when advocate-fiscal Jean Baptiste Van Slabbeeck and his successor Henri Joseph de Villers had to be replaced. In 1766, Van Slabbeeck handed in his notice, referring to his bad state of health. The sovereign accepted his resignation on the condition that he would continue to assume his responsibilities until a new advocate-fiscal had been appointed. Contrary to Jean Philippe de Wapenaert, Van Slabbeeck truly had serious medical problems and he died only a few months later, in January 1767. In the meantime, the Great Council started its quest for a new fiscal. Again for want of volunteers, it appointed four councilors *ex officio*: Nicholas Joseph Pouppez, Jean Dominique Vriesen, Joseph Wiro de Bors and Godefroid Tackoen. All four requested to be excused. The Privy Council advised the sovereign to accept their excuses as it would not be in the interest of the public or in that of the ruler herself to compel someone to fulfill the duties of public prosecutor. Moreover, a strong advocate-fiscal was needed since the current procurator-general—Henri Theodore Jacobs—had more than once proven to be a weak and cowardly figure.[165]

Yet, the Privy Council started to lose patience, criticizing the right of the Great Council to propose a *terne*. The Council even threatened to revoke this privilege, bringing to mind that the sovereign could alter the statutes of the Great Council if the occasion called for it. In a certain sense, the death of Van Slabbeeck presented a

[163] Brussels, ARA, GRO 442A, 1761: appointment record of Henri Theodore Jacobs as procurator-general. With the benefit of hindsight, we might suspect that de Waepenaert's excuses did not entirely correspond to the truth. Councilor de Waepenaert only died in 1797 and continued to occupy his seat until the very end of the Great Council in the Netherlands in 1794. Apparently he was not too ill or too blind to work for more than another thirty years as councilor after his resignation as procurator-general. Cf. infra, Chap. 4.

[164] Brussels, ARA, GRO 442A, 1761: appointment record of Henri Theodore Jacobs as procurator-general.

[165] Brussels, ARA, GRO 443A, 1767: appointment record of Henri Joseph de Villers as advocate-fiscal "… le procureur général du Grand Conseil a donné plusieurs fois des preuves de sa faiblesse et de sa pusillanimité ainsi qu'il est de la connaissance de V.A.R."

way out of the deadlock. Instead of again proceeding to a second nomination, which would undoubtedly fail once more, the Great Council suggested to first appoint someone to fill Van Slabbeeck's councilor's seat and then ask the new appointee about becoming the new advocate-fiscal. Even though the Privy Council was aware what was afoot—there was little chance the Great Council would include anyone in the *terne* who was not willing to be advocate-fiscal—it advised the sovereign to accept the solution, as it seemed the only viable one for the moment. Indeed, less than two months after his promotion to a councillorship at the Great Council, Henri Joseph de Villers was appointed advocate-fiscal. Since the Great Council needed to present a threesome and since none of the other councilors would run the risk of getting appointed, they selected Henri Chrétien Diu and Jacques Joseph de Stassart—respectively the deputy procurator-general and a regular advocate of the Great Council—to run for public prosecutor.[166] As they were at that time not yet councilors, they were never really considered.[167]

A mere four years later, Henri Joseph de Villers tendered his resignation as fiscal.[168] Again no one volunteered and again those appointed[169] asked to be excused, causing the Privy Council to once again investigate the refusals. The Council wanted to avoid 1771 turning into a copy of 1767, when de Villers accepted the position only to wait for the right opportunity to get rid of it.[170] Unsurprisingly, the Privy Council's inquiry turned out to have the exact same results as the similar survey of 1744. A mere councillorship was financially much more lucrative than a position as public prosecutor. True, the salaries of the advocate-fiscal and procurator-general exceeded those of the regular councilors by about 70 florins annually, but that could in no way compensate for the loss of income from 'report money'. The only feasible solution was to substantially increase the compensation package of the fiscals in order to make the position more attractive.

The Privy Council finally suggested raising the annual fixed income of the fiscals with 500 florins, accorded in the form of an *ad personam*.[171] The finan-

166 Brussels, ARA, GRO 443A, 1767: appointment record of Henri Joseph de Villers as advocate-fiscal.

167 Coincidence or not, both of them would later become respectively procurator-general and advocate-fiscal.

168 He more or less copied the example of Jean Philippe de Waepenaert: in his letter of resignation he referred to his bad health. However, de Villers' health was good enough to stay on as councilor until 1794. Brussels, ARA, GRO 443, 1771: appointment record of Ignace Joseph Wirix as advocate-fiscal.

169 Ignace Joseph Wirix, André Kerens and Philippe Joseph Rogez.

170 Brussels, ARA, GRO 443A, 1771: appointment record of Ignace Joseph Wirix as advocate-fiscal.

171 Brussels, ARA, GRO 443A, 1771: appointment record of Ignace Joseph Wirix as advocate-fiscal. For fear of similar demands from the other fiscals, it was decided that only the procurator-general and advocate-fiscal of the Great Council could make claims on this raise, as, according to the central government, the fiscals of the other councils could not present the same titles and worked in very different circumstances. Alternatively, it was just not as difficult to find a public prosecutor in the other provinces as was the case in Malines. For example, at the Council of Brabant, it was seemingly no problem to recruit fiscals. In fact, Gaillard mentions that the position of

cial incentive did not exactly provoke a lot of enthusiasm among the councilors, undoubtedly because the government had decided that a *médianate* of more than 133 florins would be demanded because of this rise in pay.[172] During the second nomination round, again nobody volunteered and Ignace Wirix, André Kerens and Philippe Rogez were once again nominated *ex officio*. The former was appointed, despite his objections that he was too old (60) and no longer had the resilience required to do the strenuous work of an advocate-fiscal. However, he apparently did not dare to actually turn down the offer, which was probably enough reason for the central government to appoint him.[173]

In the end, the increase in pay did have a positive effect, at least to a certain extent. When the death of Henri Jacobs vacated the seat of procurator-general, there were again no volunteers, but those appointed *ex officio* for once did not send any excuses to the central government. Henri Diu filled in the position, although—or because?—he had only been a councilor for 2 months. With his appointment, the Great and the Privy Councils tied in with the tendency to select freshly initiated members as fiscals. Contrary to Jean Philippe de Waepenaert and Henri de Villers, Diu stayed on for almost thirty years until the abolishment of the Great Council.[174] The same pattern can be observed when Wirix resigned: nobody volunteered, but those appointed did not refuse. In the end, Jacques Joseph de Stassart became fiscal alongside Diu.[175] He proved to be an excellent choice for the government, being the most vigorous and proactive advocate-fiscal the Great Council had witnessed in years.[176] After the promotion of de Stassart to the presidency of the Council of Namur, his replacement by Melchior Goubau went equally smoothly[177]—undoubtedly his exemption from paying the *médianate* helped—and was equally successful: Goubau turned out to be the energetic and trustworthy advocate-fiscal the government needed in the troublesome times of the late 1780s and early 1790s.[178]

---

procurator-general—who at the Council of Brabant was not a regular councilor—was one of the most lucrative in the province of Brabant, yielding up to 21,000 florins a year in the eighteenth century, much higher indeed than at the Great Council. Gaillard, Arthur. 1898–1902. *Le Conseil de Brabant: histoire, organisation, procédure*. Brussels: Lebègue, t. 2, p. 391.

172 Brussels, ARA, ARR 857, 1789: appointment record of Melchior Goubau as advocate-fiscal. "… il leur a été notifié par lettre du ci devant conseil des finances du 30 octobre 1771, que par rapport à cette augmentation lesdits fiscaux seraient soumis à une médianate de cent trente trois florins 6 sols huit deniers …".

173 Brussels, ARA, GRO 443A, 1771: appointment record of Ignace Joseph Wirix as advocate-fiscal.

174 Brussels, ARA, GRO 442A, 1767: appointment record of Henri Chrétien Diu as procurator-general.

175 Brussels, ARA, GRO 443B, 1778: appointment record of Jacques Joseph de Stassart as advocate-fiscal.

176 As we demonstrated in Verscuren, An. 2005. *"L'oeil et le bras du Roi?" Het vervolgingsbeleid van het officie-fiscaal van de Grote Raad van Mechelen (1767–1788)*. Unpublished Master's Thesis. Leuven: Katholieke Universiteit Leuven.

177 Brussels, ARA, ARR 857, 1789: appointment record of Melchior Goubau as advocate-fiscal.

178 Cf. infra, Chap. 5.

Indeed, if the government could choose among several candidates for the position of fiscal—which, admittedly, only seldom happened—the criteria handled were not so much family or networks, but energy, vitality and certainly also loyalty. Henri Theodore Jacobs, for example, was reproached for being 'weak and cowardly'. In contrast, the last two advocates-fiscal—Jacques Joseph de Stassart and Melchior Goubau—scored high in those areas. If only counting the number of trials he initiated[179]—by himself (14) or together with his colleague procurator-general Henri Chrétien Diu (11)—de Stassart stood out in comparison with his immediate predecessor Joseph Wiro de Bors (who prosecuted not a single trial on his own and merely three together with Diu).[180] No definite figures are available for Goubau, but the number of political trials from the period after 1789 exceeds the 25 handled by de Stassart. In that regard, loyalty to the Austrian Crown was also an important prerequisite, especially in the politically unstable circumstances in the Netherlands after the judicial and political reforms of Joseph II of 1787. Both de Stassart and Goubau were threatened, attacked and in case of the latter even imprisoned for their loyalty to the emperor.[181] Unsurprisingly, neither were 'appointed volunteers' nor were they deprived of a healthy ambition.

2.3 The Councilors' Profile

It is self-evident that the profile of the councilors largely derived from the criteria used during the nomination and appointment procedure. Therefore, we discuss the members' social backgrounds—linked to kinship and personal networks—as well as their origin, education and careers. Additionally, we investigate further developments in the councilors' professional lives, if there were any at all: was membership in the Great Council merely an intermediate stage, a stepping stone to a position in the highest ranks of the administration, or did it constitute the nadir of their careers? Throughout our discussion, this group portrait of the councilors of the eighteenth century Great Council will be compared with both that of their predecessors and that of the members of comparable tribunals.[182]

[179] Prosecuting crimes was only one of the many duties of the fiscals. Cf. Verscuren, An. 2005. *"L'oeil et le bras du Roi?" Het vervolgingsbeleid van het officie-fiscaal van de Grote Raad van Mechelen (1767–1788)*. Unpublished Master's Thesis. Leuven: Katholieke Universiteit Leuven, 19.

[180] Verscuren, An. 2006. (S)pionnen van de vorst? De fiscalen van de Grote Raad in de tweede helft van de achttiende eeuw. *Pro Memorie* 8.2: 269.

[181] Cf. infra, Chap. 5.

[182] For the late fifteenth and early sixteenth century Great Council, we make use of the doctoral study of Kerckhoffs-de Heij. Herein she reconstructs the geographical, social and cultural background of the councilors, providing us with reference material for the early history of the tribunal. It is somewhat problematic that she gives absolute numbers without mentioning for how many councilors she has been able to gather data, making it difficult to retrieve the percentages involved. Kerckhoffs-De Hey, A.J.M. 1980. *De Grote raad en zijn functionarissen, 1477–1531*.

2.3.1 Social Background

Our analysis of the nomination and appointment procedures demonstrated that having the 'right' relatives and networks highly enhanced a candidate's chances of acquiring a councillorship at the Great Council. This is certainly no surprise: especially fathers—or fathers in-law—who had already served the Crown could further a career, as they were considered a guarantee for the quality of work that could be expected from a relative.[183]

Table 2.1 indicates that the majority of the councilors' fathers—*i.e.* 70 %—were officials themselves, serving in central institutions such as the Great Council or the Accounts Chamber, in provincial courts such as the Council of Flanders, or in the local administration of cities or smaller regions. Two others pursued a military career. Five people were engaged in what we would now call a liberal profession, two of whom were medical doctors and three of whom practiced as advocates, two at a provincial council and one at the Great Council itself. Finally, the list ends with three university professors and three persons who apparently lived off the income of their estates. Unsurprisingly, none of the councilors descended from the lower classes or even the lower middle classes. The social origins of the presidents of the Great Council—which in the eighteenth century was still a prestigious position[184]—show all of them had parents serving in a provincial or central institution, except for Goswin de Fierlant. He however, could not only boast a great-grandfather who had been chancellor of the Council of Brabant,[185] but especially his marriage with the daughter of Patrice de Neny trusted him in the highest regions of the administration.

Amsterdam: s.n. The article of Thomas regarding the seventeenth century councilors, on the other hand, provides us with much more detailed information, allowing proper comparison. Thomas, Cathérine. 2013. Hommes d'Etat, hommes de loi. Les conseillers du Grand Conseil de Malines au XVIIe siècle. In *Gouvernance et administration dans les provinces belges (XVIe–XVIIIe siècles)* (Archives et Bibliothèques de Belgique 99), Eds. Claude De Morbeau de Gerbehaye e.a., 155–177. Brussels: Archives et Bibliothèqes de Belgique. Van Poelgeest's article on the eighteenth century High Council (Van Poelgeest, L. 1988. De raadsheren van de Hoge Raad van Holland, Zeeland en West-Friesland in de achttiende eeuw. *Bijdragen en mededelingen betreffende de geschiedenis der Nederlanden* 103.1: 20–51), the study of Hempenius-Van Dijck, Nieuwland and Vries on the Council of Friesland (Hempenius-Van Dijck, Barendina e.a. 1999. *De Heeren van den Raeden: biografieën en groepsportret van de raadsheren van het Hof van Friesland, 1499–1811*. Hilversum: Uitgeverij Verloren) and Gaillard's monumental three volumes on the Council of Brabant (Gaillard, Arthur. 1898–1902. *Le Conseil de Brabant: histoire, organisation, procédure*. Brussels: Lebègue) provide reference material for the situation in these councils.

[183] We limited our research to identifying the social background of fathers. Grandfathers, uncles, brothers, in-laws etc. could all play a role, but, except for a few notorious examples (Goswin de Fierlant, Martial de le Vielleuze, Robert Happart, …), there is simply not enough information on the extended family of the councilors.

[184] Contrary to the regular councilors of the Great Council, Bruneel and Hoyois rated the presidents among the high officials of the Austrian Netherlands.

[185] Stevens, Fred. 2000. Goswinus Anna Maria Felix de Fierlant (1735–1804): Een Turnhoutse bevoorrechte getuige van het einde van een tijdperk. *Taxandria: jaarboek van de Koninklijke geschied-en oudheidkundige kring van de Antwerpse Kempen* 71: 8.

Table 2.1 Councilors' paternal professional background[a]

	Nr of councilors	% known total	% overall total
Administration (All)	36	73	
Administration—Central	10	20	
Administration—Provincial	5	10	
Administration—Local	21	43	
Doctor or advocate	5	10	
Rentier	3	6	
Military	2	4	
Academia	3	6	
Total known	49	100	51
Unknown	47		49
Overall total	96		100

[a]It must be noted that there is no data available for 47—or almost 50%—of the councilors. However, we believe that the data we do possess is more or less representative, although it must be taken into account that the reason for the lack of information might be connected to their social status (there might be much less incentive to name the profession of a father when a candidate is not high born). Since the results of our analysis are similar to what Thomas has determined for the seventeenth century (cf. infra) and since some of the councilors for whom we do not possess any information are from noble descent or have other family members working in the Austrian administration, we have reasons to believe that those for whom we do not have any data are not particularly from a low background

In addition, 55 out of 96 members of the Council—or some 57%—were of noble descent.[186] This is not surprising, first because candidates of noble descent were favored by the government[187] and secondly, because sometime around 1660 hereditary nobility was officially granted to the councilors of the Great Council.[188] Since several members of the tribunal had ancestors who had served in one or another central institution, quite a few of them had already been elevated to the gentry. Those who had not yet acquired nobility obtained it for themselves and their offspring by their promotion to the Great Council. For them, membership of the Great Council was certainly a step forward on the social scale and held the promise of a future career for their children in the administration of the Netherlands. Those who were already blue blooded could receive a (supplementary) title: de Coloma, for example, became count in 1728, while de St Vaast was elevated to baron in 1767.[189]

[186] See Excel database: councilors of the eighteenth century Great Council.

[187] Cf. supra, 2.2.2.1 Family matters.

[188] An Edict of Isabelle and Albrecht of 1616 had already granted hereditary nobility to '*ceux … qui à cause de leurs estats, offices et charges … ont droit de ce faire … pourront … prendre ou s'attribuer la qualité d'escuyer …*' without however specifying who exactly was eligible. In 1660, the Privy Council confirmed that the councilors of the Great Council could pass their nobility on to their offspring. The same was true for the presidents of the provincial councils. Regular councilors of provincial courts however, had no right to such hereditary nobility (although especially those of the Council of Brabant continued to claim this); they were merely noble on a personal title. Cf. Janssens, Paul. 1993. Les charges anoblissantes dans les conseils des Pays-Bas espagnols et autrichiens. In *Beleid en bestuur in de oude Nederlanden. Liber amicorum Prof. Dr.M. Baelde*, eds. Hugo Soly and René Vermeir, 225–239. Ghent: RUG.

[189] In both cases, these titles were accorded after their career in the Great Council.

The social background of the eighteenth century members of the Great Council is to a large degree comparable to their predecessors in the previous centuries. Based on the profession of the councilors' fathers, A.J.M. Kerckhoffs-de Heij, for the late fifteenth and early sixteenth centuries and C. Thomas for the seventeenth century, determined that many councilors originated from a civil service family.[190] In the period studied by Thomas, this amounted to even 77 %.[191] Similarly, a fairly high number of the members of the sixteenth and seventeenth century Great Council were of noble descent. Councilors born into a bourgeois family whose fathers were engaged in a 'liberal profession'—advocates included—constituted a minority.[192]

The social profile of the members of the Council of Friesland[193] does not differ very much either from what we have established for the Great Council: the majority of them was born in civil servants' families and was somehow related to the 'regents' of Friesland. Only a minority had fathers with a career in the military, at the university or in trade.[194] The same is true for the councilors of the eighteenth century High Council of Holland, Zeeland and West-Friesland: no less than 70 % of the councilors had fathers who had worked in the Dutch administration; only 5 % had fathers working in a liberal profession. *Homines novi* were equally rare in the High Council: the few that did manage to make the social climb were often from Zeeland. This had everything to do with the province's specific nomination procedure, which, without entering into detail, made it possible for talented, ambitious men who did not possess the right network but did have some financial resources to buy their way into the High Council.[195] Yet, they were the exception that proved the rule. In general, the majority of the members of the provincial or central tribunals

---

[190] Kerckhoffs-De Hey, A.J.M. 1980. *De Grote raad en zijn functionarissen, 1477–1531*. Amsterdam: s.n, 76; Thomas, Cathérine. 2013. Hommes d'Etat, hommes de loi. Les conseillers du Grand Conseil de Malines au XVIIe siècle. In *Gouvernance et administration dans les provinces belges (XVIe–XVIIIe siècles)* (Archives et Bibliothèques de Belgique 99), Eds. Claude De Morbeau de Gerbehaye e.a. Brussels: Archives et Bibliothèques de Belgique, 161.

[191] In her table, Thomas mentioned only 51 %. However, if we do not take into account the number of councilors for which she does not have any data on the profession of their fathers, 73 out of 94 councilors came from a civil servant background.

[192] Kerckhoffs-De Hey, A.J.M. 1980. *De Grote raad en zijn functionarissen, 1477–1531*. Amsterdam: s.n, 76–79; Thomas, Cathérine. 2013. Hommes d'Etat, hommes de loi. Les conseillers du Grand Conseil de Malines au XVIIe siècle. In *Gouvernance et administration dans les provinces belges (XVIe–XVIIIe siècles)* (Archives et Bibliothèques de Belgique 99), Eds. Claude De Morbeau de Gerbehaye e.a. Brussels: Archives et Bibliothèques de Belgique, 161.

[193] Hempenius-Van Dijck studied all members of the Council of Friesland between 1578 and 1811.

[194] Hempenius-Van Dijck, Barendina e.a. 1999. *De Heeren van den Raeden: biografieën en groepsportret van de raadsheren van het Hof van Friesland, 1499–1811*. Hilversum: Uitgeverij Verloren, 152–155.

[195] Van Poelgeest, L. 1988. De raadsheren van de Hoge Raad van Holland, Zeeland en West-Friesland in de achttiende eeuw. *Bijdragen en mededelingen betreffende de geschiedenis der Nederlanden* 103.1: 220.

Table 2.2 Geographical origins of the councilors of the Great Council in the eighteenth century[b]

Nationality	Number	%
Brabant	31	32.3
Flanders	23	24.0
Malines	12	12.5
Hainaut	8	8.3
Luxemburg	7	7.3
Namur	3	3.1
Gelre	3	3.1
Tournai	1	1.0
Terres de Débat	1	1.0
Other[a]	7	7.3
Total	*96*	*100*

[a] Other category includes Northern Netherlands, France, Liege, Hungary, Ireland, and German Empire

[b] Place of birth has been used as the determining factor to establish the councilors' geographical origin. When determining which province a city belonged to, we evidently took into consideration the time of birth of the councilor. For example, by the late seventeenth century, Tourcoing had been permanently attached to France; at the time of birth of Philippe du Jardin however, it was still part of Flanders

were born in some "patriarchate of the State",[196] independent of the century or the council in which they served.

2.3.2 Geographical Origin

The geographical origin of the councilors was, as long as they were born within the borders of the Austrian Netherlands, not a key criterion. However, several provinces did attach some importance to being represented at the Great Council and the court itself equally benefited from having councilors of a different linguistic background: councilors who understood Dutch were always needed (Table 2.2).[197]

The predominance of Flanders and Brabant immediately attracts attention: taken together, they count for more than 50 % of the total. Of the 53 members of the Great Council originating in one of those two provinces, most have their roots in larger cities such as Brussels, Antwerp and Leuven for Brabant and Bruges and Ghent for Flanders. To be such a small seigniory, Malines as well provided a rather significant amount of councilors. This does not come as a surprise, given that several eighteenth century members of the Great Council had relatives who (had) worked at the Council (before). Moreover, the presence of the Great Council in the city also

[196] Thomas, Cathérine. 2013. Hommes d'Etat, hommes de loi. Les conseillers du Grand Conseil de Malines au XVIIe siècle. In *Gouvernance et administration dans les provinces belges (XVIe–XVIIIe siècles)* (Archives et Bibliothèques de Belgique 99), Eds. Claude De Morbeau de Gerbehaye e.a. Brussels: Archives et Bibliothèques de Belgique, 165.

[197] Cf. supra, 2.2.2.3 Geographical distribution.

attracted a whole range of other professions; advocates practicing at the tribunal are only one example.[198] The southern provinces of Hainaut, Luxemburg, Namur and Tournai—especially considering their size—were considerably underrepresented. Finally, seven out of 96 councilors were not born in the Austrian Netherlands. While foreigners were officially banned, there were certainly ways to acquire a dispensation.[199]

If the large number of councilors born in Flanders follows along the lines of expectation, the absolute preponderance of the province of Brabant seems somewhat out of the ordinary given that the Council of Brabant had not been subordinate to the jurisdiction of the Great Council since the early sixteenth century. Of course, Brabant was one of the most populated regions, but also—more importantly—dominant in both economic and political terms. Moreover, of the 31 Brabant councilors, 10 were born in Brussels. As capital of the Austrian Netherlands, the city naturally attracted many officials who served in the (central) administration, in institutions such as the Privy Council, the Council of Finance or the Council of Brabant. Looking at the known family ties of those 10 Brussels-born members of the Great Council, it is clear that many had fathers who lived in the city because of their professional occupation: Pierre Van Kerrenbroeck's father was a member of the Council of Brabant, Honoré Vanderhaeghen was the son of the Brussels treasurer, Albert de Lindicq's father served as secretary for the *Audience* etc.[200] Considering that family ties were essential in a civil servant's career, it is absolutely not surprising that many of these high officials were born in Brussels.

Hempenius-Van Dijk noticed the same phenomenon for the Council of Friesland: more than 40 % of the members of the Council of Friesland who served between 1578 and 1811 were born in Leeuwarden. Undoubtedly, this can be explained by the fact that many of the councilors were sons of high office holders who frequently stayed in the Fries capital for their work.[201] It also accounts for the relative underrepresentation of the southern provinces in the Austrian Netherlands: the career opportunities in, for example, Namur and Luxemburg were far more limited than in Brabant and Flanders.

There is a large degree of similarity between the geographical origin of the councilors of the eighteenth century Great Council and that of their predecessors of the late fifteenth, early sixteenth and seventeenth centuries. Kerckhoffs-de Hey found for the early years of the tribunal a distinct dominance of Flanders and Burgundy, followed by Brabant. Holland and Zeeland were relatively underrepresented; Ma-

198 The importance the Great Council had for the economic activity and prosperity of the city will be amply discussed in the following chapters.

199 Cf. supra, 2.2.2.3 Geographical distribution.

200 Excel database: the councilors of the eighteenth century Great Council.

201 Hempenius-Van Dijck, Barendina e.a. 1999. *De Heeren van den Raeden: biografieën en groepsportret van de raadsheren van het Hof van Friesland, 1499–1811*. Hilversum: Uitgeverij Verloren, 152.

lines itself provided only five councilors for the entire period.[202] Since Malines was, for a certain time during the period under study, not yet an administrative or judicial center—as it officially became with the permanent establishment of the Great Council after 1504—this is hardly surprising. In the seventeenth century, on the contrary, Malines provided the second largest number of members of the Great Council (22 %), preceded by Brabant (32 %) and followed at a certain distance by Flanders (15 %). Only three councilors were foreigners: all of them were born in Liège, which, although it did not officially belong to the Austrian Netherlands, was still a close neighbor.[203]

The Great Council was apparently the only high court which, as a rule, included members in its ranks who came from provinces that did not fall under its jurisdiction. For the seventeeth century at least, Thomas observed a concern to arrive at an even representation of the different provinces of the Austrian Netherlands.[204] At the Council of Friesland, however, all councilors needed to be Fries born or to have lived for an extended period of time in the province. This was the only recruitment criterion which was never ignored.[205] The High Council also (almost) exclusively accepted men who were born within the environs of Holland or Zeeland: in the eighteenth century, only one member's cradle had not been set in one of these two provinces.[206] At the Council of Brabant, two seats *could* be occupied by councilors born outside Brabant: however, especially during the eighteenth century, the Council of Brabant did its utmost to avoid that non-natives became involved in the affairs of the province.[207]

2.3.3 Education and Previous Career

In general, the career of a councilor started with studying both laws at the university. For 66 of the 96 members of the eighteenth century Great Council it has been certified that they obtained the degree of *licencié en droits*, but it can be assumed

[202] Kerckhoffs-De Hey, A.J.M. 1980. *De Grote raad en zijn functionarissen, 1477–1531*. Amsterdam: s.n, 71–76.

[203] Thomas, Cathérine. 2013. Hommes d'Etat, hommes de loi. Les conseillers du Grand Conseil de Malines au XVIIe siècle. In *Gouvernance et administration dans les provinces belges (XVIe–XVIIIe siècles)* (Archives et Bibliothèques de Belgique 99), Eds. Claude De Morbeau de Gerbehaye e.a., 155–177. Brussels: Archives et Bibliothèques de Belgique, 159.

[204] Ibidem, 160.

[205] Hempenius-Van Dijck, Barendina e.a. 1999. *De Heeren van den Raeden: biografieën en groepsportret van de raadsheren van het Hof van Friesland, 1499–1811*. Hilversum: Uitgeverij Verloren, 150.

[206] Van Poelgeest, L. 1988. De raadsheren van de Hoge Raad van Holland, Zeeland en West-Friesland in de achttiende eeuw. *Bijdragen en mededelingen betreffende de geschiedenis der Nederlanden* 103.1: 23. Van Poelgeest attributes this phenomenon to the habit in Zeeland of selling offices in het High Council to the highest bidder.

[207] Gaillard, Arthur. 1898–1902. *Le Conseil de Brabant: histoire, organisation, procédure*. Brussels: Lebègue, t. 2, p. 233.

that the 30 others also graduated in law.[208] Having a law degree was—if not in theory than certainly in practice—a prerequisite for becoming a councilor at the Great Council. Apart from two exceptions, all members earned their certificate at the *Alma Mater* in Leuven: in an attempt to prevent the spread of heresies, the decree of Philips II of 1598, repeated in 1617 by Albert and Isabella, determined that the universities of Leuven (and Douai) would suffice to educate jurists in the Southern Netherlands, turning especially Leuven into a breeding ground for high officials. Pierre Van Heydenreyck, however, preferred to enroll at the *nation flamande* of the University of Dôle.[209] Yet at the time he obtained his degree—he matriculated in 1665—the Franche-Comté was still part of the Habsburg Netherlands. Juste Jacques Bervoet, on the other hand, studied both at the University of Leuven and Douai: his choice for the latter can be explained by its geographical proximity to his hometown Veurne.

While in the late fifteenth and early sixteenth centuries, the majority of the councilors also had a degree from Leuven, the diversity of universities attended was much greater: some preferred Cologne because it was closer to where they lived; several others obtained their degree in France (Orléans, Paris or Poitiers) or in Italy (Padua, Bologna, Ferrara or Turin).[210] In the seventeeth century, the influence of the decrees of 1598 and 1617 was already clearly noticeable: the majority of law students attended the University of Leuven.[211] At other major tribunals as well—for example the High Council and the Council of Friesland—it was encouraged or even imperative that councilors held a university degree.[212]

After having obtained a degree in law, some practical experience was needed before one had a chance at becoming a councilor at the Great Council.

---

[208] ARA, MD 432.

[209] Thomas, Cathérine. 2014. *Le visage humain de l'administration: les grands commis du gouvernement central des Pays-Bas espagnols (1598–1700)*. Brussels: Académie royale, 296.

[210] Kerckhoffs-De Hey, A.J.M. 1980. *De Grote raad en zijn functionarissen, 1477–1531*. Amsterdam: s.n, 79–81.

[211] Thomas, Cathérine. 2013. Hommes d'Etat, hommes de loi. Les conseillers du Grand Conseil de Malines au XVIIe siècle. In *Gouvernance et administration dans les provinces belges (XVIe–XVIIIe siècles)* (Archives et Bibliothèques de Belgique 99), Eds. Claude De Morbeau de Gerbehaye e.a., 155–177. Brussels: Archives et Bibliothèques de Belgique, 167. Nevertheless, the University of Leiden still attracted one student from the Spanish Netherlands who later managed to secure a position as councilor at the Great Council. This was the case of President Igram Van Achelen, but he acquired his law degree in Leiden long before 1598. Born in 's Hertogenbosch, he started his career as president of the Council of Friesland but took refuge to Brabant when the rebellion broke out. Around 1586, he became councilor of the Privy Council and was appointed president of the Great Council in 1598. Cf. Stroobant, Louis. 1903. *Les magistrats du Grand Conseil de Malines*. Antwerp: De Backer, 16.

[212] Van Poelgeest, L. 1988. De raadsheren van de Hoge Raad van Holland, Zeeland en West-Friesland in de achttiende eeuw. *Bijdragen en mededelingen betreffende de geschiedenis der Nederlanden* 103.1: 25; Hempenius-Van Dijck, Barendina e.a. 1999. *De Heeren van den Raeden: biografieën en groepsportret van de raadsheren van het Hof van Friesland, 1499–1811*. Hilversum: Uitgeverij Verloren, 159.

Table 2.3 Councilors' prior career background[a]

	Nr of councilors	% known total	% overall total
Advocate Great Council	44	48	
Advocate Provincial Council	14	15	
Councilor Provincial Council	13	14	
Local administration	9	10	
Clerical	5	5	
Academic	5	5	
Registrar great council	2	2	
Total known	92	100	97.9
Unknown	2		2.1
Overall total	94		100

[a]The table is based on the data retrieved from the Excel database: councilors of the eighteenth century Great Council. We have not taken into account presidents de Fierlant and Le Clerc because they had an 'atypical' career, serving as head of the Great Council without having been a regular councilor at the tribunal first. Moreover, several councilors had multiple positions before acquiring a councillorship at the Great Council; in that case, we selected the career that seemed most relevant. For more information, see the Excel database

As Table 2.3 demonstrates, almost all members of the Great Council started their career in one or another position within the urban administration or a court of justice, except for the clergy. More than half of them (44 out of 82) were at some point in their careers employed as an advocate of the Great Council. The combination with an appointment as deputy procurator-general was an almost certain guarantee to promotion to a councillorship. Of the 14 deputies who served since 1670, ten became judges of the Great Council; three others managed to get another position in the Austrian administration.[213] Advocates practicing at a provincial council—Brabant, Flanders etc.—also formed an important recruitment pool. In addition, 13 members of the Great Council were first councilors of a provincial council before they were promoted to the Malines tribunal.

Noteworthy are the two registrars—Bruitsma and Van Volden—who eventually became councilors, respectively in 1690 and 1712. In the eighteenth century, promotion from the registry into a councillorship was not easily achieved, partly because it was often—probably wrongly—assumed that registrars had only little knowledge of the day-to-day legal practice. In fact, the Privy Council noted in 1753 "(…) *cet employ [de greffier] n'a rien de commun avec celui d'un juge*."[214] In 1793, advocate-fiscal Goubau expressed an equally low opinion of the registrars, remarking that they 'do not require any specific talents or extraordinary capabilities'.[215] We may suppose that Pierre François Du Trieu was a victim of this impression: as a registrar of the Great Council—appointed in 1737—he tried three times to become

[213] Stroobant, Louis. 1903. *Les magistrats du Grand Conseil de Malines*. Antwerp: De Backer, 121–127. Adrien Hellemans was the only one whose untimely death prevented a promotion.

[214] Brussels, ARA, GRO 443B, 1753: appointment record of Ignace Wirix.

[215] Brussels, ARA, GRMOF BD 69, f.131–134.

a councilor—in 1742, in 1753 and again in 1763—but failed each time.[216] Even his attempt to receive the title of honorary member of the Great Council in 1780 was thwarted.[217]

Clerical councilors similarly suffered from a lack of experience, whether real or perceived.[218] Clergymen were not allowed to work as an advocate at lay tribunals and over the course of the eighteenth century they were also replaced by laymen at the ecclesiastical tribunals. As a result, only a few of them had any practical legal experience. Prior to their appointments, most clerical councilors had been canon in one or another chapter and some had also taught a course at the University of Leuven; consequently, the majority of them had been even less exposed than registrar du Trieu to everyday legal practice. Only Ambroise de Smet and Jean Baptiste Van Velde had a prior career as advocates, respectively at the Council of Flanders and the Council of Brabant: they both had taken on their clerical status in later life.

No matter what kind of professional background the candidates had, several years of experience were required before their ambition to obtain a councillorship at the Great Council could be met with success. By means of the dates of birth—as far as they were available—and the dates of the actual appointment, the average age of promotion into the Council has been established at 40 (Cf. Fig. 2.1: Number of councilors by age of appointment).

Three members—Jean Baptiste de Decker, Arnould Vermeulen and Jean Jacques Marci—were only 29 when selected, and as a consequence would have gained only very little experience. At the other end of the curve, Antoine Reniers was 60 when he received his appointment. He, however, never applied for a position at the Great Council but was unilaterally appointed by the government. In the special circumstances of 1789, his age or experience were undoubtedly far less relevant than his loyalty and trustworthiness.

While throughout the eighteenth century the average age upon which a candidate was appointed did not vary much, freshly appointed members were slightly older in the late seventeenth and early eighteenth centuries than after 1730. Moreover, councilors appointed before approximately 1735 came from a more diverse set of backgrounds than those appointed after that date. Contrary to the first few decades, the bulk of the members of the late eighteenth century Great Council started their careers as advocates or urban pensionaries. Did a career in the Great Council become less interesting for civil servants who already had a more 'mature' career? Or did the criterion of having the right network and relatives, especially if compared to

[216] Brussels, ARA, GRO 443B, 1742: appointment record of Jean Jacques Marci; ARA, GRO 443B, 1753: appointment record of Ignace Wirix; Brussels, ARA, GRO 443A, 1763, appointment record of Godefroid Tackoen.

[217] Brussels, ARA, GRO 442A, 1780: advice of the Privy Council on the request of registrar du Trieu to receive an honorary councillorship. Presumably, he wanted the hereditary nobility attached to a councillorship for his family, having several sons who tried to make their career in the administration. Stroobant, Louis. 1903. *Les magistrats du Grand Conseil de Malines*. Antwerp: De Backer, 137–139.

[218] Cf. supra, 2.2.2.2 Personal merits.

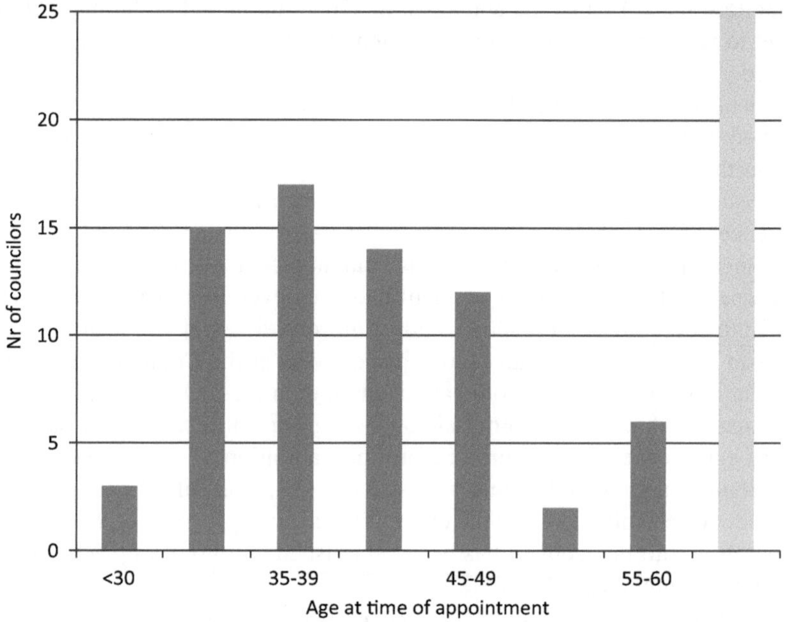

Fig. 2.1 Number of councilors by age at appointment. (The chart is based on the data retrieved from the Excel database: councilors of the eighteenth century Great Council)

the factor experience, become even more important in the course of the eighteenth century?

The presidency was only granted to senior civil servants with several years of experience in the higher administration. No exceptions were made in that regard. The first six presidents, aged between 44 and 68, came from within the Great Council and had at least 12 years of experience as a councilor; Guillaume Pycke had even been an ordinary judge for 27 years before his promotion. The last two presidents—Goswin de Fierlant and Antoine Le Clerc—were not selected among the members of the Great Council. Contrary to what we have determined for the regular councilors—who in the later eighteenth century became appointed at a younger age and came from slightly less high-profile careers—these last two presidents of the Great Council came from the top of the central administration. The former had already had a considerable career at the Privy Council; at the same time—by order of the government—he had written several tracts on the reformation of the (penal) law, when, at age 38, he was selected to be at the head of the Great Council.[219] His successor Antoine Le Clerc had also climbed the hierarchical ladder before he was appointed president of the Great Council: he had been a member of the Accounts Chamber and the Privy Council, had been selected to prepare in Vienna with Mar-

[219] Stevens, Fred. 2000. Goswinus Anna Maria Felix de Fierlant (1735–1804): Een Turnhoutse bevoorrechte getuige van het einde van een tijdperk. *Taxandria: jaarboek van de Koninklijke geschied-en oudheidkundige kring van de Antwerpse Kempen* 71: 7–20.

tini the administrative and legal reforms of Joseph II—who consequently honored him with a councillorship of the Council of State in 1787—and had occupied a seat in the *Conseil du gouvernement général*.[220] Nevertheless, Le Clerc's later career was overshadowed by his personal financial concerns. Therefore, we could wonder if his 'promotion' to the presidency of the Great Council was really a step forward in his career or rather an attempt of the Austrian Crown to put him on the sidelines.[221]

In comparison, in the late fifteenth and early sixteenth centuries, the career path a councilor followed before his promotion to the Great Council could be very diverse. As was the case in the eighteenth century, most of the laymen fulfilled a position of some kind in the judicial administration before being promoted to the Great Council—as advocate, pensionary or councilor at a provincial council. Yet, contrary to two centuries later, not only advocates but proctors as well could aspire to a councillorship. Even secretaries of provincial councils formed an important recruitment pool.[222]

In the seventeenth century, the career background of councilors of the Great Council was more similar to what we have determined for the first decades of the eighteenth century. 20 % of the seventeenth century members of the Great Council had been a councilor in one of the provincial councils of the Netherlands. Another 20 % had started their career in the urban administration of the larger cities—Antwerp, Brussels, Bruges or Malines—as member of the magistrate or as pensionary. 28 % was recruited among the body of advocates, both working in Malines and at other provincial councils. Finally, those who had worked at the Great Council from the beginning of their *cursus honorum*, be it as deputy procurator-general or as registrar, constituted a mere 6 %. While registrars were equally unlikely to be promoted to a councillorship in the eighteenth century,[223] the seventeenth century deputy procurators-general apparently had much less chance of becoming councilors than their eighteenth century colleagues.[224]

Contrary to the Great Council, the Council of Friesland explicitly imposed an age limit of 25 and demanded that all candidates should be matriculated as an advocate at the Council of Friesland. Especially the latter prerequisite was far from always

---

[220] Jacob, Steve. 1999. Jacques-Antoine Le Clerc (1731–après 1797). Un fonctionnaire au service d'une politique réformatrice. In *La haute administration dans les Pays-Bas autrichiens (Ambroise-Joseph de Herzelles, Denis-Benoît de Cazier, Jacques-Antoine Le Clerc)* (Etudes sur le XVIIIe siècle 27), eds. Hervé Hasquin and Roland Mortier, 243–354. Brussels: Université de Bruxelles; Bruneel, Claude and Hoyois, Jean-Paul. 2001. *Les grands commis des Pays-Bas autrichiens: dictionnaire biographique du personnel des institutions centrales*. Brussels: Algemeen Rijksarchief, 364–368.

[221] Cf. infra, Chap. 5.

[222] Kerckhoffs-De Hey, A.J.M. 1980. *De Grote raad en zijn functionarissen, 1477–1531*. Amsterdam: s.n, 81–84.

[223] In fact, Henri Bruitsma was promoted from registrar to councilor in 1690, so still in the seventeenth century.

[224] Thomas, Cathérine. 2013. Hommes d'Etat, hommes de loi. Les conseillers du Grand Conseil de Malines au XVIIe siècle. In *Gouvernance et administration dans les provinces belges (XVIe–XVIIIe siècles)* (Archives et Bibliothèques de Belgique 99), Eds. Claude De Morbeau de Gerbehaye e.a., 155–177. Brussels: Archives et Bibliothèques de Belgique, 169–170.

enforced. In general though, the early career path of a member of the Council of Friesland was comparable to that of a councilor of the Great Council: most of them had worked as advocates or as civil servants in the urban administration. Nevertheless, six councilors started their careers as officers in the army, even though only one of them had a law degree. Eight others were promoted to the Council of Friesland immediately after their studies at university, which of course was not only a flagrant breach of the requirement to have worked as an advocate, but also of the minimum age. Several of them were under 25; the youngest had even barely attained the age of 18. All of these appointments had been made after 1673 and prove, according to Hempenius-Van Dijck, that in the later years of the Council, the administrators of Friesland—who made the decisions—had become far more casual about the rules than in its early history.[225]

At the eighteenth century High Council on the other hand, the age limit of 25 was always respected. Moreover, all 47 councilors had practiced as an advocate, the majority of them at the High Council or at the Council of Holland. Almost 25 % of the advocates were directly promoted to a councillorship. Another quarter first worked as councilor at a provincial court—predominantly the Council of Brabant. The remaining half first moved to a position within the municipal administration, such as pensionary, before their promotion. Conspicuous by their absence are the professors of law, according to Van Poelgeest because of the absolute lack of practical applicability of the law as it was instructed at the university. The eighteenth century Great Council, on the other hand, recruited six professors, four of whom came directly from a university. It hardly comes as a surprise that they were without exception clergy, given the problems the Great Council experienced with the recruitment of clerical councilors. The High Council, of course, never had to deal with that kind of issues. More striking is that compared to the High Council, a smaller percentage of councilors at the Great Council started their career as members of a provincial council (14 % or 13 councilors). The fact that only five of these were appointed to the Great Council after 1723 is even more telling.

2.3.4 Further Career

For an overwhelming majority of the members—71 out of 94 or 75 %—their appointment as councilor, procurator-general or advocate-fiscal constituted the pinnacle of their career as civil servants. Most died in office, often at an advanced age. Several were in their seventies and Pierre Govaerts even continued to serve as a councilor until his death at 82. Not all of these 'Nestors' actually continued to perform their tasks until they died. Examples of councilors requesting to be relieved of their duties on full pay, meaning their annual salaries but also their *émoluments* and

[225] Hempenius-Van Dijck, Barendina e.a. 1999. *De Heeren van den Raeden: biografieën en groepsportret van de raadsheren van het Hof van Friesland, 1499–1811*. Hilversum: Uitgeverij Verloren, 163–165.

Table 2.4 Career after a position as councilor[a]

	Number	%
None	71	75.5
Councilor Privy Council (plus further career)[b]	10	10.6
Councilor Privy Council (final career)	6	6.4
Councilor High Council for the Netherlands (plus further career)	2	2.1
President Great Council	1	1.1
President Provincial Council	1	1.1
President Council of Finance (plus further career)	1	1.1
Episcopal see	2	2.1
Total	*94*	*100*

[a] Only the first appointment after a position as councilor on the Great Council is considered; for further career details, please consult the overall Excel dataset
[b] Or Council of State before 1725

privileges,[226] are legion throughout the entire eighteenth century.[227] For example, in 1705, Henri Chabotteau requested to be relieved from the exercise of his duties because of illness and infirmity, claiming they were due to his long and extreme dedication to his work as civil servant. Furthermore, he invoked his large family as an argument to retain his income. Finally, testimonies from councilors of the Councils of Namur, Luxemburg and Tournai confirmed that it was a common practice to award old and ill members the full enjoyment of their compensation package (Table 2.4).[228]

In most instances, these absences were rather limited, because many of the absentees were indeed seriously ill and died shortly after their *de facto* retirement. Jean Baptiste Hony proved the exception to the rule. After a stroke in December 1745, he was unable to attend the Council's sessions, but he kept his status and salary for another twenty years before he actually passed away and could be replaced.[229] At several times, however, because of the inconveniences caused by these absences and the ensuing incomplete membership, additional councilors were appointed notwithstanding the ban imposed by the procedure ordinance.[230] We have already cited the example of Jacques Joseph de Stassart and Jean Baptiste Van der

[226] Cf. infra, Chap. 3.

[227] It was not until 1781 that Joseph II introduced an official system of retirement, meaning that officials could receive a pension in line with their years of services. Galand, Michèle. 2001. Gages, honneurs, mérites: les hauts fonctionnaires dans les Pays-Bas autrichiens. *Revue belge de philologie et d'histoire* 73.2: 566.

[228] Brussels, Koninklijke Raad van Philips V (1702–1711), 19, 1705: request of Henri Chabotteau, advice of the Royal Council, final decision. Other known examples are Norbert Van Voorspoel who asked to be relieved of duty in 1719, Jean Baptiste Hony in 1745, Jean Henri Kahnn in 1753, Daniël Servaes in 1776, Gillis De Cock in 1783, Jean Dominique Vriesen in 1792 and Jean Mathias Ludovisi d'Orley in 1793 (See Excel database). In the case of Charles Otté, the Great Council itself asked to excuse him from intervening in the decisions because of his constant state of drowsiness. Cf. Gaillard, Arthur. 1900–1903. *Inventaire des mémoriaux du Grand Conseil de Malines*. Brussels: Weissenbruch, t. 2, 433, n°2518.

[229] Brussels, ARA, MD 432, biography of Jean Baptiste Hony.

[230] *ROPB,* 2ième série, t. 7, August 8, 1559, p. 461, art. I, title 7.

Fosse who in 1776 both shared the seat left vacant by the death of Philippe Rogez as long as Daniël Servaes was on 'sick leave'.[231] In 1783, after the death of councilor de Partz, François Van Volxem and Thomas Joseph Cottin themselves proposed to occupy a single position, in order to remedy the problems caused by the absence of Gillis de Cock. Obviously, they hoped that sooner rather than later a councilor would die or get promoted, so that they could both be awarded a full membership and salary. Their hope seemed justified as Van der Fosse only had to wait for two months before Servaes drew his last breath. Cottin and Van Volxem, however, were less lucky: De Cock lived for another four years, while it was not until a year later that councilor Pierre Henri Timmermans died and Van Volxem could finally enjoy full membership.[232]

Not all councilors voluntarily retired from the Great Council. In 1704, Louis de Frarin protested the attempts of his fellow councilors to have him 'silenced'. According to his colleagues, Frarin was absolutely deaf and therefore unable to actively participate in the debates, let alone to report a case. Because of the many complaints they had received, they requested that Frarin would be allowed to attend the sessions of the Great Council, but that they would no longer be required to take his opinions into account. Frarin denied these charges, claiming that there was nothing wrong with his ears and that he was still very well capable of performing his duties as a councilor. In fact, he even offered to prove this in person.[233]

Given his already advanced age in 1704—he was 74 at the time—it is very well possible that he was indeed hearing-impaired and unable to partake in the Council's activities. Yet, his protest letter makes us doubt that he was as deaf as his fellow councilors wanted the Royal Council to believe. Other members of the Great Council personally requested to be relieved from their tasks and considered it a privilege that they were allowed to retain all remunerations and benefits connected to their status.[234] A possible reason why the Great Council might have wanted to put councilor Frarin on the sidelines was the tarnishing of his name provoked by his nephew Robert Balthazar Frarin. The latter—appointed secretary of the Great Council in 1693—was condemned to death in 1702 for the (attempted) murder of his cousins, which he *nota bene* had done in the house of his uncle.[235] Knowing how much

[231] Brussels, ARA, GRO 442A, 1776: appointment record of Jean Baptiste Van der Fosse.

[232] Brussels, ARA, GRO 442A, 1783: appointment record of François Van Volxem and Thomas Joseph Cottin.

[233] Brussels, ARA, Koninklijke Raad van Filips V, 19, 1704.

[234] Galand, Michèle. 2001. Gages, honneurs, mérites: les hauts fonctionnaires dans les Pays-Bas autrichiens. *Revue belge de philologie et d'histoire* 73.2: 566.

[235] For more information on the Frarin case: Simon, Jules. 1921. La procédure criminelle sous l'ancien régime (Grand Conseil de Malines). *Handelingen van de Koninklijke Commissie voor de uitgave van oude wetten en verordeningen van België* 10: 397–437; Maes, Louis Th. 1975. Gerechtelijke beslissingen in strafzaken, 16e—18e eeuw. Een vergiftigingszaak 1697–1702. In *De besluitvorming vroeger en nu* (Algemeen rijksarchief en rijksarchief in de provinciën. Educatieve Dienst. Catalogus 49), eds. Hugo de Schepper and John Gilissen, 197–236. Brussels: Algemeen Rijksarchief.

weight the Great Council attached to its reputation—cf. the Happart case[236]—we can very well imagine that the councilors were afraid the reputation of the tribunal might suffer if councilor de Frarin, uncle of a condemned man, would continue to weigh on their decisions.

While for the majority of the councilors their seat on the Great Council formed the pinnacle of their career, some 25 % achieved higher aspirations. For them, their time in the Council merely constituted a step on the ladder. Sixteen among them were promoted to a councillorship in the Privy Council;[237] one, Guillaume Snoy, was selected to become councilor at the Privy Council, but he declined. For some of them, a position in the Privy Council was merely a passage. Both Joseph d'Olmen and Guillaume Pycke returned to the Great Council as presidents. Six were promoted to the presidency of a provincial council;[238] only Jacques Joseph de Stassart made the direct leap from a councillorship in the Great Council to the presidency of the Council of Namur. Three were called to occupy a seat in the High Council for the Netherlands. At their return, they all invariably landed a prestigious position, with de Coloma as one of the few former councilors of the Great Council—Christophe de Baillet and Augustin de Steenhault were the other two—who managed to climb to the presidency of the Privy Council, one of the most powerful functions in the Austrian Netherlands.[239]

Those who aspired to a career at the top of the administration combined their 'primary' tasks as councilor of, for example, the Privy Council with a membership of all kinds of committees (*jointes*).[240] Not only was it financially attractive to occupy a seat in one of these *jointes*, it was also regarded as an honor. Yet the most important and financially rewarding honorary title was that of councilor of the Council of State, especially after 1725 when it lost all its power to the newly established Privy Council. Awarding a civil servant a membership in the Council of State was a way for the sovereign to compensate him for his long service.[241] In the course of the

[236] Cf. supra, 2.2.3 The 'result' of the nomination procedure.

[237] Or the Council of State before 1725.

[238] Honoré Vanderhaeghen (chancellor of Brabant in 1725), Charles Philippe Pattin (president of the Council of Flanders in 1742), Pierre Claude Marie de St Vaast (chancellor of the Council of Gelre in 1748), Juste Jacques Bervoet (president of the Council of Namur in 1749), Gilles François Streithagen (chancellor of Brabant in 1763), Martial de le Vielleuze (President of the Council of Tournai in 1794).

[239] Bruneel, Claude and Hoyois, Jean-Paul2001. *Les grands commis des Pays-Bas autrichiens: dictionnaire biographique du personnel des institutions centrales*. Brussels: Algemeen Rijksarchief, 116–117 (biography of Hyacinthe Marie de Brouckhoven); Ibidem, 240–241 (biography of Honoré Henri Eesbeeck Vanderhaeghen); Ibidem, 180–181 (biography of Jean Alphonse de Coloma).

[240] Gilles de Streithagen, for example, was at different times during his career member of no less than 13 *jointes*. Bruneel, Claude and Hoyois, Jean-Paul. 2001. *Les grands commis des Pays-Bas autrichiens: dictionnaire biographique du personnel des institutions centrales*. Brussels: Algemeen Rijksarchief, 578–579.

[241] Galand, Michèle. 2001. Gages, honneurs, mérites: les hauts fonctionnaires dans les Pays-Bas autrichiens. *Revue belge de philologie et d'histoire* 73.2: 560.

eighteenth century, several (former) members and presidents of the Great Council were honored with this title.[242]

Compared to their laymen colleagues, clerical councilors were even less likely to progress. Seven out of nine died while in office. Only Felix Brenart and Jean Baptiste Van Velde moved on to higher positions, respectively as bishops of Bruges and of Roermond.[243] Jean Baptiste Hony was offered the bishopric of Roermond in 1742, but he declined.

Between the early and the later eighteenth century, there is a slight but potentially significant difference noticeable in the number of councilors for whom the Great Council was merely a means to another career.[244] Partially, this can be explained by the lack of opportunities: for those who served at the very end of the eighteenth century, the uncertain times and eventually the end of the Habsburg sovereignty in the Netherlands closed off the usual routes. Many of the higher civil servants in fact refused to change their loyalties to the new rulers: Goswin de Fierlant for example, swore the oath required of all returning immigrants in 1802, but solemnly declared in 1803 that he refused to become French, thereby forfeiting all chances at a new career.[245] It seems that all former councilors of the Great Council refused to serve under the French authority.[246] Nevertheless, some of those who had attracted the attention of the emperor because of their hard work and loyalty and who nurtured a healthy ambition did manage to further their career after their emigration. Advocate-fiscal Melchior Goubau for example, occupied several high-profile positions in the Viennese administration. Finally, with the establishment of the United Kingdom of the Netherlands he was called on by King Willem I to serve the new state.[247] Therefore, even though the post-1787 events certainly played a role in the lower incidence rate of councilors with careers surpassing the Great Council, it can not entirely account for it.

The data therefore seems to suggest that in the early eighteenth century, more councilors considered the Great Council as a springboard for a further career compared to the later period. From the 1750s on, a seat in the tribunal constituted for many civil servants a goal in itself, a position that allowed them to relax somewhat

---

[242] To name only a few: Augustin de Steenhault, Pierre Van Volden, Charles Pattin, Pierre Claude de St Vaast, Juste Jacques Bervoet, Guillaume Pycke, Gilles Streighagen etc.

[243] Previously, in 1787, Jean-Baptiste Van Velde had been appointed to take up a seat in the *Commission des fondations pieuses* associated with the *Conseil du gouvernement général*. After the Austrian restoration of 1791, he returned to his position at the Great Council. In November 1793, he was promoted to the bishopric of Roermond. He arrived in the city sometime in June 1794, but already had to leave Roermond on July 22, 1794 due to the advancing French troops, never to return again. Bruneel, Claude and Hoyois, Jean-Paul. 2001. *Les grands commis des Pays-Bas autrichiens: dictionnaire biographique du personnel des institutions centrales*. Brussels: Algemeen Rijksarchief, 622–623.

[244] See Excel database: councilors of the eighteenth century Great Council.

[245] Bruneel, Claude and Hoyois, Jean-Paul. 2001. *Les grands commis des Pays-Bas autrichiens: dictionnaire biographique du personnel des institutions centrales*. Brussels: Algemeen Rijksarchief, 255–256.

[246] Cf. infra, Chap. 5.

[247] Cf. infra, Chap. 5.

after the initial strive for a career in the central administration and one that would provide them with a noble title and a decent income until their death.[248] The examples of Jean Baptiste Hony and Guillaume Snoy who declined an offer for a bishop's seat in 1742 and a councillorship in the Privy Council in 1757 respectively corroborate this thesis.

The data for the seventeenth century also points in that direction. First of all, for the period between 1595 and 1700, Thomas identified 142 civil servants who at one point in their career occupied a seat at the Great Council.[249] In contrast, over roughly a century from the end of the seventeenth century[250] until 1797, only 94 councilors worked at the tribunal, supplemented by two external presidents. This difference can be partially explained by the somewhat longer period Thomas covers, as well as by the higher life expectancy in the eighteenth century. Nevertheless, those two elements alone cannot account for the 50 additional members that the Great Council counted in the seventeenth compared to the eighteenth century. Since the number of councilors was fixed at 16—president excluded—before the start of the seventeenth century, we are led to believe that there must have been a higher turnover rate in the 1600s compared to the 1700s.[251] The information on the careers of the councilors demonstrates that this was indeed the case.

For only half of the seventeenth century members, their position as councilor, procurator-general or advocate-fiscal was the crowning moment of their career. 27 out of 142 councilors, or some 20 %, managed to get appointed to the Privy Council, slightly more than a third of whom were again promoted to the presidency of a provincial council, the Great Council or even the Privy Council. These numbers certainly do not spectacularly differ from what we have determined for the eighteenth century. Yet, in the 1600s, nearly one fifth of the councilors moved directly to the presidency of a provincial council from the Great Council, compared to only one in the 1700s. For the clerical councilors, the situation was very similar to the eighteenth century: only four did not die in office but were awarded an Episcopal See. Finally, the seventeenth century Great Council counted four presidents who had no

[248] Cf. the above mentioned assessment by the Privy Council of a councillorship at the Great Council as a position for people who deserved some rest after a tiresome career: Brussels, ARA, GRO 442A, 1761: appointment record of Henri Theodore Jacobs: "Nous observons néanmoins que le conseiller Servaes aiant exercé pendant quinze ans le ministère public de conseiller fiscal dans la province de Flandres, a la satisfaction du gouvernement, *paroit mériter de jouir de repos auquel il est parvenu, par sa promotion a une place de conseiller du Grand Conseil.*"

[249] Thomas, Cathérine. 2014. *Le visage humain de l'administration: les grands commis du gouvernement central des Pays-Bas espagnols (1598–1700)*. Brussels: Académie royale, 159.

[250] We included all members who served during the eighteenth century, even though they were appointed some time in the seventeenth century. This is the case for 17 councilors: Frarin, de Brouchoven, du Jardin, Stalins, Van Kerrenbroeck, Van Voorspoel, Govaerts, Bruitsma, Van Heydenryck, Seghers, de Grouffe, de Vreven, Janssens d'Hujoel, Bernaerts, Van der Haeghen, Chabotteau and de Tombeur.

[251] In the first quarter of the seventeenth century, the number of councilors temporarily rose to 19. The time-frame, however, is too limited to account for the difference. Wijffels, Alain. 1994. Grote Raad voor de Nederlanden te Mechelen (ca.1445–1797). In *De centrale overheidsinstellingen van de Habsburgse Nederlanden*, ed. Erik Aerts e.a., 448–461. Brussels: Algemeen Rijksarchief, 452.

previous ties to the court; two of them were later on promoted to the chancellorship of the Council of Brabant.[252]

For the late fifteenth and early sixteenth centuries, the available data are hard to interpret, as Kerckhoffs-de Heij does not mention how many members ended their careers as councilors of the Great Council. Therefore, it is difficult to assess if the Great Council was regarded as a steppingstone to another position in the high administration or rather constituted the apogee of a career. On the other hand, the kind of careers followed by the councilors who did get a promotion are very comparable to the eighteenth century: clericals became bishops; laymen were promoted to the presidency of a provincial council or of the Great Council, to a chancellorship in the Council of Brabant, or to membership and sometimes eventually the presidency of the Privy Council. Somewhat remarkably, Kerckhoffs-de Heij considers an appointment as procurator-general of the Great Council an attractive promotion, suggesting that the position was quite prestigious during the first centuries of the Great Council.[253] The problems connected to the appointment of fiscals during the eighteenth century clearly indicate that this was no longer the case in the later years of the tribunal.

At the Council of Friesland as well, more than half of the councilors died in office. From the 63—out of 139—who did not remain at the tribunal until their death, 16 were discharged, usually for political reasons[254] rather than because of inappropriate behavior.[255] From the other 47 who voluntarily resigned, only 32 continued their professional career, some as *grietman*, some in another 'regent position' such as member of the Council of State. All in all, only 23 % moved on to a different function, which is very much comparable to the 25 % determined for the eighteenth century members of the Great Council.

The eighteenth century High Council almost always constituted the pinnacle of the career of its members. Some managed to secure a position in the Council of State, but their career path was not representative. Nevertheless, while it was not a steppingstone for individuals, it could play that role for families. Once a family member was promoted to the High Council, his descendants might be able to reach even higher. Yet, Van Poelgeest noticed a declined interest in seats at the High Council: while in the sixteenth and early seventeenth centuries, a position in the High Council was still attractive for personalities such as Oldenbarneveld and de Witt, this was absolutely no longer the case a hundred years later. To a certain extent at least, the High Council, as well as the Council of Holland, were aware of this

[252] Thomas, Cathérine. 2014. *Le visage humain de l'administration: les grands commis du gouvernement central des Pays-Bas espagnols (1598–1700)*. Brussels: Académie royale, 173–174. While in theory the Great Council was the 'first tribunal of the Netherlands', it is obvious that this position was in practice reserved for the Council of Brabant. Cf. infra, Chap. 4.

[253] Kerckhoffs-De Hey, A.J.M. 1980. *De Grote raad en zijn functionarissen, 1477–1531*. Amsterdam: s.n., 84–85.

[254] For example, in the transition to the Batavian Republic.

[255] Hempenius-Van Dijck, Barendina e.a. 1999. *De Heeren van den Raeden: biografieën en groepsportret van de raadsheren van het Hof van Friesland, 1499–1811*. Hilversum: Uitgeverij Verloren, 167.

evolution and attempted to confirm their—at least self-perceived—preponderance over other institutions in the Northern Netherlands: when in 1715, the transition of one of the councilors of the High Council to the Accounts Chamber of Holland was described as a promotion, the High Council and the Court of Holland lodged a combined protest.[256]

This declined interest in occupying positions at central 'umbrella' tribunals[257] during the eighteenth century was not merely limited to the Austrian and the Northern Netherlands. For the eighteenth century German *Reichskammergericht*, Sigrid Jahns noticed a somewhat comparable evolution.[258] Using the recruitment and staff policy of the tribunal as an indicator, she described how the *Reichskammersgericht* was unmistakably in decline during the last century of its existence. While in its early history, this high court of the German empire could still attract a large number of high-profile individuals, it became increasingly difficult to recruit personnel, especially from the early eighteenth century on. In 1570, the number of councilors had been increased from 16 to 28; in 1648, it was determined that there should be at least 50 councilors to have a smoothly running tribunal. Yet in the year 1719/1720, the *Reichskammergericht* was composed of a mere 13 councilors.[259] The candidates who did present themselves often did not have the right qualifications: they were ever younger and did not necessarily have a law degree.[260] At the same time, the members of the Council became more elitist about the social background of the candidates: for the first time, appointees from a lower social background were refused because of their humble birth. Undoubtedly connected to this evolution, ever more relatives served together at the *Reichskammergericht,* despite the prohibition against family members simultaneously occupying a seat. Certainly, German society had gradually become more closely knit. Yet, the main problem was that many

[256] Van Poelgeest, L. 1988. De raadsheren van de Hoge Raad van Holland, Zeeland en West-Friesland in de achttiende eeuw. *Bijdragen en mededelingen betreffende de geschiedenis der Nederlanden* 103.1: 37.

[257] The term 'umbrella tribunal' confers the idea of a tribunal being responsible for more than one region (contrary to provincial councils) without however necessarily taking up the position of a superior court.

[258] Jahns, Sigrid. 1990. Die Personalverfassung des Reichskammergerichts unter Anpassungsdruck. Lösungen im Spannungsfeld zwischen Modernität und Überalterung. In *Das Reichskammergericht in der deutschen Geschichte: Stand der Forschung, Forschungsperspektiven* (Quellen und Forschungen zur höchsten Gerichtsbarkeit im alten Reich 21), ed. Bernhard Diestelkamp, 59–109. Cologne: Böhlau.

[259] Jahns, Sigrid. 1990. Die Personalverfassung des Reichskammergerichts unter Anpassungsdruck. Lösungen im Spannungsfeld zwischen Modernität und Überalterung. In *Das Reichskammergericht in der deutschen Geschichte: Stand der Forschung, Forschungsperspektiven* (Quellen und Forschungen zur höchsten Gerichtsbarkeit im alten Reich 21), ed. Bernhard Diestelkamp. Cologne: Böhlau, 80.

[260] A law degree was only required for the non-noble half of the Council. Nobles (the *Ritterbürtige*) were encouraged, but were not obligated, to acquire a degree. Jahns, Sigrid. 1990. Die Personalverfassung des Reichskammergerichts unter Anpassungsdruck. Lösungen im Spannungsfeld zwischen Modernität und Überalterung. In *Das Reichskammergericht in der deutschen Geschichte: Stand der Forschung, Forschungsperspektiven* (Quellen und Forschungen zur höchsten Gerichtsbarkeit im alten Reich 21), ed. Bernhard Diestelkamp. Cologne: Böhlau, 71–73.

councilors remained for a longer period of time at the tribunal, while they also wanted to assure a good position for their offspring.[261]

Jahns identified the unwillingness and lack of interest of both the emperor[262] and the *Reichstände* (the State's Estates) to implement much-needed reforms as the main reason for this decline of the *Reichskammergericht.* Institutions age, while at the same time a society changes. Until the early seventeenth century, the emperor and the *Reichstände* were prepared to respond to the changing circumstances by imposing new decrees on the *Reichskamergericht*, but they did not continue this policy in the 1700s. Therefore, Jahns argued, while social changes and changes in mentality in the eighteenth century created an urgent need to modify the recruitment and staff policy of the *Reichskammergericht*, a normative correction remained forthcoming. Consequently, as Jahns claimed, *Den Desinteresse und erlahmende Fürsorge vor allem der mächtigeren Kräfte im Reich für die fortgesetzte Aufrechterhaltung seiner Funktionsfähigkeit mussten ein derart konstruiertes oberstes Reichsgericht in seinem Lebensnerv treffen.*[263]

Conclusion

In the eighteenth century Great Council—and by extension in all institutions of the eighteenth century high administration—family and networks, rather than competence or experience, constituted the main recruitment criteria. This invariably caused a certain form of 'inbreeding'. *Homines novi* were rare, new councilors were selected from a caste of civil servants. Especially the *droit de terne* provided the Great Council with an instrument to run a highly nepotistic recruitment policy and to consolidate the power of the incumbent elite. The sovereign certainly benefited from this approach as it created stability, which undoubtedly served him well.

In fact, ever since the sixteenth century, family relations had played an important role in the growth of state power. Wolfgang Reinhard specifically underlined the significance of family networks as well as the more artificial relationship of affinity as a source of support for a strong, centralized state. Building on this thesis, the Austrian sovereign had all reasons to appoint councilors to the Great Council

[261] Jahns, Sigrid. 1990. Die Personalverfassung des Reichskammergerichts unter Anpassungsdruck. Lösungen im Spannungsfeld zwischen Modernität und Überalterung. In *Das Reichskammergericht in der deutschen Geschichte: Stand der Forschung, Forschungsperspektiven* (Quellen und Forschungen zur höchsten Gerichtsbarkeit im alten Reich 21), ed. Bernhard Diestelkamp. Cologne: Böhlau, 104.

[262] Conspicuously, in the eighteenth century, the crown of the Holy Roman Empire was in the hands of the Austrian Habsburgs.

[263] Jahns, Sigrid. 1990. Die Personalverfassung des Reichskammergerichts unter Anpassungsdruck. Lösungen im Spannungsfeld zwischen Modernität und Überalterung. In *Das Reichskammergericht in der deutschen Geschichte: Stand der Forschung, Forschungsperspektiven* (Quellen und Forschungen zur höchsten Gerichtsbarkeit im alten Reich 21), ed. Bernhard Diestelkamp. Cologne: Böhlau, 108.

who had relatives with a good track of supporting his policies. As Reinhard noticed: "Technical qualifications and ability were less important for appointment, promotion and dismissal than birth, wealth, and above all family connections and patronage."[264] Moreover, while the sovereign only once unilaterally imposed a new councilor—Antoine Reniers in 1789—there should be no doubt that (s)he had an, albeit indirect, influence on the selection of the candidates for the *terne*. The risk connected to this intergenerational approach was of course a decline in the quality of new councilors. Nevertheless, we can conclude that competence was not the primary quality expected from a councilor at the Great Council: loyalty, trustworthiness and docility were valued much more highly.

The profile of the councilors evidently stemmed from the criteria used: the members of the Great Council all had a law degree and some years of legal experience but more importantly, they had almost all been imbedded in the civil servantcy before they became judges. In that regard, the eighteenth century members of the Great Council did not differ much from their colleagues in other, somewhat comparable tribunals, such as the High Council of Holland, Zeeland and West-Friesland and the Council of Friesland. In addition, many similarities can be found between the profile of the eighteenth century councilors of the Great Council and their predecessors in the late fifteenth, early sixteenth and the seventeenth centuries. There is however one major difference: far more members of the eighteenth century Great Council compared to their seventeenth century forerunners considered their position at the tribunal the pinnacle of their career. Only a very limited number of councilors moved on to another position in the higher administration of the Austrian Netherlands and two even refused their promotion. The turn-over rate in the eighteenth century Great Council was much more limited than it had been a hundred years before. And if we may believe the Privy Council, work at the Great Council was not exactly strenuous.

At the same time, another evolution is noticeable, which might indicate that a councillorship at the Great Council became less desirable in the eighteenth century—especially for careerists—than it had been in its previous history. In fact, over the course of the 1700s, fewer candidates came from the ranks of councilors of a provincial council, which limited the Great Council's recruitment pool to mainly its own advocates and urban pensionaries. At the same time, this suggests that the members of the tribunal became an increasingly 'closed' group, as advocates belonged to their own network. Another writing on the wall was that the provincial Estates lost interest in placing their representatives at the Great Council. Combined with the 'inbreeding' in its recruitment policy and the lack of enthusiasm displayed by the eighteenth century councilors to obtain a promotion, we can wonder if these are signs of a declining importance attached to the tribunal, or, in other words, if the councilors abandoned the tribunal to lethargy.[265]

---

[264] Reinhard, Wolfgang. 1996. Introduction. In *Power elites and state building*, ed. Wolfgang Reinhard, 8–11. Oxford: Clarendon.

[265] Bruneel, Claude and Hoyois, Jean-Paul. 2001. Les grands commis des Pays-Bas autrichiens: dictionnaire biographique du personnel des institutions centrales. Brussels: Algemeen Rijksarchief, 5.

Additionally, we have to ask the question if these phenomena were limited to the Great Council or if they can be distinguished at other tribunals in Europe as well. Hempenius-Van Dijck already noted that at the Council of Friesland, several criteria—connected to minimum age and previous career—were easily disregarded when recruiting new candidates in the late seventeenth and eighteenth centuries. Van Poelgeest, as well, identified comparable changes for the High Council, while Jahns argued that there was indeed a serious degeneration noticeable in the recruitment policy at the eighteenth century *Reichskammergericht*, caused by a lack of interest of the sovereign and the Estates to remedy the problems.

References

Archival Sources

Brussels, General State Archives

Algemene Regeringsraad
857
Collectie microfilms Wenen
II995–II996
Geheime Raad, Oostenrijkse Periode
Kartons 442A, 443A, 443B
Geheime Raad. Registers
400, 401, 419
Grote Raad van Mechelen. Registers

4–5 *Patent letters*

GRM 4–5 mainly contains the *lettres patentes* or open letters by which the employees of the Great Council—both the president, councilors and the lower personnel—were appointed into their position. Appointment letters were always standardized texts, describing the 'rights' and 'duties' of the appointee in question in which only the names and dates were changed. To a smaller extent, the patent letters also include letters of naturalization and habilitation which foreign-born candidates for a councillorship in the Great Council needed to be considered. Patent letters for the Great Council have been preserved for the period between 1686 and 1794. The appointment files, which do give ample information about a prospective candidate, can be found in the Privy Council, which was responsible for the nomination of councilors and other personnel at the royal courts.

97–98; 133; 135–140 *Correspondence*

The "recueils de la correspondance du Grand Conseil" have been preserved for the entire history of the Council, covering the period between 1464 and 1794. The correspondence of the Great Council consists of a diverse array of letters and requests sent to or by the Great Council. The central government, usually through the Privy Council, is the main correspondent, but other institutions, such as provincial councils, and even individuals figure in these registers. The subject matter ranges from orders to organize a *Te Deum*, requests of all sort of dispensations, and conflicts of jurisdiction with especially the Council of Flanders or the Magistrate of Malines, to instructions of the governor on how to respond to a potential invasion by the French. The only structure in this mishmash of documents is the date on which they were composed or received, but even this chronological criterion was not always rigorously followed. The registers provide a privileged insight into the judicial but even more into the non-judicial aspects of the Great Council's workings. However, the enormous volume of the series (consisting of 129 registers over a period of 330 years) and the lack of organization make research into the correspondence very time-consuming. The correspondence of the Great Council has its counterpart in the archives of the office-fiscal (GRMOF, Banden en Delen) which, however, suffers from the same problems.

617–620 *Distribution records ranged by province of origin*
629–633 *Distribution records ranged by reporter*
635–637 *Distribution records of the "Différends"*

The distribution books record all the lawsuits introduced at the Great Council that reached the phase of 'distribution', i.e. the stage at which the case was assigned to a reporter. There is, however, at least one exception to this rule: only a very limited number of criminal cases were recorded in the distribution books. In general, distribution books contain the date of distribution, the instance, the procedure (appeal, first instance, *différend*, …), the name of the councilor reporter and the name (and sometimes a certain qualification) of the litigants. In several cases, but far from always, they also list the name of the procurators and the decision rendered. For the eighteenth century, the archives of the Great Council hold two different types of distribution records. While the first type contains both appeals and first instance cases, the second type is exclusively reserved for those lawsuits that followed the communicatory procedure (*différends*). Consequently, procedure is the distinguishing feature. In addition, the first type can again be divided into two subcategories, which do not much differ by the information they provide as by the way the data is arranged, *i.c.* by province of origin or by name of the councilor who acted as reporter. Comparison between these two categories had demonstrated that there is a considerable overlap and that possible lacunae must be attributed to the inevitable human errors of the registrar who recorded the cases. Why there are two further subcategories within the registers containing the appeals and first instance cases following the procedure on the *rôle* is less clear. In a certain way, they seem to represent an 'incoming stream' versus an 'outgoing stream'. Indeed, the distribution books arranged by province record in which part of the jurisdiction of the Great Council the lawsuits originated and thus entered the registry. The other subcategory records to which councilor the case was distributed. Even though the files did not literally leave the Great Council, we could say that the process of allocating a lawsuit to a certain member of the

Council could be regarded as an 'outgoing stream', as the files left the registry. Possible this distinction was made as a means to keep track of all the files that were brought to the Great Council and to have an idea of the whereabouts of a certain file. The distribution records ranged by province of origin are available for the years 1613 until 1794; those ranged by councilor have been preserved for the year 1503, and then from 1542 up until 1794 with a gap between 1550 and 1601. Whether the 'missing' distribution records for the sixteenth century are lost or simply never existed, is unknown. The distribution records of the *Différends* only start at 1683. We presume that, before that date, they were recorded together with the other first instance and appeal cases, given the fact that the communicatory procedure only became popular over the course of the seventeenth century.

Grote Raad van Mechelen. Officie-fiscaal. Procesdossiers
561
Grote Raad van Mechelen. Officie-fiscaal. Banden en Delen.
69
Koninklijke Raad van Filip V
19
Manuscrits Divers
432, 860/A, 860/B
Raad van State
Portefeuilles 651, 653, 654, 655, 656
Regentschapsraad van State
285

Published and Printed Sources

Bolsée, Jean. 1969–1970. L'ordonnance du 8 août 1559 réglant le statut, le style et la manière de procéder du Grand Conseil de Malines (texte néerlandais). Handelingen van de Koninklijke Commissie voor de uitgave der Oude Wetten en Verordeningen van België 24: 77–152.

De Le Court, Jules-Victor, Gachard, Louis Prosper and Verhaegen, Paul. 1860–1942. *Recueil des ordonnances des Pays-Bas autrichiens. 3e série: 1700–1794*, 15 tomes. Brussels: Devroye.

Literature

Alix, Flore. 2009. Les critères de sélection des hauts fonctionnaires des Pays-Bas méridionaux (1700–1725). *Belgisch tijdschrift voor filologie en geschiedenis* 87: 297–348.

Bruneel, Claude, and Hoyois, Jean-Paul. 2001. *Les grands commis des Pays-Bas autrichiens: dictionnaire biographique du personnel des institutions centrales*. Brussels: Algemeen Rijksarchief.

Delporte, Laurent. 2001. *Problématique de la vénalité des offices dans les Pays-Bas autrichiens: les approches institutionnelle et discrétionnaire*, Université Libre de Bruxelles, Unpublished Master's Thesis.

De Schryver, Reginald. 1987. De Oostenrijkse aanspraken op de Spaans-Habsburgse erfenis. De Zuidelijke Nederlanden tijdens de Spaanse Successieoorlog. 1700–1716. In *Oostenrijks België 1713–1794. De Zuidelijke Nederlanden onder de Oostenrijkse Habsburgers*, ed. Hervé Hasquin, 11–36. Brussels: Gemeentekrediet van België.

Doyle, William. 1996. *Venality: the sale of offices in 18th century France*. Oxford: Clarendon.

Gaillard, Arthur. 1898–1902. *Le Conseil de Brabant: histoire, organisation, procédure*. Brussels: Lebègue.

Gaillard, Arthur. 1900–1903. *Inventaire des mémoriaux du Grand Conseil de Malines*. Brussels: Weissenbruch.

Galand, Michèle. 2001. Gages, honneurs, mérites: les hauts fonctionnaires dans les Pays-Bas autrichiens. *Revue belge de philologie et d'histoire* 73.2: 557–580.

Gilissen, John. 1980. De Grote Raad van Mechelen. Historisch overzicht. In *Miscelannea Consilii Magni. Ter gelegenheid van twintig jaar Werkgroep Grote Raad van Mechelen*, 13–43. Amsterdam: Universiteit van Amsterdam. Faculteit der rechtsgeleerdheid.

Hasquin, Hervé. 1973. Les difficultés financières du gouvernement des Pays-Bas autrichiens au début du XVIIIe siècle (1717–1740). *Revue internationale de la Banque* 6: 100–133.

Hempenius-Van Dijck, Barendina e.a. 1999. *De Heeren van den Raeden: biografieën en groepsportret van de raadsheren van het Hof van Friesland, 1499-1811*. Hilversum: Uitgeverij Verloren.

Jacob, Steve. 1999. Jacques-Antoine Le Clerc (1731-après 1797). Un fonctionnaire au service d'une politique réformatrice. In *La haute administration dans les Pays-Bas autrichiens (Ambroise-Joseph de Herzelles, Denis-Benoît de Cazier, Jacques-Antoine Le Clerc)* (Etudes sur le XVIIIe siècle 27), eds. Hervé Hasquin and Roland Mortier, 243–354. Brussels: Université de Bruxelles.

Jahns, Sigrid. 1990. Die Personalverfassung des Reichskammergerichts unter Anpassungsdruck. Lösungen im Spannungsfeld zwischen Modernität und Überalterung. In *Das Reichskammergericht in der deutschen Geschichte: Stand der Forschung, Forschungsperspektiven* (Quellen und Forschungen zur höchsten Gerichtsbarkeit im alten Reich 21), ed. Bernhard Diestelkamp, 59–109. Cologne: Böhlau.

Janssens, Paul. 1993. Les charges anoblissantes dans les conseils des Pays-Bas espagnols et autrichiens. In *Beleid en bestuur in de oude Nederlanden. Liber amicorum Prof. Dr. M. Baelde*, eds. Hugo Soly and René Vermeir, 225–239. Ghent: RUG.

Kerckhoffs-De Hey, A.J.M. 1980. *De Grote raad en zijn functionarissen*, 1477–1531. Amsterdam: s.n.

Lefèvre, Joseph. 1934. Les nominations faites dans la magistrature pendant l'occupation française, 1746–1747. *Revue belge de philologie et d'histoire* 13: 697–711.

Lefèvre, Joseph. 1939. *Documents concernant le recrutement de la haute magistrature dans les Pays-Bas autrichiens au XVIIIe siècle*. Brussels: Palais des Académies

Lefèvre, Joseph. 1975. *Documents concernant le recrutement de la haute magistrature dans les Pays-Bas, sous le régime espagnol, 1555–1700*. Brussels: Palais des Académies.

Maes, Louis Th. 1975. Gerechtelijke beslissingen in strafzaken, 16e–18e eeuw. Een vergiftigingszaak 1697–1702. In *De besluitvorming vroeger en nu* (Algemeen rijksarchief en rijksarchief in de provinciën. Educatieve Dienst. Catalogus 49), eds. Hugo de Schepper and John Gilissen, 197–236. Brussels: Algemeen Rijksarchief.

Mousnier, Roland. 1970. *La plume, la faucille et le marteau: institutions et société en France du moyen âge à la Révolution* Paris: PUF.

Reinhard, Wolfgang. 1996. Introduction. In *Power elites and state building*, ed. Wolfgang Reinhard, 8–11. Oxford: Clarendon.

Simon, Jules. 1921. La procédure criminelle sous l'ancien régime (Grand Conseil de Malines). *Handelingen van de Koninklijke Commissie voor de uitgave van oude wetten en verordeningen van België* 10: 397–437.

Swart, Koenraad. 1949. *Sales of offices in the 17th century*. Tha Hague: Martinus Nijhoff.

Stevens, Fred. 2000. Goswinus Anna Maria Felix de Fierlant (1735–1804): Een Turnhoutse bevoorrechte getuige van het einde van een tijdperk. *Taxandria: jaarboek van de Koninklijke geschied-en oudheidkundige kring van de Antwerpse Kempen* 71: 7–21.

Stroobant, Louis. 1903. *Les magistrats du Grand Conseil de Malines*. Antwerp: De Backer.

Thomas, Cathérine. 2013. Hommes d'Etat, hommes de loi. Les conseillers du Grand Conseil de Malines au XVIIe siècle. In *Gouvernance et administration dans les provinces belges (XVIe-XVIIIe siècles)* (Archives et Bibliothèques de Belgique 99), Eds. Claude De Morbeau de Gerbehaye e.a., 155–177. Brussels: Archives et Bibliothèques de Belgique.

Thomas, Cathérine. 2014. *Le visage humain de l'administration: les grands commis du gouvernement central des Pays-Bas espagnols (1598–1700)*. Brussels: Académie royale.

Vandenbulcke, Anne. 1992. *Le pouvoir et l'argent sous l'Ancien Régime: la vénalité des offices dans les conseils collatéraux des Pays-Bas espagnols (seconde moitié du XVIIe siècle)* (Standen en Landen 94). Kortrijk: UGA.

Van Poelgeest, L. 1988. De raadsheren van de Hoge Raad van Holland, Zeeland en West-Friesland in de achttiende eeuw. *Bijdragen en mededelingen betreffende de geschiedenis der Nederlanden* 103.1: 20–51.

Vermeesch, Griet. 2012. Professional lobbying in Eighteenth-century Brussels: The Role of Agents in Petitioning the Central Government Institution in the Habsburg Netherlands. *Journal of Early Modern History* 16: 95–119.

Verscuren, An. 2005. *"L'oeil et le bras du Roi?" Het vervolgingsbeleid van het officie-fiscaal van de Grote Raad van Mechelen (1767–1788)*. Unpublished Master's Thesis. Leuven: Katholieke Universiteit Leuven.

Verscuren, An. 2006. (S)pionnen van de vorst? De fiscalen van de Grote Raad in de tweede helft van de achttiende eeuw. *Pro Memorie* 8.2: 246–273.

Wijffels, Alain. 1994. Grote Raad voor de Nederlanden te Mechelen (ca.1445–1797). In *De centrale overheidsinstellingen van de Habsburgse Nederlanden*, ed. Erik Aerts e.a., 448–461. Brussels: Algemeen Rijksarchief.

Chapter 3
The Framework: Internal Organization and External Power Relations

3.1 Introduction

While it is certainly true that it was the councilors who gave the Great Council its own character and were ultimately responsible for its reputation, it should not be disregarded that they did not work in a vacuum. In fact, they were limited in their activities by two important factors. First, they had to act within a certain legal framework, established by the sovereign and regulated by decree. Throughout the early sixteenth century, several general ordinances were promulgated—in 1504, 1522 and 1531—to direct the internal organization of the Great Council, which eventually cumulated in the procedure-ordinance of 1559.[1] The latter text,[2] published by Philip II right before his departure to Spain, constituted the last all-encompassing regulation for the Great Council. Subsequent individual ordinances and decrees adjusted and changed certain parts of the text, but in essence, the 1559 ordinance determined the tasks of the members and the procedures to follow for the next 200 years until Joseph II attempted to dispose of the entire judicial organization in the Austrian Netherlands and replace it by a completely new system.[3]

Secondly, the Great Council was also embedded in the larger context of the Austrian Netherlands' society and therefore necessarily 'restricted' by its power relations. Even if the Council was at the outset established as a superior court, destined to control the administration of justice in the entire Netherlands, this position as

---

[1] Wijffels, Alain. 1994. Grote Raad voor de Nederlanden te Mechelen (ca.1445–1797). In *De centrale overheidsinstellingen van de Habsburgse Nederlanden*, ed. Erik Aerts e.a., 448–461. Brussels: Algemeen Rijksarchief. For a history of the early Great Council of Malines: Van Rompaey, Jan. 1973. *De Grote Raad van de hertogen van Boergondië en het parlement van Mechelen* (Verhandelingen van de Koninklijke Academie voor wetenschappen, letteren en schone kunsten van België. Klasse der Letteren 73). Brussels: Koninklijke Academie voor Wetenschappen, letteren en schone kunsten van België.

[2] *ROPB*, 2ième série, t. 7, August 8, 1559, pp. 461–492.

[3] Cf. infra, Chap. 5.

A. Verscuren, *The Great Council of Malines in the 18th century*,
Studies in the History of Law and Justice 3, DOI 10.1007/978-3-319-09638-4_3

'first tribunal' did not remain uncontested for very long.[4] In the eighteenth century, the Great Council's already reduced jurisdiction—if compared to the sixteenth century—was further nibbled away at when the appeals coming from the *Terres de débat* (contested territories) were no longer dealt with in Malines but divided over the Councils of Hainaut and Flanders in 1743 and even more so when the Councils of Luxemburg and Tournai received sovereignty in 1782.[5]

Jahns focused only on the personnel policy of the *Reichskammergericht* to demonstrate that it was the waning interest of the German Emperor and Estates that caused the decline of the tribunal throughout the eighteenth century. In this chapter, we investigate if this thesis can also be applied to the framework in which the Great Council worked: its internal organization on the one hand and the relations the court maintained with other actors in the eighteenth century Austrian Netherlands on the other hand. Given that the last all-encompassing ordinance regulating the workings of the Great Council dated from 1559, the question should be asked if the individual decrees of the 1600s and 1700s were sufficient to adjust the tribunal to the changed circumstances. Indeed, in 200 years, society had changed while the court had 'aged' and there should be no doubt that adaptations to the organization of the tribunal were essential to meet the changed requirements.

Moreover, the position of the Great Council in the larger society should be assessed. The Southern Netherlands constituted a 'composite state', a mosaic of heterogeneous territories, each with its own administrative institutions, traditions, customs and habits which they all defended, not only against the central government but against the other provinces as well. In theory, the Great Council, as the highest court of justice in the Netherlands represented the ideal instrument of the central government to coordinate and control the different regions and to limit the influence of local administrative and judicial institutions. On the other hand—as Van Peteghem has been able to determine for Flanders[6]—the 'divide and rule' principle as well could be a leading strategy in a ruler's attempt to achieve centralization.

Sources The 1559 procedure-ordinance constitutes the first important source for our understanding of the internal organization of the Council. This text is supplemented with the decrees of subsequent rulers of the Austrian Netherlands, with special attention to those of the eighteenth century.[7] However, both the procedure-ordinance and the later regulations only describe the 'ideal' way the Great Council was meant to function. The reality was probably, at times, far removed from this

[4] Oosterbosch, Michel. 1998. *Grote Raad voor de Nederlanden te Mechelen: procesbundels beroepen uit Vlaanderen: ordinaris processen (nr. 1–1000)*. Brussels: Algemeen Rijksarchief, 14.

[5] Wijffels, Alain. 1994. Grote Raad voor de Nederlanden te Mechelen (ca.1445–1797). In *De centrale overheidsinstellingen van de Habsburgse Nederlanden*, ed. Erik Aerts e.a., 448–461. Brussels: Algemeen Rijksarchief, 454. Cf. infra, 3.3.3 Checks and balances.

[6] Van Peteghem, Paul. 1990. *De Raad van Vlaanderen en staatsvorming onder Karel V (1515–1555): een publiekrechtelijk onderzoek naar centralisatiestreven in de XVII Provinciën*. Nijmegen: Gerard Noodt Instituut, VIII.

[7] As we elaborate on Joseph II's judicial reforms in the fourth chapter, our present scope is limited to the period before he came to power.

model. Indeed, early-modern legislation does not necessarily give an accurate idea of the real circumstances.[8] Moreover, since the actual court practice was self-evident for the councilors, we do not possess any texts that explain in detail how the tribunal functioned. Therefore, we have to use 'indirect' sources that allow us to deduce the workings of the court.

The *livres dits aux rapports* (report books)[9] are one such example. The registrars originally kept this series of several volumes to list the *épices* each councilor received for his actual work at the tribunal—independent of his annual fixed salary—in order to determine at the end of each semester what sum every single member was entitled to. Yet, not only do these registers allow us to calculate by approximation the income of the councilors from their work in the tribunal, they also make it possible to discover how the court was internally organized: the partition in two chambers, their respective workload and their changing composition (Fig. 3.1).

The *mémoriaux*[10], a series of registers containing mainly letters from the central administration to Malines and the responses—often formulated as advice—from the Great Council, offer some insight as well, especially into the larger environment in which the court had to operate. Of note are the various connections between the *mémoriaux* and the ordinances issued by the government: problems described in the *mémoriaux*, sometimes are officially 'solved' and institutionalized by a decree in the *ordonnances*.

Finally, the *consultes* (recommendations) of the Privy Council[11] supplement our understanding of the—especially discordant—relations the Great Council maintained with other players in the eighteenth century Austrian Netherlands. The series of *consultes* contain the opinions the Privy Council gave to the governor on issues of a very diverse nature, which were not necessarily related to the administration of justice. Still, the Great Council figures fairly often in the *consultes*. Every advice of the Privy Council was triggered by a request to the governor: at times, the Great Council itself sent such a petition, for instance complaining about infractions on its jurisdiction; at other moments other institutions or even individuals sent questions or grievances pertaining to the Great Council. Both parties in the discussion were 'heard' by the Privy Council, after which it formulated an often extensively motivated *consulte* to the governor. While the latter always had the final word, he only seldom went against the opinions of the Privy Coun-

[8] Van Rhee, Remco. 1997. *Litigation and legislation: civil procedure at first instance in the Great Council of for the Netherlands in Malines (1522–1559)*. Brussels: Algemeen Rijksarchief, 1.

[9] Brussels, ARA, GRM 682–694, liber primus, 1708–1788; Brussels, ARA, GRM 697–710, liber secundus, 1708–1756.

[10] Brussels, ARA, GRM 160–168G: Mémoriaux du Grand Conseil. Gaillard has composed an inventory of these *mémoriaux* up and until the year 1749. Gaillard, Arthur. 1900–1903. Inventaire *des mémoriaux du Grand Conseil de Malines*. Brussels: Weissenbruch; Brussels, ARA, GRM 141–142, Registre aux résolutions secrètes du Grand Conseil toutes chambres réunies. Even though these registers are not included among the *mémoriaux*, to their content they belong to this series.

[11] Brussels, ARA, GR, Registers 351–482. An analysis of these *consultes* for the period between 1725 and 1794 is available: De Breyne, Emile e.a. 1998. *Analyse des consultes du Conseil Privé sous le régime autrichien*. 2t. Brussels: Algemeen Rijksarchief.

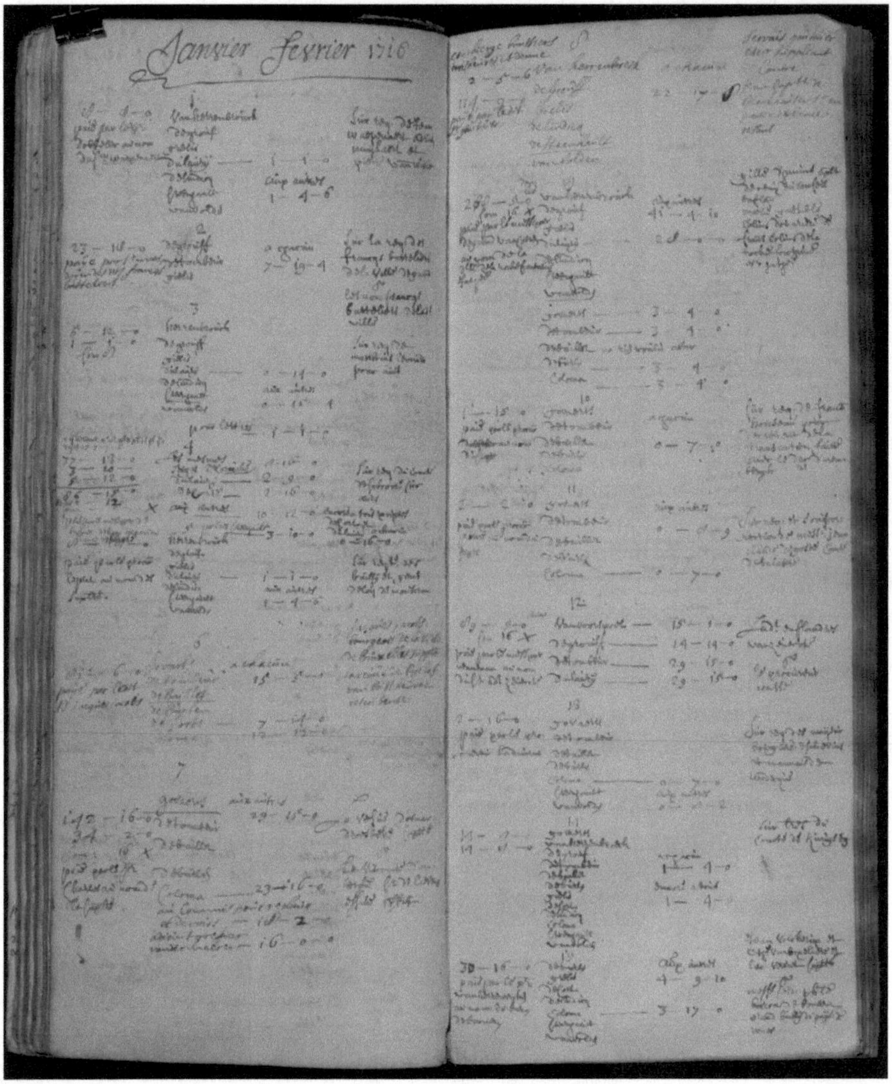

Fig. 3.1 Report book, 1713–1718. (Brussels, ARA, GRM 683. Liber primus)

cil. Since the recommendations were solely meant for the eyes of the governor, the Privy Council did not refrain from voicing its opinions on the Great Council, which were not necessarily very flattering. Additionally, the *consultes* allow us to reconstruct the eternal struggle between the 'highest court' and the highest administrative and political institution.

3.2 Internal Organization

3.2.1 The Great Council's Jurisdiction[12]

The 1559 ordinance does not expressly state the jurisdiction of the Great Council, nor do any of the previous or later ordinances. The only explicit reference to its jurisdiction is a negative one: the Great Council was not allowed to hear cases that should be dealt with by a provincial council or by another subaltern court.[13] The reason for this inexact definition of the powers of the Great Council should be at least partly looked for in the fact that the court was not the result of a deliberate act of foundation but had instead grown 'organically' within the *curia ducis*.[14] Therefore, its jurisdiction had never been though-out thoroughly. More importantly, however, this vagueness was in the interest of both the sovereign and the Council. A fixed jurisdiction hampered flexibility and would require a change in legislation whenever a modification of the council's powers was necessary. In particular the extension of these powers would invariably cause problems and be met by protest, as the lower tribunals would not accept a restriction of their own jurisdiction.[15]

Therefore, we are left to infer the jurisdiction of the Great Council from the individual ordinances the sovereigns promulgated over time and from its own legal practice. As both the Council's competences and its procedures have already been extensively studied, these parts will be predominantly based on previous literature.[16]

---

[12] In the late seventeenth or early eighteenth century, an official of the ecclesiastical tribunal of Ieper wrote a document concerning the jurisdiction, personnel, and workings of the Great Council, which can now be found at the archives of the Archbishop in Malines. The author described how the Great Council worked and added additional comments. The status of the document is unknown as it is unclear why an official of Ieper would write on the internal organization of the Great Council. Malines, AAM, Verzameling Kerk en Staat 870.

[13] *ROPB*, 2ième série, t. 7, August 8, 1559, p. 462, article 1, point 11.

[14] This phenomenon is not unique to the Great Council, but rather typical for the way in which Ancien Regime institutions came into being.

[15] Van Rhee, Remco. 1997. *Litigation and legislation: civil procedure at first instance in the Great Council of for the Netherlands in Malines (1522–1559)*. Brussels: Algemeen Rijksarchief, 27–28.

[16] No new research has been done into the procedure of the Great Council. Unless otherwise mentioned, the section 'jurisdiction' and 'procedure' are based on Gilissen, John. 1980. De Grote Raad van Mechelen. Historisch overzicht. In *Miscelannea Consilii Magni. Ter gelegenheid van twintig jaar Werkgroep Grote Raad van Mechelen*, 13–43. Amsterdam: Universiteit van Amsterdam. Faculteit der rechtsgeleerdheid, on the introduction to Oosterbosch, Michel. 1998. *Grote Raad voor de Nederlanden te Mechelen: procesbundels beroepen uit Vlaanderen: ordinaris processen (nr. 1–1000)*. Brussels: Algemeen Rijksarchief, on Van Rhee, Remco. 1997. *Litigation and legislation: civil procedure at first instance in the Great Council of for the Netherlands in Malines (1522–1559)*. Brussels: Algemeen Rijksarchief, on Van Rompaey, Jan. 1973. *De Grote Raad van de hertogen van Boergondië en het parlement van Mechelen* (Verhandelingen van de Koninklijke Academie voor wetenschappen, letteren en schone kunsten van België. Klasse der Letteren 73). Brussels: Koninklijke Academie voor Wetenschappen, letteren en schone kunsten van België and on Wijffels, Alain. 1994. Grote Raad voor de Nederlanden te Mechelen (ca.1445–1797). In

3.2.1.1 Jurisdiction as First Instance Tribunal

Van Rhee[17] mentioned eight circumstances in which the Great Council administered justice at first instance. Firstly, if privileged litigants were involved (jurisdiction *ratione personae*). Several categories of litigants, who either enjoyed the royal *sauvegarde* or who because of their position could appeal to the *privilegium fori*, were allowed to bring their disputes immediately before the Great Council, either as plaintiffs or as defendants. Members of this group included: the sovereign's household and family, knights of the Order of the Golden Fleece, the court's own personnel and their families, foreign merchants who had no fixed residence and the *miserabiles personae* such as widows and orphans.

Secondly, if the subject matter was privileged, the Great Council had jurisdiction at first instance (*ratione materiae*). For example, if the subject matter involved the interpretation and execution of administrative and legislative documents emanating from the sovereign (ordinances and patent letters) or if it concerned the rights of the sovereign (counterfeiting, *lèse majesté*, censure, …), the Great Council was competent to hear the case at first instance. Possessory actions as well—such as *complainte* and *maintenue*—could be brought directly before the Great Council. Opposition against the Great Council's open letters which were awarded on the simple request of a party without a preceding examination of the validity of the request constituted an important part of the Great Council's jurisdiction *ratione materiae*.

Other less important reasons which could bring a case to the Great Council were: if involvement of the Great Council in related matters could be demonstrated, if the applicable rules on jurisdiction made the initiation of lawsuits at several courts necessary—which was undesirable because it could result in high costs and conflicting judgments—if the defendant did not have a fixed place of residence, if courts which, according to the applicable rules on jurisdiction, should take cognizance of the case were prevented from doing so, if the defendant, originally not subject to the court's jurisdiction, had earlier submitted all his future disputes to the Great Council and if both parties had submitted an existing dispute to the Great Council.[18]

De centrale overheidsinstellingen van de Habsburgse Nederlanden, ed. Erik Aerts e.a., 448–461. Brussels: Algemeen Rijksarchief.

[17] Van Rhee extensively discussed the grounds for jurisdiction over subject matter at first instance: Van Rhee, Remco. 1997. *Litigation and legislation: civil procedure at first instance in the Great Council of for the Netherlands in Malines (1522–1559)*. Brussels: Algemeen Rijksarchief, 35–49. Van Rompaey as well dedicated a large part of his work on the early Great Council to a discussion of its jurisdiction, both at first instance and appeal. Van Rompaey, Jan. 1973. *De Grote Raad van de hertogen van Boergondië en het parlement van Mechelen* (Verhandelingen van de Koninklijke Academie voor wetenschappen, letteren en schone kunsten van België. Klasse der Letteren 73). Brussels: Koninklijke Academie voor Wetenschappen, letteren en schone kunsten van België, 271–370.

[18] Van Rhee, Remco. 1997. Litigation and legislation: civil procedure at first instance in the Great Council of for the Netherlands in Malines (1522–1559). Brussels: Algemeen Rijksarchief, 35–36.

3.2.1.2 Jurisdiction in Appeal

Already in the fifteenth century, the Great Council had dealt with appeals against sentences of other tribunals.[19] The Dukes of Burgundy had foreseen the possibility to lodge an appeal at a higher court against the sentences of a lower court with the explicit goal of limiting the authority of the local and—with regards to the Great Council—provincial institutions. By the eighteenth century, however, the Great Council had lost a lot of this jurisdiction in appeal, due to both internal and external circumstances. In the 1700s, the tribunal remained competent as a court of appeal, on the one hand for the provincial councils within its jurisdiction—the Councils of Flanders, Namur and Luxemburg (until 1782)—and on the other hand for a number of benches of aldermen which did not come under a provincial council—such as the Magistrate of Malines, the benches of aldermen of the 'Land of Dendermonde' and those of the *Terres de débat* (until 1743). In general, it is taken for granted that only sentences in civil cases could be appealed.[20] This proposition must be nuanced: at the end of the eighteenth century, some form of cassation against criminal condemnations by the Council of Flanders became possible.[21]

3.2.1.3 Other Legal Remedies

For the sake of completeness, we mention a few other legal remedies that could bring a case at the Great Council. *Evocation*—the withdrawal of an action from the tribunal from which it commenced—was in theory a privilege of the sovereign. He could decide that a lawsuit, which had originally been brought before another court, should be dealt with at the Great Council.

Secondly, the court treated cases as part of a voluntary jurisdiction: in that case, parties voluntarily agreed to be condemned to the observance of an arrangement, which could or could not be within the scope of a dispute. These voluntary condemnations had the same legal force as a regular sentence of the Great Council and all lawsuits concerning them were equally dealt with by the tribunal.[22]

---

[19] At the Great Council, there were two techniques to lodge an appeal against a judgment: appeal and reformation. Cf. infra, 3.2.2 Procedure.

[20] Pardons functioned in criminal trials as some sort of counterpart for appeal in civil lawsuits. The right to pardon a criminal was a prerogative of the sovereign and was considered to be his own personal instrument to express his dominance over the local and provincial tribunals. De Schepper, Hugo. 2006. Staatsgezag en staatsmacht in de Nederlanden. Verworvenheden en beperkingen van het Bourgondisch-Habsburgse systeem. In *Staatsvorming onder de Bourgondiërs en Habsburgers. Theorie en Praktijk*, eds. Hugo de Schepper en Jacques Geurts. Maastricht: Shaker, 25.

[21] Cf. infra, 2.3.3.1 The 'subordinate' councils. See: Monballyu, Jos. 1998. De Raad van Vlaanderen, een soevereine justitieraad in strafzaken? In *Handelingen van het tweede Hof van Holland Symposium gehouden op 14 November 1997 in de Treveszaal te Den Haag*, ed. Rob Huijbrecht, 77–90. The Hague: Algemeen Rijksarchief.

[22] The eighteenth century registers of extended judgments demonstrate that often a party did not fulfill its commitments. In that case, a regular sentence of the court was necessary, which usually foresaw in the forced sale of the property of one of the litigants to pay off his debts. Cf. Verscuren,

Finally, as a last remedy, parties could file for a revision (or *proposition d'erreur*) of a sentence by the Great Council. In that case, the contested decision was reviewed by the entire tribunal in plenary session, often supplemented—in the case of a grand revision—by additional members of a provincial council or even of the Privy Council. Revision was neither possible in possessory actions nor in intermediary sentences which still could be amended in a definitive sentence (*réparables en définitive*).

3.2.1.4 The Great Council as an Administrative Body

Apart from its functions as a tribunal, the Great Council was also an administrative body. In this regard, the Council was, among others, responsible for the publication of legislation within its jurisdiction (e.g. the seigniory of Malines, the land of Dendermonde, the *terres franches* etc). This authority led to numerous conflicts, especially with the Magistrate of Malines, which claimed to possess the privilege of publishing royal legislation within its jurisdiction.[23] Moreover, the Great Council's opinion was sometimes requested when the central government considered introducing certain judicial reforms, for example the abolition of torture.[24] However, the Great Council never boasted the right of remonstration that the *Parlement de Paris* or the Council of Brabant possessed.[25] Finally, the fiscals were not only engaged in prosecuting crimes, but also had certain administrative tasks such as the supervision of local officials working within the Council's jurisdiction, the inspection of printers, the monitoring of prisons, the responsibility for controlling waterways and roads etc.[26]

3.2.2 *Procedure*[27]

The preamble of the 1559 procedure-ordinance mentions why the sovereign considered it necessary to issue a new decree for the Great Council of Malines, even

An. 2013. *Nadere toegang op de geëxtendeerde sententies van de Grote Raad van Mechelen: 1693–1772.* Brussels: Algemeen Rijksarchief.

[23] Cf. infra, 3.3.1 "*Un corps si fort audessus d'eux*"

[24] The Great Council's advice on this matter has been preserved in the archives of the Privy Council: Brussels, ARA, GRO, Registers 464, f. 55–67, 1771.

[25] In the eighteenth century, the Council of Brabant was the only provincial council in the Austrian Netherlands which boasted the right of remonstration. This inevitably led to conflicts with the central government, especially in the seventeenth and eighteenth centuries. Cf. Put, Eddy. 2002. Gedeelde soevereiniteit? De dubbelrol van de Raad van Brabant. In *Politieke representatie*, eds. Henk de Smaele and Johan Tollebeek, 226–229. Leuven: Universitaire Pers Leuven.

[26] See: Verscuren, An. 2005. *"L'oeil et le bras du Roi?" Het vervolgingsbeleid van het officie-fiscaal van de Grote Raad van Mechelen (1767–1788)*. Unpublished Master's Thesis. Leuven: Katholieke Universiteit Leuven.

[27] For more information on the procedure used at the Great Council: Oosterbosch, Michel. 2001. Appelprocedure, dossierbehandeling en registervoering bij de Grote Raad van Mechelen. In: Voortschrijdend procesrecht. Een historische verkenning, eds. Fred Stevens, Ernest Persoons and

though the previous instructions dated from a mere 30 years earlier. Indeed, following a recommendation of the Privy Council, Philip II had ordered the president and councilors of the Great Council to send him all the previous ordinances and add suggestions for improved methods to administer justice more briefly in the future.[28]

Lengthy lawsuits had been a persistent problem since the early sixteenth century. Already in 1540, the Great Council, the Councils of Brabant, Flanders and Artois and the Court of Holland were requested to voice their opinions on a draft for an Abbreviation Ordinance. Nothing came of the plan, partly due to the reluctance of the Great Council, which considered the intended legislation not necessary; the procurator-general and the president, at least, claimed that there had never been any complaints about the court's procedure. Yet, many of the rules incorporated in the 1559 ordinance can be traced back to the Abbreviation Project.[29]

Despite the new regulations governing case duration, the problem persisted. In the eighteenth century, several complaints[30] and new decrees demonstrated that the issue had not been solved at all. In 1708, the future Charles VI published a reminder of and a minor adjustment to the regulations[31] in order to remedy the many delays in procedure which were detrimental to both the plaintiff and the defendant, but also to the good administration of justice. Some of these delays had to be attributed to the councilors: every time a member was absent, the entire discussion of the previous

---

Remco Van Rhee, 3–25. Leuven: Universitaire Pers Leuven; Van Rhee, Remco. 1997. Litigation and legislation: civil procedure at first instance in the Great Council of for the Netherlands in Malines (1522–1559). Brussels: Algemeen Rijksarchief; Van Rompaey, Jan. 1977. De procedure in beroep bij het Parlement van Mechelen. In Consilium magnum, 1473–1973: herdenking van de 500e verjaardag van de oprichting van het Parlement en de Grote Raad van Mechelen, 371–381. Brussels: Algemeen Rijksarchief; Oosterbosch, Michel. 1998. Grote Raad voor de Nederlanden te Mechelen: procesbundels beroepen uit Vlaanderen: ordinaris processen (nr. 1–1000). Brussels: Algemeen Rijksarchief.

28 *ROPB*, 2ième série, t. 7, August 8, 1559 p. 461:"… nous, par l'advis de nos très chiers et féaulx, les chief président et gens de nostre Privé Conseil et autres noz conseillers, ayons entre autres mandé et ordonné aux président et gens de nostre Grand Conseil résident à Malines de nous envoyer et apporter les institutions et ordonnances autrefois faictes par noz prédecesseurs et y adjouster ce que leur sembleroit pouvoir servir davantaige à la briefe et bonne expédition et administration d'icelle, pour après le tout estre visité et examiné par ceulx de notre Conseil estant lez nous et en estre faict comme pour le bien de justice se trouveroit convenir, …"

29 Van Rhee, Remco. 1997. *Litigation and legislation: civil procedure at first instance in the Great Council of for the Netherlands in Malines (1522–1559)*. Brussels: Algemeen Rijksarchief, 313–318. For more information on the problem of the duration of lawsuits, see: Van Rhee, Remco. 1998. Snelheid en efficiency in hoger beroep (civiele procedures, 16de eeuw). In *Handelingen van het tweede Hof van Holland Symposium gehouden op 14 November 1997 in de Treveszaal te Den Haag*, ed. Rob Huijbrecht, 21–37. The Hague: Algemeen Rijksarchief and Van Rhee, Remco ed. 2010. *Within a reasonable time: the history of due and undue delay in civil litigation* (Comparative studies in continental and Anglo-American legal history 28) Berlin: Duncker and Humblot.

30 E.g. Brussels, ARA, GRM 162, mémoriaux, f. 77, 1716: "Touchant les débats pour les clauses". This is a complaint about the duration of the debates at the Great Council and about the fact that the councilors do not follow the 'old style' anymore.

31 *ROPBA*, t. 2, pp. 179–180, November 8, 1708: "Etant informé qu'en notre grand conseil il s'est introduit quelques usages par où l'expédition des procès est fort retardé, au grand préjudice des parties et de la bonne administration de justice, …"

meeting had to be repeated, which of course was rather time-consuming. Therefore, the sovereign decided that councilors who had not been present during the entire decision process, should be excluded from any further intervention in that particular case.

Deliberately or not, the litigants also slowed down the course of a lawsuit, for example by introducing a *requête civile*, an instrument a litigant needed to present new facts or new titles after the therefore specifically dedicated moment had passed. The future Charles VI tried to solve this problem by raising the amount of the fine for *requêtes civiles* with 50–100 florins, depending on the phase of the lawsuit.[32] This decree did not solve the issue of timeliness either. In 1725, the governor of the Austrian Netherlands—Count de Daun—sent a request for advice to the Great Council, suggesting that it might be necessary to draw up some new ordinances to reduce the length of the procedure, especially in criminal cases.[33] Advocates and proctors were considered to be the main perpetrators as they were the benefactors of longer-lasting lawsuits. By introducing ever more paperwork, opening new debates, requesting postponements etc. the lawyers continually raised their profits. Despite the plethora of ordinances[34]—issued not only by the government but also by the Great Council itself and by several provincial councils—the problem persisted for at least a few decades. From the 1740s onwards, complaints from litigants about the delays gradually seem to have disappeared.[35]

While it is certainly true that abuses existed and that the councilors were probably not always as industrious as they should have been, the procedure did not favor a quick expedition of justice either. Each lawsuit was a complicated process, with different steps that had to be rigorously followed by all parties involved. Even the smallest side-issue which was not directly connected to the principal cause—such as the consignation of money—could evolve into an elaborate and time-consuming debate. The defendant also could default up to three times and each time the entire process of re-adjournment would be repeated. Consequently, the 1559 ordinance—despite its goal of achieving a 'brief administration of justice'—did not solve the issue.

[32] *ROPBA*, t. 2, pp. 179–180, November 8, 1708.

[33] Brussels, ARA, GRM 141, registre aux résolutions sécrètes, f. 33v, March 13, 1725. "Messieurs, sa majesté impériale et catholique etant informé des longueurs avec lesquelles se traitent les affaires de justice en ces Pays-Bas tant civiles que criminelles, et voulant y remedier pour le plus grand bien et soulagement de ses bons et fidels sujets, nous vous faisons la présente pour vous ordonner en son royal nom et de sa part de nous informer s'il ne convient pas de faire a ce sujet quelques nouvelles ordonnances pour en abroger les longueurs, notamment au criminel…"

[34] E.g: *ROPBA*, t. 1, p. 667, December 24, 1705; *ROPBA*, t. 2, p. 111, January 11, 1708; *ROPBA*, t. 2, p. 433, October 12, 1712; *ROPBA*, t. 3, p. 46, December 24, 1716; etc.

[35] It must be noted that when in 1782, Joseph II awarded sovereignty to the Council of Luxemburg, the duration of the appeal procedure at the Great Council was cited as one of the main reasons. Cf. infra, 3.3.3.1, The 'subordinate' councils.

3.2.2.1 First Instance Procedure[36]

In general, first instance lawsuits at the Great Council followed one of three patterns: the procedure on 'the *rôle*', the 'communicatory' procedure or the procedure before commissioners.[37] Theoretically, criminal trials would be conducted according to a separate criminal procedure, but depending on the kind of crime involved, they could take on the pattern of a civil case.[38] Every civil lawsuit started with a petition (*requête de venue en cour*) submitted to one of the secretaries of the court by the plaintiff. A councilor, charged with handling the petitions, investigated if the Great Council had the authority to deal with the request, subsequently marked it with an apostil and returned it to the secretary who executed the decision of the councilor. If the councilor issued a summons, one of the bailiffs took it to the counterparty.

The civil procedure: the rôle Originally, the procedure on the *rôle* was by far the most commonly used at the Great Council. On Thursday, Friday and Saturday mornings, two councilors,[39] appointed for the period of 1 month, chaired the *rôle* sessions, assisted by a registrar who made notes and a bailiff who was responsible for calling the litigants and keeping order. Once the parties appeared in court, the lawsuit was recorded on the *rôle*. Before the actual proceedings started, the defendant could try to avoid the litigation by challenging the authority of the court (*exception déclinatoire*), by evoking reasons to reject the lawsuit, for example because the claim had become barred by lapse of time, (*exception péremptoire*) or by asking for a delay (*exception dilatoire*).

If none of these exceptions were valid, the plaintiff (*demandeur*) formulated his demands, to which the defendant (*défendeur*) could respond with an answer. This could be countered by a reply of the plaintiff, followed by a *duplique* of the defendant, a *triplique* of the plaintiff etc. These exchanges could go as far as a *sex-*

[36] First instance procedure was used for both first instance and reformation cases.

[37] The term *procédure communicatoire* was not commonly used at the Great Council. Oosterbosch, Michel. 2006. Archief of niet? De procesdossiers van de Grote Raad voor de Nederlanden te Mechelen. In *Hoge rechtspraak in de oude Nederlanden*, eds. Hugo de Schepper and René Vermeir. Maastricht: Shaker, 67. Van Rhee only briefly discusses this procedure, when he mentions that petitions for a *provision de justice* sometimes contained an *apostille* by which the bailiff was not ordered to serve the summons on the defendant, but only commissioned to show him the petition and await an answer. In the sixteenth century, this procedure was merely reserved for distinguished persons or institutional parties. Van Rhee, Remco. 1997. *Litigation and legislation: civil procedure at first instance in the Great Council of for the Netherlands in Malines (1522–1559)*. Brussels: Algemeen Rijksarchief, 82–83. It is not surprising that Van Rhee does not extensively discuss the communicatory procedure as he limits his description of the first instance procedure to the period between 1522 and 1559, while the communicatory procedure only gained popularity in later centuries.

[38] Cf. infra, the criminal procedure.

[39] Only lay councilors could chair the *rôle*, clericals were excluded as well as the president. Since the fiscals had to act as prosecutors in criminal cases, neither the advocate-fiscal nor the prosecutor-general were allowed to act as chairman. *ROPB, 2ième série*, t. 7, August 8, 1559, title 8, pp. 477–478.

tuplique. One attempt to reduce the length of the lawsuits consisted in limiting the number of procedural acts to four: the plaintiff could make a demand and respond with a reply, the defendant could introduce an answer to the demand and then a *duplique* to the reply.[40]

In order to determine what exactly was contested, every fact or argument advanced by one of the parties was presented to the counterparty, which would admit or deny it (procedure *per verbum credit vel non credit*). Afterwards, the court ordered the litigants to provide proof of their claims by written documents, titles or witnesses, which again could be disputed by the counterparty and lead to another series of pleas. Once the case was sufficiently argued, the court instructed both parties to *fournir* (furnish) all their records together with the mandate of their proctor and an inventory of all pieces included. The files were placed in two bags and handed to the registrar who was responsible for checking the contents and passing them to the president. Afterwards, the latter distributed the files to one of the councilors who acted as reporter (*distribution*).

In theory, the litigants were kept in the dark about who reported their lawsuit: the registrar was not allowed to reveal which councilor took on the case.[41] In practice, we may assume that the parties often did know the identity of the reporter.[42] Gaillard as well mentions that at the Council of Brabant the litigants were originally not allowed to know the name of the reporter of their case—in order to prevent corruption or manipulation—but that this disposition was abolished as being impractical.[43] It is very likely that the same was true for the Great Council.

After having examined the lawsuit, the reporter gave an account of it in his chamber—or, if it was an important case, in a plenary session—where all councilors voiced their opinions[44] and then passed judgment. The sentence also included the condemnation to the costs of the trial.

---

[40] *ROPBA*, t. 12, pp. 552–568, November 3, 1786.

[41] *ROPB, 2ième série*, t. 7, August 8, 1559, title 1, point 31. Van Rhee mentions that the *rapporteur* ought to remain unknown, and if, inadvertently, his identity became known to the parties, a new *rapporteur* was to be appointed. Van Rhee, Remco. 1997. *Litigation and legislation: civil procedure at first instance in the Great Council of for the Netherlands in Malines (1522–1559)*. Brussels: Algemeen Rijksarchief, 193.

[42] Brussels, ARA, GRM 163, mémoriaux, f. 50–55, November 12, 1712: César-Eléazar Buor, the plaintiff in a lawsuit before the Great Council, requested the court to replace councilor Guillaume Gielis, who had so far been reporting his case, by another, more 'mature' and established councilor; Brussels, ARA, GRM 168B, mémoriaux, f. 70–73, May 21, 1745: in this case, one of the parties asked to add two judges to help councilor Charles de Partz who was reporting the lawsuit. The plaintiff wished to come to a brief expedition of justice, given the fact that the case had been dragging on for such a long time and that the costs were simply skyrocketing.

[43] Gaillard, Arthur. 1898–1902. *Le Conseil de Brabant: histoire, organisation, procédure*. Brussels: Lebègue, t. 2, 267.

[44] Some of these opinions have been preserved in the archives of the Great Council. So far, they have not been integrated in an official inventory, but a series *recueils et opinions* is available. From the limited sample for the eighteenth century we have been able to investigate, it seems that first the reporter gave his opinion, followed by the clerical councilor and then the other councilors of the chamber in descending order of seniority. The last member to give his views, however, was

The civil procedure: The communicatory procedure Apart from the procedure on the *rôle*, the Great Council also conducted lawsuits—called *différends*—using the communicatory procedure (*procédure communicatoire*). Contrary to the *rôle*, cases following the communicatory procedure were entirely written in nature. From 1683 onwards, these *différends* were recorded in a register apart from the other first instance lawsuits and from the appeal cases.[45] They are easily recognizable because the parties are designated by the terms *suppliant* and *rescribent* instead of *demandeur* and *défendeur*.[46]

Rather than summoning the parties, the apostil on the first petition contained an order to show the request to the counterparty (*soit [icelle requeste] monstrée à partie*), who then replied to it, also in writing. The parties never appeared in court and never saw each other. The councilor responsible for their case acted as an intermediary between the plaintiff and the defendant, receiving and sending their respective writings: the entire trial was conducted by mail. Once the councilor judged the case to be complete, it was handled as on the *rôle*: the parties had to furnish their files, a reporter was appointed and a sentence pronounced. The increased popularity of the communicatory procedure is apparent from the greater amount of *différends* compared to the number of procedures on the *rôle*. Of the approximately 5600 recorded eighteenth century first instance lawsuits,[47] more than 4300 followed the communicatory procedure. According to Gaillard, the popularity of the communicatory procedure should at least partially be attributed to the fact that—contrary to the lawsuits on the *rôle*—the councilors continued to deal with these cases during the holidays of the court, permitting a much more speedy settlement of the action.[48]

---

again one of the more senior councilors. The High Council as well had a fixed sequence: first the reporter gave his opinion, followed by the most senior councilor and then his younger colleagues in ascending order of seniority. Van Poelgeest, L. 1988. De raadsheren van de Hoge Raad van Holland, Zeeland en West-Friesland in de achttiende eeuw. *Bijdragen en mededelingen betreffende de geschiedenis der Nederlanden* 103.1: 39.

[45] All first instance lawsuits, following the procedure on the *rôle*, as well as the appeal cases are recorded in registers arranged according to the province of origin of the lawsuits, or according to the councilor who reported these cases. Brussels, ARA, GRM 617–620: "distribution par province du ressort" 1680–1794; Brussels, ARA, GRM 629–633: "distribution par conseiller" 1680–1794. The *différends* however were separately recorded: Brussels, GRM 635–637: "différends distribués" 1683–1788. Cf. infra, Chap. 3.

[46] According to Van Rhee, in the sixteenth century the term *suppliant* was used to denote the plaintiff in the early stages of the proceedings, because he commenced the action by way of a petition. A plaintiff who had acquired leave to commence an action was termed *impétrant*, while the plaintiff who had made his appearance at the cause-list sitting was referred to as *demandeur*. Van Rhee, Remco. 1997. *Litigation and legislation: civil procedure at first instance in the Great Council of for the Netherlands in Malines (1522–1559)*. Brussels: Algemeen Rijksarchief, 7. This however does not apply to the eighteenth century. The difference in denomination does not refer to the stage the lawsuit was in but rather to the procedure used to deal with the case.

[47] That is to say: first instance lawsuits that reached the distribution phase. Cf. Excel database: distribution records of the eighteenth century Great Council.

[48] Gaillard, Arthur. 1898–1902. *Le Conseil de Brabant: histoire, organisation, procédure*. Brussels: Lebègue, t. 2, 140.

The civil procedure: proceedings before commissioners Proceedings before commissioners have been scantily researched for the Great Council. According to Van Rhee, it was the president of the court who would appoint commissioners to perform specific tasks before a legal action had been commenced, during the proceedings in court and after final judgment was passed. In the first case, two commissioners—usually a councilor and a secretary—were deputized at the request of the parties in an attempt to find an amicable settlement of the dispute, the proceedings *at accordandum*. After an action had been commenced, a commissioner's task consisted in leading an *enqueste*, such as the hearing of witnesses. Finally, after the final judgment had been passed, a commissioner would be appointed to prepare the case in such a manner that the judgment could be enforced, for example by determining the value of a property. While some commissioners had the power to decide the issues brought before them (*commissarissen om te decideren*), others merely had the authority to effect an investigation and report to the court on their findings (*commissarissen van refereren*). Subsequently, the court decided the issue.[49]

For the Council of Brabant, E. Put remarked that the procedure before commissioners developed into some sort of 'extraordinary *rôle* procedure'. Initially, the ordinances prescribed that these proceedings had to be limited to urgent matters and disputes which were better not dealt with on the public *rôle*, such as lawsuits between close family members. In the course of time, the proceedings before commissioners developed into some sort of 'luxury procedure': not only was it faster, more discrete and more efficient, it was also much more expensive.[50] It is important to stress that, contrary to the situation at the Council of Brabant, parties seem to have been unable to commence an action before commissioners at the Great council. In fact, it was always a decision of the court to have commissioners handle a case, which originally was conducted on the *rôle* or followed the communicatory procedure.

The Criminal Procedure[51] The prosecution of a crime did not necessarily follow the criminal procedure. In general, civil offenses, i.e. those that could only be

---

[49] Van Rhee, Remco. 1997. Litigation and legislation: civil procedure at first instance in the Great Council of for the Netherlands in Malines (1522–1559). Brussels: Algemeen Rijksarchief, 300–303.

[50] Put, Eddy. 1995. *Inventaris van het Archief van de Raad van Brabant. Deel 1: Archief van de griffies*. Brussels: Algemeen Rijksarchief, 29–30.

[51] This paragraph is extracted from Monballyu's article on the criminal procedure in Flanders: Monballyu, Jos. 2001. De hoofdlijnen van de criminele strafprocedure in het graafschap Vlaanderen (16de tot 18de eeuw). In *Voortschrijdend procesrecht. Een historische verkenning*, eds. Fred Stevens, Ernest Persoons and Remco Van Rhee, 63–108. Leuven: Universitaire Pers Leuven, from Put's description of the procedure at the Council of Brabant: Put, Eddy. 1995. *Inventaris van het Archief van de Raad van Brabant. Deel 1: Archief van de griffies*. Brussels: Algemeen Rijksarchief, 32–33 and from Simon's article on the criminal procedure during the Ancien Régime in general, and at the Great Council in particular: Simon, Jules. 1921. La procédure criminelle sous l'ancien régime (Grand Conseil de Malines). *Handelingen van de Koninklijke Commissie voor de uitgave van oude wetten en verordeningen van België* 10: 397–437. All three councils more or less followed the same procedure in criminal cases, most likely because they had no specific guidelines

punished with a non-capital penalty—such as a fine or a short banishment—were conducted according to one of the above-explained civil procedures. On the other hand, severe crimes that could lead to banishment for life, a corporal punishment or the death penalty were prosecuted using the criminal procedure.[52] In the course of the lawsuit, civil cases could be 'criminalized' and criminal cases 'civilized' as the tribunal saw fit. Only a small part of the 1559 ordinance is dedicated to the criminal procedure. In 1570, a general criminal ordinance was established, but its legitimacy was not undisputed.[53]

One of the principal characteristics of the criminal procedure was its secrecy: often the accused was barely aware of the charges. Moreover, the suspect did not have the right to demand a proctor or advocate for his defense; the decision to receive legal aid was entirely left to the discretion of the court.[54] Even in the eighteenth century, the rights of the defense continued to be rather limited.[55]

Before the Great Council decided to put the suspect on trial, one of the fiscals—usually the procurator-general—had to perform a preliminary investigation into the offenses, the *informations préparatoires*. Based on this file, the court could either dismiss the case or decide that there was enough ground to issue a summons or take the suspect into custody (*prise de corps*).

In case a summons was ordered, the accused had to appear before the Great Council on the day indicated. If the interrogation gave reason to believe that a severe crime had been committed, the suspect was taken prisoner. Once in custody, two commissioners interrogated the accused—in principle within 3 days—using a questionnaire the fiscals had compiled. Provided that the suspect admitted his crimes, the fiscals concluded the case and urged the court to pronounce a sentence. If, on the other hand, the suspect denied the facts, the fiscals requested permission to interrogate the prisoner, interview potential witnesses and confront them with the accused. If necessary, the fiscals could ask for an interlocutory sentence to extract a declaration of guilt by subjecting the prisoner to torture (*examen extraordinaire*).

---

for criminal procedures and effectively relied on the 1570 ordinance. It must however be noted that the jurisdiction of the Great Council in criminal cases was rather limited.

[52] Yet, in practice, the distinction was not so straightforward. In the records of the office-fiscal, a distinction was made between *grand et petit criminel*, a difference which we assume is based on the procedures used. Experience has proven that similar crimes could be catalogued both as 'grand' and as 'petit criminel', and therefore could be prosecuted under either the criminal or the civil procedure. Cf. infra, Chap. 3.

[53] Monballyu, Jos. 2001. De hoofdlijnen van de criminele strafprocedure in het graafschap Vlaanderen (16[de] tot 18[de] eeuw). In *Voortschrijdend procesrecht. Een historische verkenning*, eds. Fred Stevens, Ernest Persoons and Remco Van Rhee, 63–108. Leuven: Universitaire Pers Leuven, 69.

[54] According to Simon, once the accused had answered all questions asked by the councilor-commissioner on the case—so in fact after the most essential parts of the trial were over—he could be assisted by legal counsel. Simon, Jules. 1921. La procédure criminelle sous l'ancien régime (Grand Conseil de Malines). *Handelingen van de Koninklijke Commissie voor de uitgave van oude wetten en verordeningen van België* 10: 404.

[55] Monballyu, Jos. 2001. De hoofdlijnen van de criminele strafprocedure in het graafschap Vlaanderen (16de tot 18de eeuw). In *Voortschrijdend procesrecht. Een historische verkenning*, eds. Fred Stevens, Ernest Persoons and Remco Van Rhee, 63–108. Leuven: Universitaire Pers Leuven, 73.

Every confession thus made, had to be repeated outside the torture chamber. If the suspect still denied the facts, the 1559 ordinance prescribed absolution. If he did confess, the case was furnished and a councilor was nominated to report to the entire chamber, which then proceeded to assessing the punishment.

As the lack of enthusiasm for the function of fiscal already suggested, criminal trials were absolutely unpopular among the councilors of the Great Council. The reason for their reluctance to prosecute crimes—in the latter half of the eighteenth century, the councilors regularly decided not to take on a trial after the fiscals had composed their *informations préparatoires*[56]—was of a financial nature: suspects were more often than not insolvent and the sovereign could not or would not compensate the councilors for their work done. At the same time, the *caisse des exploits*—which in theory could be used for this sort of expenditure—was frequently empty, as it was already overburdened with other expenses.[57] It is not hard to imagine that abuses occurred. In fact, since it was so difficult to retrieve the legal costs in a criminal trial, the prosecuting officer sometimes gave way to the inclination to make an arrangement with the suspect, who then could buy off the prosecution (*composer*). The criminal ordinance of 1570 specifically prohibited this practice in real criminal cases, i.e. when the accused could be sentenced to a corporal or capital punishment, and probably forbade it even when the crimes could only be penalized by a fine.[58]

It is unknown if this prohibition was actually put into practice or rather remained dead letter. The eighteenth century ordinances, at least, demonstrate that criminal justice continued to be a source of concern for the central government. In 1753, the problem of prosecuting officers cutting a deal with criminals resurfaced. Again, the prohibition to accept a fine without going to court for crimes punishable by a corporal penalty or banishment was repeated. At the same time, the sentiment within the Privy Council was that this decree should not be published since they feared

56 Verscuren, An. 2005. *"L'oeil et le bras du Roi?" Het vervolgingsbeleid van het officie-fiscaal van de Grote Raad van Mechelen (1767–1788)*. Unpublished Master's Thesis. Leuven: Katholieke Universiteit Leuven, 57.

57 Gaillard noticed the same phenomenon at the Council of Brabant. Gaillard, Arthur. 1898–1902. *Le Conseil de Brabant: histoire, organisation, procédure*. Brussels: Lebègue , t. 2, 283. At the Brabant court, it was always the most junior councilor who had to report criminal trials. While this sort of arrangement did not exist for the Great Council (cf. infra, Chap. 3), we can easily assume that the majority of the councilors did not exactly burn with enthusiasm to take on these cases. Simon also noticed in this regard that there was little to be gained from being a reporter in a criminal trial, which is why the task was usually bestowed upon junior councilors. Simon, Jules. 1921. La procédure criminelle sous l'ancien régime (Grand Conseil de Malines). *Handelingen van de Koninklijke Commissie voor de uitgave van oude wetten en verordeningen van België* 10: 407: "Le rôle effacé du conseiller commissaire le protégeait contre toute déformation de sa mentalité de juge, mais en revanche, ses fonctions, mettant leur titulaire peu en relief, étaient peu recherchées. Elles incombaient généralement aux conseillers les moins anciens et par conséquent les moins expérimentés."

58 Van Rompaey, Jan. 1961. Het compositierecht in Vlaanderen van de veertiende tot de achttiende eeuw. *Tijdschrift voor rechtsgeschiedenis* 29:70; 76.

that the public might criticize the prosecuting officers.[59] In 1762, Maria Theresa, in an official decree, prescribed the fiscals to exactly observe the ordinances on the administration of criminal justice and ensure a speedy expedition.[60]

In theory, it was not possible to appeal against criminal sentences, except against those that inflicted a simple fine.[61] The privilege the sovereign had to pardon a convict was considered to be a substitute for the non-existence of appeal against criminal condemnations.[62] Nevertheless, in practice, the issue was somewhat less straightforward. For example, in 1716 at the Council of Namur, a trial was held in appeal against a sentence of the bench of aldermen of Namur which had condemned the accused, Jeanne Servais, to 3 months in prison and eternal banishment for allegedly having plundered the inheritance of her recently deceased master.[63] The fact that the prosecutor did not protest this appeal, but decided to enter an appeal *a minima* in order to obtain a more severe punishment, indicates that this practice must have been institutionalized.

The prosecutor's attempt to lodge an appeal against the sentence of the Council of Namur, however, was rebuffed by the central government; appealing against a criminal sentence of a provincial council was apparently still impossible. Yet, even that was not absolute. As Monballyu has demonstrated, the Council of Flanders lost some of its sovereignty in criminal affairs to the Great Council in the early 1770s.[64] While it was still not feasible to actually appeal against a criminal sentence that did not merely condemn the suspect to a fine, it became possible to demand the nullification of such a sentence, based on procedural technicalities, comparable to some sort of appeal at the court of cassation *avant la lettre*.[65]

[59] *ROPBA*, t. 7, pp. 268–269, October 31, 1753, footnote (1): "Le conseil privé ne fut pas d'avis de publier ce décret dans la forme accoutumée: voici en effet ce qu'on lit dans sa consulte à la date du 9 octobre 1753: 'Quoique ce projet tel il est conçu, ait la forme d'une ordonnance à publier partout, un des membres du conseil est de sentiment qu'il ne faut et qu'il ne convient pas de faire cette publication dans les formes ordinaires, parce qu'on y décrédite publiquement la conduite des officiers. Il est donc de sentiment qu'il suffira d'envoyer l'ordonnance a tous les tribunaux supérieurs de justice et à ceux de la chambre des comptes, chargeant ceux-ci de la lire à tous les officiers comptables et de leur en donner un exemplaire en leur ordonnant de l'enregistrer dans les registres de leurs offices.'"

[60] *ROPBA*, t. 8, pp. 476–477, August 9, 1762.

[61] Given the nature of the punishment, these lawsuits had been conducted according to the civil procedure and were therefore appealable.

[62] De Schepper, Hugo. 2006. Staatsgezag en staatsmacht in de Nederlanden. Verworvenheden en beperkingen van het Bourgondisch-Habsburgse systeem. In *Staatsvorming onder de Bourgondiërs en Habsburgers. Theorie en Praktijk*, eds. Hugo de Schepper en Jacques Geurts, 13–50. Maastricht: Shaker, 25.

[63] Brussels, ARA, GRM 163, Mémoriaux, 1710–1720, f. 347–365.

[64] Monballyu, Jos. 1998. De Raad van Vlaanderen, een soevereine justitieraad in strafzaken? In *Handelingen van het tweede Hof van Holland Symposium gehouden op 14 November 1997 in de Treveszaal te Den Haag*, ed. Rob Huijbrecht, 77–90. The Hague: Algemeen Rijksarchief.

[65] As can be expected, the Council of Flanders did its utmost to reverse this decision. Cf. infra, 3.3.3.1 The 'subordinate' councils.

3.2.2.2 Procedure in Appeal[66]

There were two ways to protest a sentence: reformation and appeal. While the aggrieved party had 1 year and 1 day to ask for reformation of a judgment, an appeal had to be entered within 10 days. Another difference between the two, as is often claimed, is that in case of reformation the sentence was executed, while the execution was suspended in case of appeal. Nevertheless, appeal did not automatically postpone the implementation of a sentence. At the Great Council, a difference was made between a 'simple appeal' and an 'appeal with clauses'. The former did not suspend the sentence; the latter did, but often only until the first day of the trial when the appellant had to request an extension of the suspension.[67] Moreover, as appears from the distribution registers, reformation at the Great Council was reserved for protesting sentences by the Magistrate of Malines. It does not seem to have been possible to enter a reformation against the judgments of a provincial tribunal: those could only be appealed.[68]

While reformations followed one of the procedures of first instance, appeals had their own *modus operandi*. After the sentence of the lower tribunal had been pronounced, the offended party had 10 days to lodge an appeal. If the Great Council acknowledged the appeal as valid, the appellant had 3 months to 'elevate' his appeal (*lever son appel);* during this period he had to summon the judges *a quo*—to defend their judgment[69]—and signify the counterparty (*intimé*). Moreover, he needed to pay 60 florins security deposit for the penalty for *fol appel* in case he lost the lawsuit before the Great Council. Nevertheless, not all appeals were treated the same way. The procedures differed depending on the question if the Great Council qualified the lawsuit in the previous instance as a written case (*procès par écrit*) or not. In the latter instance, the lawsuit did not follow the classical procedure for appeal, but by analogy with reformation, was conducted according to the first instance procedure.

---

66 This paragraph is to a large extent based on the introduction to Oosterbosch, Michel. 1998. *Grote Raad voor de Nederlanden te Mechelen: procesbundels beroepen uit Vlaanderen: ordinaris processen (nr. 1–1000)*. Brussels: Algemeen Rijksarchief, 14–17. For more information on the procedure in appeal: Van Rompaey, Jan. 1973. *De procedure in beroep bij het Parlement van Mechelen*. In *Consilium magnum, 1473–1973: herdenking van de 500e verjaardag van de oprichting van het Parlement en de Grote Raad van Mechelen*, 371–381. Brussels: Algemeen Rijksarchief.

67 Brussels, ARA, MD 2968: "Instructions et forme de procéder au Grand Conseil de Sa Majesté imperiale roiale etc etc avec deux tables des matières y continues alphabétisés. 1794." F. 59: 'manière de procéder au Grand Conseil.'

68 Since the Great Council was the last step in an entire judicial pyramid, some of the appeals against sentences of a provincial council were double or even triple appeals. For example, the Great Council could deal with an appeal against a sentence of the Council of Flanders, which was pronounced in a reformation against the sentence of the Magistrate of Ghent.

69 In practice, as can be inferred from the extended sentences, the judges of the previous instance did not partake in the proceedings. Yet, in some cases, judges of a lower tribunal could be condemned for making a 'bad' decision. E.g., Brussels, ARA, GRM 975, f. 308–455, October 4, 1738: Extended sentence in the lawsuit between Guilliam Damerin and Michiel Vraem concerning the testamentary dispositions regarding the movable property of canon Zannequin. There are no known examples of the Great Council condemning the councilors of a provincial council to a fine for making the 'wrong' judgment.

If the lawsuit was received as a *procès par écrit*, the appellant had to have the written file transferred from the previous instance(s). In principle, the Great Council decided the appeal based on the same set of documents as the subordinate court (*ex eisdem actis*) in order to asses if the judges at first instance had or had not pronounced the correct sentence (*an bene vel male (judicatum)*). However, it appears from the extended sentences that both the appellant and the *intimé* regularly deviated from the normal procedure to introduce new evidence.

When all proceedings were concluded, each party placed its documents, including an inventory signed by its proctor, in a bag and deposited it at the registry. The president of the Council designated a councilor responsible to report the case, after which it was discussed in the entire chamber. Finally, a sentence was passed. If the sentence of the subordinate tribunal was confirmed, the appellant did not only have to pay the costs of the appeal, but also the penalty of *fol appel*. If, on the contrary, the court decided in the appellants' favor, the *intimé* would pay the costs, often both of the first instance and of the appeal case. Sometimes, the councilors divided the costs over both parties, especially if they were high. While this practice was condemned by the government, it was often used as a means to secure payment.

3.2.2.3 Revision (or proposition d'erreur)[70]

Since the Great Council was a tribunal of last instance, appeals against one of its sentences was not possible. The last resort for those parties who felt they had been treated unfairly was to ask for a revision of their lawsuit. A request for revision had to be made within 2 years after the sentence. The security deposit for a revision was 120 florins, much more than for *fol appel*. This is partly attributable to the higher cost for revision and was partly meant to discourage the all too extensive use of the procedure. Revisions were always handled by a plenary session of the Great Council. However, after 1762, the fiscals could no longer intervene.[71] In case of a so called grand revision, judges from other—often provincial—tribunals were added.[72] After the revision, the losing party had exhausted all legal remedies and had no other option than to submit to the judgment of the Council. At least in theory, the Great Council was the superior court of the Netherlands and the last resort for all parties.[73]

[70] For more information on the procedure used for revisions: Koster-Van Dijk, Joke M.I. and Wijffels, Alain. 1990. Les procédures en révision au Grand Conseil de Malines (1473–1580). *Publications du Centre Européen d'Etudes Bourguignonnes* 30: 67–97.

[71] *ROPBA*, t. 8, p. 449, February 3, 1762.

[72] While there were no fixed regulations concerning the choice of supplementary councilors, certain criteria were handled to select them, such as their field of specialization as well as their knowledge of languages. In general, if the revision concerned an appeal against a sentence of a provincial council, members of that particular council would usually not be selected. Koster-Van Dijk, Joke M.I. and Wijffels, Alain. 1990. Les procédures en révision au Grand Conseil de Malines (1473–1580). *Publications du Centre Européen d'Etudes Bourguignonnes* 30: 82–83.

[73] Nevertheless, H. de Schepper has called into question this status of the Great Council as the highest legal institution of the Netherlands. In two articles, (1978 and 1998), he claimed that the

3.2.3 The Great Council's Inner Workings

3.2.3.1 Division into Chambers

The councilors of the Great Council were allocated to two chambers, each working separately from the other.[74] Only for matters of great importance—such as revisions, advice to the governor, conflicts of jurisdiction or the selection of a *terne*—the two chambers would confer together. The 1531 ordinance specifically mentioned this "bi-chamberalism" and ordered that each chamber should be composed of at least five to six members;[75] the procedure ordinance of 1559, however, did not repeat this rule. Moreover, any instructions on how the two chambers should be organized are entirely lacking. Although several eighteenth century decrees indirectly refer to the existence of two chambers, they do not supply any information about their composition either. For the members of the Council, the rules governing this bi-chamberalism may have been so obvious at the time that they did not feel the need record them.

In addition, there are no specific written guidelines to determine how lawsuits were distributed over the chambers. The only sources that explain how this may have worked, are the *livres dits aux rapports* (report books), and even then only

---

Privy Council had the highest judicial authority, even though it only seldom used it and most often referred lawsuits to the Great Council or another competent court. His thesis has certainly not remained uncontested. We will debate his theory when discussing the relations between the Great Council and the Privy Council. Cf. infra, 3.3.4 Status anxiety. De Schepper, Hugo. 1978. De Grote Raad van Mechelen, hoogste rechtscollege in de Nederlanden? *Bijdragen en Mededelingen betreffende de Geschiedenis der Nederlanden* 93: 358–376 and De Schepper, Hugo. 1998. De Geheime Raad als hoogste rechtscollege in de Nederlanden (1504–1580). In *Handelingen van het tweede Hof van Holland Symposium gehouden op 14 November 1997 in de Treveszaal te Den Haag*, ed. Rob Huijbrecht, 39–48. The Hague: Algemeen Rijksarchief.

[74] Gilissen believed that both chambers had different competences. The second chamber examined the case file and prepared the sentence; afterwards the lawsuit was sent to the first chamber where the advocates held their pleadings and the sentence was drafted and pronounced. Gilissen, John. 1980. De Grote Raad van Mechelen. Historisch overzicht. In *Miscelannea Consilii Magni. Ter gelegenheid van twintig jaar Werkgroep Grote Raad van Mechelen*, 13–43. Amsterdam: Universiteit van Amsterdam. Faculteit der rechtsgeleerdheid, 35. We, however, have found no data that support this hypothesis. Van Rhee as well takes the view that the division of the lawsuits over both chambers was in no way associated to the stage of the procedure. Van Rhee, Remco. 1997. *Litigation and legislation: civil procedure at first instance in the Great Council of for the Netherlands in Malines (1522–1559)*. Brussels: Algemeen Rijksarchief, 194.

[75] Ordonnances, statuts, stile, et manière de procéder, faits et decretez par le roi Don Philippe II pour son Grand Conseil le 8 août 1559 avec les éclaircissements sur lesdites ordonnances émanés du même conseil. L'institution d'icelui, par le duc Charles de Bourgogne en l'an 1473. Celle de l'archiduc Philippe du janvier 1503 et l'ordonnance par l'empereur Charles V du 26 octobre 1531. 1721. Brussels: t'Serstevens, 218: "Voulons et ordonnons aussi que nosdits présidents et conseillers du Grand Conseil entendent en deux Chambres à la visitation, et decision des matières, procès et affaires pendans audit Grand conseil, et iceux procès, et affaires puissent resoudre, arrester et conclure, estans six ou du moins cincq en chascune chambre, si ce ne sont matières de tant grande importance et considération, ou si difficiles à déterminer, qu'il semblast besoing les décider en plein conseil (…)"

indirectly.[76] In fact, the information the report books supply is predominantly financial: they list the remuneration of the councilors for each case whether as reporter or as a regular judge. Since the report books clearly demonstrate a distribution of the councilors over two separate groups, we assume that these groups correspond in fact to the two chambers.

As far as can be derived from the report books, the 'grand' chamber (*grande chambre)* usually consisted of nine councilors, while the 'small' chamber (*petite chambre*) was composed of eight judges.[77] The two clerical councilors and the two fiscals normally did not sit together in the same chamber, given that neither the clerical councilors nor the fiscals were allowed to perform certain tasks. Neither could judge criminal cases, the former because they could not pronounce the death penalty, the latter because they acted as prosecutors in criminal trials. Moreover, the fiscals were not permitted to report cases, as they were often absent due to their large variety of tasks.[78] Therefore, putting fiscals and clericals together could inconvenience the expedition of justice.

Furthermore, relatives never occupied a seat in the same chamber. According to the procedure ordinance, they were not even allowed to be councilors in the Great Council simultaneously.[79] Given the intrinsically intertwined relationships between officials in the higher administration, relatives did end up occupying seats in the Great Council, most often in a father-in-law—son-in-law relationship.[80] In order to meet the objections that might rise from having two family members together in the Great Council, they were put in different chambers to keep interactions to a minimum. However, problems could arise when, in matters of great importance, the two chambers convened. The logical solution would be to forbid one of the two relatives—probably the most junior—to attend these plenary sessions. Nevertheless, from the samples we investigated, it seems that this was not the case. In all instances, even when the candidates for a new councillorship needed to be assessed, both family members were admitted to the collective deliberations.[81]

---

[76] Brussels, ARA, GRM 682–694, liber primus, 1708–1788; Brussels, ARA, GRM 697–710, liber secundus, 1708–1756. We do not exactly know the difference between the liber primus and the liber secundus, as they both list the *épices* of the councilors in the two chambers at the same time. It might have been connected to the functioning of the registry. Given that there were two registries—one 'upper' and one 'lower' registry—it might have been possible that the two books—primus and secundus—were kept by two different registrars.

[77] This is the terminology used in a sixteenth century document: Brussels, ARA, Audiëntie 1419/4, 1553: investigation into the behavior of procurator-general de Cocq. The 'grand' chamber is the 'presidential' chamber. Despite what the qualification between 'grand' and 'small' chamber might suggest, both had probably equal authority and jurisdiction.

[78] The same was true for the president. Cf. supra, Chap. 2.

[79] This prohibition was repeated several times, up until the end of the eighteenth century. *ROPBA*, t. 10, p. 330, January 13, 1773.

[80] This was the case with Van Voorspoel and de Decker, O'Donnogue and Richterich, Bervoet and Happart, de Potter and Marci and Deudon and de le Vielleuze, who all served together during a certain time. De Laing and president Leclerc were brothers-in-law. Cf. supra, Chap. 2.

[81] For example, this was the case in 1740 with Richterich and O'Donnogue and in 1750 with de Potter and Marci. Brussels, ARA, GRM 707, liber secundus, 1737–1740; Brussels, ARA, GRM

The report books also demonstrate that the chambers were often incomplete during the decisive phase of a lawsuit. This was because councilors were sometimes absent due to duties connected with other cases, such as a *vue-de-lieu* or the interrogation of witnesses who were unable to make the journey to Malines. Moreover, once a councilor had been absent during the reporting phase of a lawsuit, he was no longer allowed to intervene, so as not to slow down the expedition of justice. The only exception to this rule was if the councilor had a legitimate reason to be absent—for example, in case of sickness—and the president deemed his presence useful.[82]

Based on the report books, it has not been possible to distinguish a definitive pattern in the composition of the two chambers or in the way the councilors were allocated to them. At the Council of Brabant, the 'low chamber' (*la chambre basse*) or chancellor's chamber was always composed of three senior and four junior members, and the advocate-fiscal. The 'high chamber' (*la chambre haute*) consisted of four junior and four senior councilors—the oldest member of the Council included. In order to maintain the right proportion between junior and senior members in one chamber, the composition changed after the death or resignation of a councilor.[83]

A similar model could not be established for the Great Council. On the contrary, the impression is that both chambers were almost entirely randomly arranged. The president, for instance, regularly switched chambers. In January and February 1710, one chamber was composed of president Stalins and councilors Govaerts (as clerical councilor), Van Voorspoel, Seghers, de Tombeur, de Baillet (as fiscal), de Burlen, Gielis and de Corte. The other chamber consisted of councilors de Coriache (as clerical councilor), Van Kerrenbroeck (as fiscal), Heijdenreijck, de Grouff, Janssens, Vanderhaeghen, du Laury and de Lindicq. However, in the same months of that same year, the president regularly changed chambers, while the rest of the composition of the chambers stayed exactly the same.[84]

Councilors as well could move from one chamber to the other, although this happened less frequently. For instance, in the months November and December of 1710, the president stayed put, but councilor de Burlen changed chambers several times.[85] Yet, at no time in the year 1710 did a member leave or get added to the Council. The *mémoriaux* confirm that it was not unusual for councilors to transfer from one chamber to another.[86]

709, liber secundus, 1747–1751.

[82] *ROPBA*, t. 2, pp. 179–180, November 8, 1708.

[83] Gaillard, Arthur. 1898–1902. *Le Conseil de Brabant: histoire, organisation, procédure*. Brussels: Lebègue, t. 2, 128–129.

[84] Brussels, ARA, GRM 682, liber primus, January–February 1710; Brussels, ARA, GRM 697, liber secundus, January–February 1710.

[85] Brussels, ARA, GRM 682, liber primus, November–December 1710.

[86] In 1714, the plaintiff in an inheritance conflict asked if councilor Remi Albert du Laury, who had intervened in the decision of an earlier lawsuit between the same parties, could also take part in the decision of their present case despite the fact that he had switched chambers. Brussels, ARA, GRM 163, Mémoriaux, 1710–1720, f. 142–144.

This pattern of apparent randomness repeated itself in the samples we have taken throughout the eighteenth century.[87] The only exception is the year 1785, when apparently there was no second chamber. In all instances, de Fierlant presided while the composition of the chamber barely changed. Sometimes, a certain councilor was absent, or another one was added, but only one chamber consistently counted nine of the same members more or less (president de Fierlant, councilors Van Volxem (as clerical councilor), Vriesen, Tackoen, Ludovisi, de Stassart (as fiscal), Van der Fosse, Ghison and de Cock). From time to time, Douglas and Cottin appeared instead of Van der Fosse and Vriesen, while Diu sometimes replaced de Stassart as fiscal and Van Velde Van Volxem as clerical, but unless the entire council convened for matters of great importance, de Villers, de Laing, de Waepenaert and Wirix never acted as members of a reporting chamber.[88]

We have not (yet) been able to explain this anomaly,[89] nor have we found a rationale that underlied the composition of the chambers. It is safe to assume that it was normally the president who decided on the composition of the chambers, but his motives to assign a councilor to a specific chamber or to have councilors change chambers remains unknown. Unlike the situation at the Council of Brabant, seniority does not seem to have played any role. Geographical origin was not a determining element either: while it is true that the councilors of Brabant and Flanders were rather equally allocated to the two chambers, the data is not distinct enough to ascertain that geography was a decisive factor.

The hypothesis that there was some sort of functional distribution might be more fruitful. In that case, the chambers could be composed of people from different backgrounds with different specialties. For example, while one councilor might have had experience in dealing with land matters, another could have earned his merits in inheritance issues, while a third may be considered a specialist in settling possessory claims. A reasonable solution would be to assemble people with different specialties in the same chamber, in order to cover the greatest possible diversity of subject matters in one chamber. The fact that the two clerical councilors sometimes sat together in one single chamber—when, as we can suppose, a lawsuit with a religious slant to it was covered—seems to nourish this assumption. Additionally, cases that were redistributed—because, for example, the initial reporter was ill, had died, had moved to another position or lacked the time—were not necessarily assigned to a councilor who occupied a seat in the same chamber as the original reporter.[90]

---

[87] The samples are chosen according to the availability and completeness of the data. For liber primus, we have investigated the years 1710, 1720, 1730, 1740, 1765 and 1785. For liber secundus, we have done the same thing for the years 1710, 1720, 1730, 1740, 1745, 1750 and 1755.

[88] Brussels, ARA, GRM 694, liber primus, 1782–1788, 1785.

[89] Potentially, this has to do with the incompleteness of the sources as we do not possess the *liber secundus* for the year 1785.

[90] This information could be retrieved by combining the data with regards to redistribution in the distribution books with the data concerning the division of the councilors over the chambers in the report books. The sample that could be examined was rather small but clearly indicated that approximately 50% of the cases were redistributed to a new reporter who occupied a seat in the same chamber as the initial one.

What we do know for certain is that the chamber in which the president occupied a seat always handled the majority of the cases, independent of its composition. Although the president never received as much 'report money' as the regular councilors, he had reason to ensure that he was chairing the chamber sentencing the most complicated—and thereby usually lucrative—lawsuits, which could have motivated his decision to regularly switch chambers.

3.2.3.2 Keeping up Appearances? The Relations Between the Court's Personnel

The relationships between the Council's members are not easy to document, as official sources do not divulge their day-to-day interactions and ego-documents are lacking. To the extent that there was a hierarchy among the councilors, seniority was the determining factor. In the absence of the president, the most senior councilor fulfilled his duties—unless this was the procurator-general or advocate-fiscal who could not preside over the Council. On the other hand, each councilor had its own rank, even though, as far as we know, this did not have any practical consequences in the eighteenth century.[91] It may have been connected to a certain seat in the chamber itself, but it was in any case entirely independent of seniority. In fact, when a councilor died, his successor also always succeeded him in his rank.[92]

Given that the (financial) stakes were sometimes high, we can assume that frictions must have existed. Gaillard cited numerous examples of conflicts between the members of the Council of Brabant, usually when money was involved.[93] For the Great Council, we have very little evidence of serious frictions. However, this does not necessarily mean that it was all roses there. The members of the Council might have had every reason to be discreet. Yet, they also may have wished to limit internal strife as much as possible: the councilors formed such an intricate social network through familial and other relations that they could not afford too much internal dissent, especially not out in the open. Either way, the available records[94] mention very few issues between the members of the Great Council: the Happart case is one of the few examples we could find of serious internal conflict.[95] Obviously, any member who threatened to stain the prestige of the court could not count on much sympathy from his colleagues.

---

[91] Only MD 860/B refers to this rank, but does not explain what exactly it consisted of or if there were any practical consequences associated with it.

[92] For example, Pierre Jacques Van Heydenreyck was the 22nd councilor of the first rank, taking the place of Jean François Colins who was the 21st councilor of the first rank. Brussels, ARA, MD 860/B, f. 18r.

[93] Gaillard, Arthur. 1898–1902. *Le Conseil de Brabant: histoire, organisation, procédure*. Brussels: Lebègue, t. 2.

[94] Records consulted include the *Mémoriaux*, the *consultes* of the Privy Council, the criminal case files of the Great Council and the recommendations of the fiscals.

[95] Cf. supra, Chap. 2.

Apart from their tribunal's reputation, the councilors also jealously guarded what they saw as their privileges: at least, they certainly did not hesitate to denounce the president's behavior to the central government when he attempted to increase his own power by infringing on their rights. In November 1709 while Jacques Stalins was president, a conflict arose concerning the admission of new proctors. In a letter from the councilors to the central government, they revealed that the president appointed proctors on his own account, without consulting the councilors and without submitting the candidates to the designated exam. The problem was not new: in the seventeenth century, a series of incidents had led to the decree of May 11, 1690 which determined the procedure for the admission of proctors and limited their number to 16.[96] Moreover, president Hyacinthe de Brouchoven also had attempted to establish his authority on the matter, but had been rebuffed by the Council. Stalins refused to listen to his colleagues and appointed proctors at his own will, even accepting money from the candidates.

When it became clear that the reprimand of the Privy Council of November 1709 did not have the desired effect, the members of the Great Council sent another complaint in February 1710. The issue had come to the forefront when—after the death of proctor Hasart—the president had dismissed a suitable candidate without consulting his colleagues in the Council, instead announcing that he would appoint his own selection for proctor. As a result, an official decree was issued in the name of the future Charles VI, declaring that the Great Council had to comply with the instructions of May 11, 1690.[97] Moreover, a letter would be sent to the president, informing him that he had to conform to these rules on pain of his decisions being null and void. As for the proctors who had already been admitted, those who had taken the exam could continue to perform their functions. Those who been appointed by the president without having previously taken the test as well as all other candidates who believed they had the right competences, were allowed to present themselves to be examined by the councilors. Afterwards, a plenary session of the Great Council would decide, with a majority of the votes, who to admit.

While it was obvious that president Stalins had failed to garner more influence, he did not give in easily. In 1713, a second conflict arose as the result of a new attempt by the president to increase his own authority. Given how he played off the councilors against one another, he might be even suspected of having tried to sow discord between the members of the Council in order to accumulate more power in his own hands. In a letter from the councilors to the sovereign, they denounced the behavior of the president and his attempts to change certain customs that had been in use for centuries.[98]

The councilors argued it was custom at the Great Council to have the councilor-reporter handle the effective liquidation of the goods in a lawsuit concerning a forced public auction (*sentence de décret*). Yet, since the appointment of the new

---

[96] Brussels, ARA, GRM 141, Registre aux résolutions secrètes, f. 13v, November 1709; f. 14v–15, February 1710.

[97] *ROPBA*, t. 2, pp. 284–285, February 5, 1710.

[98] *ROPBA*, t. 2, pp. 476–477, September 16, 1713, footnote.

president, the execution of the sentence had been referred to the *rôle*. This caused several inconveniences as the commissioners on the *rôle* changed monthly or sometimes even weekly. Subsequently, they were not always well-informed about every lawsuit. And while the letter did not mention it explicitly, it undoubtedly also meant a serious loss of income for the original reporter.

Secondly, after having noted his apostil on a *requête civile*, the president could give it to any councilor instead of to the reporter of the case. As a consequence, many of these *requêtes civiles* finished up on the *rôle* instead of with the reporter, which caused constant delays in the decision of the lawsuits. Thirdly, the procurator-general had always intervened in the examination of prospective proctors, notaries and bailiffs until the new president decided that it should be left to one single councilor. As a result, the members of the Great Council requested the central government to remedy such deviations to the customs and to order Stalins to abide by the rules. The result of these complaints was a new decree, which redressed all the complaints of the members of the Council in the exact way they had requested it. President Stalins again saw his attempts to increase his own authority rebuffed by an official ordinance.[99] After his death in 1714, conflicts between the president and the councilors seem to have ceased.

Together, the councilors and the president formed the core or the 'inner circle' of the Great Council. All other employees in one way or another were at their service, making their work possible or facilitating it. Their position within the Council was not always clear-cut. For example, a request of Hubert de Tombeur in 1712[100] gave rise to a discussion concerning the question if registrars did or did not belong to the 'inner circle' of the Council. The advocates of their inclusion argued that—according to article 3 of the procedure ordinance[101]—it was indisputable that registrars belonged to this 'inner circle', even though they were subordinate to the councilors. Furthermore, the procedure ordinance laid down the same rules for the nomination of registrars and councilors: the Great Council also had the *droit de terne* when a vacancy for the registrar's office opened up. On the other hand, the registrars' tasks were entirely different from those of the regular councilors: they had to draft the extended sentences, send out the ordinances, open letters and apostils the councilors requested them to etc., and, more vitally, they lacked a voice in the Council.

To complicate matters further, both registrars were secretaries, but not all secretaries were registrars. The six secretaries who were not registrars were part of a 'second circle'. The deputy procurator-general as well belonged to this second circle, although his position was sometimes as ambiguous as that of the registrars. In fact, his duties were limited to those of the public ministry; he could not re-

[99] *ROPBA*, t. 2, pp. 476–477, September 16, 1713.

[100] In 1712, Hubert de Tombeur sent a request to the sovereign asking permission to apply for the vacancy of registrar at the Great Council. Given that his father was at that time a councilor, the question was if he did or did not need a dispensation. ARA, Regentschapsraad van State 285, 1712.

[101] *ROPB*, 2*ième* série, t. 7, August 8, 1559, p. 462, title I, n°3: "Que nos dicts président, conseilliers, advocat fiscal, procureur général et greffier de nostre dict Grand Conseil ne pourront prendre et avoir aulcuns gaiges ou pensions de ce que ce soit autres que de nous…"

place the procurator-general in his position as councilor. On the other hand, when the procurator-general was absent, he assumed the latter's responsibilities in the prosecution of crime. Furthermore, the deputy did not participate in the debates and, contrary to the councilors, he was allowed to supplement his modest salary with a practice as advocate. Additionally, the nomination procedure for the deputy procurator-general was—at least in the eighteenth century—exactly the same as that of the regular councilors[102] and, contrary to most registrars and certainly the secretaries, they usually had further careers as councilors of the Great Council or of a provincial council.[103]

The bailiffs and the *chauffe-cire* ('wax heater') constituted the 'outer circle' of the Great Council. The latter was responsible for the material infrastructure of the Council: he took care of the building, the heating, the lighting etc. The former acted on the one hand as messengers of the Great Council, serving summons on the litigants, supervising auctions, delivering notifications etc. On the other hand, they were responsible for the good order in the courtroom. The ordinary bailiffs lived in Malines, the extraordinary were posted in one of the provinces subjected to the jurisdiction of the Great Council.[104]

The president, the councilors, the registrars, the secretaries, the deputy procurator-general, the ordinary bailiffs and the *chauffe-cire* held more or less permanent positions and received—except for the registrars[105]—a fixed salary. Somewhat more loosely connected to the Great Council were the advocates and proctors. Although they needed to be admitted to plead at the Great Council and although they enjoyed the *privilegium fori*, they were not strictly spoken members of the court.

The relationships the councilors maintained with the other members of the Council are as hard to establish as those among the councilors themselves. It is however a given that the councilors were responsible for all contraventions made by or against the tribunal's members, including advocates and proctors. For example, the Great Council was competent to deal with bailiffs who failed to renew their security bond at the first session after Easter[106] or who did not show during the execution of a

[102] When in 1683, the Great Council proposed a *terne* for the position of deputy procurator-general, the Council of State wrote in its advice to the governor that the Great Council had no right to nominate three candidates for that position. Brussels, ARA, RvSt 651, 1683: appointment record of Norbert Van Voorspoel as deputy procurator-general. In 1723, however, when a new deputy procurator-general had to be appointed, a new *terne* was proposed without any problems. In fact, the Council of State remarked that 'as the custom goes', the Great Council had nominated three candidates for the position of deputy procurator-general. Brussels, ARA, RvSt 651, 1723: appointment record of de Robiano as deputy procurator-general.

[103] Cf. supra, Chap. 2.

[104] *ROPB,* 2ième série, t. 7, pp. 470–475, title VI, August 8, 1559.

[105] The registrars do not figure in the *Listes des gages du grand conseil,* while all other personnel, including the Augustinian Friars who celebrated Mass for the Great Council, are included. Brussels, ARA, GRM 3102, liste des gages du grand conseil, 1744; 1749–1769. This item does not figure in the inventory of Van den Bussche but can be consulted at the State Archives on special request.

[106] Brussels, ARA, GRMOF, BD 91, f. 149–150, July 21, 1781: advice of the Great Council on the request of extraordinary bailiff Mersch to be reinstated.

criminal sentence.[107] Because of the *privilegium fori,* advocates who, for instance, had been involved in a bar fight were equally punished by the Great Council.[108] On the other hand, the tribunal also took legal action against those who insulted or used force against the lower personnel of the Council. Bailiffs in particular, were often subject to insults, threats and violence when serving summons or executing a sentence of the Great Council.[109] At the same time, the records mention several civil suits in which one of the tribunal's members was involved.

Yet, the relations between the councilors and the lower personnel of the Great Council were not always entirely harmonious, especially when the latter suspected the former of 'stealing' their rightful share. The most notorious example of this was a drawn-out discussion between the councilors and the secretaries in the early years 1740 concerning the question of who was responsible for making copies of the reports, inquiries etc. which were drawn up in the proceedings before commissioners.[110] A similar dispute in the late seventeenth century had led to the decree of 1705, attributing these duties to the secretaries.

The councilors, however, ignored the provisions of the 1705 decree and usually assigned these tasks to their own domestic servants. Presumably, this enabled them to pocket part of the profits. In the 1740s, the secretaries brought the matter to the attention of the central government. The secretaries accused the councilors of 'stealing', valuing their loss of income at some 400 florins annually. The councilors, however, claimed that the secretaries wildly exaggerated their loss of earnings, estimating the total value of the copy-making at some 15 florins a year. Moreover, they claimed that it was impractical to have the secretaries make copies of reports etc. in the proceedings before commissioners, and added that many of them were bad writers, that they did not understand or speak any French—while this was the only language used at the Great Council—and that they consistently unnecessarily enlarged their handwriting in order to maximize their own profits.

The examples of internal conflicts cited here, are only those which were important enough to bring to the attention of the central government. Undoubtedly, much of the dirty laundry was not washed in public and certainly not recorded. When the internal conflicts did come out, they were always related to either financial issues or privileges, as was the case for the Council of Brabant.

---

107 Brussels, ARA, GRM 1044, 1770–1779, June 15, 1776: dictum in the lawsuit of procurator-general Diu against bailiff Fourny for failing to be present at the public execution of counterfeiter Herweig.

108 Brussels, ARA, GRMOF 65, 1778: the fiscals against advocate d'Haenens for assault on his colleague, advocate Bertrand; Brussels, ARA, GRMOF 504, 1784: the fiscals against advocate Posson for the insult and provocation of his colleague, advocate Scheppers.

109 For example: Brussels, ARA, GRMOF 406, 1779: trial against Francois-Joseph and François-Joachim Lepeucq for threatening bailiff Meisner.

110 Brussels, ARA, GR Register 408, f. 77–122, July 10, 1745.

3.2.3.3 Money Matters: Financial Sacrifices and Rewards

Financial Sacrifices

Since 1651,[111] the payment of a *médianate*[112]—which was considered to be a non-reimbursable loan—was an essential condition to acquire a councillorship at the Great Council. While in the early eighteenth century, the amount fluctuated and a 'gift' was often added—influenced by the government's need for money during the war[113]—the *médianate* was fixed in a decree of 1719, not only for the Great Council, but also for the provincial councils.[114] The amount to be paid was supposedly in line with the income the future councilors would receive. For a councillorship at the Council of Gelre, for example, a candidate had to pay 2000 florins, a rather limited amount, which must be explained by the fact that in the early eighteenth century the provincial Council of Gelre had lost the bulk of its jurisdiction. To become a member of the Councils of Luxembourg or Namur, the bill amounted to 5000 florins while a nominee in the Council of Hainault had to come up with 6000 florins. Finally, the *médianate* for a councillorship at the Councils of Brabant and Flanders, as well as at the Great Council, amounted to no less than 8000 florins. That a councillorship at the Great Council did not cost more than one at the Councils of Flanders or Brabant—even though it was supposed to be the 'highest' court of the Netherlands—probably signifies that the members of all three councils had a comparable annual income.

For many prospective councilors, the *médianate* constituted a serious burden and several apparently attempted to avoid paying it. In 1735, governess Maria-Elisabeth raised the matter with the different provincial councils. As a result, a new ordinance determined that secretaries and registrars were prohibited to register the patent letters and commissions of those who could not prove that they had already paid the amount due. Moreover, if the prospective councilors were unable to show a receipt for payment, they should not be allowed to take the oath. If someone still managed to slip through the net, his wages would be withheld.[115]

Over the course of the eighteenth century, the government apparently began to acknowledge that candidates experienced difficulties securing the necessary funds. In 1742, Maria Theresa decided that councilors could deduct the sum they had paid for a previous office from the *médianate* of their new appointment.[116] In 1743,

---

[111] Thomas, Cathérine. 2013. Hommes d'Etat, hommes de loi. Les conseillers du Grand Conseil de Malines au XVIIe siècle. In *Gouvernance et administration dans les provinces belges (XVIe-XVIIIe siècles)* (Archives et Bibliothèques de Belgique 99), Eds. Claude De Morbeau de Gerbehaye e.a., 155–177. Brussels: Archives et Bibliothèques de Belgique.

[112] For more information about the *médianate*, see: Vandenbulcke, Anne. 1992. *Le pouvoir et l'argent sous l'Ancien Régime: la vénalité des offices dans les conseils collatéraux des Pays-Bas espagnols (seconde moitié du XVIIe siècle)*. Kortrijk: UGA.

[113] Cf. supra, Chap. 2.

[114] *ROPBA*, t. 3, p. 175, September 30, 1719.

[115] *ROPBA*, t. 6, pp. 43–44, May 31, 1735.

[116] *ROPBA*, t. 5, pp. 477–480, April 24, 1742.

Königsegg reduced by half the amount of the *médianate* for those of the nobility who, after having obtained a law degree, were accepted into a councillorship. Once the circumstances allowed it, the government intended to diminish the *médianate* for every candidate.[117] Nevertheless, it was not until 1782 that Joseph II decreed to cut in half the *médianate* for councilors in the provincial councils. The emperor understood that the burden for people with only modest means was far too heavy and that it discouraged qualified persons from a poorer background from applying for a councillorship.[118] In 1792, however, Governors Albert and Marie-Christine reversed Joseph's decision and reestablished the *médianate* to the same level as before the 1782 decree.[119]

On top of the *médianate*, a newly appointed councilor had to pay several fees—e.g. for the sealing and registration of his patent letters—to the Privy Council, the Council of Finance and the Accounts Chamber.[120] Additionally, for the Council of Brabant, Gaillard mentioned the existence of yet another sum the councilors had to give before they could occupy their positions. Every councilor had to reimburse a part of the forced loan of the year 1690, amounting to 960 florins, to the widow or the heirs of his predecessor.[121] While we have not been able to ascertain if the same rule applied to the councilors of the Great Council, we have reason to believe that they as well were obliged to pay this sum to their predecessors or heirs. Therefore, the total sum a councilor had to pay before he was allowed to take the oath might have been up to 10,000 florins.

Financial Rewards

The councilors' financial rewards consisted of three main categories. First, they received their wages, which were fixed at a certain level and paid by the collector of East Flanders every 6 months.[122] Secondly, they shared in the 'report money' (*épices*) every time they were engaged in the decision of a lawsuit. This source of

[117] *ROPBA*, t. 5, p. 583, December 20, 1743.

[118] *ROPBA*, t. 12, p. 169, June 10, 1782.

[119] *ROPBA*, t. 14, p. 75, February 8, 1792.

[120] Gaillard, Arthur. 1898–1902. *Le Conseil de Brabant: histoire, organisation, procédure*. Brussels: Lebègue t. 2, 321.

[121] Gaillard, Arthur. 1898–1902. *Le Conseil de Brabant: histoire, organisation, procédure*. Brussels: Lebègue, t. 2, 323: "Chaque conseiller devait, en outre, en entrant en fonction, se substituer aux droits de son prédécesseur en lui remboursant sa part dans l'emprunt forcé de l'année 1690 s'élévant à 960 florins de change ou 1120 florins argent courant. Il n'était mis en possession de sa charge qu'après avoir justifié, par quittance, du versement de cette somme entre les mains de la veuve ou des héritiers de son prédécesseur." At the Privy Council, a similar system seems to have existed. In 1726, the widow of the former president of the Privy Council Albert de Coxie claimed from the newly appointed president of the Privy Council Christophe de Baillet the payment of two sums her late husband had loaned to the government in the late seventeenth century. Brussels, ARA, GRM 165, mémoriaux, f. 479–481, August 1726.

[122] These payments can be retrieved from the archives of the Accounts Chambers.

income was not set and fluctuated according to the quantity and the complexity of the lawsuits the councilors dealt with as well as to the number of times a member of their chamber was appointed reporter of a lawsuit. Finally, they also enjoyed certain privileges and exemptions on taxes, which represented a rather significant extralegal advantage. Therefore, at least in theory, once the councilors had taken up their positions, they should have been able to relatively easy recoup their initial investment.[123]

Wages (fixed income) Several sources[124] give us an idea of the fixed pay of the councilors. Even though the information is not complete—and especially for the end of the eighteenth century almost entirely lacking—it provides us with a general impression of what the usual wages were for the members of the Great Council. In the first half of the eighteenth century, wages were recorded and paid following a bi-annual system, at least in theory. Every 6 months, a detailed overview was sent to the Great Council, enumerating the earnings of each member. The president had the highest fixed income, consisting of 1920 florins every 6 months or 3840 florins yearly. The councilors were, at least in theory, paid per day: a clerical councilor received 24 *stuivers* a day, a layman 28 *stuivers* and both fiscals 32 *stuivers*.[125] In practice, this amounted respectively to 1138, 1211 and 1284 florins a year.[126] In the early 1740s, a certain percentage called *arrha*—first it was 5 %, but from 1744 on, it amounted to 10 %—was deducted from the wages of both the president and the councilors. Since this reduction was not matched by an equal rise in their pay

[123] Councilors were in fact explicitly supposed to recover their initial investment. When in 1730 Charles de Partz succeeded to Adrien Casselot—who died after a mere six months in office—he apparently was obliged to cede during 12 years half of his salary to the widow of Casselot as a compensation for the *médianate* her husband had paid for an office he had only enjoyed for such a short period of time. Brussels, ARA, MD 432, N°314: biography of Charles de Partz.

[124] Brussels, ARA, GRM 734, émoluments divers, déclarations bis annuels, 1690–1729; Brussels, ARA, GRM 3102, listes des gages du Grand Conseil, 1744 and 1749–1769; Brussels, ARA, RK 2039–2053: 1769–1783.

[125] Each florin was worth 20 *stuivers* and each *stuiver* 12 *denieren artois.* For more information on monetary systems in the Ancien Régime Netherlands, see: Lemmens, Karel. 1998. Rekenmunt en courant geld. *Jaarboek van het Europees genootschap voor munt-en penningkunde* 4:19–52.

[126] Brussels, ARA, GRM 3102: list of the salaries of the councilors per trimester. Each trimester, the president, clerical councilors, layman councilors and fiscals earned respectively 960 florins, 284 florins and 16 *stuivers*, 302 florins and 15 *stuivers* and 321 florins. In comparison: around 1730, an unskilled farm laborer in Antwerp earned on average 12 (in the winter 10 and in the summer 14) *stuivers* a day. Since the number of days he worked during the year fluctuated from 250 to 270, his annual income amounted to roughly 156 florins. In the late eighteenth century, a skilled bricklayer in Antwerp could earn up to 24 *stuivers* a day, amounting to an annual income of roughly 312 florins. Verlinden, Charles and Scholliers, Etienne eds. 1959–1973. *Dokumenten voor de geschiedenis van prijzen en lonen in Vlaanderen en Brabant.* Brugge: De Tempel, t. 2, p. 988 and 977. In Antwerp, an average income of 10 *stuivers* a day, Sunday included, was needed to be able to feed bread to a family of four in normal years. In crisis years, this was insufficient. In Malines, the prices of bread were probably somewhat lower. Craeybeckx, Jan. 1958. Brood en levensstandaard. Kritische nota betreffende de prijs van het brood te Antwerpen en te Brussel in de 17de en 18de eeuw. *Bijdragen tot de prijzengeschiedenis* 3: 135.

per day, the councilors experienced a *de facto* decrease of their yearly wages.[127] In 1749, the *arrha* was adjusted to the size of the officials' fixed income:[128] it was reduced for the councilors and the president of the Great Council to 5 and 8%, respectively.[129]

From at the latest 1750 on, the wages were listed and paid every 3 months. In real terms, they did not increase until at least 1765, the latest date for which we have concrete numbers. Only president Pycke apparently received a raise in comparison to president de Poederlé. While the latter obtained the usual 3840 florins yearly as president of the Great Council and an extra 1200 florins for his councillorship of the Council of State—by then a merely honorary title—the former received 1750 florins every quarter, adding up to a total of 7000 florins a year. Moreover, on top of his usual wages, he also received a certain amount for his membership of the Council of State. In addition, Pycke was engaged in several *jointes* and was the president of the *Monts de Piété*, for which he was undoubtedly also awarded recompense. The increase in income for president Pycke also produced an increase in the *arrha*: his wages were again taxed at 10%.[130]

After 1769, the accounts of the Great Council no longer provide any detailed information. From 1769 to 1783,[131] we can rely only on the most basic data in the archives of the Accounts Chamber. These merely state how much the 'general collector of the domains and finances of the sovereign' spent on the wages of the Great Council. As these accounts indicate, not much changed between 1769 and 1783, as the annual amounts distributed for the payment of the wages of the members of the Great Council[132] fluctuated between 24,300 florins (in 1774) and 26,555 florins (in 1775).[133] As a result, given that from the 1740s on the *arrha* was deduced from the councilors' wages, their total fixed income dropped rather than rose over the course of the eighteenth century. We even have reason to assume that their salary did not significantly change after 1623, when they received a collective raise of 700 florins a year.[134] Nevertheless, we can suspect that the cost of living over more than a century increased due to inflation.[135]

---

[127] The president now earned 3456 florins a year, the clerical councilors *grosso modo* 1025 florins, the laymen 1088 florins and the fiscals 1155 florins.

[128] Galand, Michèle. 2001. Gages, honneurs, mérites: les hauts fonctionnaires dans les Pays-Bas autrichiens. *Revue belge de philologie et d'histoire* 73.2: 561.

[129] Brussels, ARA, GRM 3102, listes des gages du Grand Conseil, 1749. The 'listes des gages du Grand Conseil' do not figure in the inventory of Van den Bussche but they can be consulted at the State Archives on special request.

[130] Brussels, ARA, GRM 3102, listes des gages du Grand Conseil, 1760.

[131] After 1783, we have not been able to find any data at all.

[132] These numbers also include the pay of the secretaries, the deputy procurator-general, the warden etc.

[133] The fluctuations can be explained by the fact that the Great Council was often incomplete due to the lapse between the death or departure of a councilor and the appointment of his successor.

[134] Brussels, ARA, GRM 734, déclarations bis annuels, 1690–1729.

[135] Cf. Scholiers, Etienne and Vandenbroeke, Christian. 1977–1983. Structuren en conjuncturen in de Zuidelijke Nederlanden 1480–1800. In *Algemene Geschiedenis der Nederlanden*, eds. Walter

Yet, compared to the members of the Councils of Flanders or Brabant, the councilors of the Great Council had a rather generous fixed income. While for the year 1773, the Great Council received 25,000 florins to spend on wages, the Council of Flanders only had 9919 florins available for the payment of its members.[136] Even though we can presume that the Great Council employed more personnel, it is still very likely that councilors in Malines were much better paid than in Flanders. The members of the Council of Brabant were even less well off, despite its status as a sovereign council. In 1781, it could spend 7788 florins on the wages of its members, while the Great Council received that same year 26,216 florins.[137] Obviously, the members of the Great Council obtained a much higher fixed income than their colleagues in the provincial Councils of Brabant and Flanders, even though the *médianate* for all three tribunals was determined at 8000 florins. Given that the *médianate* was in principle proportionate to the revenue the councilors could expect, we can assume that the councilors of Brabant and Flanders had a much more elevated variable income.[138]

Despite these rather decent wages, the councilors constantly complained about their income, not so much about the amount as about the delay in payment. Already in 1700, the sovereign sent—in answer to a complaint of the Great Council—an order to the Council of Finance to pay the wages in arrears to the members of the Great Council in preference to those of the Privy Council.[139] In 1707, the councilors again aired their grievances, but only in 1710—after the councilors had informed the government that they had not been paid for 4 years—did the central government try to remedy the problem.[140]

Although it seems possible that this problem was related to the confusing circumstances of the early eighteenth century, the same issue reoccurred several years later in 1724 when the Austrian monarchy had more or less firmly established its authority. Again the councilors complained that their wages had not been paid for almost 3 years. Moreover, they felt that they were being treated unfairly. According to the councilors, the other tribunals had small arrears if any; the members of the Great Council could not imagine that 'the sovereign wanted the 'principal seat' of justice in the country to be frustrated in the payment of its wages'.[141] Furthermore,

---

Prevenier e.a, t. 5, 252–310. Haarlem: Fibula-Van Dishoeck.

[136] Brussels, ARA, RK 2043, f. 174v—175r : "Recette générale des finances pour l'année 1773 par van Overstraten." Originally, the wages of the Council of Brabant were paid by the collector of the domains of Brussels. From 1779 on, they were charged on the *recette générale des finances,* just as was the case for the other tribunals of the Austrian Netherlands.

[137] Brussels, ARA, RK 2051, f. 134v: "Recette générale compte XXIV du consr receveur general Van Overstraeten pour 1781". In fact, the annual salary of a councilor of the Council of Brabant was fixed at a mere 438 florins. Gaillard, Arthur. 1898–1902. *Le Conseil de Brabant: histoire, organisation, procédure*. Brussels: Lebègue, t. 2, 234.

[138] Cf. infra, *Epices*.

[139] Brussels, ARA, GRM 162, mémoriaux, f. 39, 1700.

[140] Brussels, ARA, GRM 162, mémoriaux, f. 54r and f. 57r, 1710.

[141] It is highly unlikely that the councilors of the other tribunals had no or only small arrears. In fact, Gaillard mentioned that the payment to the members of the Council of Brabant was also often

the councilors maintained that the other courts had several advantages the Great Council did not enjoy, such as frequent commissions and presentations. On top of all that, they earned more per hour than the councilors of the Great Council. The councilors claimed that the situation had become so dire that they no longer could keep up the standing that was expected from them. Indeed, for the president, his wages constituted up to two thirds of his total income and for the councilors up to one third.[142] Apparently, the problems were not solved: in 1728, the Great Council again implored the governess, with the same arguments as 4 years earlier, to see to it that their wages would be promptly and regularly paid.[143] Despite all complaints and appeals to the sovereign, the payment of the councilors' wages continued to cause pressing difficulties until at least the 1750s.[144]

Epices (variable income) The fixed revenues of the councilors only constituted a part of their income. In fact, according to the members of the Great Council, one third of the president's income and two thirds of the councilors' came from other sources.[145] The *épices*—the allowances they received for their work on a specific case—were not only an important addition to their wages but even surpassed them. Detailed information about the amount each councilor annually received can be retrieved from the report books.[146] These sources list for each case—lawsuits as well as recommendations to the governor or discussions on certain internal issues—the fee each councilor obtained. The report books demonstrate that the reporter usually did not reap more *épices* than his colleagues. In fact, unless there was some special task connected to the case, he received the same amount as the other regular councilors. As a rule, the president and the fiscals earned less, probably because they could never act as reporters. The same was true for the clerical councilors: they were neither allowed to preside over the *rôle* nor to judge in a criminal trial.

While the report books provide us with data for each individual case, the *billets des rapports* record the entire amount for each councilor for every 2 months.[147] Unfortunately, the archives only contain the *billets* for the period from 1746 to

delayed. Gaillard, Arthur. 1898–1902. *Le Conseil de Brabant: histoire, organisation, procédure*. Brussels: Lebègue, t. 2, 300. The same is true for the members of the *conseils collatéraux*. By 1736, the payment of their wages was delayed by up to 30 months. Galand, Michèle. 2001. Gages, honneurs, mérites: les hauts fonctionnaires dans les Pays-Bas autrichiens. *Revue belge de philologie et d'histoire* 73.2:561.

142 Brussels, ARA, GRM 162, mémoriaux, f. 150–153; f. 159–161, 1724.

143 Brussels, ARA, GRM 165, mémoriaux, f. 643–646, 1728.

144 Brussels, ARA, GRM 3102, Liste des gages du Grand Conseil: during the entire period between 1745 and 1748, no wages were paid. In 1753 a new complaint was made. After that date, we have no information on any other problems concerning the payment of wages, but this might be due to a lack of sources.

145 Cf. supra, Wages.

146 Brussels, ARA, GRM 682–693, Livres dits aux rapports, liber primus, 1708–1788; Brussels, ARA, GRM 697–710, Livres dits aux rapports, liber secundus, 1708–1756.

147 Brussels, ARA, GRM 3032–3056, billets des rapports, 1746–1770. The billets des rapports do not figure in the inventory of Van den Bussche, but they can be consulted at the State Archives on special request.

Table 3.1 Variable income in 1730 for a selection of councilors. (In the chamber with de Coriache, Keyaerts and de Waepenaert, the president earned 576 florins. In the other chamber—with de Smet, de Beeckman and de Decker/de Potter—the president had a variable income of 1250 florins)

1730	Florins
President Van Volden	1826
Coriache (clerical)	1857
de Smet (clerical)	1982
Keyaerts (proc-gen)	1857
de Decker/de Potter (adv-fisc)	1585
de Waepenaert	2397
de Beeckman	1984

1770. Before this time, we have to use numbers that are only roughly correct, since it implies manually adding up every single *épice* for a group of councilors. In order to have representative results for the early eighteenth century, we chose the year 1730.[148] In this year, we investigated the income from the *émoluments* for seven different persons: president Pierre van Volden, clerical councilors Aimé de Coriache and Ambroise de Smet, procurator-general Jean Ferdinand Keyaerts and advocate-fiscal Jean Baptiste de Decker,[149] and two laymen councilors Charles Philippe de Waepenaert and Philippe de Beeckman (Table 3.1).[150]

If we look at the numbers and compare them to the fixed wages of the members of the Great Council, it is clear that the *épices* indeed constituted one third of the president's income while they more or less accounted for two thirds of the councilors' pay. These numbers also confirm the validity of the fiscals' complaint: even though they had a larger fixed income, this did not compensate for the losses they suffered from being unable to act as a reporter. It is evident that for more work they received less pay. Since the wages of the councilors remained at the same level throughout the eighteenth century—and even slightly decreased in real terms due to the *arrha*—and inflation was not corrected for, only a raise in income from the *épices* could have caused a de facto increase in revenue.[151]

[148] Given that the first two decades were rather turbulent with constantly changing and often confusing political circumstances, we have focused on a time when the situation was stabilized. Moreover, in practical terms, both the *liber primus* and *liber secundus* provide us with complete data for 1730.

[149] De Decker died in October 1730, but was replaced shortly afterwards by Guillaume de Potter; once the latter takes over, his statistics are compiled into the data for accuracy.

[150] The choice for these councilors was prompted by their function in the council—the fiscals, two clericals, two laymen and the president—and by their distribution over the different chambers. The first two months of 1730, de Coriache, Keyaerts and de Waepenaert are to be found in one chamber and de Smet, de Beeckman and de Decker in the other. The president switched regularly, and analysis revealed that de Coriache and de Smet often changed chambers. The other councilors usually stayed in their own chamber, even though there are certain exceptions.

[151] Evidently, the *épices* were linked to the number of lawsuits that were brought before the Great Council (and reached the judgment phase) and/or to the advice obtained from the Council. Therefore, the amount of income stemming from the *épices* might be indicative for the workload of the Great Council in the eighteenth century. Yet, an increase in the *épices* is not necessarily the result of a higher number of lawsuits. In fact, it might also mean that the councilors voluntarily extended

Table 3.2 Variable income in 1750 and 1765 for a selection of councilors

1750	Florins	1765	Florins
President d'Olmen de Poederlee	1468	President Pycke	1783
Van Slabbeeck (adv-fisc)	1536	Brenart (clerical)	2290
de Waepenaert (proc-gen)	1395	Jacobs (proc-gen)	1637
Goubau	1941	Van Slabbeeck (adv-fisc)	1947
de Partz	2069	de Waepenaert	2196
		Tackoen	2195
		Exploits	1522

As points of comparison, we opted for the years 1750 and 1765.[152] We proceeded in the same manner as we did for 1730, focusing, if possible, on the president, the two clerical councilors, the procurator-general and advocate-fiscal and two laymen councilors, who are divided over two different chambers. For the laymen councilors, we deliberately opted for one councilor with a certain seniority and another rather recent appointee.[153] The results are more or less in line with what we found for 1730 (Table 3.2):

While the figures from 1750 show a small decline in the overall amount—which could have been caused by the recent return of the Great Council to Malines after its exile to Echternach—the year 1765 demonstrates a restoration to the prewar level and a more or less *status quo* in comparison to 1730. Overall, the differences in variable income between 1730 and 1765 are almost negligible.

If we add their wages and their *épices*, the councilors seem to have had a very decent annual income situated *grosso modo* for the president between 5300 and 5600 florins, for the clerical councilors between 2900 and 3400 florins, for the fiscals between 2700 and 3200 florins and for the laymen councilors between 3100 and 3600 florins. On top of these sums, they also received certain extraordinary revenues.[154] Chances are that their real income was even higher. For the Council of Brabant,

the duration of the lawsuits in order to draw more income or that they managed to obtain a raise in their *épices*. The number of lawsuits brought before the Great Council in the eighteenth century will be examined in Chap. 4.

[152] This choice has been predominantly made from a practical point of view. From 1744 on, we have the *billets* at our disposal, which list the entire amount of *épices* for every councilor for the period of two months instead of for each case separately. This of course eliminates the necessity of the very labor-intensive work of adding up every individual *épice*. Furthermore, 1750 and 1765 provide us with the largest range possible, since the data for 1770 are not complete and we do not possess any complete information after that date. The *billets* do not allow a breakdown of the president's income according to chamber.

[153] In practice, we did the counting for president Joseph d'Olmen, procurator-general Jean Philippe de Waepenaert, advocate-fiscal Jean Charles Van Slabbeeck and councilors Charles Henri Goubau and Charles de Partz for 1750 (in 1750, there were no clerical councilors at the Great Council—cf. supra, Chap. 2) and president Guillaume Pycke, clerical councilor Felix Brenart, procurator-general Henri Theodore Jacobs, advocate-fiscal Jean Charles Van Slabbeeck, and councilors Jean Philippe de Wapenaert and Godefroid Tackoen for 1765. In May 1765, Hyacinthe de Partz was appointed clerical councilor. However, for reasons of convenience, we did not take him into account

[154] Brussels, ARA, GRM 162, mémoriaux, f. 104–113.

Gaillard calculated, based on the available information, that a regular councilor could earn some 1734 florins a year. In reality however, a personal account made up by one of the members of the Council of Brabant, testified that between 1781 and 1787, he had an average annual income of about 6741 florins.[155] While we can imagine that a councilor from the Council of Brabant had a larger income stemming from *épices* than his colleagues at the Great Council, it is very much possible that the revenues of the members of the Great Council were in actuality somewhat higher than what we have projected.

Despite their seemingly decent income, the councilors complained at various times about their financial situation. In 1740, in response to a letter from the sovereign asking the Great Council to explain the recent lack of good candidates for the vacancies and to propose means to remedy this problem, the councilors took the opportunity to raise the issue. The reply was one long lament about the complete inadequacy of their earnings.[156]

The councilors believed that the reasons why the vacancies were so difficult to fill were manifold. First of all, after one had made a lot of sacrifices and expenses to arrive at the point where it was possible to apply for a councillorship, it became clear that the financial rewards were undeniably inadequate. While it was barely possible to sustain oneself and one's family appropriately, it was utterly unfeasible to save money for one's children. As a result, candidates from a more modest background refrained from applying, and settled for an inferior position that promised equal benefits without the need to make the same expenses. Secondly, because the Great Council was unable to rely exclusively on candidates from Malines and needed to attract people from other provinces, many councilors were forced to live far from their own properties and affairs. Therefore, they constantly had to employ other people to manage their business, often at great expenses. Moreover, the delay in payment was a recurring problem. On top of that, the deduction of the *arrha* notably diminished their pay. These two combined made it sometimes impossible for the councilors to support themselves.

The councilors complained that not only the revenues were inadequate, but that the *médianate* for a councillorship constituted a considerable burden, forcing the majority of the applicants to loan a certain amount at interest. Furthermore, many already had paid a *médianate* for a position of city pensionary or similar. It was only normal that those who had acquired a good employment without the initial investment of a *médianate* as well as lawyers, who often had a very lucrative office, would never be willing to spend a sum that could seriously inconvenience their family.

To the members of the Great Council, the solution to the problem of the scarcity of candidates was clear: money. First of all, their wages and *épices* needed to be increased in order to enable them to live according to their standing while not being forced to consume their entire fortune. As the members of the Great Council were

---

[155] Gaillard, Arthur. 1898–1902. *Le Conseil de Brabant: histoire, organisation, procédure*. Brussels: Lebègue, t. 2, 325.

[156] Brussels, ARA, GRM 168C, mémoriaux, f. 18v–21v, 1740.

worse off than their inferiors, capable people were deterred from applying for a position. Moreover, it was necessary to indemnify councilors for the losses they suffered from being away from their own businesses and affairs. Furthermore, it was absolutely adamant that the wages should be paid on time and that nothing should be deducted. Even though the decree restricted the deductions to only 4 years, it would be favorable to eradicate all doubts and fears on this point.[157] Finally, the *médianate* should be reduced to an amount that would not constitute an insurmountable obstacle for potential candidates; it would also be wise to allow new councilors to subtract the *médianate* they had paid for a previous position from the amount they needed to come up with for their position at the Great Council. The members of the Great Council assured the sovereign that all their recommendations needed to be implemented in order to attract decent candidates for a future contest.

As far as is known from the *mémoriaux* and the *ordonnances*, the only recommendation that was actually implemented was the last one, i.e. the possibility to deduct the sum of a previously paid *médianate* from the new one.[158] Unsurprisingly, new complaints were raised. In 1757, the councilors requested the governor once again raise their income, referring to the increase in *épices* the councilors of several provincial councils, even those subjected to the tribunal's jurisdiction, had received.[159] Given that the Great Council was one of the *conseils collatéraux* and the first corps of justice in the country, the councilors believed they should be able to distinguish themselves from the provincial councils both by their privileges and by their wages and *épices*. Moreover, the councilors argued that over the years, the cost of living had increased—especially for food and other basic necessities—which, in combination with the changes in the country's currency,[160] had considerably diminished the value of their revenues. Once again the councilors claimed that if the government wished to attract the best judges for the Great Council, their revenues needed to be seriously augmented. The governor eventually consented to a small raise to be paid for the councilors' work in the Council or at home; however, there would be no increase of the fees for *verbaux* or travel.

Given that the councilors' wages remained at their seventeenth century level and that there was no substantial raise in *épices*[161] while life costs did not stay stable, it is true that the financial situation of the members of the Great Council relatively de-

157 As far as we have been able to determine, the deduction was never abolished.

158 This was decided in 1742. Cf supra, 3.2.3.3.1 Financial sacrifices.

159 Brussels, ARA, GR Register 440, f. 228–230, April 20, 1757.

160 There is not much information given about what happened to the currency of the Austrian Netherlands, except that there was a *haussement des monnoies*. Brussels, ARA, GR Register 440, f. 228–230, April 20, 1757. A reform in the price of silver was introduced in 1755, but it is unclear how that might have affected the councilors' revenues. Cf. Janssens, Valery. 1957. *Het geldwezen in de Oostenrijkse Nederlanden* (Verhandelingen van de Koninklijke Vlaamse academie voor wetenschappen, letteren en schone kunsten van België. Klasse der Letteren 29). Brussels: Paleis der Academiën, 125–137.

161 As we have noticed, the small raise the councilors received for their work at the Council or at home in 1757 was not reflected in a substantially higher income from *épices* in 1765. The effect of the raise must therefore have been erased by another factor. Cf. infra, Chap. 3.

teriorated over the course of the eighteenth century. Therefore, the councilors might have had legitimate reasons to complain. Galand as well acknowledged that even the high officials in the Austrian administration—councilors of the Privy Council or the Council of Finance—absolutely needed a considerable personal fortune in order to lead a comfortable life. There should be no doubt that this also applied to the members of the Great Council. In addition, the increase in the costs of life—especially after 1766—constituted an important deterioration in the material conditions of even the highest officials.[162] In that regard, the councilors of the Great Council were fortunate to be located in Malines, as the city was less expensive to live in than, for example, Brussels.

Privileges Apart from their wages and *épices*, the councilors also enjoyed several benefits and exemptions of all kinds of taxes. First, once they were appointed to the Great Council, the councilors acquired nobility, as did their descendants.[163] Since a noble title still opened doors and often came accompanied with several advantages—such as a reduction of the *médianate*—it was considered an important privilege. The fact that the members of the Great Council jealously guarded this privilege is demonstrated by the protest lodged by the advocate-fiscal of the Great Council in 1716 against a decree of the Council of State of 1713, which awarded hereditary nobility to the councilors of the Council of Flanders.[164] According to the Great Council, only the sovereign possessed the right to assign nobility and neither the councilors of Flanders nor those of any other provincial council had ever obtained a noble title for their children. Minister plenipotentiary Königsegg followed the Great Council's argumentation and ordered that the decree should be disregarded.

More tangible benefits were the exemptions from all sorts of taxation—both municipal and provincial. Even though an exhaustive enumeration of all these exemptions is not available, the infractions that gave reason to many complaints, offer us a certain idea of the extent of these privileges. For example, the councilors were exempted from the taxes for crossing a bridge; when in 1788 the toll collector of Rillaar charged councilor Vriesen with the regular tax, and, on top of that, failed to show the necessary respect, the procurator-general of the Great Council implored the Council of Brabant to force the toll collector to repay the full amount and to offer his apologies to councilor Vriesen.[165] A similar infraction on privileges happened to registrar du Trieu: when he had a hay cart transported from Charleroi, both the collector of the sixtieth tax of Charleroi and the barrier guard of Lodinsart charged him despite his certificate of exemption.[166]

[162] Galand, Michèle. 2001. Gages, honneurs, mérites: les hauts fonctionnaires dans les Pays-Bas autrichiens. *Revue belge de philologie et d'histoire* 73.2: 562.

[163] Janssens, Paul. 1993. Les charges anoblissantes dans les conseils des Pays-Bas espagnols et autrichiens. In *Beleid en bestuur in de oude Nederlanden. Liber amicorum Prof. Dr.M. Baelde*, eds. Hugo Soly and René Vermeir, 225–239. Ghent: RUG. Cf. supra, Chap. 2.

[164] Brussels, ARA, GRM 162, mémoriaux, f. 70v, August 15, 1716.

[165] Brussels, ARA, GRM 141, registre aux résolutions secrètes, f. 151–152, July 11, 1788.

[166] Brussels, ARA, GRM 141, registre aux résolutions secrètes, f. 157v–158r, March 12, 1776.

The councilors of the Great Council, their widows and children also benefitted from the dispensation of the *droit d'issue*[167] and of consumption taxes, such as on wine, beer and grain.[168] In general, the members of the Great Council wished to enjoy the same privileges and exemptions as those of the Privy Council.[169] Discussions about which members of the Council should be considered to be privileged were legion. Usually, it was assumed that the councilors, the registrars, the secretaries, the deputy procurator-general and the ordinary bailiffs could claim a right to these exemptions.[170]

The councilors' benefits and exemptions led to many frictions with the Magistrate of Malines.[171] In fact, the aldermen had to tolerate in their midst a not inconsiderable group of privileged people who did not contribute much to the city's treasury. The multiple conflicts demonstrate that the Great Council jealously guarded its privileges against any attempts by the Magistrate to limit or abolish them. No doubt these exemptions were responsible for a considerable part of their revenue and became even more important over the course of the eighteenth century, given that the councilors experienced a relative decline in the two other aspects of their income. In addition, any attempt to question their privileges was also perceived as an attempt to undermine their social standing.

3.3 Strategy of Confrontation? The Great Council's Struggle to Hold its Ground

So far, we have predominantly examined the internal framework of the Great Council, in order to evaluate how the Council was organized and how the councilors organized themselves during the eighteenth century. The position the tribunal occupied within the larger society of the Austrian Netherlands is equally important to assess the workings of the court and even more so to estimate to what extent the central government was still willing to support the tribunal. In fact, initially established as a superior court, destined to control the administration of justice, the Great Council necessarily interacted with other institutions in the Austrian Netherlands society. Even though these interactions were undoubtedly various in nature, we will mainly focus on the conflicts the Great Council had with the city of Malines, the Church, the provincial councils and the Privy Council, as these discordant relations often involved the interference of the central government.

[167] The *droit d'issue* was a tax the city council levied on the inheritance bequeathed by a burgher to a non-burgher of the city.

[168] Brussels, ARA, GRM 168B, mémoriaux, f. 100, March 1750.

[169] Brussels, ARA, GRM 141, registre aux résolutions secrètes, f. 160–162, 1779; *ROPBA*, t. 9, p. 273, June 11, 1766.

[170] Brussels, ARA, GRM 142, registre aux résolutions secrètes, f. 8–9, 1781.

[171] Cf. infra, 2.3.1 "*Un corps si fort audessus d'eux*".

Confronted with an ever shrinking jurisdiction coupled with constant pressure from concurring institutions which attempted to expand their own influence at the Great Council's expense, the court often seemed to have felt the need to display its self-declared power and prestige. To a large extent, these conflicts molded and influenced its (self)image. In addition, the 'collisions' the Great Council had, will enable us to examine if, during the eighteenth century, centrifugal rather than centripetal forces were at work. Did the central government support the Great Council in its attempts to maintain (or rather re-establish?) its authority, or did the government make it ever more difficult for the tribunal to play the role of watchdog it was originally destined to?

Certainly, the sources that document the relations between the Great Council and the other players in the eighteenth century Austrian Netherlands are legion, not only in the archives of the Great Council itself but also in the records of the provincial councils, the city of Malines and the Archdiocese.[172] However, we predominantly made use of the *mémoriaux* of the Great Council and of the *consultes* of the Privy Council, mainly because the discussion of an issue at such a high level is already indicative of the seriousness of a conflict. In general, the central administration wanted to prevent official institutions and authorities from fighting out their differences in public.[173]

3.3.1 "Un corps si fort audessus d'eux":[174] Conflicts with the Magistrate of Malines

Unlike all other central institutions, such as the Privy Council or the Council of Finance, the Great Council did not have its seat in Brussels, the governmental center of the Austrian Netherlands, but in the relatively modest town of Malines. While in the fifteenth and early sixteenth centuries, Malines had been the political center of the Netherlands, the transfer of most central councils to Brussels after the death of Margareth of Austria in 1530 had given a serious blow to the image and prosperity of the city. The explosion of the munitions depot at the Zandpoort in 1543, destroying or severely damaging entire neighborhoods, reduced the city to a second- or, arguably, third-rate provincial town. In the eighteenth century, only—or at least,

[172] For the Council of Flanders, see: Buntinx, Jan. 1964–1977. *Inventaris van het archief van de Raad van Vlaanderen.* 8t. Brussels: Algemeen Rijksarchief; for the Arbischopric, see: Poukens, Johan. 2010. *Inventaris van de verzameling Kerk en Staat in het Aartsbisschoppelijk Archief te Mechelen (16de–18de eeuw).* Brussels: Algemeen Rijksarchief; for the city of Malines, see: Hermans, Victor and Van Doren, Pierre.-Joseph. 1859–1896. *Inventaire des archives de la ville de Malines.* Malines: Van Velsen.

[173] Brussels, ARA, GR Register 454, f. 226–230, November 29, 1765: conflict of jurisdiction regarding the question if the heirs of the councilors' children had to pay the *droit d'issue.* Advice of the governor: "Son Altesse aiant voulu par sa roiale dépêche du 18 février 1756 communiquer au conseil par decret du 28 après, qu'on évite autant qu'il sera faisable de renvoier les corps et administrations publiques en justice reglée."

[174] Brussels, ARA, GRM 168F, mémoriaux, f. 1–29, 1749.

principally—the presence of the Great Council and of the Archdiocese still added some luster to Malines.

Why the Great Council did not make the move to Brussels together with the *conseils collatéraux* remains unclear, but it might be connected to the reasons why—according to Van Rompaey—the court was initially established in Malines: first, because the city was centrally located, and secondly, because Malines enjoyed a special status as a seigniory independent from the powerful provinces of Brabant and Flanders.[175] Whatever the reason, the eighteenth century councilors of the Great Council were very self-conscious about the fact that their tribunal did not have its residence in the capital where the *conseils collatéraux* had their seat.[176] This inferiority complex made the Great Council determined to establish and defend its superior status over the aldermen, which resulted in several conflicts with the Magistrate of Malines over rather petty issues.

Protocol for example, was extremely important to the members of the Great Council as a constant reminder to the aldermen of Malines that they were subordinate to the tribunal. When in 1717, the Great Council and the Magistrate had to coordinate the celebrations of the Austrian victory over the Turks, the mayor and the pensionary declined to take their swords off when arriving at the Great Council's premises, even though a seventeenth century ordinance determined that anybody entering the judges' chambers had to leave their weaponry with the baillifs.[177] While the mayor and pensionary eventually yielded, the issue resurfaced again some years later: this time, the councilors accused the Magistrate of attempting to extract itself from the submission to the authority of the sovereign 'which resided in the Great Council'.[178]

Allegedly wrongfully used titles and terms of address were considered important enough to bring to the attention of the Privy Council. In 1756, the members of the Great Council claimed that pensionary Vriesen had no right to use the title *conseiller pensionnaire* (councilor pensionary) because he did not have the privilege to identify himself as a councilor.[179] When the Magistrate complained to the Privy Council, the latter rebuffed the Great Council's claims, asserting that it had been merely out of jealousy that the councilors had raised the matter, anxious as they were about their own honors and privileges.

Privileges in particular were very much cherished by the members of the Great Council, but were at the same time a thorn in the flesh of the Magistrate. These

[175] Van Rompaey, Jan. 1977–1983. De Bourgondische staatsinstellingen. In *Algemene Geschiedenis der Nederlanden*, eds. Walter Prevenier e.a. Haarlem: Fibula-Van Dishoeck, t. 4, 147. Moreover, the question might be asked to what extent the Great Council was located in Malines to prevent constant confrontations with the Council of Brabant.

[176] Brussels, ARA, GRM 168D, mémoriaux, f. 8, December 1740: "En effet aiant l'honneur d'être le premier corps de justice dont sa majesté est le premier et souverain chef, suivant la teneur expresse de ses institutions et ceux, qui le composent étant reputés ses serviteurs et domestiques non obstant que leur séance se tient à Malines …"

[177] Brussels, ARA, GRM 162, mémoriaux, f. 122, September 3, 1717.

[178] Brussels, ARA, GRM 168D, mémoriaux, f. 5, December 1740.

[179] Brussels, ARA, GR Register 437, f. 2–5, April 5, 1756.

privileges and especially the exemptions of all kinds of taxes formed without a doubt an important part of the income of the councilors.[180] As a result, the members of the Great Council ferociously defended their rights against the multiple attempts of the Magistrate to curtail them. The favorite strategy of the councilors when addressing the Privy Council about the issue was to remind the aldermen that Malines benefited highly from the presence of the tribunal: the choice for Malines as capital of justice had been inspired, not so much by its central location, but rather by 'the desire to pull the city out of its misery'. Nevertheless, the councilors argued, despite the many advantages the Great Council brought to Malines, the Magistrate was ungrateful and constantly tried to infringe on their privileges.

In 1749, an especially fierce discussion broke out between the councilors and the aldermen.[181] This time, the Magistrate wanted to compel the Great Council to contribute new taxes to pay off the debts from the previous war. Finding itself in a very difficult situation, the city had no choice but to impose new taxes, for which no exceptions would be made for the privileged. The councilors had no intention to cooperate, and using the deputy procurator-general as their mouthpiece, accused the Magistrate of deliberately taking advantage of the circumstances of the war to finally execute a premeditated plan to abolish the privileges of the members of the Great Council.

The deputy procurator-general claimed that the aldermen not only pled the extortions made by the French as an excuse, but also abused the fact that the Great Council could not dispose of its records, which had been moved to Douai during the French occupation and had not yet been returned. Nevertheless, the Magistrate did not have a leg to stand on: the sovereign himself had awarded the councilors their privileges and exemptions at the establishment of the Great Council and the Magistrate itself had promised in 1585—when they had begged the Council to return to Malines after its stay in Namur—that the members would be forever exempted from all taxes.

Moreover, the deputy added, the city should not forget the many advantages it drew from the presence of the Great Council, which it would not have if the tribunal should take its seat elsewhere. According to him, the Great Council directly and indirectly supported more than 200 households. If all these people moved away, much of the business of the city would decline and eventually disappear. Furthermore, the deputy reminded the Magistrate that the Council attracted many foreign families to Malines. As these people were often well-off and voluntarily spent their income in Malines, the Magistrate should be grateful that the Great Council had its residence in the city. Punishing its members with taxes would in the end prove to be counterproductive.

Despite these arguments—and many more—the governor decided that for this one time, because of the special circumstances, the councilors had to contribute in the new taxes, at least for a period of 6 years. However, he also reproached the

[180] Cf. supra, 3.2.3.3.2 Financial rewards.

[181] Brussels, ARA, GRM 168F, mémoriaux, f. 1–29, 1749. This was shortly after the Great Council had returned from its exile in Echternach.

Magistrate of Malines for the lack of respect towards the Great Council it had demonstrated in its requests.[182]

The fact that the Great Council also had some jurisdiction over the seigniory of Malines and acted as court of appeal for the sentences of the Magistrate certainly did not improve relations. The aldermen not only challenged the privileges of the individual councilors, but also questioned the authority of the tribunal as a corpus. First, the Magistrate tried to break away from the jurisdiction the Great Council had in administrative affairs. Already in the late seventeenth and early eighteenth centuries, the aldermen contested the right of the councilors to send ordinances from the central government using the terms *de par l'empereur* as well as the habit of the Council to end its letters with the formula *car ainsi nous plait-il*.[183] In addition, the fact that the Magistrate was ranked among the *juges subalternes* of the Great Council was a thorn in its flesh.[184] Until the very end of the court's existence, these issues continued to be a point of discussion and were even used by the Magistrate as a *quid pro quo* when the government needed it to award extraordinary subsidies in 1788.[185]

The conflicts of jurisdiction in legal matters were even more important. In 1723, the Great Council attempted to appropriate the right to deal with appeals against criminal sentences of the Magistrate of Malines, even though the latter was—just as the provincial councils—sovereign in criminal affairs.[186] Citing procedural er-

---

[182] *ROPBA*, t. 6, p. 424, June 17, 1749. This is only one example of the many conflicts over privileges and exemptions the Great Council had with the Magistrate. Others include a dispute over the exemptions on wine, beer and grain in 1750 (Brussels, ARA, GRM 168B, mémoriaux, f. 100, 1750), over a tax on olive oil in 1762 (*ROPBA*, t. 8, p. 495, November 24, 1762) and again over a new tax on beer and wine in 1764 (Brussels, ARA, GRM 141, registre des résolutions secrètes, f. 149–150, 1764).

[183] Malines, Stadsarchief Mechelen, Archives de la ville de Malines, affaires civiles et ecclésiastiques 23, 1698, 1708 and 1710. It must be noted that the numbers of the records in this archival fund do not correspond anymore to those mentioned in the inventory: Hermans, Victor and Van Doren, Pierre.-Joseph. 1859–1896. *Inventaire des archives de la ville de Malines*. Malines: Van Velsen, t. 6. The new numeration can only be found in the adapted inventory available in the reading room of the *Stadsarchief*. Also: Brussels, ARA, GRM 165, mémoriaux, f. 406–432, June 18, 1725. The file contains a remarkable comment about the archives of the Great Council. At a certain point, the councilors admitted that there were many gaps in the records they used to support their argument, especially for the period between 1661 and 1690. Even though they were convinced that in that particular period they had often written to the Magistrate, the volumes could not be retrieved from their archives. The councilors could only conclude that they must have been stolen. This comment demonstrates that the records of the Great Council were already incomplete during the working years of the tribunal.

[184] Malines, Stadsarchief Mechelen, Archives de la ville de Malines, affaires civiles et ecclésiastiques 23, April 5, 1788.

[185] Malines, Stadsarchief Mechelen, Archives de la ville de Malines, affaires civiles et ecclésiastiques 23, November 22, 1788. The Magistrate was however rebuffed. Cf. infra, Chap. 4.

[186] Malines, Stadsarchief Mechelen, Archives de la ville de Malines, affaires civiles et ecclésiastiques 23, 1723: "Le magistrat contre le grand conseil au sujet de lettres de reformation contre une sentence rendue en matière criminelle." Brussels, ARA, GRM 141, registre aux résolutions secrètes, f. 480–498, 1723. The case in question is somewhat peculiar. The letters of reformation had been requested by a former beguine of Malines, Pétronille Basyn. For some unknown reason, Basyn had been expelled from the beguinage of Malines. Being without means in a city unfamiliar to her—she was originally from Antwerp—she had found shelter in the house of baker Joseph

rors—the imprisonment of the female suspect had been disproportionately severe to the crime she had committed, her interrogation had only been conducted by one instead of two aldermen, the accused had not had access to legal counsel although that was the standard procedure, etc.—the Great Council was convinced that it had reasonable grounds to review the case. While the decision of the central government in this case is unknown, we do suspect that the Great Council's request was turned down. In fact, we have not been able to find a trace of this specific lawsuit, neither in the distribution books nor in the fiscals' records.[187]

The Magistrate and the Great Council also regularly collided over the question of which of the two had the authority over the Malines prison and its guard. After a complaint against the prison's guard in 1779,[188] the Magistrate requested the governor settle this conflict of jurisdiction once and for all. The governor, following the Privy Council's recommendation, decided that the prison and its guard fell under the authority of the Great Council and that the Magistrate should not be involved in any issues surrounding the prison. Even more important for the Great Council than having won this struggle with the Magistrate, was that the Privy Council specifically reminded the aldermen that they were subordinate to the Great Council.

The attempts of the Magistrate of Malines to contest the jurisdiction of the Great Council and to assert its authority over the city are legion. The Great Council itself, on the other hand, constantly referred to its superior position—*un corps si fort audessus d'eux*[189]—and to the respect the Magistrate was due to pay. The central government's attitude towards the two institutions was somewhat ambiguous. On the one hand, the governor sometimes reprimanded the Magistrate for not displaying enough reverence towards the Great Council and underlined that the latter was absolutely superior to the former. For example, when the Privy Council decided in 1786 that while a certain case involving the daughter of the late director of the *Mont de Piété* of

Everaerts and his wife. While she originally slept on a stack of hay in the stable, the baker and his wife invited her to sleep in their bed after she had started suffering from a severe cold. Although Everaerts' wife had always slept between Basyn and her husband, the former had admitted that at a certain point he had touched her throat and her breasts. On account of adultery, the Magistrate of Malines convicted Basyn to two weeks in prison on a harsh regime. Given that the baker had more or less confessed and considering that there were several witnesses to the crime, we might assume that the Great Council merely wanted to dispute the Magistrate's dealing with the case because it constituted a good occasion to challenge the aldermen's sovereignty in criminal affairs.

[187] We are aware that 'negative evidence' is merely indicative and that the case file might simply have been lost or misplaced.

[188] Brussels, ARA, GR, Register 475, f. 231–241, August 4, 1779. In 1779, when the widow of a certain Broers complained about the amount of freedom the guard granted to prisoner Schoel—who was awaiting trial for extorting her—she first addressed the Great Council in order to reprimand the guard. When this had no effect, the widow sent a new protest to the Magistrate. The actions the aldermen undertook against the guard caught the attention of the Great Council, which demanded an explanation from the Magistrate for overstepping its authority. Instead of responding to this request, the aldermen plainly informed the fiscals that they had brought the matter to the attention of the government.

[189] Brussels, ARA, GRM 168F, mémoriaux, f. 1–29, 1749: "… pour marquer la déférence qu'ils doivent à un corps si fort audessus d'eux…" "… la déférence qu'ils doivent à ce premier tribunal de justice des Pays-Bas…"

Malines should have been introduced at the Magistrate instead of at the Great Council, the plaintiff should still be allowed to continue her business at the Great Council. Referring her to the Magistrate of Malines would be 'disgraceful'.[190] On the other hand, the Privy Council and the governor also sometimes sided with the Magistrate, as if they deliberately tried to keep a certain balance of power in Malines.[191]

3.3.2 The State Versus the Church: Conflicts with Ecclesiastical Authorities[192]

In the eighteenth century, the relations between the Great Council and the Church—which was particularly powerful in Malines through the presence of the archbishop—were influenced by the larger context of 'Regalism/Gallicanism' and of the Jansenist-Ultramontanist conflict in the Austrian Netherlands.[193] As long as Archduchess Maria-Elisabeth was governess, the Ultramontanists—who favored a strong central and hierarchically organized Church led by the Pope—had free game. In order to promote Ultramontanism, she defied the opposition of the councils of justice and outwardly ignored the orders of her brother Charles VI.

Immediately after the death of Maria Elisabeth, the Privy Council in particular began to steer a more regalist course, which promoted the preponderance of the national church and the autonomy of the local bishops, and endorsed a close cooperation between the royal and the clerical authorities. The Council even attempted to reverse some of Maria Elisabeth's decisions. These efforts were renewed and intensified after the restoration of the Austrian authority in 1749. Especially the president of the Privy Council de Neny showed himself a staunch advocate of a 'Belgian Church', arguing that secular tribunals had the competence to determine the extent

---

190 Brussels, ARA, GR Register 482, f. 17–19, April 3, 1786.

191 For instance in the case of the beguine Pétronille Basyn.

192 For information on the church and (ecclesiastical) justice in general, see: De Brouwer, Jozef. 1971–1972. *De kerkelijke rechtspraak en haar evolutie in de bisdommen Antwerpen, Gent en Mechelen tussen 1570 en 1795.* Tielt: Veys; Put, Eddy. 2005. Standenongelijkheid in strafzaken: geestelijke voor Zuid-Nederlandse en Luikse officialiteiten (16de–18de eeuw). In *Recht in geschiedenis: een bundel bijdragen over rechtsgeschiedenis van de Middeleeuwen tot de hedendaagse tijd*, eds. Jozef Janssens e.a., 291–302. Leuven: Davidsfonds; Roegiers, Jan. 1980. *Kerk en Staat in de Oostenrijkse Nederlanden.* In In *Algemene Geschiedenis der Nederlanden*, eds. Walter Prevenier e.a, t. 9, 361–375. Haarlem: Fibula-Van Dishoeck; Van De Wiel, Constant. 1976. Recours aux tribunaux laics en matière ecclésiastique vers 1720. In *Mélanges Mgr Wagnon. Etudes d'histoire et de droit*, 416–436. Louvain-la-Neuves: Faculté internationale de droit canonique; Wauters, Bart. 2004. La jurisdiction contentieuse du nonce de Flandre (XVIIe–XVIIIe). *Zeitschrift der Savigny Stiftung für Rechtsgeschichte* 90: 430–455."; Wauters, Bart. 2005. *Recht als religie: canonieke onderbouw van de vroegmoderne staatsvorming in de Zuidelijke Nederlanden.* Leuven: Universitaire Pers.

193 Roegiers, Jan. 1980. *Kerk en Staat in de Oostenrijkse Nederlanden.* In In *Algemene Geschiedenis der Nederlanden*, eds. Walter Prevenier e.a, t. 9. Haarlem: Fibula-Van Dishoeck, 361.

of the ecclesiastical immunity.[194] Moreover, in the course of the eighteenth century, the clergy took ever more recourse to secular courts, at least as far as civil justice was concerned.[195] Conflicts of jurisdiction between secular and clerical tribunals were the order of the day. Especially the Council of Brabant willingly got involved in all sorts of conflicts between Church and State, but the Great Council too regularly collided with the ecclesiastical authorities, and in particular with the chapter of Saint Rombout and the Archbishop of Malines, who in the eighteenth century was invariably an Ultramontanist.

Especially in lawsuits related to the appointment of clergymen, the lower clergy made use of the *recursus ad principem* to pass over the clerical courts and introduce their cases at a secular tribunal.[196] In at least one instance, the Archbishop, Philippe d'Alsace, was involved in what he considered to be an infringement by the Great Council on the exclusive domain of the Church.[197] In this case, the tribunal had awarded *lettres de maintenue* to Charles Leijdecker, temporary assistant priest in the parish of Saint Rombout in Malines, even though he had been forbidden to continue his functions since he had failed the mandatory exam. Not only did d'Alsace condemn the intervention of the Great Council as an illicit intrusion on what should be considered the exclusive domain of ecclesiastical jurisdiction, but he also personally attacked the members of the Great Council. Firstly, the Archbishop claimed that the lawsuit had not been properly conducted—thereby casting doubt on the competence of the councilors. Secondly, he was convinced that the councilors would never have taken on the case had it not been for the absence of the president—thereby suggesting that the councilors knew they were doing something inappropriate, which their president Christophe de Baillet would not approve of.

The members of the Great Council responded in kind. They claimed that the court did have the jurisdiction to issue *lettres de maintenue*, if only to prevent the (arch)bishop(s) from acting autocratically. If the royal councils were deprived of their jurisdiction, lower-ranked clericals would be liable to the arbitrary decisions of ecclesiastical authorities without any means of defense. Therefore, it was absolutely mandatory that the Great Council—and other superior tribunals—could award *lettres de maintenue* as a form of royal protection from the bishops' despotism.

[194] Put, Eddy. 2005. Standenongelijkheid in strafzaken: geestelijke voor Zuid-Nederlandse en Luikse officialiteiten (16de–18de eeuw). In *Recht in geschiedenis: een bundel bijdragen over rechtsgeschiedenis van de Middeleeuwen tot de hedendaagse tijd*, eds. Jozef Janssens e.a. Leuven: Davidsfonds, 286.

[195] Van De Wiel, Constant. 1976. Recours aux tribunaux laics en matière ecclésiastique vers 1720. In *Mélanges Mgr Wagnon. Etudes d'histoire et de droit*, 416–436. Louvain-la-Neuves: Faculté internationale de droit canonique.

[196] The eighteenth century extended sentences of the Great Council contain several cases related to the appointment of clergy: Brussels, ARA, GRM 973, f. 330–355, February 10, 1727; GRM 975, f. 518–553, March 4, 1744; GRM 976, f. 436–441, April 21, 1762; GRM, 976, f. 352–435, March 29, 1760; GRM 976, f. 436–441, April 21, 1762. See: Verscuren, An. 2013. *Nadere toegang op de geëxtendeerde sententies van de Grote Raad van Mechelen: 1693–1772.* Brussels: Algemeen Rijksarchief.

[197] Brussels, ARA, GRM 164, mémoriaux, f. 618–630, 1723–1725.

Apart from the question of jurisdiction, the councilors vigorously denied the archbishop's claim that president de Baillet would never have approved of their behavior in this case. In order to protect the honor of the Great Council and its members, the councilors felt compelled to emphasize that the archbishop's implications were simply untrue.[198]

Throughout the 1720s the figure of Maria Elisabeth and her Ultramontanist tendencies loomed large, but the regalist trend gained importance after her death, and even more so after Patrice de Neny became president of the Privy Council. Even though Empress Maria Theresa and Chancellor Kaunitz were hesitant at first about de Neny's ideas on a 'Belgian Church'—mostly because they did not want to offend Rome—their attitude drastically changed around the late 1760s.[199]

In 1768, Maria Theresa sent a letter to the presidents of the Great Council and the provincial councils requesting them to secretly—with the intervention of only two or three trustworthy councilors—give their advice on a proposal on how to avoid future conflicts of jurisdiction between the secular and the ecclesiastical authorities.[200] Her suggestion amounted to nothing less than limiting the authority of the Church to pure spiritual matters. The power of the Church should be confined to the preaching of the Gospel, the administration of sacraments and the preservation of its internal order. According to Maria Theresa, even decisions on dogma, cult and discipline did not exclusively belong to the domain of the Church. Since these issues had repercussions for the entire society, the sovereign, as head of state as well as protector of the Church, could not permit that these matters would be left to clerical authority alone. The empress hereby limited the jurisdiction of the ecclesiastical courts and claimed that it was her right and even her duty to interfere in the internal affairs of the Church.

The fact that the State attempted to further impose its authority was no surprise, given the numerous conflicts it had had with the Church in the previous years on the ecclesiastical right of asylum,[201] but also on the prosecution of crimes committed

[198] While we do not know what came of the case, it might be true that de Baillet would have been reluctant to infringe on what could be considered a purely ecclesiastical authority. In any case, it has been assessed that as president of the Privy Council, he never attempted in any way to oppose Maria Elisabeth's ultramontanist policies. Roegiers, Jan. 1980. *Kerk en Staat in de Oostenrijkse Nederlanden.* In In *Algemene Geschiedenis der Nederlanden*, eds. Walter Prevenier e.a, t. 9. Haarlem: Fibula-Van Dishoeck, 363.

[199] Roegiers, Jan. 1980. *Kerk en Staat in de Oostenrijkse Nederlanden.* In In *Algemene Geschiedenis der Nederlanden*, eds. Walter Prevenier e.a, t. 9. Haarlem: Fibula-Van Dishoeck, 364–368.

[200] Brussels, ARA, GRM 142, registre aux résolutions secrètes, f. 4v–5, 1768: letter of Maria Theresa to the provincial councils of the Austrian Netherlands.

[201] Several ordinances limited this right of asylum, as a result of a number of incidents, e.g: *ROPBA*, t. 5, pp. 475–476, April 10, 1742; *ROPBA*, t. 7, p. 270, October 31, 1753. AAM, Verzameling Kerk en Staat 181, 1719: correspondence between president de Baillet of the Great Council and archbishop d'Alsace concerning the question of which institution was responsible for matters regarding the right of asylum. In the early eighteenth century, procurator-general of the Great Council Du Jardin was even excommunicated for having violated the ecclesiastical jurisdiction on the right of asylum and it was not until 1703 that his excommunication was withdrawn. Malines, AAM, Verzameling Kerk en Staat 327, 1700–1703. For more information on the right of asylum:

by clergy. Indeed, while many clergymen found their way to the secular tribunals for civil jurisdiction, they continued to take recourse to the *privilegium fori* to have their criminal trials judged by an ecclesiastical court. This was only logical given that ecclesiastical tribunals were far more lenient than their secular counterparts.[202]

The clerical authorities actively cooperated with this policy, undoubtedly as an act of defiance against the secular courts of justice. In late 1749, for instance, the Great Council summoned both the president of the episcopal seminary of Malines and the archbishop on account of the prosecution of a theologian, who had killed two colleagues and wounded a third one in the seminary.[203] In order to keep the crime hidden from the state authorities, the president had the two bodies secretly buried in the seminary's chapel. He also made sure that the perpetrator—a theologian named Van Meir—was transported to Sint Truiden, a city in the diocese of Liège, and accordingly out of reach of the Great Council's jurisdiction, and of any other court in the Austrian Netherlands. When first the bailiff of Malines and later the fiscals of the Great Council got wind of the crime, the archbishop refused to let them interrogate witnesses or to cooperate in any other way with the investigation.

The governor authorized the fiscals not only to request the extradition of Van Meir, but also to prosecute those who had helped him escape from the city of Malines, without distinguishing between the laity and clergy. Even Archbishop d'Alsace was suspected of having had a hand in—or at least knowledge of—the transport of Van Meir to Sint Truiden. Although d'Alsace vigorously protested the actions of the fiscals, citing the immunity of clericals against prosecution by the Great Council, the right of asylum which Van Meir enjoyed, and the fact that it had been an act of charity to have him transported to the diocese of Liège, the governor commissioned the fiscals to act.

Whilst most numerous, disputes between the Great Council and the Church in Malines were not limited to conflicts of jurisdiction. Far more trivial questions caused tensions between the two institutions. In 1741, both the Great Council and the chapter of Saint Rombout claimed that they had the privilege to organize the official commemoration of the death of Charles VI in the city.[204] According to the chapter of Saint Rombout, this was a purely ecclesiastical matter; consequently, it had the sole right to compose the program and to stipulate the time and date for the memorial services. The chapter went back as far as archdukes Albert and Isabella to prove that it had always been the canons who organized these commemorations. The Great Council on the other hand, asserted that the practical arrangements had

---

Proost, Jean-Joseph-Eugène. 1870. *Histoire du droit d'asile religieux en Belgique*. Ghent: Hebbelynck.

[202] Put, Eddy. 2005. Standenongelijkheid in strafzaken: geestelijke voor Zuid-Nederlandse en Luikse officialiteiten (16de–18de eeuw). In *Recht in geschiedenis: een bundel bijdragen over rechtsgeschiedenis van de Middeleeuwen tot de hedendaagse tijd*, eds. Jozef Janssens e.a. Leuven: Davidsfonds, 286.

[203] Brussels, ARA, GR, Register 413, f. 206–212, December 21, 1749; Brussels, ARA, GR, Register 414, f. 54–55, January 30, 1750; Id, f. 68, February 3, 1750; Id, f. 143–152, March 10, 1750. Advice of the Privy Council on the murders by and escape of theologian van Meir.

[204] Brussels, ARA, GRM 168D, f. 4–60, January–May 1741.

always been its duty, while it was left to the chapter to actually celebrate Mass. Given that they were the representatives of the sovereign in Malines, the councilors maintained that they should determine date and time in the same way relatives did for a deceased family member. The discussion was even brought before the governor, and while both contestants continued to bombard each other with arguments and Bible quotes, he decided that at least this time, the Great Council had the right to organize the commemorations.[205]

Finally, how did the clerical councilors behave in these matters? It is likely that they had mixed loyalties, being members of the Church while also serving on the Great Council and subsequently serving the sovereign. It is not hard to imagine that Maria Theresa's comment on the 'two or three trustworthy councilors' to examine her proposal intended to exclude the clerical councilors from the discussions. In all respects, the Great Council itself tried to avoid to have clerical councilors in its midst.[206]

The example of councilor Brenart demonstrates that certainly not all clericals felt much attachment to their former employers, especially not when their benefits were at stake.[207] In 1759, shortly after the appointment of Brenart to the Great Council, the sovereign granted him letters of *significamus*, allowing Brenart to maintain his income from his dignity as dean at the Saint Gummarus church in Lier, even though he no longer lived or worked there. When the chapter of Lier sent a letter of complaint, Brenart requested the sovereign to allow him the continued receipt of his benefits, thereby directly contravening his ecclesiastical superiors. Most clerical councilors—who in principle were appointed for life, received a decent wage from the state, enjoyed various benefits and held a position that probably brought more standing than one as member of a chapter—seemed to have easily switched their loyalties to their new employer. And at least Brenart did not hesitate to go as far as to take legal action against his former brothers of the chapter.

All these examples confirm the impression that the State in the eighteenth century did not hesitate to confront the Church. In many of the arguments the Great Council—and other provincial councils for that matter—had with the ecclesiastical authorities, the Privy Council, at least after 1740, sided with the courts against the Church and did not hesitate to support charges against the Archbishop himself. There should be no doubt that the State used the Great Council as an instrument to assert its power and authority over the Church, which especially in the eighteenth century was ever more on the defensive.

[205] It was not until 1765 that the matter was finally settled with the decision that in all future events, the councilors of the Great Council should make arrangement for official celebrations. Brussels, ARA, GRM 168G, mémoriaux, f. 4, October 1765.

[206] Cf. supra, Chap. 2.

[207] Brussels, ARA, GR Register 445, f. 365–369, August 6, 1759; Register 448, f. 177–196, November 3, 1760.

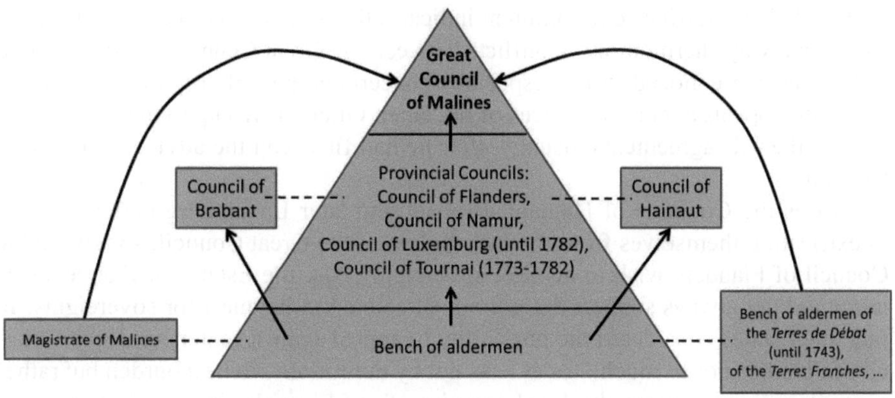

Fig. 3.2 Judicial structure of the eighteenth century Austrian Netherlands. (The figure is only a schematic showing simplified representations of the relations between the different tribunals in the eighteenth century Austrian Netherlands)

3.3.3 Checks and Balances: Conflicts with the Provincial Councils

3.3.3.1 The 'Subordinate' Councils

As the 'superior' court of the Austrian Netherlands, the Great Council constantly maintained intense relations with the provincial councils, especially with those that fell under its jurisdiction: the Councils of Flanders, Luxemburg[208] and Namur (Fig. 3.2). Unsurprisingly, these relations often took the form of conflicts as the subordinate councils constantly attempted to extend their own influence and to explore the limits of authority the Great Council could wield in the eighteenth century.

The Council of Flanders[209] In the eighteenth century, the Council of Flanders provided the majority of the appeals dealt with at the Great Council.[210] The tribunal's subordination to Malines was a constant thorn in its side, even more so after the Council of Luxemburg acquired sovereignty in 1782. In 1785, the Council of Flanders remarked that the Great Council derived its sole existence from its competence as appeal judge for the province of Flanders; Namur was too small to be signifi-

[208] Until 1782, when Joseph II awarded sovereignty to the Council of Luxemburg.

[209] For a more elaborate analysis of the relations between the Great Council and the Council of Flanders, we refer to Verscuren, An. 2012. The interactions between the Council of Flanders and the Great Council of Malines in the eighteenth century. In *Intermediate institutions in the County of Flanders in the Late Middle Ages and the Early Modern Era*, eds. Georges Martyn e.a., 139–153. Brussels: Algemeen Rijksarchief. Given that we formulated in this paper some hypotheses which might explain the lack of sovereignty of the Council of Flanders, we do not further discuss the matter here.

[210] Almost 60 % of the appeal cases came from Flanders. Cf. infra, Chap. 4.

cant.[211] This somewhat sour comment indicates that relations between the tribunals were not always harmonious. Conflicts between the Great Council and the Council of Flanders were indeed legion, especially concerning the authority of the former to deal with appeals against sentences of the latter. Often, it was up to the governor to resolve their disagreements, usually after he had first won the advice of the Privy Council.

Just as the Councils of Hainaut, Brabant and later Luxemburg had succeeded in extricating themselves from the jurisdiction of the Great Council, so too did the Council of Flanders wish to achieve sovereignty. Yet, the Estates of Flanders certainly did not always support the provincial council in its quest for sovereignty. In fact, the Estates considered the possibility to appeal against sentences of the Council of Flanders not so much—or at least not by definition—to be a burden but rather a privilege guaranteeing the legal security of the Flemish citizens. For instance, in January 1714, the Estates of Flanders protested an ordinance of the Council of State, which had conferred to the Council of Flanders the right to judge by arrest in order to speed up the settlement in a specific case concerning two merchants,[212] thereby depriving the losing party of his fundamental right to appeal the sentence. Moreover, the Estates of Flanders themselves also at times made use of the right to appeal against sentences of the provincial council.[213]

During the greater part of the eighteenth century, the two councils also disagreed on their respective (geographical) jurisdiction. At several instances in 1729, 1732, 1750 and 1751,[214] the authority over the land and town of Dendermonde was contested. On March 20, 1751, it was decided that—at least provisionally—the Great Council was competent to deal with criminal cases, police matters and violations of the ordinances, while the Council of Flanders judged civil cases.[215] Despite this ordinance, the discussions on Dendermonde were reopened in 1763[216] and it was not until 1775 that the matter was settled to the advantage of the Great Council.[217]

Especially in the second half of the eighteenth century, the governor—usually following the advice of the Privy Council—supported the Great Council in its constant conflicts with the Council of Flanders. More importantly, the central government often rebuffed the *conduite irrégulière* of the Flemish councilors in their dealings with the Great Council. For instance, in 1750, a conflict arose between the two courts as a result of an appeal against a sentence of the Magistrate of Tournai,

[211] Brussels, ARA, GR Registers 481, f. 197–203, August 1785: "… quoiqu'il n'appartienne pas aux exposans d'approfondir les motifs qui determinent sa majesté à laisser subsister le Grand Conseil presque pour la seule province de Flandres…"

[212] Brussels, ARA, GRM 163, mémoriaux, f. 121–132, January 18, 1714.

[213] Cf. Excel Database: distribution records of the eighteenth century Great Council.

[214] Brussels, ARA, GRM 166, mémoriaux, f. 61–78, June 3, 1729; Brussels, ARA, GRM 167, mémoriaux, f. 115–130, April 1732; Brussels, ARA, GR, Register 414, f. 119, February 25, 1750; Brussels, ARA, GRM 141, registre aux résolutions secrètes, f. 125–126, March 24, 1751.

[215] *ROPBA*, t. 7, p. 16, March 20, 1751.

[216] Brussels, ARA, GRM 140L, file 17: conflict of jurisdiction between the Great Council and the Council of Flanders on Ertbrugge.

[217] Brussels, ARA, GRM 141, registre aux résolutions secrètes, f. 153–157r, May 10, 1775.

which in 1744 had been dealt with in Flanders but which after the French conquest had been moved to Douai.[218] When in 1750 the case had not yet been decided, the question arose over which tribunal should be authorized to judge the lawsuit: the Council of Flanders or the Great Council? Even though eventually the Council of Flanders won the argument, the dispute had gradually turned more into a discussion on the haughtiness with which the Council of Flanders had treated the Great Council than into a debate on the original conflict of jurisdiction.

Instead of answering two different letters from the Great Council, dated on September 5th and 25th, the councilors of Flanders merely had informed the litigants on September 30th that they should continue their lawsuit before their court, under the penalty of a fine of 100 silver coins. The Great Council considered this sort of behavior as an assault on its jurisdiction, and as an attempt to rearrange the entire judicial hierarchy and to proclaim the Council of Flanders an independent and sovereign court. Therefore, the Great Council requested the governor to take action. In his decision, the governor made known to the Council of Flanders that this behavior was absolutely beyond the pale. On matters of justice, Flanders was completely subject to the Great Council, and, instead of acting haughtily, it should have responded to the Great Council's letters. Still, this was not the end of the affair for Flanders. With two official ordinances—one of May 5, 1751 and one of December 7, 1752[219]—Charles of Lorraine emphasized the subordination of the Council of Flanders to the Great Council.

In the second half of the century, the Great Council not only succeeded in firmly establishing its superiority in civil cases but also managed to infringe on the Council of Flanders' authority in criminal affairs. More specifically, the impossibility to appeal against criminal sentences became contested. The dispute dated back to the seventeenth century: in 1665, Don Francisco de Moura y Cortereal, governor of the Spanish Netherlands, decided by provisionary decree that the Great Council was only competent to deal with appeals against criminal sentences of the Council of Flanders, if the punishment was limited to a simple fine. Additionally, the appeal could not suspend the execution of the sentence.[220]

Nevertheless, the disagreement resurfaced in the eighteenth century. In the early 1750s, in the context of the prosecution initiated by the Great Council's fiscals against one of the registrars of the Council of Flanders, the provincial council wrote—and published in print!—a lengthy and extensively argued defense of its sovereignty in criminal matters.[221] Apparently, the Council of Flanders won the ar-

---

[218] Brussels, ARA, GRM 168F, mémoriaux, f. 130–132v, October 5, 1750.

[219] *ROPBA*, t. 7, pp. 24–25, May 5, 1751; *ROPBA*, t. 7, pp. 180–181, December 7, 1752.

[220] For more information on the seventeenth century conflict: Monballyu, Jos. 1998. De Raad van Vlaanderen, een soevereine justitieraad in strafzaken? In *Handelingen van het tweede Hof van Holland Symposium gehouden op 14 November 1997 in de Treveszaal te Den Haag*, ed. Rob Huijbrecht, 77–90. The Hague: Algemeen Rijksarchief.

[221] Exposition historique et juridique des privilèges de la province de Flandres et des prérogatives du Conseil provincial par les président et gens du même conseil de Sa Majesté l'Impératrice Reine, comtesse de Flandres etc. ordonné en Flandres contre les président et gens du Grand Conseil de Sa Majesté à Malines. 1752. Ghent: J.J. Bauwens.

gument, because nothing came of the case. At least not until some 20 years later, when the Great Council issued letters of appeal against a criminal sentence of the Council of Flanders condemning Pieter Joseph Keppens, parish priest of Bavikhove, to being discharged and to a fine of 100 florins because of his constant quarrels with the sacristan and 'other excesses'.[222] Not surprisingly, the Council of Flanders protested this course of events, invoking the decree of April 7, 1665.

According to the Great Council, the decree of 1665 was not applicable: there was no conflict of jurisdiction, since Keppens did not simply appeal to the Great Council, but resorted to a superior court in order to receive the nullification of a criminal sentence. In other words, the appeal was not directed against the substance of the case, but against procedural errors. By awarding letters of appeal, the Great Council did not judge the merits of the case, but merely declared that Keppens should get the opportunity to explain why the trial before the Council of Flanders was invalid.[223] The governor agreed with the arguments of the Great Council.[224]

Soon, it became clear that the governor's decision of 1774 had established an important precedent. In 1782, a comparable dispute arose when Orbain Van Heulendoncq appealed to the Great Council against a criminal sentence of the Council of Flanders.[225] Originally, Van Heulendoncq had been arrested by the aldermen of Boekhoute. His complaints against this apprehension—according to Van Heulendoncq, the officer had refused to interrogate witnesses *à décharge*—resulted in the evocation of the trial by the Council of Flanders. However, the latter decided that the officer of Boekhoute was above reproach and sent the case back to the aldermen, condemning Van Heulendoncq to pay the costs. It was against this sentence of the Council of Flanders that Van Heulendoncq appealed to the Great Council. When the Council of Flanders refused to accept the appeal, the Great Council brought the matter to the attention of the Privy Council.

The Privy Council acknowledged that, as a rule, the Great Council did not have the authority to deal with appeals against criminal sentences of the Council of Flanders. However, if the appeal attacked the sentence because of formal inconsistencies or errors, and therefore was aimed at receiving nullification of the procedure, the Great Council did have the competence to take up the case. Since Van Heulendoncq only appealed against the decision of the Council of Flanders not to consider his objections against his arrest and refer him back to the aldermen of Boekhoute, it was obvious that this was not a criminal case and that the Great Council—as superior court—could deal with the matter. Moreover, the Privy Council judged that the analogies with the Bavikhove case of the previous decade were too striking to ig-

222 Brussels, ARA, GR Register 469, f. 407–409. Monballyu extensively discussed this case in his article *De Raad van Vlaanderen, een soevereine justitieraad in strafzaken?*

223 Brussels, ARA, GRM 168G, mémoriaux, f. 54–58, 1774.

224 Brussels, ARA, GR Register 469, f. 407r–409v, December 5, 1774.

225 Brussels, ARA, GR Register 479, f. 263–269, August 23, 1783. Also: Monballyu, Jos. 1998. De Raad van Vlaanderen, een soevereine justitieraad in strafzaken? In *Handelingen van het tweede Hof van Holland Symposium gehouden op 14 November 1997 in de Treveszaal te Den Haag*, ed. Rob Huijbrecht, 77–90. The Hague: Algemeen Rijksarchief.

nore. Therefore, the Privy Council as well as the governor concurred with the Great Council and forced the Council of Flanders to send the file to Malines.

As a result, even though it was still impossible to actually appeal against a criminal sentence that did not merely condemn the suspect to a fine, it became feasible to demand the nullification of such a sentence, based on procedural technicalities, comparable to some sort of appeal to the Court of Cassation *avant la lettre*. The Keppens case signified a turning point for the Council of Flanders. In the years to come, several other criminal sentences were 'appealed' against at the Great Council for procedural errors. Even though the Council of Flanders brought the matter before the Privy Council every single time, as far as known, it was never put in the right.[226]

The above cited examples suggest that the Privy Council, the governor and even the sovereign supported the Great Council in thwarting the ambitions of the Council of Flanders to acquire sovereignty, a privilege all other important provincial councils in the Austrian Netherlands enjoyed. Moreover, the central government did not try to prevent the Great Council from overstepping its own jurisdiction by accepting appeals against criminal sentences—even if it was only on formal grounds—but even resolved these conflicts in favor of the Great Council. As a result, the Council of Flanders saw its jurisdiction limited over the course of the eighteenth century rather than extended.

The Council of Luxemburg The Council of Luxemburg was responsible for the second highest number of appeal cases at the Great Council.[227] Still, in the first half of the eighteenth century, the Great Council had far less conflicts with the Council of Luxemburg than with its Flemish counterpart. In fact, the Malines tribunal sometimes even sided with the Council of Luxemburg, even if this meant that the councilors forfeited the chance of demonstrating their authority, a behavior that was almost unimaginable in their dealings with the Council of Flanders. For example, in 1723, the Abbot of *Saint Hubert en Andenne*, who had taken up the case of Jean François Le Febvre, wished to appeal to the Great Council against the personal citation of Le Febvre by the Council of Luxemburg, arguing that it had no jurisdiction over Saint Hubert.[228] As the Great Council did not have the authority to deal with appeals in criminal cases, it refused to issue the necessary letters of appeal. The request of the abbot to the central government again met with a refusal of the Great Council to either issue letters of appeal or even deal with the case at first instance. The councilors argued that *évocation* was only possible when the lawsuit in question was related to another matter that was being dealt with at the Great Council. Since this condition was not fulfilled, the Great Council redirected the Abbot of Saint Hubert to the Council of Luxemburg.

226 E.g. Brussels, ARA, GR Register 482, f. 46, November 17 1786; GRM 138, correspondances, August 3, 1791; GRM 140, correspondances, August 11, 1793; GRM 140, correspondances, April 3, 1794.

227 Cf. infra, Chap. 4 for concrete numbers.

228 Brussels, ARA, GRM 164, mémoriaux, f. 338–352, November 20, 1723.

Nevertheless, once the Great Council felt seriously threatened in its jurisdiction over the Council of Luxemburg, the conflicts multiplied and became far more fierce and sustained. Indeed, while the Great Council apparently did not attempt to extend its jurisdiction over the Council of Luxemburg—contrary to its attitudes toward the Council of Flanders—there could be no question that its authority over the province would be seriously limited or even completely abolished.

Contrary to the Estates of Flanders, the Estates of Luxemburg were not exactly satisfied with the possibility their inhabitants had to appeal to the Great Council against sentences of the Council of Luxemburg. In fact, they attempted to extract as much jurisdiction as possible from the Great Council. In 1755, the Estates of Luxemburg made a first appeal to the central government to detach the Council of Luxemburg from Malines.[229] Somewhat surprisingly, it was the Magistrate of Malines—much more so than the Great Council itself—that wrote a fierce letter to the government opposing the sovereignty of the Council of Luxemburg, arguing that it would mean "*la ruïne inévitable de la ville et province de Malines ... [vu] que le grand conseil s'occupe au moins un tiers de l'année pour vuider et juger les procès qui lui sont dévolus par voie d'appel des sentences portées par ledit conseil de Luxembourg ...*"[230]

While the request of the Luxemburg Estates was not granted, the Council of Luxemburg did receive more authority to judge by arrest over the course of the eighteenth century. In 1768 and 1771, two separate decrees stipulated that it was no longer possible to appeal to the Great Council against a sentence of the Council of Luxemburg in legal proceedings concerning communities and guilds, unless their members appealed in their own name and not as a body. The rationale behind this law was to avoid the degradation of the communal forests, caused by the numerous and expensive lawsuits in which the communities of Luxemburg all too easily engaged. To put a stop to this practice, it had already been decided in 1754 that a lawsuit could not be initiated without the authorization of the provincial council. By appealing to the Great Council against the decisions of the Council of Luxemburg, the parties bypassed this decree, thereby again getting engaged in an endless judicial tug-of-war.

The legislation of 1768 and 1771 closed that loophole. It was against these decrees that the Great Council vehemently protested to the Privy Council.[231] The letter not only contained an enumeration of the reasons why this specific legislation was unnecessary and even detrimental for the communities of Luxemburg, but the mem-

[229] *ROPBA*, t. 7, p. 497, August 2, 1755.

[230] Malines, Stadsarchief Mechelen, Archives de la ville de Malines, affaires civiles et ecclésiastiques 138, "Conseil de Luxembourg", 1755. The letter demonstrates that the Magistrate of Malines had very ambiguous feelings towards the Great Council. On the one hand, the aldermen were constantly quarrelling with the Great Council over the privileges and exemptions of its members and its jurisdiction over the Magistrate of Malines. On the other hand, they were very well aware that the economic prosperity of their city depended to a high extent on the presence of the tribunal in Malines. In 1789, when the Brabant Revolution *de facto* abolished the Great Council, the Magistrate of Malines would again express its worries about the economic consequences of the disappearance of the Great Council for the city. Cf. infra, Chap. 5.

[231] Brussels, ARA, GRM 232, f. 5–18, June 3, 1771.

bers of the Great Council, close to panic-stricken, also expressed their worries that these decrees were the first step towards the complete annihilation of their tribunal. Moreover, the councilors argued, the prospect that the Council might disappear had also enormously alarmed the burghers of Malines, who were entirely dependent for their prosperity—and their ability to pay taxes—on the presence of the Great Council in their city.

In their advice, the members of the Privy Council described the document as a pompous display of the Great Council's self-declared importance and its services to the public. The first seven pages were entirely filled with an exposition of the alleged plans formed against the Great Council with the goal of silently obliterating the tribunal.[232] The Privy Council was assured that these protestations were exclusively motivated by the self-interest of the councilors, who indeed saw their sphere of influence slightly reduced. However, the advantages of the decrees more than outweighed their perceived disadvantages and the Privy Council was convinced that they would not reduce the councilors of the Great Council to the dole. An additional advantage was that, since they would not be occupied with the trifles of these lawsuits from Luxemburg, they could work on other, more important cases, which would lead to the speedier expedition of justice.[233]

Finally, in 1782, Joseph II converted the Council of Luxemburg into a sovereign council, thereby depriving the Great Council of its geographically largest and in terms of workload second largest jurisdiction.[234] Unsurprisingly, the Great Council protested this serious curtailment of its jurisdiction, however to no avail.[235] We can only guess why exactly Joseph II awarded sovereignty to the Council of Luxemburg and not, for example, to the Council of Flanders. The reasons cited—distance, translation issues, the export of finances and the delay in the settlement of the case—were at least partially applicable to the situation in Flanders. Either way, it is obvious that while the central government supported the Great Council's attempts to extend its jurisdiction at the expense of the Council of Flanders, it adopted a

[232] Brussels, ARA, GR Register 466, f. 89–96, March 14, 1772. "La représentation ci-jointe, que le Grand Conseil a adressée à votre altesse royale et qu'elle nous a remise par decret du 13 juin dernier pour la consulter sur ce qui en fait le sujet, annonce de la part de ce tribunal une terreur panique sur son anéantissement, dont nous ne voyons ni sujet, ni apparance. Un étalage pompeux de son établissement, de son importance, de ses services; une exposition pathétique des prétendus orages qui se seroient formés contre lui et d'un prétendu plan qui sembleroit subsister encore pour le sapper et l'anéantir à la sourdine, remplissent les sept premiers pages de cette pièce."

[233] Brussels, ARA, GR Register 466, f. 89–96, March 14, 1772.

[234] *ROPBA*, t. 12, pp. 189–191, August 1, 1782.

[235] We have not been able to retrieve the Great Council's original protest letter. However, Hubert in his account of the voyage of Emperor Joseph II in the Netherlands, recounted parts. Unfortunately, his reference to 'Secretairerie d'Etat et de Guerre, liasse 623' turned out to be a dead end, potentially because the *liasses* in the *Secretairerie* have been renumbered. Cf. Hubert, Eugène. 1900. *Le voyage de l'empereur Joseph II dans les Pays-Bas (31 mai 1781–27 juillet 1781): etude d'histoire politique et diplomatique*. Brussels, Lebègue, 162, footnotes 1–4. Nevertheless, we do possess a document from 1791 in which the Great Council explained its arguments for reintegrating the Council of Luxemburg into its jurisdiction. Brussels, ARA, GRM 138, Correspondances, f. 25–40, February 24, 1791. Given that this episode is part of the reform policy of Joseph II, we will this discuss the matter in detail in Chap. 5.

completely opposite policy towards the Great Council's authority over the Council of Luxemburg.

The Council of Namur The Council of Namur was in terms of workload far less important than the Council of Flanders and the Council of Luxemburg.[236] Accordingly, the number of conflicts the Great Council had with the Council of Namur were relatively limited. Yet, they were not insignificant. In one of these conflicts, the Great Council attempted to extend its jurisdiction in criminal matters at the expense of the Council of Namur. The story started in August 1716, when the bench of aldermen of Namur convicted Jeanne Servais, a servant, to 3 months in prison and eternal banishment from the city for robbing her recently deceased master Jacques Burlet.[237] Although it is often claimed that appeals against criminal sentences in the Austrian Netherlands were not possible, Jeanne Servais was able to appeal against her conviction to the Council of Namur. The prosecutor in the case—mayor Jean François d'Hinslin—also lodged an appeal against the judgment of the aldermen, in his case because he was convinced that the punishment was far too lenient.

On March 13, 1717, after a thorough investigation of the trial and some additional inquiries, the Council of Namur acquitted Jeanne Servais of all charges and ordered mayor d'Hinslin to pay the costs of the prosecution. Two days later, Servais requested the Council of Namur to order d'Hinslin to release her. The prosecutor however, refused to accept her acquittal and appealed against this sentence to the Great Council of Malines. The tribunal also got itself involved in the discussion and supported the reasoning of d'Hinslin that the impossibility to appeal against a criminal sentence by the Council of Namur did not apply to the prosecuting officer. The discussion was only settled a year later by the Austrian Emperor, who officially decreed that the sentence was not appealable[238]—thereby indirectly rebuffing the efforts of the Great Council to display its superiority over the Council of Namur.

Despite this setback, the Great Council continued to claim a certain authority in the matter. When the Burlet brothers—who had denounced Jeanne Servais—saw themselves condemned to pay the procedural costs and damages, they appealed against this sentence to the Great Council. This time, the argument was decided in the Great Council's favor.[239] Compared to the ordinance of March 5, 1718, which confirmed that it was impossible to appeal against the Council of Namur's judgment, the central government's opinion that the Great Council was competent to deal with the appeal against the condemnation to pay the expenses seems rather inconsistent. Indeed, Jeanne Servais herself again ran the risk to foot the bill—it

---

[236] Cf. infra, Chap. 4.

[237] Brussels, ARA, GRM 162, mémoriaux, f. 121v: July 1717 and f. 126v: April 1718; GRM 163, mémoriaux, f. 318 and f. 347–365, April 1717. The case of Jeanne Servais also figured prominently in a paper we presented at the 20th British Legal History Conference (Cambridge, July 2011) carrying the title: *The humanization of criminal justice in the early eighteenth century Austrian Netherlands: Enlightenment or struggle for power?*

[238] *ROPBA*, t. 3, pp. 54–56, April 20, 1717.

[239] Cf. Excel database: distribution records of the eighteenth century Great Council. June 1723: "Antoine Burlet appellant de Namur contre Jeanne Servais et le mayeur dudit Namur."

was rather rule than exception that an acquitted accused in a criminal trial had to pay the costs. While there might have been good reason connected to the case to make this ruling, it is not inconceivable that the government allowed the Great Council to deal with the lawsuit in order to give the councilors an opportunity to reaffirm their authority over the Council of Namur, in some sort of semi-conscious *divide et impera* strategy.

3.3.3.2 The Sovereign Councils of Brabant and Hainaut

Contrary to the Councils of Flanders, Luxembourg and Namur, the Councils of Brabant and Hainaut were not subjected to the authority of the Great Council. Ever since the early sixteenth century, both courts sentenced by arrest, which made it impossible to appeal against their judgments. Even though they had in principle less need to interact with the Great Council, conflicts of jurisdiction were nevertheless numerous.

Almost all confrontations with the Council of Brabant can be brought down to inheritance disputes. Each time a (former) president or councilor of a governmental council died in Brussels or in another city of Brabant, the same question arose: which council was authorized to deal with possible disputes among the heirs, or with the appointment and supervision of one or several guardians when minors were involved? Both the Council of Brabant and the Great Council often disputed their reciprocal jurisdiction. Since the Great Council could not assert any rights based on territory, everything depended on the question if the deceased had been counted among the *escrous*, if this status was still valid after his death, if his widow and/or his children continued to enjoy the privileges associated with this position, etc. The status of the heirs was also important, since some of them could equally claim membership of the Order of the Golden Fleece or some other aspect which may have entitled them to bring their claims before the Great Council. The matter was often even further complicated by the presence of—by times numerous—creditors who had their own reasons to prefer one or the other tribunal.

Whenever the Council of Brabant and the Great Council were unable to solve the jurisdiction dispute—which seemed to have happened rather frequently[240]—the case was presented to the central government in order to have the matter settled. In these disputes, they bombarded each other—and the Privy Council/the governor—with precedents and jurisprudence. In addition, the Great Council complained

[240] For example: Brussels, ARA, GRM 163, mémoriaux, f. 11–15, 1711: conflict of jurisdiction between the Council of Brabant and the Great Council on the inheritance of Pierre François de Blondel, baron d'Oudenhove Sainte-Marie, president of the Privy Council; Brussels, ARA, GRM 166, mémoriaux, f. 277–296, 1729–1730: conflict of jurisdiction on the inheritance of Jean, comte de T'Serclaes-Tilly and Marie-Françoise de Montmorency; Brussels, ARA, GRM 167, mémoriaux, f. 18–34, 1728–1732: conflict of jurisdiction on the inheritance of councilor de Lindicq; Brussels, ARA, GR Register 147, f. 82–96, 1751: conflict of jurisdiction on the inheritance of count de Fraula; Brussels, ARA, GR Register 455, f. 50–70, February 13, 1766: conflict of jurisdiction on the guardianship of the underaged children of councilor de Coloma; etc.

about the attitude of the councilors of Brabant. And indeed, certain examples seem to suggest that the latter were at times simply obnoxious.[241]

When deciding these conflicts of jurisdiction, the Privy Council sometimes sided with the Council of Brabant, while at other times it settled the issue in favor of the Great Council. Just as was the case with the conflicts between the Great Council and its subordinate tribunals, this might have been a well-considered strategy of the central government in order to prevent one of the councils from accumulating too much power.

The Great Council had as many conflicts of jurisdiction with the Council of Hainaut as it had with the Council of Brabant, but they were of a more territorial nature. Several villages situated in the present province of Hainaut were in the eighteenth century seigniorial domains, which enjoyed full jurisdiction and which for historical reasons were not subjected to any provincial council. As a rule, all areas that did not answer to a provincial court belonged to the authority of the Great Council. The Council of Hainaut, in its attempt to establish its jurisdiction over these domains, often clashed with the Great Council.[242] The inhabitants of these regions regularly played a major role in these conflicts, as they were usually the ones who requested the Great Council to become involved in the debates.

The majority of the conflicts of jurisdiction between the Great Council and the Council of Hainaut dealt with the so-called *terres de débat* or 'contested territories'. These consisted of seven villages—Flobecq, Wodecq, Ellezelles, Lessines, Bois-de-Lessines, Papignies and Ogy—which took their nickname from the fact that in the Middle-Ages they had been contested between the Count of Flanders and the Count of Hainaut. Since the dispute was never really solved—although from the Burgundy period on, both regions belonged to the same sovereign—Charles V's decree of December 15, 1515 'temporarily' assigned the jurisdiction over these contested villages to the Great Council of Malines. In the early eighteenth century, the situation stood at what had been established 200 years earlier, meaning that the Great Council

[241] For instance, in one of the conflicts of jurisdiction with the Great Council, the councilors of Brabant brushed the Great Council's arguments aside by simply claiming that the examples the Great Council cited of the period after 1727 should be considered as pure usurpations of the Council of Brabant's jurisdiction: ARA, GRM, 168C, mémoriaux, f. 55–84, 1743: conflict of jurisdiction between the Council of Brabant and the Great Council on the inheritance of the registrar of the Council of Finance de Francquen. In the seventeenth century as well, the councilors of the Council of Brabant had deliberately tried to humiliate the members of the Great Council by awarding them the same honorarium to act as supplementary judges in revision cases as the members of the Councils of Flanders and Luxemburg, who were obviously subordinate to them. Gaillard, Arthur. 1898–1902. *Le Conseil de Brabant: histoire, organisation, procédure*. Brussels: Lebègue, t. 2, 279.

[242] E.g. In 1715, both councils claimed the jurisdiction over the village of Pipaix. Brussels, ARA, GRM 163, mémoriaux, f. 188–199, 1715. In 1757, a comparable conflict arose about the village of Lembeek. Brussels, ARA, GR Register 466, f. 132–143, November 17, 1759. In this case, the central government decided to divide the jurisdiction between the two councils. *ROPBA*, t. 8, p. 343, November 28, 1759.

was qualified for the *terres de débat* in exclusion of the Council of Hainaut (as well as of the Council of Flanders).[243]

Inevitably, this led to various conflicts of jurisdiction in which the inhabitants of the contested territories invariably complained about infractions on their rights by the Council of Hainaut.[244] Since these kinds of infringements on the authority of the Great Council regularly happened and forced the inhabitants of the *terres de débat* to denounce this violation of their rights, often at great cost, the Great Council pleaded for a decree that would put an end to it.[245]

The solution to the eternal problem of which court could exercise authority over the *terres de débat*, was probably not exactly the answer the Great Council had had in mind when urging the central government for a permanent arrangement in 1723. In 1737, the tribunal received a request to give its advice on a proposition for a new jurisdiction in the contested territories, worked out by the Council of Flanders and the Council of Hainaut.[246] Both courts had decided to bury the hatchet and to divide between them the authority the Great Council had had for several centuries. Officially, the Councils of Flanders and Hainaut wished to offer relief to the inhabitants of these *terres de débat*, who had always been forced to seek justice in a 'foreign country' (Malines) and put an end to the constant conflicts of jurisdiction. Therefore, the Councils of Flanders and Hainaut proposed to assign the two largest villages—Flobecq and Ellezelles—to Flanders and the other five—Lessines, Wodecq, Bois de Lessines, Ogy and Papignies—to Hainaut. This division was only valid as far as the Great Council had had authority over these territories, meaning in criminal and personal cases. For all real actions, the Council of Hainaut retained jurisdiction over all seven villages. This way, the century long debate would finally be solved to the advantage of both the inhabitants and the two councils.

It should be no surprise that the Great Council was not thrilled with the deal worked out by Flanders and Hainaut. In their advice, the councilors did their best to invalidate the arguments of the two provinces. First, the Council argued that all territories that did not belong to a province came under the Great Council. Since both councils admitted that the seven villages were only neighboring, it was obvious that the Great Council was responsible. Secondly, according to the councilors, the Council of Flanders had never exercised any jurisdiction at all in these regions.

---

243 For more information see: Cauchies, Jean Marie. 1974. Le Grand Conseil des ducs de Bourgogne, le Parlement de Malines et les 'terres de débat' (Lessines-Flobecq): à propos de publications récentes. *Bulletin du cercle royal d'histoire et d'archéologie d'Ath et de la région et musée athois* 8: 346–350; Cauchies, Jean Marie, Desmaele, Bernard and Mariage, Florian. 2009. *Les institutions publiques régionales et locales en Hainaut et Tournais-Tournaisis sous l'Ancien Régime*. Brussels: Algemeen Rijksarchief.

244 E.g, Brussels, ARA, GRM 165, mémoriaux, f. 671–675, 1727: conflict of jurisdiction between the Great Council and the Council of Hainaut over Flobecq.

245 Brussels, ARA, GRM 164, mémoriaux, f. 402–407, 1721–1723: conflict of jurisdiction between the Great Council and the aldermen of Mons over Wodecq.

246 Brussels, ARA, GRM 168A, mémoriaux, f. 457–485, 1737–1740: Dossier relatif à un projet de partage de la terre de Lessines entre la Flandre et le Hainaut, présenté par les conseils de justice de ces deux provinces.

Accordingly, it could not claim any authority solely based on a dispute with Hainaut several centuries ago. Furthermore, the Great Council continued, it was not the privilege of the provincial councils to determine this conflict of jurisdiction. Only the sovereign had the power to change anything about the present circumstances. Since the two provincial councils acknowledged that the knot had become ever more inextricable as time had passed, the sovereign might consider it wiser to leave the issue at its present state.

Moreover, it was obvious to the Great Council that Flanders and Hainaut only served their own interests and not those of the sovereign or those of the people of the *terres de débat*, who, after all, had never complained about the arrangement. Apart from that, the councilors also saw several inconveniences the new settlement would bring about. First of all, it would only be another temporary solution and would necessarily produce other conflicts of jurisdiction, this time between the Council of Hainaut and the Council of Flanders. But more importantly, since Flobecq and Ellezelles would now resort to the Council of Flanders, the inhabitants of these villages would have to deal with an extra instance. After the case had been treated in Ghent, the final stage still remained Malines. Not only would that in no way solve the problem of distance, but it would also cause additional costs for the parties while lawsuits would drag on for an even longer time.

In order to know the opinion of the authorities of the seven villages, the Great Council sent them the proposal for the new settlement. Apparently, Flanders and Hainaut had not bothered to consult the people involved when working out the agreement. In the next few years, several officials, such as the intendant of the dame of Lessines and Flobecq, Elisabeth of Lorraine, the bailiff of Flobecq and Lessines, the aldermen of Ellezelle and Papignies, the lord of Wodecq and the aldermen of Bois de Lessines sent their advice to the Great Council. Except for the lord of Wodecq who did not really have strong opinions on the matter, all those concerned were absolutely ill-disposed towards the proposal of Flanders and Hainaut.

The Great Council sent these replies together with its own advice to the Privy Council. If the sovereign felt the need to change anything at all about the present situation, the Great Council thought it would be better to assign all the *terres de débat* to one single council, preferably the Council of Hainaut.[247] Despite the negative advice of the contested territories and of the Great Council, the Count of Königsegg sanctioned the agreement between the Council of Flanders and the Council of Hainaut with an official ordinance on March 26, 1743.[248] Thereby the governor not only finally solved a matter that had dragged on ever since the sixteenth century, but he also deprived the Great Council of another part of its jurisdiction. While the *terres de débat* were in terms of quantity of lawsuits rather insignificant, this further loss of jurisdiction must have come as a serious (psychological) blow to the councilors. Indeed, to what extent was the central government still willing to support the Great

[247] This might sound somewhat contradictory, but we presume that the Great Council assumed that the Council of Flanders would never agree to such a solution and that in the end, nothing would change.

[248] *ROPBA*, t. 5, pp. 540–541, March 26, 1743.

Council in its status as superior council of the Netherlands, if it sanctioned the limitation of its jurisdiction by the Council of Hainaut?

3.3.3.3 Other Tribunals

Except for interactions with the major provincial councils, the Great Council also came in regular contact with smaller tribunals, such as for example the Magistrate of Brussels,[249] the Council of Tournai or the Council of Gelre. The status of the latter was somewhat ambiguous. While, according to Berkvens, the Council was sovereign[250]—which was also corroborated by the ordinance of 1737, introducing a new judicial organization in Roermond[251]—and it enjoyed the right *de non evocando* the distribution records indicate that some parties in Gelre still took their cases to the Great Council.[252]

In the early eighteenth century, the Austrian government had considered depriving the Council of Gelre of its sovereign status and integrating the tribunal within the jurisdiction of the Great Council. Nevertheless, because of the importance of the free seigniories—Weert, Wessem, Nederweert, Meyel, Obbicht and Pappenhoven—which were connected to the Austrian part of Gelre,[253] the High Council of the Netherlands eventually advised Charles VI to maintain the Council of Gelre as a sovereign court and to appoint a trustworthy chancellor at its head. Yet, given the small jurisdiction the Council of Gelre had and the related limited income the councilors received, it proved to be very difficult to find suitable candidates for the councilors' seats and even more so for the position of chancellor.[254] As a result, parties regularly challenged (several of) the councilors either because they were considered to be prejudiced or because they were suspected to be incompetent.[255] Consequently, while the Council of Gelre in theory enjoyed the right of *de non evocando*, the Privy Council often had no other choice than to approve the request

[249] Brussels, ARA, GRM 164, mémoriaux, f. 615–618: conflict of jurisdiction with the Magistrate of Brussels on the arrest of the bailiff of the Great Council Jean Van Steijnemeulen.

[250] Berkvens, Aloyisus M.J.A. 1990. 'Un emploi de haut nom et d'une rapport modique'. De benoeming van kanseliers van het Oostenrijks Hof van Gelre. *Maaslands Mélange* 14: 55–65.

[251] *ROPBA*, t. 5, pp. 191–193, October 2, 1737.

[252] Cf. Excel database: distribution records of the eighteenth century Great Council.

[253] See: Wassink, Jos F.A. 2005. *Van stad en buitenie: een institutionele studie van rechtspraak en bestuur in Weert 1568–1795*. Hilversum: Verloren.

[254] Berkvens, Aloyisus M.J.A. 1990. 'Un emploi de haut nom et d'une rapport modique'. De benoeming van kanseliers van het Oostenrijks Hof van Gelre. *Maaslands Mélange* 14: 59.

[255] Examples of lawsuits that were treated by the Great Council after *évocation*: Brussels, ARA, GR Register 356, f. 389–401, August 26, 1730. Case of Guillaume Adrien de Freneau, councilor of the Council of Gelre, asking *évocation* of his case to the Great Council because of the multiple errors made during his lawsuit; Brussels, ARA, GR Register 361, f. 78–81, June 22, 1731: *évocation* of all lawsuits concerning the 'Land of Daelembroek' from the Council of Gelre to the Great Council after the plaintiff had challenged six out of seven judges of the Council of Gelre; Brussels, ARA, GR Register 427, f. 162–168, August 14, 1753: *évocation* of all the lawsuits concerning the legacy of the marquis de Schenck from the Council of Gelre to the Great Council.

for *évocation*. Moreover, tying the Council of Gelre to the Great Council by means of *évocation* could have been a strategy to keep a certain form of control over this rather remote province, which shared several borders with non-Austrian territory, including the Prince-Bishopric of Liège, certain German states and the Republic.

Another tribunal with a rather ambiguous relationship to the Great Council was the Council of Tournai.[256] In 1716, the Superior Court of Justice of Tournai was abolished and its jurisdiction transferred to the Council of Flanders. In practice, this meant that Flanders would deal with all appeal cases against the sentences of the Magistrate of Tournai and of the *officiers du bailliage*.[257] The distribution books, however, demonstrate that from that time on, many inhabitants of Tournai also directly appealed to the Great Council. Moreover, in 1773, in order to end the multiple conflicts of jurisdiction and to speed up the settlement of the lawsuits, Empress Maria Theresa abolished the *siège royal du bailliage* and instead established the provincial Council of Tournai. The sentences of the latter tribunal could be directly appealed against at the Great Council without the intermediary of the Council of Flanders.[258] In 1782, an official decree again transferred the jurisdiction over Tournai, this time to the Council of Hainaut,[259] meaning that the Great Council lost once again a small though not inconsiderable part of its jurisdiction. In practice however, certain appeals from Tournai continued to be brought before the Great Council.

This, for example, happened in November 1783, when Pierre Joseph du Fermond requested to appeal to the Great Council against a criminal sentence—pronounced by the Council of Tournai—condemning him to several years of banishment. The principal question was if appeal against criminal judgments of the Council of Tournai was possible at all. According to the councilors of Tournai, they had always judged by arrest in criminal trials. The Great Council on the other hand, claimed that appeal was possible, at least to suspend the execution of the judgment. In this particular case, the Great Council considered itself competent to deal with the appeal, because firstly, it was not clear if the Council of Tournai had been authorized to take on the trial, and secondly, because it was obvious—at least according to the accused—that several mistakes had been made by the councilors of Tournai. In other words, the Great Council wanted to accept the appeal on pure formal grounds.

The Privy Council in its advice to the governor noticed that it would be inconsequent to admit an appeal against a criminal sentence while at the same time have it executed. After all, when a judgment was appealed, the supposition was that the judges who rendered it were not entirely to be trusted and that they had made a mistake. However, it was absolutely absurd to have the condemned undergo an

[256] Cf. Cauchies, Jean Marie, Desmaele, Bernard and Mariage, Florian. 2009. *Les institutions publiques régionales et locales en Hainaut et Tournais-Tournaisis sous l'Ancien Régime*. Brussels: Algemeen Rijksarchief.

[257] *ROPBA*, t. 3, p. 36, August 19, 1716.

[258] Brussels, ARA, GRM 138, correspondances, f. 26–40, February 24, 1791. This change is also reflected in the distribution records. In the years 1770, the number of appeals from Tournai in Malines is considerable. Cf. Excel database: distribution records of the eighteenth century Great Council.

[259] *ROPBA*, t. 12, pp. 216–217, November 22, 1782.

execution of the sentence—which by definition could not be repaired—before the appeal judge was able to review the trial. Moreover, if it was decided that the sentence should be reviewed, this would only create a general popular disturbance. What was the point of giving someone who was condemned to death the right to appeal against a sentence if, despite the appeal, he had to undergo the judgment? The Privy Council did admit that the practice existed in Flanders, but added that the jurisprudence in Tournai had changed. Therefore, du Fermont should endure his punishment.[260]

This example demonstrates that the central government thought it wise to have the Great Council accept appeals against criminal sentences of the Council of Flanders but not of the Council of Tournai. Obviously, the Privy Council—and the governors—used two standards to decide what in practice amounted to the same question. Especially since Tournai had at least for a while appealed to Flanders, it seems that the central government had some ulterior motives than just 'to conserve the customs and habits of Tournai'. The arguments used by the Privy Council in the du Fermont case—that it would be inconsistent to admit an appeal against a criminal sentence while at the same time executing it—were equally applicable to the Keppens and other related cases coming from the Council of Flanders. Potentially, the Privy Council and the government may have considered it more important to keep the Council of Flanders under their control than the smaller and less powerful Council of Tournai. Moreover, this policy of allowing the Great Council to deal with appeals against criminal sentences from one provincial council but not from another might have fitted perfectly in the central government's divide and rule strategy.

3.3.4 Status Anxiety?: Relations with the Privy Council

The position the Great Council held towards the Privy Council is not undisputed: not at present, considering the ideas of de Schepper,[261] and not in the past given the countless conflicts of jurisdictions between the two institutions.[262] In two articles—one from 1978 and one more nuanced from 1998—de Schepper argued that not the Great Council but rather the Privy Council was the highest tribunal of the Netherlands. According to de Schepper, the ordinances of 1531 and 1540, which had explicitly removed the administration of justice from the responsibilities of the

[260] Brussels, ARA, GR, Register 479, f. 274–278, September 1, 1783.

[261] De Schepper, Hugo. 1978. De Grote Raad van Mechelen, hoogste rechtscollege in de Nederlanden? *Bijdragen en Mededelingen betreffende de Geschiedenis der Nederlanden* 93: 358–376 and De Schepper, Hugo. 1998. De Geheime Raad als hoogste rechtscollege in de Nederlanden (1504–1580). In *Handelingen van het tweede Hof van Holland Symposium gehouden op 14 November 1997 in de Treveszaal te Den Haag*, ed. Rob Huijbrecht, 39–48. The Hague: Algemeen Rijksarchief.

[262] Oosterbosch, Michel. 2001. *Appelprocedure, dossierbehandeling en registervoering bij de Grote Raad van Mechelen*. In: *Voortschrijdend procesrecht. Een historische verkenning*, eds. Fred Stevens, Ernest Persoons and Remco Van Rhee. Leuven: Universitaire Pers Leuven, 5.

Privy Council, remained a dead letter. Throughout the sixteenth century, the latter dealt with ever more cases which had originally been reserved for the Great Council or the provincial tribunals, and appropriated the jurisdiction over the *escroux*, the treatment of *casus reservati* and the settlement of conflicts (of jurisdiction) between several institutions. Based on counts in the Privy Council's dicta and the Great Council's extended sentences, de Schepper calculated that the Privy Council handled up to 30 % of all lawsuits. Moreover, the Privy Council possessed the prerogative of granting pardon and could interfere in pending lawsuits with all sorts of suspending measures.

In addition, de Schepper argued, while the Great Council remained the main tribunal for appeal cases, the Privy Council could revise the arrests of the Great Council as well as those of other sovereign tribunals. On the other hand, the Great Council did not have any competence to deal with appeals against the Privy Council's sentences. Finally, the Privy Council enjoyed the right to award *lettres d'évocation* which, in theory, it could use to its own advantage. However, de Schepper admitted that in practice the Council almost never made use of the privilege and waited for a request of the parties to withdraw a lawsuit from the competent court.

Right after the first lecture of de Schepper on the matter,[263] several critiques were formulated. His more nuanced contribution of 1998[264] did not remain undisputed either.[265] While we have no intention of reopening the discussion, we would like to make some additional comments on de Schepper's ideas. First, the numbers on which de Schepper relied in order to argue that the Privy Council dealt with ever more lawsuits in comparison to the Great Council are somewhat misleading. In fact, de Schepper compared the number of extended sentences pronounced at the Great Council with the number of dicta he could find for the Privy Council. Not only do these dicta contain, apart from definitive sentences, several provisional dispositions—which means that two or even more dicta can relate to one single lawsuit—but they also have an entirely other status than the extended sentences. While we can reasonably assume that most lawsuits ended in a dictum,[266] extended sentences represented only a fraction of all sentences pronounced.[267] Moreover, de Schepper only investigated the sixteenth century until 1580. The eighteenth century, however, presents a somewhat different picture. For example, while de Schepper argued that the Privy Council became more or less the tribunal by default to deal with

[263] In 1974 on the occasion of the 'celebration' of 500 year Great Council of Malines.

[264] De Schepper, Hugo. 1998. De Geheime Raad als hoogste rechtscollege in de Nederlanden (1504–1580). In *Handelingen van het tweede Hof van Holland Symposium gehouden op 14 November 1997 in de Treveszaal te Den Haag*, ed. Rob Huijbrecht. The Hague: Algemeen Rijksarchief, 39.

[265] Oosterbosch, Michel. 2001. *Appelprocedure, dossierbehandeling en registervoering bij de Grote Raad van Mechelen*. In: *Voortschrijdend procesrecht. Een historische verkenning*, eds. Fred Stevens, Ernest Persoons and Remco Van Rhee. Leuven: Universitaire Pers Leuven, 5–6.

[266] At least, if they were prosecuted until the end.

[267] As we will demonstrate in Chap. 4, the extended sentences represented only the tip of the iceberg.

the *escroux*, the distribution records demonstrate that even councilors of the Privy Council introduced their lawsuits at the Great Council in the eighteenth century.[268]

Nevertheless, it is certainly true that in the 1700s as well, the relationship between the Privy Council and the Great Council was rather complex. On the one hand, both councils shared their origins and some of their members—a seat in the Privy Council was an interesting career move for the councilors of the Great Council—but on the other hand, the Privy Council had, at least indirectly, a certain authority over the Great Council. It was the Privy Council which advised the government on the new councilors to appoint, which consulted the governor in conflicts of jurisdiction between the Great Council and other tribunals and which also had a certain authority to interfere with the expedition of justice by according suspension of the execution of a sentence.

In their relations with the members of the Privy Council, the councilors of the Great Council seemed to have suffered from some sort of 'inferiority complex'. Indeed, the Great Council often felt the need to remind the Privy Council of their common origins—even though they dated back to the late fifteenth century—and underlined that the tribunal was not in any way inferior or subordinate to the Privy Council in the expedition of justice. Undoubtedly, this sense of inferiority was also connected to their place of residence: the Privy Council had its sessions in the former palace of the dukes of Brabant on the *Koudenberg* in Brussels, located near the governor's residence and close to the power base of the Austrian Netherlands, while the Great Council assembled in the former palace of Margaretha of Austria, which, admittedly, was somewhat prestigious, but still in Malines. And their place of residence—given that it used to be the seat of the central government in the early sixteenth century—might actually have worked as a constant reminder of the perished glory of the now merely second rate city.

Their wish to uphold their importance, as a result of some sort of collective 'status anxiety', influenced the many conflicts the members of the Great Council had with their colleagues on the Privy Council. When defending its rights against the attempts of infringement by the Privy Council, the Malines tribunal often had to request the assistance of the governor, thereby already betraying its weak position. Moreover, the governor was far from always willing to support the Great Council and, on certain occasions, the councilors' protests against the 'usurpation' of their authority even backfired.

This was especially the case in 1737, when the Privy Council, on the request of Frédéric count d'Eynatten, awarded the suspension of the execution of a sentence, pronounced by the Great Council, in a lawsuit against his mother-in-law.[269] The councilors were furious, first of all because it was clear that the Privy Council interfered with their jurisdiction: the latter often granted suspensions of sentences of the Great Council on the simple demand of one of the parties, without being

[268] Cf. Excel database: distribution records of the eighteenth century Great Council. For example: "Le seigneur conseiller au conseil privé, de Robiano, et consors supls contre Chretien Alexandre de la Croix escr seigr de Manbraij rescribent". Lawsuit distributed on June 4, 1740.

[269] Brussels, ARA, GRM 168A, mémoriaux, f. 259–271, July 20, 1737.

familiar with all the circumstances of the lawsuit. According to the councilors, this was an outward assault on the status of the Great Council. Moreover, the councilors argued, Charles V himself had ordered the Great Council in 1517 not to defer to any attempts to hamper the course of justice.

The Great Council was also convinced that the members of the Privy Council had abused the clause *à la délibération du lieutenant, gouverneur et capitaine général*: it could hardly be true that Governess Maria-Elisabeth had consented to such an injurious suspension of the normal administration of justice of the 'Majesty's first council in the Austrian Netherlands'. According to the Great Council, the Privy Council abused this clause to extend its power beyond the limits of its jurisdiction. The councilors feared that if they had to obey this suspension decree, the Privy Council would easily be able to entirely subordinate the Great Council to its authority, something it had already unsuccessfully attempted in the past. Therefore, the Great Council was convinced that the governess should forbid the Privy Council to issue any suspensions in the future or in any other way hamper the administration of justice.

To their surprise, the members of the Great Council were reproached by Maria-Elisabeth regarding their disobedience of what was apparently an order she had personally approved of. By a decree of August 6, 1737, she compelled the councilors to erase their complaint from their registers and to personally give proof that they had carried out her order. The Great Council immediately responded with an apology, claiming that it had never had the intention to disobey a direct order from the governess or to disrespect her authority. From the moment the members knew that Maria-Elisabeth herself had decreed the suspension, it was implemented. Therefore, the councilors added, they hoped that she would excuse them from erasing their opinions, as it would be a disgrace for the Great Council and constitute a pretext for the Privy Council to accuse them of defying the orders of the governess.

The Great Council even sent delegates to plead its cause with Maria Elisabeth.[270] She consented to excuse the councilors from the personal appearance, but insisted on the erasing of their notes. Nevertheless, she also granted the councilors the opportunity to present a memorandum in order to explain their position with regards to the Privy Council and to protest the constant interference of the latter with their jurisdiction. Based on this memo, the governess could decide for herself which of the two councils constantly overstepped the boundaries of its authority.

Little more than a month later, the councilors presented a letter several pages long that reads as a lengthy apology of their behavior and a denunciation of the Privy Council's attitude.[271] After all, the councilors complained, the Privy Council constantly tried to interfere with the administration of justice, even though the Great Council was in no way subordinate to the Privy Council. Despite the ordinance of 1725, which specifically determined that all legal disputes had to be sent to the Great Council, the Privy Council continued to infringe on the Great Council's do-

[270] Brussels, ARA, GRM 168A, mémoriaux, f. 333–335, September 26, 1737.

[271] Brussels, ARA, GRM 168A, mémoriaux, f. 291–308v, November 5, 1737.

main. According to the councilors, it was clear that the Privy Council's only goal was to completely subdue the Great Council.

When only a short time later, the Privy Council again suspended the execution of a sentence of the Great Council, the latter urged Count Frederik d'Harrach—temporary representative of the Austrian government in Brussels—to settle the dispute once and for all. Finally, in December 1738, it was decided that in the future no suspensions could be issued unless they had been signed by the governor.[272] Nevertheless, this did not entirely stop the Privy Council from interfering in the Great Council's matters. Only after the death of governess Maria-Elisabeth, an ordinance of Maria Theresa of 1744[273] put an end to what the Great Council considered to be the constant mingling of the Privy Council with the administration of justice.[274] This time, the decree apparently did not remain a dead letter. In fact, the distribution records demonstrate that, after 1743, the Privy Council stopped sending lawsuits close to conclusion to the Great Council just to draw up the final judgment; at the same time, the Privy Council would no longer demand from the Great Council to have a specific lawsuit forwarded for further treatment at its own institution.[275]

This however did not signal the end to the stormy relations between the Great Council and the Privy Council. The latter merely moved its sphere of action to another area: finances. A decree from 1760 obliged the councilors of the Great Council to have their expenses inspected.[276] From 1760 on, the Great Council could only freely spend its financial resources on lighting, paper, small repairs and the payment of report money in criminal cases. The new rule had been implemented as a reaction against what was considered the Great Council's squandering of public means on unnecessary conflicts of jurisdiction, on payments for messengers who were sent to Brussels to collect the councilors' salary, or on presents given to, for example, the primus of the University of Leuven. The president of the Great Council considered this new rule to be an unacceptable limitation of an authority it had always enjoyed. After all, in all conflicts of jurisdiction, the defense of the sovereign's rights stood central. The many disputes the councilors had with other tribunals to preserve their privileges should be considered a service to the sovereign. According to the presi-

---

[272] Brussels, ARA, GRM 168A, mémoriaux, f. 308v–310r, December 12, 1738

[273] *ROPBA*, t. 5, pp. 591–592, January 22, 1744.

[274] The Privy Council did not only hamper the administration of justice at the Great Council. Gaillard described that one of the biggest problems of the Council of Brabant was the constant interference of the central government in the administration of justice. Gaillard, Arthur. 1898–1902. *Le Conseil de Brabant: histoire, organisation, procédure*. Brussels: Lebègue, t. 2, p. 116: "Les gouverneurs généraux intervinrent dans l'administration de la justice, soit sur les instigations du conseil privé, soit à la requête d'un plaideur mécontent, cherchant à vexer ses juges ou à obtenir, par voie détournée, le redressement d'une décision défavorable à ses prétentions. Le conseil dut à tout instant se justifier, réfuter des plaintes non fondées ou des allégations diffamatoires."

[275] Cf. Excel database: distribution records of the eighteenth century Great Council. Cases sent from the Privy Council are usually indicated as "*du conseil privé*". If the Privy Council demanded to have a lawsuit sent for treatment, the remark mentions: "*envoyé au conseil privé*". For example: May 10, 1698, the burghers of Ostend against Arnould Mintens: "*envoyé au conseil privé ensuite de ses lettres du premier febvrier de la mesme année*".

[276] Brussels, ARA, GR Register 463, f. 86–94, February 24, 1770.

dent, asking permission in advance would not solve the problem, since it would only increase the costs as well as the length of the disputes.

The Privy Council on the other hand, defended the supervision of the Great Council's spending as a well thought-out policy. Without any form of control, abuses abounded. If, on the contrary, the courts were obliged to ask for permission before they started disputing each other's jurisdiction or defending their privileges, then they would think twice before plunging into another lengthy and expensive lawsuit. That the law had positive effects, the Privy Council added, could be easily derived from the steady decrease in conflicts of jurisdiction between the Great Council on the one hand and especially the Council of Flanders or the Magistrate of Malines on the other.[277]

The Privy Council also did not shy away from using its direct line of communication with the governor to control the Great Council and even sometimes 'humiliate' the court. Almost every time the latter addressed the governor on some matter or another, the request was sent to the Privy Council for advice. In at least one instance, the Privy Council recommended the governor not to answer the question because it would be 'beneath his dignity'. In 1765, the councilors of the Great Council were divided over the question if they were still competent to judge the lawsuit between Jean Louis de Carondelet and the Jesuits of Tournai in relation to certain lands which had belonged to the Netherlands before the War of the Austrian Succession, but which were now in French territory.[278] The main problem was that the original lawsuit dated from the late seventeenth century, when the domain still fell under the jurisdiction of the Great Council. Since the Peace Treaty ending the War of the Austrian Succession did not really answer the question and the councilors could not arrive at unanimity, they addressed the governor to decide the matter.

The latter sent the request to the Privy Council, which in its advice expressed its surprise that the issue could have ignited such a conflict of opinion among judges who were supposed to be enlightened and well versed in the administration of justice. The Privy Council observed that it was even more astonishing that in order to reach an agreement, they had considered it necessary to turn to the central government for what was really a very simple legal question. Since this was a case in which territory was involved, and since some of those lands were now part of the Kingdom of France, it was clear that the French tribunals were competent for the domains under French rule, while the Great Council should judge over those that still belonged to the Austrian Netherlands. The Peace Treaty was not an argument in this rather simple question. Nevertheless, the Privy Council remarked, it could not advise the Great Council on this matter, as the administration of justice was outside of its jurisdiction … Therefore, the Privy Council recommended the governor—who conformed to it—not to respond and to have the Great Council, which in the end was the superior tribunal of the Netherlands, settle the matter for itself.

[277] If this was truly the case can be doubted. In fact, the conflicts between the Great Council and the Council of Flanders and the Magistrate of Malines continued to arise until the 1790s. Cf. infra, Chap. 5.

[278] Brussels, ARA, GR Register 453, f. 216–223, 1765.

Returning to de Schepper's thesis, we have to agree that for some time the Privy Council did constantly interfere in the administration of justice of the Great Council—and not only of the Great Council. However, several ordinances of the late 1730s and early 1740s seriously limited the influence of the Privy Council in this regard and this time the law did not remain a dead letter. Nevertheless, the Privy Council continued to dominate the Great Council and articulate its superiority in various ways. The fact that most interactions between the governor and the Great Council happened through the agency of the Privy Council gave the latter an important advantage in terms of influence, which it gleefully used to its own benefit.

Conclusion

Can we conclude from our analysis of the 'framework' of the Great Council that the central government still actively intervened in the Great Council's organization and supported its position with regards to other institutions in the Austrian Netherlands or do we have to decide that it merely left the tribunal to languish? There are arguments for both hypotheses. The procedure-ordinance of 1559 was indeed the last all-encompassing ordinance organizing the Great Council's workings, but several individual decrees in the seventeenth and eighteenth centuries attempted to remedy recurring problems. Other issues were solved almost 'organically', without the explicit intervention of the central government: the time-consuming procedure on the *rôle* gradually gave way to the more expedient communicatory procedure.

On the other hand, there were also certain consistent difficulties that the central government did not attempt to rectify. In this regard, we have to especially mention the declining income of the members of the Great Council, an issue of which they regularly bitterly complained to the central government. And while there was undoubtedly a certain amount of exaggeration in their lamentations, it is true that they at least relatively impoverished throughout the eighteenth century as their sources of income were not adjusted to match inflation: their fixed wages had not been increased since the early seventeenth century and their *épices* were only marginally raised. In addition, they had to allow the curtailment of their privileges during certain periods, such as after the French occupation of 1746–1748. As a result, it became ever more difficult to recruit the 'best and the brightest'.

The central government was equally Janus-faced with regards to the position of the Great Council in the Austrian Netherlands. There should be no doubt that the Magistrate of Malines as well as the provincial councils attempted to extend their authority at the expense of the Great Council. At the same time, the latter also tried to increase its control over certain areas and in particular over the domain of criminal justice. For the Magistrate of Malines, the Council of Flanders, the Council of Namur and the Council of Tournai we have examples that prove that the Great Council attempted to extend its jurisdiction to appeals against criminal sentences, while these were at least in theory unappealable. It is telling that the Great Council only succeeded in this attempt with regards to the Council of Flanders.

In general, the central government did not pursue a consistent policy: at times it supported the Great Council in its conflicts with its subordinate tribunals, at other times it ruled against the Malines tribunal. The same is true for its relations with the sovereign councils of Hainaut and Brabant. While it is not clear cut that this was a very well thought-out policy, there are reasons to assume that the government was guided by a semi-conscious *divide et impera* strategy in playing off the different institutions in the Austrian Netherlands' society against each other. Only in its conflicts with the ecclesiastical authorities did the central government consistently support the Great Council, especially after 1740. Yet, this attitude fitted entirely in the general policy of the central government to curtail the power of the (Ultramontane) Church.

The relations with the central government itself—predominantly with or at least through the agency of the Privy Council—were equally complicated. Certainly, as de Schepper has indicated, the Privy Council stepped on the domain of the Great Council. Yet, it did so rather by indiscriminately awarding suspensions of the latter's sentences than by actually taking over the administration of justice. However, the interference of the Privy Council in that regard was seriously limited in the 1740s and eventually even quasi-abolished. On the other hand, after that date, the Privy Council was allowed to move its authority over the Great Council to the domain of finances. Apparently, the governor and/or the sovereign used the same *divide et impera* strategy to play off the Privy Council and the Great Council against each other as the Privy Council used in deciding on the conflicts between the Great Council and the provincial tribunals.

It is also most obvious in its conflicts with the Privy Council that the members of the Great Council suffered from some sort of 'inferiority complex' and of a collective status anxiety. In fact, they constantly felt the need to underline their importance as the 'first tribunal of the Austrian Netherlands' and to remark that they were in no way subordinate to the Privy Council, having the same origins and enjoying the same privileges. In that regard, we can also wonder if the seemingly relative lack of internal dissent—at least compared with, for example, the Council of Brabant—is in any way connected to their multiple 'external' conflicts with the Magistrate of Malines, the Church, the provincial councils and the Privy Council. Were the councilors of the Great Council so concerned with their status and position in the larger society that they attempted to keep internal strife as limited as possible? In other words: did they suffer from such a collective status anxiety that they deliberately attempted to remain as close knit as possible as a corpus in order to be well armed to fight their battles with concurring institutions?

And secondly: why did they consider it necessary to so vigorously defend their tribunal? Had the Great Council really become so superfluous—as the Council of Flanders suggested—that the councilors needed to worry that they would indeed be condemned to the dole? Certainly, the loss of jurisdiction over the *terres de débat* and the Councils of Luxemburg and Tournai must have been a serious psychological blow, but was its effect on the quantity of cases dealt with really that significant? In fact, how much work did the court have in the eighteenth century? If we should believe the councilors of Flanders, the tribunal's sole reason of existence was its function as appeal court for the sentences of the Council of Flanders. On the other hand: in case we presume that there is a connection between the number of lawsuits the councilors dealt with and the amount of *épices* they received, the almost negligible differences in income between 1730 and 1765—even corrected for the small raise in *épices* they were awarded—do not seem to suggest a decline in activity of the Great Council. In order to assess how much work the Great Council had in the eighteenth century, we will examine the volume of litigation at the tribunal in the next chapter.

References

Archival Sources

Brussels, General State Archives

Audiëntie
1419/4
Geheime Raad. Registers
351, 352, 356, 358–361, 366, 369, 373, 399–401, 404, 406, 408, 413, 414, 416, 417, 419, 420, 423, 424, 426–428, 430, 432, 435, 437, 439–441, 443–446, 448, 449–457, 459, 460, 463, 464, 466–470, 473, 475, 476, 478–482, 484
Grote Raad van Mechelen. Registers

97–98; 133; 135–140 *Correspondence*

The "recueils de la correspondance du Grand Conseil" have been preserved for the entire history of the Council, covering the period between 1464 and 1794. The correspondence of the Great Council consists of a diverse array of letters and requests sent to or by the Great Council. The central government, usually through the Privy Council, is the main correspondent, but other institutions, such as provincial councils, and even individuals figure in these registers. The subject matter ranges from orders to organize a *Te Deum*, requests of all sort of dispensations, conflicts of jurisdiction with especially the Council of Flanders or the Magistrate of Malines, to instructions of the governor on how to respond to a potential invasion by the French. The only structure in this mishmash of documents is the date on which they were composed or received, but even this chronological criterion was not always rigorously followed. The registers provide a privileged insight into the judicial but even more into the non-judicial aspects of the Great Council's workings. However, the enormous volume of the series (consisting of 129 registers over a period of 330 years) and the lack of organization make research into the correspondence very time-consuming. The correspondence of the Great Council has its counterpart in the archives of the office-fiscal (GRMOF, Banden en Delen) which, however, suffers from the same problems.

141–142 Secret resolutions

The name given to these registers—*Registre aux résolutions secrètes du Grand Conseil toutes chambres réunies*—does not cover their content. In fact, even though GRM 141–142 are not included among the mémoriaux, to their content they belong to this series and the information they contain is as secret or public as that of the *mémoriaux*. This seemingly wrong identification of the documents did not happen in modern times but in fact dates from the eighteenth century. Why the series is only available for the eighteenth century—GRM 141 covers the period between 1700–1756 and the year 1788 while GRM 142 starts on November 26, 1756 and runs until 1791—is equally unclear. The issues discussed in these registers range from conflicts of jurisdiction with several kinds of institutions—provincial tribunals, the Council of Finance, military tribunals etc. -, requests for pardon, (infractions made on) privileges of the councilors, to letters from the central government announcing the appointment of a new governor or minister plenipotentiary. Together with the correspondence and the mémoriaux, these registers constitute the ideal source of information for the issues the Great Council dealt with outside the purely judicial domain.

160–168G *"Mémoriaux"*

The mémoriaux of the Great Council (GRM 143–168G) cover—albeit with certain gaps—the period between 1503 and 1781. The numbers 160–168G are relevant for the eighteenth century. An inventory by Gaillard is available for most of the mémoriaux, but for some unknown reason the numbers 168A until 168G—which are titled *Correspondances: mémoriaux*—are not included. Similarly, it remains unclear why GRM 162 is named *Registre aux résolutions secretes du Grand Conseil* but is still ranged within the series of the mémoriaux. It does however suggest that the two series are interrelated. The mémoriaux mainly consist of letters from the central administration to Malines and the responses, often formulated as advice, from the Great Council. They as well offer some insight into the larger environment in which the court operated throughout its existence. Of note are the various connections between the *mémoriaux* and the ordinances issued by the government: problems described in the *mémoriaux* are sometimes officially solved and then institutionalized by a decree. As was the case for the *Correspondence*, the information in the *mémoriaux* is chronologically ordered but this arrangement is once again not rigorously followed. The inventory of Gaillard, however, makes research much less time-consuming and difficult for those registers covered by it.

231–232 *Miscellaneous*

The "miscellaneous" category in Van den Bussche's inventory (consisting of the numbers 231–261/3) is indeed a collection of unrelated documents that do not really fit anywhere else. It consists mostly of marriage contracts, last wills and 'letters written by famous people that have been extracted from their case files'. The numbers 231 and 232, however, are even in this "miscellaneous" category somewhat "outsiders". Van den Bussche describes GRM 231 as cahier portant des annotations au sujet de certains faits auxquels le grand conseil s'est trouvé mêlé ou qui l'ont mis dans le cas de devoir prendre une délibération ou une consulte officieuse (1701–1800). In practice, the first part of this register is indeed an overview of unofficial decisions taken by the Great Council, mostly with regards to their ceremonial duties (such as congratulating a newly appointed governor or organizing a holy mess for the sovereign's health). The second part, however, mostly deals with the first invasion of the French in 1792 and describes in great detail the decisions regarding the stay of the Council in Düsseldorf and the councilors' dissatisfaction with this 'exile'. Finally, the register also includes the documents regarding the awarding of the title of 'Councilor of State' to the senior councilor of the Great Council in 1794. If the description of GRM 231 does not entirely cover its content and is probably an artificially put together collection, this is equally true for GRM 232. While the register is described in the inventory as Recueil des documents concernant le personnel du Grand Conseil, particulièrement les secrétaires, et diverses pièces touchant le rétablissement du siège en 1791, not many documents about any of those two subjects are included. Even though there is a long complaint by the secretaries denouncing the fact that, in violation of all ordinances, councilors 'steal' their work (and thereby their income) by awarding copying jobs to their personal assistants and a document describing the re-erection of the Great Council after the Brabant Revolution, the main part of the register is filled with a long letter of the councilors of the Great Council, dated in 1771, denouncing the ever growing jurisdiction of the Council of Luxemburg. As a rule, a wealth of information is often hidden behind inadequate descriptions, in the archives of the Great Council.

617–620 *Distribution records ranged by province of origin*
629–633 *Distribution records ranged by reporter*
635–637 *Distribution records of the "Différends"*

The distribution books record all the lawsuits introduced at the Great Council that reached the phase of 'distribution', i.e. the stage at which the case was assigned to a reporter. There is, however, at least one exception to this rule: only a very limited number of criminal cases were recorded in the distribution books. In general, distribution books contain the date of distribution, the instance, the procedure (appeal, first instance, *différend*, …), the name of the councilor reporter and the name (and sometimes a certain qualification) of the litigants. In several cases, but far from always, they also list the name of the procurators and the decision rendered. For the eighteenth century, the archives of the Great Council hold two different types of distribution records. While the first type contains both appeals and first instance cases, the second type is exclusively reserved for those lawsuits that followed the communicatory procedure (*différends*). Consequently, procedure is the distinguishing feature. In addition, the first type can again be divided into two subcategories, which do not much differ by the information they provide as by the way the data is arranged, i.e. by province of origin or by name of the councilor who acted as reporter. Comparison between these two categories had demonstrated that there is a considerable overlap and that possible lacunae must be attributed to the inevitable human errors of the registrar who recorded the cases. Why there are two further subcategories within the registers containing the appeals and first instance cases following the procedure on the rôle is less clear. In a certain way, they seem to represent an 'incoming stream' versus an 'outgoing stream'. Indeed, the distribution books arranged by province record in which part of the jurisdiction of the Great Council the lawsuits originated and thus entered the registry. The other subcategory records to which councilor the case was distributed. Even though the files did not literally leave the Great Council, we could say that the process of allocating a lawsuit to a certain member of the Council could be regarded as an 'outgoing stream', as the files left the registry. Possible this distinction was made as a means to keep track of all the files that were brought to the Great Council and to have an idea of the whereabouts of a certain file. The distribution records ranged by province of origin are available for the years 1613 until 1794; those ranged by councilor have been preserved for the year 1503, and then from 1542 up until 1794 with a gap between 1550 and 1601. Whether the 'missing' distribution records for the sixteenth century are lost or simply never existed, is unknown. The distribution records of the *Différends* only start at 1683. We presume that, before that date, they were recorded together with the other first instance and appeal cases, given the fact that the communicatory procedure only became popular over the course of the seventeenth century.

682–694 *Report Books. Liber Primus*
697–710 *Report Books. Liber Secundus*

The *livres dit aux rapports* (GRM 667–710) or report books list the *épices* each councilor received for his actual work at the tribunal, independent of his annual fixed salary. The information the report book supply is predominantly financial: they list the remuneration of the councilors for each case whether as reporter or as a regular judge. The report books clearly demonstrate a distribution of the councilors over two separate 'groups' which, as can be assumed, probably correspond to the two chambers of the Great Council. It is unknown what exactly the difference is between the liber primus and the liber secundus as they both list the épices of the councilors in the two chambers at the same time. It could have been connected to the functioning of the registry. Given that there were two registries—one 'upper' and one 'lower' registry—it might have been possible that the two books—primus and secundus—were kept by two different registrars. For the *liber primus*, the report books are available for the years 1661 until 1794, although there are a few gaps in the late seventeenth century. The *liber secundus* is preserved for the period between 1681 and 1752, with the exception of the years 1686–1707 which are missing. Apart from the *liber primus* and *secundus*, the archives of the Great Council also contain a series *rapports anciens* (GRM 667–678, 1564–1646) and *livres dits 'journaliers'* (GRM 711–720, 1619–1654) which also provide financial information, but as they do not pertain to the eighteenth century, they were not used in this research. While these financial sources make it possible to calculate by approximation the income of the councilors from their work in the tribunal, they also make it possible to discover how the court was internally organized: the partition in two chambers, their respective workload and their changing composition.

734 *Déclarations bis annuelles*

GRM 734 (1690–1729) provides for each councilor the official salary earned over a period of 6 months. The source can be used together with the *listes des gages du Grand Conseil* to reconstruct the fixed income of the members of the Great Council. The *Déclarations bis annuelles* (GRM 731–734) are available for the period between 1596 and 1729.

790–976 Extended sentences

Within the archives of the Great Council, the extended sentences (GRM 790–976) constitute a separate series, which—contrary to many others—is fairly exhaustive. The registers cover a period of some 300 years in which only the last two decades of the eighteenth century are missing. The absence of a register for the period between 1773 and 1794 can be explained by the specific manner in which these registers were compiled. In fact, they were originally written on separate quires and only after a certain period of time bound together into a single register. It is reasonable to presume that there were just not enough extended sentences in the last 20 years of the eighteenth century to bind together into a register. Further examination of the records of the Great Council has corroborated this theory; the archives contain a few separate extended sentences drafted in the period after 1772.
Every register until 1690—except for a limited period of time in the first half of the seventeenth century—contains one's year worth of extended sentences. In reality, this is not always the case: certain years are missing. Some of these turned out to be included in the register of the previous year, but others are completely absent. This probably does not mean that not a single extended sentence was registered in that specific year, but rather that the registers have gone astray in one of the different 'wanderings' of the archives. According to the procedure-ordinance of 1559 and a 'special' instruction for the redaction of extended sentences, it was the register or clerk who was responsible for recording these judgments. Based on certain documents in the case file, the registrar reconstructed in their case, after which a councilor proofread and corrected the text. In the eighteenth century, the extended sentences—drafted and pronounced in the name of the emperor—contained five elements: (1) the identification of the parties, including possible changes during the lawsuit (e.g. due to the death of one of the parties); (2) the subject of the dispute, often formulated at the request of the plaintiff; (3) an account of the progress of the case with a description of the principal acts of both litigants; (4) the primary arguments of the plaintiff and the defendant; (5) the decision. In case of appeal, accounts of all legal acts in the previous instance(s) were included as well as a summary of the appealed judgment.

It is unclear what purpose exactly the extended judgments had. Most cases in fact, were decided by a dictum while extended sentences were rather rare, probably because they were expensive to draft. Given that dicta were often short and lacked any detail about the parties or the case, it is likely that extended sentences functioned primarily as a 'title', as evidence for the future.

1029–1045 *Dicta*

The series of registers of dicta comprises 70 volumes, covering the period from 1475 to 1480 and then from 1502 until 1794. For the seventeenth and eighteenth centuries, there are even two parallel series, one of the *minutes* containing the 'rough versions' of the dicta (GRM 1047–1115) and one of the faire copies (GRM 977–1045). Unlike the extended sentences, the dicta were directly recorded in the registers, first as a draft and later copied out. Compared to the extended sentences, the number of dicta is much higher and they also have a much smaller informative value. In fact, a dictum does not provide any insight into the subject of a case or into the arguments used: it is merely a concise disposition, drafted by the reporting councilor, which mainly contains the names of the litigants, the procedure and the decision of the court. It is important to note that the dicta registers contain, apart from the final decisions in a case, all provisional dispositions. It might seem evident that these decisions would be readily available for anyone with some interest in the case. Certain dicta, however, make mention of a 'secret resolution', especially when directions were given to the councilor-reporter as to what questions he had to ask the litigants, what actions he had to take depending on their answers etc.

3102 "Listes des gages du Grand Conseil"

The listes des gages are not described in the inventory of Van den Bussche but can be consulted at the State Archives on special request. These registers record the fixed salary each member of the Great Council earned for his work for every 6 months. These listes des gages are a supplement to the déclarations bis annuelles

Grote Raad van Mechelen. Officie-fiscaal. Procesdossiers.
65; 406; 504
Grote Raad van Mechelen. Officie-fiscaal. Banden en Delen.
91
Manuscrits Divers
432, 860/B, 2968
Raad van State
Portefeuilles 651
Rekenkamer
2039–2053

Malines, Archives of the Archdiocese

Verzameling Kerk en Staat
870

Malines, City Archives

Archives de la ville de Malines: affaires civiles et ecclésiastiques
23, 129/5, 138

Published and Printed Sources

De Le Court, Jules-Victor, Gachard, Louis Prosper and Verhaegen, Paul. 1860–1942. *Recueil des ordonnances des Pays-Bas autrichiens. 3e série: 1700–1794*, 15 tomes, Brussels: Devroye.

Exposition historique et juridique des privilèges de la province de Flandres et des prérogatives du Conseil provincial par les président et gens du même conseil de Sa Majesté l'Impératrice Reine, comtesse de Flandres etc. ordonné en Flandres contre les président et gens du Grand Conseil de Sa Majesté à Malines.1752. Ghent: J.J. Bauwens.

Ordonnances, statuts, stile, et manière de procéder, faits et decretez par le roi Don Philippe II pour son Grand Conseil le 8 août 1559 avec les éclaircissements sur lesdites ordonnances émanés du même conseil. L'institution d'icelui, par le duc Charles de Bourgogne en l'an 1473. Celle de l'archiduc Philippe du janvier 1503 et l'ordonnance par l'empereur Charles V du 26 octobre 1531. 1721. Brussels: t'Serstevens.

Literature

Berkvens, Aloyisus M.J.A. 1990. 'Un emploi de haut nom et d'une rapport modique'. De benoeming van kanseliers van het Oostenrijks Hof van Gelre. *Maaslands Mélange* 14: 55–65.

Buntinx, Jan. 1964–1977. *Inventaris van het archief van de Raad van Vlaanderen*. 8t. Brussels: Algemeen Rijksarchief.

Cauchies, Jean Marie. 1974. Le Grand Conseil des ducs de Bourgogne, le Parlement de Malines et les 'terres de débat' (Lessines-Flobecq): à propos de publications récentes. *Bulletin du cercle royal d'histoire et d'archéologie d'Ath et de la région et musée athois* 8: 346–350.

Cauchies, Jean Marie, Desmaele, Bernard, and Mariage, Florian. 2009. *Les institutions publiques régionales et locales en Hainaut et Tournais-Tournaisis sous l'Ancien Régime*. Brussels: Algemeen Rijksarchief.

Craeybeckx, Jan. 1958. Brood en levensstandaard. Kritische nota betreffende de prijs van het brood te Antwerpen en te Brussel in de 17de en 18de eeuw. *Bijdragen tot de prijzengeschiedenis* 3: 133–162.

De Breyne, Emile e.a. 1998. *Analyse des consultes du Conseil Privé sous le régime autrichien*. 2t. Brussels: Algemeen Rijksarchief.

De Brouwer, Jozef. 1971–1972. *De kerkelijke rechtspraak en haar evolutie in de bisdommen Antwerpen, Gent en Mechelen tussen 1570 en 1795*. Tielt: Veys.

De Schepper, Hugo. 1978. De Grote Raad van Mechelen, hoogste rechtscollege in de Nederlanden? *Bijdragen en Mededelingen betreffende de Geschiedenis der Nederlanden* 93: 358–376.

De Schepper, Hugo. 1998. De Geheime Raad als hoogste rechtscollege in de Nederlanden (1504–1580). In *Handelingen van het tweede Hof van Holland Symposium gehouden op 14 November 1997 in de Treveszaal te Den Haag*, ed. Rob Huijbrecht, 39–48. The Hague: Algemeen Rijksarchief.

De Schepper, Hugo. 2006. Staatsgezag en staatsmacht in de Nederlanden. Verworvenheden en beperkingen van het Bourgondisch-Habsburgse systeem. In *Staatsvorming onder de Bourgondiërs en Habsburgers. Theorie en Praktijk*, eds. Hugo de Schepper en Jacques Geurts, 13–50. Maastricht: Shaker.

Gaillard, Arthur. 1898–1902. *Le Conseil de Brabant: histoire, organisation, procédure*. Brussels: Lebègue.

Galand, Michèle. 2001. Gages, honneurs, mérites: les hauts fonctionnaires dans les Pays-Bas autrichiens. *Revue belge de philologie et d'histoire* 73.2: 557–580.

Gilissen, John. 1980. De Grote Raad van Mechelen. Historisch overzicht. In *Miscelannea Consilii Magni. Ter gelegenheid van twintig jaar Werkgroep Grote Raad van Mechelen*, 13–43. Amsterdam: Universiteit van Amsterdam. Faculteit der rechtsgeleerdheid.

Hermans, Victor and Van Doren, Pierre.-Joseph. 1859–1896. *Inventaire des archives de la ville de Malines*. Malines: Van Velsen.

Hubert, Eugène. 1900. *Le voyage de l'empereur Joseph II dans les Pays-Bas (31 mai 1781–27 juillet 1781): etude d'histoire politique et diplomatique*. Brussels, Lebègue.

Janssens, Valery. 1957. *Het geldwezen in de Oostenrijkse Nederlanden* (Verhandelingen van de Koninklijke Vlaamse academie voor wetenschappen, letteren en schone kunsten van België. Klasse der Letteren 29). Brussels: Paleis der Academiën.

Koster-Van Dijk, Joke M.I. and Wijffels, Alain. 1990. Les procédures en révision au Grand Conseil de Malines (1473–1580). *Publications du Centre Européen d'Etudes Bourguignonnes* 30: 67–97.

Lemmens, Karel. 1998. Rekenmunt en courant geld. *Jaarboek 1998 van het Europees genootschap voor munt-en penningkunde* 4:19–52.

Monballyu, Jos. 1998. De Raad van Vlaanderen, een soevereine justitieraad in strafzaken? In *Handelingen van het tweede Hof van Holland Symposium gehouden op 14 November 1997 in de Treveszaal te Den Haag*, ed. Rob Huijbrecht, 77–90. The Hague: Algemeen Rijksarchief.

Monballyu, Jos. 2001. De hoofdlijnen van de criminele strafprocedure in het graafschap Vlaanderen (16de tot 18de eeuw). In *Voortschrijdend procesrecht. Een historische verkenning*, eds. Fred Stevens, Ernest Persoons and Remco Van Rhee, 63–108. Leuven: Universitaire Pers Leuven.

Oosterbosch, Michel. 1998. *Grote Raad voor de Nederlanden te Mechelen: procesbundels beroepen uit Vlaanderen: ordinaris processen (nr. 1–1000)*. Brussels: Algemeen Rijksarchief.

Oosterbosch, Michel. 2001. *Appelprocedure, dossierbehandeling en registervoering bij de Grote Raad van Mechelen*. In: *Voortschrijdend procesrecht. Een historische verkenning*, eds. Fred Stevens, Ernest Persoons and Remco Van Rhee, 3–25. Leuven: Universitaire Pers Leuven.

Oosterbosch, Michel. 2006. Archief of niet? De procesdossiers van de Grote Raad voor de Nederlanden te Mechelen. In *Hoge rechtspraak in de oude Nederlanden*, eds. Hugo de Schepper and René Vermeir, 65–78. Maastricht: Shaker.

Poukens, Johan. 2010. *Inventaris van de verzameling Kerk en Staat in het Aartsbisschoppelijk Archief te Mechelen (16de–18de eeuw)*. Brussels: Algemeen Rijksarchief.

Proost, Jean-Joseph-Eugène. 1870. *Histoire du droit d'asile religieux en Belgique*. Ghent: Hebbelynck.

Put, Eddy. 1995. *Inventaris van het Archief van de Raad van Brabant. Deel 1: Archief van de griffies*. Brussels: Algemeen Rijksarchief.

Put, Eddy. 2002. Gedeelde soevereiniteit? De dubbelrol van de Raad van Brabant. In *Politieke representatie*, eds. Henk de Smaele and Johan Tollebeek, 221–229. Leuven: Universitaire Pers Leuven.

Put, Eddy. 2005. Standenongelijkheid in strafzaken: geestelijke voor Zuid-Nederlandse en Luikse officialiteiten (16de–18de eeuw). In *Recht in geschiedenis: een bundel bijdragen over rechtsgeschiedenis van de Middeleeuwen tot de hedendaagse tijd*, eds. Jozef Janssens e.a., 291–302. Leuven: Davidsfonds.

Roegiers, Jan. 1980. *Kerk en Staat in de Oostenrijkse Nederlanden*. In *Algemene Geschiedenis der Nederlanden*, eds. Walter Prevenier e.a, t. 9, 361–375. Haarlem: Fibula-Van Dishoeck.

Scholiers, Etienne and Vandenbroeke, Christian. 1977–1983. Structuren en conjuncturen in de Zuidelijke Nederlanden 1480–1800. In *Algemene Geschiedenis der Nederlanden*, eds. Walter Prevenier e.a, t. 5, 252–310. Haarlem: Fibula-Van Dishoeck.

Simon, Jules. 1921. La procédure criminelle sous l'ancien régime (Grand Conseil de Malines). *Handelingen van de Koninklijke Commissie voor de uitgave van oude wetten en verordeningen van België* 10: 397–437.

Vandenbulcke, Anne. 1992. *Le pouvoir et l'argent sous l'Ancien Régime: la vénalité des offices dans les conseils collatéraux des Pays-Bas espagnols (seconde moitié du XVIIe siècle)*. Kortrijk: UGA.

Van De Wiel, Constant. 1976. Recours aux tribunaux laics en matière ecclésiastique vers 1720. In *Mélanges Mgr Wagnon. Etudes d'histoire* et de droit, 416–436. Louvain-la-Neuves: Faculté internationale de droit canonique.

Van Peteghem, Paul. 1990. *De Raad van Vlaanderen en staatsvorming onder Karel V (1515–1555): een publiekrechtelijk onderzoek naar centralisatiestreven in de XVII Provinciën*. Nijmegen: Gerard Noodt Instituut.

Van Poelgeest, L. 1988. De raadsheren van de Hoge Raad van Holland, Zeeland en West-Friesland in de achttiende eeuw. *Bijdragen en mededelingen betreffende de geschiedenis der Nederlanden* 103.1: 20–51.

Van Rhee, Remco. 1997. *Litigation and legislation: civil procedure at first instance in the Great Council of for the Netherlands in Malines (1522–1559)*. Brussels: Algemeen Rijksarchief.

Van Rhee, Remco. 1998. Snelheid en efficiency in hoger beroep (civiele procedures, 16de eeuw). In *Handelingen van het tweede Hof van Holland Symposium gehouden op 14 November 1997 in de Treveszaal te Den Haag*, ed. Rob Huijbrecht, 21–37. The Hague: Algemeen Rijksarchief.

Van Rhee, Remco ed. 2010. *Within a reasonable time: the history of due and undue delay in civil litigation* (Comparative studies in continental and Anglo-American legal history 28) Berlin: Duncker and Humblot.

Van Rompaey, Jan. 1961. Het compositierecht in Vlaanderen van de veertiende tot de achttiende eeuw. *Tijdschrift voor rechtsgeschiedenis* 29: 43–79.

Van Rompaey, Jan. 1973. *De Grote Raad van de hertogen van Boergondië en het parlement van Mechelen* (Verhandelingen van de Koninklijke Academie voor wetenschappen, letteren en schone kunsten van België. Klasse der Letteren 73). Brussels: Koninklijke Academie voor Wetenschappen, letteren en schone kunsten van België.

Van Rompaey, Jan. 1977–1983. De Bourgondische staatsinstellingen. In *Algemene Geschiedenis der Nederlanden*, eds. Walter Prevenier e.a, t. 4, 136–155. Haarlem: Fibula-Van Dishoeck.

Van Rompaey, Jan. 1977. *De procedure in beroep bij het Parlement van Mechelen*. In *Consilium magnum, 1473–1973: herdenking van de 500e verjaardag van de oprichting van het Parlement en de Grote Raad van Mechelen*, 371–381. Brussels: Algemeen Rijksarchief.

Verlinden, Charles, and Scholliers, Etienne eds. 1959–1973. *Dokumenten voor de geschiedenis van prijzen en lonen in Vlaanderen en Brabant*. 4t. Brugge: De Tempel.

Verscuren, An. 2005. *"L'oeil et le bras du Roi?" Het vervolgingsbeleid van het officie-fiscaal van de Grote Raad van Mechelen (1767–1788)*. Unpublished Master's Thesis. Leuven: Katholieke Universiteit Leuven.

Verscuren, An. 2012. The interactions between the Council of Flanders and the Great Council of Malines in the eighteenth century. In *Intermediate institutions in the County of Flanders in the*

Late Middle Ages and the Early Modern Era, eds. Georges Martyn e.a., 139–153. Brussels: Algemeen Rijksarchief.

Verscuren, An. 2013. *Nadere toegang op de geëxtendeerde sententies van de Grote Raad van Mechelen: 1693–1772*. Brussels: Algemeen Rijksarchief.

Wassink, Jos F.A. 2005. *Van stad en buitenie: een institutionele studie van rechtspraak en bestuur in Weert 1568–1795*. Hilversum: Verloren.

Wauters, Bart. 2004. La jurisdiction contentieuse du nonce de Flandre (XVIIe-XVIIIe). *Zeitschrift der Savigny Stiftung für Rechtsgeschichte* 90: 430–455.

Wauters, Bart. 2005. *Recht als religie: canonieke onderbouw van de vroegmoderne staatsvorming in de Zuidelijke Nederlanden*. Leuven: Universitaire Pers.

Wijffels, Alain. 1994. Grote Raad voor de Nederlanden te Mechelen (ca.1445–1797). In *De centrale overheidsinstellingen van de Habsburgse Nederlanden*, ed. Erik Aerts e.a., 448–461. Brussels: Algemeen Rijksarchief.

Chapter 4
Administering Justice: Volume and Nature of Litigation

4.1 Introduction

In 2007, in an article on the uses of judicial records, H. Piant observed that in legal history only scant attention had been devoted to the archives produced by the *Ancien Régime* civil courts.[1] Until then, much of the historical research in this area had been case driven, marked by a preoccupation with 'famous trials', as well as by a predominant focus on criminal justice. Piant remarked that civil justice largely remained *terra incognita*: the sheer volume of the court records—with, according to Piant, almost 20 times more civil suits than criminal trials—renders research difficult. At the same time, it made a quantitative approach all the more necessary and useful.

Four years later, M.-C. Le Bailly made a comparable remark.[2] She noticed that the tendency—which has its origins in the late medieval period—to bring ever more interpersonal conflicts to court, has been observed for the *Parlement de Paris*, the English superior courts, the *Reichskammergericht*, the Great Council of Malines and several regional tribunals such as the Council of Holland, but that a firm quantitative basis to study this phenomenon over a longer period of time is entirely lacking. As far as materials are available, the research is predominantly focused on civil justice in the fifteenth and sixteenth centuries and on criminal justice during the eighteenth century. It is well known that the superior tribunals handled the bulk of the civil cases in the late sixteenth century, after which the volume seriously declined in the seventeenth century. What happened to (and in) these tribunals after 1700, is not as clear.

As Le Bailly observed, a quantitative approach to legal history does not only enable us to lay bare certain patterns or ask new questions, but it also allows us to map the increase in scale and reach of princely jurisdiction. In fact, the literature

[1] Piant, Hervé. 2007. Des procès innombrables. Eléments méthodologiques pour une histoire de la justice civile d'Ancien Régime. *Histoire et mesure* 22.2: 13–39.

[2] Le Bailly, Marie-Charlotte. 2011. Langetermijntrends in de rechtspraak bij de gewestelijke hoven van justitie in de Noordelijke Nederlanden van ca. 1450 tot ca. 1800. *Pro Memorie* 13: 30–67.

A. Verscuren, *The Great Council of Malines in the 18th century*,
Studies in the History of Law and Justice 3, DOI 10.1007/978-3-319-09638-4_4

points to the expansion of princely jurisdiction as an indicator of centralization and the creation of a unified state. As far as the Great Council is concerned, this was certainly true for the fifteenth and early sixteenth centuries: the Dukes of Burgundy had specifically 'established' the tribunal as a means of unifying their very disparate possessions in the Netherlands. The question should therefore be asked: what was the volume of litigation at the eighteenth century Great Council? And to what extent did this affect the government's use of the court as a means of centralization and unification in the eighteenth century?

For the first part of our analysis—assessing the volume of litigation at the Great Council, its 'breakdown' by province, the tribunal's accumulated caseload and the distribution of the lawsuits over the councilors—we adopted a predominantly quantitative approach. As Piant rightfully recognized, the first obstacle for this method lies in the compilation of a corpus. In this case, that is indeed a significant challenge.

In fact, in comparison to criminal trials, the volume of civil cases is absolutely massive. Civil litigation constituted more than 90 % of the activity at most European tribunals;[3] in the case of the Great Council this percentage may be even higher, as its jurisdiction in criminal justice was very limited. Moreover, the records also impose certain limitations: many series have lacunas and/or are badly inventoried. The present condition of the archives of the Great Council prevents us from even merely counting the number of eighteenth century civil case files; not only is there no inventory available for the majority of these files, an additional problem is that they are not chronologically arranged, making it impossible to easily identify those belonging to the eighteenth century. As such, in order to create an image as accurate as possible of the level of activity of the Great Council and its members during the last 100 years of its existence, we selected several complementary sources: the extended sentences,[4] the dicta,[5] the distribution registers[6] and the criminal case files.[7]

As far as the analysis of the subject matter treated at the Great Council is concerned, a primarily qualitative approach was used. As the dicta and the distribution books give only very scant information—if any at all—about the subject of the case, we made use of a different array of sources: apart from the extended sentences, we analyzed the collection entitled 'lawsuits concerning prominent families',[8] and the eighteenth century collections of case law.[9]

[3] Piant, Hervé. 2007. Des procès innombrables. Eléments méthodologiques pour une histoire de la justice civile d'Ancien Régime. *Histoire et mesure* 22.2: 15.

[4] Brussels, ARA, GRM, 790–976.

[5] Brussels, ARA, GRM, 1029–1045.

[6] Brussels, ARA, GRM, 617–620; 629–633; 635–637.

[7] ARA, GRMOF, case files. An inventory has been published by Put, Eddy. 1995. *Officie-fiscaal van de Grote Raad van Mechelen: werkbeschrijvingen.* Brussels: Algemeen Rijksarchief.

[8] Put, Eddy. 1995. *Grote Raad van Mechelen. Processen van aanzienlijke families (Reeksen A en B)*: werkbeschrijvingen. Brussels: Algemeen Rijksarchief. The original descriptions were made in the 1860s by H.F. D'Hoop, L. Galesloot and M. Van Hollebeke.

[9] De Saint Vaast, Pierre and Du Laury, Remi Albert. La jurisprudence des Pais-Bas autrichiens établies par les arrêts du Grand Conseil de Sa Majesté Impériale et Catholique, résident en la ville de Malines, auxquels sont ajoutés quelques Décrets portés au Conseil Privé de Sadite Majesté,

4.2 The Volume of Litigation

4.2.1 Civil Litigation: Corpus and Research Results

The core of our corpus consists of three main sources: the extended sentences, the dicta and the distribution registers. Naturally, these are not the only sources available to measure the number of civil lawsuits the tribunal dealt with during the eighteenth century. First, the registers of the *rôle* have also been preserved in the archives of the Great Council:[10] they contain every lawsuit that followed the procedure on the *rôle* with a description of all proceedings and sometimes even the outcome of the case.[11] Yet, given that this procedure was less popular in the eighteenth century and that ever more lawsuits were dealt with following the communicatory procedure, the *rôle* registers only provide a very partial view of the number of lawsuits treated at the Great Council in the eighteenth century.[12] Moreover, counting lawsuits in these registers is problematic, as the same cases reappear on various dates.

The *registres aux causes jugés* could also provide an idea of the volume of civil litigation at the Great Council.[13] These registers record all lawsuits which reached judgment and state for each one the number of bags, the names of the litigants and the procedure (first instance or appeal).[14] In addition, they contain an indication in the margin of what happened to the litigants' files: were they returned to the tribunal *a quo* or handed back to the parties or their proctor? Given that the information in these registers overlaps to a large extent with what can be found in the distribution records, we preferred not to use them for our quantitative analysis. This does not mean that they are entirely redundant. On the contrary: based on the information these registers provide, it should be possible—at least in theory—to discover if documents associated with a lawsuit are still present in the Great Council's archives.

Finally, from the 1.4 linear kilometer records on the Great Council that are preserved at the State Archives, 1.1 km consists of case files.[15] For want of inventories,

---

Brussels, 1717; De Coloma, Jean Alphonse and Hony, Jean Baptiste. Arrêts du Grand Conseil de Sa Majesté Impériale et Royale, séant en la ville de Malines, 2 tomes, Malines, 1781.

[10] For the eighteenth century: Brussels, ARA, GRM 517–608.

[11] The registers are divided into two columns: the right column contains the identification of the proctor, the litigants and the case; the left column is reserved for the description of the proceedings and at times also the outcome of the case. Usually, the lawsuits presented by the procurator-general were handled first, followed by those in which he was the defending party and finally all cases in which other proctors litigated.

[12] Cf. supra, Chap. 3.

[13] For the eighteenth century: Brussels, ARA, GRM 1134 (différends), 1129 (débats), 1152–1158 (procès).

[14] Oosterbosch, Michel. 2006. Archief of niet? De procesdossiers van de Grote Raad voor de Nederlanden te Mechelen. In *Hoge rechtspraak in de oude Nederlanden*, eds. Hugo de Schepper and René Vermeir. Maastricht: Shaker, 72.

[15] This corresponds to approximately 30,000–50,000 files. Oosterbosch, Michel. 2006. Archief of niet? De procesdossiers van de Grote Raad voor de Nederlanden te Mechelen. In *Hoge rechtspraak in de oude Nederlanden*, eds. Hugo de Schepper and René Vermeir. Maastricht: Shaker, 65.

a good part of this series of files is still not available for systematic study, and to some extent even remains entirely inaccessible.[16] Subsequently, not nearly all files of proceedings have been preserved in the archives. Some files were sent back to the tribunal *a quo*, others were removed by the litigants themselves.[17] As a consequence, systematic research in this series is not only difficult, but there is also no way of knowing what percentage of the files has been preserved.

While there are certainly other sources available in the archives of the Great Council, we selected the extended sentences, the dicta and the distribution registers, because we believe that they will supply—despite their limitations—a fairly accurate image of the eighteenth century Great Council's caseload.

4.2.1.1 Extended Sentences (Fig. 4.1)[18]

Typology Within the archives of the Great Council, the extended sentences constitute a separate series, which—contrary to many others—is fairly exhaustive.[19] The registers cover a period of some 300 years in which only the last 2 decades of the eighteenth century are missing. The absence of a register for the period between 1773 and 1794 can be explained by the specific manner in which these registers were compiled. We may indeed assume that they were originally written on separate

[16] Wijffels, Alain. 1989. Legal Records and Reports in the Great Council of Malines (fifteenth to eighteenth century). In *Judicial Records, Law Reports and the Growth of Case Law*, ed. John H. Baker, 181–206. Berlin: Duncker und Humblot.

[17] In theory, the parties should have extracted their files from the Great Council's records. However, many of them preferred not to do so for a variety of reasons: e.g., because they lost interest in the case or in their files, because the lawsuit never ended etc. For more information on the status of these files, see: Put, Eddy. 2000. In de zak? De archiefstatus van procesdossiers uit het ancien régime. In *Door de archivistiek gestrikt: liber amicorum prof. dr. Juul Verhelst* (Archiefinitiatie(f) 4), eds Gustave Janssens e.a., 187–196. Brussels: VUBpress and Oosterbosch, Michel. 2006. Archief of niet? De procesdossiers van de Grote Raad voor de Nederlanden te Mechelen. In *Hoge rechtspraak in de oude Nederlanden*, eds. Hugo de Schepper and René Vermeir, 65–78. Maastricht: Shaker.

[18] For more information on the redaction and the significance of the extended sentences of the Great Council, see a. o.: Wijffels, Alain. 1997. Grand Conseil de Malines: la rédaction des sentences étendues et le recueil de jurisprudence de Guillaume de Grysperre. In *Case law in the making: the techniques and methods of judicial records and law reports (Comparative studies in continental and Anglo-American Legal History* 17) v.1, ed. Alain Wijffels, 299–316. Berlin: Duncker und Humblot; a similar article has been published about the extended sentences of the Parlement of Flanders (Douai): Michel, Sabrina. 2009. Les 'arrêts étendus' du Parlement de Flandre: etude d'une spécificité juridique locale. *Revue du Nord* 91.4: 745–761. A detailed description of the extended sentences and their use can be found in the introduction to Verscuren, An. 2013. *Nadere toegang op de geëxtendeerde sententies van de Grote Raad van Mechelen: 1693–1772.* Brussels: Algemeen Rijksarchief.

[19] Brussels, ARA, GRM, 790–976.

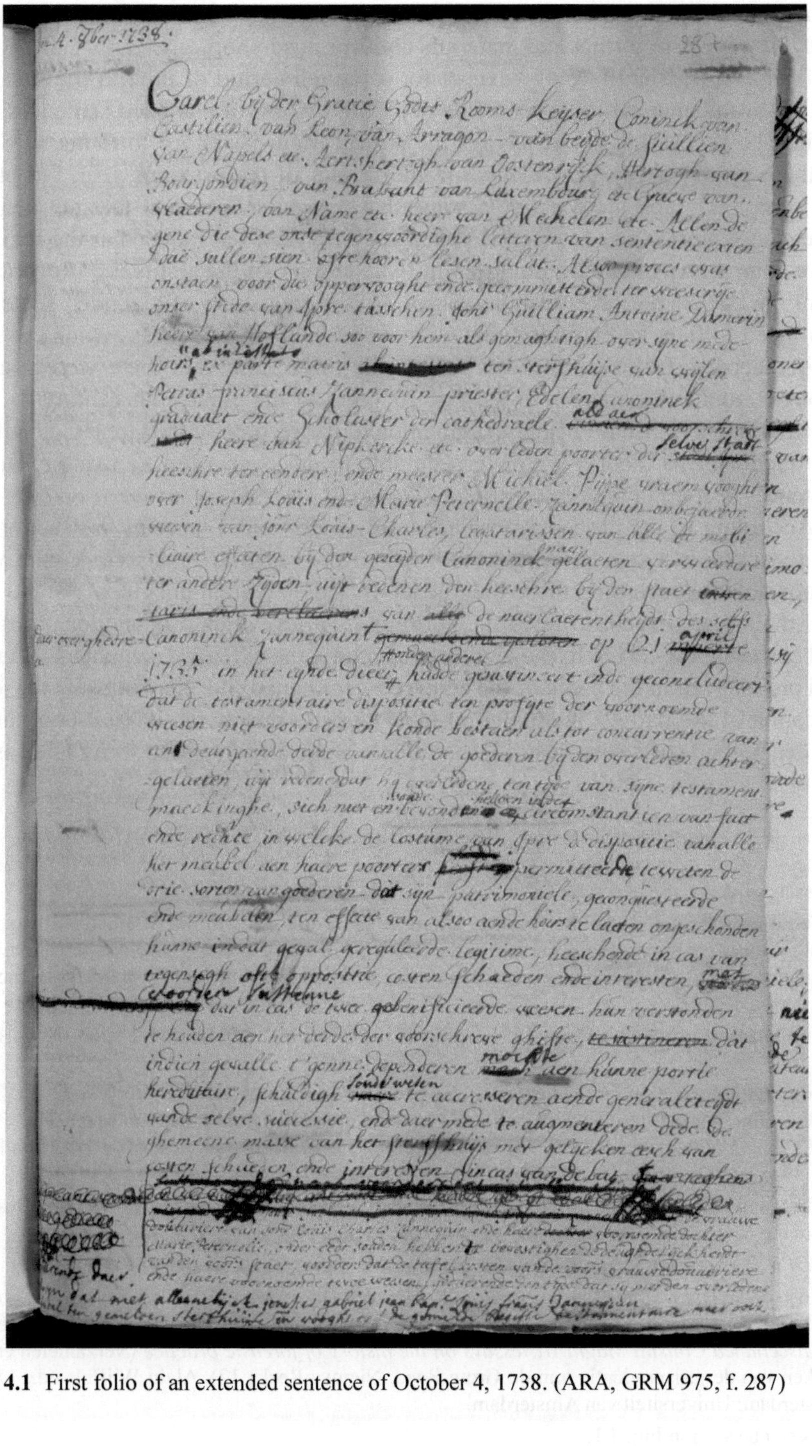

Fig. 4.1 First folio of an extended sentence of October 4, 1738. (ARA, GRM 975, f. 287)

quires, and only after a certain period of time bound together into a single register.[20] The differences in format and materials confirm this hypothesis.

Every register until 1690—except for a limited period of time in the first half of the seventeenth century—contains one year's worth of extended sentences.[21] In reality, however, this is not always the case: certain years are 'missing'.[22] Some of these turned out to be included in the register of the previous year, but others are completely absent. We may assume that this does not mean that not a single extended sentence was registered in that specific year, but rather that the registers have gone astray in one of the different 'wanderings' of the archives.[23] Regardless, from the end of the seventeenth century on, the frequency of extended sentences continued to flag, an evolution that culminated in the last register, which covers 2 entire decades. It therefore seems reasonable to presume that there were just not enough extended sentences in the last 20 years of the eighteenth century to bind together into a register. Further examination of the records of the Great Council has corroborated this theory; we have been able to discover a few separate extended sentences drafted in the period after 1772.[24]

According to the procedure-ordinance of 1559[25] and a 'special' instruction for the redaction of extended sentences,[26] it was the registrar or his clerk who were responsible for recording these judgments. Based on certain documents in the case file, the registrar reconstructed the entire case, after which a councilor proofread and corrected the text.[27] In the eighteenth century, the extended sentences—drafted and pronounced in the name of the emperor—contained five elements: (1) the identification of the parties, including possible changes during the lawsuit (e.g. due to the death of one of the parties); (2) the subject of the dispute, often formulated as the

[20] Van Rhee made the same remark: Van Rhee, Remco. 1997. *Litigation and legislation: civil procedure at first instance in the Great Council of for the Netherlands in Malines (1522–1559).* Brussels: Algemeen Rijksarchief, 206.

[21] Yet, it must be noted that the registers comprising several years in the first half of the seventeenth century are almost twice the size of the holdings for a single year. Therefore, the diminished frequency in registers does not necessarily indicate a diminished number of extended sentences in that period of time.

[22] The 'missing years' are: 1580, 1581, 1596, 1613, 1620, 1621, 1642, 1643, 1663, 1665, 1681, and 1687.

[23] For more information on the history of the Great Council's archives, see: Verscuren, An. 2014. Archieven in oorlog, speelbal van politiek. Het archief van de Grote Raad van Mechelen (1746–1869)'. In *Macht en Onmacht. De rol van archieven in oorlog en bij rechtsherstel,* eds. Ron Blom e.a., 49–59. 's-Gravenhage: Stichting Archiefpublicaties.

[24] These individual extended sentences are included neither in the inventory of Van den Bussche nor in the *Nadere Toegang.*

[25] *ROPB*, 2ième série, t.7, August 8, 1559, p. 461–492.

[26] Koster-Van Dijck edited this instruction: Koster-Van Dijck, Joke M.I. 1988. Instruction pour le greffier du Grand Conseil concernant la rédaction des sentences (Introduction et édition du texte). In *Miscellanea Consilii Magni III: essays on the history of forensic practice* (Verzamelen en bewerken van de jurisprudentie van de Grote Raad. Nieuwe Reeks 12), Alain Wijffels ed., 17–41. Amsterdam: Universiteit van Amsterdam.

[27] As can be seen in Fig. 4.1.

request of the plaintiff; (3) an account of the progress of the case with a description of the principal acts of both litigants; (4) the primary arguments of the plaintiff and the defendant; (5) the decision. In case of appeal, accounts of all legal acts in the previous instance(s) were included as well as a summary of the appealed judgment.

An essential difference between *Ancien Régime* (extended) sentences and contemporary judgments lies, as is well known, in the complete absence of any form of judicial motivation in the former. Legal decisions were never motivated and the judges were even forbidden to unveil potential divergent opinions among them.[28] Given that the councilors were obliged to keep their deliberations secret, they were equally forced to refrain from revealing arguments invoked during their conclusive debates.[29] Some qualification is however warranted: A. Wijffels for example argued that judgments which discussed the scope or the interpretation of a judicial source—e.g. an ordinance—did contain a certain motivation.[30] Moreover, the selection of arguments the registrar made while drafting the sentence may shed some light on those pieces of evidence that were considered to be of overriding importance.[31] Nevertheless, these are only indirect indications: the extended sentences were certainly never intended to motivate a judgment.

What purpose the extended judgments did have, remains open for discussion. Since both a registrar and a councilor spent several hours or even days drafting and proofreading these sentences, there should be no doubt that it was a rather expensive affair. We may assume that the party who did request these extended judgments—this was *de facto* always the 'winning' party—had a good reason to do so, since he was the one who had to foot the bill.[32] Both A. Wijffels and S. Michel argued that an extended sentence functioned primarily as a 'title', as evidence for the future. In fact, a *dictum* was not detailed enough to fulfill that purpose, as it only mentioned the names of the litigants and the verdict, but not the subject of the dispute. In order for a sentence to guarantee judicial security in the future and prevent the losing party from taking the same matter to court twice, the identity

---

[28] The fact that the councilors often disagreed and even at times had outwardly contradictory opinions on the same case can be seen in the limited number of *recueils et opinions* that have been preserved in the records of the Great Council. These *recueils et opinions* do not figure in the inventory of Van den Bussche but can be consulted at the State Archives on special request.

[29] Dauchy, Serge and Demars-Sion, Véronique. 2006. Argumentation et motivation dans les recueils d'arrêts des cours souverianes de France. L'exemple du Parlement de flandre (fin XVIIe—début XVIIIe siècle). In *Juristische Argumentation, Argumente der Juristen*, ed. albrecht Cordes, 127–152. Cologne: Böhlau Verlag.

[30] Wijffels, Alain. 1997. Grand Conseil de Malines: la rédaction des sentences étendues et le recueil de jurisprudence de Guillaume de Grysperre. In *Case law in the making: the techniques and methods of judicial records and law reports (Comparative studies in continental and Anglo-American Legal History* 17) v.1, ed. Alain Wijffels. Berlin: Duncker und Humblot, 300.

[31] This is also the opinion of Verkerk: Verkerk, Cornelis L. 1977. Onderzoek naar motivering in rechte bij de Grote Raad van Mechelen. In *Consilium magnum, 1473–1973: herdenking van de 500ᵉ verjaardag van de oprichting van het Parlement en de Grote Raad van Mechelen*, 287–291. Brussels: Algemeen Rijksarchief.

[32] *ROPB*, 2ième série, t.7, p. 467, title 'greffiers'.

of the litigants, the subject matter and the arguments had to be clearly specified.[33] Buntinx suggested that the extended sentences played a role in the implementation and execution of a judgment.[34] This was certainly true for the so called *sentences de decrét* (sentences of decree)[35] which figure prominently in the eighteenth century registers of extended sentences. It seems plausible that forced sales were—maybe not obligatory but certainly by preference—settled using a *sentence de décret* given that it provided the buyer with a proof of ownership in case the debtor would later try to dispute the agreement.

Research Results In the past, significant effort has been devoted to making the registers with the extended sentences readily accessible for users. Between 1966 and 1988, the Dutch research group dedicated to the Great Council under the direction of J. Th. de Smidt published a 6-volume series *Chronologische lijsten van de geëxtendeerde sententiën berustende in het archief van de Grote Raad van Mechelen* (Chronological lists of the extended sentences in the archives of the Great Council), covering the period between 1465 and 1580. J. Monballyu described the sentences in Dutch of the decade between 1581 and 1590;[36] C. Douxchamps-Lefèvre[37] and Ph. Godding[38] studied the rulings in French. The recently published *Nadere Toegang*[39] deals with the extended sentences from the period between 1693 and 1772. Despite the differences in methodological approach, these publications offer an excellent source for a first quantitative measurement of the workload of the Great Council as well as a helpful means for comparison.[40] For the period not covered by these publications—*i.e.* from 1591 to 1692—we counted the number of extended sentences directly in the registers, making it possible to map the evolution in the number of extended sentences throughout the entire history of the Great Council.

[33] Wijffels, Alain. 1997. Grand Conseil de Malines: la rédaction des sentences étendues et le recueil de jurisprudence de Guillaume de Grysperre. In *Case law in the making: the techniques and methods of judicial records and law reports (Comparative studies in continental and Anglo-American Legal History* 17) v.1, ed. Alain Wijffels. Berlin: Duncker und Humblot, 302.

[34] Buntinx, Jan. 1964–1977. *Inventaris van het archief van de Raad van Vlaanderen.* 8t. Brussels: Algemeen Rijksarchief, t1, 66–67.

[35] These *sentences de décret* settled forced sales.

[36] Monballyu, Jos. 1998. Chronologische Lijst van de Nederlandstalige geêxtedeerde sententiën van de Grote Raad van Mechelen (1581–1590). *Handelingen van de Koninklijke Commissie voor de uitgave der Oude Wetten en Verordeningen van België* 39: 79–146.

[37] Douxchamps-Lefevre, Cécile. 2003. Les sentences du Grand Conseil de Malines en appel d'instances namuroises (1582–1590). *Handelingen van de Koninklijke Commissie voor de uitgave der Oude Wetten en Verordeningen van België* 44: 59–136.

[38] Godding, Philippe and Petit, Roger. 2001. Les sentences du Grand Conseil de Malines relatives au duché de Luxembourg (1582–1590). *Handelingen van de Koninklijke Commissie voor de uitgave der Oude Wetten en Verordeningen van België* 42: 63–201.

[39] Verscuren, An. 2013. *Nadere toegang op de geëxtendeerde sententies van de Grote Raad van Mechelen: 1693–1772.* Brussels: Algemeen Rijksarchief.

[40] For the period between 1470 and 1580, we made use of the counts done by M.-C. Le Bailly in the *chronologische lijsten* published under the direction of de Smidt.

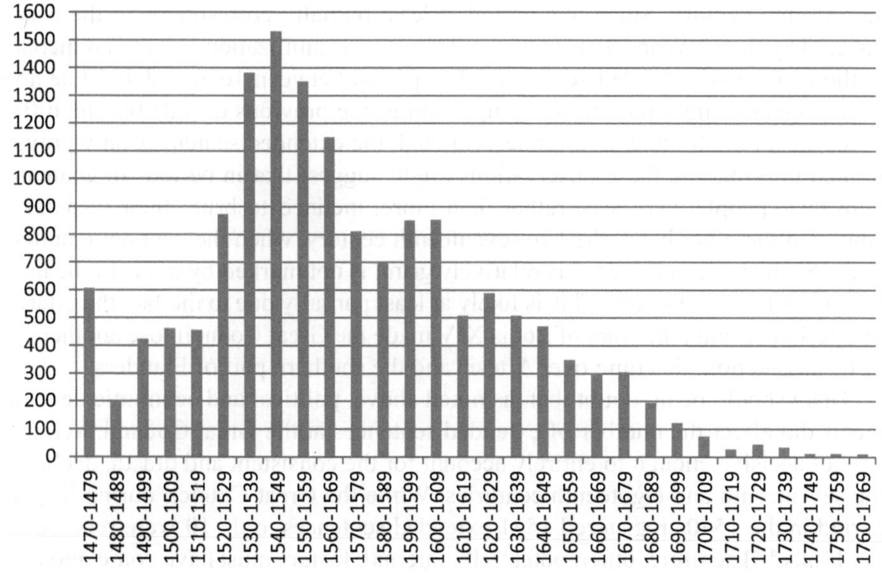

Fig. 4.2 Number of extended sentences of the Great Council of Malines (1470–1769)

Figure 4.2[41] clearly demonstrates that the Great Council registered a fairly high number of extended sentences in the 40 years between 1530 and 1569. A rather steep decline follows in the 1570s and 1580s: given the highly insecure political situation of the time, the Dutch Revolt and the exile of the Great Council to Namur in the years 1580–1585, this is certainly no surprise. Moreover, after the *de facto* secession of the Northern Netherlands, the Great Council could no longer assert its authority over almost half its former jurisdiction. Especially the Council of Holland—which was responsible for the counties of Holland, Zeeland and West-Friesland—provided a fairly large number of appeal cases to the Great Council.[42] The fact that the number of extended sentences in the late sixteenth and early seventeenth centuries never attained its previous levels is in that regard only logical.

Less easy to explain by referring to external circumstances is the second, relatively drastic decrease in the number of extended sentences in the early years of the

[41] Since there is no register for the extended sentences for the period between 1772 and 1794, we do not have any data after 1772. In order not to distort the analysis we did not include the period between 1770 and 1779. It is also important to mention that we made projections about the number of extended sentences in some missing years, *in casu* 1613, 1620 and 1621. We know for certain that the registers for these years are lacking and have not been incorporated in the registers of the previous years. Moreover, the absence of data for these years has a considerable impact on the overall picture. Therefore, we decided to fill in these missing years by using the average number of extended sentences for the decade in question. Since for other missing years a correction would not change the overall pattern in essence, we preferred not to make any potentially ill-founded projections.

[42] Le Bailly, Marie-Charlotte. 2001. *Recht voor de Raad: rechtspraak voor het Hof van Holland, Zeeland en West-Friesland in het midden van de vijftiende eeuw*. Hilversum: Uitgeverij Verloren, 109.

seventeenth century. Since this period at least partially corresponds to the period covered by the 12 Years' Truce, we would expect a stabilization or even an increase in the number of extended sentences. The period between 1620 and 1629 demonstrates again a slight pick-up in comparison to the previous decade but the differences are all in all rather negligible. Although the extended sentences only provide limited information, these observations might suggest that in periods of economic buoyancy, people were less, rather than more, inclined to bring their disputes to court. On the other hand, the late seventeenth century, when the economic outlook in the Spanish Netherlands was relatively grim, is not marked by a rise in the number of extended sentences. This is likely at least partially due to the fact that, during this period of time, the wars of Louis XIV made the Great Council lose another part of its jurisdiction, this time over Artesia and the southern part of Flanders.

There should be no doubt that, as noted above, political and economic developments did affect the number of extended sentences at the Great Council. Yet, they are not decisive enough to entirely account for the consistent and drastic decline in the seventeenth and eighteenth centuries. While the Great Council during its peak period in the 1540s registered 1531 extended sentences, only 10 were recorded in the 1760s.[43] Therefore, other, potentially internal, factors must have come into play.

Possibly, the explanation should be looked for in the motivations the parties had to request an extended judgment. Without a doubt, extended sentences were relatively expensive to obtain; moreover, we can assume that costs were calculated based on the number of hours that the registrar and the councilor spent drafting and proofreading their text—which of course was linked to the number of folios. By analyzing the eighteenth and late seventeenth century registers of extended sentences, we were able to determine that, from the 1740s on, both the legal acts and the arguments of the parties were described in much more detail than before. Whereas at the end of the seventeenth century a register contained more than 40 sentences comprising an average of 15 folios, during the course of the eighteenth century this number declined to ±25 judgments, a few of which were spread out over more than 100 folios. The *sentences de décret* seem to be the only kind of judgments that were not subject to this evolution; they continue to be abundantly present in the registers and almost never exceed 10 folios. It is indeed conspicuous that the percentage of sentences of decree in the sixteenth century registers was far more limited than in those of the late seventeenth and eighteenth centuries: while in the earlier period the sentences of decree comprised on average 4% of all extended sentences, this percentage increased to an average of 30% in the last century of the Great Council's existence.[44]

Considering this, we may presume that certain parties refrained from requesting an extended sentence because of the skyrocketing costs. Possibly, the winning party

[43] We only found three extended sentences in the 1770s, but that number is incomplete given that the last extended sentence registered dates from 1772.

[44] These percentages were calculated based on 15 sample years in de Smidt's *Chronologische Lijsten* (1510, 1515, 1520 etc until 1580) and on the information of our analysis from the late seventeenth and early eighteenth century extended sentences.

Table 4.1 Number of extended sentences of the eighteenth century Great Council

1700–1709	73
1710–1719	27
1720–1729	44
1730–1739	34
1740–1749	11
1750–1759	11
1760–1769	10
1770–1772	3

judged that the benefits of an extended judgment no longer outweighed the costs. This might also explain the relatively high percentage of *sentences de décret* in the eighteenth century registers. Since these judgments were, as a rule, rather limited in size, they were not too expensive and they might have remained in high demand. If, as Buntinx suggested, forced sales were by definition passed by an extended sentence, the high incidence rate of *sentences de décret* can be easily explained.

Regardless of the reasons for the decrease, it is undeniable that the number of extended sentences passed by the Great Council in the eighteenth century is extremely limited in general (cf. Table 4.1). Moreover, there is also a noticeable decline over the course of the century. During the first decade, the Great Council still registered 73 extended sentences. This number sharply declined over the next 10 years to a mere 27 extended judgments. We can assume that the complicated political situation in the second decade of the eighteenth century was at least partially responsible for this decrease. The next 2 decades do indeed show a slight recovery. The steepest drop is situated in the 1740s, which to a large extent must be attributed to the Great Council's exile in Echternach between 1746 and 1749; in this period, not a single extended sentence was recorded. However, there was no recovery in the number of extended judgments after 1749: in the following decades the quantity of extended sentences stabilized around 10/11 per decade.[45] In this case, there does not seem to be a political or economic explanation for the decline: the years 1750–1770 were a period of relative peace and internal stability in the Austrian Netherlands, assured by the moderate and appeasing policy of Empress Maria Theresa.

Does this mean that we have to conclude that the workload of the Great Council dramatically declined over the course of time, to an absolute low at the end of the eighteenth century? Based on the information provided by the extended sentences, we could answer this question affirmatively. Nevertheless, only a limited subset of lawsuits was concluded by an extended judgment. In the eighteenth century, judgments in criminal trials, for example, were never recorded as an extended sentence. The same is true for several civil lawsuits as it was usually—although not necessarily—one of the litigants who had to specifically request an extended sentence. Moreover, the status of these extended sentences and their importance for the litigants remains somewhat unclear and may have changed over the course of the centuries.

[45] It must be noted that there are several years in which not a single extended sentence was recorded.

Therefore, the extended sentences probably constitute merely the tip of the iceberg and the insight they provide must be supplemented by other data.

4.2.1.2 Dicta[46] (Fig. 4.3)

Typology The series of registers of *dicta* comprises 70 volumes, covering the period from 1502 to 1794.[47] For the seventeenth and eighteenth centuries, there are even two parallel series, one of the *minutes* containing the 'rough versions' of the dicta, and one of the fair copies. Unlike the extended sentences, the dicta were directly recorded in the registers, first as a draft and later copied out. As a consequence, we may assume that we possess a high percentage of all dicta that have been registered until the final working day of the Great Council.[48] Nevertheless, samplings have demonstrated that the registers of extended sentences contain decisions that are not contained in the registers of dicta.

So far, dicta have not yet been frequently used in studies of legal history. This can be easily explained: not only is the number of dicta (usually) much higher than the number of extended sentences—and therefore harder to process—but the dicta also have a much smaller informative value. Contrary to an extended sentence, a dictum does not provide any insight into the subject of a case or into the arguments used: it is merely a concise disposition, drafted by the reporting councilor, which mainly contains the names of the litigants, the procedure and the decision of the court.[49] It is important to note that the dicta registers contain, apart from the final decisions in a case, all provisional dispositions. It might seem evident that these decisions would be readily available for anyone with some interest in the case. Certain dicta, however, make mention of a 'secret resolution', especially when directions were given to the councilor-reporter as to what questions he had to ask the litigants, what actions he had to take depending on their answers etc.[50]

The presence of both preliminary and final judgments in the dicta registers also had repercussions for our attempt to count the dicta. In order to achieve a reliable estimate of the number of lawsuits that were judged in last instance by the Great Council, we had to distinguish between final and preliminary judgments. Separating these two did not turn out to be as straightforward as might be assumed: through a

[46] Contrary to the extended sentences, we counted the eighteenth century dicta but did not exhaustively study all of them. Instead, we worked with four sample years: 1701, 1731, 1761 and 1791. Our choice of these data is motivated by the fact that they allow the widest possible range using 30-year increments.

[47] There are also registers for the years 1475–1480.

[48] Cf. infra, Chap. 5.

[49] Wijffels, Alain. 1989. Legal Records and Reports in the Great Council of Malines (fifteenth to eighteenth century). In *Judicial Records, Law Reports and the Growth of Case Law*, ed. John H. Baker. Berlin: Duncker und Humblot, 184.

[50] E.g. Brussels, ARA, GRM 1030, January 15, 1701; February 3, 1701; August 25, 1701; etc.

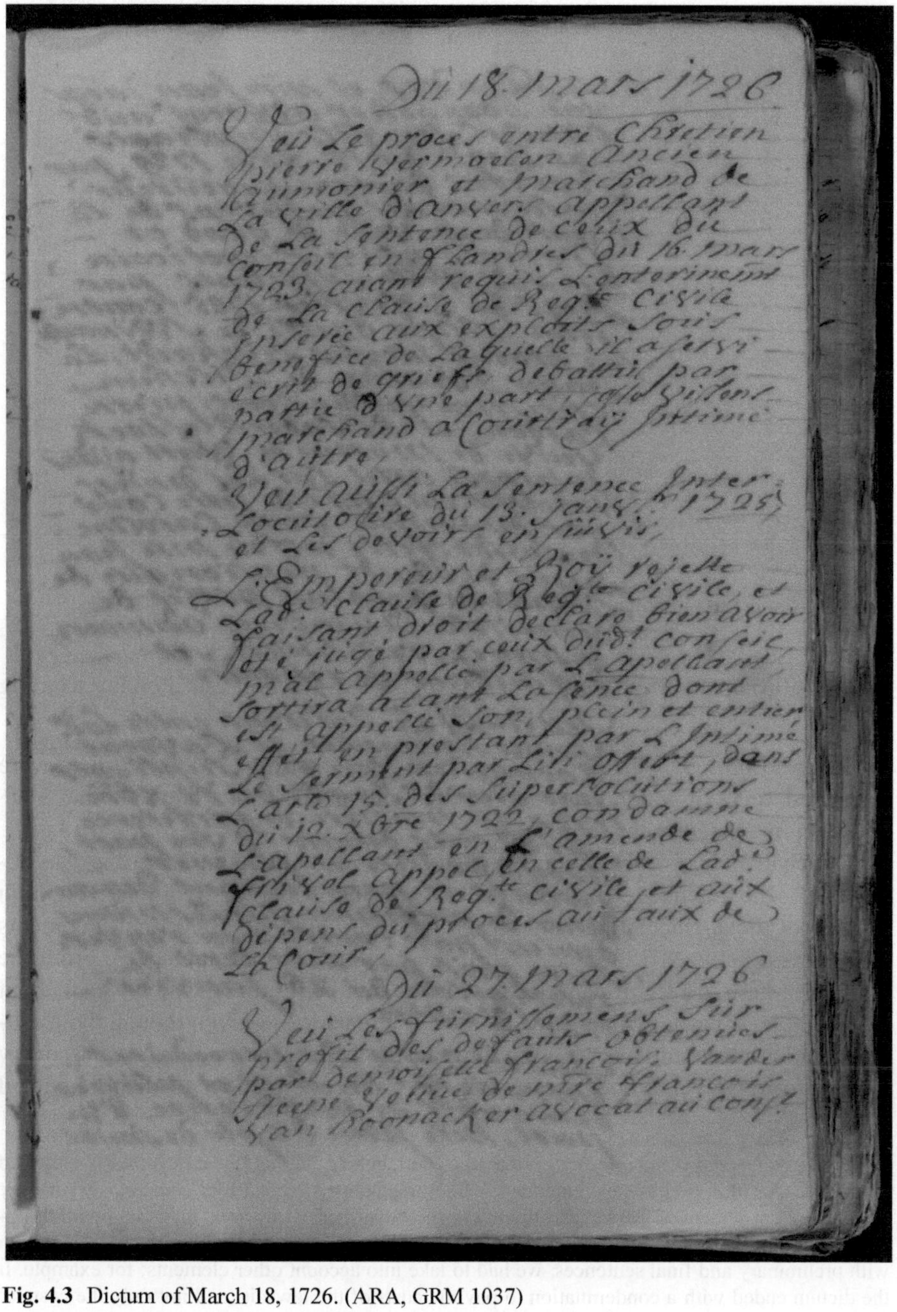
Du 18 mars 1726

Veu le proces entre Chretien Pierre Vermaelen ancien aumonier et marchand de la ville d'anvers appellant de la sentence de ceux du conseil en flandres du 16 mars 1723 aiant requis l'enterinement de la clause de Reqte civile inseree aux exploits sous benefice de laquelle il a servi escrit de griefs debattus par partie d'une part, [illegible] marchand a Courtray intimé d'autre.

Veu aussi la sentence interlocutoire du 13 janvier 1725 et les devoirs ensuivis,

L'Empereur et Roy rejette lad. clause de Reqte civile, et faisant droit declare bien avoir esté jugé par ceux dud. conseil, mal appellé par l'appellant, ordonne que la sentence dont est appellé sortira son plein et entier effet, en prestant par l'intimé le serment par lui offert, dans l'art. 15 des [illegible] du 12 Xbre 1722, condamne l'appellant en l'amende de fol appel, en celle de lad. clause de Reqte civile et aux depens du proces au taux de la Cour.

Du 27 mars 1726

Veu les fournissemens sur profit des defauts obtenus par demoiselle Françoise Vander Steene vefue de Mre François van Roonacker avocat au consl

Fig. 4.3 Dictum of March 18, 1726. (ARA, GRM 1037)

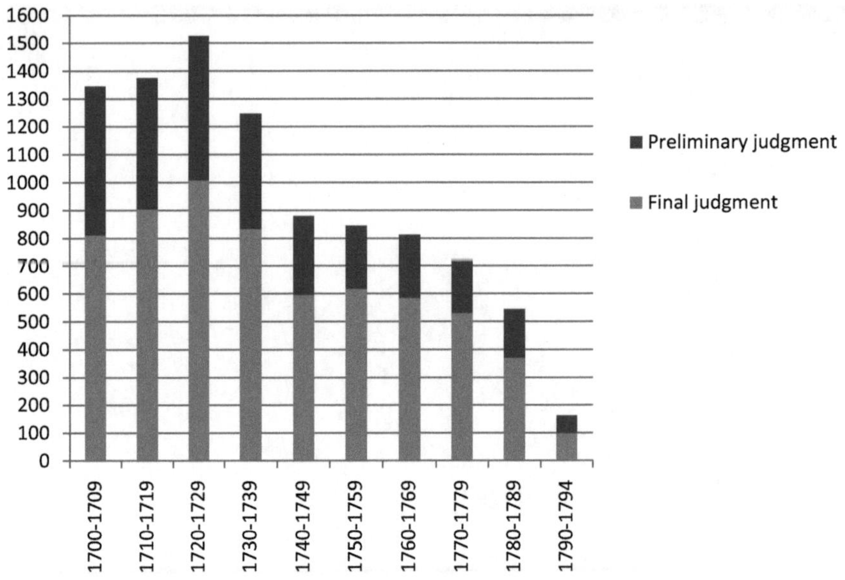

Fig. 4.4 Number of preliminary and final judgments in the dicta registers (1700–1794)

process of trial and error, we were able to make a distinction based on the wording of the disposition.[51]

Research Results For the entire period between 1700 and 1794, 9457 dicta were registered, 6352 of which proved to be final judgments, while the remaining 3105 are preliminary sentences (Fig. 4.4[52]).

The chart mapping the dicta demonstrates an evolution similar to the one observed for the extended sentences: the early period is marked by a relatively high number of dicta, fluctuating between *grosso modo* 800 and 1000 final judgments in 10 years (between 1240 and 1530 if the preliminaries are included). From the 1740s on, there is a significant decrease in the number of dicta, which was without a doubt at least partially instigated by the Echternach exile. Even though the political situation returned back to normal in the 1750s, there are no signs of recovery to the pre-war level. Nonetheless, after the 1740s, the number of dicta remained

[51] The phrase *La cour avant que de disposer* (the court, before judging [the case]) clearly indicated that we dealt with a preliminary judgment, while judgments preceded by *l'empereur et roi* were obviously final sentences. However, in between these two lies a grey area, made up by all dispositions starting with the simple two words *la cour*. Since this wording could be associated both with preliminary and final sentences, we had to take into account other elements: for example, if the dictum ended with a condemnation to pay the costs of the lawsuit (and not only the costs of e.g. a *requête civile*) we considered it to be a final judgment. Nevertheless, a certain error rate is unavoidable.

[52] It is important to note that the last period described only comprises 5 years, two of which the Great Council remained in exile. The decrease in the number of dicta is therefore not as drastic as it seems.

stable throughout a period that more or less coincides with the reign of Maria Theresa: from 1750 to 1779, the number of final judgments fluctuated between 530 and 620. The 1780s however, show another rather steep decline. Even though the significant drop in the number of dispositions can at least partially be explained by the loss of jurisdiction over the Councils of Luxemburg and Tournay as well as by the complicated circumstances of the time—the (legal) reforms of Joseph II and the consequent rebellion in the Netherlands—there is undeniably a consistent pattern of decline in the output of the Great Council over the course of the eighteenth century. An average of 37 dicta per year in the 1780s, divided over 14–16 councilors, does not paint a picture of a thriving tribunal, but rather of an institution that is slowly but certainly fading away, assisted in its death throes by the circumstances.

Our previous research into the prosecution policy of the fiscals has demonstrated that several—at least criminal—cases in which sentences were unmistakably pronounced[53] proved to be absent from the dicta. In fact, of the 31 trials conducted between 1767 and 1788 for which the sentences were preserved in the files, only 8 sentences were recorded in the dicta.[54] So far, we have been unable to determine why certain judgments are missing. Without a doubt, a certain fraction has to be attributed to human error—e.g. during the copying phase—but it seems unlikely that the registrar accidentally forgot to record 23 criminal sentences. Considering that we do not know the exact percentage of 'missing dicta', that we have no idea if our findings for the fiscal files are also applicable in civil cases, that it is uncertain how many lawsuits were terminated before there was a judgment, and that we are unable to provide any reason for the absence of certain dispositions in the registers of the dicta, we have to conclude that the dicta only present a partial view of the caseload of the Great Council and even of the number of cases judged.

4.2.1.3 Distribution Records[55] (Fig. 4.5)

Typology While so far we have mainly examined the 'output' of the Great Council—i.e. the number of lawsuits in which a sentence was effectively pronounced—the distribution records allow us to have some idea of the 'input'.[56] For the eighteenth

[53] Many criminal case files contain the sentence of the trial. A possible explanation for this phenomenon is that files preserved in the archives of the fiscals were considered to be the 'property' of the office-fiscal.

[54] Verscuren, An. 2005. *"L'oeil et le bras du Roi?" Het vervolgingsbeleid van het officie-fiscaal van de Grote Raad van Mechelen (1767–1788)*. Unpublished Master's Thesis. Leuven: Katholieke Universiteit Leuven, 54. Conversely, we were also able to retrieve three dicta of trials that did not correspond to a case file in the archives. Given the large number of un-inventoried civil case files and the several dozens of meters of archives waiting for an inventory in the *varia*, it is possible that these criminal files will turn up in the future.

[55] Brussels, ARA, GRM 617–620; Brussels, ARA, GRM 629–633; Brussels, ARA, GRM 634–637.

[56] That is to say: an idea of the number of lawsuits that reached the distribution phase. We can be fairly certain that a certain percentage of cases introduced at the Great Council were never

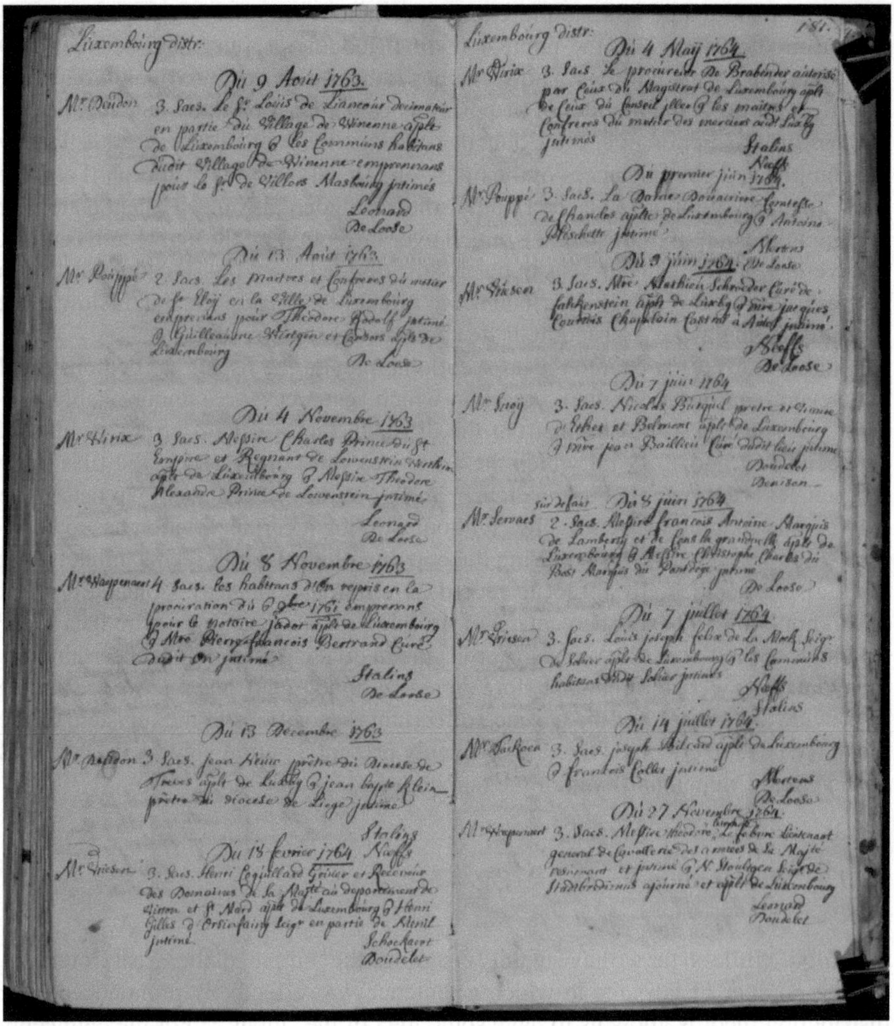

Fig. 4.5 Distribution record arranged by province of origin. (ARA, GRM 619)

century, the archives of the Great Council hold two different types of distribution records. While the first type contains both appeals and first instance cases, the second type is exclusively reserved for those lawsuits that followed the communicatory procedure (*différends*). Consequently, procedure is the distinguishing feature.[57] In

distributed.

[57] This is true for the late seventeenth and eighteenth century. From 1683 on, there are separate distribution records listing the *différends*. Before that date, we can assume that they were recorded together with the other first instance and appeal cases. Given that the communicatory procedure became popular only over the course of the seventeenth century, this is no surprise.

addition, the first type can again be divided into two subcategories, which do not so much differ by the information they provide as by the way the data is arranged, *i.c.* by province of origin or by name of the councilor who acted as reporter.[58] Comparison between these two categories has demonstrated that there is a considerable overlap and that possible lacunae must be attributed to the inevitable human errors of the registrar who recorded the cases.[59]

The division between the different types and subtypes of distribution records is not the result of any *post factum* intervention in the archives, but was already applied during the active phase. Exactly as with the dicta, the registrars recorded the lawsuits directly in the distribution books instead of putting together the registers afterwards. Given that, at least in the eighteenth century, procedure was the determining factor for categorizing incoming cases—as mentioned, appeals and first instance cases that were handled on the *rôle* were registered separately from the *différends*—it must have played an important role in the workings of the Great Council.

Why there are two further subcategories within the registers containing the appeals and first instance cases following the procedure on the *rôle*, is less clear. In a certain way, they seem to represent an 'incoming stream' versus an 'outgoing stream'. Indeed, the distribution books arranged by province record in which part of the jurisdiction of the Great Council the lawsuits originated and thus entered the registry. The other subcategory records to which councilor the case was distributed. Even though the files did not literally leave the Great Council, we could say that the process of allocating a lawsuit to a certain member of the Council could be regarded as an 'outgoing stream', as the files left the registry. Possibly, the distinction was made as a means to keep track of all the files that were brought to the Great Council and to have an idea of the whereabouts of a certain file.

Contrary to the dicta and the extended sentences, the distribution records not only report those cases that were eventually judged, but all the lawsuits that reached the phase of 'distribution', i.e. the stage at which the case was assigned to a reporter. There is, however, at least one exception to this rule: only a very limited number of criminal cases were recorded in the distribution books. Barely four out of the more than 200 eighteenth century criminal trials could be retrieved; all four fall within the *petit criminel* category, which probably means that they followed the civil procedure.[60]

As it was not unusual for litigants to discontinue their legal actions, many of the cases recorded in the distribution books never reached the judgment phase; indeed, observations such as *[sacs] rendu, l'appellant ayant desisté* are legion. Therefore, it

---

[58] This is true from 1613 on. Before that date, only distribution records arranged by name of the reporter are available.

[59] In addition, a small number of errors might be due to the inevitable limitations of our own work copying and analyzing the data. Given the massive amount of data, it is virtually unavoidable that a minor number of inaccuracies have crept into our analysis (although clearly not to such an extent that they could realistically be expected to alter our overall conclusions).

[60] Cf. supra, Chap. 3.

is important to stress that the distribution records provide a dataset that is essentially different from the one gathered from the registers of the extended sentences or from the dicta. The lawsuits listed in the distribution records have reached the final stage before judgment, but many of them will never be sentenced for a variety of reasons: for instance, because one of the parties died, or because the litigants had reached a mutual agreement outside court, or because the parties lost interest in their original claims etc.

The time frame we are dealing with in the distribution records is also different from the dicta and the extended sentences: the sentence could be pronounced within a few weeks or months after the distribution, but the case could also drag on for another few years. In one case, it took 65 years to reach a final judgment after the case had been distributed.[61] As a consequence, comparing data gathered from the distribution records on the one hand and from the dicta and the extended sentences on the other is a somewhat complicated endeavor.

Given that it could take several years before the councilors reached a final disposition, there is inevitably a certain amount of overlap in the cases recorded in the distribution books. Naturally, there is not a single councilor who lived long enough to be solely responsible for a case that took over 60 years to be sentenced. Certain lawsuits were passed on from one councilor to another, for instance because of the death of the first reporter, or because he moved on to another career, or even because he was challenged as a judge by (one of) the litigants. Consequently, as cases were reshuffled after a certain time, the distribution records contain several identical lawsuits with different dates of distribution. As a result, when 'counting' the number of lawsuits in the distribution records, we have to take into account that a not inconsiderable part of the cases returned once, twice or even more.

Methodology The wealth of data the distribution records provide, allows for a wide range of analyses that are not possible using the information of the dicta or the extended sentences. For the purpose of assembling a database of all the cases distributed at the Great Council during the timeframe selected, we started with the information provided by the distribution records organized by the name of the councilor-reporter. This approach was motivated by pragmatic considerations: given that we wanted to have an overview of all cases reported by councilors who lived during the eighteenth century—even though they had already been appointed in the previous century and had reported several cases by 1700—the most straightforward way was to start our search based on the name of the reporter instead of on the region of origin. All these data were brought together in a Microsoft Excel spreadsheet[62] with the following fields: (1) date of distribution, (2) instance (first instance, appeal from Flanders, Luxembourg, Namur etc.), (3) the description of the litigants (the subject of the lawsuit is usually not mentioned in the distribution records) and the number of bags, (4) the name of the reporting councilor, (5) if present, the names of the proctors, and (6) possible other 'observations' such as the restitution of the files to

[61] Cf. infra, 4.5.1.1 Duration of lawsuits.

[62] See: Excel database: distribution records of the eighteenth century Great Council.

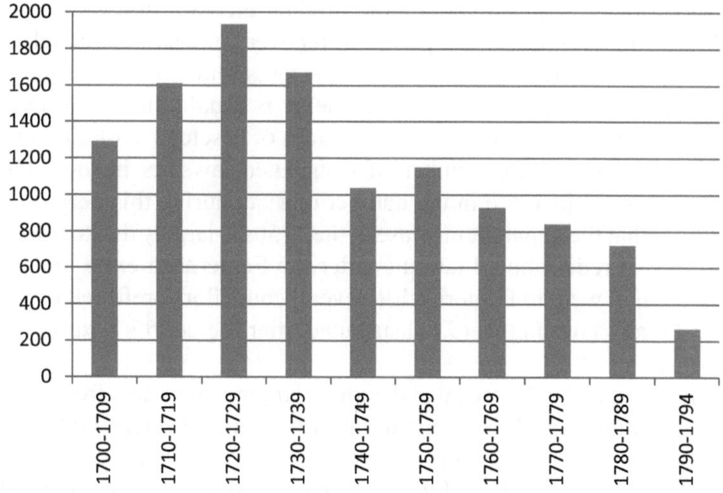

Fig. 4.6 Distributed lawsuits between 1700 and 1794

the litigants, the handing over of a case of one councilor to another or—most importantly—the judgment date. After we had thus assembled a database, we matched and cross-checked our data using the distribution books arranged by province of origin. As we had, at this stage, only included appeals and first instance cases that followed the procedure on the *rôle*,[63] we completed our data collection effort using data from the distribution books listing the *différends*. As a result, we were able to compile an Excel database with 13,152 records spread out over a period of more than hundred years, ranging from 1680 to 1794.[64]

Research Results A first glance at Fig. 4.6[65] suffices to notice that the evolution in the number of lawsuits distributed in the eighteenth century is similar to the one observed for the dicta. The first decades of the eighteenth century are marked by a gradual increase with a peak in the 1720s. The 1740s display a serious dip—there is a difference of more than 600 distributed cases between the 1730s and the 1740s connected to the Great Council's 'exile' in Echternach—followed by a slight recovery in the 1750s and then a progressive decline until 1794. Apart from the fact that

---

[63] Several first instance cases were categorized by the term *matière crue*. However, not all *matière crue* lawsuits proved to be first instance cases: certain appeals were also categorized as such. The status of these *matières crue* lawsuits remains somewhat in the dark, but a valid hypothesis might be that appeals that did not have a written case file—and therefore followed again the first instance procedure at the Great Council—were equally designated as *matières crues*.

[64] Cf. Excel database: distribution records of the eighteenth century Great Council.

[65] Source: Excel database: distribution records of the eighteenth century Great Council. We have not taken into account the period before 1700 as the dataset for this period is incomplete. In fact, we only incorporated those lawsuits distributed to members of the Great Council that were still active in the eighteenth century. Therefore, the chart does not show the 13,152 entries for the entire period between 1680 and 1794 but only the 11,448 lawsuits that were introduced after 1700.

the number of dicta demonstrated a more gradual increase in the early 1700s and that the 1750s did not constitute a period of recovery, the two charts tell an almost identical story. This conclusion was to be expected: although distribution by definition precedes the judgment of a case, this delay is usually not significant enough to create a major difference in the overall pattern of caseload evolution over time.

Only the recovery in the number of distributed lawsuits in the 1750s is not matched by a similar increase in the number of dicta during this period. There is a real possibility that the apparent increase in the 1750s is largely due to a significantly higher number of redistributed lawsuits after the Echternach exile. Indeed, only a 'truncated' council went to Echternach—several councilors preferred to stay in Malines[66]—and many lawsuits were redistributed after the court's return to its hometown.

Either way, it must be stressed that detailed comparison of data from the dicta and from the distribution records is always a somewhat delicate enterprise because of the time lags—which could range from a single day to several decades[67]—between the date of distribution and the date of the sentence. Yet, some entries in the distribution records were labeled as *jugé rendu*.[68] Therefore, to make a comparison between the data retrieved from the distribution records and those from the dicta, we counted the number of cases—distributed between 1700 and 1794—listed as 'judged'.

Theoretically, the results of these calculations should be more or less equal to the number of final dicta we found for the same period. Nevertheless, a certain level of discrepancy is inevitable as we have only taken into account the period between 1700 and 1794: there should be no doubt that several lawsuits distributed in the 1690s and even the 1680s were sentenced several decades later. Moreover, we can assume that the recording of judgments in the distribution books was far from perfect; in fact, the judgment date was not yet known at the time the distribution of the case was recorded and therefore always had to be added *post-factum*. Eventually, we were able to retrieve 5914 sentences for cases distributed between 1700 and 1794. The difference between this number and the 6352 final sentences registered in the dicta can, in our opinion, be explained by these two observations.[69]

The distribution records do not only mention the 'actual' sentences, where the court delivered its judgment, but also record if and when the parties reached a mu-

---

66 Cf. infra, 4.5.2 Caseload of individual councilors.

67 Cf. infra, 4.5.1.1 Duration of lawsuits.

68 Sometimes, but by no means always, the date the sentence was pronounced is included as well.

69 It is also interesting to note that several cases recorded in the dicta cannot be recovered from the distribution records. For the 4 years we researched in detail—1701, 1731, 1761 and 1791—we consistently identified a certain number of dicta that could not be matched to a distributed case. In 1701 and 1731 this was the case for a rather high proportion of the dicta, respectively 29 and 13 %, while in 1761 and 1791 only 4 % of the dicta could not be retrieved in the distribution records. To a certain extent, this phenomenon can be explained by the fact that preliminary sentences were also recorded in the dicta and that the parties involved were not necessarily the same as in the 'main' case: for example, in case of a debate, the parties involved might have another status, or they might even be different from the original parties, making it impossible to retrieve the case in the distribution records. Probably we must also take into account a certain carelessness and sloppiness of the registrars. Yet, there might be other reasons—not known to us—that can explain the absence of certain cases from the distribution records.

tual agreement or when the plaintiff decided to abandon his lawsuit. The former happened rather frequently: in approximately[70] 850 cases, the parties were *accordé* or *transigé*.[71] In fact, as a rule, the councilor-reporter always had to try to accommodate the litigants first. Apart from that, in roughly 120 instances, the plaintiff declared that he wished to abandon the lawsuit (*desisté*); in addition, we encountered several cases designated as *cessé, rendu*, which probably means that the case was abandoned and that the bags were returned to the registrar. Moreover, it is often mentioned that the lawsuit was *remis*—returned—sometimes with the additional clarification *faute de poursuite* (by lack of further proceeding). Finally, it is very likely that for the last 4–5 years (i.e., roughly between 1789 and 1794)—being the chaotic time of the revolution and the French invasions—the data set is lacunal, if only because many lawsuits were distributed too late to be sentenced.

Taking into account all of these limitations, we know for certain what happened to approximately 8000 out of 11,448 lawsuits (or some 70 %) distributed between 1700 and 1794.[72] A certain percentage of the remaining 3000 cases are probably 'doubles', lawsuits that have been redistributed at least once, but sometimes even multiple times, to other councilors. Therefore, we can estimate that the number of 'original' lawsuits distributed in the eighteenth century (until 1794) should be somewhere between 8500 and 10,000.

4.2.2 Criminal Litigation: Corpus and Research Results

So far, we have almost exclusively focused our attention on civil litigation at the Great Council. While it was less far-reaching than its authority in civil affairs, the Great Council's administration of justice in criminal matters constituted an integral part of its jurisdiction. Especially during the fifteenth and sixteenth centuries, criminal justice was a crucial aspect of modern state formation. Indeed, only when sovereigns succeeded in removing the punishment of offenses from the private sphere and managed to transfer the prosecution of crimes to their own tribunals, did it become possible to build a unified state.[73] In the eighteenth century as well, criminal jurisdiction remained a crucial aspect of state building, although in a somewhat different form.[74] Therefore, the question is: to what degree was the Great Council willing and allowed to play a role in this process?

[70] It is impossible to calculate the exact numbers, as these remarks are often rather randomly included and phrased in several different ways. Therefore, the results are always only approximate.

[71] *Transigé* means: concluded before an arbiter. Cf. Kaiser, Colin. 1980. The deflation in the volume of litigation at Paris in the Eighteenth Century and the waning of the old judicial order. *European Studies Review* 10.3: 311.

[72] We have not taken into account the period before 1700 as these numbers are incomplete. In fact, we only incorporated those lawsuits distributed to members of the Great Council that were still active in the eighteenth century.

[73] Levy, René and Rousseaux, Xavier. 1992. Etats, justice pénale et histoire: bilan et perspectives. *Droit et société* 20 21: 249.

[74] In the eighteenth century, this took on the form of attempts by 'enlightened' rulers to impose a unified penal code for all their possessions. Levy, René and Rousseaux, Xavier. 1992. Etats, justice

The archives of the office-fiscal contain four registers with criminal sentences from the eighteenth century.[75] In theory, these registers could form the ideal instrument to count the number of criminal trials in the eighteenth century Great Council. However, earlier research into the prosecution policy of the eighteenth century office-fiscal has demonstrated that only a small percentage of all criminal convictions have been recorded in these registers.[76] The same is true for the fiscal *rôle*:[77] samplings have proven that only a very limited number of criminal trials have been recorded on the *rôle*.[78]

While the series 'recommendations and correspondence of the office-fiscal' contain a few descriptions of criminal trials—though mostly by way of indirect reference—they mainly record advice from the fiscals in response to questions or orders from the government, and to requests from individuals. Given that there have been 60 registers preserved for the eighteenth century and given the large number of entries in these registers as well as their chaotic organization, combing through these records in search of information on criminal trials would be tantamount to searching for a needle in a haystack. Eventually, the criminal case files proved to provide the most accurate information on the prosecution policy of the Great Council.

4.2.2.1 Criminal Case Files[79]

Typology Contrary to the civil case files, the criminal case files have been entirely inventoried, probably during the eighteenth or the early nineteenth century.[80] It turned out to be difficult to pinpoint the exact date when the inventory was first compiled. Between approximately 1750 and 1780 several attempts were undertaken to arrange the archives of the office-fiscal—which were described as 'in great num-

pénale et histoire: bilan et perspectives. *Droit et société* 20–21: 264.

[75] Brussels, ARA, GRMOF, BD 96–99. Register 96 is entirely dedicated to the prosecution of the turmoil in Malines of 1720. Registers 98 and 99 turned out to be copies of register 97.

[76] Verscuren, An. 2005. *"L'oeil et le bras du Roi?" Het vervolgingsbeleid van het officie-fiscaal van de Grote Raad van Mechelen (1767–1788)*. Unpublished Master's Thesis. Leuven: Katholieke Universiteit Leuven, 41. Those sentences that are recorded are elaborately described, as well as their execution. For example, the hanging of counterfeiter Herweig in 1776 is depicted in great detail. Brussels, ARA, GRMOF, BD 97, May 25, 1776.

[77] Brussels, ARA, GRMOF, BD 94, rôle fiscal de 9 avril 1701 à 1794.

[78] The fiscal *rôle* mainly contains descriptions of the annual presentation of bailiffs. Every year the bailiffs of the Great Council had to present themselves and provide surety bonds at the first session of the Great Council after Easter break. Failing to do so resulted in a (temporary) suspension until all requirements were fulfilled. This for example happened to bailiff Mersch. Brussels, ARA, GRMOF, BD 91, f.°149–150, July 21, 1781.

[79] The criminal case files are to be found in the archives of the fiscals: Brussels, ARA, GRMOF.

[80] Brussels, ARA, INV 102. This inventory has later been published by Put, Eddy. 1995. *Officie-fiscaal van de Grote Raad van Mechelen: werkbeschrijvingen*. Brussels: Algemeen Rijksarchief. We based our research on the 'old' inventory as the published version describes the trials in less detail and only mentions the currently 'missing' files without disclosing their content.

ber and without any order or arrangement'—and to compose an inventory.[81] The inventory the archives currently hold might in fact be the result of these efforts; this hypothesis is supported by the conclusion that it mentions several files, which by now have disappeared from the archives. On the other hand, the inventory is remarkably complete, listing trials up and until 1794, while the assignment to assemble an inventory had been given sometime during the early 1750s. Moreover, all descriptions seem to have been written down in the same handwriting. That said, it is still possible that this inventory is a fair copy of an initial draft made by these eighteenth century 'archivists' of the fiscal papers.

It can be assumed that the surviving case files make it possible to draw a fairly representative picture of the prosecution policy of the Great Council. In civil suits, litigants were allowed to collect their files, at least after they had forfeited the possibility of revision and after they had paid a certain fee. As a consequence, merely counting the number of case files would certainly only give a very partial idea of the real scale of civil litigation at the Great Council. As far as criminal trials are concerned, the situation is somewhat different. These were files composed by the procurator-general and advocate-fiscal and were therefore probably considered to be property of the Great Council's office fiscal.[82] Contrary to the civil case files, which were composed by the advocates and proctors of the litigants and often contained important documents belonging to the plaintiff and/or defendant—such as titles—the criminal files consisted entirely of documents collected by one or both fiscals: interrogations, testimonies, etc. Even the sentence was often included. As a consequence, given that the defendants did not own the documents and were therefore not allowed to remove them, we do believe that the number of case files gives a representative—although certainly not entirely complete[83]—image of criminal litigation at the Great Council.[84]

Research Results According to the old inventory, the archives of the office-fiscal once held 287 criminal case files for the entire eighteenth century,[85] subdivided in

[81] Brussels, ARA, GRM 175/10 (19c): archives du Grand Conseil. Classement de l'office fiscal.

[82] The records of the office-fiscal are not part of the main archive of the Great Council. They were in fact separately preserved in the fiscals' quarters. At present, they are still stored separately from the tribunal's records.

[83] There can be no doubt that a certain percentage of the criminal case files have been lost, especially in the period after 1790 when the papers of the office-fiscals were often moved. Moreover, the series first instance cases also contain a few criminal case files that have not been preserved in the archives of the office-fiscal. The real number of criminal cases will therefore be higher than the estimated number of 287.

[84] For more information on the status of case files in the archives of tribunals, see: Put, Eddy. 2000. In de zak? De archiefstatus van procesdossiers uit het ancien régime. In *Door de archivistiek gestrikt: liber amicorum prof. dr. Juul Verhelst* (Archiefinitiatie(f) 4), eds Gustave Janssens e.a, 187–196. Brussels: VUBpress and Oosterbosch, Michel. 2006. Archief of niet? De procesdossiers van de Grote Raad voor de Nederlanden te Mechelen. In *Hoge rechtspraak in de oude Nederlanden*, eds. Hugo de Schepper and René Vermeir, 65–78. Maastricht: Shaker.

[85] In counting the number of criminal trials and in arranging them by decade, we always took into account the latest date mentioned, as some criminal cases started in the seventeenth century but

grand and *petit criminel* trials as well as in so called political lawsuits. The first two categories cover a great variety of crimes. We may presume that the difference between *grand* and *petit criminel* is one of procedure in which those trials categorized under the label *grand criminel* followed the criminal procedure while the *petit criminel* suits were conducted according to the civil procedure.[86]

In practice,[87] at least for the period between 1767 and 1788, half of the trials dealt with contraventions against authority. In this category, we put all forms of aggression—both verbal and physical—against authorities, such as insulting behavior towards a councilor or aggression against a bailiff. Some 20 % of the trials relate to misconduct by officials in the execution of their duties. A third category includes offences against persons who were not acting in their capacities as Great Council officials at the time the crime was committed: a street fight between two advocates can be found in this category.[88] Finally, contraventions against property constitute the last category. These include thefts of all kinds as well as a trial against the alleged attempt of some fishmongers to acquire a monopoly on the herring sale in the city of Malines.[89] Lastly, the *procès politiques* refer to those trials connected to the rebellious times of 1786–1794.[90]

Figure 4.7 mapping the spreading of criminal lawsuits over time, shows that there is a substantial peak in the 1720s and a pronounced dip in the 1760s. To a large extent, the peak in the 1720s can be explained by the trials in the wake of the 1718 uprising in Malines:[91] 38 of the 74 criminal cases dealt with by the Great Council during this time are connected to the prosecution of people accused of having participated in the upheaval. This leaves 36 regular trials, a number in line with the previous 2 decades.

The dip in the 1760s seems harder to explain. However, in our earlier research on the prosecution policy of the office-fiscal between 1767 and 1788, we suggested that the number of criminal actions at the Great Council depended to a large extent

continued in the eighteenth century.

86 Our research in 2005 has in any case demonstrated that two very comparable lawsuits may be catalogued in different categories. See: Verscuren, An. 2005. *"L'oeil et le bras du Roi?" Het vervolgingsbeleid van het officie-fiscaal van de Grote Raad van Mechelen (1767–1788)*. Unpublished Master's Thesis. Leuven: Katholieke Universiteit Leuven, 65.

87 See: Verscuren, An. 2005. *"L'oeil et le bras du Roi?" Het vervolgingsbeleid van het officie-fiscaal van de Grote Raad van Mechelen (1767–1788)*. Unpublished Master's Thesis. Leuven: Katholieke Universiteit Leuven, 53.

88 Brussels, ARA, GRMOF 504: case file of the trial against advocates Posson and Scheppers (1783).

89 Brussels, ARA, GRMOF 536, 1766–1771: the fiscals against Pierre François and Corneil Joseph Poullet, Pierre and Jacques Morissons, the widow of Antoine Morissons and the widow of Matthieu Verhuyck, all fishmongers in the city of Malines.

90 However, closer examination has revealed that some other, unrelated trials, were included as well. Probably, all trials of this period have been indiscriminately grouped into this category for convenience reasons.

91 Tambuyser, Raphaël. 1953. Sociale troebelen te Mechelen in 1718. *Handelingen van de Koninklijke Kring voor Oudheidkunde, Letteren en Kunst van Mechelen* 57: 188–203.

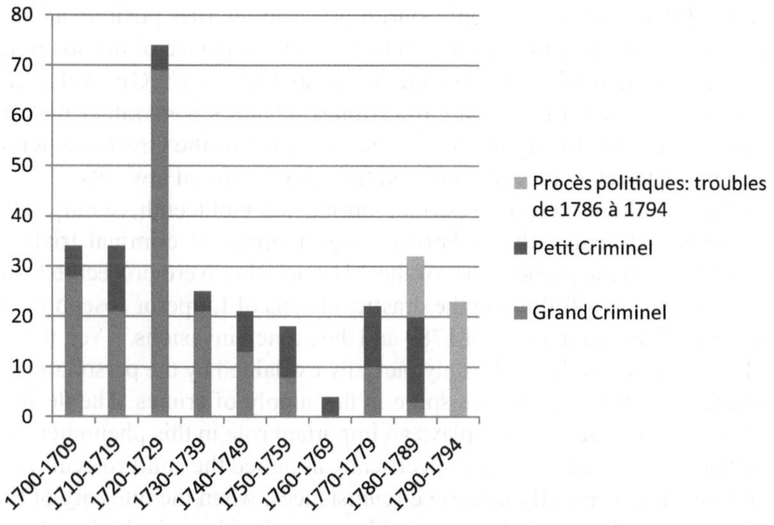

Fig. 4.7 Criminal case files at the great council of Malines (1700–1794)

on the personalities of the prosecutors.[92] Many fiscals were appointed more or less against their own will and turned out to be less than perfectly diligent prosecutors of crime. Three of them—Henri Jacobs (prosecutor-general between 1761 and 1767), Jean-Baptiste van Slabbeeck (advocate-fiscal between 1744 and 1766) and Henri-Joseph de Villers de Fourneau (advocate-fiscal between 1767 and 1771)—were 'active' during the 1760s, accounting for the very small number of criminal trials during this period. Once Henri Chrétien Diu (prosecutor-general between 1767 and 1794) took over and especially when Jacques Joseph de Stassart became his colleague (between 1778 and 1789), the number of prosecutions rose again and came close to matching the number of the first 2 decades of the eighteenth century. De Stassart's successor Melchior Goubau took his duties as prosecutor-general to heart as well.[93] This phenomenon at least partially explains why from the 1770s on, the activity levels of criminal trials show an evolution opposite to that observed for civil lawsuits: while there is a consistent decline in the latter, the former slightly picks up.

Compared to civil proceedings, the number of criminal cases is almost negligible.[94] The main reason for this is the very restricted criminal jurisdiction of the Great Council. The tribunal was only competent to deal with offences by its own personnel and by those persons who were counted among the *escroux*, as well as with all crimes that encroached on the sovereign's authority. Furthermore, it is important to

---

[92] Verscuren, An. 2005. *"L'oeil et le bras du Roi?" Het vervolgingsbeleid van het officie-fiscaal van de Grote Raad van Mechelen (1767–1788)*. Unpublished Master's Thesis. Leuven: Katholieke Universiteit Leuven, 86–87.

[93] Cf. infra, Chap. 5.

[94] It does not mean that crime in the jurisdiction of the Great Council was negligible: this number only represents the number of crimes prosecuted by the Great Council; most were brought before the bench of aldermen of Malines.

keep in mind that fiscals could only start a prosecution after positive advice from the councilors of the Great Council or following an ordinance of the sovereign, the governor, the Council of Finance or the Accounts Chamber.[95] Given that criminal trials were in general not financially rewarding—chances were rather high that the accused were not able to pay the bill[96]—the members of the Great Council can be suspected of some reluctance to taking on too many criminal lawsuits.

Nevertheless, there were two periods during the eighteenth century when the Great Council did deal with a relatively large number of criminal trials: firstly, around 1720, when the perpetrators of the 1718 uprising were prosecuted, and secondly, during the years following the drastic reforms of Emperor Joseph II, starting around 1786, the Brabant revolt of 1789 and the French invasions.[97] Yet, this sudden rise in the number of trials can be only partially explained by the personalities of the prosecutors or even by the sudden spike in the supply of crimes. The desire of the Great Council to showcase itself plays an important role in this phenomenon, especially because the government had specifically assigned the court to deal with these political trials. It was exactly in these circumstances, when the integrity of the state was in danger, that the Great Council could assume its role as the highest tribunal of the Austrian Netherlands, defending the authority of the Austrian sovereigns, proving that it was *par excellence* the 'Emperor's Court'.[98]

4.3 Types of Civil Litigation

In origin, the Great Council was first and foremost an appeal court: while its jurisdiction in first instance was somewhat limited, the Great Council could hear appeals against sentences of the majority of the provincial councils in the Netherlands. As

[95] *ROPB,* 2ième série, t.7, August 8, 1559, title II, article 4.

[96] In general, fiscals could not be ordered to pay the costs of a criminal trial. Cf. *ROPB,* 2ième série, t.7, August 8, 1559 title II, article 10. While it once in a while happened that the advocate-fiscal and procurator-general were ordered to pay the costs (e.g. Brussels, ARA, GRMOF 536, 1766–1771), it was often the defendant who had to pay the bill, even if he was acquitted. If the accused was insolvent, it regularly happened that the councilors attempted to recover the costs from the *caisse des exploits*. Given that the funds in the *caisse* were not always sufficient, the councilors' work in criminal trials could remain unrewarded.

[97] The 38 criminal cases of 1720 connected to the prosecution of people accused of having participated in the upheaval and the 35 *procès politiques* of the period between 1786 and 1794 still constitute a small number compared to the number of trials that were dealt with at other tribunals. For example, over a period of 40 years in the second half of the eighteenth century, the Council of Namur conducted 378 criminal trials. Dupont-Bouchat, Marie-Sylvie and Page-Steffens, Marie-Paule. 2006. Des délits et des peines: l'activité pénale du Conseil Provincial de Namur au XVIIIe siècle. In *La Belgique criminelle: droit, justice, société (XIVe-XXe siècles)*, eds. Marie-Sylvie Dupont-Bouchat and Xavier Rousseaux, 273–316. Louvain-la-Neuve: Academia-Bruylant.

[98] Cf. infra, Chap. 5.

Table 4.2 Ratio appeals versus first instance cases in the sixteenth and eighteenth century extended sentences

	# Appeals	# First instance
1510	19	19
1515	25	14
1520	31	20
1525	39	19
1530	49	39
1535	80	59
1540	74	49
1545	49	64
1550	79	74
1555	39	32
1560	55	50
1565	88	58
1570	49	38
1575	53	28
1580	9	2

	# Appeals	# First instance
1693-1702	47	37
1703-1712	17	40
1713-1722	10	25
1723-1732	19	19
1733-1742	16	14
1743-1752	3	9
1753-1762	6	3
1763-1772	9	1

Table 4.2[99] indicates, analysis of the sixteenth century extended sentences has indeed revealed that during the first century of its existence, the Malines tribunal usually dealt with substantially more appeal cases than first instance lawsuits.[100] While the special nature of the extended sentences might have somewhat colored this observation—there could have been reasons to more readily require an extended sentence for an appeal case than for a first instance lawsuit—a comparable analysis of the eighteenth century extended sentences has revealed that at times, especially in the first half of the century, there were more first instance cases than appeals; when the opposite was true, the difference was only small.

[99] Source for the sixteenth century: De Smidt, Jacobus et al. eds. 1966–1988. *Chronologische lijsten van de geëxtenderdeerde sententiën berustende in het archief van de Grote Raad van Mechelen*, 6 volumes. Brussels: Koninklijke Commissie voor de uitgave der oude wetten en verordeningen van België. Source for the eighteenth century: Verscuren, An. 2013. *Nadere toegang op de geëxtendeerde sententies van de Grote Raad van Mechelen: 1693–1772*. Brussels: Algemeen Rijksarchief.

[100] We have counted the number of appeal and first instance cases in de Smidt's *Chronologische Lijsten* carrying out a sample survey at 5 year intervals (1510, 1515, 1520 and so on until 1580). Gilissen claimed that analysis of the *Chronologische Lijsten* has revealed that there is an almost even split between first instance lawsuits and appeals. Cf. Gilissen, John. 1980. De Grote Raad van Mechelen. Historisch overzicht. In *Miscelannea Consilii Magni. Ter gelegenheid van twintig jaar Werkgroep Grote Raad van Mechelen*. Amsterdam: Universiteit van Amsterdam. Faculteit der rechtsgeleerdheid, 33. Based on our observations, we believe that this is not the case. In fact, only in 1545 did the Council deal with more first instance cases than appeals.

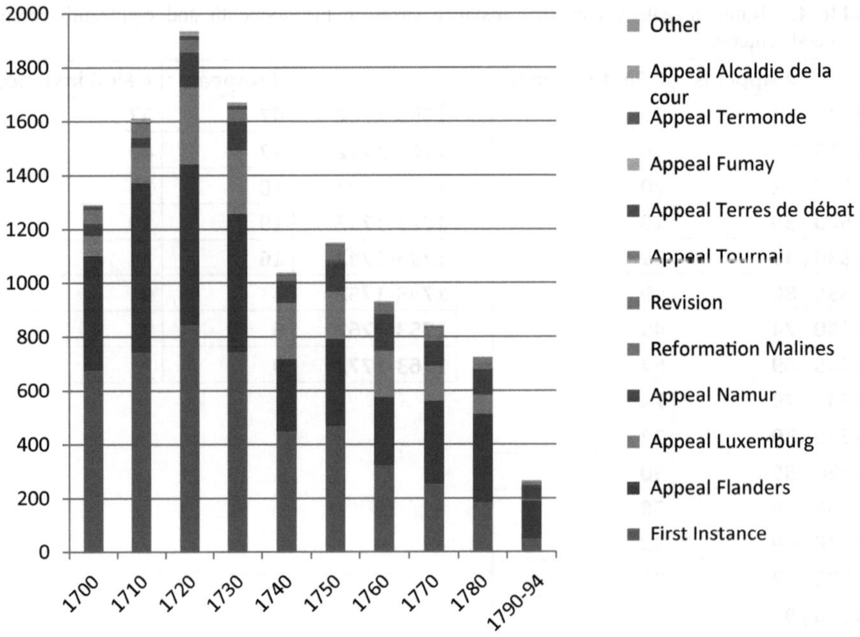

Fig. 4.8 Breakdown of distributed lawsuits by instance and by province of origin

For the eighteenth century, we can compare the data from the extended sentences with those provided by the distribution books. Not only does this make it possible to determine if the information from the extended sentences is representative—at least for the eighteenth century—it also allows for a much more detailed analysis of the breakdown of civil litigation at the Great Council.

The following table and chart show the number of distributed lawsuits arranged by instance and, as far as the appeals are concerned, by province of origin (Fig. 4.8).

Unsurprisingly, first instance cases[101] and appeals from Flanders, Luxembourg and Namur—which constitute the core of the jurisdiction of the Great Council—account for 95 % of the total number of eighteenth century (civil) lawsuits. The preponderance of first instance cases largely confirms our preliminary findings from the extended sentences: although in aggregate the number of appeals exceeds the number of first instance cases, the latter in itself accounts for 41 % of the total.[102] The high incidence rate of first instance lawsuits in the eighteenth century compared to appeals can to some extent be attributed to the restricted jurisdiction of the

[101] When breaking down these first instance cases according to procedure into *différends* versus lawsuits on the *rôle*, it turned out that some 78 % belonged to the first category, indicating the predominance—and increasing popularity—of the communicatory procedure over the procedure on the *rôle*. Cf. Excel database: distribution records of the eighteenth century Great Council.

[102] The fact that the number of first instance cases in the extended sentences exceeds the number of appeals can be largely attributed to the high incidence rate of *sentences de decret*. Cf. supra.

Great Council in appeal during the last century of its existence. Given that for the greater part of the eighteenth century, the tribunal was only competent for the Councils of Flanders, Namur and Luxemburg and the Magistrate of Malines, it is natural that the proportion of appeals should be much smaller than in the sixteenth century.

Additionally, the high incidence rate of first instance cases may also indicate that litigants regularly turned to the Great Council as first instance tribunal. This may seem at odds with the court's jurisdiction in first instance, which remained limited to cases involving privileged persons or privileged subject matter.[103] The explanation may lie in the fact that much of the Great Council's activity in first instance was connected to the opposition against 'open letters' (*lettres patentes)* which the tribunal awarded on simple request of a party without any preceding examination of the validity of the request or of the question whether it was competent to deal with the matter. It is possible that the Great Council indirectly and stealthily did increase its jurisdiction in first instance in this way, maybe even as a deliberate attempt to compensate for its loss of jurisdiction in appeal. No matter what the explanation of the phenomenon might be, it is clear that the function of the Great Council evolved somewhat over the course of its existence from a court of appeal to a not unimportant first instance tribunal. At the very end of the eighteenth century however, this evolution turned around again.

Observations on the Ratio of First Instance versus Appeal Cases As Table 4.3[104] indicates, Flanders was the major provider of appeals. This was to be expected: if not the largest in terms of territory, it was the most densely populated and wealthy region within the jurisdiction of the Great Council. What catches the eye is the increase in the number of appeals coming from Flanders in the 1770s and 1780s compared to the period before. In fact, the trend is exactly opposite to the developments we noticed in the number of first instance cases. After a distinct dip in the 1740s—during its exile in Echternach, the Great Council handled only certain first instance cases and appeals from Luxembourg—the appeals from Flanders display some recovery. When looking at the figures for Namur, we notice a similar development: a dip in the 1740s—although not as distinct as in the case of Flanders—followed by an increase. During the last 4 years of the Great Council's active existence, even more appeals from Namur were distributed than first instance cases.

The number of appeals from Luxemburg does not appear to follow the same pattern. Unsurprisingly, there was no drastic decrease during the 1740s: in fact, Luxemburg was the only region over which the Great Council kept its jurisdiction

[103] Cf. Chap. 3 for the overview of the jurisdiction of the Great Council in first instance.

[104] Source: Excel database: distribution records of the eighteenth century Great Council. We again used the 11,448 lawsuits, even though there is inevitably a number of double-counted cases. However, since it is not easy to distinguish between the original cases and the doubles and since these doubles will not profoundly affect the evolution or the break-down in regions of origin, we decided to take our original count as a starting point. Moreover, as was the case for the chart mapping the dicta, the final period described (1790–1794) only comprises 5 years, including 2 years during which the Great Council had to go into exile. The decrease in the number of distributed lawsuits is therefore not as drastic as it might seem at first glance.

Table 4.3 Breakdown of distributed lawsuits by instance and by province of origin

INSTANCE	1700	1710	1720	1730	1740	1750	1760	1770	1780	1790	TOTAL
First Instance	677	744	844	745	448	470	322	254	185	49	4,738
Appeal Flanders	424	629	597	512	270	321	253	306	327	141	3,780
Appeal Luxemburg	76	130	287	236	208	175	173	132	71	5	1,493
Appeal Namur	45	37	129	108	82	121	137	92	97	53	901
Reformation Malines	45	32	32	30	15	40	25	17	21	10	267
Revision	7	16	11	12	3	15	10	5	2		81
Appeal Tournai		3	3	2	2		1	26	20	2	59
Appeal *Terres de débat*	12	8	16	14	3						53
Appeal Fumay	1	6	7								14
Appeal Dender-monde						3	3	4		1	11
Appeal *Alcaldie de la cour*	1	2	5								8
Other	*2*	*3*	*4*	*11*	*5*	*5*	*5*	*4*	*1*	*3*	*43*
TOTAL	1290	1610	1935	1670	1036	1150	929	840	724	264	11,448

throughout the entire period of the French invasion and occupation. The number of appeals from Luxemburg did diminish after the 1740s, but not as dramatically as the number of first instance cases. It is also notable that there were still 71 appeals from Luxembourg distributed over the 1780s and five in the 1790s, even though the Council of Luxemburg had been awarded sovereignty in 1782. This must be explained by the delay between the introduction of a case at the Great Council and its distribution. The fact that there were still 71 appeals from Luxembourg ongoing in the 1780s—a relatively high number, as we can assume that almost no new cases were introduced after 1782—indicates that Luxembourg did not exhibit an entirely different development from Namur and Flanders.

In summary, the number of first instance cases and the number of appeals show an almost opposite evolution. While the former demonstrated a persistent decline after 1740—the revival in the 1750s was almost negligible—the latter showed at most a small decrease, and in case of Flanders and especially Namur, even a renewed rise in the late eighteenth century.

This observation is not easy to explain. The figures seem to suggest that, contrary to what happened at the Great Council, the number of first instance cases at the Councils of Flanders and Namur (and potentially Luxembourg) did not decline,

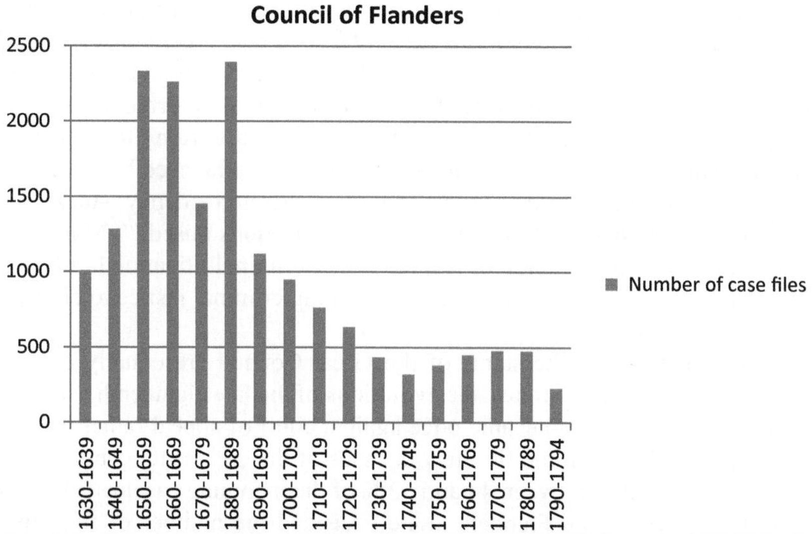

Fig. 4.9 Number of case files in the council of flanders (1630–1790)

but instead slightly rose towards the end of the eighteenth century, at least if we assume that there is a correlation between the number of first instance and appeal cases. Since no thorough quantitative research has yet been done on the provincial councils of the Netherlands, numbers are rare. However, for the Council of Flanders some information is available: based on the inventory of Buntinx, M.-C. Le Bailly has counted the number of case files in the archives of the Council of Flanders for the period between the 1630s and 1790s[105] (See Fig. 4.9[106]).

In general, the overall evolution is marked by a steady decrease in the number of case files starting in the late seventeenth century. It is however remarkable that a small—but not inconsiderable—increase can be noticed in the 1750s, to a large extent corresponding to the slight rise in the number of appeals coming from Flanders at the Great Council. Both the time frame and the increase are far too limited to draw any significant conclusions, but it does raise some questions: in fact, if a comparable evolution could be determined at the Councils of Namur and Luxemburg, the constant decline in the number of first instance cases at the Great Council would be more exception than rule in the Netherlands.

None of these questions are easy to answer and the lack of available data for comparison does not help. So far, C. Kaiser, in his study on the *Parlement de Par-*

[105] M.-C. Le Bailly has produced these figures in the context of a research proposal, and was kind enough to allow us to use them. Of course, the absolute numbers should not be compared to any of the data we have available for the Great Council; in fact, they reflect the number of **case files** left in the archives of the Council of Flanders, a data set that for practical reasons we did not investigate for the Great Council.

[106] The numbers for the 1790s only comprise 5 years until 1794.

is, is the only author who has used distribution records to systematically map the number of lawsuits or any evolutions herein.[107] As a result, certain studies, which do examine longitudinal developments[108] only provide a high-level picture but do not offer any breakdown by instance (first instance, appeal, reformation etc.). Since our analysis has proven that there might be variations according to instance—for the Great Council it is obvious that the general trend is influenced by the decline in first instance cases, but that the appeals follow a different tendency—these general studies will only partially help in answering the questions raised.[109] Moreover, for other councils—e.g. the Council of Namur—only criminal litigation has been subject to research.[110] Extrapolating numbers regarding criminal justice to civil justice is obviously problematic.

The consequences for the status of the Great Council are equally difficult to assess. As Table 4.3 demonstrates, the evolutions of the late eighteenth century suggest that the Great Council became once again a court of appeal rather than a first instance tribunal. While in the first few decades of the eighteenth century, first instance cases constituted between 44 and 52 % of the incoming caseload at the Great Council, the appeals from Flanders alone exceeded the number of first instance lawsuits from the 1770s on. In the 1790s, the number of appeals provided by the Council of Namur even surpassed the number of first instance cases introduced at the Great Council. A larger supply of lawsuits at the provincial councils is at the basis of these evolutions. On the one hand, this suggests that the Great Council lost its attraction for litigants as first instance court. On the other hand, the court might have been able to strengthen its grip—albeit to a limited extent given the very small overall number of cases introduced in the period between 1770 and 1794—on the tribunals subordinate to its authority.

Miscellanea The remaining numbers in Table 4.3 appear to follow the normal pattern. Before 1740, there is an increase in the number of lawsuits with a peak around the 1720s, when the chaotic situation in the Southern Netherlands caused by the death of Charles II had more or less settled down and the new Austrian rulers were steadily imposing their authority. The relatively limited number of appeals from the Councils of Luxembourg and Namur in the first 2 decades of the eighteenth century

[107] Kaiser, Colin. 1980. The deflation in the volume of litigation at Paris in the Eighteenth Century and the waning of the old judicial order. *European Studies Review* 10.3: 309–336.

[108] Cf. Le Bailly, Marie-Charlotte. 2011. Langetermijntrends in de rechtspraak bij de gewestelijke hoven van justitie in de Noordelijke Nederlanden van ca. 1450 tot ca. 1800. *Pro Memorie* 13: 30–67; Champion, W.A. 1998. Recourse to the Law and the meaning of the Great Litigation Decline. In *Communities and courts in Britain, 1150–1900*, eds. Christopher Brooks and Michael Lobban, 179–198. Rio Grande: Hambledon Press; Horwitz, Henry and Polden, Patrick. 1996. Continuity or change in the Court of Chancery in the seventeenth and eighteenth centuries? *Journal of British Studies* 35.1: 24–57.

[109] Cf. infra, 3.7 Explaining the ‘great litigation decline’.

[110] Dupont-Bouchat, Marie-Sylvie and Page-Steffens, Marie-Paule. 2006. Des délits et des peines: l’activité pénale du Conseil Provincial de Namur au XVIIIe siècle. In *La Belgique criminelle: droit, justice, société (XIVe-XXe siècles)*, eds. Marie-Sylvie Dupont-Bouchat and Xavier Rousseaux, 273–316. Louvain-la-Neuve: Academia-Bruylant.

can be traced back to the War of the Spanish Succession: when in 1708 'enemy' troops occupied Malines, Philips V assigned the jurisdiction over Luxembourg and Namur to the Provincial Council of Hainaut.[111] When 3 years later, Mons was captured as well, Maximilien Emmanuel de Bavière decided that the Council of Luxemburg would function as court of appeal for sentences of the Council of Namur and vice versa.[112] It was only in 1714 that Königsegg reassigned the authority to hear appeals from the Councils of Luxembourg and Namur to the Great Council, at least for those cases that had not yet been distributed.[113]

The small number of revisions is also in line with what one might expect. As revisions were the last resort for litigants who did not agree with a Great Council ruling, they would in theory simply constitute the final stage in their proceedings. In practice, however, revisions were a considerably expensive step to take in litigation, since they always required a joined session of the Council's chambers, supplemented with external judges: for these additional councilors, the litigants not only had to pay the regular *épices* but also their travel and accommodation expenses. It is not hard to imagine that after having run through a number of instances which may have lasted for several years, most of the litigants decided to submit to the verdict of the court.

Table 4.3 also illustrates that the decision of 1743 to assign the jurisdiction over the *Terres de débat* to the Councils of Flanders and Hainaut[114] was implemented despite the Great Council's opposition.[115] Indeed, appeals coming from the *Terres de débat* suddenly taper off in the 1740s. Although they were never very prominent—the region is only small in size—there were consistently at least some cases originating from these 'contested territories' during the first 3 decades of the eighteenth century. We can make a similar observation for Tournai: in 1773, the jurisdiction over the Council of Tournai was assigned to the Great Council, but in 1782[116] the Great Council lost it again to the Council of Hainaut. The handful of lawsuits that were still being distributed in the 1780s and 1790s can be mainly explained by the delay between the introduction of a case at the Great Council and that case entering the reporting phase.[117]

Finally, a very small percentage of the total number of cases distributed at the Great Council is made up of appeals coming from small seigniories which were independent from any provincial council and therefore took directly to the Great Council.[118]

---

[111] *ROPBA*, t.2, pp. 110–111, January 10, 1708.

[112] *ROPBA*, t.2, pp. 377–379, September 3, 1711.

[113] *ROPBA*, t.2, pp. 375–376, December 2, 1714.

[114] *ROPBA*, t.5, pp. 540–541, March 26, 1743.

[115] Cf. supra, Chap. 3.

[116] *ROPBA*, t.12, pp. 216–217, November 22, 1782.

[117] Still, as we have demonstrated in Chap. 3, some lawsuits originating from Tournai were newly introduced after 1782.

[118] We have discussed the case of Dendermonde in Chap. 3.

4.4 The Nature of Litigation

4.4.1 Sources

Literature on the Great Council often repeats the usual commonplaces about the jurisdiction of the court, without however exactly specifying the kind of cases treated.[119] Only the—often lacunal—sources on the actual administration of justice can shed some light on the nature of litigation at the Great Council. The reality is that the means available to investigate the subject matter handled at the tribunal are very sparse and only indirect. As neither the dicta nor the distribution registers mention the subject of the lawsuits, we can only guess what the cases described were about. We can, for example, reasonably assume that lawsuits between two individuals who are both listed as heirs of the same testator deal with inheritance questions—but neither the dicta nor the distribution records provide enough information to know for certain.

The case files could potentially be useful, but given that only a small part of the files has been subject to inventory—at least as far as civil litigation is concerned—and that there is no chronological order in the files preserved in the archives, the use of these dossiers is rather limited. Moreover, as the inventories of Oosterbosch demonstrate,[120] several of these files are incomplete, containing sometimes barely one or two documents, making it complicated to determine the exact subject of the lawsuit. Despite these obstacles, inventories pertaining to certain parts of the enormous number of case files are available. For instance, the collection of lawsuits regarding 'prominent families' has been described sometime during the nineteenth century. In addition, the nature of litigation at the Great Council is analyzed using the extended sentences and the eighteenth century collections of case law.

In order to get a grasp of what sort of lawsuits litigants brought before the Great Council, we selected only first instance cases.[121] The reason we did not include appeals is twofold. Firstly, since we aimed to examine what kind of lawsuits litigants brought *directly* before the Great Council, taking appeals into consideration would have little benefit for our analysis.[122] In addition, appeals from Flanders,

[119] Van Rhee, Remco. 1997. *Litigation and legislation: civil procedure at first instance in the Great Council of for the Netherlands in Malines (1522–1559)*. Brussels: Algemeen Rijksarchief, 35.

[120] Oosterbosch, Michel. 1998. Grote Raad voor de Nederlanden te Mechelen: procesbundels beroepen uit Vlaanderen: ordinaris processen (nr. 1–1000). Brussels: Algemeen Rijksarchief.; Oosterbosch, Michel. 2006. Inventaris van het archief van de Grote Raad voor de Nederlanden te Mechelen: procesbundels beroepen uit Holland 1460–1740. Brussels: Algemeen Rijksarchief.

[121] The only exception to this rule are the recueils d'arrêts, as these sources often did not allow us to distinguish the first instance cases from the appeals.

[122] Additionally, investigating the subjects of appeal cases would lead us too far and reveal more about the competence of the lower tribunals than about the jurisdiction of the Great Council. We do admit that in practice, the Great Council dealt with a wider range of subject matters than what will be discussed in this subsection because of its competence as a court of appeal. On the other hand, the jurisdiction of the provincial tribunals in first instance is somewhat comparable to that of the Great Council.

Luxemburg, and Namur and reformations from Malines were handled by the Great Council primarily because it was the dedicated court of appeal for these tribunals and not because it had any special competence to deal with the litigants or subjects in question. Moreover, if a written case file was available, the Great Council in theory used the same set of documents as the subordinate court *(ex eisdem actis)* and only assessed whether or not the judges in first instance had pronounced the correct sentence (*an bene vel male (judicatum))*.[123]

4.4.1.1 The Collection of Case Files Concerning Prominent Families[124]

Most likely, the collection of case files concerning prominent families—*in casu* the nobility—were assembled during the nineteenth century from various different sources—first instance cases, appeals, etc.—and artificially put together into one collection. We can indeed assume that the archives of the Great Council were initially arranged according to the origin of the case files, and that the collection prominent families was compiled post-factum to meet a nineteenth century interest. Regardless, the inventory provides us with a first idea of the nature of the lawsuits in which these noble families acted as plaintiffs or defendants.[125]

346 out of the more than 1380 case files described in the A series of the inventory were identified as eighteenth century dossiers; 330 of these are first instance cases. The bulk of these cases deal with debts in the broadest sense of the word: unsettled accounts, outstanding interests, servants complaining about unpaid salaries, or just unspecified claims … causing in the worst case scenario the (forced) sale of properties, ranging from land and individual properties to entire seigniories. These so-called *sentences de décret* constitute the largest category.

An extreme example of this compulsory sale of properties, including entire seigniories and manors, is the liquidation of the estate of the Prince of Steenhuize. In the early eighteenth century, several creditors of the deceased prince brought multiple claims before the Great Council in order to have his properties sold and his debts paid off. During these auctions, several domains changed hands: Lembeek, Steenhuize, Avelgem, Muncken, Tiltenhove, Gruithuize, Arzele and Dottenijs.[126]

[123] Although it must be said that, in practice, many litigants introduced new facts and documents during an appeal procedure.

[124] Put, Eddy. 1995. *Grote Raad van Mechelen. Processen van aanzienlijke families (Reeksen A en B)*: werkbeschrijvingen. Brussels: Algemeen Rijksarchief. The original descriptions were made in the 1860s by H.F. D'Hoop, L. Galesloot and M. Van Hollebeke.

[125] This is only true for the 'A' series. In the inventory of the 'B' series only the names and the capacities of the litigants are mentioned.

[126] Brussels, ARA, GRM, Processen aanzienlijke families, Reeks A, N°869, 885, 891, 905, 909, 936. The inventory mentions the city of Ottignies as one of the properties to auction. However, Ottignies is not located in the surroundings of any of the other manors and it is therefore very unlikely that it was part of the estate of the Prince of Steenhuize. Moreover, the extended sentences mention a domain named Dottignies—in Dutch: Dottenijs—instead of Ottignies. The information provided by the latter source also informs us that even more properties than hereto mentioned

A sale of a manor also included the transfer of the seignorial rights and privileges attached to it to the new owner.

The importance of these rights and privileges to the prominent families involved is clearly brought out by their regular quarrels about them, even independent from any auctions or sales of property. In most cases, the legal authority over a certain territory was disputed: e.g. between the Prince of Orange and the Abbot and Prince of Stavelot in the 1750s over the judicial rights and the allocation of the mayor of St.-Vith[127] or between the Duke of Corswarem-Looz and the de Piret family in the 1750s and 1760s concerning the jurisdiction over the *ban* of Tourtru, situated between Hachy and Villers.[128] While the right to administer justice was without a doubt the most significant of all seigniorial rights, noble families did not hesitate to start lengthy lawsuits over far more basic issues as well, such as the right to cut timber.[129]

Another considerable category of first instance lawsuits between prominent families consists of all sorts of disputes connected to wills and testaments. In these lawsuits the inheritors were usually pitched against various creditors, but it also occurred rather frequently that siblings sued each other or that sons contested their mothers' claims. Family members who were in dispute about the guardianship of a deceased's children have also been included in this category.[130] In some instances, the fiscals interfered in the assignment of custody or in the way guardians managed the estates of their protégés.[131]

In general, the lawsuits concerning prominent families constituted an important part of the jurisdiction of the Great Council, especially as some of these nobles had the status of Knights of the Golden Fleece[132] for whom the Malines court was exclusively responsible.[133] In practice this meant that several of these prominent families enjoyed the privilege of being able to directly take their disputes to the Great Council, without passing through any of the subordinate local and/or provincial

were auctioned: Tombreu, Berchem (Oudenaarde), Heestert, Boekem, Waarmaarde and Otegem. Brussels, ARA, GRM 971, f.424–431, f.432–443, f.444–457, f.458–474, f. 475–486, f.487–496, f.497–508, f.601–614, f.615–626.

[127] Brussels, ARA, GRM, Processen aanzienlijke families, Reeks A, N°1244.

[128] Brussels, ARA, GRM, Processen aanzienlijke families, Reeks A, N°1370.

[129] Brussels, ARA, GRM, Processen aanzienlijke families, Reeks A, N°914.

[130] For example, in 1727 Marie-Thérèse de Bette, dowager of Bornem and Steenhault was engaged in a lawsuit against Anne-Marie de Croy, dowager of Lede, over the guardianship of the young marquis de Lede. Brussels, ARA, GRM, Processen aanzienlijke families, Reeks A, N°212.

[131] This was for instance the case in 1732 when the procurator-general acted as defendant against both the Count of Merode and the Prince of Rubempré about the guardianship of the children of the count of Westerlo. Brussels, ARA, GRM, Processen aanzienlijke families, Reeks A, N°1107.

[132] The Knights of the Golden Fleece are mentioned as individuals—by definition belonging to prominent families—who enjoyed the privilege, among others, to take their lawsuits to the Great Council. More information on the Knights of the Golden Fleece and a membership list can be found in Pauwels, Henri ed. 1962. *Het Gulden Vlies: vijf eeuwen kunst en geschiedenis*. Brugge: Stad Brugge.

[133] Apart from these large categories, there are some individual cases. As these are not exactly representative for the general nature of litigation between noble families we do not mention them.

tribunals. To be sure, this was not only important for the families involved but also for the Great Council itself, as it could thereby distinguish itself from the provincial tribunals, including the Council of Brabant.

4.4.1.2 Extended Sentences

As a considerable percentage of the parties litigating at the Great Council were noblemen, quite a few of the previously discussed subject matters return in the extended sentences. Nevertheless, given that the judgments incorporated in the registers were not restricted to lawsuits concerning prominent families, it is possible to widen our scope and investigate other kinds of litigants and subject matters at the Council. The extended sentences—because of their special status[134]—inevitably still provide a somewhat biased image: considering the high cost associated with these judgments, we can assume that only those lawsuits in which the stakes were high enough found their way into the registers.

Of the 280 extended sentences we investigated,[135] 157 proved to be judgments in first instance lawsuits.[136] In 94 of these cases, one or both of the litigants were of noble blood. Another well-represented social class is the clergy: both clerical institutions—such as chapters—and individual clergy often acted as plaintiffs or defendants before the Great Council. Advocates, proctors, bailiffs and other personnel of the Great Council can also be regularly found among the litigants as well as the Magistrate of Malines. In addition, a limited number of other administrative bodies—such as the bench of aldermen of Kortrijk or Harelbeke—also took some of their actions directly to the Great Council.[137] Finally, several private individuals, who seemingly did not enjoy any special status or stood out by their occupation, were engaged in first instance actions before the Council.

Given that in the majority of the extended sentences at least one party belonged to the nobility, the breakdown into different categories should more or less correspond to the conclusions drawn from the collection of lawsuits concerning prominent families. Indeed, the bulk of the first instance cases mentioned in the extended sentences consists of *sentences de décret*.[138] In terms of content, these sentences of

[134] Cf. infra, 4.2.1.1 Extended sentences.

[135] Brussels, ARA, GRM, 969–976 (1693–1774). See Verscuren, An. 2013. *Nadere toegang op de geëxtendeerde sententies van de Grote Raad van Mechelen: 1693–1772.* Brussels: Algemeen Rijksarchief.

[136] The other 123 extended sentences were judgments in appeal brought before the Great Council. 105 of these were originally from Flanders, 6 from Luxembourg, 6 from Malines, 5 from Namur and 1 from the *Terres de débat*.

[137] These city councils did not have any privilege—at least as far as we know—to litigate directly before the Great Council. The reason why they appeared as litigants in first instance cases must have been connected to the subject matter or some other unknown external factor.

[138] There are certain overlaps in the sentences of decree described in the extended sentences and in the inventory listing the lawsuits concerning the prominent families: for example, the actions with regards to the estate of the Prince of Steenhuize can be retrieved from the extended sentences.

decree are rather repetitive and merely indicate which properties changed hands in a forced sale. In addition, arguments about inheritances and testamentary dispositions abound. Unsurprisingly, the nobility played a role in the majority of these types of action as their estates were considerable enough to be worth a lengthy lawsuit and to have the judgment of the Great Council written down as an extended sentence. Slightly less significant—at least in terms of numbers—are the cases dealing with all sorts of rights and privileges. Often these were seigniorial rights, which were passed on together with the manors, making noblemen again the primary litigants in such lawsuits.

Actions dealing with all sorts of debts—unsettled accounts, outstanding interests, etc.—are much less prominently present.[139] The few cases of *maintenue* that found their way into the registers demonstrate that lawsuits could be directly introduced at the Great Council—even if neither the litigants nor the subject matter were privileged—when open letters, which had been awarded by the tribunal on simple request, were disputed.[140] Since the Great Council did not investigate the merits of the case or examine if it was at all competent to deal with it when granting these open letters, this was a means of indirectly extending its competence beyond the limits of its usual jurisdiction.

Lastly, the final important category consists of 'actions regarding procedure', which unlike the other categories does not correspond to any counterpart in the lawsuits concerning prominent families; in the majority of the cases, noblemen were not involved.[141] The registers of extended sentences contain a few of these

However, there are many other forced sales of properties listed in the inventory that cannot be matched with an extended sentence. This would suggest that—contrary to our earlier hypothesis—*sentences de décret* did not necessarily have to be settled by an extended sentence. The high incidence rate of these sentences of decree among the extended sentences probably means (1) that people often preferred to have the judgment in an auction written down as an extended sentence but that they were not obligated to do so and (2) that the eighteenth century witnessed a very large number of these forced sales, as the 92 known cases from the extended sentences are potentially only the tip of the iceberg.

[139] Compared to the somewhat repetitive *sentences de décret*, these judgments often deal with almost elementary issues. For example, in 1694, the inheritors of advocate Coolman—two of whom were advocates of the Council of Flanders—went to court against Anne Josine Le Poivre, widow of Gerard de Villers and a creditor to the same Coolman. The discussion involved the way in which debts had to be divided over the inheritors of the debtor. More specifically: were all inheritors jointly responsible for the debts of the testator—meaning that in case of insolvency of one of the heirs, *i.c.* their mother, the others had to make an additional payment—or if each was only severally liable for his or her own share? The Great Council finally judged that the plaintiffs were indeed accountable for the entire sum of the debt: they were allowed to identify both liquid and fixed assets of their mother on which her part of the debt could be recovered. Nevertheless, if that did not suffice, they were obligated to pay the remaining sum of their mother's share. ARA, GRM 969, July 14, 1694; Another example can be found in Brussels, ARA, GRM 971, March 7, 1709.

[140] Brussels, ARA, GRM 973, February 19, 1927: Contestation of the nomination to a prebendaryship at the Cathedral Chapter of Tournai.

[141] This is for instance true for a lawsuit, dating from 1704, which pitched Jan de Termer, a bargeman from Zoutleeuw, against Guilliam Vandewinckel, a priest and procurator in the monastery of Hanswijk in Malines. The plaintiff wished to force Vandewinckel to confirm before a judge that

lawsuits that started out as dealing with a very specific concern, such as the question which language should be used in court proceedings,[142] that led the Great Council to express very general legal principles as part of its judgment. Possibly the Great Council itself considered these lawsuits important enough to integrate them in the register of extended sentences, as they might be used as precedents in the future.[143]

4.4.1.3 Recueils d'arrêts

In 1970, Ph. Godding remarked that historians thus far had not shown much interest in compilations of case law; in fact, even an inventory of the—very numerous—manuscripts was not yet available.[144] Thirty-five years later, Dauchy made a comparable observation: while the *recueils d'arrêts* constitute one of the sources most frequently used by legal historians and form the basis of many studies, only scant research has been dedicated to these collections of case law. In 2005 an exhaustive list of the *recueils* that had been published in print was still not available, let alone an overview of the many manuscripts hidden in archival institutions and libraries.[145]

---

the two parcels of contraband, found on his ship and sent to the defendant by his brother-in-law, were the defendant's property, and that he, as bargeman could not be held responsible for these forbidden goods. This lawsuit, which originally had started as an almost trivial case, eventually evolved into the discussion of an important principle of law, *i.c.* the protection against self-incrimination. The Great Council itself summarized the subject of this action as: "*Qu'on n'est obligé de donner temoignage contre soij meme ny contre ses proches parens.*" Brussels, ARA, GRM 971, August 22, 1704.

[142] Brussels, ARA, GRM 970, May 19, 1696. The lawsuit started off as a discussion between two suspects accused before a local court and their prosecuting officer about the language—Dutch or French—in which the witnesses should be interrogated, only to evolve into a general discussion about the use of language in court.

[143] In the previously mentioned 'language' case, the extended sentence is written down in French while the plaintiffs—who won the case before the Great Council and were therefore the only ones with a reason to request an extended sentence—were Dutch speakers and had brought proceedings precisely in order to be allowed to have their witnesses interrogated in their native language, instead of the French spoken by the prosecutor and the lord of the seigniory. Therefore, we wonder whether the judgment found its way into the registers of extended sentences, not so much because the plaintiffs had requested it, but in order to have a detailed account of the judgment for internal use and for instruction of the—usually French speaking—prosecuting officers.

[144] Godding, Philippe. 1970. L'origine et l'autorité des recueils de jurisprudence dans les Pays-Bas Méridionaux (XIIIe-XVIIIe siècles). In *Rapports belges au VIIIe congrès international de droit comparé.* Brussel: CIDC, 1 Godding noticed that Simon is the only author who has written about these *recueils d'arrêts*, and then only specifically about those of the Great Council: Simon, Jules. 1907. Les recueils d'arrêts du Grand Conseil de Malines. *Handelingen van de Koninklijke Commissie voor de uitgave van oude wetten en verordeningen van België* 10: 265–256. Maes more or less repeated Simon's conclusions in his study: Maes, Louis Th. 1949. De Grote Raad der Nederlanden en zijn arrêtisten. *Tijdskrif vir hedendaagse Romeins-Hollandse Reg* 12: 58–76.

[145] Dauchy, Serge. 2005. Introduction. In *Les recueils d'arrêts et dictionnaires de jurisprudence: XVIe-XVIIIe siècles*, eds. Serge Dauchy and Véronique Demars-Sion. Paris: La mémoire du droit, 10.

Although Dauchy's comment was specifically meant to describe the situation in France, the parallels with the state of affairs in present-day Belgium are legion. As studies are so scarce, we heavily draw upon the collection of essays edited by S. Dauchy and V. Demars-Sion for our discussion of the status and importance of these *recueils*. For specific information about the *recueils* collected by practitioners or councilors in the Austrian Netherlands, we will rely on the—still unique although somewhat outdated—study of Godding, on the few remarks A. Wijffels made about these compilations following his edition of the *recueils d'arrêts* of Guillaume de Grysperre[146] and on his discussion of the major *arrestographes* of the Great Council in his essay on the sources available to study case law at the Great Council of Malines.[147]

Typology From the sixteenth century on,[148] several collections of case law were gathered in the different tribunals of the Southern Netherlands, with the exception of the Council of Flanders. The lack of *recueils d'ârrets* for the Council of Flanders—at least for the one situated in the Netherlands[149]—is not hard to explain: as it was always possible to appeal against Flemish sentences at the Great Council of Malines, the Council of Flanders could not pronounce *arrêts* in a civil case.[150] The Council of Hainaut does boast a collection of *recueils d'arrêts*, but not a single one has appeared in print; all have remained in the form of manuscripts in the archives of the tribunal. On the other hand, all known *recueils d'arrêts* for the Council of

[146] Wijffels, Alain. 1997. Grand Conseil de Malines: la rédaction des sentences étendues et le recueil de jurisprudence de Guillaume de Grysperre. In *Case law in the making: the techniques and methods of judicial records and law reports (Comparative studies in continental and Anglo-American Legal History* 17) v.1, ed. Alain Wijffels. Berlin: Duncker und Humblot, 304–312.

[147] Wijffels, Alain. 1989. Legal Records and Reports in the Great Council of Malines (fifteenth to eighteenth century). In *Judicial Records, Law Reports and the Growth of Case Law*, ed. John H. Baker, 181–206. Berlin: Duncker und Humblot.

[148] Godding distinguished 'two periods' in the *recueils d'arrêts* compiled in the Netherlands: 1. the period between the thirteenth and fifteenth century, when the judgments of the local tribunals—especially of the benches of aldermen—were gathered 2. the period from the sixteenth until the end of the eighteenth century, when the focus of the *arrestographes* lay on the higher tribunals. In our discussion we only focus on the second period.

[149] Godding remarked that after the conquest by Louis XIV of a part of Flanders, several compilations of judgments were published for the *Parlement de Flandres*—successively located in Tournai, Cambrai and Douai—as new councilors had to adopt customs and habits they were not familiar with. E.g. Dubois d'Hermaville, Augustin, De Baralle, Ladislas, De Blye, Jean-Baptise and De Flines, Séraphin eds. 1773. *Recueil d'arrêts du Parlement de Flandres*. Lille: C.F.J. Lehoucq. According to Demars-Sion and Dauchy, this was also the reason why so many of these *recueils* contain the motivation of the judges. Dauchy, Serge and Demars-Sion, Véronique. 2006. Argumentation et motivation dans les recueils d'arrêts des cours souverianes de France. L'exemple du Parlement de flandre (fin XVIIe—début XVIIIe siècle). In *Juristische Argumentation, Argumente der Juristen*, ed. albrecht Cordes, 127–152. Cologne: Böhlau Verlag.

[150] Godding, Philippe. 1970. L'origine et l'autorité des recueils de jurisprudence dans les Pays-Bas Méridionaux (XIIIe-XVIIIe siècles). In *Rapports belges au VIIIe congrès international de droit comparé.* Brussel: CIDC, 25.

Brabant have been published.[151] In France, *recueils d'arrêts* were even more plentiful as councilors in almost all the important provincial courts had been busy collecting compilations of case law applying to their jurisdiction.[152]

Within the Great Council of Malines as well, several councilors had been active as *arrestographes*. The first published collection of case law for the Southern Netherlands was of the hand of Paulus Christinaeus (1553–1631), who worked at the Great Council as an advocate. All other collections compiled in Malines were the work of councilors: Guillaume de Grisperre (c. 1544–1622), Pierre Cuvelier (?-1628), Claude de Humyn (c. 1582–1639), Nicolas du Fief (1578–1651), Jean Charles Roose (?-1694), Louis-Marie Frarin (1630–1706), Remy-Albert du Laury (1664–1716), Jean Alphonse de Coloma (1677–1739) and Jean-Baptiste Hony (1693–1765). Some of these *recueils* appeared over the course of the eighteenth century as posthumous editions.[153] The kind of cases that are compiled in these collections, and therefore the subject matter treated, depends on the target group and on the objectives the 'authors' of the *recueils d'arrêts* envisioned. Consequently, we first discuss their status and their use before looking at the nature of the litigation reflected in these collections. The focus of this discussion will be on the work of the eighteenth century *arrestographes*.[154]

First of all, it is important to note that several *arrestographes* not only collected contemporary cases but also integrated lawsuits from earlier periods, when they had not yet been councilors. This is, for example, true for the collection of Remy-Albert Du Laury, edited and published under the auspices of Pierre Claude Marie de Saint Vaast. For the earlier period, Du Laury drew heavily on the—by then still unpublished—work of du Fief. Furthermore, apart from *arrêts*, he also integrated recommendations of the Great Council following questions for advice from the Privy Council. De Coloma and Hony on the other hand, strictly limited themselves to integrating cases that were

---

[151] Godding, Philippe. 1970. L'origine et l'autorité des recueils de jurisprudence dans les Pays-Bas Méridionaux (XIIIe-XVIIIe siècles). In *Rapports belges au VIIIe congrès international de droit comparé*. Brussel: CIDC, 26. E.g: Stockmans, Petrus. 1670. *Decisionum curiae Brabantiae sesquicenturia*. Brussels: Franciscum Foppens; De Wynants, Goswin. 1744. *Supremae curiae Brabantiae decisiones*. Brussels: Petrum Foppens.

[152] For a comprehensive list of the *recueils d'arrêts* collected at a number of French tribunals, see: Dauchy, Serge and Demars-Sion, Véronique eds. 2005. *Les recueils d'arrêts et dicitionnaires de jurisprudence: XVIe-XVIIIe siècle*. Paris: La mémoire du droit, 455–464.

[153] Wijffels, Alain. 1989. Legal Records and Reports in the Great Council of Malines (fifteenth to eighteenth century). In *Judicial Records, Law Reports and the Growth of Case Law*, ed. John H. Baker, 181–206. Berlin: Duncker und Humblot, 186–187. The manuscripts of these *recueils* can be found in the archives of the Great Council, in the *Manuscrits divers* collection at the State Archives in Brussels, in the archives of the City of Malines, and in the Belgian Royal Library.

[154] For the eighteenth century, we have two *recueils d'arrêts* at our disposal: De Saint Vaast, Pierre Claude Marie and Du Laury, Remi Albert. 1717. *La jurisprudence des Pais-Bas autrichiens établies par les arrêts du Grand Conseil de Sa Majesté Impériale et Catholique, résident en la ville de Malines, auxquels sont ajoutés quelques décrets portés au Conseil Privé de Sadite Majesté*. Brussels: t'Serstevens; De Coloma, Jean Alphonse and Hony, Jean-Baptiste. 1781. *Arrêts du Grand Conseil de Sa Majesté Impériale et Royale, séant en la ville de Malines (2v.)*. Malines: P.J. Hanicq.

judged during their time at the Council. The difference is not unimportant, not only because of reasons of reliability but also because the *arrestographes* who integrated earlier sentences were not always able to convey the motivation behind certain decisions, while this is often considered to be one of the primary goals of gathering case law.[155]

Most authors do indeed agree that the *recueils d'arrêts* were not so much the 'expression of the ambition of the councilors or of the vanity of a parliamentary corpus'—they were not destined for the larger public—but supposed to be guidelines for all kinds of practitioners in order to familiarize themselves with the jurisprudence of their tribunal.[156] Therefore, the *recueils d'arrêts* were primarily intended to fill a need felt by many young advocates and members of provincial councils who were not accustomed to the specific jurisprudence of the tribunals they worked at. As the universities taught almost exclusively Roman and Canon Law, young practitioners needed other resources to learn, understand and interpret the law they were supposed to apply. Indeed, their education had not prepared them for any sort of legal practice, be it as an advocate or as a member of a provincial council. In that regard, the inclusion of the motivation behind a decision—completely absent in the sentence—and sometimes even of the opinions voiced by the different judges on the case, was essential. As A. Wijffels remarked: "*Le principal apport d'un tel recueil est de fournir des informations sur les motifs juridiques ayant, le cas échéant, emporté la décision.*"[157]

For Godding, the usefulness of these compilations of case law consisted in 'avoiding that certain parties start futile actions, facilitating the settlement of certain questions which have already been treated by other councils, providing an insight in 'modern legal practice' etc.'. Moreover, Godding argued that—albeit unintentionally—the *recueils d'arrêts* made it possible to achieve a far more stable jurisprudence.[158] In France, the *Edit de Saint Germain* of 1679, which reformed

[155] Dauchy, Serge and Demars-Sion, Véronique. 2006. Argumentation et motivation dans les recueils d'arrêts des cours souverianes de France. L'exemple du Parlement de flandre (fin XVIIe—début XVIIIe siècle). In *Juristische Argumentation, Argumente der Juristen*, ed. albrecht Cordes. Cologne: Böhlau Verlag, 128. "C'est la raison pour laquelle [the absence of a motivation in judgments] les cours souveraines ont accepté puis encouragé la réalisation de recueils d'arrêts qui, à la faveur du développement de l'imprimerie, assureront à la fois la publicité des décisions et la révélation de leurs motifs."

[156] Dauchy, Serge. 2005. Introduction. In *Les recueils d'arrêts et dictionnaires de jurisprudence: XVIe-XVIIIe siècles*, eds. Serge Dauchy and Véronique Demars-Sion.. Paris: La mémoire du droit, 10. According to Dauchy, many *arrestographes* have become celebrities despite themselves. Most of them never envisaged the publication of their work but compiled collections of case law primarily for their own use and that of their successors. Their manuscripts were often posthumously published, not seldom by one of their inheritors, be it their descendants or their former (younger) colleagues.

[157] Wijffels, Alain. 1997. Grand Conseil de Malines: la rédaction des sentences étendues et le recueil de jurisprudence de Guillaume de Grysperre. In *Case law in the making: the techniques and methods of judicial records and law reports (Comparative studies in continental and Anglo-American Legal History* 17) v.1, ed. Alain Wijffels. Berlin: Duncker und Humblot, 309.

[158] Godding, Philippe. 1970. L'origine et l'autorité des recueils de jurisprudence dans les Pays-Bas Méridionaux (XIIIe-XVIIIe siècles). In *Rapports belges au VIIIe congrès international de droit comparé.* Brussel: CIDC, 33–34.

the legal education at the universities, even institutionalized the use of the *recueils d'arrêts*.[159] Even though collections of case law never received the same status in the Southern Netherlands, we may assume that they had a large impact on the practical training of young advocates and councilors. The fact that they were first and foremost supposed to be for internal use only, explains why many of them remained unpublished manuscripts for so long, and why these manuscripts, which were constantly copied, had—at least according to Godding—an equally large influence as their published counterparts.[160]

Since the *recueils d'arrêts* were primarily intended to be educational tools, we can assume that the recorded case law did not—or at least not principally—consist of judgments in 'exotic' cases. Hilaire remarked that there certainly were *arrestographes* who preferred to include 'rare and singular sentences', but that in general they wished to convey the normal jurisprudence.[161] Wijffels arrived at a similar conclusion in his edition of Grysperre's *recueils d'arrêts*: apart from a selection based on the author's own participation in the settlement of the lawsuit, he noticed a tendency to include cases that established important legal precedents.[162] For example, many of the judgments apply to matrimonial law and to the laws of inheritance—two subject matters that, based on the *extended sentences* and on the lawsuits concerning prominent families, have already been identified as being of primary importance in the jurisprudence of the Great Council. Finally, according to Dauchy, the publishers often played a key role: since they wanted to reach a public as large and diverse as possible, they tried to influence the content of these collections of case law.[163]

The question might be asked to what degree the *recueils d'arrêts* had an influence on the formation of the law, considering that some judgments apparently

---

[159] Dauchy, Serge. 2005. Introduction. In *Les recueils d'arrêts et dictionnaires de jurisprudence: XVIe-XVIIIe siècles*, eds. Serge Dauchy and Véronique Demars-Sion. Paris: La mémoire du droit, 13. It must be said that this reform was especially intended to enhance the control of the central government on legal education. In the eighteenth century, the *recueils d'arrêts* were more and more replaced by so called *dictionnaires* which were often regarded as the first step towards codification, an evolution finalized with Napoleon's codification efforts.

[160] Godding, Philippe. 1970. L'origine et l'autorité des recueils de jurisprudence dans les Pays-Bas Méridionaux (XIIIe-XVIIIe siècles). In *Rapports belges au VIIIe congrès international de droit comparé.* Brussel: CIDC, 25. According to Godding, within the circle of councilors and practitioners, the published collections of case law did not necessarily wield more influence than the unedited manuscripts.

[161] Hilaire, Jean. 2005. Questions autour de la jurisprudence des arrêts. In *Les recueils d'arrêts et dictionnaires de jurisprudence: XVIe-XVIIIe siècles*, eds. Serge Dauchy and Véronique Demars-Sion. Paris: La mémoire du droit, 31.

[162] Wijffels, Alain. 1997. Grand Conseil de Malines: la rédaction des sentences étendues et le recueil de jurisprudence de Guillaume de Grysperre. In *Case law in the making: the techniques and methods of judicial records and law reports (Comparative studies in continental and Anglo-American Legal History* 17) v.1, ed. Alain Wijffels. Berlin: Duncker und Humblot, 309.

[163] Dauchy, Serge. 2005. Introduction. In *Les recueils d'arrêts et dictionnaires de jurisprudence: XVIe-XVIIIe siècles*, eds. Serge Dauchy and Véronique Demars-Sion. Paris: La mémoire du droit, 16.

conveyed a certain legal authority. Even in the eighteenth century, legislation by the sovereign was not yet the primary source of law. Therefore, we could assume that these collections of judgments, which presented solutions in day-to-day cases, were considered to be precedents, thereby influencing the decision-making of future similar lawsuits. Dauchy believed that in France, jurisprudence, as manifested by these collections of case law, did to a certain extent serve as a form of inspiration for the legislator. And even if the *recueils d'arrêts* did not immediately become a source of law, they often constituted an important source of discussion of the law.[164]

As far as the Southern Netherlands are concerned, Wijffels is less convinced that these *recueils d'arrêts* had a decisive impact on how councilors would evaluate a similar case in the future: Hony himself had observed that the diversity of opinions uttered by the councilors did not allow him to determine whether any principle was established by the judgment.[165] Wijffels also argued that the judges of the supreme courts did not consider themselves bound in any way by their own precedents as they believed that circumstances were essential and doctrine constantly evolved.[166] Godding remarked that the *arrestographes* themselves intended the solutions, applied by the superior courts, to have force of law, at least as far as the subordinate jurisdictions were concerned. He himself doubted that these *recueils d'ârrets* had that kind of authority and viewed their influence as limited to being a source of information about the jurisprudence of the principal courts of the Netherlands.[167]

Finally, to what extent are these compilations of case law reliable? Several introductions to published *recueils d'arrêts* criticized the work of predecessors as being at best mediocre. It is indeed true that some critics doubted the trustworthiness of the information provided by the *recueils*. Many of the decisions the *arrestographes* incorporated in their works were never verified at the clerk's office. Certainly the methods used to compile the judgments were inevitably error-prone. Collecting the data for a *recueil d'arrêts* was an enormous task. More often than not, authors copied entire parts of the work of their predecessors without verifying its reliability, thereby magnifying the chances of mistakes. This also meant that they themselves had not been present during the handling of the case or the deliberations, and that they were entirely dependent for the quality of their own work on the diligence of their predecessors. Moreover, as many collections were often only posthumously published, there was always another party—a descendant, a colleague from a later period or even merely a printer-publisher[168]—dealing once again with the material. They often adjusted the original work to their own ideas or needs, and regularly

164 Ibidem, 18.

165 Wijffels, Alain. 1989. Legal Records and Reports in the Great Council of Malines (fifteenth to eighteenth century). In *Judicial Records, Law Reports and the Growth of Case Law*, ed. John H. Baker. Berlin: Duncker und Humblot, 200.

166 Ibidem, 203.

167 Godding, Philippe. 1970. L'origine et l'autorité des recueils de jurisprudence dans les Pays-Bas Méridionaux (XIIIe-XVIIIe siècles). In *Rapports belges au VIIIe congrès international de droit comparé.* Brussel: CIDC, 36.

168 For example, in 1774, the printer Henry published the *recueils d'arrêts* of Grysperre and Cuvelier who compiled their collection during the late sixteenth and early seventeenth centuries.

decided to publish only part of the original compilation. Despite all these shortcomings, Dauchy believed that most *recueils d'arrêts* are reliable sources.[169]

The eighteenth century recueils d'arrêts of the Great Council Many of the characteristics of the compilations of case law—as identified by literature—can be directly applied to the two *recueils d'arrêts* collected and published by eighteenth century members of the Great Council: the first one by councilor and procurator-general du Laury, adapted and published under the auspices of his fellow-councilor and protégé de St Vaast, and the second one by councilors de Coloma and Hony, published posthumously by the Malines printer Hanicq.

The first edition of du Laury's work, which appeared in 1717, contained 200 *arrêts*, although—according to de St Vaast—du Laury's notes would have been sufficient to furnish content for 'four fat volumes.'[170] In 1761, a new edition appeared, this time printed by the Brussels bookseller Morris. He augmented the number of judgments to 219.[171]

Du Laury's collection of case law consists only partially of judgments contemporary to his activities in Malines. Many of the decisions rendered date from the late seventeenth century, when Du Laury was still working as an advocate at the Council of Flanders. Moreover, the *recueil* does not exclusively contain arrests from the Great Council, but also incorporates a significant number of resolutions by the Privy Council or the Council of State, taken after advice from the Great Council;[172] other entries are merely answers—based on doctrine or on the work of previous *arrestographes*—to notable questions without any reference to a decision from the Great Council.[173] Furthermore, many of the *arrêts* compiled by du Laury are barely 'legible', as references to earlier collections of case law—amongst others by his predecessor Christinaeus—abound and surpass the description of the case or of du Laury's own evaluation. He only gave scant information about the discussions

[169] Dauchy, Serge. 2005. Introduction. In *Les recueils d'arrêts et dictionnaires de jurisprudence: XVIe-XVIIIe siècles*, eds. Serge Dauchy and Véronique Demars-Sion. Paris: La mémoire du droit, 13.

[170] Wijffels, Alain. 1989. Legal Records and Reports in the Great Council of Malines (fifteenth to eighteenth century). In *Judicial Records, Law Reports and the Growth of Case Law*, ed. John H. Baker, 181–206. Berlin: Duncker und Humblot. Also: De Saint Vaast, Pierre Claude Marie and Du Laury, Remi Albert. 1717. *La jurisprudence des Pais-Bas autrichiens établies par les arrêts du Grand Conseil de Sa Majesté Impériale et Catholique, résident en la ville de Malines, auxquels sont ajoutés quelques décrets portés au Conseil Privé de Sadite Majesté*. Brussels: t'Serstevens, 'Au lecteur' "[du Laury a laissé] suffisamment de la matière pour fournir à quatre gros volumes."

[171] De Saint Vaast, Pierre Claude Marie and Du Laury, Remi Albert. 1761. La jurisprudence des Pais-Bas autrichiens établies par les arrêts du Grand Conseil de Sa Majesté Impériale et Catholique, résident en la ville de Malines, auxquels sont ajoutés quelques décrets portés au Conseil Privé de Sadite Majesté. Brussels: Jean Moris.

[172] E.g. Du Laury, Arrêt XVII, 24: *Que la remission d'homicide commis en Flandre par un Flamand obtenue en Brabant a effet en Flandre.*

[173] Dauchy, Serge and Demars-Sion, Véronique. 2009. A propos d'un 'recueil d'arrêts' inédit: la jurisprudence du Parlement de Flandre de Georges de Ghewiet. *Tijdschrift voor Rechtsgeschiedenis* 77: 165.

within the Great Council and motivations of any kind are often completely absent. Finally, any form of organization, be it chronologically or thematically, is lacking.

In 1781, the Malines printer Hanicq—who called himself 'printer of the Great Council'[174]—published the sentences collected by the late councilors de Coloma and Hony, supplemented with several 'interesting pieces' compiled by the former. No member of the Great Council was involved in this publication; apparently Hanicq set out to compile it on his own accord.[175] Contrary to du Laury, both de Coloma and Hony only collected sentences in cases contemporary to their activities at the court. Although de Coloma usually offered answers to generally formulated questions—as did du Laury—he identified the parties and the circumstances in the corresponding proceedings, even in criminal trials.[176] Instead of merely using doctrine or earlier jurisprudence, de Coloma heavily relied on precedents. Moreover, he regularly voiced his own opinions as well as those of his colleagues, and, more often than not, motivated the judgment passed in that specific case. Although he also relied on earlier *recueils d'arrêts* or writings of other legists—Van Espen for instance—his arrests are far more readable than those of du Laury. Finally, unlike du Laury's, de Coloma's collection of case law—as well as Hony's—is chronologically ordered. Wijffels suspected this chronological arrangement to be the work of printer Hanicq, as it is not followed in the manuscript he consulted.[177]

---

[174] This is mentioned on the first page of the edition:"A Malines, chez P.J. Hanicq, imprimeur du Grand Conseil de Sa Majesté."

[175] In his foreword, Hanicq summarized his motivation for publishing this compilation of case law: first, the *recueils d'arrêts* of sovereign courts are known to be useful instruments for the public. These works instruct the parties about what they can expect from their claims, teach the advocates what advice to give to their clients while the judges will find elucidation in them in order to sentence similar cases in full confidence. These considerations in combination with his own desire to place himself at the service of the public persuaded him to publish this collection of case law. What follows next, is a long praise of the Great Council, a sovereign court which 'has always been composed of distinguished magistrates, known for their brilliant insights and ennobled by their long experience' and of de Coloma in particular, who is described as one of the 'most famous legists of his time', having fulfilled different positions within the Austrian Netherlands. Still, even though de Coloma did have a long and outstanding career, he was never president of the Great Council as Hanicq claimed. Hony is equally mentioned as a 'wise legist', but it seems that he is considered to be of lesser importance. What does make him stand out is his position as a clerical councilor; his rather short active career at the Great Council—Hony never returned after a stroke in 1745—without a doubt explains the rather limited number of judgments he compiled. "Avertissement du libraire au public." De Coloma, Jean Alphonse and Hony, Jean-Baptiste. 1781. *Arrêts du Grand Conseil de Sa Majesté Impériale et Royale, séant en la ville de Malines (2v.).* Malines: P.J. Hanicq, 3–8

[176] For example, when discussing the kind of evidence necessary to condemn a man to torture or to the death penalty, he used a specific case as precedent, *i.c.* the case of the procurator-general against Vincent R. accused of having murdered the secretary of the Great Council Eynatten, this despite the fact that the suspect in question was later acquitted of all charges. De Coloma, v.1, Arrêt 22, February 12, 1713.

[177] Wijffels, Alain. 1989. Legal Records and Reports in the Great Council of Malines (fifteenth to eighteenth century). In *Judicial Records, Law Reports and the Growth of Case Law*, ed. John H. Baker. Berlin: Duncker und Humblot, 199, footnote 124.

The number of arrests collected by Hony (21) is limited compared to that of du Laury (±200) and de Coloma (84+29 'interesting questions'). Like de Coloma, Hony extensively described the circumstances of the lawsuit—often cases in which he himself acted as a reporter—and identified the litigants.[178] Although he sometimes reported the views of his colleagues, he seldom expressed his own opinions. Contrary to both du Laury and de Coloma, Hony made only limited use of earlier legists and was weary of relying on foreign jurisprudence, believing that, for example, French jurisprudence was not applicable in the Austrian Netherlands as it went against common law.[179] All in all, he seemed to doubt that there were any fixed principles or rules in certain instances and was apparently not convinced that—due to the diversity of opinions expressed by the councilors or *in casu* by advocates when asked for advice—it was possible to establish any legal principle based on the judgments.[180]

Research Results What these *recueils d'arrêts* all have in common, despite their different format and approach, is the nature of the litigation they discuss.[181] Analysis of the *recueils* confirms the thesis that the authors rarely dealt with exotic lawsuits and that the bulk of the case law reflect relatively standard issues. As a consequence, we may assume that these compilations of case law provide a more or less accurate idea of the nature of litigation at the Great Council.

While *sentences de décret* frequently appeared in the extended sentences and in the lawsuits concerning prominent families, they are not so plentiful in the *recueils d'arrêt*. This is not surprising, considering their standard pattern and their limited substantive value. Nevertheless, they do appear occasionally: du Laury in particular discussed the sale—forced or not—of properties and the conditions associated with such transactions.[182] Debt-related issues of all kinds are also treated in the collections of case law—including questions of interest and taxes—although this subject

[178] For example, *Arrêt* number 11 relates a case in which his colleague Kahnn acted as a litigant. Hony, Arrêt 11, pp. 284–287.

[179] Hony, Arrêt 11, p. 287: "Il est vrai, que les auteurs français sont plus rigoureux sur la révocabilité des traités de mariage; mais leur jurisprudence ne peut avoir force de loi à notre égard, où le droit commun est contraire ...".

[180] Wijffels, Alain. 1989. Legal Records and Reports in the Great Council of Malines (fifteenth to eighteenth century). In *Judicial Records, Law Reports and the Growth of Case Law*, ed. John H. Baker. Berlin: Duncker und Humblot, 200.

[181] In order to investigate what kind of cases the *arrestographes* deal with, we classified them along the same lines as we did for the extended sentences and the lawsuits involving prominent families. We should note that in the *recueils d'arrêts* both first instance cases and appeals are discussed. Since especially du Laury did not mention the circumstances of the case, it is not always possible to identify the first instance lawsuits. As such, we decided to examine both first instance and appeal cases, firstly because of practical reasons and secondly because we have reasons to believe that the themes discussed were commonly considered by the Great Council, be it in appeal or in first instance.

[182] E.g. Du Laury, Arrêt XLVI, p. 73: "Acheteur des biens par décret chargé de rentes, n'est pas tenu personnellement".

is not as widespread as in the other sources we used.[183] 'Rights and privileges' are similarly prevalent in the *recueils d'arrêts* and in the lawsuits involving prominent families.[184] What stands out most is the number of *arrêts* that deal with the rights of the Church or its representatives.[185]

Among the most commonly discussed issues are questions involving matrimonial law and the—often connected—laws of succession. Given that all three *arrestographes* extensively deal with these two themes, much doubt and uncertainty must have surrounded jurisprudence related to matrimony and inheritance. Some of the issues discussed are rather basic questions regarding disinheritance or the limitation of the legal portion,[186] responsibility for children after a separation,[187] or whether the laws favoring children of a first marriage were still applicable. The ability of (members of) the Church to pass down or inherit assets—especially property[188]—also figure in the *arrêts*.[189]

In addition, several of the *arrêts* deal with regulations or customs that are regionally specific. Du Laury, for example, tackled the question if citizens of the city of Ghent were allowed during their marriage to mutually benefit each other in their testaments with properties situated in the province of Brabant.[190] In another *arrêt*, he commented on the validity—or rather the lack thereof—of the Brabant *Bulle*

---

[183] Du Laury, Arrêt LVI, p. 88: "Si la moindre partie des créanciers d'un homme faille peut être contraint à se conformer au plus grand nombre, ayant accordé moderation, ou attermination."; Arrêt LXXXVIII, p. 158: "Que les grands adherités d'un poldre sont solidairement obligés, et exécutables pour les dettes du poldre."; De Coloma, v.1, Arrêt 2, January 11, 1712: "Que celui qui est condamné à une somme de 50,000 fl. ne peut pas contraindre son créancier de recevoir en paiement des lettres de change, ou bien un autre débiteur en sa place."

[184] E.g. Du Laury, Arrêt CXIII, p. 217: "Un seigneur n'ayant pas de moulin banal en sa terre, ne peut empêcher un meunier étranger d'y chercher moûture."

[185] For example, du Laury discussed the right of a bishop to exempt a provost of a church from his residency requirement even though he was responsible for the spiritual care of his flock and even though he had a canonship. Du Laury, Arrêt CXL, p.275: "Que l'évêque peut donner dispense de non résider à un prévôt d'une église collegiale, ayant charge d'âmes, et un canonicat y annexé, pour le terme d'un an."

[186] Du Laury, Arrêt XLIV, p. 66: "Que l'aieule maternelle peut exhereder son petit fils, pour s'être marié à son insû, et contre son gré."; Arrêt LIX, p. 93: "Le fils d'un gentilhomme titré, ayant atteint l'âge de vingt-cinq ans, ne peut être réduit par ses père et mère à sa légitime, pour avoir épousé sans leur consentement, et sans avoir demandé leur avis, une fille d'extraction noble."

[187] De Coloma, v.1, Arrêt 20, January 12, 1713: "Quand les conjoints par marriage sont séparés, qui des deux doit nourrir et entretenir les enfans communs?" The case in question was between councilor Pierre Albert Van Kerrenbroeck and his wife Maria Anna Hougaerts.

[188] Hony, Arrêt 20, October 1745: "Du leg des immeubles fait à un couvent."

[189] Except for these general issues, some of the sentences deal with seemingly very specific matters. De Coloma, for instance, discusses the necessary conditions for the testament of a blind person to be valid. However, closer inspection reveals that he does not necessarily refer to a person who is literally blind, but rather to someone who is incompetent, for instance because he or she cannot read. De Coloma, v.1, Arrêt 16, July 6, 1712: "Ce qui est requis pour la validité du testament d'un aveugle."

[190] Du Laury, Arrêt II, p. 3: "Que bourgeois de la ville de Gand conjoints par mariage se peuvent avantager respectivement pendant leur mariage par testament des biens situés en Brabant."

d'or ('Golden Bull') in Flanders.[191] De Coloma as well discussed a certain law of succession which was only valid in Namur and which had no repercussions in any of the other provinces of the Austrian Netherlands.[192] The same is true for Hony, who included several specifically Flemish and Namur customs.[193] The lawsuits, to which these *arrêts* refer, were of course never introduced as first instance cases and explain customs and habits that were valid in territories within the jurisdiction of the Great Council.

Finally, by far most recurring in the *recueils d'arrêts* of du Laury and de Coloma are all matters concerning procedure and (conflicts of) jurisdiction/authority. While they are also marginally present in the two sources discussed before, these questions take up almost half of all the *arrêts* in the collections of case law. In fact, some of the judgments even read as a chapter in a manual for young practitioners. Which judge should execute a sentence, the one judging in first instance or in appeal?[194] Can a party requesting a revision ask to be judged by the Great Council without the addition of accessory councilors?[195] Is it possible to challenge a sentence in revision by claiming it is null and void?[196] Is a judge allowed to request reference to another court if not asked for by one of the litigants?[197] …

Within these procedural questions, several issues concerning criminal law are dealt with—although the Great Council had only limited jurisdiction in criminal matters—laying bare the need to clarify and exemplify that area of the law. Even very fundamental issues such as 'whether the Great Council is always competent to deal with crimes committed against its members?'[198] can be found among the *arrêts*. This fuels the idea that these *recueils d'arrêts* were indeed primarily intended as guidelines for (young) councilors.

---

[191] Du Laury, Arrêt CLXXXIX, p. 420: "Que la Bulle d'or des Brabançons n'a pas lieu en Flandre, pour y empêcher les arrêts sur leurs personnes, ou biens."

[192] De Coloma, vol 2, Arrêt 79, March 27, 1724: "Suivant la coutume de Namur, il suffit en succession collatérale, que l'on soit le plus proche du tronc, dont viennent les biens; sans qu'il soit nécessaire d'être descendu de l'acquéreur."

[193] E.g. Hony, Arrêt 13, October 1735: "De l'effet de purgement fait par un créancier personnel de la saisine d'un crédirentier, selon la coutume de Namur"; Arrêt 14: "Si selon les coutumes de Flandre le mari par contrat de mariage peut donner l'usufruit entier de ses fiefs."; Arrêt 15: "Si selon les coutumes de Flandre, lorsqu'après sept ans d'absence on a partagé les biens d'un absent, ceux qui ont obtenu la jouissance, en transmettent le droit et propriété, en cas de non retour, à leurs hoirs? Ou si la jouissance d'iceux passe au plus proche de l'absent?"

[194] Du Laury, Arrêt VII, p. 12: "Par quel juge se doit faire l'exécution d'une sentence, ou par celui *à qua* ou bien par celui *ad quem*."

[195] Du Laury, Arrêt XIV, p. 21: "Si un impétrant de revision est recevable à demander droit pardevant ceux du Grand Conseil sans intervention d'aucuns ajoints."

[196] Du Laury, Arrêt CXVI, p. 230, "Si l'on peut impugner un arrêt revisionel du chef de nullité?"

[197] De Coloma, vol 1, Arrêt 5, February 5, 1712: "Qu'un juge ne peut point demander le renvoi sans en être requis par partie."

[198] De Coloma, v.1, Arrêt 18, November 12, 1712: "Si le Grand Conseil est toujours juge compétent des crimes contre ses membres?"

4.4.2 Some General Observations

In general, the type of litigants that brought their cases to Malines drove the nature of civil litigation at the Great Council. In fact, the jurisdiction *ratione personae* seems to be more determining than the jurisdiction *ratione materiae* for the subject matter treated at the tribunal. The Great Council was *par excellence* a court for the privileged. As some noble families had the right to plea before the Great Council, it is unsurprising that many of the lawsuits dealt with rights and titles. The same is true for the *sentences de décret* and most other property transactions, whether or not as part of an inheritance. In addition, by the late eighteenth century, several noble families had apparently accumulated large debts and the obvious—and often only—way to pay them off was by selling off their estates. The connection with litigation about certain provisions in testaments or prenuptials—usually of a financial kind—is easily made.

Another considerable portion of first instance cases involved personnel of the Great Council or their families. They were primarily responsible for cases concerning conflicts of jurisdiction or procedure. Debt issues—if we only think about the many lawsuits involving councilor Happart[199]—were also prevalent. A third important category consists of clergy or clerical institutions, which often argued—as plaintiff or defendant—with their flock and other parties about tithes, contributions to repairs to the church or the payment of an extra (assistant) priest. The residual category is composed of a mishmash of individuals and organizations of the city of Malines: the Magistrate, the guilds, local merchants, etc., who brought their disputes about privileges, jurisdiction, outstanding accounts, etc., to the Great Council.

Only in lawsuits that were the result of opposition against open letters awarded by the Great Council did the jurisdiction *ratione personae* play no role. Indeed, these could involve a wide variety of litigants and subjects, which were not by definition privileged. *Maintenue* cases were especially common in this category.

Yet, the Great Council was in the first place a court for the higher social strata in the society of the Austrian Netherlands. In that regard, M. Van Dijck's idea that citizens looking for justice were consumers with the capacity and possibility to choose between different suppliers of justice must be qualified.[200] While this might have been true for the privileged—who had the right but were not obligated to bring their cases before the Great Council—this was certainly not the case for those who did not enjoy a privileged status. They had no choice but to get their right at a local tribunal and could only through the way of appeal have their cases eventually settled by the Great Council—at least if they had the necessary funds. As a result, the majority of the 'consumers' of the Great Council were by definition privileged.

[199] Cf. supra, Chap. 2. Councilor Happart was frequently engaged in lawsuits before the Great Council in order to settle his many debts.

[200] Van Dijck, Maarten. 2009. *Towards an economic interpretation of justice? Conflict settlement, social control and civil society in urban Brabant and Mechelen during the late Middle Ages and the early modern period*. In *Serving the Urban Community. The rise of public facilities in the Low Countries*, eds. Martijn Van der Burg et al., 62–88. Amsterdam: Aksant.

4.5 The Great Council's Caseload in the Eighteenth Century

4.5.1 Caseload of the Tribunal as a Whole

The analysis of the data derived from the extended sentences, from the dicta and from the distribution books has demonstrated that, throughout the eighteenth century, the Great Council experienced a serious decline in the number of civil lawsuits. Yet, it must be stressed that these numbers only measure the output—in case of the extended sentences and the dicta—and the input—in case of the distribution books—of the lawsuits at the Great Council, but that they do not necessarily provide an accurate image of the cumulative caseload of the tribunal.

In Chap. 3 we observed that, over the course of the eighteenth century, the councilors did not experience a substantial decrease in their revenues from the *épices*, at least not in nominal terms.[201] Admittedly, in 1757 they did receive a raise for some of their work. However, even if that is taken into account, the stability or even slight rise in their income from the *épices* between 1730 and 1765 is not congruent with the considerable decrease in the number of lawsuits that were distributed at the Great Council. Indeed, based on the *épices*, there is no immediate evidence that would suggest that the councilors had much less case-work to deal with by the late eighteenth century.

One explanation for this observation could lie in the duration of the lawsuits. If the councilors spent a much longer time handling their cases, assuming that this was accompanied by a corresponding proliferation of the number of legal acts deemed necessary, they could charge more than if they dealt with their lawsuits quickly and efficiently. The extended sentences already provide some indication that this was indeed the case: if a late seventeenth century register contained some 40 extended sentences with an average of 15 folia per sentence, that number dropped in the middle of the eighteenth century to approximately 25 extended sentences, some of which fill over 100 folia.[202] Therefore, in order to get an accurate impression of the caseload of the Great Council, the length of the lawsuits—in other words, the time they continued to remain 'active' at the tribunal—must be taken into account.

4.5.1.1 Duration of Lawsuits

Complaints about the length of the procedure were legion, as were the efforts of the central government to rectify the problem,[203] but specific numbers were never given. While the data set provided by the distribution books does not allow us to

[201] Cf. supra, Chap. 3. In real terms however, the purchasing power from their income undoubtedly fell over the course of the eighteenth century due to inflation.

[202] Verscuren, An. 2013. *Nadere toegang op de geëxtendeerde sententies van de Grote Raad van Mechelen: 1693–1772.* Brussels: Algemeen Rijksarchief.

[203] Cf. supra, Chap. 3.

follow an entire lawsuit from the day of its introduction to the day the sentence was pronounced,[204] it does make it possible to calculate the time span between the lawsuit's distribution and its eventual end date. In general, a case could be finalized in three ways: when a sentence was pronounced, when the parties were accommodated or when the plaintiff decided to abandon the lawsuit.

For 6107 cases, the distribution books provide the information necessary to estimate their duration, i.e., the dates—sometimes by approximation—on which the lawsuits were distributed and on which they ended.[205] At the low end of the spectrum, 156 lawsuits were finalized on the very same day they were distributed. At the other end, over 65 years passed by between the distribution of one specific case and its judgment.[206] Given that extreme examples on both sides would drastically distort the overall average case duration, we calculated both the median and an adjusted average with outliers excluded, to get a sense for the typical length of a case.[207] In this way, we estimated that the median duration of the lawsuits distributed at the Great Council in the eighteenth century was 214 days, while the 'adjusted' average duration was approximately 334 days.

Methodology The 6107 cases were selected from a total of 13,152 distributed cases or an estimated 9000–10,000 after accounting for redistributions and other forms of double-counting. We selected all lawsuits for which we have knowledge of the (approximate) date on which they were judged, on which they were abandoned, or on which the litigants were accommodated. If it is known that a lawsuit has been redistributed—whether only once or repeatedly—we used the date that it was first distributed combined with the date that it ultimately ended.[208]

It should also be emphasized that we only used the subset of lawsuits for which the end date is actually available, although in reality the councilors also worked for some time on all those other cases (which probably ended at some point before 1794 but never received an official end date in the distribution records). However, given that taking them into account—for instance, by artificially setting their end date to 1794—would drastically distort the results, we opted to work with the 6107 lawsuits mentioned above. As these represent close to half of all distributed lawsuits at the Great Council[209]—and closer to 60–65 % when accounting for redistributed

[204] The extended sentences do provide this information, but we preferred not to use this data as it might give a distorted image because of its 'special' status.

[205] See Excel database: distribution records of the eighteenth century Great Council.

[206] The lawsuit in question was an appeal against a sentence of the Council of Flanders between the *maîtres des pauvres du Saint Esprit* of the *Saint Sauveur* Church in Bruges and the prior of the Carmelites of Bruges, distributed in February, 1695 and judged on May 20, 1760.

[207] We opted to define outliers as cases with durations in the lowest and highest 10 % of the sample of 6107 cases considered. In practice, this means that all lawsuits that lasted less than 30 or more than 1369 days were not taken into account for calculation of the adjusted average.

[208] If the specific day of the month is not provided, we fixed the distribution date and/or the end date to the 15th of the ending month. As a result of this assumption and approximation, the table shows peaks in the number of lawsuits that ended every 30 or 31 days after their distribution date. Therefore, the results of our analysis are only an approximation of the reality.

[209] It also must be noted that several cases are marked as judged in the distribution records, which, however, do not have a judgment date.

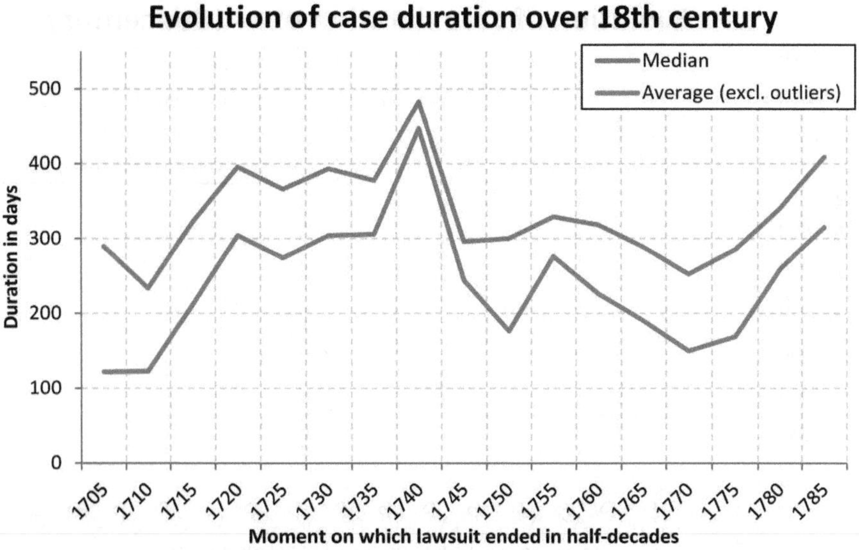

Fig. 4.10 Evolution of case duration throughout the eighteenth century

cases or other forms of double-counting—we believe that our numbers will be representative estimates for the overall set of cases distributed over the course of the eighteenth century.

In order to get a sense for the evolution of the median and average duration of a lawsuit throughout the eighteenth century, we calculated these metrics in 5-year increments. Figures. 4.10 and 4.11, which map the evolution of case duration over the eighteenth century, both show the adjusted average and median number of days a lawsuit lasted for each 5-year period. In addition, Fig. 4.11 also includes the evolution of the highest and lowest quintiles: the dotted lines in this chart indicate how the top 20 % highest and lowest case durations (within each 5-year window) change over time.

To determine which 5-year period a case is assigned to for this purpose, we rounded down its actual end date. For example, if a lawsuit ended in 1742, this was rounded down to 1740. It is important to emphasize that, at least for Figs 4.10 and 4.11, our analysis is indeed based on the *end dates*[210] of the lawsuits, as opposed to, for instance, the distribution date.[211] For instance, a lawsuit that ended between 1720 and 1724 lasted an adjusted[212] average of 395 days after it had been

[210] As explained before, a case could be finalized in three ways: when a sentence was pronounced, when the parties were accommodated or when the plaintiff decided to abandon the lawsuit. Obviously, we define the end date of a case used for this analysis accordingly, i.e., as the judgment date, settlement date or case withdrawal date.

[211] The chart based on the distribution date of the lawsuits demonstrates a similar pattern—though somewhat more distinct—with of course a small time difference. See Excel database: distribution records of the eighteenth century Great Council.

[212] As noted above, we define adjusted average as the average excluding outliers, that is, cases with a duration in the lowest and highest 10 % of the sample of 6107 cases considered (which works out

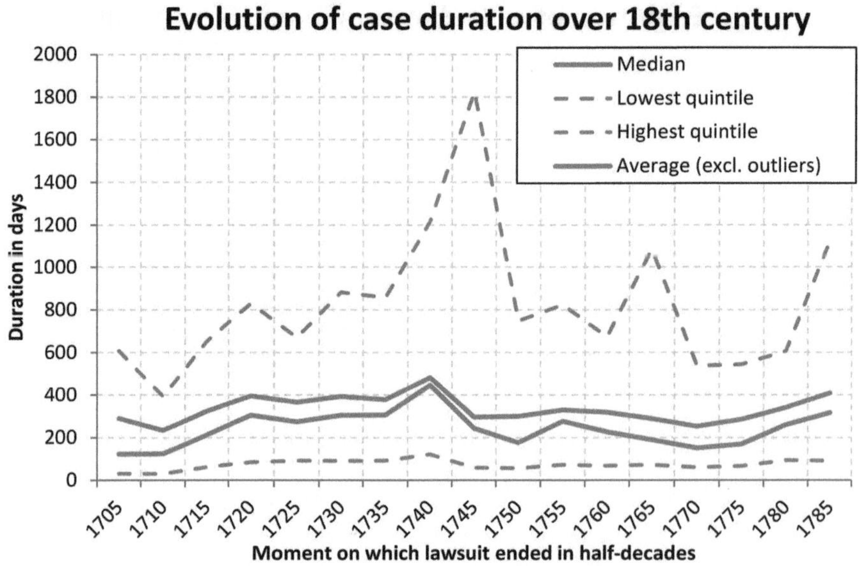

Fig. 4.11 Evolution of case duration throughout the eighteenth century with lowest and highest quintile

distributed. The first 5 years of the eighteenth century were left out in Figs. 4.10 and 4.11, because several lawsuits from the late seventeenth century will have had their end-date in that period and the data for cases distributed in the 1680s and 1690s are incomplete. We also left out the last decade of the century because—due to the revolutionary period ending in the *de facto* abolition of the tribunal—many of the lawsuits distributed in this period were never finalized.

It must be noted that the estimated case duration evolution shown in Figs. 4.10 and 4.11 might to some extent be distorted by variations in data availability over time.[213] For lawsuits distributed between 1700 and 1750 and again in the 1790s, we could identify an end date for less than 50 % of the cases. For the period between 1750 and 1790 on the other hand, between 60 and 75 % of the distributed cases have a known end date. We can think of two possible explanations for this observation: either a larger percentage of lawsuits reached a conclusion—as opposed to remaining 'pending' indefinitely—after 1750 than before (i.e., the effect is real), or the registrars of the first half of the century were simply less diligent when recording the end date of lawsuits in the distribution records than those of the second half of the century (i.e., the effect is an artificial result of changes in recordkeeping). If the latter is the case, the estimated case duration and its evolution might be affected to the extent that there is a correlation between registrar diligence and case duration.

to less than 30 or more than 1369 days).

[213] See Excel database: distribution records of the eighteenth century Great Council. Chart "Fraction of cases with known end date by distribution year" in tab "Duration by half decade start date".

For example, there is some evidence that registrars only began to consistently record end dates in the 1740s;[214] in addition, we can reasonably assume that long-running cases may have been particularly badly affected by this poor pre-1740s record-keeping.[215] The result of this would be that pre-1740s case duration averages are artificially biased lower, whereas for cases ending in the 1750s and later there would be no such effect. To the extent that this is the case, the drop in average case duration between 1720 and 1745 on the one hand, compared to 1750–1770 on the other, shown in Figs. 4.10 and 4.11 may even understate the real shortening of case length.

Analysis Results Figure 4.10 demonstrates that both the average and median duration of a lawsuit increased between 1710 and 1740. The distinctive peak in the year 1740 is particularly remarkable: lawsuits that were finalized in the half decade between 1740 and 1745 lasted on average 483 days, as if the councilors decided in 1740 to clean the Augean stables and put an end to several lawsuits that had been lying around for quite some time.[216] Figure 4.11, which outlines the highest and lowest quintiles together with the adjusted average and median, demonstrates that one fifth of the lawsuits that ended between 1745 and 1749 had lasted more than 5 years. This indeed seems to imply that, for some reason, the decision was taken around 1740 to tackle the Great Council's long-lasting lawsuits, a task that took some 5–10 years to accomplish and that ended with the completion of the lengthiest—and most complicated?—lawsuits in the late 1740s.

This raises the question why it was precisely around 1740 that the councilors started to deal with cases that had been dragging on for quite some time. One hypothesis might be that an order had come from the Privy Council or even the governor himself to speed up the completion of lawsuits at the Great Council because of an extreme backlog. While we have no direct knowledge of such an order, it is true that the last complaint about the excessive length of lawsuits at the Great Council dates from 1745—exactly around the time it was occupied with some very long

[214] There are indications that this was indeed the case. Based on the number of finalized lawsuits in the distribution books, we would think that a comparable number of cases ended in the first and the second half of the century (for example, both in 1710 and in 1777 the number of finalized lawsuits stands at 63). Nevertheless, if we look at the number of dicta in the eighteenth century, it becomes immediately evident that many more judgments were passed in the first half of the century than in the second half. Cf. Chart 3.2 versus the chart mapping the number of cases finalized by year (for the latter, see Excel database: distribution records of the eighteenth century Great Council).

[215] This assumption does seem intuitively plausible: it is certainly less cumbersome for registrars to record the end date for a case distributed fairly recently (which may have been recorded only a few pages back in the distribution books) than for one distributed years ago (for which the original entry may well be in an entirely different volume).

[216] In 1740, two lawsuits ended that had been distributed in 1726, one that been distributed in 1728, one from 1732, five from 1736, four from 1737 and one from 1738. In addition, 18 lawsuits that lasted around a year or less were judged or finalized in some other way. In comparison, in 1720—when a lawsuit lasted on average 395 days, which is still above the overall average of 334 days—one lawsuit ended that had been distributed in 1715, three that had been distributed in 1717, eight that had been distributed in 1718 and 18 that had been distributed in 1719.

cases.[217] Although the subsequent lack of criticism is by no means proof of such a hypothesis, it does provide some indication that something happened around 1740. Potentially this might have been the result, not so much of a top down order, but rather of a bottom up effort: in that scenario, several litigants at the Great Council may have complained to the government about the procedural tardiness of the late 1730s and early 1740s.

Certainly, the War of the Austrian Succession might have played a role in the timing as well: while in 1740 the theatre of war was still far off in Silesia, it is possible that several litigating parties at the Great Council saw the storm coming and wished to see their cases settled before the conflict moved to the Austrian Netherlands. Additionally, it is remarkable that exactly in 1740 the number of cases finalized is also relatively low.[218] Only 29 lawsuits were concluded, a number that climbs steeply towards 79 in 1744, fueling the hypothesis that there was some government interference in urging the Great Council to finalize more lawsuits.

Besides any outside interferences with the Great Council's handling of cases, there might also have been an internal dynamic at work. In May 1739, a new president—Joseph d'Olmen de Poederlé—was appointed to the Great Council. Possibly, he decided to stimulate (some of) his colleagues to clean up their backlogs.

The War of the Austrian Succession caused a disruption in this pattern of dealing with ever longer-lasting lawsuits. It should not come as a surprise that only two cases were finalized in the latter half of 1746, only one in 1747 and only six in 1748. Input as well as output was very limited during this period of time. Probably, several cases simply could not have come to a conclusion because only a truncated Great Council made the move to Namur and Echternach.[219] Moreover, the Great Council had been able to take only a limited number of case files with it when leaving Malines.[220] The fact that the average duration of a lawsuit judged in the early 1750s

---

[217] Brussels, ARA, GRM 168B, f.70–73, May 1745: request of both litigants—Charles Claude de Namur vicomte d'Elzée and the widow of Charles Edmond Dossain dit de Jemeppe—in a lawsuit before the Great Council to have the reporter of their case, assisted by two additional commissioners, judge their lawsuits without intervention of the entire Council. To motivate their request, they cite the enormous costs of the debates they have already had before the Great Council as well as the sheer lengthiness of the proceedings at the tribunal. According to the request, the latter was caused by the exceptional amount of work the councilors had at that time. "… considerans combien il seroit encore fraieux de laisser juger lesdits debats pardevant ledit grand conseil comme les autres ont été jugés ci devant, et en outre combien il seroit difficile d'obtenir un prompt jugement par rapport a la grande multitude desdits debats nés et a naitre et a la grande quantité d'autres affaires et proces qui occuperoient extraordinairement ledit grand conseil …".

[218] Cf. Excel database: distribution records of the eighteenth century Great Council, tab 'number of cases finalized by year'. Some qualification is necessary: the numbers are based on the information provided by the distribution records. Potentially, the data for 1740 were somehow badly registered, causing an apparent dip when in reality there was no major change. However, the number of dicta in 1740 is also relatively low—47—compared to the years before and after.

[219] Cf. supra, Chap. 3. Several, especially more senior councilors preferred to stay in Malines during the French occupation.

[220] The Great Council had not yet left Malines when the French entered it in 1746. While the French permitted the councilors to leave the city, they put serious restrictions on the documents the councilors were allowed to take with them. Cf. infra, Chap. 5.

is short is also unsurprising, given the limited influx of new cases during the Echternach period. Moreover, as explained above, several very lengthy cases had been finalized in the 1740s. With most of these long-lasting cases gone, it is only natural that the duration of a typical case would significantly drop in the early 1750s.

In addition, part of the reason for this drop may also relate to the situation of the Great Council's case records in the early 1750s. In 1746, the French had a large part of the records pertaining to the conquered territories of the Austrian Netherlands transported to the *Parlement de Flandres* in Douai.[221] Not only can we be sure that numerous cases that were originally introduced at the Great Council were finished in Douai, it also took several years before the archives were ultimately returned to Malines. A small part of those documents were restituted around 1750—which can indeed be seen in the eight cases distributed in 1750 and 1751 at the Great Council coming from Douai—but the Council had to wait until the *Traité des limites* was signed in Versailles in May 1769 before the mutual exchange of archives between France and the Austrian Netherlands became official. It was not until a year later that the remaining documents were finally sent back to Malines.[222] And indeed, in 1770, one lawsuit that had originally been introduced at the *Parlement de Flandres* in Douai was distributed at the Great Council.[223]

Still, only ten lawsuits originally handled in Douai in the period between 1746 and 1749 were eventually distributed at the Great Council. As this can certainly not be the real number of lawsuits pertaining to the occupied territories within the jurisdiction of the Great Council in this time period, we can assume that many lawsuits were eventually 'lost' for the Great Council—judged by the *Parlement* of Douai or simply abandoned.

After a slight increase in 1755, the average duration of lawsuits judged at the Great Council consistently declined. This might mean that the councilors had become more efficient—at least relatively speaking—in dealing with lawsuits. Was it perhaps the central government—now firmly in the hands of Empress Maria Theresa—which urged them to handle cases more swiftly as part of its general effort to improve government efficiency?

Whatever the reason, after 1770, the average and median durations consistently rose again to reach a new peak around 1785. Why the case duration increased again is unclear. One hypothesis might be that around 1770 the councilors acknowledged

[221] Brussels, ARA, GRMOF, BD 43, 1744–1750, f. 306–307, January 5, 1750: request of Robiano and du Trieu to be refunded for their travels to Douai. See also: Brussels, ARA, INV 42.

[222] Brussels, ARA, GRM 175/10, May 18, 1770: Mémoire of the Comte de Wijnants. This file also includes an inventory of the records that were restituted. Part of the archives, however, stayed behind in France, cf. Lorgnier, Jacques. 1988. Les procédures du Grand Conseil de Malines conservés à Lille (série V B des archives du Nord—présentation, inventaire et index pour les XVe et XVIe siècles). In *Miscellanea Consilii Magni III: essays on the history of forensic practice* (Verzamelen en bewerken van de jurisprudentie van de Grote Raad. Nieuwe Reeks 12), Alain Wijffels ed., 43–110. Amsterdam: Universiteit van Amsterdam.

[223] See: Distribution Records of the eighteenth century Great Council. The case was distributed on November 21, 1770 to councilor Rogez: Jacques François de Poucques ec[uie]r et consors appls de ceux de la gouvernance de Douai au parlement illec contre Pierre François Huvenne intimé; renvoié ceans ensuite du Traité des Limites.

that the decline in the number of cases distributed at the Great Council was dramatic. Therefore, they had plenty of incentive to let cases drag on in order to amass more work—and income. Moreover, they might have been concerned that an obvious lack of work would have a negative impact on their status, or even that the very reason of existence of the court could be questioned.

It is worth noting here that the Great Council was not the only central court that procrastinated in the settlement of cases: at the Court of Chancery in England, the proportion of suits lasting more than two years also increased over time. While at the seventeenth century Court of Chancery, almost nine-tenths of the cases were either dropped or judged within 2 years, that proportion had fallen to roughly three-quarters by 1785. Conspicuously, it was estate cases especially that lasted ever longer: in these lawsuits, the Court took the entire estate under its administration and therefore profited from its income.[224]

In addition to this question of incentives, we also need to examine why the councilors apparently had the opportunity to extend the duration of the lawsuits from roughly 1770 onwards. Did the appointment of Goswin de Fierlant as the new president of the Great Council in 1773 have any effect on this? Was he less impervious to the councilors' complaints than his predecessors? Or was he an absentee president who was so engaged in his other projects that he refrained from interfering with the day-to-day business at the Council? Or should we look for the real reason higher in the echelons of the government? Could the central government—the Privy Council and/or the governors—no longer be bothered to do something about overly long-lasting lawsuits at the Great Council (and potentially at other tribunals), because either they simply lost interest in the existing judicial system or possibly even wished to deliberately aggravate the litigants in order to make reforms easier to stomach?

Duration according to Instance Finally, in order to investigate if instance had any impact on the duration of the lawsuits, we analyzed the median and adjusted average duration[225] of first instance cases, revisions, reformations from Malines and appeals from Flanders, Luxemburg and Namur.

Table 4.4[226] demonstrates that the median duration of an appeal against a sentence of the Council of Luxemburg was twice as long as that of a reformation against a sentence of the Magistrate of Malines or a revision of a judgment of the Great Council itself. Even though the adjusted average figures show smaller differences—as, unlike the median, it is still somewhat influenced by the outliers—it remains obvious that litigants appealing against sentences from the Council of Luxemburg had to wait the longest to have their case concluded. Not only did it take the Great Council on average 370 days, or more than a year, to deal with an appeal from Luxemburg after distribution, in 20 % of the lawsuits the councilors needed

[224] Horwitz, Henry and Polden, Patrick. 1996. Continuity or change in the Court of Chancery in the seventeenth and eighteenth centuries? *Journal of British Studies* 35.1: 53–55.

[225] Again, we left out the highest and lowest 10 % of the sample of 6107 cases considered.

[226] 953 cases were available to calculate the average and median duration of first instance cases, 3055 for appeals from Flanders, 962 for appeals from Luxemburg, 671 for appeals from Namur, 257 for reformation of Malines and 73 for revision.

Table 4.4 Duration according to instance (in days)

Instance	Median	"Adjusted" average	Lowest quintile	Highest quintile
First Instance	214	334	51	877
Appeal Flanders	213	322	61	649
Appeal Luxemburg	330	370	91	1129
Appeal Namur	242	344	73	792
Reformation Malines	153	296	42	480
Revision	151	262	64	447

(more than) 1129 days—or over 3 years—to reach a decision. Compared to this, appeals from Flanders—which on average ended after 322 days while the duration of the 20 % longest lawsuits was 'only' 649 days or more—found, in general, a much speedier conclusion. Based on this analysis, the argument—used when awarding sovereignty to the Council of Luxemburg in 1782—that decisions in Luxemburg lawsuits became extremely delayed if sent to Malines, seems to be sound, and certainly more valid than in the case of Flanders.[227]

4.5.1.2 Accumulated Number of Lawsuits

The case duration analysis is interesting in itself, but also a tool that can be used to determine the accumulated caseload of the Great Council. While the charts picturing the evolution of the number of distributed cases[228] merely show how many new cases were allocated to the councilors, they do not take into account the total, cumulative number of lawsuits the councilors were dealing with at a certain moment. In order to get an approximate idea of the total caseload of the court—which is understood as the total number of lawsuits that were 'pending' at any given time—we calculated for every day of the eighteenth century how many lawsuits were newly distributed on that day as well as how many earlier lawsuits were still being worked on at that time. The results of these calculations were then averaged by month to arrive at the average cumulative case-load for that month.

Figure 4.12[229] shows that the caseload of the Great Council was at its absolute peak in 1742 (206 active cases). This is the logical outcome of the durational

[227] Cf. supra, Chap. 3.

[228] Cf. supra, Figs. 4.6 and 4.8.

[229] In order to construct this chart, we not only used the 6107 lawsuits for which we have some kind of end date, but also all lawsuits of which we are certain that they were redistributed at a certain point. For these cases, we considered the last date on which the case was redistributed as the end date. While this is not an accurate representation of the entire duration of the lawsuit in question, it does give us an approximate idea of at least its minimum length. For example: in 1761, the appeal of Louis Claude Joseph de Rahier against a sentence of the Council of Luxemburg, was distributed at the Great Council to Ignace Wirix. In 1771, the same case was redistributed to councilor Daniël Servaes. Given that we know that the case remained 'pending' at the Great Council for at least 10 years, we integrated this information into the chart and considered the case to have a 10-year duration for this purpose. Still, the chart only represents part of the real caseload, since in

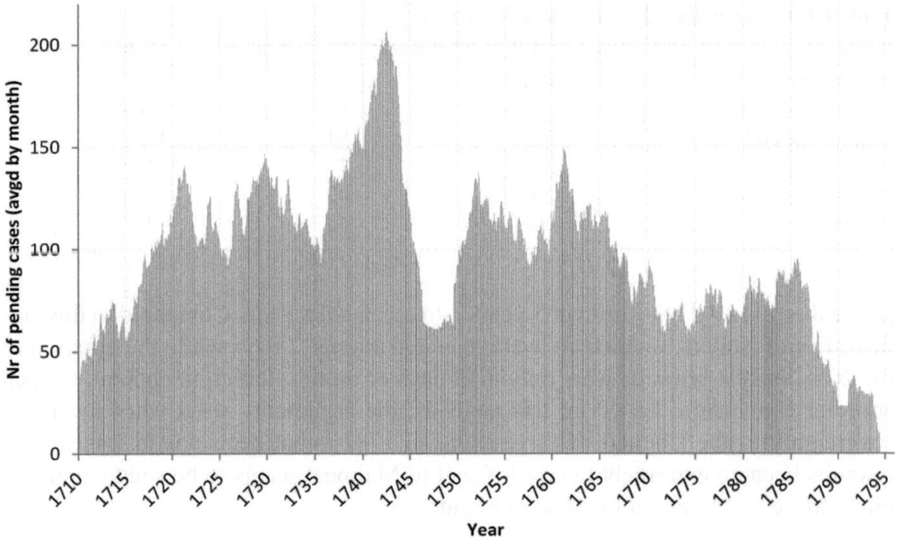

Fig. 4.12 Civil case workload evolution over time (1710–1794)

analysis: as explained above, in the early 1740s, the lawsuits with the longest (on average) durations were eventually finalized. The fact that many lengthy lawsuits had been concluded in the early 1740s, combined with the lack of newly introduced cases during the Echternach period and the temporary displacement of part of the Great Council's archives to Douai explain the subsequent dip in the latter half of the 1740s. Another modest peak in 1761 is followed by a more or less consistent decline until approximately 1770.

Particularly interesting is the observation that, contrary to what Figs. 4.6 and 4.8 suggested, the number of cases the councilors were working on in the period between roughly 1770 and 1787—i.e. the year of the drastic judicial reforms of Joseph II—stabilized and, ultimately, even rose slightly. In 1785, the number of active lawsuits at the Great Council stood at approximately 94, which was more or less the level that the Great Council attained in 1717 (95) and 1725 (100). In contrast,

reality work on the case clearly continued after 1771, although we do not know for how long given that the ultimate judgment date is not provided. In addition, for many other lawsuits we have neither an end date nor a redistribution date. These cases were obviously active for some time before they started to gather dust at the registry because none of the parties could be bothered to follow through. Alternatively, a sentence was pronounced (or the litigants were accommodated) but the registrar failed to include the date in the distribution records. Since simply assuming that all of these cases remained 'pending' until 1794 is senseless, we decided not to include these cases in the chart. For these reasons, the estimated caseload shown in the chart will inevitably underestimate the Council's actual caseload and should not be relied upon as an accurate approximation of the Council's work load in absolute terms; it does, however, show a fairly accurate picture of how the Council's caseload evolved over time.

however, in 1717 and 1725 respectively 170 and 187 cases[230] were distributed at the tribunal, while in 1785 only 57 lawsuits were divided over the councilors. This evolution confirms our earlier conclusions: from 1770 on, the average length of the lawsuits started to increase, causing a rise in the number of lawsuits that were active at the Great Council in spite of the flow of incoming new cases gradually drying up.

In summary, the accumulated caseload of the councilors did not consistently decline throughout the eighteenth century, as the number of extended sentences, dicta and distributed lawsuits would suggest. A decrease after roughly 1750[231] was followed by a recovery from 1770 on, not so much because more cases were introduced—rather the opposite—but because the average duration of lawsuits considerably lengthened. While we have no direct proof for our hypothesis forwarded in subsection 3.5.1.1, we believe that it is possible that the councilors deliberately let cases drag on, multiplying the number of 'acts'—*enquêtes*, *verbaux*, etc.—to keep their incomes from dropping too steeply. Alternatively, it could be that the councilors lost interest in their work at the Council and that they were just lazy, considering it unnecessary to spend much time reporting lawsuits as it was no longer financially lucrative. In that regard, the reforms of 1787 might have been a serious wake-up call, especially since afterwards the government again started to rely more heavily on the Great Council to advance its own policies.[232]

The consequences of this observation are interesting as well. Did the length of the average lawsuit at the Great Council—and the higher costs that were probably associated with this longer duration—deter potential litigants from bringing their cases to court? Or was it the other way around? Or, were both dynamics at play, resulting in a vicious circle: did the declining number of lawsuits prompt the councilors to let them drag on longer, in turn making potential litigants ever more reluctant to go to court?

4.5.2 Caseload of Individual Councilors[233]

During the last 100 years of the tribunal's existence, 94 councilors were active at the Great Council, all but one of whom effectively reported lawsuits.[234] 93 councilors

[230] The reason that the number of distributed cases in 1717 and 1725 is higher than the number of active cases is that we have only taken those cases into account that have a known end date or redistribution date.

[231] The low number of cases between 1746 and 1749 is due to special circumstances connected to the Echternach exile and is therefore not taken into consideration here.

[232] Cf. infra, Chap. 5.

[233] The information in this paragraph is entirely based on the data provided by the distribution records. See: Excel database: distribution records of the eighteenth century Great Council.

[234] Henri Diu was the only member of the Great Council to whom not a single case was distributed. Since he started his career in 1767 at the level of procurator-general and remained in this position until 1794, he never acted as a regular councilor and was therefore not allowed to handle a case as reporter. Cf. supra, Chap. 2.

dealing with 13,152 cases[235] means that on average every councilor was responsible for 141 lawsuits. Naturally, this figure is entirely meaningless[236] given that the number of cases a councilor reported strongly depended on his overall career—the duration of his service at the Great Council, if he made it to fiscal or even president during his career, if he was a clerical or a layman councilor, etc.—and at what point during the eighteenth century he was employed at the tribunal.

The declining overall number of lawsuits distributed at the Great Council throughout the eighteenth century obviously affected the caseload of each individual councilor as well. Councilors in the late eighteenth century reported a much smaller number of cases than those with a similar number of active years in the early decades of the century. For example, Charles Philippe de Waepenaert, who had a 12-year career spanning the period between 1724 and 1735, was a reporter for 242 cases, or, on average 20 per year. By contrast, Jacques Joseph Ghison, who entered the Great Council in 1783 and remained councilor until the very last day of the tribunal's existence—in total some 12 years—was a reporter for only 59 lawsuits, an average of barely five per year. These men had very comparable careers: they both started as advocates at the Great Council and never received a promotion or took on the role of fiscal. This demonstrates that the determining factor for the number of cases they reported was indeed linked to the time frame in which they worked, rather than, for instance, their personality or descent.

Indeed, far more than the councilors' capabilities or experience, the overall circumstances at the Great Council as a whole were paramount in determining their workload. We can find an excellent example of this in the period between 1746 and 1749, when the Great Council went into exile, first to Namur and then to the city of Echternach in Luxemburg. Not only did this period constitute a dramatic drop in the number of cases the councilors could deal with—a decline of which the Great Council never really recovered—but the distribution of lawsuits over the different councilors also indicates that several members of the Great Council declined to make the journey: Guillaume de Potter, Charles de Partz, Joseph Richterich, Jean Baptiste Hony,[237] Guillaume Snoy and François de Meuldre apparently preferred to remain in Malines. Naturally, their absence from the Great Council during that period put a considerable damper on the number of cases they reported. The junior councilors—not necessarily in age, but in seniority—did follow the Council in exile: Jean François Lamosnier (appointed in 1738), Charles Thomas Caimo (1741), Gilles Streithagen (1741), Pierre Deudon (1741), Jean Jacques Marci (1741) and Charles Henri Goubau (1744).[238]

[235] These 13,152 lawsuits include the 1704 cases distributed before 1700, as the councilors who reported them continued their careers in the eighteenth century.

[236] The numbers vary widely, ranging from 3 cases reported by councilor Casselot to 365 by councilor A.D. de Steenhault.

[237] Hony stayed on as a councilor until 1765, but he became ill in 1745 and never returned to take his seat. It is therefore evident that he remained in Malines.

[238] Although we are not entirely certain that the president (d'Olmen de Poederlé), the advocate-fiscal (Van Slabbeeck) and the procurator-general (Sotteau) followed the Council into exile, we

While the time period a councilor was active was certainly crucial, it is clear that various other factors, some of which may be hard to identify, also influenced how many lawsuits he would report. This can be illustrated by the contrasting experiences of councilors Augustin de Steenhault and Philippe de Beeckman. While both were appointed around the same time—in 1712 and in 1716 respectively—and while de Beeckman had a much longer career at the Great Council—25 years compared to 15 for de Steenhault—the former reported almost 50 lawsuits less than the latter (286 versus 365).[239]

The underlying reason for this notable difference in workload is unclear. In theory, the president of the Great Council was responsible for the distribution of lawsuits: "*Item, tous procès, après qu'ilz seront instruictz, seront mis au greffe et le president les distribuera à son plaisir ...*"[240] Although the qualification '*à son plaisir*' is primarily intended to formally establish the monopoly of the president over the distribution process, to a certain extent it does go further than that: indeed 'at his pleasure' seems to suggest that his discretion was not necessarily restricted by any rules or need for rational motivation. This could be one explanation for large and seemingly arbitrary differences in workload, such as those observed between councilors de Steenhault and de Beeckman. That said, however, we can realistically assume that in most cases the president likely did use certain criteria when assigning a specific case to a specific councilor, even if they were not specified in any regulations.

At the Council of Brabant, it was the secretaries and registrars who often personally distributed the cases, even though in theory this was the privilege of the chancellor. The most important and most voluminous—and therefore the most financially rewarding—files in particular were distributed by the secretaries and registrars under the pretext that these lawsuits were related to another earlier case that a certain specific councilor had reported. Apparently, the councilors also sometimes appointed themselves as reporters, even though this was strictly forbidden. Finally, at times, the litigants had some say in the choice of the reporter of their case: while they could not request the chancellor to assign their case to their hand-picked councilor, they could ask him *not* to have a certain councilor report it, even if they did not have sufficient grounds to officially challenge him.[241] For the High Council, Van Poelgeest observed that the councilors took turns when the most lucrative lawsuits were distributed in order to avoid internal strife.[242]

---

do assume that especially the former two did. Sotteau died in 1747 during the exile. However, we have no information on his location at that time.

239 For exact numbers, see the distribution of the number of lawsuits over the different councilors in the Excel database: distribution records of the eighteenth century Great Council.

240 *ROPB*, 2ième série, t.7, p. 463, August 8 1559, title 1, art. 36.

241 Gaillard, Arthur. 1898–1902. *Le Conseil de Brabant: histoire, organisation, procédure*. Brussels: Lebègue, 265–268.

242 Van Poelgeest, L. 1988. De raadsheren van de Hoge Raad van Holland, Zeeland en West-Friesland in de achttiende eeuw. *Bijdragen en mededelingen betreffende de geschiedenis der Nederlanden* 103.1: 37.

For the Great Council, we do not know if such a rotation system existed or if the councilors managed in one way or another to influence the distribution process. In the sixteenth century, complaints were voiced within the Great Council about the registrars' interference with the distribution of lawsuits.[243] Given that we have no evidence to the contrary for the eighteenth century, we assume that it was the president who assigned certain cases to certain councilors.[244] An analysis of the allocation of the lawsuits over the councilors provides some hypotheses as to the criteria used when appointing a reporter.

4.5.2.1 Criteria used for the Distribution of Lawsuits[245]

The 'Type' of Lawsuit Not a single member of the Great Council had such a degree of specialization that he dealt with only one type of cases: they all handled both first instance cases and appeals coming from different provincial councils.[246] In practice many of them did tend to focus on specific types of lawsuits, which was at least partly the result of the general case workload of the Council as a whole. With only a few exceptions, all councilors until Wirix (appointment in 1753) predominantly judged first instance cases, followed by appeals coming from Flanders. Beginning with councilor van Goethem (who started his career in 1755), the pattern changed: the majority of the councilors now primarily handled appeals from Flanders, with first instance cases ranking second; in the last decade, the latter fell even further behind and was often preceded by appeals coming from Namur. Evidently, this pattern corresponds entirely to the previously discussed ratio of first instance versus appeal cases at the Great Council.[247]

Nevertheless, the number of appeals coming from Flanders exceeded the number of first instance cases for a few councilors active in the first half of the eighteenth century, *i.c.* Jean Thadée de Grouff, Josse Bernaerts, Remy du Laury, Jean Baptiste de Decker, Guillaume de Potter and Ambroise de Smet. In addition, for councilors Jacques Stalins, Joseph de Corte, Charles Philippe Pattin, Pierre Claude de St. Vaast and Guillaume Pijcke, the number of appeals from Flanders came close to matching their first instance cases. Every single one of these councilors—except for Josse Bernaerts—was born in the region of Flanders. This means that for 10 out of 16 councilors born in Flanders who were predominantly active in the first half of the eighteenth century—when first instance cases constituted the most important category of the overall case inflow—appeals coming from their own region

[243] Brussels, ARA, Audiëntie 1419/4, 1553: the comment was made in the margin of an investigation into the behavior of procurator-general de Cocq.

[244] Although we admit that, since the bags with the litigants' files had to be deposited at the court registry, the registrars had plenty of opportunity to take control of the distribution process.

[245] Source: Excel database: distribution records of the eighteenth century Great Council

[246] There is only one exception to this rule: councilor Timmermans exclusively dealt with appeals coming from Flanders, but he was active at the Great Council for only a little over a year.

[247] Cf. 4.3 Types of civil litigation.

made up for a disproportionately large part of their workload. As for the six others, four of them—Guillaume Gielis Hujoel, Charles Otté, Juste Bervoet and Charles de Partz—still spent a relatively large amount of their time dealing with appeals from Flanders. Only Philippe Du Jardin and Charles Philippe de Waepenaert did not stand out in this regard.

As far as the councilors from Namur, Luxemburg or Malines are concerned, there are no indications that they reported more appeals coming from their province of origin than other members of the Great Council, even when corrected for the small amount of lawsuits that these regions supplied. Councilor Jean Henri Kahnn is the only exception: he in fact did primarily deal with lawsuits from Luxemburg. Nevertheless, there are too many counterexamples to conclude that there is a systematic connection between a councilor's provenance and the type of cases he reported.

On the other hand, the fact that many Flemish members of the Great Council did predominantly handle appeals from Flanders and that Kahnn's main workload consisted of lawsuits coming from his own region, Luxemburg, is too striking to ignore. There is clearly no doubt that those councilors were familiar with the specific laws and customs of their respective provinces and that this played an important role in considering a case.[248] The Estates of Flanders even used it as its major argument when campaigning for more Flemish councilors at the Great Council. However, this observation does not explain why Brussels-born Bernaerts also primarily handled appeals from Flanders. Possibly, the determining factor was not—or not in the first place—familiarity with specific customs, but knowledge of the languages spoken in a specific province.

Language As the Great Council based its own judgments in essence on the written files compiled in lower tribunal(s), the members of the Great Council had to understand the language used in these documents. Since Dutch was the predominant language in Flanders and a considerable percentage of files coming from Luxemburg must have been in German, reporters who had some knowledge of these languages were a must. In fact, in 1787, after the death of Gillis de Cock and with several of the councilors engaged in Brussels, de Fierlant urged the *Conseil du gouvernement général* to speedily appoint a new councilor who was fluent in Flemish because *ce vuide le gène dans la distribution des causes flamandes*.[249]

We can assume that most members who were born in Flanders were well-versed in Dutch, which might not have been true for their colleagues from Namur or Luxemburg, let alone from abroad. Councilor Philippe Rogez for example, openly admitted that his Dutch needed some improvement and we can presume that Jacques de Stassart also had problems understanding cases that were not in French.[250] The same is true for Luxemburg: councilor Christophe de Baillet was born in Latour, a small community near Virton, in the present-day Belgian province of Luxemburg,

[248] Cf. supra, Chap. 3.

[249] Cf. supra, Chap. 2. Brussels, ARA, ARR 857, Letter of de Fierlant to the *Conseil du gouvernement général*, November 1787.

[250] Cf. supra, Chap. 2.

where French was without a doubt the dominant if, not the only, language spoken. Jean Henri Kahnn on the other hand was born in the current capital of the Grand-Duchy of Luxembourg, where German was widespread. Moreover, his last name leads us to suspect that he was himself a German-speaker or that he was at least of German ancestry. Therefore, it stands to reason that he was the principal reporter for appeals coming from Luxemburg that were not written in French.[251]

Connections to Previous Lawsuits Gaillard suggested that, at the Council of Brabant, a councilor was more likely to be appointed reporter of a lawsuit if there was a demonstrable connection to a previous case he had handled.[252] While the information provided by the distribution records does not directly allow us to determine such a relationship, we can assume that different cases introduced by the same litigant—or his family members—were often related to previous lawsuits, especially if noble families were involved. In fact, since the latter were so frequently engaged in lawsuits related to their patrimony,[253] there must certainly have been identifiable connections to previous cases at various points, providing a clear rationale to assign the bulk of the cases to the same councilor. Given the enormous amount of data available, we selected a sample of six families who were frequent 'customers' of the Great Council in order to verify this hypothesis, *i.c.* Arenberg, Egmont, Nassau, d'Ursel, d'Isenghien and Looz-Corswarem. Each of these parties brought over 40 actions to the court during the eighteenth century; for the d'Isenghien family we counted over 80 lawsuits.[254]

There are indeed several clear examples of certain councilors consistently dealing with lawsuits introduced by one of these litigants. The pattern is most visible for the Nassau family. For example, in 9 out of 11 lawsuits in which the Nassaus served as plaintiffs or defendants in 1700 and 1701, councilor Henri Bruitsma acted as reporter. Between 1701 and 1707, Jacques Stalins was allocated 7 out of 8 of the lawsuits concerning the family. In the period between 1708 and 1720, councilor Guillaume Gielis Hujoel appeared as the main reporter in the actions of the Nassau's. Jean O'Donnogue was dominant in the late 1730s and early 1740s, while Charles de Partz took over his role in 1742.

Although less obvious, our dataset reveals a comparable pattern for the other families: for the Arenberg's, councilors Charles Pattin and Charles Philippe de Waepenaert divided among the two of them the 10 cases distributed in 1729 and 1730,[255] while Joseph Richterich was the leading reporter in the early 1740s. The lawsuits of the de Looz-Corswarem family were often reported by Juste Bervoet in the late 1720s and early 1730s[256] whereas François de Meuldre was the councilor-reporter

---

[251] It must however be noted that many cases from Luxemburg were probably translated into French. Cf. supra, Chap. 3.

[252] Gaillard, Arthur. 1898–1902. *Le Conseil de Brabant: histoire, organisation, procédure*. Brussels: Lebègue, 265

[253] Cf. supra, 4.4 The nature of litigation.

[254] Source: Excel database: distribution records of the eighteenth century Great Council.

[255] There is only one exception: in 1729, de Potter reported one *différend*

[256] Between 1727 and 1735 Bervoet was responsible for 6 out of 9 cases.

of choice in the period between 1738 and 1752 and in the years 1757–1761.[257] For the Egmont's Henri Bruitsma and Jacques Stalins accounted for the bulk of the cases distributed between 1690 and 1707 and Jean O'Donnogue and Charles de Partz for those distributed between 1739 and 1742.[258] For the d'Isenghien family we observed a similar dominance of certain councilors during a given period of time. The d'Ursel family constitutes somewhat of an exception.

Even if, as illustrated above, there are certain identifiable relationships between a particular councilor and a litigant for some specific families at specific points in time, we should not overestimate their importance in general. First of all, those councilors who reported five or more lawsuits involving the same family were rather the exception than the rule.[259] Secondly, most councilors who handled five or more of such lawsuits did so within 1 or 2 years.[260] Furthermore, the relationship between a certain councilor and a particular family is more obvious in the early eighteenth century than in the late eighteenth century; in fact, when the Council's case inflow dropped and lawsuits involving the same family became more scattered over time, different lawsuits of the same litigants were generally spread out over multiple councilors. As a consequence, even though there are strong indications that a connection to a previous lawsuit—especially one concluded in the recent past—was one of the criteria for distribution, its importance should not be overrated.

Financial Concerns Given that a reporter at the Great Council—contrary to one at the Council of Brabant[261]—only very seldom received more *épices* for his work than the other members of his chamber, apart from the president and the fiscal(s), it is unlikely that financial concerns were a major criterion when assigning a lawsuit to a certain councilor. Only when the case was particularly complicated and required special procedures—such as *enquêtes* or *verbaux*—could a reporter realistically hope to increase his income in comparison to his colleagues, but this was rather the exception than the rule. Therefore, it was often less important for a councilor to be

---

[257] Between 1738 and 1752 de Meuldre acted as a reporter in 10 out of 15 lawsuits. Between 1757 and 1761 he was the sole reporter, dealing with no less than 5 cases.

[258] Between 1690 and 1707 Bruitsma and Stalins dealt with 19 out of 26 relevant lawsuits, for the period between 1739 and 1742 O'Donnogue and de Partz acted as reporters for 10 out of 12 cases. It is conspicuous that these four councilors were also the primary reporters for the cases involving the Nassau family.

[259] For example: for the 64 cases between 1692 and 1787 in which members of the de Looz-Corswarem family acted as plaintiffs or defendants we counted 24 different councilors. François De Meuldre, Jean Vriesen and Juste Bervoet respectively dealt with 15, 7 and 6 lawsuits but on the other hand, 12 others (Bruitsma, de Steenhault, de Potter, d'Olmen, C.P. de Waepenaert, Hony, Pouppez, Goubeau, Van Goethem, Brenart, de Laing and Ludovisi d'Orley) only appeared once as a reporter. This observation is even more distinct for the d'Arenberg family: no less than 32 different councilors handled 59 lawsuits in the period between 1700 and 1793. While C.P. de Waepenaert and Richterich dealt with several of Arenberg's cases, more than half of the reporters only reported just one case.

[260] For instance, C.P. de Waepenaert's activity for the Arenberg's is concentrated in 1729 and 1730. Likewise, Bruitsma dealt with all of his 9 cases for the Nassau family in 1700 and 1701.

[261] Gaillard, Arthur. 1898–1902. *Le Conseil de Brabant: histoire, organisation, procédure*. Brussels: Lebègue, t.2, 274.

a reporter himself than to have a seat in the chamber which handled the majority of the cases. Financial concerns might have played a role, but not so much on the level of the individual councilors as of the chamber as a whole.

Workload and Career Path Finally, the president might have tried to even out the amount of work on each councilor's plate, taking into account the quantity as well as the quality of the lawsuits. Indeed, if a councilor already had several complicated and time-consuming cases to report, he may not have been able to take on any additional caseload.[262] Moreover the councilor's career path might have been a determining factor as well. While there is no obvious overall pattern in the highs and lows of a councilor's career, quite a few members of the Great Council seem to have had the apex of their careers—at least in terms of number of cases to report—during their early years at the Great Council.

The seniority of a councilor was probably especially decisive when criminal trials were distributed. We might assume that in general, given that criminal trials were not very popular, they were allocated to relatively recently appointed councilors.[263] This hypothesis is largely confirmed by our analysis of the criminal case files:[264] many councilors who reported the *grand criminel* cases were fairly 'junior' members of the Great Council; on average, they had just 5 years of seniority. Only a few had been active for more than 10 years in the Council when dealing with a trial categorized as *grand criminel*.[265]

For the *petit criminel*, the reporter's seniority was typically higher—on average 9 years—and several councilors still dealt with these sorts of lawsuits when they

---

[262] Potentially, in addition to having insufficient time to take on any more caseload, a councilor in this situation might have been unwilling to report more cases given that his position as reporter did not yield much extra revenue. To what extent being a reporter was regarded as a prestigious, sought-after position is not known.

[263] At the Council of Brabant, it was usually the most junior councilor who was entrusted with the reporting of criminal trials.

[264] Since the old inventory does not mention which councilor acted as reporter of the trial, we investigated every single one of the 280 case files still present in the archives (seven of the files described in the inventory are missing) in order to retrieve the name of the councilor-reporter. In 94 instances we were not able to identify the reporter, often because a case was introduced by the fiscals but was never followed up by the Great Council. Sometimes, the file had been transmitted from another provincial or city council—e.g. dossier nr 169 was sent from the Council of Luxembourg (Brussels, ARA, GRMOF 169 (1700–1701))—and only contained documents from that particular council. For 186 trials however, we do know who acted as reporter. In the period between 1700 and 1794, 56 members of the Great Council dealt with a criminal case file, the majority of them only once or twice; only seven members handled six or more. One councilor—A.D. de Steenhault—stands out: he reported 41 trials in the period between 1713 and 1725, adding to his already impressive 365 civil lawsuits. In fact, he singlehandedly dealt with all cases related to the prosecution of the 1718 Malines revolt, which means that in 1720 alone, he worked as a reporter in 34 criminal trials on top of the 18 civil lawsuits distributed to him during that same year.

[265] This included A.D. de Steenhault, Vanderhaeghen (13), Gieilis Hujoel (14), Tackoen (14), Marci (13), Deudon (11) and Van Voorspoel (19).

had been at the Great Council for 20 years and more.[266] Since these cases presumably followed the civil procedure and were therefore offenses usually punished by a fine, they were probably considered to have the same status as civil cases and did not generate much less revenue than a regular civil suit. In fact, we were even able to retrieve a few of these *petit criminel* lawsuits in the distribution records.[267] As for the 34 *procès politiques*, which dealt with the revolts of 1786–1794, they were most likely too numerous to be distributed among the recently appointed councilors. Instead, it appears they have been rather indiscriminately divided over the qualified (non-clerical) councilors available during that period.

4.5.2.2 Case Turnaround Time for Individual Councilors

Irrespective of what allocation criteria were used for the distribution of lawsuits to the different councilors, it is clear that some councilors received many more cases to report than others. Nevertheless, just as we observed for the caseload of the tribunal as a whole, the workload of each individual councilor was not only determined by the number of lawsuits he had to report but also by their complexity and duration. In order to examine if the time spent on a case differed much between individual councilors, we calculated the case turnaround time for each councilor.

Figure 4.13[268] maps the case turnaround time for each councilor, confirming the earlier observations concerning case duration at the Great Council as a whole. Councilors Richterich, Lamosnier and de Meuldre, who all had a high median and average turnaround time, were active during the late 1730s and early 1740s, at the exact same time that many long-lasting lawsuits ended.[269] It is notable, looking at the 'highest quintile' data in Fig. 4.13, that one fifth of the lawsuits reported by Richterich lasted more than 1808 days (about 5 years); for de Meuldre, the corresponding figure is 1452 days (about 4 years).[270]

---

[266] J.Ch. de Waepenaert (29), Van Voorspoel (26), Deudon (29), Gielis Hujoel (23), Vriesen (27), Tackoen (23), Richterich (22) and Kahnn (27).

[267] Brussels, ARA, GRMOF 448, 466, 496 and 558.

[268] We only have data for 92 councilors; none of the lawsuits distributed to councilor Van Cutsem were ever concluded (or at least the distribution records do not indicate their ending date). In general, we have information on the end date for almost half of the cases distributed to each councilor. The pale pink bar indicates the adjusted average case turnaround time for each councilor.As noted in subsection 4.5.1.1 Duration of lawsuits, we define adjusted average as the average excluding outliers, that is, cases with a duration in the lowest and highest 10 % of the sample of 6107 cases considered. The top and the bottom of the blue line refers to respectively the highest and the lowest quintile in the range of turnaround times for each councilor, with the blue dot marking the median of that range.

[269] Cf. supra, 4.5.1.1 Duration of lawsuits.

[270] It is important to note that the majority of the lawsuits Richterich and de Meuldre reported were 'original' cases, i.e. cases that were initially distributed to them, and were therefore not lawsuits that had been redistributed from another councilor. While both did deal with a few redistributed cases, these could not have had any major influence the statistics. Cf. Excel database: distribution records of the eighteenth century Great Council.

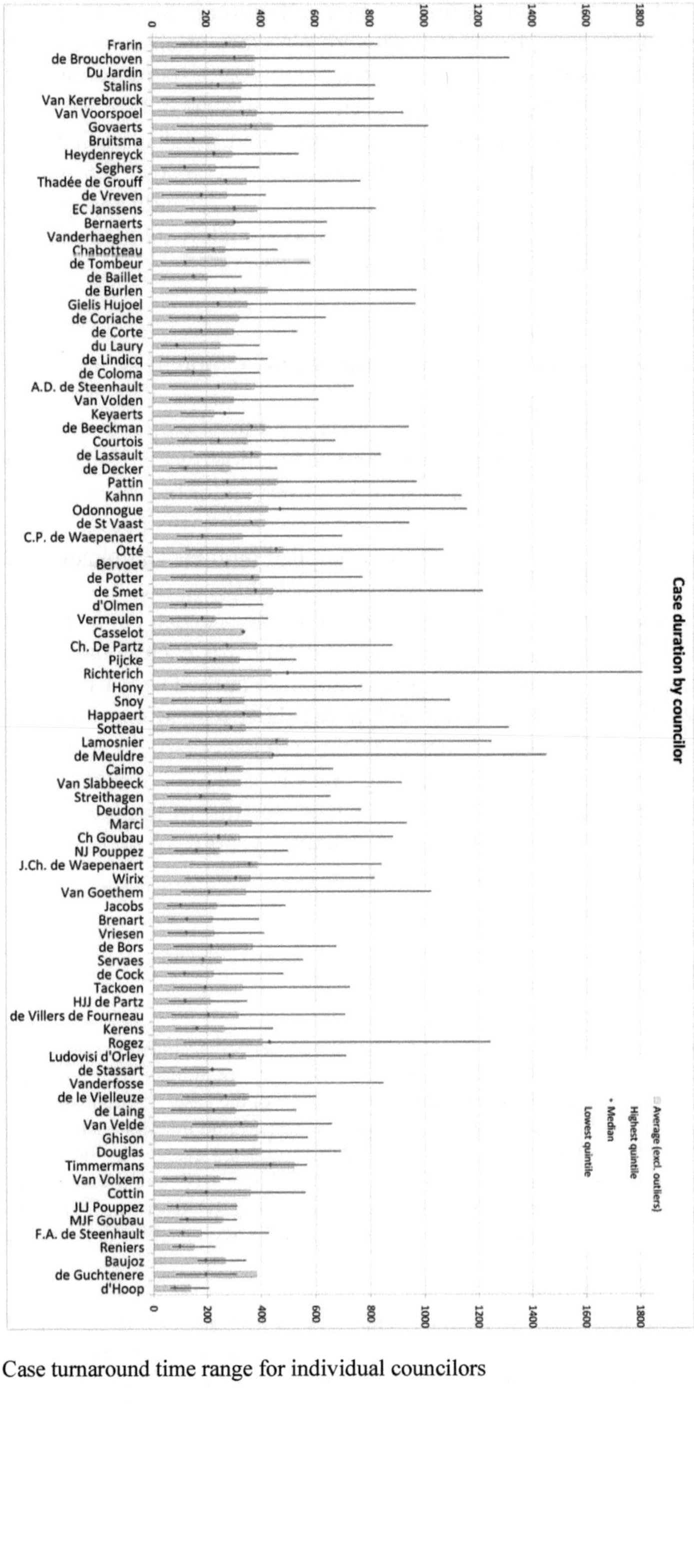

Fig. 4.13 Case turnaround time range for individual councilors

Unfortunately, the information available does not allow us to determine if these councilors were specifically appointed to deal with extremely complicated matters—perhaps as part of a 'grand plan' to clean up some of the most long-running cases still pending in the early 1740s—if they were merely inefficient or sluggish, or if they deliberately let many of their cases drag on for a long time for some other reason. In any case, it is clear that these councilors are to a large extent responsible for the longevity of the lawsuits judged in the period between 1740 and 1750. The cut-off again seems to be around 1740. Councilors who were appointed shortly after that date—such as Streithagen, Van Slabbeeck and Deudon—all dealt relatively quickly with their lawsuits, keeping their median turnaround time around 200 days.

Even apart from the somewhat special case of the 1740s, some individual councilors spent a long time handling their lawsuits, however without meaningfully influencing the general average and median throughput times for the tribunal as a whole. Councilors Van Voorspoel, Pattin, Otté, de Smet and Rogez are a case in point. Again, it is not clear if they, for some unknown reason, were appointed to report especially complicated cases or if they prolonged their caseload on purpose. The reason that councilors active around the end of the eighteenth century had a short turnaround time is certainly not related to their efficiency, but rather to developments at the Council as a whole: in practice, the *de facto* abolition of the tribunal in 1794 also marked the end to any long-lasting lawsuits they might have been working on.

4.5.3 Concluding Remarks

Even though the accumulated caseload of the Great Council did not decline as consistently as the steep drop in distributed lawsuits shown in Fig. 4.8 might suggest, councilors active in the later period of the eighteenth century inevitably had less work than their predecessors. Therefore, the question that gave cause to our analysis of the accumulated caseload of the Great Council—why is it that the councilors active towards the end of the Council's existence did not suffer from a substantial decrease in their revenues from the *épices*?—is not entirely answered.

A few other hypotheses come to mind. First of all, many cases introduced at the court might never have reached the distribution phase. If the percentage of cases introduced but never distributed was higher in the late than the early eighteenth century, then this could explain the fact that the amount of *épices* the councilors received remained more or less at the same level throughout the eighteenth century. Another option is that more legal acts were performed—and thus more income was generated—but that this had no effect on the duration of the lawsuits.

Finally, it is likely that the data available simply does not allow us to evaluate if the same sort of lawsuit was as expensive in the early as in the late eighteenth century. The report books do not provide any information at all about the subject of the lawsuit and, besides, they are incomplete after 1769.

4.6 A Comparative Perspective

"By and large drawn to the political chronicle of the *parlements* and the social history of their members, scholars have usually either neglected the question of volume or dealt with it by hasty generalization."[271] C. Kaiser made this remark in 1980, in a paper discussing the deflation in the volume of litigation at the *Parlement* of Paris during the eighteenth century. According to him, no historian had ever bothered to investigate the—completely unfounded—assessment of François Bluche from 1960 that the volume of litigation at the *Parlement de Paris* had remained constant throughout its existence.

Kaiser's observations suggest that the lack of quantitative data does not only apply to the Austrian Netherlands, but is to a large extent also an issue for other parts of Europe. Fortunately, over the past 30 years, a few scholars have attempted to investigate—and quantify—the volume of litigation at different European courts, enabling us to compare the situation at the Great Council with a number—albeit limited—of other European tribunals.

For a substantial part of the quantitative data on several of these European courts, we are indebted to M.-C. Le Bailly and G. Vermeesch, who allowed us to use the numbers they collected.[272] In addition, we made use of the data assembled by C. Kaiser and D. Feutry in their respective articles on litigation in the eighteenth century *Parlement de Paris,*[273] by H. Horwitz and P. Polden on the Court of Chancery of London,[274] by W.A. Champion on the Shrewsbury Local Courts[275] and by M.-C. Le Bailly on the major tribunals of the Northern Netherlands.[276] It must be noted from the outset that we focused our analysis on trends, as opposed to absolute figures. As

[271] Kaiser, Colin. 1980. The deflation in the volume of litigation at Paris in the Eighteenth Century and the waning of the old judicial order. *European Studies Review* 10.3: 309.

[272] Both researchers assembled numbers on different councils in the context of an application for funding for a project, intended to investigate and explain the decline of litigation in the eighteenth century.

[273] Kaiser, Colin. 1980. The deflation in the volume of litigation at Paris in the Eighteenth Century and the waning of the old judicial order. *European Studies Review* 10.3: 309–336; Feutry, David. 2012. The historian's mountain of paper. *French history* 26.3: 277–297.

[274] Horwitz, Henry and Polden, Patrick. 1996. Continuity or change in the Court of Chancery in the seventeenth and eighteenth centuries? *Journal of British Studies* 35.1: 24–57.

[275] Champion, W.A. 1998. Recourse to the Law and the meaning of the Great Litigation Decline. In *Communities and courts in Britain, 1150–1900*, eds. Christopher Brooks and Michael Lobban, 179–198. Rio Grande: Hambledon Press.

[276] Le Bailly, Marie-Charlotte. 2011. Langetermijntrends in de rechtspraak bij de gewestelijke hoven van justitie in de Noordelijke Nederlanden van ca. 1450 tot ca. 1800. *Pro Memorie* 13: 30–67. Le Bailly collected data for the Council of Holland, Zeeland and West-Friesland, the High Council of Holland, Zeeland and West-Friesland, the Council of Friesland, the Council of Utrecht, the *Etstoel* of Drenthe, the Council of Gelre in Roermond and in Venlo, the 'Northern' Council of Brabant and the 'Northern' Council of Flanders. The addition 'Northern' to the latter two councils is used to indicate the difference between the Councils of Brabant and Flanders in the Austrian Netherlands and the Councils of Brabant and Flanders in the Northern Netherlands founded after the Revolt.

the procedures as well as the sources available to quantify the volume of litigation were different for every court, the numbers for each tribunal represent a different reality and are therefore not directly comparable.[277] Nevertheless, the general trends and evolutions depicted by these numbers could be meaningfully compared in most cases.

In order to measure the volume of litigation at the *Parlement de Paris*, Kaiser made use of the registers which describe the distribution of actions to the councilors.[278] In doing so, he made a distinction between the *jugés*, appeals against sentences of lower tribunals that were dealt with by the chambers of the *Parlement* staffed by its more junior members, and the *instances appointées*, appeals heard before the councilors of the *grand'chambre*.[279] Despite the lacunae in the sources,[280] it is evident that the number of civil appeals steadily dwindled.

For the *jugés* this decline started probably in the late 1680s; for the *appointées* it began in the earlier part of the decade. Despite these small variations, a common pattern emerges: a steep drop in volume in the first decade of the eighteenth century, followed by short periods of recovery in the 1720s and 1740s and again in the 1770s—consistent with political changes in eighteenth century France. Yet, despite these intermittent revivals, there was unmistakably an overall, steady decline in the number of civil lawsuits brought before the *Parlement*.[281] The pattern observed for the criminal trials is somewhat different: here Kaiser observed a dip in the 1680s, but the number of criminal cases appeared to level off in the first half of the eighteenth century; from the 1760s on, it began to climb steadily and continued to do so until the French Revolution.[282]

In a recent article on litigation at the *Parlement* of Paris,[283] D. Feutry contested Kaiser's conclusions, claiming that the sources he used only record a very small part of the total number of lawsuits at the *Parlement*. First of all—according to Feutry—

[277] For example: the volume of litigation at the Great Council for almost its entire history can be quantified by using the extended sentences. However, in terms of absolute numbers, this would provide a different image of the volume of litigation at the Great Council than if we had used the distribution records or if we had counted the case files, as has been done in the case of the Council of Flanders. Nevertheless, as we have shown earlier in this chapter, all of these different metrics do point towards the same broad trends in the volume of litigation at the Great Council over time.

[278] Kaiser, Colin. 1980. The deflation in the volume of litigation at Paris in the Eighteenth Century and the waning of the old judicial order. *European Studies Review* 10.3: 311. We assume that these registers are very similar to the distribution records that we used to quantify the volume of litigation at the Great Council in the eighteenth century.

[279] Kaiser, Colin. 1980. The deflation in the volume of litigation at Paris in the Eighteenth Century and the waning of the old judicial order. *European Studies Review* 10.3: 312.

[280] Kaiser only had data for the period between roughly 1670 and 1788.

[281] Kaiser, Colin. 1980. The deflation in the volume of litigation at Paris in the Eighteenth Century and the waning of the old judicial order. *European Studies Review* 10.3: 312–313; charts on p. 331.

[282] Kaiser, Colin. 1980. The deflation in the volume of litigation at Paris in the Eighteenth Century and the waning of the old judicial order. *European Studies Review* 10.3: 320; chart on 332.

[283] Feutry, David. 2012. The historian's mountain of paper. *French history* 26.3: 277–297.

the distribution records[284] only registered the written cases dealt with by the Chambers of Inquests, while failing to take into account the lawsuits heard orally at the Grand Chamber. Moreover, these registers were not official records that the registrars were obliged to keep up to date. Finally, Feutry claimed that "a fall in the activity in the clerks' registers does not necessary reflect (…) a fall in the actual activity of the Parlement. On the contrary, it could indicate that it was piling up, and that clerks with too much to do in the Parlement no longer took care to keep the registers tidy."[285] Therefore, the author suggested using official records—without however exactly specifying which records could properly be labeled official—and to count their number, measure their thickness and count the number of *actes* they contain. Based on this method he came to the conclusion that "one thing is absolutely clear: an increase in the Parlement's activity. (…) The number of registers, their width and the number of acts produced by the Parlement demonstrate consistently that the institution's activity was constantly growing."[286]

As a consequence, Feutry entirely contradicted Kaiser's earlier observations on the 'great litigation decline' at the *Parlement de Paris* during the eighteenth century. He claimed that instead of a decrease in activity, there was a considerable increase. While we acknowledge that Feutry's approach has its merits, we also have some concerns about his methodology. First, an increase in the number of registers and in their thickness does not necessarily imply that the *Parlement* dealt with more lawsuits. In fact, these two observations could simply indicate that the registrars wrote less per page or that the councilors extended the duration of the lawsuits, thereby multiplying the *actes* for each case. At the Great Council at least, the smaller number of extended sentences recorded in an eighteenth century register compared to a seventeenth century register did not have much effect on the thickness of the registers.[287] Secondly, Feutry made the leap from *actes* to judgments. He defined an *acte* as a 'decision of one of the *Parlement's* chambers at whatever stage in a case (…) This yields the total number of judgments, whether civil, interlocutory (pending further information on a case) or final …" Not only do *actes* usually cover a wide range of legal actions in addition to just judgments, but it also means that Feutry did not actually count the number of lawsuits at the *Parlement*, as Kaiser attempted to do. Given that Feutry also included interlocutory judgments in his calculations, he counted different *actes* that may belong to one and the same lawsuit.

Therefore, Feutry measured the workload of the *Parlement* instead of identifying the inflow of new cases at the *Parlement*. It is very much possible that the judges created additional work by letting cases drag on, thereby increasing their caseload and their income, similar to what we observed for the Great Council. For that reason, Feutry's conclusion that the councilors of the *Parlement* did not reap less *épices* in the course of the eighteenth century might well be true, but that does not

[284] Feutry called them the 'registers of allocation'. Feutry, David. 2012. The historian's mountain of paper. *French history* 26.3: 285.

[285] Feutry, David. 2012. The historian's mountain of paper. *French history* 26.3: 285–286.

[286] Feutry, David. 2012. The historian's mountain of paper. *French history* 26.3: 288.

[287] Verscuren, An. 2013. *Nadere toegang op de geëxtendeerde sententies van de Grote Raad van Mechelen: 1693–1772.* Brussels: Algemeen Rijksarchief.

necessarily mean that the number of lawsuits introduced at the *Parlement* increased. As a consequence, the fact that Feutry analyzed the total accumulated caseload of the tribunal rather than merely the number of lawsuits introduced at the *Parlement* constitutes the main merit of his approach. This does not, however, necessarily invalidate the thesis of Kaiser, who observed a decrease in the number of **new** cases distributed at the *Parlement* over the course of the eighteenth century.

For the Court of Chancery, Horwitz and Polden made use of the number of bills of complaints submitted and the number of entries for suits recorded in the Court's book of orders for nine sample years between 1609 and 1785.[288] The data shows that the Chancery's caseload of **active** cases was at its highest level in the second quarter of the seventeenth century, but then steadily decreased towards the end of the eighteenth century. The final year, 1784–1785, was an exception, and witnessed a slight surge in the number of active cases.[289]

However, Horwitz and Polden also counted the number of **new** bills introduced and determined that there was a sharper proportionate fall in new suits than in active cases in the mid- and late-eighteenth century. In fact, these numbers seem to indicate, again, that the court took ever more time to deal with its cases so as to reduce the impact of a dwindling inflow of new cases on their workload and incomes.[290] From their observations, Horwitz and Polden drew the conclusion that—given that the "overall fall in business in Chancery was in large part a result of the increasing avoidance of the central court by provincials"—the explanation for the diminishing caseload should be looked for in the provinces.[291]

Building at least partially on Horwitz's and Polden's work, Champion investigated the volume of litigation in the Shrewsbury local courts, amongst others the *curia parva* which dealt with civil litigation, and the *curia magna* which also handled criminal trials.[292] Unfortunately, Champion did not explicitly state which sources he used to determine the volume of civil litigation at the Shrewsbury *curia parva*.

The table included in his article, showing the "average annual number of actions by decade", demonstrates a peak in litigation in the period between 1570 and

[288] Horwitz, Henry and Polden, Patrick. 1996. Continuity or change in the Court of Chancery in the seventeenth and eighteenth centuries? *Journal of British Studies* 35.1: 29–31. They also added a tenth sample for the year 1819/1820, but as this is beyond the scope of our research (and is specific to the English situation since England did not have an entire reorganization of its judicial system as was the case on the continent), we decided to limit our comparison to the period 1609–1785.

[289] Horwitz, Henry and Polden, Patrick. 1996. Continuity or change in the Court of Chancery in the seventeenth and eighteenth centuries? *Journal of British Studies* 35.1: 31, Table 4.2.

[290] Horwitz, Henry and Polden, Patrick. 1996. Continuity or change in the Court of Chancery in the seventeenth and eighteenth centuries? *Journal of British Studies* 35.1: 31, Table 4.3. This conclusion is very comparable to what we have determined for the Great Council, and what Feutry found for the *Parlement* of Paris.

[291] Horwitz, Henry and Polden, Patrick. 1996. Continuity or change in the Court of Chancery in the seventeenth and eighteenth centuries? *Journal of British Studies* 35.1: 57.

[292] Champion, W.A. 1998. Recourse to the Law and the meaning of the Great Litigation Decline. In *Communities and courts in Britain, 1150–1900*, eds. Christopher Brooks and Michael Lobban. Rio Grande: Hambledon Press, 179–180.

1630—with a minor slump between 1590 and 1600.[293] During the rest of the seventeenth century and in the early eighteenth century,[294] there was a steady, continuous decline in the number of cases treated at the Shrewsbury *curia parva*. While at its peak in 1580–1590, the court dealt with almost 1600 lawsuits on average a year, the number dramatically dropped to a mere hundred in the third decade of the eighteenth century.

A similar evolution can be noticed in the number of criminal trials, conducted at the Shrewsbury *curia magna*. Champion made use of the number of fines (and from 1660 on, of private presentments) for affrays and bloods to get an approximate idea of the criminal workload of the *curia magna* and especially of its developments over time. A very distinct peak is noticeable in the number of criminal trials—or at least of the fines paid—in the period between 1610 and 1639. Afterwards, a drastic decline set in, with the frequency of private presentments in the second decade of the eighteenth century dropping to just one every 2.5 years on average.[295]

In conclusion, the evolution in caseload at the Shrewsbury local courts more or less followed the developments described for the Court of Chancery in London. As a consequence, Horwitz's and Polden's idea that the province would provide answers for the decline in litigation at the Chancery seems not particularly fruitful. Even though it is possible that there was a flight from provincials away from the central courts in London, they apparently did not take refuge to the local courts. And indeed, figures for the important borough courts also demonstrate that "by 1750 the totals of actions in these jurisdictions were also only about 5–20% of those recorded in the late sixteenth and early seventeenth centuries."[296]

M.-C. Le Bailly analyzed the long-term trends in the administration of justice at the provincial courts in the Northern Netherlands for the period between ca. 1450 and 1800.[297] She correctly described her study as 'work in progress', acknowledging the problem that she did not have the same kind of data at her disposal for all tribunals: some of her data are based on a counting of (extended) sentences, some on the number of case files preserved in the archives, some on the dicta, etc. Moreover, lacunae in the source materials are legion. Nevertheless, even though

293 Champion, W.A. 1998. Recourse to the Law and the meaning of the Great Litigation Decline. In *Communities and courts in Britain, 1150–1900*, eds. Christopher Brooks and Michael Lobban. Rio Grande: Hambledon Press, 181, Fig. 11.1.

294 The data only reach until 1730.

295 As there are no data available for the years after 1719, we do not know if the Shrewsbury *curia magna* experienced a renewed surge in the number of criminal trials at the end of the eighteenth century.

296 Champion, W.A. 1998. Recourse to the Law and the meaning of the Great Litigation Decline. In *Communities and courts in Britain, 1150–1900*, eds. Christopher Brooks and Michael Lobban. Rio Grande: Hambledon Press, 179.

297 Le Bailly, Marie-Charlotte. 2011. Langetermijntrends in de rechtspraak bij de gewestelijke hoven van justitie in de Noordelijke Nederlanden van ca. 1450 tot ca. 1800. *Pro Memorie* 13: 30–67. Her research is strictly speaking not entirely limited to the Northern Netherlands: she also took into account the Council of Gelre in Roermond, which answered to the Spanish and later to the Austrian Crown. However, as she rightly noted, it would not make much sense to discuss the evolution of litigation at the Council of Gelre in Venlo without considering its counterpart in Roermond.

the numbers extracted from these different sources do not allow for comparison in absolute terms, they do provide a clear overview of the general trends.[298]

The trends in litigation volumes observed for the Northern Netherlands are certainly in line with the conclusions reached by Kaiser, Champion, and Horwitz and Polden. In accordance with the European context, civil litigation at the Dutch courts boomed during the sixteenth and seventeenth centuries. Specific to the Dutch situation is that the apex differed according to the dates the courts were created: the tribunals that came into being in the fifteenth century—such as the Council of Holland, Zeeland and West-Friesland—had their high point around 1590[299] while the courts established after the Revolt—such as the 'Northern' Council of Flanders—reached theirs around 1660.

Nevertheless, in both instances, a steady decrease set in around the end of the seventeenth century at the latest; by the late eighteenth century all Dutch courts processed only a fraction of the caseload in civil litigation they had dealt with in earlier centuries.[300] The number of criminal trials[301] showed far more transitory fluctuations, probably connected to political developments in the provinces. Although it is impossible to identify one single pattern for the different courts, the data clearly points to an increase in the number of criminal trials by the end of the eighteenth century, thereby confirming the insights gained from the *Parlement* in Paris.[302]

Due to the absence of a thorough study on the volume of litigation at the Council of Brabant, concrete numbers are lacking. However, there are some qualitative indicators. When in January 1788 Joseph II decided to create a third chamber with seven additional councilors—with the goal of assuring the support of the majority of the Council—the members of the Council of Brabant immediately raised several objections. One of these concerned the decline in the number of lawsuits at the Council of Brabant: adding members to the court would be useless—at least according to the councilors of Brabant—as there was hardly enough work to keep the existing staff busy.[303] While this remark must be seen in context and might be

[298] Le Bailly, Marie-Charlotte. 2011. Langetermijntrends in de rechtspraak bij de gewestelijke hoven van justitie in de Noordelijke Nederlanden van ca. 1450 tot ca. 1800. *Pro Memorie* 13: 33, chart 1.

[299] At the Great Council, which in the sixteenth century still had jurisdiction over a large part of the Dutch territory, the peak was reached even earlier, in the decade between 1540 and 1549. The sudden drop afterwards should to a large degree be attributed to the ongoing war and the separation of the Northern Netherlands from the Spanish Crown.

[300] Le Bailly, Marie-Charlotte. 2011. Langetermijntrends in de rechtspraak bij de gewestelijke hoven van justitie in de Noordelijke Nederlanden van ca. 1450 tot ca. 1800. *Pro Memorie* 13: 65–67.

[301] It must be noted here that criminal jurisdiction was different for the various tribunals, some having very extended (e.g. the Council of Holland) and others only very limited authority (e.g. the Council of Gelre) in criminal matters.

[302] Le Bailly, Marie-Charlotte. 2011. Langetermijntrends in de rechtspraak bij de gewestelijke hoven van justitie in de Noordelijke Nederlanden van ca. 1450 tot ca. 1800. *Pro Memorie* 13: 66.

[303] Gaillard, Arthur. 1898–1902. *Le Conseil de Brabant: histoire, organisation, procédure*. Brussels: Lebègue, t.1, p. 415. "… la diminution constante du nombre des procès assurait à peine une besogne régulière aux conseillers actuels."

slightly exaggerated, it may be assumed that the Council of Brabant also experienced a considerable drop in the volume of litigation.

Finally, the numbers provided by Vermeesch and Le Bailly allow us to say a few words about the quantitative workload of the *Reichskammergericht* and the Chancery of Valladolid in the period between roughly 1500 and 1700.[304] Data from cases in advanced stages has been used for the *Reichskammergericht*, while the *cartas ejecutorias* provide the figures for the Chancery of Valladolid. Unsurprisingly, the caseload of both courts exhibited an evolution comparable to the one identified in the tribunals described above: a peak in the caseload around 1580–1590, followed by a more or less consistent—although interrupted occasionally by a transient recovery—decrease over time towards the eighteenth century.

In summary, given the recurrence of the same patterns at all these courts, we believe that we can truly speak of a Pan-European phenomenon: an apogee in civil litigation at the end of the sixteenth century followed by a steady fall. In the eighteenth century, all of these tribunals dealt with only a fraction of the civil lawsuits they had handled two centuries earlier. This does not necessarily mean that the combined caseload of the councils decreased as dramatically. In fact, for the Great Council as well as for the Court of Chancery it has been established that the number of active cases—those newly introduced as well as those 'pending' judgment—declined much more gradually. Feutry claimed that the number of active cases at the *Parlement* de Paris even increased. Either way, there should be no doubt that at all European tribunals for which we have data available, there was a pronounced decrease in the number of newly introduced cases. When it comes to criminal jurisdiction, the image is less clear. Still, the data suggests that there was a comparable decrease in the number of criminal trials in the seventeenth century, while the latter half of the eighteenth century witnessed a recovery.

4.7 Explaining the Great Litigation Decline?

4.7.1 State of the Art

Contemporaries are known to have noticed the diminished workload and even complained about it, predominantly out of financial concerns. According to Kaiser, the collapse in volume at the *Parlement de Paris* caused the abolition of several positions while at the same time the prices of masterships of requests and councillorships plummeted. The lawyer Barbier reported that masterships "*ne rapportent*

[304] Vermeesch and Le Bailly have derived their data for the *Reichskammergericht* from Ranieri, Filippo. 1985. *Recht und Gesellschaft im Zeitlter der Rezeption: eine rechts-und sozialgeschichtliche Analyse der Tätigkeit des Reichskammergerichts im 16. Jahrhundert*. Cologne: Böhlau. For the Chancery of Valladolid, they used the study of Kagan, Richard. 1981. *Lawsuits and litigants in Castile, 1500–1700*. Chapel Hill: University of North Carolina Press.

rien".[305] Yet, while the afflicted professionals voiced their concerns about the repercussions of the decreasing workload, they remained absolutely silent on the reasons behind it. In literature, several hypotheses have been put forward in order to provide an explanation, but an entirely satisfying answer is still lacking.

Kaiser identified the causes of the fluctuations in volume as a "mixture of the obvious and the mysterious".[306] He believed that "when the variations are measured against the political and economic chronology of the age, certain correlations immediately come to mind". First of all, political events could have caused a rise or fall in the number of cases handled, such as the 'Maupeou episode'[307] in France. Economic conditions played a role as well. Kaiser cited the economic crisis starting at the end of the seventeenth century as an important trigger to the volume deflation: "The combination of war taxation and mediocre revenues may have forced much of the social elite, which was also the most litigious class, out of the tribunals."[308] Thirdly, Kaiser identified certain 'institutional' causes which provoked litigants to take their business elsewhere. For the *Parlement* in particular, the establishment and proliferation of the urban courts of commerce in the early eighteenth century had serious consequences for the quantity of appeals.[309] Finally, Kaiser believed that the faster rate of decrease noticed for the chambers of *enquêtes* in comparison to the *grand'chambre* indicates that litigants were discouraged by the unreliability of the young judges—the average age of a new lay councilor had fallen to approximately 23 years old—who had limited education and even less experience. For the *Reichskammergericht*, as well, Jahns noticed a similar evolution towards younger and less

---

[305] Kaiser, Colin. 1980. The deflation in the volume of litigation at Paris in the Eighteenth Century and the waning of the old judicial order. *European Studies Review* 10.3: 326–328. Feutry acknowledged that in 1756 64 offices of councilor and two Chambers of Inquests were abolished. He, however, believed that the rise in the number of lawsuits dealt with by the Grand Chamber amply compensated for the declined workload of the Chambers of Inquests. Feutry, David. 2012. The historian's mountain of paper. *French history* 26.3: 294.

[306] Kaiser, Colin. 1980. The deflation in the volume of litigation at Paris in the Eighteenth Century and the waning of the old judicial order. *European Studies Review* 10.3: 313.

[307] The 'Maupeou' episode is a period of time between 1770 and 1774 when the then chancellor—Maupeou—tried to break the resistance of the *Parlements* against his attempts at reform by *de facto* abolishing them and sending the magistrates into exile. Afterwards, he attempted to install an entirely new judicial system. The death of Louis XV, however, marked the end of his chancellorship and of his reforms; shortly after his accession to the throne, Louis XVI reinstated the *Parlements* and their officials. For more information, see: Doyle, William. 1970. The Parlements of France and the breakdown of the Old Régime 1771–1778. *French Historical Studies* 6: 415–458.

[308] Kaiser, Colin. 1980. The deflation in the volume of litigation at Paris in the Eighteenth Century and the waning of the old judicial order. *European Studies Review* 10.3: 314

[309] As these courts of commerce were allowed to act as sovereign judges in all civil suits in which the claims of the parties were worth not more than 500 livres, they constituted a serious threat for the *Parlement de Paris*. Moreover, staffed by merchants and former consuls, the courts of commerce must have been a lot more attractive to the trading classes than the tribunals in the hands of *robins*. In fact, the *juges-consuls* had a "reputation for rapidity of procedure and modicity of fees—not at all the image of the typical Ancien Régime judge." Kaiser, Colin. 1980. The deflation in the volume of litigation at Paris in the Eighteenth Century and the waning of the old judicial order. *European Studies Review* 10.3: 315–316.

experienced councilors, which not only weighed on the court's prestige but—according to her—also deterred litigants from introducing lawsuits.[310]

Horwitz and Polden were somewhat vague when it comes to determining the causes of the drop in litigation activity at the Court of Chancery in London. They believed that the key to solving the puzzle lies in "reformulating the question and hence redirecting the search for answers". In fact, their findings suggest that the fall in business in Chancery was largely the result of the increasing avoidance of the central courts by provincials. Therefore, attention should be directed to the provinces as it is "now evident that the answers do not lie at the center."[311]

This hypothesis, however, is to a large extent invalidated by the research of Champion, who determined that the local tribunals at Shrewsbury experienced an evolution comparable to that of the central courts. According to Champion, the causes for the decline in litigation should be looked for principally in the changes English urban society went through over the course of the eighteenth century. Champion argued that "it was not that personal interactions (…) had necessarily diminished, but that to a significant extent they now took place outside of the old modes of court monitoring, as previous institution-like forms of communal supervision in local societies broke down."[312] On top of that, he identified the bureaucratic and cost factors—not only the court fees but also the increase in the councilors' salaries—as contributing factors to the process; although the lengthier procedure and higher costs did not directly cause the decline in litigation, they certainly added to it.[313]

The numbers provided by Le Bailly for the Council of Flanders also suggest that the answer should not necessarily be looked for at the provincial courts.[314] She believed that the question regarding the litigation decline in the eighteenth century can also be turned around: why did so many people find their way to the tribunals in the sixteenth century, compared to the earlier and later centuries? In fact, the fifteenth and predominantly the sixteenth centuries were marked by a substantial increase in civil litigation. Demographic factors apparently did not come into play, as there is no direct correlation between population size and litigation levels. Other

---

[310] Jahns, Sigrid. 1990. Die Personalverfassung des Reichskammergerichts unter Anpassungsdruck. Lösungen im Spannungsfeld zwischen Modernität und Überalterung. In *Das Reichskammergericht in der deutschen Geschichte: Stand der Forschung, Forschungsperspektiven* (Quellen und Forschungen zur höchsten Gerichtsbarkeit im alten Reich 21), ed. Bernhard Diestelkamp. Cologne: Böhlau, 86–87.

[311] Horwitz, Henry and Polden, Patrick. 1996. Continuity or change in the Court of Chancery in the seventeenth and eighteenth centuries? *Journal of British Studies* 35.1: 57.

[312] Champion, W.A. 1998. Recourse to the Law and the meaning of the Great Litigation Decline. In *Communities and courts in Britain, 1150–1900*, eds. Christopher Brooks and Michael Lobban. Rio Grande: Hambledon Press, 197.

[313] Champion, W.A. 1998. Recourse to the Law and the meaning of the Great Litigation Decline. In *Communities and courts in Britain, 1150–1900*, eds. Christopher Brooks and Michael Lobban. Rio Grande: Hambledon Press, 191.

[314] Cf. supra. Fig. 4.9. Le Bailly's counting of the case files projects an image of the evolution of civil litigation at the Council of Flanders which is very comparable to the one observed for the central courts, such as the Court of Chancery and the *Parlement de Paris*.

explanations can be looked for in the advancing process of state formation and centralization in the late fifteenth and early sixteenth centuries, the introduction of academically educated jurists in the tribunals, the expansion of the economy and political developments.[315] In theory, a change in these factors could also explain the decline in litigation during the eighteenth century.

Le Bailly suggested external factors such as socio-political developments, the economic downturn and the ensuing flight from the city as possible explanations for the decrease—or rather as hypotheses that need to be further investigated. If people did leave the city in response to the shrinking economy, then maybe local tribunals in the countryside gained popularity. Another suggestion is to look for factors inherent to the eighteenth century judicial system: did the ever higher costs and the much longer procedures—consequences of the changes within the administration of the tribunals—cause a contraction in the caseload at the central and provincial courts? Yet, just as Champion, Le Bailly believed that the lengthy procedure and high costs—although many complaints were lodged about it[316]—cannot be the only cause for the dramatic decline in civil litigation. In fact, during the sixteenth and seventeenth centuries, when the central and provincial courts were at their peak, litigants also complained about the costs and duration of the proceedings, but this was obviously no impediment to litigation.[317]

It has often been suggested that litigants took their business elsewhere in order to reach a settlement outside the sphere of contentious jurisdiction. Le Bailly did some research for the Council of Holland, Zeeland and West-Friesland in the registers used to record voluntary jurisdiction. There she found several indications that litigants searched for a cheaper solution via arbitration. While the number of civil lawsuits experienced a serious decline over the course of the eighteenth century, the system of voluntary jurisdiction—in which parties subjected themselves to a mutually pre-agreed order executed by a judge without actually going to court—was on the rise, especially in the last quarter of the eighteenth century.[318] In that regard, notarial deeds might also constitute an interesting source to investigate: instead of taking their matters to a tribunal altogether, parties might have preferred to make their settlements before a notary.

Although the question to what degree voluntary jurisdiction replaced (part of) the contentious jurisdiction may be interesting enough to warrant further research, it is doubtful that this phenomenon could be the sole explanation for the complete collapse in newly introduced cases at the central and provincial courts over the course of the eighteenth century. Le Bailly therefore believed that research into a possible

[315] Le Bailly, Marie-Charlotte. 2011. Langetermijntrends in de rechtspraak bij de gewestelijke hoven van justitie in de Noordelijke Nederlanden van ca. 1450 tot ca. 1800. *Pro Memorie* 13: 65.

[316] That there was indeed an increase in the duration of lawsuits over time has been determined by Horwitz, Henry and Polden, Patrick. 1996. Continuity or change in the Court of Chancery in the seventeenth and eighteenth centuries? *Journal of British Studies* 35.1: 55.

[317] Le Bailly, Marie-Charlotte. 2011. Langetermijntrends in de rechtspraak bij de gewestelijke hoven van justitie in de Noordelijke Nederlanden van ca. 1450 tot ca. 1800. *Pro Memorie* 13: 66.

[318] Le Bailly, Marie-Charlotte. 2011. Langetermijntrends in de rechtspraak bij de gewestelijke hoven van justitie in de Noordelijke Nederlanden van ca. 1450 tot ca. 1800. *Pro Memorie* 13: 36.

shift in the nature and subject matter of lawsuits might be fruitful.[319] Given that it is complicated to derive the subject matter from the available sources, only scant attention has so far been paid to this aspect of litigation.

Hortwitz and Polden are the only hitherto discussed authors who have attempted to look at the nature of litigation. For the Court of Chancery, they used their sample cases[320] and divided them into five—artificially constructed—categories: business transactions, debts and bonds, *inter vivos* trusts, landholding and estate matters. Their analysis demonstrated an interesting shift in the dominant subject matter over time. While in 1627, questions concerning landholding took up the majority of the cases closely followed by debts and bonds, the ratio had shifted in 1785 to a preponderance of estate questions with matters regarding landholding following second at a considerable distance.

However, in terms of proportion, the sharpest proportional increase across a century and a half was in business cases (by almost threefold), while the sharpest proportional decrease was in debts and bonds. In addition, the proportion of estate cases almost doubled, while the proportion of questions regarding land fell by almost one-quarter.[321] Although Horwitz and Polden did offer an explanation for some of these developments, they had to admit that they were unable to provide any clear-cut answers to the question why these shifts in subject matter occurred. Moreover, they acknowledged that their analysis does not explain the collapse of the caseload in the Court of Chancery or in other central courts throughout the eighteenth century.

In a final effort to find an explanation for the 'great litigation decline', Horwitz and Polden investigated the identity of the litigants who figured in Chancery cases, hoping to establish patterns of presence or absence among various types of litigants.[322] Although the identification of the litigants was at times rather problematic—for example, for reasons of clarity Horwitz and Polden chose to almost completely exclude women—the authors were able to distinguish four major categories: gentlemen, farmers, commercial and artisanal tradesmen, and professionals. What immediately caught the eye when comparing the data from the 1627 sample and the 1818/1819 sample—the authors did not include any data from the late seventeenth or the eighteenth century—was the sharp decline in the categories of gentlemen and farmers, and the steep proportional increase in the category of commercial and

[319] Le Bailly, Marie-Charlotte. 2011. Langetermijntrends in de rechtspraak bij de gewestelijke hoven van justitie in de Noordelijke Nederlanden van ca. 1450 tot ca. 1800. *Pro Memorie* 13: 66.

[320] The authors used 291 cases from 1627, 251 cases from 1685, 299 cases from 1735, 143 cases from 1785 and 152 cases from 1818/1819. Horwitz, Henry and Polden, Patrick. 1996. Continuity or change in the Court of Chancery in the seventeenth and eighteenth centuries? *Journal of British Studies* 35.1: 33.

[321] Horwitz, Henry and Polden, Patrick. 1996. Continuity or change in the Court of Chancery in the seventeenth and eighteenth centuries? *Journal of British Studies* 35.1: 35. Table 6+Table 7 (36).

[322] In order to discover the identity of the litigants, Horwitz and Polden relied on the pleadings, given that in these legal acts, the parties were required to give some indication of their status and occupation. Horwitz, Henry and Polden, Patrick. 1996. Continuity or change in the Court of Chancery in the seventeenth and eighteenth centuries? *Journal of British Studies* 35.1:42.

artisanal litigants (and, to a smaller extent, within the group of professionals).[323] To a certain degree, these changes in the status of the litigants paralleled the socioeconomic trends of the era, predominantly the growth of trade and industry.

Subsequently, Horwitz and Polden matched litigants with their geographical origin. This analysis laid bare that, proportionally, the number of people coming from the English provinces dramatically decreased over time.[324] As the impact of distance on costs did not change significantly between the early 1600s and the late 1700s, Horwitz and Polden did not believe that the added expenses involved in conducting a lawsuit at a distance deterred provincial plaintiffs. Other available data—predominantly from Brooks—confirmed that the growth in the proportion of metropolitan plaintiffs was not unique to the Court of Chancery, but was also visible in the Common Pleas and the King's Bench.[325] Based on these observations, Horwitz and Polden came to the conclusion that the explanation for the drastic decline in the number of lawsuits in the eighteenth century should be looked for in the provinces.[326]

M.-C. Le Bailly and G. Vermeesch also believed that socio-economic circumstances were at least partially responsible for the decrease in civil litigation.[327] While they agreed that the changes identified by historians so far—in mentality, in the institutional framework of credit and contracts, in economic performance and demography, and in legal administration—have contributed to the 'great litigation decline', they ascertained that the 'proletarianization' of the 'middling groups' during the Early Modern period was an essential factor in explaining the deflation in the volume of litigation in the eighteenth century. Based on the observation that wage dependent households rarely went to court to have their disputes settled, Le Bailly and Vermeesch suggested that the relative impoverishment of the regular sixteenth century customers—the lower middling groups—led to a decline in litigation. While in the late sixteenth and early seventeenth centuries these lower middling groups went to court in order to protect their imperiled economic independence—for which credit relations and therefore credibility were essential, hence the large number of defamation suits—they had lost this battle by the end of the seventeenth and early eighteenth centuries. Being condemned to wage dependency,

[323] Horwitz, Henry and Polden, Patrick. 1996. Continuity or change in the Court of Chancery in the seventeenth and eighteenth centuries? *Journal of British Studies* 35.1: 46.

[324] Horwitz, Henry and Polden, Patrick. 1996. Continuity or change in the Court of Chancery in the seventeenth and eighteenth centuries? *Journal of British Studies* 35.1: 50, Table 17.

[325] Horwitz, Henry and Polden, Patrick. 1996. Continuity or change in the Court of Chancery in the seventeenth and eighteenth centuries? *Journal of British Studies* 35.1: 51. The reference they make to Brooks: Brooks, Christopher. 1989. *Interpersonal conflict and social tension: civil litigation in England, 1640–1830.* In *The first modern society. Essays in English history in honour of Lawrence Stone*, eds. David Cannadine et al., 357–399. Cambridge: Cambridge University Press.

[326] Nevertheless, as we have already pointed out, numbers for the Shrewsbury local courts have indicated that this was not the case.

[327] Le Bailly, Marie-Charlotte and Vermeesch, Griet. Explaining the great litigation decline. *To be published.*

they stopped taking recourse to the courts, thereby bringing about the decline in litigation.

4.7.2 Discussion and Further Observations[328]

The above overview suggests that there is not one single cause that can explain the decline in litigation of the seventeenth and, in particular, eighteenth centuries. Any explanation must consist of a combination of factors of both internal and external origin. The repercussions of the late seventeenth century economic crisis, the changes in the social fabric, shifting political circumstances, higher procedural costs, the tardiness of the courts in dealing with lawsuits, … all of these factors contributed to the drop in litigation over the course of the eighteenth century. Considering that this dramatic decrease in the number of civil lawsuits is clearly a pan-European phenomenon, explanations should not be looked for in local circumstances, specific to a certain province or even country, but in conditions and trends that were present in most if not all European countries.

Therefore, in what follows, we will look for pieces of the puzzle in (1) the changed socio-economic features of the regular customers of the early modern tribunals; (2) the problems connected to the procedure used; (3) the profile of the judges; (4) the knowledge of precedents; and (5) government policy (or rather the lack thereof).

4.7.2.1 The Litigants

Le Bailly and Vermeesch identified the proletarianization of the lower middling groups as one of the major causes of the decline in litigation. However, given that members of the lower middling groups only rarely figure among the parties engaged in civil litigation at the Great Council, it seems unlikely that this could sufficiently explain the decreasing number of lawsuits at the Malines tribunal. Although we did not systematically study the social background of the litigants at the Great Council—of the sources used, only the extended sentences would provide enough information for such an analysis—we do know that the tribunal functioned in first instance as a court for the privileged. Therefore, in order to investigate whether the profile of the regular customers of the Great Council changed and, if so, whether this can indeed be an explanatory factor, an analysis should be made of those groups that were higher up on the social scale. Kaiser already remarked that the social elite—which according to him was the most litigious class—was forced out of the tribunals because of economic circumstances.[329]

[328] Our observations are specifically based on our knowledge of the situation at the eighteenth century Great Council.

[329] Kaiser, Colin. 1980. The deflation in the volume of litigation at Paris in the Eighteenth Century and the waning of the old judicial order. *European Studies Review* 10.3: 314.

The limited analysis we did based on the data in the eighteenth century distribution registers[330] demonstrates that more than one third of the plaintiffs belonged to the nobility. Moreover, the inventory of the collection of lawsuits concerning noble families indicates that the number of lawsuits in which a member of the nobility acted as plaintiff—against both noble and non-noble parties—proportionally declined from a high point of 83 % in 1730 to less than 40 % in the 1780s.[331] This means that more noblemen were passively forced to go to court as defendants instead of actively choosing to litigate as plaintiffs. While this is only circumstantial evidence, it could be fruitful to analyze over a longer period of time the relative proportion of the gentry to the total number of litigants as well as the identity of the nobility who came to court. In fact, if the (economic) situation of the gentry became ever more problematic over the course of the eighteenth century, this might explain their absence at the provincial and central courts, which in turn could be part of the answer to the question of the great litigation decline.

4.7.2.2 Procedure

Going to court in the *Ancien Régime* was almost always a complicated and long process. At the Great Council, once a lawsuit was in the reporting phase, it had an average duration of 214 days.[332] The top 15 % lengthiest lawsuits, however, dragged on for more than 1000 days (roughly 3 years) after their distribution. Not only does this number exclude the period before the case was distributed to a reporter, but—in case the lawsuit was an appeal against a sentence of a lower tribunal—it does not take into account the time it took to pass through the lower instance(s). Feutry as well has demonstrated by his analysis of the number of acts at the *Parlements de Paris* that procedure at France's highest court could be long and often consisted of a multitude of legal actions.[333] As a consequence, the establishment and proliferation of urban courts of commerce in early eighteenth century France is only logical:[334] the merchant class was especially in need of speedy litigation.

As we can assume that the duration of a case was to a certain extent related to the number of legal acts and that this in turn had an influence on the costs of the

[330] For five sample years—1700, 1720, 1740, 1760 and 1780—we calculated the proportion of noblemen acting as plaintiffs, which fluctuated between 32 and 38 % of all litigants.

[331] Based on the inventory, we calculated the number of lawsuits in any given decade, and divided them into cases in which a member of the nobility acted as a plaintiff (against non-nobility), as a defendant (against non-nobility) and as both plaintiff and defendant.

[332] This is the 'adjusted' average, with the outliers (highest and lowest 10 % of the sample of 6107 cases considered) excluded. As noted in subsection 3.5.1.1, this works out to cases with a duration of less than 30 or more than 1369 days.

[333] Cf. supra 4.6 A comparative perspective. It must be noted again that Feutry himself did not directly state that he did not measure the input of the number of lawsuits at the *Parlement de Paris* but rather the tribunal's accumulated caseload.

[334] Kaiser, Colin. 1980. The deflation in the volume of litigation at Paris in the Eighteenth Century and the waning of the old judicial order. *European Studies Review* 10.3: 315–316.

procedure, it is very likely that during the eighteenth century going to court was expensive. Not only did the court fees rise, but advocates and proctors also charged extra for performing all sorts of acts, such as composing and signing legal documents.[335] If it is true that the economic situation of the regular customers of the European tribunals had deteriorated by the eighteenth century, the high costs of litigation might have deterred them—much more than in previous centuries—from litigating.[336]

While it is certainly true, as Le Bailly and Vermeesch have stated, that complaints about the length and costs of legal procedures were not limited to the eighteenth century but surfaced recurrently throughout the Ancien Régime, it is possible that the cost of going to court constituted a bigger problem for the litigants in the 1700s than in previous centuries. In that regard, it might be interesting to calculate the actual inflow of new cases: Le Bailly and Vermeesch put forward the idea that the increase in litigation costs did not necessarily scare people away from starting a lawsuit, as that was fairly affordable. Legal fees only started to add up when lawsuits reached advanced stages. Therefore, starting a lawsuit might even have served as a means of mounting pressure on the defendant to reach an informal settlement.[337] If this hypothesis is true, it might mean that the total number of newly introduced lawsuits was much higher than the total number of distributed lawsuits, which in turn could lead to the conclusion that the number of introduced cases did not decrease over time but rather that a smaller proportion reached an advanced stage. Further research into this hypothesis is therefore warranted.

4.7.2.3 The Judges

In addition to procedural problems and the changed social background of the litigants, the evolving profile of the judges themselves might also have contributed to the decline in litigation at many European courts. As an example, Kaiser attributed the more pronounced decrease in litigation at the chamber of *enquêtes* in comparison to the *grand'chambre* of the *Parlement de Paris* to the unreliability of the young judges staffing the former. Jahns as well believed that the evolution towards ever younger and less experienced councilors negatively affected the prestige of the *Reichskammergericht.*[338]

At the Great Council, the profile of the judges only slightly changed over the course of the eighteenth century and it is not clear to what extent this could have had any influence on the willingness of parties to go to court. Moreover, the direction

---

[335] Champion, W.A. 1998. Recourse to the Law and the meaning of the Great Litigation Decline. In *Communities and courts in Britain, 1150–1900*, eds. Christopher Brooks and Michael Lobban. Rio Grande: Hambledon Press, 184–185.

[336] And here again, we run into the Catch 22 mentioned before: was it the high cost of litigation that discouraged potential litigants from taking their disputes to court, or was it that the court and probably the proctors and advocate charged more because the number of lawsuits decreased?

[337] Le Bailly Marie-Charlotte and Vermeesch, Griet. Explaining the great litigation decline. *To be published.*

[338] Cf. supra, Chap. 2.

of any causal link is again unclear. Did the inexperienced councilors discourage the parties from litigating, or did the diminished caseload of the tribunal discourage more experienced people from aspiring to a councillorship?

4.7.2.4 Precedents

Legal precedents as well as increased regulation may also have played a role in the decline in litigation. Le Bailly and Vermeesch pointed to institutional changes that regulated credit relations and reduced the need for litigation. In other words, and loosely speaking: precedents from and regulatory changes prompted by litigation in the early seventeenth century made litigation after 1640 unnecessary.[339] Indeed, the proliferation of case law compilations in the eighteenth century led to a widespread knowledge of legal precedents on an entire array of subjects, including testamentary causes, estate-related questions and matrimonial law. Godding too believed that the usefulness of the compilations of case law consisted in "avoiding that certain parties start futile actions, facilitating the settlement of certain questions which have already been treated by other councils (…)".[340]

Even printer Hanicq, in his foreword to the publication of the recueils d'arrêts of Coloma and Hony, pointed out that, "pareils ouvrages instruisent les parties de ce qu'ils peuvent espérer de leurs prétentions: les avocats y voient ce qu'ils peuvent répondre aux parties qui les consultent."[341] Given that if not the litigants themselves, at least their advocates and proctors must have had some knowledge of these recueils d'arrêts, it is possible that they discouraged certain parties to go to court over disputes that had already been settled by a sentence in an earlier, similar, lawsuit. While we can assume that advocates and proctors were, in general, eager to take on as many cases as possible, we can also imagine that reputation-wise they were reluctant to deal with lawsuits that they were likely to lose.

4.7.2.5 Government Policy

Based on the personnel policy of the *Reichskammergericht*, Jahns identified the unwillingness and the lack of interest of both the emperor and the *Reichstände* to implement much-needed reforms as the main reason for the decline of the

[339] Le Bailly Marie-Charlotte and Vermeesch, Griet. Explaining the great litigation decline. *To be published.*

[340] Godding, Philippe. 1970. L'origine et l'autorité des recueils de jurisprudence dans les Pays-Bas Méridionaux (XIIIe-XVIIIe siècles). In *Rapports belges au VIIIe congrès international de droit comparé.* Brussel: CIDC, 33–34.

[341] "Avertissement du libraire au public". De Coloma, Jean Alphonse and Hony, Jean-Baptiste. 1781. *Arrêts du Grand Conseil de Sa Majesté Impériale et Royale, séant en la ville de Malines (2v.).* Malines: P.J. Hanicq, 3.

tribunal.[342] As far as Castille was concerned, Richard Kagan asserted that the high litigation rates of the sixteenth century must be partly attributed to the attention Charles V and Philips II paid to high-quality justice. Their successors on the other hand, were much less interested in this aspect of their administration.[343]

In Chap. 2, we demonstrated that during the eighteenth century the Austrian government was no longer concerned about the internal workings of the Great Council and pursued a 'divide and rule' policy regarding the tribunal's conflicts (of jurisdiction) with other players in the Austrian Netherlands. In addition, it is clear that the Great Council, due to a lack of government support in terms of new regulations and legislation, was no longer adapted to the changed circumstances of the eighteenth century. If the government had shortened and simplified the procedure, reduced the costs, if it had given the tribunal the means to attract experienced and well trained personnel, and if it had actively promoted the courts as the forum of choice for dispute resolution, the downward slide in litigation might have been turned around. Until the reign of Joseph II, not much reform was introduced at all. On the flipside, Joseph II's eradication of the existing judicial system and replacement by an entirely new one was simply too radical and abrupt to be acceptable.

As mentioned before, the dissemination of royal jurisdiction is often regarded as a measure of centralization. Charles Tilly considered the settlement of disputes as one of the most important activities of a state.[344] In theory, this would mean that—given the remarkable decrease in the volume of litigation at, especially, the royal courts—the degree of centralization must have been steadily declining during the latter part of the Ancien Régime. The reality of royal absolutism, however, teaches us differently. All over Europe, rulers tried to accumulate as much power as possible into their own hands, often under the flag of Enlightenment. Did sovereigns in Europe deliberately let the central courts languish? In fact, whereas the Great Council and other central tribunals had once been tools in the hands of the fifteenth and sixteenth century rulers trying to unite their disparate territories, were they now rather impediments on the road to absolutism? Had they become so obsolete that, in the eighteenth century, they acted more as a counterweight to than as a catalyst for centralism? Maybe, the eighteenth century sovereigns had good reasons to discourage litigation at the central and provincial courts or at least not to intervene in their

342 Jahns, Sigrid. 1990. Die Personalverfassung des Reichskammergerichts unter Anpassungsdruck. Lösungen im Spannungsfeld zwischen Modernität und Überalterung. In *Das Reichskammergericht in der deutschen Geschichte: Stand der Forschung, Forschungsperspektiven* (Quellen und Forschungen zur höchsten Gerichtsbarkeit im alten Reich 21), ed. Bernhard Diestelkamp, 59–109. Cologne: Böhlau.

343 Kagan, Richard. 1981. A golden age in litigation: Castile, 1500–1700. In *Disputes and settlements. Law and human relation in the west*, ed. John Bossy. Cambridge: Cambridge University Press, 160. Cf. Le Bailly, Marie-Charlotte and Vermeesch, Griet. Explaining the great litigation decline. *To be published.*

344 Tilly, Charles. 1992. *Coercion, Capital and European States, AD 990–1992.* Cambridge: Blackwell, as cited in Le Bailly, Marie-Charlotte. 2011. Langetermijntrends in de rechtspraak bij de gewestelijke hoven van justitie in de Noordelijke Nederlanden van ca. 1450 tot ca. 1800. *Pro Memorie* 13: 66.

decline? Was their lack of interest in supporting the tribunals and adjusting them to the demands of the time a well thought-out policy?

That the eighteenth century *Parlements* of France were considered to have too much power is well known.[345] Nevertheless, unlike their French counterparts, the provincial and central councils in the Austrian Netherlands had no—or only very limited—political power.[346] Their sphere of influence was therefore much more restricted. Yet, Maria Theresa absolutely did not attempt to boost the authority of these tribunals—a strategy we might have expected had she actively sought to increase her grip on the Austrian Netherlands through these courts. Joseph II went even further: he limited the scope of the Great Council even more by removing the Councils of Luxemburg and Tournai from its sphere of influence. Moreover, in 1787, he attempted to completely eradicate the existing system and replace it by an entirely different one, certainly not just to improve efficiency but first and foremost to extend his own power and control over the judicial system. Centralization for the emperor was not a matter of strengthening the existing tribunals. The failure of this attempt was not so much due to the resistance of the councilors of the Great Council, but rather to the opposition of the members of the provincial Estates, in particular of Brabant and Hainaut.[347]

4.7.3 Consequences of the Great Litigation Decline

While literature usually offers several—albeit divergent—explanations for the waning litigation volumes in the seventeenth and eighteenth centuries, it generally remains silent on the consequences of this decline. However, it is not hard to imagine that there were institutional, social and political repercussions: courts lost their prestige, a career in the judiciary became much less attractive for young talents, fewer options remained available for the socially mobile, councilors suffered from

---

345 Doyle, William. 1970. The Parlements of France and the breakdown of the Old Régime 1771–1778. *French Historical Studies* 6: 416. We must however mention that Doyle puts certain question marks to this idea of the *parlements* as hotbeds of resistance. In fact, he believed that they did not have much power; otherwise they would not have felt the need to call for the Estates-General to assemble.

346 The Council of Brabant had some political authority. (See: Put, Eddy. 2002. Gedeelde soevereiniteit? De dubbelrol van de Raad van Brabant. In *Politieke representatie*, eds. Henk de Smaele and Johan Tollebeek, 226–229. Leuven: Universitaire Pers Leuven) The Great Council on the other hand, had almost none. In that regard, the remark of Wijffels that the Council of Brabant rather than the Great Council was the real supreme court of the Austrian Netherlands is absolutely correct. Wijffels, Alain. 1997. Grand Conseil de Malines: la rédaction des sentences étendues et le recueil de jurisprudence de Guillaume de Grysperre. In *Case law in the making: the techniques and methods of judicial records and law reports (Comparative studies in continental and Anglo-American Legal History* 17) v.1, ed. Alain Wijffels. Berlin: Duncker und Humblot, 312: "Il est en tout cas frappant que ce fut le Conseil de Brabant, sans doute la cour supérieure de justice des Pays-Bas méridionaux …"

347 Cf. infra, Chap. 5.

job insecurity and potentially from loss of income.[348] Kaiser believed that, while the flagging caseload in Parisian courts was not so much a crisis in itself, its consequences "traced one of the routes which led France to revolution".

Most authors do not go as far as Kaiser in drawing a direct line from the decline in litigation to the end of the *Ancien Régime.* Jahns showed how councilors at the *Reichskammergericht* became embittered by the weakness of their tribunal and argued that the fall in court cases was at least indicative for the fact that centrifugal forces in the German *Reich* gained strength.[349] For the Austrian Netherlands as well, we believe that the decline in litigation was at least symptomatic of the 'decay' of the *Ancien Régime* model. The fact that central governments across continental Europe were apparently undisturbed by these evolutions—let alone stepped in to remedy problems at their tribunals—might be a sign that they were preparing for a new social order, albeit in a form completely different from what the revolutionaries had in mind. It is also notable that in the Southern Netherlands the first signs of dissent were directed against the attempts by Joseph II to implement reforms, among others in the judicial system, which aimed at more centralization.

4.8 Litigation on the Rise: Criminal Trials

In one area of the administration of justice, several European tribunals did become more active in the second half of the eighteenth century than they had been in the first. Contrary to civil litigation, the number of criminal trials increased towards the end of the eighteenth century. At the *Parlement de Paris*, Kaiser noticed that from the 1760s on, the number of criminal trials began to climb steadily and continued to do so until the end of the monarchy. [350] Le Bailly has established a comparable growth in criminal trials at the courts of the Northern Netherlands by the end of the eighteenth century.[351] While Kaiser believed that these rising numbers should be attributed to an intensification of the prosecution policy, Le Bailly argued

[348] Kaiser believed this was the case at the *Parlement de Paris*; Feutry however disagreed with this thesis, as he is convinced that the volume of litigation did not so much decrease as increase. At the Great Council, the councilors' fixed salary as well as their income from *épices* remained more or less stable, but we can assume that, due to inflation, the councilors did see their incomes dwindle in real terms throughout the eighteenth century.

[349] Jahns, Sigrid. 1990. Die Personalverfassung des Reichskammergerichts unter Anpassungsdruck. Lösungen im Spannungsfeld zwischen Modernität und Überalterung. In *Das Reichskammergericht in der deutschen Geschichte: Stand der Forschung, Forschungsperspektiven* (Quellen und Forschungen zur höchsten Gerichtsbarkeit im alten Reich 21), ed. Bernhard Diestelkamp. Cologne: Böhlau, 60; 107.

[350] Kaiser, Colin. 1980. The deflation in the volume of litigation at Paris in the Eighteenth Century and the waning of the old judicial order. *European Studies Review* 10.3: 320.

[351] For example, the Council of Friesland witnessed a serious increase in the number of criminal cases from the 1770s on (countings based on case files). For the Council of Utrecht, this process started somewhat later in the 1780s. Le Bailly, Marie-Charlotte. 2011. Langetermijntrends in de rechtspraak bij de gewestelijke hoven van justitie in de Noordelijke Nederlanden van ca. 1450 tot ca. 1800. *Pro Memorie* 13: 45 chart 6 and 48 chart 7.

that, at least in the Republic, they point to a rising crime rate towards the end of the eighteenth century. Potentially, the backdrop of continued economic deterioration played a significant role in this process.[352]

A similar phenomenon can be distinguished at the Great Council: the number of criminal case files climbed from four in the 1760s, to 22 in the 1770s, to 32 in the 1780s to 23 in the first half of the 1790s.[353] The majority of the cases of the 1780s and 1790s are the so-called political trials, dealing with the aftermath of the revolution and the French occupation. These 2 decades were certainly characterized by a rising 'crime' rate. At the same time, it is remarkable that exactly in this period the ratio of the *grand* and *petit criminel* cases turned around; especially in the 1780s the latter considerably outnumbered the former. This observation, as we have already determined, had as much to do with the personality of the prosecuting officers as with a rise in crime rates within the jurisdiction of the Great Council.[354]

In the late 1780s, it was the government that urged the Great Council to prosecute the insurgents and 'revolutionaries'. The same was true in 1718, when the tribunal became responsible for bringing the instigators of the Malines revolt to trial. These two examples suggest that in times of crisis the government did still use the Great Council as an instrument of its policies.[355] Nevertheless, given that the volume of criminal litigation at the Great Council is almost negligible—in absolute numbers but especially compared to the volume of civil litigation—the importance of these two episodes should not be overstated. It is obvious that during the eighteenth century, the tribunal no longer played the same role in the government's centralization schemes as it had done in the fifteenth and sixteenth centuries.

Conclusion

Even though the data available to measure the volume of litigation at the Great Council is incomplete and 'colored' by record-keeping practices, it is undeniable that the number of civil cases exhibits an almost consistent decline from the late sixteenth towards the eighteenth century. Certain political or economic circumstances were responsible for temporary recoveries in the number of lawsuits handled by the Council, but these were merely fluctuations in an otherwise almost linear downward trajectory.

[352] Le Bailly, Marie-Charlotte. 2011. Langetermijntrends in de rechtspraak bij de gewestelijke hoven van justitie in de Noordelijke Nederlanden van ca. 1450 tot ca. 1800. *Pro Memorie* 13: 66.

[353] Cf. supra, Fig. 4.7.

[354] Indeed, once de Stassart came at the helm of the office-fiscal, there was a surge in the numbers of criminal cases dealt with at the Great Council. Therefore, both the increased 'crime' rate and the more hands-on prosecution policy were responsible for the rise in the number of criminal trials at the Great Council.

[355] We will investigate the attitude of the Great Council towards the central government in the period between 1787 and 1797 in Chap. 5.

It must be noted, however, that our data could be influenced by the way records were created in the Ancien Régime and especially by the evolutions and changes herein. If registrars in the sixteenth century were more diligent in keeping records than their colleagues in the eighteenth century, this could have a considerable impact on the apparent evolution of the Great Council's caseload. In the case of the extended sentences, for instance, it is a certainty that a much broader array of lawsuits found their way into the sixteenth century registers than into those of the eighteenth century. In fact, these differences are clearly laid bare by comparing the sixteenth century *Chronologische lijsten*[356] to the list of the eighteenth century extended sentences.[357] Still, even though we have to take into account a certain error rate due to potentially evolving record-keeping practices, it is indisputable that the Great Council experienced a declining litigation rate over time. This became particularly distinct during the eighteenth century: apart from the purely quantitative data, the complaints voiced by the late eighteenth century councilors about the declining caseload point in the same direction.

The breakdown by instance of litigation at the Great Council allowed us to establish that this downward trend was especially visible in the declining number of first instance cases. Until 1760, they constituted the largest single category, but were then surpassed by the appeals from Flanders and in the period between 1790 and 1794 even by the appeals from Namur. This gradual growth in the number of appeals from Flanders towards the end of the eighteenth century was matched by a comparable rise in the number of first instance cases dealt with by the provincial council.[358] As a consequence, it is highly unlikely that the declining number of appeals coming from Flanders in the first half of the century is attributable to some sort of provincial reflex of the litigants. Rather, we believe it was driven by a decline in the number of lawsuits introduced at the Council of Flanders, equivalent to the evolution witnessed at the Great Council itself. In addition, the decrease in the number of lawsuits dealt with at the Malines tribunal was exacerbated by the dwindling inflow of appeals from the *Terres de débat* from 1743 on, and from the Councils of Luxemburg and Tournai from 1782 on.

While the number of distributed lawsuits showed a pattern of consistent decline, the accumulated caseload of the Great Council suggests a somewhat less bleak image. The link with the duration of the lawsuits is obvious: the longer the cases lasted, the more work the tribunal—and some individual councilors—had at any given time. The accumulated caseload of the Great Council demonstrated a notable peak around the early 1740s, which was indeed matched by a high point in the

---

[356] De Smidt, Jacobus et al. eds. 1966–1988. *Chronologische lijsten van de geëxtenderdeerde sententiën berustende in het archief van de Grote Raad van Mechelen*, 6 volumes. Brussels: Koninklijke Commissie voor de uitgave der oude wetten en verordeningen van België.

[357] Verscuren, An. 2013. *Nadere toegang op de geëxtendeerde sententies van de Grote Raad van Mechelen: 1693–1772.* Brussels: Algemeen Rijksarchief.

[358] Further research is warranted to investigate if this additional caseload at the end of the eighteenth century at the provincial councils is caused by a rise in first instance lawsuits—in which case the Great Council would be the exception to the rule—or rather by an increase in appeals from subordinate courts.

average and median length of the lawsuits concluded between 1740 and 1750. A period characterized by more efficiency followed after the Echternach exile, which does suggest that it was indeed the government—perhaps prompted by exasperated litigants—which had ordered the Great Council to arrive at a speedier conclusion. In 1770, however, this trend towards more efficiency turned around again: in the 1770s and 1780s, the average duration of a lawsuit started to climb once more. Was this because the central government no longer could be bothered to intervene in the Great Council's inner workings, thus providing the councilors with a new opportunity to let cases drag on for an extended period of time? Or was the government, by the late 1770s, already planning on eventually abolishing the Great Council or even entirely transforming the judicial structure of the Austrian Netherlands?

In truth, by the eighteenth century, the Great Council had changed almost unrecognizably from the tribunal that was established in the early sixteenth century as a superior court to provide a check on the provincial councils by its jurisdiction in appeal. Not only had several provincial courts managed to extract themselves from its sphere of influence over the course of time, the Great Council also almost never dealt with interprovincial conflicts anymore.[359] Most of the first instance lawsuits heard by the court concerned debts, testamentary dispositions, marital arrangements, and rights and privileges. In summary, the tribunal was mostly engaged in restoring credit and other relations between individual litigants. From time to time, towns and communities brought their internal conflicts to the Great Council, but even then, these cases only seldom involved disputes between litigants from different provinces. In fact, these sorts of lawsuits were often appeals against sentences from, for example, the Council of Flanders.

Comparing our observations on litigation at the Great Council—especially in terms of volume—with several other European central, provincial and local courts, allowed us to draw some parallels. The decline in litigation was a phenomenon that can be clearly observed at other European tribunals. The starting point in time, as well as the scale of the decline, might have differed between tribunals, but in general, the number of civil lawsuits these central and provincial courts were dealing with exhibited a consistent and unmistakable downward trend. Explaining the causes of this decrease proved to be difficult and a definitive explanation is still lacking. Undoubtedly not one single factor but rather a combination of mutually reinforcing elements was responsible.

---

[359] According to Oosterbosch, the Great Council's role as judge in interprovincial conflicts was already played after the death of Charles V. Oosterbosch, Michel. 2001. *Appelprocedure, dossierbehandeling en registervoering bij de Grote Raad van Mechelen*. In: *Voortschrijdend procesrecht. Een historische verkenning*, eds. Fred Stevens, Ernest Persoons and Remco Van Rhee. Leuven: Universitaire Pers Leuven, 6. One of the few exceptions in the eighteenth century seems to be the discussion surrounding the jurisdiction over the *Terres de débat* in the late 1730s and early 1740s (cf. supra, Chap. 2). However, this was not in the margin of a lawsuit brought before the Great Council. Moreover, we can presume that the tribunal was asked for advice not so much because it was the 'superior court' of the Netherlands, which had to judge interprovincial conflicts, but rather because the Great Council itself was an interested party.

It is only in the area of criminal litigation that we can identify a noticeable increase at several European courts. At the Great Council, this rise can, to some extent, be explained by a more hands on prosecution policy of the fiscals, but a rise in crime rates is also an important contributing factor—especially crimes connected to the reforms introduced by Joseph II, the insurrection of 1789 and the invasions of the French revolutionaries. In these turbulent times at the end of the eighteenth century, the government relied heavily on the Great Council to organize the prosecutions, exactly as it had done in 1718.

Nevertheless, criminal litigation was only a fraction of the total caseload—and jurisdiction—of the Great Council. The general picture is one of a court in decline, which the central government was no longer investing in. Moreover, by the eighteenth century, it had obviously played it historical role as an instrument of centralization and unification. However, the question must be asked if the same was true for periods of crisis, when the government needed a loyal and trustworthy instrument to rely on. The role of the Great Council during these times of turmoil—which were omnipresent during the last ten years of the *Ancien Régime*—is discussed in Chap. 4.

References

Archival Sources

Brussels, General State Archives

Audiëntie
1419/4
Grote Raad van Mechelen. Registers

160–168G "*Mémoriaux*"

The mémoriaux of the Great Council (GRM 143–168G) cover—albeit with certain gaps—the period between 1503 and 1781. The numbers 160–168G are relevant for the eighteenth century. An inventory by Gaillard is available for most of the mémoriaux, but for some unknown reason the numbers 168A until 168G—which are titled *Correspondances: mémoriaux*—are not included. Similarly, it remains unclear why GRM 162 is named *Registre aux résolutions secretes du Grand Conseil* but is still ranged within the series of the mémoriaux. It does however suggest that the two series are interrelated. The mémoriaux mainly consist of letters from the central administration to Malines and the responses, often formulated as advice, from the Great Council. They as well offer some insight into the larger environment in which the court operated throughout its existence. Of note are the various connections between the *mémoriaux* and the ordinances issued by the government: problems described in the *mémoriaux* are sometimes officially solved and then institutionalized by a decree. As was the case for the

Correspondence, the information in the *mémoriaux* is chronologically ordered but this arrangement is once again not rigorously followed. The inventory of Gaillard, however, makes research much less time-consuming and difficult for those registers covered by it.

175/10 Decrees and Ordonnances

Number GRM 175/10 is ranged under the heading *Edits, Placards et Ordonnances* (comprising GRM 169–175/11). This series contains, at least in theory, a list of all ordinances and decrees that the Great Council had to publish—or at least give the order to have them published—in its jurisdiction, predominantly for the second half of the eighteenth century, although some earlier periods are also included. However, the title is somewhat misleading; in fact the inventory specifies for this specific number that it deals with the judicial administration for the period 1789–1794 in addition to information about residences of the Great Council outside of Malines, ceremonial issues, relations with other institutions and procedure for the period between 1466 and 1794. In practice, number 175/10 is not a register but a 'file' filled with a mishmash of documents with little or no internal connection. Documents concerning the period between 1789 and 1795—the official act that abolished the Great Council in 1789 can be found here—are included, as well as descriptions of the paintings that are hanging in the premises of the Great Council. In addition, the move of the Great Council to Namur in 1746 is extensively described. Moreover, the file also contains several documents about the archives of the Great Council that were not necessarily written during the Ancien Régime: e.g. the letter of P.J. L'Orye from 1830, criticizing Audoor's report on the archives of the Great Council, an overview of the documents of the Great Council that were eventually returned by the French in 1770 and several accounts of the chaotic situation the archives of the office-fiscal were in. Finally, the file contains a separate subfile that deals with the problems concerning the jurisdiction of the Council of Luxemburg. It is obvious that a wealth of information is hidden behind an inadequate description.

517–608 *Rôle*

The registers of the *role* have been preserved in the archives for almost the entire period from 1474 to 1794 (GRM 302–608), with only a few gaps predominantly in the late fifteenth and early sixteenth century. The registers contain every lawsuit that followed the procedure on the *rôle* with a description of all proceedings and sometimes even the outcome of the case. The registers are divided into two columns: the right column contains the identification of the proctor, the litigants and the case; the left column is reserved for the description of the proceedings and at times also the outcome of the case. Usually, the lawsuits presented by the procurator-general were handled first, followed by those in which he was the defending party and finally all cases in which other proctors litigated. The use of these registers in research is somewhat problematic because of the massive amount of data they contain. Even simply counting cases is difficult as the same lawsuits reappear on various dates.

617–620 Distribution records ranged by province of origin
629–633 Distribution records ranged by reporter
635–637 Distribution records of the "Différends"

The distribution books record all the lawsuits introduced at the Great Council that reached the phase of 'distribution', i.e. the stage at which the case was assigned to a reporter. There is, however, at least one exception to this rule: only a very limited number of criminal cases were recorded in the distribution books. In general, distribution books contain the date of distribution, the instance, the procedure (appeal, first instance, *différend*, …), the name of the councilor reporter and the name (and sometimes a certain qualification) of the litigants. In several cases, but far from always, they also list the name of the procurators and the decision rendered. For the eighteenth century, the archives of the Great Council hold two different types of distribution records. While the first type contains both appeals and first instance cases, the second type is exclusively reserved for those lawsuits that followed the communicatory procedure (*différends*). Consequently, procedure is the distinguishing feature. In addition, the first type can again be divided into two subcategories, which do not much differ by the information they provide as by the way the data is arranged, *i.c.* by province of origin or by name of the councilor who acted as reporter. Comparison between these two categories had demonstrated that there is a considerable overlap and that possible lacunae must be attributed to the inevitable human errors of the registrar who recorded the cases. Why there are two further subcategories within the registers containing the appeals and first instance cases following the procedure on the *rôle* is less clear. In a certain way, they seem to represent an 'incoming stream' versus an 'outgoing stream'. Indeed, the distribution books arranged by province record in which part of the jurisdiction of the Great Council the lawsuits originated and thus entered the registry. The other subcategory records to which councilor the case was distributed. Even though the files did not literally leave the Great Council, we could say that the process of allocating a lawsuit to a certain member of the Council could be regarded as an 'outgoing stream', as the files left the registry. Possible this distinction was made as a means to keep track of all the files that were brought to the Great Council and to have an idea of the whereabouts of a certain file. The distribution records ranged by province of origin are available for the years 1613 until 1794; those ranged by councilor have been preserved for the year 1503, and then from 1542 up until 1794 with a gap between 1550 and 1601. Whether the 'missing' distribution records for the sixteenth century are lost or simply never existed, is unknown. The distribution records of the *Différends* only start at 1683. We presume that, before that date, they were recorded together with the other first instance and appeal cases, given the fact that the communicatory procedure only became popular over the course of the seventeenth century.

790–976 Extended sentences

Within the archives of the Great Council, the extended sentences (GRM 790–976) constitute a separate series, which—contrary to many others—is fairly exhaustive. The registers cover a period of some 300 years in which only the last 2 decades of the eighteenth century are missing. The absence of a register for the period between 1773 and 1794 can be explained by the specific manner in which these registers were compiled. In fact, they were originally written on separate quires and only after a certain period of time bound together into a single register. It is reasonable to presume that there were just not enough extended sentences in the last 20 years of the eighteenth century to bind together into a register. Further examination of the records of the Great Council has corroborated this theory; the archives contain a few separate extended sentences drafted in the period after 1772.

Every register until 1690—except for a limited period of time in the first half of the seventeenth century—contains one's year worth of extended sentences. In reality, this is not always the case: certain years are missing. Some of these turned out to be included in the register of the previous year, but others are completely absent. This probably does not mean that not a single extended sentence was registered in that specific year, but rather that the registers have gone astray in one of the different 'wanderings' of the archives. According to the procedure-ordinance of 1559 and a 'special' instruction for the redaction of extended sentences, it was the register or clerk who was responsible for recording these judgments. Based on certain documents in the case file, the registrar reconstructed in their case, after which a councilor proofread and corrected the text. In the eighteenth century, the extended sentences—drafted and pronounced in the name of the emperor—contained five elements: (1) the identification of the parties, including possible changes during the lawsuit (e.g. due to the death of one of the parties); (2) the subject of the dispute, often formulated at the request of the plaintiff; (3) an account of the progress of the case with a description of the principal acts of both litigants; (4) the primary arguments of the plaintiff and the defendant; (5) the decision. In case of appeal, accounts of all legal acts in the previous instance(s) were included as well as a summary of the appealed judgment.

It is unclear what purpose exactly the extended judgments had. Most cases in fact, were decided by a dictum while extended sentences were rather rare, probably because they were expensive to draft. Given that dicta were often short and lacked any detail about the parties or the case, it is likely that extended sentences functioned primarily as a 'title', as evidence for the future.

1029–1045 *Dicta*

The series of registers of dicta comprises 70 volumes, covering the period from 1475 to 1480 and then from 1502 until 1794. For the seventeenth and eighteenth centuries, there are even two parallel series, one of the *minutes* containing the 'rough versions' of the dicta (GRM 1047–1115) and one of the faire copies (GRM 977–1045). Unlike the extended sentences, the dicta were directly recorded in the registers, first as a draft and later copied out. Compared to the extended sentences, the number of dicta is much higher and they also have a much smaller informative value. In fact, a dictum does not provide any insight into the subject of a case or into the arguments used: it is merely a concise disposition, drafted by the reporting councilor, which mainly contains the names of the litigants, the procedure and the decision of the court. It is important to note that the dicta registers contain, apart from the final decisions in a case, all provisional dispositions. It might seem evident that these decisions would be readily available for anyone with some interest in the case. Certain dicta, however, make mention of a 'secret resolution', especially when directions were given to the councilor-reporter as to what questions he had to ask the litigants, what actions he had to take depending on their answers etc.

Grote Raad van Mechelen. Processen aanzienlijke families. Reeks A
212, 869, 885, 891, 905, 909, 914, 936, 1107, 1244, 1370

Grote Raad van Mechelen. Officie-fiscaal. Procesdossiers.
30, 34–40, 52–54, 58–66, 69, 73–82, 86–129, 142, 144–147, 152, 168–178, 194, 197, 200, 205, 213, 217, 220, 228, 230, 232, 234, 235, 237, 239, 248, 255, 257, 261, 271, 278, 289, 297–299, 304, 339, 351–352, 354–358, 361–364, 367–371, 374–380, 383, 385–387, 400, 405, 406, 411–413, 417–432, 440–445, 448, 458, 459, 461, 462, 464, 466–472, 474, 477, 479–482, 484, 487–489, 492–496, 502, 504, 505, 510, 514, 516, 519, 523–525, 530, 532–534, 536–548, 550–564, 717–751

Grote Raad van Mechelen. Officie-fiscaal. Banden en Delen.
43, 91, 96–99

Inventarissen van de Derde Afdeling
42, 102

Published and Printed Sources

De Saint Vaast, Pierre Claude Marie and Du Laury, Remi Albert. 1717. La jurisprudence des Pais-Bas autrichiens établies par les arrêts du Grand Conseil de Sa Majesté Impériale et Catholique, résident en la ville de Malines, auxquels sont ajoutés quelques décrets portés au Conseil Privé de Sadite Majesté. Brussels: t'Serstevens.

De Saint Vaast, Pierre Claude Marie and Du Laury, Remi Albert. 1761. La jurisprudence des Pais-Bas autrichiens établies par les arrêts du Grand Conseil de Sa Majesté Impériale et Catholique, résident en la ville de Malines, auxquels sont ajoutés quelques décrets portés au Conseil Privé de Sadite Majesté. Brussels: Jean Moris.

De Coloma, Jean Alphonse and Hony, Jean-Baptiste. 1781. Arrêts du Grand Conseil de Sa Majesté Impériale et Royale, séant en la ville de Malines (2v.). Malines: P.J. Hanicq.

De Wynants, Goswin. 1744. Supremae curiae Brabantiae decisiones. Brussels: Petrum Foppens.

Dubois d'Hermaville, Augustin, De Baralle, Ladislas, De Blye, Jean-Baptise and De Flines, Séraphin eds. 1773. Recueil d'arrêts du Parlement de Flandres. Lille: C.F.J. Lehoucq.

Stockmans, Petrus. 1670. Decisionum curiae Brabantiae sesquicenturia. Brussels: Franciscum Foppens.

Literature

Brooks, Christopher. 1989. Interpersonal conflict and social tension: civil litigation in England, 1640–1830. In *The first modern society. Essays in English history in honour of Lawrence Stone*, eds. David Cannadine et al., 357–399. Cambridge: Cambridge University Press.

Buntinx, Jan. 1964–1977. *Inventaris van het archief van de Raad van Vlaanderen*. 8t. Brussels: Algemeen Rijksarchief.

Champion, W.A. 1998. Recourse to the law and the meaning of the great litigation decline. In *Communities and courts in Britain, 1150–1900*, eds. Christopher Brooks and Michael Lobban, 179–198. Rio Grande: Hambledon Press.

Dauchy, Serge. 2005. Introduction. In *Les recueils d'arrêts et dictionnaires de jurisprudence: XVIe-XVIIIe siècles*, eds. Serge Dauchy and Véronique Demars-Sion, 9–20. Paris: La mémoire du droit.

Dauchy, Serge and Demars-Sion, Véronique. 2006. Argumentation et motivation dans les recueils d'arrêts des cours souverianes de France. L'exemple du Parlement de flandre (fin XVIIe—début XVIIIe siècle). In *Juristische Argumentation, Argumente der Juristen*, ed. albrecht Cordes, 127–152. Cologne: Böhlau Verlag.

Dauchy, Serge and Demars-Sion, Véronique. 2009. A propos d'un 'recueil d'arrêts' inédit: la jurisprudence du Parlement de Flandre de Georges de Ghewiet. *Tijdschrift voor Rechtsgeschiedenis* 77: 157–189.

De Smidt, Jacobus et al. eds. 1966–1988. *Chronologische lijsten van de geëxtenderdeerde sententiën berustende in het archief van de Grote Raad van Mechelen*, 6 volumes. Brussels: Koninklijke Commissie voor de uitgave der oude wetten en verordeningen van België.

Douxchamps-Lefevre, Cécile. 2003. Les sentences du Grand Conseil de Malines en appel d'instances namuroises (1582–1590). *Handelingen van de Koninklijke Commissie voor de uitgave der Oude Wetten en Verordeningen van België* 44: 59–136.

Doyle, William. 1970. The Parlements of France and the breakdown of the Old Régime 1771–1778. *French Historical Studies* 6: 415–458.

Dupont-Bouchat, Marie-Sylvie and Page-Steffens, Marie-Paule. 2006. Des délits et des peines: l'activité pénale du Conseil Provincial de Namur au XVIIIe siècle. In *La Belgique criminelle: droit, justice, société (XIVe-XXe siècles)*, eds. Marie-Sylvie Dupont-Bouchat and Xavier Rousseaux, 273–316. Louvain-la-Neuve: Academia-Bruylant.

Feutry, David. 2012. The historian's mountain of paper. *French history* 26.3: 277–297.

Gaillard, Arthur. 1898–1902. *Le Conseil de Brabant: histoire, organisation, procédure*. Brussels: Lebègue.

Gilissen, John. 1980. De Grote Raad van Mechelen. Historisch overzicht. In *Miscelannea Consilii Magni. Ter gelegenheid van twintig jaar Werkgroep Grote Raad van Mechelen*, 13–43. Amsterdam: Universiteit van Amsterdam. Faculteit der rechtsgeleerdheid.

Godding, Philippe. 1970. L'origine et l'autorité des recueils de jurisprudence dans les Pays-Bas Méridionaux (XIIIe-XVIIIe siècles). In *Rapports belges au VIIIe congrès international de droit comparé*, 1–37. Brussel: CIDC.

Godding, Philippe and Petit, Roger. 2001. Les sentences du Grand Conseil de Malines relatives au duché de Luxembourg (1582–1590). *Handelingen van de Koninklijke Commissie voor de uitgave der Oude Wetten en Verordeningen van België* 42: 63–201.

Hilaire, Jean. 2005. Questions autour de la jurisprudence des arrêts. In *Les recueils d'arrêts et dictionnaires de jurisprudence: XVIe-XVIIIe siècles*, eds. Serge Dauchy and Véronique Demars-Sion, 21–40. Paris: La mémoire du droit.

Horwitz, Henry and Polden, Patrick. 1996. Continuity or change in the Court of chancery in the seventeenth and eighteenth centuries? *Journal of British Studies* 35.1: 24–57.

Jahns, Sigrid. 1990. Die Personalverfassung des Reichskammergerichts unter Anpassungsdruck. Lösungen im Spannungsfeld zwischen Modernität und Überalterung. In *Das Reichskammergericht in der deutschen Geschichte: Stand der Forschung, Forschungsperspektiven* (Quellen und Forschungen zur höchsten Gerichtsbarkeit im alten Reich 21), ed. Bernhard Diestelkamp, 59–109. Cologne: Böhlau.

Kagan, Richard. 1981. A golden age in litigation: Castile, 1500–1700. In *Disputes and settlements. Law and human relation in the west*, ed. John Bossy, 145–166. Cambridge: Cambridge University Press.

Kagan, Richard. 1981. *Lawsuits and litigants in Castile, 1500–1700*. Chapel Hill: University of North Carolina Press.

Kaiser, Colin. 1980. The deflation in the volume of litigation at Paris in the Eighteenth Century and the waning of the old judicial order. *European Studies Review* 10.3: 309–336.

Koster-Van Dijck, Joke M.I. 1988. Instruction pour le greffier du Grand Conseil concernant la rédaction des sentences (Introduction et édition du texte). In *Miscellanea Consilii Magni III: essays on the history of forensic practice* (Verzamelen en bewerken van de jurisprudentie van de Grote Raad. Nieuwe Reeks 12), Alain Wijffels ed., 17–41. Amsterdam: Universiteit van Amsterdam.

Le Bailly, Marie-Charlotte. 2001. *Recht voor de Raad: rechtspraak voor het Hof van Holland, Zeeland en West-Friesland in het midden van de vijftiende eeuw*. Hilversum: Uitgeverij Verloren.

Le Bailly, Marie-Charlotte. 2011. Langetermijntrends in de rechtspraak bij de gewestelijke hoven van justitie in de Noordelijke Nederlanden van ca. 1450 tot ca. 1800. *Pro Memorie* 13: 30–67.

Le Bailly, Marie-Charlotte and Vermeesch, Griet. Explaining the great litigation decline. *To be published.*

Levy, René and Rousseaux, Xavier. 1992. Etats, justice pénale et histoire: bilan et perspectives. *Droit et société* 20–21: 249–279.

Lorgnier, Jacques. 1988. Les procédures du Grand Conseil de Malines conservés Ã Lille (série V B des archives du Nord—présentation, inventaire et index pour les XVe et XVIe siècles). In *Miscellanea Consilii Magni III: essays on the history of forensic practice* (Verzamelen en bewerken van de jurisprudentie van de Grote Raad. Nieuwe Reeks 12), Alain Wijffels ed., 43–110. Amsterdam: Universiteit van Amsterdam.

Maes, Louis Th. 1949. De Grote Raad der Nederlanden en zijn arrêtisten. *Tijdskrif vir hedendaagse Romeins-Hollandse Reg* 12: 58–76.

Michel, Sabrina. 2009. Les 'arrêts étendus' du Parlement de Flandre: etude d'une spécificité juridique locale. *Revue du Nord* 91.4: 745–761.

Monballyu, Jos. 1998. Chronologische Lijst van de Nederlandstalige geëxtedeerde sententiën van de Grote Raad van Mechelen (1581–1590). *Handelingen van de Koninklijke Commissie voor de uitgave der Oude Wetten en Verordeningen van België* 39: 79–146.

Oosterbosch, Michel. 1998. *Grote Raad voor de Nederlanden te Mechelen: procesbundels beroepen uit Vlaanderen: ordinaris processen (nr. 1–1000)*. Brussels: Algemeen Rijksarchief.

Oosterbosch, Michel. 2006. Archief of niet? De procesdossiers van de Grote Raad voor de Nederlanden te Mechelen. In *Hoge rechtspraak in de oude Nederlanden*, eds. Hugo de Schepper and René Vermeir, 65–78. Maastricht: Shaker.

Oosterbosch, Michel. 2006. *Inventaris van het archief van de Grote Raad voor de Nederlanden te Mechelen: procesbundels beroepen uit Holland 1460–1740*. Brussels: Algemeen Rijksarchief.

Pauwels, Henri ed. 1962. *Het Gulden Vlies: vijf eeuwen kunst en geschiedenis*. Brugge: Stad Brugge.

Piant, Hervé. 2007. Des procès innombrables. Eléments méthodologiques pour une histoire de la justice civile d'Ancien Régime. *Histoire et mesure* 22.2: 13–39.

Put, Eddy. 1995. *Grote Raad van Mechelen. Processen van aanzienlijke families (Reeksen A en B)*: werkbeschrijvingen. Brussels: Algemeen Rijksarchief.

Put, Eddy. 1995. *Officie-fiscaal van de Grote Raad van Mechelen: werkbeschrijvingen*. Brussels: Algemeen Rijksarchief.

Put, Eddy. 2000. In de zak? De archiefstatus van procesdossiers uit het ancien régime. In *Door de archivistiek gestrikt: liber amicorum prof. dr. Juul Verhelst* (Archiefinitiatie(f) 4), eds Gustave Janssens e.a, 187–196. Brussels: VUBpress.

Put, Eddy. 2002. Gedeelde soevereiniteit? De dubbelrol van de Raad van Brabant. In *Politieke representatie*, eds. Henk de Smaele and Johan Tollebeek, 221–229. Leuven: Universitaire Pers Leuven.

Ranieri, Filippo. 1985. *Recht und Gesellschaft im Zeitlter der Rezeption: eine rechts-und sozialgeschichtliche Analyse der Tätigkeit des Reichskammergerichts im 16. Jahrhundert.* Cologne: Böhlau.

Simon, Jules. 1907. Les recueils d'arrêts du Grand Conseil de Malines. *Handelingen van de Koninklijke Commissie voor de uitgave van oude wetten en verordeningen van België* 10: 265–256.

Tambuyser, Raphaël. 1953. Sociale troebelen te Mechelen in 1718. *Handelingen van de Koninklijke Kring voor Oudheidkunde, Letteren en Kunst van Mechelen* 57: 188–203.

Tilly, Charles. 1992. *Coercion, Capital and European States, AD 990–1992.* Cambridge: Blackwell.

Van Dijck, Maarten. 2009. *Towards an economic interpretation of justice? Conflict settlement, social control and civil society in urban Brabant and Mechelen during the late Middle Ages and the early modern period.* In *Serving the Urban Community. The rise of public facilities in the Low Countries*, eds. Martijn Van der Burg et al., 62–88. Amsterdam: Aksant.

Van Poelgeest, L. 1988. De raadsheren van de Hoge Raad van Holland, Zeeland en West-Friesland in de achttiende eeuw. *Bijdragen en mededelingen betreffende de geschiedenis der Nederlanden* 103.1: 20–51.

Verscuren, An. 2005. *"L'oeil et le bras du Roi?" Het vervolgingsbeleid van het officie-fiscaal van de Grote Raad van Mechelen (1767–1788).* Unpublished Master's Thesis. Leuven: Katholieke Universiteit Leuven.

Verscuren, An. 2013. *Nadere toegang op de geëxtendeerde sententies van de Grote Raad van Mechelen: 1693–1772.* Brussels: Algemeen Rijksarchief.

Verscuren, An. 2014. Archieven in oorlog, speelbal van politiek. Het archief van de Grote Raad van Mechelen (1746–1869)'. In *Macht en Onmacht. De rol van archieven in oorlog en bij rechtsherstel*, eds. Ron Blom e. a., 49–59. 's-Gravenhage: Stichting Archiefpublicaties.

Wijffels, Alain. 1989. Legal Records and Reports in the Great Council of Malines (15th to 18th century). In *Judicial Records, Law Reports and the Growth of Case Law*, ed. John H. Baker, 181–206. Berlin: Duncker und Humblot.

Wijffels, Alain. 1997. Grand Conseil de Malines: la rédaction des sentences étendues et le recueil de jurisprudence de Guillaume de Grysperre. In *Case law in the making: the techniques and methods of judicial records and law reports (Comparative studies in continental and Anglo-American Legal History* 17) v.1, ed. Alain Wijffels, 299–316. Berlin: Duncker und Humblot.

Chapter 5
Closing Time: The 'Fortunes' of the Great Council at the Turn of the Century

5.1 Introduction[1]

Did the Great Council outlive its usefulness? Was this once-prestigious tribunal nothing more than an archaic reminder of past glories which only survived into the eighteenth century because institutions were seldom abolished during the Ancien Régime? Or was the final decade of its existence—marked by serious internal turmoil in the Southern Netherlands and external threats from the French revolutionary armies—different from the rest of the eighteenth century? Given that the Great Council was one of the central government's few remaining loyal agents in the Austrian Netherlands, it might have used the court to reinforce its authority. Therefore, this chapter examines if, at the very end of the Ancien Régime, the Great Council could once again take up its almost forgotten function as the government's instrument of power.

It could be argued that in a way—completely independent from the events in France—the demise of the Ancien Régime in the Austrian Netherlands started with the death of Maria Theresa and the ascension to the throne of her eldest son, Joseph II, in 1780. For the first time, the sovereign did not merely act as a preserver of laws and customs, but rather became a reforming legislator,[2] who attempted to introduce into the Austrian Netherlands a uniform, centralized, homogeneous form of government, thereby aiming to overturn the entire way of living by arranging every aspect of life—from religion to education and leisure to administration and justice—according to his image of the perfect enlightened society. To a large extent, Joseph II's

[1] A master's thesis has already been written on the subject of the 'final years and disappearance' of the Great Council: Vervondel, Eva. 2004. *De Grote Raad van Mechelen van 1780 tot 1797. De laatste jaren en de verdwijning.* Leuven, Unpublished Master's Thesis. Katholieke Universiteit Leuven. While there is unmistakably a certain overlap in the purely factual information, this chapter provides, aside from several corrections and additional data, a deeper understanding of the events at the end of the eighteenth and the beginning of the nineteenth centuries.

[2] Dhondt, Luc. 1993. *Verlichte monarchie, Ancien Regime en revolutie.* Ghent: RUG, t.VII, 572.

A. Verscuren, *The Great Council of Malines in the 18th century,*
Studies in the History of Law and Justice 3, DOI 10.1007/978-3-319-09638-4_5

reforms—although vilified in his own Belgian provinces[3]—corresponded with the demands of the French revolutionaries in the late 1780s.[4] Both shared the objective of creating a rational, unified state in which particularistic interests had no place. Their means, however, were entirely different: Joseph II wished to accomplish this program through the exact form of government the revolutionaries reacted against: enlightened despotism.

The Years Prior to 1787[5] Before introducing his general scheme for centralization and uniformity, Joseph II wanted to personally have a taste of the Southern Netherlands. He waited until the death of Governor Charles of Lorraine to embark on his almost two-month voyage throughout the Low Countries (May 31, 1781 to July 27, 1781).[6] His trip made him the first ruler since Philip II to set foot in the Netherlands. Although his Belgian subjects were enthusiastic at first, Joseph II was not exactly impressed with what he witnessed. All sorts of complaints, written down in petitions addressed to the emperor, completed the appalling picture he had already formed of the Netherlands. Many petitioners addressed the judicial problems, criticizing the slowness of civil justice, the swiftness which characterized the system of criminal justice, the impunity of crimes that were supposed to be prosecuted by lords, but also the excessive number of advocates, lengthy procedures, exorbitant legal costs, irrational laws which made it possible to appeal *ad infinitum* in a civil case but did

[3] In this chapter, we will often make use of the term 'Belgian provinces' to refer to the Austrian Netherlands. While this may sound somewhat anachronistic, it is frequently used in the eighteenth century sources to indicate the Austrian possessions in the Netherlands.

[4] Hasquin, Hervé. 1987. Slotbeschouwingen. Jozef II en de Franse Revolutie: punten van overeenkomst en breuk. In *Oostenrijks België 1713–1794: de Zuidelijke Nederlanden onder de Oostenrijkse Habsburgers*, ed. Hervé Hasquin, 533–534. Brussels: Gemeentekrediet van België.

[5] Given that Joseph II and different aspects of his reforms in the Austrian Netherlands have already been amply studied, we give only a short overview, based on literature, of the most relevant information. See: Beales, Derek. 2009. *Joseph II. Vol II: Against the World.* Cambridge: Cambridge University Press; Bérenger, Jean. 2007. *Joseph II d'Autriche: serviteur de l'Etat.* Paris: Fayard; Blanning, Timothy. 1994. *Joseph II.* London: Longman; Blitz, Rudolph. 1989. The religious reforms of Joseph II (1780–1790) and their economic significance. *Journal of European Economic History* 18.3: 583–595; Hasquin, Hervé. 2007. *Joseph II: catholique antéclerical et réformateur impatient 1741–1790.* Brussels: Racine; Laenen, Joseph. 1905. *Etude sur la suppression des couvents par l'empereur Joseph II dans les Pays-Bas autrichiens et plus spécialement dans le Brabant (1783–1794).* Antwerp: Van Hille-De Backer; Roegiers, Jan. 1980. *Kerk en Staat in de Oostenrijkse Nederlanden.* In In *Algemene Geschiedenis der Nederlanden*, eds. Walter Prevenier e.a, t.9, 361–375. Haarlem: Fibula-Van Dishoeck; Szantay, Antal.2005. *Regionalpolitik im Alten Europa: die Verwaltungsreformen Josephs II in Ungarn, in der Lombardei und in den Österreichischen Niederlanden 1785–1790.* Budapest: Akadémiai Kiadó; Vandermeersch, Bernard. 2010. *Comme il importe au bien de l'Eglise et de l'Etat...: l'opposition de l'épiscopat 'Belgique' aux réformes ecclésiastiques de Joseph II (1780–1790).* Louvain-la-Neuve: Collège Erasme.

[6] Hubert wrote an interesting account of this trip, based on a wide range of archival sources. Although his work is somewhat tedious because of the inclusion of irrelevant details (e.g., a description of Joseph II's horse!), it is a good source to gain some insight into the emperor's movements around the Netherlands and the impressions he must have gained from the land and its people. Hubert, Eugène. 1900. *Le voyage de l'empereur Joseph II dans les Pays-Bas (31 mai 1781–1727 juillet 1781): etude d'histoire politique et diplomatique.* Brussels, Lebègue.

not allow an appeal when a man's head was at stake, lack of uniformity in procedure and habits, ignorance of the judges on the countryside, etc.[7] As if the emperor needed any more arguments for a thorough redesigning of the judicial landscape, the judges themselves also complained, first of all about their meager pay, but also about the frequent conflicts of jurisdiction that slowed down the pace of justice.

Already during his stay in the Austrian Netherlands, Joseph II had private conversations with, among others, Goswin de Fierlant, president of the Great Council at that time, to discuss some of his designs for the complete reformation of the judicial system.[8] For now, the sovereign left the development of a new scheme for both the civil and criminal administration of justice, including the redaction of an entirely new procedural code, to a commission. In the meantime, he made two preliminary adjustments: first, in June 1782, he reduced the *médianate* to one half of the original amount for all people aspiring to a councillorship in a superior court of justice.[9] Secondly, in respectively August and November of that same year, he detached the Councils of Luxemburg and Tournai from the Great Council, giving the former the status of a sovereign court and making the sentences of the latter appealable to the Council of Hainaut.[10] Unsurprisingly, the Great Council was not amused with this further reduction of its jurisdiction; yet, the councilors limited their reaction to an official protest letter.[11]

In the early years of his reign, Joseph II engaged in reforming the cultural and religious sphere—seriously restraining the power of the Church—rather than in implementing his ideas on a thorough reorganization of the judicial and administrative domains. While these ordinances were greeted by a torrent of denunciations and protests by ex-Jesuits and the religious authorities, the general population did not see enough cause to rally against the emperor. And while surely many of his measures were hardly popular—like the limitation of the number of religious holidays, the suppression of the brotherhoods, the restriction of public processions to two a year and the decision that *kermesses* and other festivals had to be celebrated in each locality on the same day of the year—they did not generate more than a stir.

Misjudging the depth and potential explosiveness of the popular discontent based on these previous experiences, Joseph II proceeded in 1786 with the establishment of a general seminary in Leuven—with a satellite in Luxemburg—thereby extracting the education of the clergy from the control of the bishops. Initially, the

[7] Hubert, Eugène. 1900. *Le voyage de l'empereur Joseph II dans les Pays-Bas (31 mai 1781–1727 juillet 1781): etude d'histoire politique et diplomatique*. Brussels, Lebègue, 130–131.

[8] Hubert, Eugène. 1900. *Le voyage de l'empereur Joseph II dans les Pays-Bas (31 mai 1781–1727 juillet 1781): etude d'histoire politique et diplomatique*. Brussels, Lebègue, 59. Hubert recounted that de Fierlant responded by disapproving of certain of Joseph II's plans as he foresaw some 'unpleasant consequences'. As Bosch has pointed out, this is rather implausible as de Fierlant is known to have been a loyal subject and as there were no other signs of discord between the emperor and the president of the Great Council. Cf. Bosch, J.W. 1965. Keizer Joseph II en de president Goswin de Fierlant. *Tijdschrift voor Rechtsgeschiedenis* 33.2: 283–289.

[9] *ROPBA*, t. 12, p. 169, June 10, 1782.

[10] *ROPBA*, t. 12, pp. 189–191, August 1, 1782; *ROPBA*, t.12, pp. 216–217, November 22, 1782.

[11] Cf. supra, Chap. 3.

protests of Archbishop Frankenberg from Malines and the other bishops were to no avail, but from the pulpit, the clergy aroused the hearts and minds of their flocks, discrediting the new institution by questioning its discipline and the orthodoxy of its doctrines. Revolts broke out among students. What started out on December 5 as a demonstration turned into a riot. Military units were brought in to restore order, but by the end of January 1787, only about 20 students remained at the school. By then Joseph II had already put the final spark to the tinder by alienating another influential segment of the population with the publication of his plans for judicial and administrative reforms. Soon, these two groups—the government's officials and the clergy—found each other in their struggle against a common enemy, culminating in the Brabant Revolution of 1789.

Sources Due to the uncertain times at the end of the eighteenth century, official record keeping at the Great Council was somewhat patchy. Especially for the periods of exile following the Brabant Revolution and the first French invasion—respectively during the greater part of 1790 and between roughly November 1792 and February 1793—only a few odd documents are available.[12] To study the time frames in which the Great Council was functioning more or less normally in Malines, we made use of the correspondence of the Great Council itself[13] and of the 'recommendations and correspondence' of its office-fiscal.[14] The former consists of all kinds of letters and requests sent to or by the Great Council. The central government, usually through the Privy Council, is the main correspondent, but other institutions—such as provincial councils—and even individuals also figure in these registers. The subject matter ranges from orders to organize a *Te Deum*, requests for all sorts of dispensations, conflicts of jurisdiction with especially the Council of Flanders or the Magistrate of Malines, to instructions of the governor on how to respond to a potential invasion by the French.

The registers containing the recommendations and correspondence of the fiscals are somewhat similar in terms of content: advice given by the fiscals alternates with correspondence of the governor, letters of the Privy Council, requests of private persons and complaints of subordinates. The only structure in this mishmash of documents is the date on which they were composed or received, but even this chronological criterion was not rigorously followed.[15]

Reconstructing the period after 1794 is even more complicated. With the dissolution of the Belgian institutions, the usual official sources dried up: the last entry

[12] Brussels, ARA, GRM 3, Documents relatifs aux archives du Grand Conseil pendant et après la révolution brabançonne et les invasions françaises, 1789–1794; GRM 175, Edits, placards et ordonnances, 1788; GRM 231, Cahier portant des annotations au sujet de certain faits auxquels le grand conseil s'est trouvé melé ou qui l'ont mis dans le cas de devoir prendre une délibération ou une consulte officieuse, XVIIIe siècle; GRM 232, Recueil de documents concernant le personnel du grand conseil, particulièrement les secrétaires, et diverses pièces touchant le rétablissement du siège en 1791.

[13] Brussels, ARA, GRM 135–140, Correspondance du Grand Conseil de Malines, 1787–1794.

[14] Brussels, ARA, GRMOF, BD 65–70, Recueils d'avis 1787–1794.

[15] For example, there are no less than three volumes in which the correspondence of the year 1777 is registered. Cf. ARA, GRMOF, BD, 57, 80 and 91.

in both the correspondence of the Great Council and the recommendations of the fiscals is dated June 18, 1794; the last dictum is registered on June 25th and ends in the middle of a sentence, as if the registrar suddenly had to close his books when he was recording what was probably the final decision of the tribunal as an institution.[16] Apart from some official ordinances—which do not provide much specific information on the Great Council or its members—the regular sources leave us somewhat in the dark from the summer of 1794 onwards.

For the period after the second French invasion, the requests for pensions filed by the Belgian *émigrés*—conserved in the *Finanz-und Hofkammerarchiv* in Vienna—constitute an important source and provide particular information on the fate of individual councilors of the Great Council.[17] Some of these files contain requests with a more or less detailed account of the further endeavors and travels of the members of the Great Council; others are empty covers which merely mention the amount of the pension to which the petitioner was entitled. Apart from these requests, the *Haus- Hof- und Staatsarchiv* preserves a file on the 'emigrated Great Council', with some information on the whereabouts of the councilors and especially on how they were treated by the Austrian government.[18]

One of the few sources available in Brussels that lifts the veil of what happened after 1794, not merely with (the members of) the Great Council but also with other institutions and functionaries of the Austrian Netherlands, can be found in the archives of the *Departement des Pays-Bas de la chancellerie de Cour et d'Etat* (Department of the Netherlands of the Chancellery of the Court and the State). In fact, the records of the Department hold the protocols of the deliberations of the *Comité établi provisoirement pour la liquidation des affaires financières belgiques* (the Provisional Committee for the Liquidation of the Belgian Financial Affairs).[19] Established on February 1, 1797 in Vienna, this Committee was responsible for the current accounts and all other financial matters that remained unresolved after the government left the Austrian Netherlands. Only the affairs concerning the Belgian pensions remained outside the Committee's jurisdiction; these would be handled as before by the *Directoire générale des finances allemandes* (the General Council of German Finances). Former councilor of the Council of Finance and the Council of State Limpens was appointed president of the Committee; he was assisted in his duties by former councilors of the Council of Finance Ransonet and Barbier, for-

16 Brussels, ARA, GRM 1045, Dicta 1780–1794.

17 Vienna, FHKA, Österreichische Kamerale 2308, 2309, 2310.

18 Vienna, HHStA, Belgien DDB rot 80 (alt 53). The postscript on the cover mentions that this file originally belonged to President Le Clerc's personal papers but was 'returned'—to the Austrian government?—after his death, by Goubau on April 12, 1813.

19 For more information, see: Laloire, Emile. 1914. Comité de liquidation des affaires belgiques de 1797 à 1804. In *Mélanges d'histoire offerts à Charles Moeller à l'occasion de son jubilé de 50 années de professorat à l'Université de Louvain*, 521–526. Leuven: Bureaux de Recueil; *Van Honacker*, Karin. 1994. Tijdelijk comité voor de vereffening van de Nederlandse financiële kwesties te Wenen (1797–1804). In *De centrale overheidsinstellingen van de Habsburgse Nederlanden*, ed. Erik Aerts e.a., 144–148. Brussels: Algemeen Rijksarchief.

mer councilor of the Privy Council Pouppez,[20] former advocate-fiscal of the Great Council Goubau and some lower functionaries.[21]

In its seven-year-long existence—the Committee was dissolved in February, 1804—it discussed a wide range of financial issues, predominantly requests for one or another form of support, but also the settlement of accounts in favor of the Austrian government as well as matters pertaining to the preservation of the records of the dissolved institutions of the Netherlands. The members of the Great Council figure in these documents at various instances—mostly because they claimed to be entitled to a higher pension or to the payment of overdue accounts—making it possible to shed some light on their whereabouts and activities after their exile from the Austrian Netherlands. In addition, these registers confirm and complete the information found in the Viennese archives. In fact, while the records in the *Haus- Hof- und Staatsarchiv* and in the *Finanz- und Hofkammerarchiv* constitute the prime source for the whereabouts of the Council and its members from 1794 up until early 1796, the archives of the Committee for the Liquidation of the Belgian Financial Affairs shed some—however partial—light on what happened to them after 1797.

5.2 Endgame: The Demise of a 300-year-old Tribunal

5.2.1 The Build-up: January, 1787–December, 1789

The imperial decrees of January 1, 1787[22] announcing several thorough legal and administrative reforms did not come out of the clear blue sky. Over the past few years, the reforms had been meticulously discussed and prepared by different committees and officials. In the end, however, Joseph II unilaterally imposed his own ideas; he wanted nothing less than a standard administrative and legal system directed from Vienna and completely amenable to the sovereign will. Finding people who shared his enthusiasm for this design and who agreed without any objections to his idea for an extreme *tabula rasa* turned out to be much more complicated.[23]

The different stages that eventually led to the promulgation of the 1787 edicts are well known.[24] What concerns us in particular, is the relative absence of the

[20] Before his promotion to the Privy Council in May 1794, Pouppez had been a member of the Great Council.

[21] Brussels, ARA, DeptNed 952/1, f.1–6.

[22] *ROPBA*, t. 13, pp. 3–4, January 1, 1787.

[23] **Tesch,** Marie-Eve. 2004. La réforme de la justice de l'empereur Joseph II dans les Pays-Bas autrichiens. Le séjour à Bruxelles du baron Karl Anton von Martini. 29 novembre 1786–1731 mai 1787. In *Bruxellois à Vienne, Viennois à Bruxelles*, ed. Bruno Bernard, 113–161. Brussels: Universiteit Brussel. According to Tesch, even Martini had serious doubts about the feasibility of Joseph's reform plans.

[24] Originally, in 1782, Joseph II assigned the reform work to a *Jointe*, presided by president of the Council of Brabant de Crumpipen and composed of president of the Great Council de Fierlant, councilor of the Great Council de Waepenaert, chancellor of the Council of Gelre Tackoen, coun-

Great Council in the entire process. In fact, the Council and its president were only indirectly involved in the redaction of the new procedural code and had no say at all in the new administrative or judicial structures. Instead of choosing de Fierlant as president of the Great Council—allegedly still the first tribunal of the Netherlands—Joseph II specifically appointed the chancellor of the Council of Brabant, Joseph de Crumpipen, to preside over the different *Jointes* and Committees to prepare the legal reforms.

Admittedly, the Great Council was asked for its opinion on the first draft of the new procedure—written by de Crumpipen together with de Robiano, one of his colleagues at the Council of Brabant—but this was not an exclusive privilege awarded to the Malines tribunal. In fact, all sovereign councils were invited to make comments and suggestions. Moreover, de Fierlant rather than de Crumpipen would have been the obvious choice to prepare a thorough procedural and institutional reform. Not only was he known to be a loyal subject of the Austrian government—like his father-in-law de Neny had been—but he was also particularly competent to work on a new legal procedure as he already had some experience with legal reforms: he was involved in several attempts to rewrite the law under Maria Theresa and drew up two memoranda on the abolition of torture and on the need to eradicate corporal punishments.[25] There could be no doubt that he was the perfect man for the job; and yet, Joseph II preferred to appoint the chancellor of the Council of Brabant to direct his legal reforms. Presumably, the sovereign rightfully identified the Council of Brabant as the most powerful and influential tribunal in the Austrian Netherlands, wielding not only legal but also some political power.[26] Furthermore, Joseph II might have hoped that the Council of Brabant would more easily accept its *de*

cilors of the Council of Brabant de Robiano and Charlier and councilor of the Privy Council Le Clerc. Even before the *Jointe* could do any work, Joseph II decided to give the assignment solely to de Crumpipen and de Robiano. Their project would afterwards be presented to the other sovereign councils (Malines, Hainaut, Luxemburg), which were then allowed to give comments. Eventually, Joseph II decided to ignore the work done and introduce into the Austrian Netherlands a structure comparable to the one he imposed in his other possessions. In order to prepare this reform, Le Clerc was sent to Vienna to confer with Martini who was eventually responsible for launching the new judicial structure and legal procedure in the Austrian Netherlands. Cf. Tesch, Marie-Eve. 2004. La réforme de la justice de l'empereur Joseph II dans les Pays-Bas autrichiens. Le séjour à Bruxelles du baron Karl Anton von Martini. 29 novembre 1786–1731 mai 1787. In *Bruxellois à Vienne, Viennois à Bruxelles*, ed. Bruno Bernard, 113–161. Brussels: Universiteit Brussel; Van Hille, Philippe. 1973. *De gerechtelijke hervorming van Keizer Jozef II*. Tielt: Veys. Gaillard as well provides an excellent overview of the legal reforms of 1787, although with an emphasis on the consequences for the Council of Brabant: Gaillard, Arthur. 1898–1902. *Le Conseil de Brabant: histoire, organisation, procédure*. Brussels: Lebègue, t.1, 335–365.

[25] On de Fierlant and his work, e.g. Monballyu, Jos. 2000. L'idée d'un code criminel chez Goswin de Fierlant. *Tijdschrift voor Rechtsgeschiedenis* 68: 281–300; Stevens, Fred. 2000. Goswinus Anna Maria Felix de Fierlant (1735–1804): Een Turnhoutse bevoorrechte getuige van het einde van een tijdperk. *Taxandria: jaarboek van de Koninklijke geschied-en oudheidkundige kring van de Antwerpse Kempen* 71: 7–21.

[26] In the eighteenth century, the Council of Brabant was the only provincial council in the Austrian Netherlands which boasted the right of remonstration. This inevitably led to conflicts with the central government, especially in the seventeenth and eighteenth centuries. Cf. Put, Eddy. 2002.

facto abolition from its own chancellor—whose loyalty to the Habsburg Crown was also unquestionable—than from the president of the Great Council.

Reactions to the new legal and administrative structures were not long in coming. Especially the Estates of the different provinces were furious: the January 1 decrees effectively signed their death sentences. The provincial councils' reaction was more restrained at first, but prodded by the Estates' deputies, they also took to the offensive, with the Council of Brabant at the forefront. As far as the sources reveal anything about the position of the Great Council, its members seem to have acted subserviently, even though the Council was also scheduled to disappear on May 1, 1787. The last session of the Great Council was probably held on or about April 20, 1787 when an inventory of all 'pending' cases was drawn up,[27] ready to be sent to the new tribunals.

The fact that the majority of the Great Council's members were awarded other positions in the new legal structure undoubtedly helped in securing their support. For most of them, in terms of prestige and status, their new functions were a promotion compared to their councillorships in the Great Council or at least maintained the status quo. The top position in the hierarchy—*i.e.,* the presidency of the Sovereign Council of Justice—was awarded to Joseph de Crumpipen, which was no surprise as Joseph II had initially preferred him to draw up the reform plans. De Fierlant had to be satisfied with the presidency of the Court of Appeal in Brussels; councilors Vriesen, Tackoen, de Villers and Diu were among his colleagues. Councilors Van der Fosse and de Laing occupied a seat in the Sovereign Council of Justice while Ludovisi d'Orley was awarded the presidency of the Court of Appeal in Luxemburg. Others fared less well: Cottin was appointed president of the Court of First Instance in Kortrijk, Douglas became his colleague in Ieper, de Waepenaert in Malines—he was the only member of the Great Council to remain in the city—de Stassart in Namur[28] and Ghison in Tournai.[29]

So far, four members of the Great Council remain unaccounted for: de Cock, Wirix, Van Velde, and Van Volxem. The first one probably did not take up any post, as he had already been on leave because of sickness; in fact, he died sometime in 1787. Councilor Wirix as well had already reached an advanced age (74) in 1787 and might have preferred to retire instead of having to move to a new position and, potentially, a new city. Councilor Van Velde left the judicial domain for a seat in the *Commission des fondations pieuses* (Commission of Pious Foundations) associated

Gedeelde soevereiniteit? De dubbelrol van de Raad van Brabant. In *Politieke representatie*, eds. Henk de Smaele and Johan Tollebeek, 226–229. Leuven: Universitaire Pers Leuven.

[27] Brussels, ARA, INV 48. The arrangement of the cases in this inventory is somewhat peculiar: the basic distinction is not made between first instance versus appeal, but according to province of origin. The cases in each province are subsequently subdivided in 'appeals' and 'first instance cases'.

[28] Van Hille, Philippe. 1973. *De gerechtelijke hervorming van Keizer Jozef II*. Tielt: Veys, 59–227. Van Hille compiled lists enumerating the members of the new tribunals. Most of the other employees of the Great Council—registrars, secretaries etc—were awarded a position at the Court of first instance in Malines.

[29] Brussels, ARA, GRM 5, f.77–78. Patent letter of Ghison.

with the *Conseil du gouvernement général* (Council of General Government).[30] He would not return to the Great Council until after 1789 when the *Conseil* was abolished and again replaced by the three *Conseils Collatéraux*. Van Volxem's fate is entirely unknown, but his background as a clerical councilor might have negatively affected his chances to be offered a new councillorship.

The appointment of several councilors as examiners of the prospective candidates for positions in the new first instance tribunals also demonstrate that the government made extensive use of the members of the Great Council to put the new structure in place. All applicants had to show a thorough knowledge of, for example, the new civil code that was bound to become operative on May 1st. Councilors Van der Fosse, Van Velde and de Laing were made responsible for respectively Flanders, Limburg and Gelre, and Namur and Malines.[31] Obviously, Joseph II was confident that the councilors of the Great Council were capable (and trustworthy) enough to select his future judges.

Contrary to their Brabant and Flemish colleagues, the members of the Great Council who were relocated never refused to take on their functions when the new tribunals were supposed to open their doors on May 1, 1787. Attempts to placate the recalcitrant members of the provincial councils failed and massive resistance from predominantly Hainaut and Brabant forced Governors Albert and Marie-Christine to suspend—at least temporarily—the new legal system on May 14th;[32] the equally loathed administrative subdivision of the Austrian Netherlands in *intendances* soon followed.[33]

On that very same May 14th, the governors ordered de Fierlant to return to his position as president of the Great Council and to call on all other members—with the exception of de Laing and Van der Fosse who were still in government service—to take back their seats.[34] On May 17th, de Fierlant replied with a request

---

[30] Bruneel, Claude and Hoyois, Jean-Paul. 2001. *Les grands commis des Pays-Bas autrichiens: dictionnaire biographique du personnel des institutions centrales*. Brussels: Algemeen Rijksarchief, 622–623; Lefevre, Joseph. 1928. *Le conseil du gouvernement général.* Brussels: Lamertin, 86–87.

[31] *ROPBA*, t. 13, pp. 15–16, February 17, 1787. De le Vielleuze received the same assignment for Hainaut and Tournai, de Robiano for Brabant and Gerden for Luxembourg.

[32] *ROPBA*, t. 13, p. 79, May 14, 1787. It should be noted that this ordinance did not come from Joseph II: at that time he was completely unaware of the situation in the Netherlands, as he himself was on a diplomatic mission to Russia. Also Gaillard, Arthur. 1898–1902. *Le Conseil de Brabant: histoire, organisation, procédure*. Brussels: Lebègue, t.1, 376–383; the establishment of the new tribunals in Hainaut had already been called off on May 7: *ROPBA*, t. 13, p. 75, May 7, 1787. It is not clear when the same ordinance was issued for Luxemburg.

[33] *ROPBA*, t. 13, p. 84, May 30, 1787. This *dépêche* for Brabant was followed by similar *dépêches* throughout June for the other provinces (e.g., June 4 for Flanders (*ROPBA*, t. 13, p. 86, June 4, 1787) June 5 for Malines (*ROPBA*, t. 13, p. 87, June 5, 1787), June 6 for Hainaut (*ROPBA*, t. 13, pp. 87–88, June 6, 1787), etc.)

[34] Brussels, ARA, GRM 135, Correspondances du Grand Conseil, f.205, May 14, 1787. The Sovereign Council of Justice continued to exist—albeit with extremely limited authority—until the end of October 1787. Cf. Lefevre, Joseph. 1928. *Le conseil du gouvernement général.* Brussels: Lamertin.

for further instructions: should he recall Van Velde, who was still working for the *Conseil du gouvernement général* and what would the policy be towards councilor Ludovisi, given that the Court of Appeal of Luxemburg had not been included in the ordinance of May 14th and was supposedly still functioning? Moreover, de Fierlant also wanted the case files which had been sent to Brussels on April 20th, including the inventory, to be returned to Malines.[35] On May 18th, the president officially announced that the Great Council had resumed its tasks.[36] Six days later, the first new lawsuits were distributed.[37] Officially, the Great Council had only been abolished for 2 weeks[38] and seemed to have smoothly returned to 'business as usual' a mere 10 days after the revocation of the new legal system. In October, councilors Van der Fosse and de Laing also returned to the Great Council, leaving only Van Velde's seat empty.[39]

Nevertheless, appearances are deceptive: for the entire period up until 1794, a return to normality was never achieved. While the *Correspondances* of the Great Council may abound in the discussion of petty issues—such as the succession of the *chauffe-cire* or the *épices* the councilors were entitled to for working a revision case—there were unmistakable signs that several provincial Estates and councils, as well as an ever larger part of the general population, were still in a rebellious mood. In those insecure times, the Great Council was one of the few courts of justice the government could still rely on. Inevitably, the Council's steadfast loyalty to the sovereign had repercussions on its reputation to the general public, and contributed to the continued erosion of the court's popularity.

When over the course of 1788, the inhabitants of Malines became increasingly aware of the Great Council's role as loyal agent of the Austrian Emperor, they responded by directing their anger at its members. As a result of an order of the Great Council to some seminarians to leave the Archbishopric Seminary—the issue of the General Seminary still aroused the spirits—a mob avenged itself on the councilors on August 2, 1788. Advocate-fiscal de Stassart in particular took a serious beating: not only was he himself physically attacked, but his home was completely ransacked. While the councilors might have been unwavering in their loyalty, they also feared for their own safety, especially since they had become responsible for the prosecution of the August 2 rebellion, and rumors were flying that the garrison in Malines would be reduced.[40] Trauttmansdorff himself reassured the members of the Great Council that there would be no reduction in the number of troops and that the government was well aware, in the present circumstances, of the need for protection for the Great Council.[41] Multiple case files in the archives of the office-fiscal

[35] Brussels, ARA, GRM 135, Correspondances du Grand Conseil, f.207, May 17, 1787.

[36] Brussels, ARA, GRM 135, Correspondances du Grand Conseil, f.220, May 18, 1787.

[37] Cf. Excel database: distribution records of the eighteenth century Great Council.

[38] In practice, it was probably closer to 3 weeks, given that the councilors had to pack up their files and move to their new assignments.

[39] Brussels, ARA, GRM 135, Correspondances du Grand Conseil, f.276, October 20, 1787.

[40] Brussels, ARA, GRM 136, Correspondances du Grand Conseil, f.102–103, September 5, 1788.

[41] Brussels, ARA, GRM 136, Correspondances du Grand Conseil, f.104, September 7, 1788.

prove that the Great Council did in fact follow orders and prosecuted several of the troublemakers.[42]

While all this was going on, the Council also had to deal with opposition from its subordinate tribunals. Both the Magistrate of Malines and the Council of Flanders continued—as they had done in previous times[43]—to question the jurisdiction of the Great Council. The former, boasting some old privileges, claimed that it only had to publish ordinances that came directly from the government and not those that reached the Magistrate by way of the Great Council.[44] The aldermen even took advantage of the extraordinary circumstances to attempt to convince the central government of the absolute necessity of this measure: on one occasion, the Magistrate informed the government that it was willing to provide some additional funds that had been requested, but argued that first certain concessions were needed to persuade the guilds in the *Breede Raad* (Large Council).[45] If the Magistrate of Malines was again allowed to publish ordinances and decrees without the intervention of the Great Council, it could easily win over the guilds to award the requested money.[46] The government, however, would not budge.

The Council of Flanders, on the other hand, refused multiple times to send files from appeal cases to the Great Council, arguing that, in those specific lawsuits, appeal was, by definition, not possible.[47] Every single time, the Great Council had to petition the government in order to establish its jurisdiction, spending a lot of time (and money!) asserting its authority against the claims of its subordinate tribunals.[48]

---

[42] Brussels, ARA, GRMOF 719, procès contre André Stevens, dit Verbiest—Affaire du 2 août 1788; GRMOF 720, Procès contre Rombaut De Ry—Affaire du 2 août 1788; GRMOF 721, Procès contre Jean-Baptiste Everaerts—Affaire du 2 août 1788; GRMOF 722, Procès contre Gilles Broers—Affaire du 2 août 1788; GRMOF 724, Affaire du Grand Séminaire Archiépiscopal de Mechelen, du 2 août 1788; GRMOF 726, Procès contre Joseph van Eesbeecke (ex-séminariste) (Affaire du Grand Séminaire); GRMOF 727, Procès contre Nicolas Peeters (Affaire du Séminaire, 2 août 1788); GRMOF 1728, Procès contre Rombaut van den Avont, dit *Lummen majoor* (Affaire du 2 août 1788).

[43] Cf. supra, Chap. 2.

[44] Brussels, ARA, GRM 135, Correspondances du Grand Conseil, f.277, October 1787; f.289, October 28, 1787; GRM 136, f.106–107, September 23, 1788; GRM 137, f.3, January 20, 1789.

[45] The *Breede* Raad of Malines consisted of the Magistrate supplemented with representatives of the city's guilds.

[46] Malines, Stadsarchief Mechelen, Archives de la ville de Malines, affaires civiles et ecclesiastiques 23, November 22, 1788. The numbering of the records in this archival fund no longer corresponds to that mentioned in the inventory: Hermans, Victor and Van Doren, Pierre.-Joseph. 1859–1896. *Inventaire des archives de la ville de Malines*. Malines: Van Velsen. The new numbering can only be found in the adapted inventory available in the reading room of the *Stadsarchief.*

[47] E.g., Brussels, ARA, GRM 136, Correspondances du Grand Conseil, f.1, January 8, 1788; f.201–202, November 8, 1788; GRM 137, f.20–29, February 9, 1789; f.95, June 7, 1789.

[48] In 1791 the Great Council sent an overview of all conflicts of jurisdiction it had been engaged in since October 1788, requesting the government to refund the costs. Not only does this list demonstrate that the majority of the conflicts of jurisdiction were fought out with the Council of Flanders, but also that the expenses were relatively high, amounting to slightly more than 451 florins. See: Brussels, ARA, GRM 138, Correspondances du Grand Conseil, f.58–59.

Nevertheless, in these times, the Great Council generally received full support of the Privy Council.[49]

The government's reliance on the Great Council as a bulwark against attempts by the provincial councils and Estates to expand their authority became even more evident on June 6, 1789, when Joseph II abolished the Council of Brabant and transferred its jurisdiction to the Great Council.[50] Two additional chambers were to be established in Brussels, composed of a few councilors of the Great Council in addition to selected members of the Council of Brabant who had been loyal to the emperor.[51] Several rebellious councilors of the Council of Brabant were incarcerated in the citadel of Antwerp;[52] Chancellor de Crumpipen retreated to his castle in Temse.[53] On June 20th, the new councilors of the Great Council were sworn in by president de Fierlant, *i.c.* Duchesne, Orts, de Villegas de Pellenberg, Anthonis, Van Langhendonck, Staquet and (Jean François) de Fierlant.[54] They were joined by councilors Van der Fosse, Ghison, Goubau, de Laing, Diu and Cottin from Malines;[55] de Fierlant personally presided over the Brussels sessions, which *de facto* reduced the 'original' Council of Malines to a mere satellite of its Brussels counterpart. These events clearly underscore the emperor's wish to have a tribunal in Brabant he could truly rely on.

Over the course of 1789, the Great Council—both in Malines and in Brussels—received ever more powers to fight the imminent rebellion. When on July 26, 1789, secretary Reiniers and his family, as well as the rector of the university Van Leempoel were attacked in Malines, the Great Council was allowed to prosecute the case with only five members, if needed, although for a *grand criminel* trial, seven coun-

---

[49] Brussels, ARA, GRM 135, Correspondances du Grand Conseil, f.277, October 1787; f.289, October 28, 1787; GRM 136, f.106–107, September 23, 1788; f.1, January 8, 1788; f.201–202, November 8, 1788; GRM 137, f.3, January 20, 1789; f.20–29, February 9, 1789; f.95, June 7, 1789.

[50] *ROPBA*, t. 13, p. 301, June 6, 1789. The Great Council did not take over the jurisdiction over Limburg and Overmaas. The Council of Limburg was awarded sovereignty. ARA, ARR 857, sessions of July 6 and August 24, 1789.

[51] Unsurprisingly, with the exception of councilor Staquet, all had been appointed by Joseph II in January, 1788 in his attempt to introduce some loyal figures into the Council of Brabant by adding an extra chamber. Cf. *ROPBA*, t. 13, p. 142, January 12, 1788; Gaillard, Arthur. 1898–1902. *Le Conseil de Brabant: histoire, organisation, procédure*. Brussels: Lebègue, t.1, 415.

[52] Lefevre, Joseph. 1928. *Le conseil du gouvernement général.* Brussels: Lamertin, 163.

[53] Petit, Jean-Luc. 1986. Joseph de Crumpipen (1737–1789), les idées d'un haut fonctionnaire et magistrate des Pays-Bas autrichiens sur la justice de son temps. *Tijdschrift voor Rechtsgeschiedenis* 54: 132. Certainly, de Crumpipen was not counted among the disloyal members of the Council of Brabant. However, de Fierlant, as president of the Great Council, was now president of the two chambers in Brussels and it is very unlikely that de Crumpipen was willing to serve as a regular councilor under de Fierlant, opting instead to retire.

[54] Brussels, ARA, ARR 858: patent letters for the personnel of the Great Council of Malines in Brussels as well as a list of all aspirants for a position in the Council. The majority of the latter were victims of the abolition of the new judicial structure.

[55] Gaillard, Arthur. 1898–1902. *Le Conseil de Brabant: histoire, organisation, procédure*. Brussels: Lebègue, t.1, 426. The presence of both Diu and Goubau is somewhat remarkable, as it means that both the procurator-general and the advocate-fiscal moved to Brussels.

cilors were usually the minimum. Moreover, councilor de Steenhault was assigned to temporarily act as deputy procurator-general in order to deal with the enormous amount of criminal trials flooding the tribunal.[56] On August 12th, an order reached the Great Council, both in Brussels and in Malines that an adequate number of councilors had to remain in office during the upcoming holiday period to deal with criminal trials.[57] On October 8th, procurator-general Diu was made exempt from assisting in the regular sessions of the Great Council for 6 weeks, with preservation of *épices*, in order to speed up his work on the large amount of extraordinary affairs.[58] On October 29th, an additional deputy procurator-general was nominated to the Great Council—advocate de Swerte—with the specific assignment to assist the *markgraaf* of Antwerp in the prosecution of '*cas royaux*', so that the Magistrate of Antwerp—which was clearly untrustworthy—would not deal with them.[59]

A letter procurator-general Diu wrote late November 1789 to advocate-fiscal Goubau illustrates that the fiscals of the Great Council worked tirelessly to root out rebellion. In a rather personal message to his colleague he confides his frustrations about his incapacity to deal with the—by now fugitive—Cardinal of Malines and enumerates the actions he is undertaking to prosecute suspected patriots, such as the parish priest of *Sint Jan* and the secretaries of the Magistrates of Reet and Rumst. Yet, Diu was also aware of the potential futility of their efforts: as an example, he mentioned that, although the Magistrate of Malines was prepared to set up a paling to protect the city from a possible patriotic invasion, it claimed to be unable to find any workers who were willing to erect the palisades. In fact, the only people the Magistrate managed to recruit were 'handicapped'.[60]

Diu turned out to be right: his letter is the last entry in the *Correspondances* of the Great Council until October 16, 1790. Trautmansdorff's attempt to completely reverse the vindictive policies of the latter half of 1789 by reinstating all privileges of the provincial Estates and Councils was to no avail. By late November, the patriotic army was victorious in its first battles. On December 12th, the Austrian troops were forced to leave Brussels. Four days later the Provisional Committee of Malines suspended the Great Council and ordered all former members of the tribunal to turn in their documents pertaining to undecided lawsuits.[61] Contrary to the provincial councils, there was no question that the Great Council could continue its work because it had discredited itself too much. Apart from that, it was also highly doubtful that many members would be willing to switch loyalties from the Austrian Emperor to their former nemeses.

Why did the members of the Great Council never openly protest any of the decisions of the Austrian Emperor—although it is hard to imagine that none of them nurtured any doubts about the complete reorganization of the judicial administra-

[56] Brussels, ARA, GRM 137, Correspondances du Grand Conseil, f.153, July 29, 1789.

[57] Brussels, ARA, GRM 137, Correspondances du Grand Conseil, f.163, August 12, 1789.

[58] Brussels, ARA, GRM 137, Correspondances du Grand Conseil, f.187, October 8, 1789.

[59] Brussels, ARA, GRM 137, Correspondances du Grand Conseil, f. 202, October 29, 1789.

[60] Brussels, ARA, GRM 137, Correspondances du Grand Conseil, f. 209–210, November 23, 1789.

[61] *ROPBA*, t. 13, p. 390, December 16, 1789.

tion in early 1787—and even actively supported its policies? The most important reason is undoubtedly the special position the Great Council occupied in the Austrian Netherlands: contrary to the Councils of Brabant, Hainaut, Flanders, Namur etc., the Great Council was not associated with provincial Estates and had not sworn an oath to uphold the customs of any specific province; therefore, it was not subject to political pressure from any one interest group. Moreover, the councilors of the Great Council owed their careers, status, position and income solely to the central government; they were neither pressured nor supported by provincial Estates. That said, the majority of them probably genuinely believed in the legitimacy of Austrian rule and saw it as their duty to defend and enhance it. Either way, from 1787 to 1789, the tribunal had proved to be first and foremost the Emperor's Council.

5.2.2 Revolution[62] and Restoration: December 1789–November 1792

With its statement of December 16, 1789, the Provisional Committee of the city of Malines declared the Great Council to be deprived of its jurisdiction, not so much because it had been formally abolished but because it was in the first place the 'Emperor's Council' and its members were still bound by their oath. Given that the Belgian provinces no longer acknowledged Joseph II as their rightful sovereign, the Great Council had lost its reason to exist. As a consequence, the members had to turn in the papers they still had in their possession and give up all privileges and exemptions they had enjoyed before being suspended. In the same breath, the Provisional Committee declined every responsibility for the pillaging of certain councilors' houses, an action inspired by the 'hatred of the people' on the first day of the Revolution.[63]

Yet, even if it was out of the question that the Great Council in its present form could continue to operate, the members of the Provisional Committee soon became anxious to re-establish a new sovereign council in Malines, this time with jurisdiction over *all* Belgian provinces. Representatives were sent to Brussels to present and defend such a project to Van der Noot en Van Eupen. The need to maintain the prosperity of the city of Malines was the only argument they could put forward in

[62] For information on the Brabant Revolution, see e.g.: Cosemans, A. 1955. De Brabantse Omwenteling en de vestiging van een nieuw bewind in de Zuidelijke Nederlanden. In *Algemene Geschiedenis der Nederlanden*, eds. Jacob Presser e.a., t.8, 170–194. Zeist: De Haan; Craeybeckx, Jan. 1967. De Brabantse Omwenteling: een conservatieve opstand in een achterlijk land? *Tijdschrift voor geschiedenis* 80, 303–330; De Gryse, Piet, Lefèvre, Patrick and Lorette, Jean eds. 1984. *Handelingen van het colloquium over de Brabantse Omwenteling, 13–14 Oktober 1983*. Brussels: Koninklijk Legermuseum; Heirwegh, Jean-Jacques. 1987. Het einde van het Ancien Régime en de revoluties. *Oostenrijks België 1713–1794: de Zuidelijke Nederlanden onder de Oostenrijkse Habsburgers*, ed. Hervé Hasquin, 467–504. Brussels: Gemeentekrediet van België; Janssens, Paul, Roegiers, Jan and Vanhemelryck, Fernand. 1990. *Revolutie in Brabant 1787–1793*. Brussels: UFSAL; Tassier, Suzanne. 1989. *Les démocrates belges de 1789*. Brussels: Hayez.

[63] Brussels, ARA, GRM 175/10, 1789–1790, suppression.

favor of a revived 'Great Council', invested with an even more extended authority than the former one.[64] Apparently, the inhabitants of Malines were suddenly aware of the importance of the detested Great Council for the economic welfare of their city. It is unknown what came of this proposition, but given the provinces' desire for sovereignty and independence, and their wish to keep common coordinating institutions to a strict minimum, it is virtually impossible that they would consider such a new council.

Either way, the Provisional Committee did not spend any time debating this question before dismantling the Great Council. On December 17, 1789, two aldermen of Malines and a former clerk of the Great Council were delegated to procure the keys to the tribunal's premises from the porter and to seal its chambers as well as the president's residence. The entrance to the fiscal chamber had to be forcibly opened, as well as that to the registry, since the porter did not have access to these locations. In the days and weeks to come, several people—mostly former proctors, secretaries or notaries of the Great Council—were busy making an inventory of the papers and transporting several of the more interesting documents to the city hall. Moreover, the Great Council's stock of candles and wood was confiscated. Finally, the Provisional Committee's delegates paid a visit to several councilors' homes such as Pouppez', Diu's, Vanderfosse's, Van Volxem's, de Laing's, and Goubau's to assemble and remove files in their possession. When this operation was finished, around the end of January 1790, the chambers of the Great Council were entirely sealed off. Only once were they reopened again, when on September 24, 1790 the porter informed the Provisional Committee that a shutter of the fiscal chamber had sprung open and that people were throwing stones at the windows. After that, no one entered the grounds until December, 1790.[65]

The fate of the councilors of the Great Council during the Brabant Revolution is much harder to reconstruct. It is certain that they did not go into exile as a corpus. The majority probably followed the government to Luxemburg or abroad. Access to the president's house, for instance, was in his absence given by one of his domestics. Goubau too was almost certainly away from Malines: it was his servant Joannes Guilliams who was interrogated by the provisional bailiff of the city about what might be found in the advocate-fiscal's home.[66] But where exactly did Goubau go during the revolution? Many officials sat out the insurrection in Cologne, but it seems unlikely that Goubau went there as well.[67] Is it possible that the advocate-fiscal failed

64 Brussels, ARA, GRM 175/10, 1789–1790, addendum 2. Malines, February 26, 1790.

65 Brussels, ARA, GRM 3: Documents relatifs aux archives du Grand Conseil, pendant et après la révolution brabançonne et les invasions françaises, 1789–1794, f.1–75.

66 Brussels, ARA, GRM 3, f.2 and f.72.

67 In an account of his adventures during the 1789 Revolution, deputy procurator-general de Vivario relates that, after he accompanied the rest of the governmental councils in their escape from Brussels to Luxemburg and later to Cologne, he stayed in the company of procurator-general Diu. Not only does he not mention Goubau, but he specifically states that both fiscals were in Düsseldorf during the first French invasion, thereby implying that Goubau was not in Cologne in 1790. "Tout cela est si vrai, qu'au cas que votre excellence puisse se former le moindre doute sur ce que j'ai l'honneur de lui représenter, elle pourra très facilement s'en convaincre par les conseillers

to escape in time and that he was captured by the revolutionaries in 1789? In 1796, Goubau himself claimed that he was imprisoned in 1790.[68] Yet, he also mentioned that his emigration of 1794 was the third one since 1790. Maybe he was released after spending time in prison and decided to flee the Netherlands after all?

Similar doubts about his whereabouts surround councilor Pouppez. It seems that he decided to remain in Malines as he himself opened the door to the delegates of the Provisional Committee searching for papers of the Great Council.[69] Yet, in 1795, proctor Benckendorff claimed that he spent the majority of his emigration in 1790 in the company of Pouppez.[70] Potentially, Pouppez initially preferred to stay in Malines, but changed his mind when the scale of the rebellion became clear to him. Indeed, not only Goubau, but also Benckendorff and de Vivario mentioned the persecutions of all loyal subjects at the hands of the insurgents, not to mention the losses and damages in terms of property they all suffered.

We can assume that particularly those councilors who were members of the Great Council of Malines for Brabant had every reason to go into exile, as they were most presumably still in Brussels at the time of the Revolution—and therefore close to the rest of the government which left the country—and were almost certain to incur the wrath of the people if they stayed put. There can be no doubt that they, as the preeminent agents of the emperor's policies against the Brabant privileges and liberties, were very much disliked by the inhabitants of the capital.

Of those members of the Great Council who did prefer to remain in Malines, only councilor Douglas was found prepared to work for the temporary government and swear the patriotic oath. Stressed as he was by his financial problems, having only limited personal funds, no income from his councillorship and a wife and seven children to take care of—or at least, that was the official explanation afterwards—he had accepted the position of pensionary to the city of Malines.[71] The sources do not reveal if he might have had any sympathies at all for the patriots and their fight for independence from the Austrian crown.[72] Regardless, his infidelity

---

fiscaux du Grand Conseil, dont le conseiller et procureur-général Diu a été également à Trèves, tous les deux à Düsseldorf ..." Vienna, FHKA, Österreichische Kamerale 2309, N°15: request of deputy procurator-general de Vivario. Würzburg, April 27, 1795.

[68] Vienna, FHKA, Österreichische Kamerale 2309, N°12. Request of Goubau for an increase of his pension. Regensburg, December 28 1795. He repeated these allegations in another request on January 9, 1796.

[69] Brussels, ARA, GRM 3, f.25, January 16, 1790.

[70] Vienna, FHKA, Österreichische Kamerale 2309, N°23. Request of proctor Benckendorff, Regensburg, December 10, 1795.

[71] Brussels, ARA, GRM 232, f.19: observations sur le rétablissement du Grand Conseil.

[72] Being of Hungarian descent, he seems to be the least likely suspect among the councilors to have had any other motives than strictly financial ones to serve the patriotic cause. Nevertheless, certain highly placed officials in the Austrian administration did agree with the principles of the Revolution. One of the most famous examples is without a doubt Edouard Walckiers, member of the Council of Finance in 1784 and later the financier of the group connected to Vonck. Cf. Bruneel, Claude. 2001. Le personnel de la chambre des comptes des Pays-Bas face à la Révolution Belgique (1787–1792). *Handelingen van de Koninklijke Commissie voor Geschiedenis* 156: 1–252.

would not be held against him, because 'everyone' testified that, in as much as it had been in his power, he had used his influence for the greater good.[73]

The 'United Belgian States' only lasted for some 11 months before crumbling down, mainly due to internal strife and lack of external support. While Van der Noot never lost hope that he could rally the support of especially Prussia and the United Provinces, it was Emperor Leopold II who in the end was specifically backed up by those two countries as well as by Great Britain. On October 14, Leopold II proclaimed that he would again recognize the laws and privileges of the Netherlands as they had been in force under Maria Theresa and that he would grant a general amnesty. If, however, the patriots did not voluntarily surrender, he would send his armies.[74] In late November 1790, the Austrian troops marched into the Southern Netherlands, encountering almost no resistance from the remaining badly equipped and incompetently led patriotic army. Early December, the Austrians reoccupied Brussels, marking the beginning of the first restoration.[75]

On January 17, 1791, the new minister plenipotentiary Mercy-Argenteau commissioned de Fierlant to summon the members of the Great Council to resume their office.[76] Councilor Douglas, as well as all other personnel of the Council who had taken the patriotic oath, were to be reintegrated on the express condition that they would renew their allegiance to the emperor. Van Velde, who had been called to Brussels in 1787, also had to return to his position at the tribunal.[77] Given that de Fierlant was still absent from Malines, de Waepenaert as senior councilor administered the oath to Douglas, Rijckaert, Van Provijn and Picard and announced that the Council would reassemble on January 26th and have its first day of pleadings within 3 days.[78]

Although the members of the Great Council expressed their joy at the restoration of the Austrian authority and declared they would be willing to forget all the insults and violence they had endured because of their loyalty to the Austrian Crown, their devotion was not unconditional.[79] They claimed that the difficult times they had

---

[73] Brussels, ARA, GRM 232, f.19.

[74] *ROPBA*, t. 13, pp. 605–609, October 14, 1790.

[75] L. Dhondt remarked that while the revolution seemingly failed, the insurgents did manage to achieve their goals through the restoration by Leopold II. Dhondt, Luc. 1993. *Verlichte monarchie, Ancien Regime en revolutie*. t.7. Ghent: RUG, 580.

[76] Before the councilors resumed their activities, an extensive inquiry was made into what had happened to the archives of the Great Council during the revolutionary period. This investigation revealed that the majority of the Great Council's documents had remained at the tribunal and that its chambers had been sealed. Some papers, however, had been transported to the city hall, but they apparently had remained untouched during the entire period. Brussels, ARA, GRM 3, f.1–75.

[77] Brussels, ARA, GRM 138, Correspondances du Grand Conseil 1790–1791, f.9–10, January 13, 1791.

[78] Brussels, ARA, GRM 138, Correspondances du Grand Conseil 1790–1791, f.11, January 19, 1791.

[79] Brussels, ARA, GRM 138, Correspondances du Grand Conseil 1790–1791, f.15, February 1, 1791. Copy of a letter from the councilors of the Great Council to Governors Albert and Marie-Christine.

recently gone through had forced them to make even larger expenses than normal. In addition, they had not received their salary or the usual income they gained from their work as councilors. Therefore, they asked Governors Albert and Marie-Christine for full compensation of their damages. As their annual salary stood at 1200 florins and they had not been paid from the first of November, 1789 up until January 31, 1791, they should receive 1500 florins each. Moreover, in an average year, their *émoluments* added up to 2800 florins, which for the same period meant a loss of 3000 florins. They claimed that, altogether, each councilor should be paid 4500 florins in outstanding salary and *emoluments*. Even though they acknowledged that, strictly spoken, they were not entitled to this payment, they hoped that their loyalty and faithfulness to the emperor would work in their favor.[80]

Apparently, the Austrian government was in no hurry to compensate the councilors. In December 1791, the latter repeated their request and once again reminded the governors of all the offenses, humiliations and even fear for their very lives they had suffered out of devotion to the emperor. The councilors repeated that they were unable to bear the financial losses which, as already mentioned, amounted to 4500 florins. This time, however, they acknowledged that several members—both among those who had gone abroad and those who had stayed at home—already had received either 2700 or 2250 florins, but they considered those payments as compensation for their sufferings rather than as an attempt to compensate their lost revenues.[81] Whether their request was ever granted is unknown; the fact that there are no more petitions does suggest that they were at least partially refunded.

Another controversial issue after the Restoration was the question of how far the implications of the promised return to the situation at the end of Maria Theresa's reign would reach. For the Great Council, it was especially important to know if it also meant that the Councils of Luxembourg and Tournai would fall again under its jurisdiction. Already in 1782, the Great Council had protested its loss of authority over both councils[82] and it now saw an opportunity to repeat its plea.[83]

First, the councilors noted, the Great Council had been established in the fourteenth century [*sic*] to support the 'supreme authority' of the sovereign; accordingly, every assault on its jurisdiction should be regarded as some sort of indirect challenge to his authority. In the case of the Council of Tournai in particular, they claimed that there could be no doubt that the late Emperor Joseph II had made a poorly informed

[80] Brussels, ARA, GRM 138, Correspondances du Grand Conseil 1790–1791, f.17, February 12, 1791. Copy of a letter from the councilors of the Great Council to minister plenipotentiary Mercy-Argenteau.

[81] Brussels, ARA, GRM 138, Correspondances du Grand Conseil 1790–1791, f.127–128, December 17, 1791.

[82] We have not been able to retrieve the Great Council's original protest letter. However, Hubert in his account of the voyage of Emperor Joseph II in the Netherlands, recounts parts of it. Unfortunately, his reference to 'Secretairerie d'Etat et de Guerre, liasse 623' turned out to be a dead end, potentially because the *liasses* in the Secretairerie have been renumbered. Cf. Hubert, Eugène. 1900. *Le voyage de l'empereur Joseph II dans les Pays-Bas (31 mai 1781–1727 juillet 1781): etude d'histoire politique et diplomatique*. Brussels, Lebègue, 162, footnotes 1–4.

[83] Brussels, ARA, GRM 138, Correspondances du Grand Conseil, f.25–40, February 24, 1791.

choice when he decided to remove it from the jurisdiction of the Great Council and make the Council of Hainaut responsible for dealing with appeals against its sentences. In fact, the main reason for the transfer of jurisdiction from Malines to Mons had been the proximity and close relationships between Hainaut and Tournai. However, the councilors maintained, except for some small parts of Tournai bordering Hainaut, there were almost no links between the two provinces: Hainaut had its own charters which did not have a single connection to any laws of the other Belgian provinces, while Tournai's customs were comparable to those of Flanders.[84] As a consequence, the Great Council argued, the judges in Mons were absolutely unfit to deal with appeals from the Council of Tournai as they were only acquainted with their own particular customs. Moreover, the Malines councilors were assured that the inhabitants of Tournai wished for no more than to be able again to appeal to the Great Council. Finally, they wondered why the Great Council—a tribunal which was not associated with any specific province, which was bound by an oath to the sovereign and which had never quivered in its loyalty—should be less worthy than a provincial council to regain its former jurisdiction.

According to the members of the Great Council, the consequences of the sovereignty awarded to the Council of Luxemburg were even graver than those of the incorporation of the Council of Tournai into the jurisdiction of the Council of Hainaut. While the councilors admitted that some of the issues addressed by the *lettres patentes* of August 1, 1782[85] were legitimate—there was a considerable distance between Luxemburg and Malines, certain case files had to be translated, there was a certain amount of export of financial resources from the province to Malines and the possibility to appeal certainly prolonged the settlement of a case—they argued that the drawbacks of Luxemburg's sovereignty were far greater.

First, the inhabitants of Luxemburg had lost the opportunity to take their appeals to a judge who was not a native of their own province: given that the members of the Council of Luxemburg were obligated to understand and speak German, they were all by definition born there. Moreover, according to the Great Council, almost all councilors of the Council of Luxemburg came from the capital, as there were no decent candidates in the countryside. As a result, the recruitment policy inevitably led to some degree of bias in the sentences of the Council of Luxemburg and made the ability to appeal to the Great Council even more essential.

Secondly, the councilors maintained that the distance between Luxemburg and Malines was, if anything, a counter-argument to letting the Council of Luxemburg keep its sovereign status: the further a provincial tribunal was removed from the direct supervision of the government, the more need there was for a superior court to control its actions and sentences. According to the Great Council, recent events had demonstrated that overly cozy relationships between provincial Estates and councils

---

[84] For more information on institutions in Tournai and Hainaut, see: Cauchies, Jean Marie, Desmaele, Bernard and Mariage, Florian. 2009. *Les institutions publiques régionales et locales en Hainaut et Tournais-Tournaisis sous l'Ancien Régime*. Brussels: Algemeen Rijksarchief.

[85] These patent letters had officially granted sovereignty to the Council of Luxemburg. Cf. supra, Chap. 3.

could prejudice the interests of the sovereign.[86] Thirdly, the Malines councilors reasoned that both the costs and the translation issues were less than dramatic: only 16 to 17 appeals from Luxemburg were handled at the Great Council each year[87] and the parties only seldom came to Malines in person, while councilors equally rarely went to Luxemburg on a commission. Moreover, less than a third of those 16 Luxemburg cases had to be translated, so the expenses were very limited, while delays were short and mistakes so far had never occurred. Furthermore, the Great Council asserted that the financial outflow from Luxemburg to Malines—another argument used in 1782 to grant sovereignty to the Council of Luxemburg—amounted to a mere 7000 à 8000 florins each year, while in several cases the litigants were not even inhabitants from the province but merely went to court over properties they had in Luxemburg. As a result, the money drain was almost negligible.

Finally, the Great Council certainly had to admit that appeals caused delays to the final settlement of the case.[88] Nevertheless, according to the councilors, this was not a sufficient reason to let the Council of Luxemburg keep its sovereignty: the possibility to appeal against a sentence was a basic right and a necessary guarantee for an individual's civil liberties. Therefore, the disadvantages in no way outweighed the advantages. The Great Council argued that the small number of appeals each year proved that people did not frivolously exercise their right to take their cases to a superior judge. If need be, adjustments could be made to the appeal procedure, such as determining a minimum stake. Either way, the councilors concluded, it was obvious that in the interest of both the public and the sovereign, the Councils of Luxemburg and Tournai should again fall under the jurisdiction of the Great Council.

Although we have no official response from the government, we may well presume that the Great Council's request was not granted, if only because it would have produced an official ordinance revoking the 1782 decree. The sovereign status of the Council of Luxemburg was probably one of the few reforms of Joseph II that did survive the ravages of time.[89] There is a certain irony to this, given that it increased the autonomy of a province instead of reducing it, as foreseen in the emperor's grand scheme of abolishing all provincial councils and bringing the locally based first instance tribunals under the jurisdiction of a central court of appeal, and eventually under the sovereign Council of Justice.

That the Great Council was not restored to its pre-1782 jurisdiction does not mean that the authorities stopped using it as the instrument of sovereign power it had proved to be in the build-up to the Brabant Revolution. Certainly, the Great Council

[86] The memorandum of the Great Council, however, fails to mention that the Estates and the Council of Luxemburg were the only ones to stay loyal to the Austrian Emperor.

[87] This seems to be a more or less accurate estimate. In the 1760s, an average of 17.3 appeals from Luxemburg a year was handled at the Great Council. During the 1770s, this number decreased to 13.2. Cf. Excel database: distributions books of the eighteenth century Great Council.

[88] Cf. supra, Chap. 4. We demonstrated that, on average, appeals coming from Luxemburg were the lengthiest lawsuits dealt with at the Great Council.

[89] The *médianate* was also restored to its pre-Josephian rate on February 8, 1792. *ROPBA*, t. 14, p. 75, February 8, 1792.

lost its jurisdiction over Brabant: the restoration provided for the reinstatement of the provincial Council of Brabant.[90] Nevertheless, several members of the Great Council were called forward to take up a seat in provincial commissions, established in Namur and Flanders, which had to deal with compensation requests for damages done during the Brabant Revolution.

The government was somewhat bothered by these claims for indemnification: on the one hand, Leopold II had proclaimed a general amnesty, but on the other hand, he could not ignore the losses of property suffered by subjects loyal to the Austrian Crown. Given that it was deemed unwise to have the provincial councils deal with demands for compensation—it was feared that it might again arouse spirits—commissions were established in the different provinces in order to quietly handle these cases trough reconciliation. The most important task of the commission members was to accommodate the parties and to determine a reasonable compensation for the losses suffered; hopes were high that in this non-confrontational manner, claims could be settled as quietly as possible. In Namur, councilors Ghison and de Steenhault had a seat in the commission, next to a member of the Council of Namur and an alderman of the city;[91] in Flanders, councilors de Laing and Reniers were appointed, together with two members of the Council of Flanders.[92] Additionally, the Great Council as a corpus received jurisdiction over those claims the Namur commission could not settle amicably; in the case of Flanders, the Great Council did not have such an authority.[93]

Apart from these institutionalized commissions, the Great Council also had to deal with individual demands, often from subordinate officers who had been mistreated by the revolutionaries in their hometown and were now unable to return to their former positions because they had made themselves *persona non grata* in the eyes of the residents of the locality where they used to hold office. Apparently, the amnesty of the Austrian government at times went so far that it would not reinstate a former officer who, because of his loyalty to the emperor, had discredited himself in the eyes of his fellow townsmen, but would instead prefer to relocate him to a different city. This, for example, was the case of J.B. Pansius, the former bailiff

[90] On February 15, 1791, the Council of Brabant was officially re-established and de Crumpipen was restored as its chancellor. *ROPBA*, t. 14, pp. 10–11, February 25, 1791. The restoration, however, did not go smoothly. For several months, even up until the French invasion of November 1792, the government and the Brabant Estates bickered over the composition of the Council: should the seven members who had served in the Great Council in Brussels be reintegrated—which was unacceptable to the Estates—and/or could the five members who had been appointed by the patriots in 1789–1790 remain in their seats—which was unacceptable to the government? Cf. Gaillard, Arthur. 1898–1902. *Le Conseil de Brabant: histoire, organisation, procédure*. Brussels: Lebègue, t.1, 442–459.

[91] Brussels, ARA, GRM 139, Correspondances du Grand Conseil, f.18–21, February 14, 1792.

[92] Brussels, ARA, GRM 139, Correspondances du Grand Conseil, f.64–68, April 23, 1792.

[93] In Brabant, attempts were made to establish a similar commission; however, the Estates of Brabant were obstructive and refused to provide the necessary funds. Either way, no member of the Great Council would ever have occupied a seat in this commission as they all had to come from the Council of Brabant. The same is true for Hainaut, where a commission was established in late 1791. Cf. Brussels, ARA, GR, Register 482, f.344–349, October 8, 1791.

of Heist-op-den-Berg. He claimed that, as a commissioner for the *intendant*,[94] he had been maltreated and even imprisoned because he had been loyal to his rightful sovereign. Since he had now lost the 'public trust' of the people of Heist, he could not return to his former post. Exalting his many accomplishments for the Austrian regime—he had been a recruiter for the government and had stood his ground during all times, even when 'surrounded by his enemies'—he requested the fiscals to be transferred to the now vacant position of bailiff of Malines.[95]

In addition, the fiscals of the Great Council were again at the forefront of the continuing fight against patriotic tumult, although much less so than in the period from 1787 to 1789. It seems that the Austrian government's strategy during this first restoration consisted in frantically attempting to avoid a new rebellion by not antagonizing dissenting voices and by steering clear of actions that could again arouse a rebellious fervor. In February 1791, minister plenipotentiary Mercy-Argenteau ordered advocate-fiscal Goubau to investigate the rumors concerning the existence of a certain patriotic bureau in Dendermonde and to examine if there were indeed a patriotic flag and some fire-arms lying around in the city hall. Nevertheless, while the minister plenipotentiary clearly wanted the advocate-fiscal to act against any patriotic feelings there might be in Dendermonde, he also explicitly mentioned that the investigations into the matter should be carried out in secrecy.[96]

All in all, both the *Correspondances* of the Great Council and the recommendations of the fiscals give the impression of a certain level of normality: they abound in the usual conflicts over jurisdiction, especially with the Council of Flanders, in requests from civilians to be appointed to certain positions or to get age dispensations, in the presentation of candidates for a new position at the Great Council, etc. Only a few examples can be found of direct orders to take action against suspected patriots[97] or (former) French soldiers roaming the Netherlands.[98] The only entry in the fiscals' recommendations that more or less stands out, is an order to bring proceedings against all the people who challenged judges because they were loyal to the emperor—which, of course, they had to be.[99]

---

[94] For more information on the *intendances*, see Kisters, Frédéric. 1996. Les intendances instituées par Joseph II en 1787. *Revue belge de philologie et d'histoire* 74.3–4: 761–803.

[95] Brussels, ARA, GRM 138, Correspondances du Grand Conseil, f.58–60, May 28, 1791. Apparently, he was eventually appointed bailiff of Malines. The *Correspondances* contain a request from the bailiff of Malines Pansius, dated November 14, 1793, to be refunded for his travel costs from Düsseldorf to Malines. Brussels, ARA, GRM 140, Correspondances du Grand Conseil, 1793–1794, f.249–250, November 14, 1793. The bailiff of Kalken had a similar experience: the Council of Flanders, after having declared its sovereignty, had him dismissed and even instigated criminal proceedings against him. Brussels, ARA, GRM 138, f.203, November 15, 1791.

[96] Brussels, ARA, GRMOF, BD 66, f.39–50, February 26, 1791.

[97] E.g. Brussels, ARA, GRMOF, BD 68, f.11–16, January 16, 1792.

[98] Brussels, ARA, GRMOF, BD 67, f.13–19, July 25, 1791.

[99] Brussels, ARA, GRMOF, BD 68, f.136, April 25, 1792.

On April 23, 1792, the French declared war on the Austrian Empire.[100] This proclamation caused serious unrest among the members of the Great Council. Even though the councilors claimed that they were 'assured' that the efforts of the French to invade the Netherlands would remain fruitless, they addressed a letter to the governors in early May asking for instructions in case of a French take-over.[101] The Great Council wished to avoid a scenario comparable to 1746, when it had been reproached for not having taking any precautions in case of a French invasion. In addition, the councilors reminded the governors that clear instructions—especially with regards to their archives—were even more necessary now, as in the event of an invasion by the French, they would be surrounded by domestic enemies who were to be feared even more than the French troops.

In their reply 3 days later, the governors assured the councilors in Malines that instructions would be given on time; meanwhile however, they should start packing in utmost secrecy the papers of the fiscal chamber as well as those documents that were deemed essential for the sovereign.[102] The next entry in the recommendations is the directive of the governors of November 7, to, if need be, follow the government into exile to Roermond. Preparations should be made, and horses and carriages procured in order to retreat from Malines—with all the essential archives—at the first signal from the government.[103] That order came the very next day, when it was announced that the withdrawal from the Belgian provinces was scheduled on the morning of November 9th.[104]

5.2.3 *'Liberation', Restoration, Annexation: November, 1792–June, 1794*

5.2.3.1 French Invasion and Exile

On the same November 8th, the governors announced their retreat to Roermond, assigned the administration of the country to the Provincial Estates and the City Magistrates, and ordered them to look after the government's interests.[105] They also offered the members of the provincial councils of justice the choice between continuing to perform their duties under French rule or withdrawing to any other city under Austrian authority, with a certain preference for the former solution.[106] Again on November 8th, the commander of the French 'Liberation' Army Dumouriez pro-

[100] A small French army crossed the border in June 1792, but had to withdraw soon afterwards for fear of an Austrian encirclement and due to a lack of support from the Belgian population. Polasky, Janet. 1985. *Revolution in Brussels 1787–1793*. Gembloux: Duculot, 208–209.

[101] Brussels, ARA, GRMOF, BD 68, f.143, May 3, 1792.

[102] Brussels, ARA, GRMOF, BD 68, f.144, May 6, 1792.

[103] Brussels, ARA, GRMOF, BD 68, f.145, November 7, 1792.

[104] Brussels, ARA, GRMOF, BD 68, f.146, November 8, 1792.

[105] *ROPBA*, t. 14, p. 145, November 8, 1792.

[106] *ROPBA*, t. 14, pp. 145–146, November 8, 1792.

claimed that the Belgian people were now freed from Austrian rule and promised that the French would not annex the Southern Netherlands or in any other way tamper with the country's own chosen form of government. Nevertheless, he warned that any village or city that might not enthusiastically embrace the 'liberty' offered by the French would be destroyed.[107]

The Great Council preferred not to await the French take-over of Malines and left the city at half past three on the morning of November 9, together with its most important records. Contrary to what happened in 1789, not a single member stayed behind in Malines; some did leave their families in the city, others brought them along. Their journey took them to Louvain, Tirlemont—where the army unit of *dragons de Latour* that had accompanied them parted—Saint-Trond, Tongres and Maastricht.[108] On November 11th, the councilors finally arrived in the city of Roermond where they were accommodated by the Magistrate in the homes of local bourgeois. Four days later, the royal treasury restituted the expenses made for the move from Malines to Roermond and paid the councilors their salaries until the end of January.

On November 16th, the members of the Great Council left Roermond for Düsseldorf, where they arrived the very next day.[109] Minister Plenipotentiary Metternich explicitly ordered the councilors to remain in Düsseldorf as private citizens and to avoid giving a hint of holding office, let alone of composing an active tribunal: that was the condition the Palatine court had stipulated before agreeing to house the members of the Great Council in Düsseldorf. The other governmental councils, such as the Privy Council, stayed behind in Roermond and continued their work from there.[110] It is not hard to imagine that the Great Council's stay in Düsseldorf must have felt as banishment from the center of activity in Roermond.

The representations made by the members of the Great Council to the minister plenipotentiary indeed reveal that they were not exactly happy—neither with their exile to Düsseldorf nor with the restrictions imposed. First of all, they requested an additional allowance on top of their regular salary: according to the councilors, Düsseldorf turned out to be a far more expensive city than Malines and their usual income of 4000 florins a year, which could barely cover their costs at home if they lived modestly, was absolutely inadequate to keep themselves and their families afloat in Düsseldorf. Additionally, a list was attached to the letter with the names of the employees of the Great Council who were responsible for the transport of the Council's archives and cash reserves, and who should receive a salary proportionate to their responsibilities and qualities. The councilors expressed the hope that—

---

[107] *ROPBA*, t. 14, pp. 147–148, November 8, 1792.

[108] Brussels, ARA, GRM 231, letters from the governors general and from Metternich-Winnebourg to the president of the Great Council, November, 1792.

[109] Councilor de Villers did not immediately accompany the rest of the members on their trip to Düsseldorf as he had fallen ill on his voyage to Roermond. He remained there for another month before he joined the Council. Vienna, HHStA, Belgien DDB rot 80 (alt C53). Request from de Villers to remain in Malines, July 3, 1794.

[110] Brussels, ARA, GRM 231, letters from the governors general and from Metternich-Winnebourg to the president of the Great Council.

given their unrelenting loyalty and dedication—the minister plenipotentiary would be willing to improve their sorry fate.[111]

Metternich replied that the Great Council should consider a move to a different city if Düsseldorf was too expensive, preferably to someplace where they would be able to continue their usual sessions, such as Duisburg, Rees or Emmerich in Prussian territory or Neuss or Gremberg in the Electorate of Cologne. On November 30th, president de Fierlant brushed that proposition aside. Possibly the Great Council felt that another move to a new city, different from the one in which the other governmental councils resided, was simply not worth the trouble? Not that de Fierlant explicitly mentioned the Great Council's 'expulsion' from the center of activity as a reason to stay put; he rather used an entire array of different arguments: in fact, during a meeting, he had decided together with councilors Van Velde, Ghison, Douglas, Pouppez, Goubau, de Steenhault, and de Guchtenaere that an assembly of the Great Council on foreign territory could not have any legal force. Given that the Great Council only had jurisdiction in a region ruled by the Austrian Crown and that it was for now impossible to move the tribunal to such a location, de Fierlant argued that continuing its sessions was impossible and should therefore not be taken into account as a reason for a move away from Düsseldorf. According to the Council's president, the only two arguments that should be considered were the safety of the Great Council's members, records and cash reserves, and financial concerns.

Bearing in mind these two requirements, the members of the Council were convinced that remaining in Düsseldorf was the best solution. Not only would another move inevitably generate additional expense, the councilors claimed that it was also better to be located on the right instead of on the left bank of the Rhine; in fact, the French were already threatening both the Cologne and Prussian territories. De Fierlant added that if Düsseldorf fell prey to the French troops, the councilors could sail up the Rhine to Nijmegen, either to stay there or to disperse and retreat to Bergen-op-Zoom, 's Hertogenbosch, Breda or any other city where they could survive on a tight budget.[112]

It appears that the government tried once more to persuade the Great Council of the advantages of a move to a different location; on December 8, 1792, de Fierlant explained in yet another letter why the councilors preferred to remain in Düsseldorf. First, the coming winter made travel more dangerous, while it was far from certain that a better refuge might be found, given the great number of French emigrants on the move. Secondly, the councilors maintained that the Council's records could not be safer elsewhere than in a city with a garrison, located on the right bank of the Rhine, in a territory belonging to a neutral power. As a result, the members of the Council were convinced that the present circumstances warranted a prolonged stay in Düsseldorf, especially since winter was bound to slow down the military operations of the French, the Palatine court still remained neutral and the Prussian king was starting to regain some territory. The councilors did not doubt that, if the situation changed, the minister plenipotentiary would warn them as soon as possible,

[111] Brussels, ARA, GRM 231, letter from the Great Council to Metternich-Winnebourg.

[112] Brussels, ARA, GRM 231, letter from president de Fierlant to Metternich, November 30, 1792.

and indicate a new safe haven to retreat to with their records and consigned cash reserves.[113] Until that moment, which they hoped would never come, the members of the Council preferred to remain in Düsseldorf.[114]

In the meantime, the city of Malines had fallen to the French who—as promised—had handed over their powers to an elected temporary authority.[115] On December 22, 1792, several representatives of the Magistrate made their way to the premises of the Great Council in order to secure its records, which were considered to be of great value. The library, the fiscal chamber, the registry, the entrance to the chapel and the *parquet*, ... were all closed off and sealed by mayor Van den Bossche, aldermen Burlet and de Vijlder and registrar Verlinden; sometime later, French commissioners superimposed their own seal. The warden of the Great Council Van den Eynde handed over—for the second time in 3 years—all the keys in his possession, but contrary to the patriots of 1789, the representatives of the Magistrate did not remove any documents or effects.[116]

The French commissioners were less amenable where the homes and properties of the emigrated councilors were concerned. In early January 1793, alarming reports started to leak through to Düsseldorf. On January 23rd, president de Fierlant informed Metternich of a letter advocate-fiscal Goubau had received from his wife: despite the opposition of the temporary Magistrate, French commissioners had started to seal off the homes of several councilors and had an inventory made of both their movable and immovable properties. At a later stage, all furniture, linens, silverware etc. would be sealed, except for what the individuals who lived in these houses needed. Rather panicky, de Fierlant added that unless a sufficient number of Austrian troops arrived to oust the French, the Belgian provinces would be completely crushed (*écrasées*).[117]

Three days later, the president of the Great Council wrote another letter to Metternich, informing him that the French had already taken stock in the homes of advocate-fiscal Goubau, procurator-general Diu, clerical councilor Van Volxem and others. The houses in which neither wife nor husband were present had been put under seal. Wives had been informed that if their husbands did not return within 2 months, everything would be confiscated.[118] The many messages de Fierlant sent to Metternich—another one was written on January 29th—betray his nervousness about the situation in the Austrian Netherlands. Metternich, on the other hand, never really responded to these panic-stricken letters. On February 11th, he simply notified the president of the Great Council that he had just returned from a trip to

[113] Fiscal Goubau was responsible for the conservation of the consigned cash. Cf. Brussels, ARA, DeptNed 953, f.1278, N°701, July 31, 1798.

[114] Brussels, ARA, GRM 231, letter from de Fierlant to Metternich, December 8, 1792.

[115] *ROPBA*, t. 14, pp. 196–197, November 27, 1792 and p. 205, November 29, 1792.

[116] Brussels, ARA, GRM 3, f.76–93, April 1793.

[117] Brussels, ARA, GRM 231, letter from de Fierlant to Metternich, January 23, 1793. The Austrian government and its officials had by now moved from Roermond to the city of Wesel, some 60 km north of Düsseldorf on the right bank of the Rhine.

[118] Brussels, ARA, GRM 231, letters from de Fierlant to Metternich, January 26 and 27, 1793.

Coblenz and that he merely wanted to let him and his fellow councilors know that the Privy Council had resumed its usual sessions in Wesel.[119]

Around the same time, the French started to encounter fierce resistance from the Belgian population as they gradually changed their policy. Instead of merely liberating the country and then handing it over to the nationals, they began to interfere ever more in Belgian affairs. By now there could be no doubt that—apart from a small group of Jacobines—there was not much enthusiasm among the general populace to support the war against the Austrians with either funds or manpower. When it became clear that the majority of the Belgians were actively turning against the French, the Austrians saw an opportunity to regain Belgian support. Encouraged by the resistance, Austrian troops crossed the Ruhr on March 1, 1793; the French troops—or what was left of them—retreated, but not before pillaging villages along their path, angered by the refusal of the Belgian citizens to support them. As if he wanted to mark the contrast to the harsh French treatment, Emperor Francis II promised the Belgian people that he would protect the *Joyeuse Entrée*, the Catholic Church and the Belgian traditions. Within a few weeks, Austrian troops triumphantly entered Brussels.[120]

5.2.3.2 Business as Usual?

On April 2nd, Metternich informed the members of the Great Council that the French had been ousted from the Netherlands and that they could return to Malines to resume their normal activities. Apparently, the councilors were in a hurry to go back to their homes, because only 6 days later, senior councilor de Waepenaert announced that the Great Council would hold its first session on Thursday, April 11th and that the first day of pleadings was scheduled for Saturday April 20th. President de Fierlant, however, would not return: he had in the meantime been appointed to the presidency of the Privy Council.[121] It took another 3 months, until early July, before the new president, Jacques Antoine Le Clerc, was inaugurated in Malines.[122]

---

[119] Brussels, ARA, GRM 231, letter from Metternich to de Fierlant, February 11, 1793.

[120] Polasky, Janet. 1985. *Revolution in Brussels 1787–1793*. Gembloux: Duculot, 237–260.

[121] Brussels, ARA, GRM 231, letter from Metternich to de Fierlant, April 2, 1793, and announcement from de Waepenaert, April 8, 1793.

[122] Brussels, ARA, GRM 231, account of the inauguration of Le Clerc as president of the Great Council, July 7, 1793. Le Clerc had been a high profile civil servant before, especially under Joseph II, when he was sent to Vienna to confer with Martini on the reforms to be implemented (although it must be mentioned that he was only third in line: de Crumpipen was ill while councilor de Reuss as second choice could not go, since he was replacing de Crumpipen; Le Clerc was the only other possible candidate who spoke German). Le Clerc later also acted as commissioner in the *Conseil du gouvernement général*, responsible for religious affairs, education and censure. It is somewhat surprising that after such a promising start, he ended up as president of the Great Council. However, the option of making him president of 'some council' had already been suggested in 1788 when his removal from the *Conseil du gouvernement général* was requested due to his unpopularity with the general public. Additionally, Le Clerc was a notorious debtor, which also might have affected his career prospects. Lefevre, Joseph. 1928. *Le conseil du gouvernement général.*

During this interval, de Waepenaert as senior councilor did the honors: the Great Council desired to return to 'business as usual' as quickly as possible.

Once again, that idea would prove illusory. First of all, the Austrian government suffered from a chronic shortage of funds. While the members of the Great Council were hoping to recuperate the costs spent on transport when returning from Düsseldorf, the amount they could request was restricted to a maximum of 200 florins for councilors and even less for registrars, clerks or secretaries.[123] Another sign of this financial distress was the sale of the position of registrar at the Great Council. The office had already been vacant since October, 1792. At that time, three candidates had offered respectively 3600, 4000 and 10,000 florins. When the treasurer had requested advocate-fiscal Goubau's advice on the matter, he had replied that the position should be sold to the highest bidder—i.c. advocate Van Grootven—given that a registrar 'did not require any specific talents or extraordinary qualities'.[124]

The French invasion must have left the matter unresolved, because in July 1793, the government informed the Great Council that it should proceed to a new nomination of three candidates. The only condition stipulated was that the candidates should be prepared to offer at least 10,000 florins, and preferably even more, as the cost of the war against the French and the need to protect the Belgian provinces against the 'tyranny of the enemy' warranted a considerable contribution to the treasury.[125] In August, the Great Council could do nothing else but notify the government that no one was willing to pay over 10,000 florins for the vacancy; there was no other solution than to dig up Van Grootven.[126]

In December 1793, the Austrian government addressed the provincial Estates and Councils—including the Great Council—with an appeal to provide the treasury with 'voluntary patriotic gifts'. Additional funds were necessary in order to protect the country against French despotism and to preserve Catholicism. Consequently, the government called on the people of the Austrian Netherlands in general, and on their representatives in particular, to donate money, but also gold or even silverware, as a gift or loan for the duration of the war.[127] There could not have been much doubt in the minds of the councilors that, for them, there was nothing voluntary about the gift: a few days after the appeal, the members of the Great Council replied that they 'wanted nothing more' than to contribute to the defense of the Belgian provinces.

Brussels: Lamertin, 159; Bruneel, Claude and Hoyois, Jean-Paul. 2001. *Les grands commis des Pays-Bas autrichiens: dictionnaire biographique du personnel des institutions centrales*. Brussels: Algemeen Rijksarchief, 364–368; Jacob, Steve. 1999. Jacques-Antoine Le Clerc (1731-après 1797). Un fonctionnaire au service d'une politique réformatrice. In *La haute administration dans les Pays-Bas autrichiens (Ambroise-Joseph de Herzelles, Denis-Benoît de Cazier, Jacques-Antoine Le Clerc)* (Etudes sur le XVIIIe siècle 27), eds. Hervé Hasquin and Roland Mortier, 243–354. Brussels: Université de Bruxelles.

123 Brussels, ARA, GRM 140, Correspondances du Grand Conseil 1793, f.21, May 13, 1793.

124 Brussels, ARA, GRMOF, BD 69, f.131–134.

125 Brussels, ARA, GRM 140, Correspondances du Grand Conseil, f.31, July 3, 1793.

126 Brussels, ARA, GRM 140, Correspondances du Grand Conseil, f.39, August 8, 1793.

127 Brussels, ARA, GRM 140, Correspondances du Grand Conseil, f.93–97, December 23, 1793.

Therefore, the president and councilors had agreed to each donate respectively 800 and 400 florins from their annual salaries for the duration of the war.[128]

Still, the finances of the Great Council itself were also less than healthy. At almost the exact same time that the government asked for a voluntary gift, the Great Council sent a request for financial support: around late December 1793, the total amount in the Council's *caisse des exploits* stood at 35 florins, while the expenses that still needed to be paid—for the services of the bailiffs but also for torches, paper, candles, wood, etc.—amounted to 4587 florins.[129] It is uncertain if the government was willing to provide the necessary funds.

The Council of Finance, in any case, refused to refund the expenses from the different conflicts of jurisdiction the Great Council had with the Council of Flanders during the early 1790s. The Great Council protested to the governor, complaining that the Council of Flanders obstinately persisted in refusing to defer to the letters of appeal awarded by the Great Council in cases of the nullification of a criminal sentence.[130] According to the councilors, the refusal of the Council of Finance to pay for the expenses incurred by these conflicts of jurisdiction would only serve to undermine the power entrusted to the Great Council to preserve the authority of the sovereign in the provinces. The Great Council feared that, given the provincial councils' constant aspirations to extend their rights and privileges at the expense of the emperor's, they would become ever bolder in their attempts to undermine the Great Council's jurisdiction—and thereby indirectly the government's authority—if they knew that their challenges to the Great Council's authority would go unpunished.[131]

5.2.3.3 The Central Government's Carrot-and-Stick Policy

In general, the policy of the government towards the Great Council seemed somewhat equivocal and it is doubtful that it had any well thought-out or uniform strategy on how to use the Council for its own purposes. On the one hand, the central government drew extensively on the Malines tribunal in its fight against its internal enemies—and would do so again—but on the other hand, there was often a lack of support when the Great Council attempted to consolidate or expand its own authority. The issues surrounding the payment of the councilors' work on conflicts of jurisdiction with the Council of Flanders were one example; the failure to get the Great Council designated as the superior court for the newly conquered region around Valenciennes was another one.

---

[128] Brussels, ARA, GRM 140, Correspondances du Grand Conseil, f.98–99, December 24, 1793.

[129] Brussels, ARA, GRM 140, Correspondances du Grand Conseil, f.102, December 26, 1793.

[130] The Great Council refers here to the decision in the case involving the parish priest of Bavikhove, which constituted the first blow to the sovereignty of the Council of Flanders in criminal cases. Cf. supra, Chap. 3.

[131] Brussels, ARA, GRM 140, Correspondances du Grand Conseil, f.131–132, April 3, 1794.

The city of Valenciennes and its surroundings were part of the Spanish Netherlands until the Treaty of Nijmegen of 1678 transferred the sovereignty over the area to the Kingdom of France. In the wake of the conquest of the Netherlands in early 1793, the Austrians managed to get hold again of Valenciennes and its surrounding territories. Anticipating the need to administer this region, the members of the Great Council offered their services as superior judges, founding their claims on seventeenth century precedents.[132] Yet, the Great Council was not the only contender; the Councils of Hainaut and Tournai also believed they had reason to demand the jurisdiction over the newly-won territory. Given that Valenciennes had been conquered only recently, this discussion seemed somewhat premature, but the Privy Council considered it important enough to address a very lengthy and well-argued advice to the governor, based on the observations of the *Jointe* for Valenciennes.[133]

The Council of Tournai's claims over the jurisdiction of the recently seized territories were not based on any legal precedents, but rather on its geographic proximity and consequently on the easy access the new subjects would have to a superior tribunal. Nevertheless, Tournai did not pretend to be entitled by custom or by law to the jurisdiction over this region. The Council of Hainaut, on the other hand—supported by its Estates—did not demonstrate any moderation in its demands. According to the councilors of Hainaut, the conquest of this 'district of Hainaut' had *de facto* reunited it to the province and therefore also subjected it in law to the jurisdiction of the provincial council. The Council of Hainaut claimed that the fundamental rule concerning the indivisibility of the province of Hainaut left no doubts about the claims it had on the newly conquered territories. Not awarding the jurisdiction to Hainaut would be an assault on the constitutions of the province—which went back to the year 1200—and an infraction on the inaugural oath the sovereign had sworn to the Estates of Hainaut.

In short, the Privy Council saw itself confronted with three claims: two based on historical and/or legal precedents, and one on geographic proximity and accessibility. An additional element that complicated matters and made the return to the old order somewhat problematic, was that the French, since they had come into possession of Valenciennes and its surroundings in 1678, had introduced an entirely new set of laws and habits that no longer conformed to any customs in vigor in

[132] Brussels, ARA, GRM 140, Correspondances du Grand Conseil, f.33, July 23, 1793. In its argumentation, the Great Council referred to a list of sentences from the seventeenth century found in its archives as well as to a dissertation by former councilor de Coloma (compiler of one of the eighteenth century *recueils d'arrêts* of the Great Council).

[133] Brussels, ARA, GR, Register 484, f.42–71, October 14, 1793. The *Jointe pour l'administration provisoire du pays conquis,* also known as the *Jointe de Valenciennes* (after its later location in the city of Valenciennes) was established in late June 1793 in order to administrate the newly conquered territories. Jacques Le Clerc, who had only recently been inaugurated as the new president of the Great Council (July 7, 1793), was appointed chairman of the *Jointe.* In June 1794, Le Clerc was replaced by councilor of the Privy Council Martial de le Vielleuze. Only a few weeks later, the *Jointe* was *de facto* abolished due to the conquest of Valenciennes by the French revolutionary armies. Van Honacker, Karin. 1994. Jointe voor het voorlopig bestuur van het op Frankrijk veroverde land (Jointe te Valencijn) (1793–1794). In *De centrale overheidsinstellingen van de Habsburgse Nederlanden*, ed. Erik Aerts e.a., 360–366. Brussels: Algemeen Rijksarchief.

the Austrian Netherlands. When asked for its opinion on the issue, the *Jointe* for Valenciennes advocated for awarding the jurisdiction to the Council of Hainaut.[134]

In its recommendation to the governor, the Privy Council expressed its concerns about Hainaut's pretentions. Certainly, they were absolutely absurd to begin with, but the main problem was that it seemed imprudent to award the Council of Hainaut jurisdiction over Valenciennes and its surroundings without stipulating any conditions. It was clear to the Privy Council that the Council of Hainaut had no intention of upholding any customs or laws that the French had introduced, but merely wanted to return to the ancient charters that had been in effect before the initial dismemberment of the territories in 1678. The Privy Council worried that any dispositions made for this region by the sovereign or the *Jointe* that in any way went against the charters of Hainaut, would be regarded as infractions against the privileges of the province and would therefore be ignored. As such, the Privy Council warned that if the jurisdiction was to be awarded to the Council of Hainaut—by preference only provisionally at first—it should be made clear from the outset that the Council must follow the prevailing customs of the conquered territories as well as any new laws that the sovereign or the *Jointe* prescribed. Referring to its own privileges and charters was out of the question. Obviously, the Privy Council had not forgotten about Hainaut's rebellions in previous years.

In the end, the Privy Council recommended to divide the jurisdiction. Aware of the sensitivities of the Great Council's members, and fully conscious of the importance of not disappointing them given their loyalty to the government, the Privy Council advised the governor to restore the jurisdiction the Great Council had exercised before 1678 over the city of Valenciennes and its immediate surroundings. The authority over the remaining areas should be given to the Council of Hainaut, with the exception of the territories that had fallen under the jurisdiction of the Council of Tournai before their transfer to France. The latter would now again be allowed to administer justice in those parts.[135]

In his unusually detailed and well-argued decision, Governor Charles Louis d'Autriche only partially agreed with the Privy Council. While he understood the importance of placating the Great Council, he dismissed the idea of having the tribunal act as a superior court for even a part of the conquered territories. Indeed, the governor believed that the Great Council was probably even less accustomed to their laws than the Council of Hainaut. Moreover, he was apprehensive that assigning the jurisdiction over Valenciennes to a tribunal so far in the interior of the country would be too clear an indication that the Austrian government intended on retaining these recent conquests. Nevertheless, he instructed the Privy Council to clearly explain the reasons behind this decision to the Great Council and assure the Malines tribunal that this temporary provision would in no way prejudice its rights once time had consolidated the new acquisition. Furthermore, there could be no

[134] Brussels, ARA, GR Registers 484, f.42–71, October 14, 1793.

[135] The Privy Council's decision to award a part of the jurisdiction of the newly won territories to the Council of Tournai is somewhat unexpected, as it was not actually a sovereign council but was subjected to the Council of Hainaut.

question of a division of jurisdiction between the Councils of Tournai and Hainaut: the governor decided to solely award the jurisdiction to the latter council—at least for now—but with the express demand that its members submitted to the conditions stipulated by the government.

In short, once again, while Charles d'Autriche had certainly displayed some sympathy for the Great Council, the councilors' request was rebuffed. The fact that exactly the Council of Hainaut—one of the most rebellious tribunals—saw its authority and power extended must have added insult to injury for the Great Council, which had always taken pride in its loyalty to the emperor.[136]

Perhaps the resolution of April 27, 1794 to award the position of councilor of State to the senior councilor of the Great Council was connected to the need the Austrian government felt to compensate the Great Council and please its members.[137] While in the eighteenth century, the Council of State no longer had any real power or participation in policy-making, membership was highly regarded and certainly financially rewarding. In his award letter, Trauttmansdorff explicitly mentioned that this honor was bestowed upon the Great Council for its unrelenting loyalty and devotion to the government's cause. It is easy to imagine that it was also intended as a form of compensation for the disgrace of losing the dispute over Valenciennes to Hainaut.

5.2.3.4 Return of the French

De Waepenaert was the sole councilor who ever enjoyed this privilege. By late April and early May, it had become clear that the Austrian authority in the Netherlands was hanging by a thread, despite the efforts of the government to root out pro-French sentiments. Contrary to the first restoration period when the governors and minister plenipotentiary had not really used much repression in fear of antagonizing the population, the second period of restoration[138] was marked by much more control and restraint, especially against non-natives.[139] Shortly after the re-establishment of

---

[136] Ironically, one of the arguments that might have convinced Charles d'Autriche to award the jurisdiction to the Council of Hainaut was exactly that the Council and the Estates of Hainaut had proved troublesome in the past. The government feared that if the Council of Hainaut was rebuffed in its claims, irritation might grow in the Hainaut Estates, which could have fiscal consequences. The fact that the government's attempts to placate the Council and Estates of Hainaut went quite far is demonstrated by the observation that, since the Council did not acknowledge the *Jointe*, all orders and instructions concerning the newly conquered territories were sent by the Privy Council instead. Van Honacker, Karin. 1994. Jointe voor het voorlopig bestuur van het op Frankrijk veroverde land (Jointe te Valencijn) (1793–1794). In *De centrale overheidsinstellingen van de Habsburgse Nederlanden*, ed. Erik Aerts e.a.. Brussels: Algemeen Rijksarchief, 365.

[137] Brussels, ARA, GRM 140, Correspondances du Grand Conseil, f.144, April 27, 1794.

[138] It must be noted that, similarly to the first restoration period, a general amnesty was proclaimed in the Netherlands.

[139] A mutual fear of a new French invasion brought the government and the conservatives together. Dhondt, Luc. 1989. De conservatieve Brabantse omwenteling van 1789 en het proces van revolutie en contrarevolutie in de Zuidelijke Nederlanden tussen 1780 en 1830. *Tijdschrift voor Geschiedenis* 92: 446.

the Austrian authority in 1793, the fiscals of the Great Council were swamped with instructions on how to proceed against the so called *clubs de Jacobins* or *sociétiés des soi-disants amis de la liberté*, and on how to monitor French—and other—*émigrés* who roamed around in the Netherlands without a passport.[140] In December, a three-day-long round-up had been organized throughout the entire country in order to arrest as many unwanted persons as possible.[141]

By spring, this nervousness had degenerated into real panic behavior. The *Breede Raad* of Malines made thankfully use of the circumstances to finally deprive the members of the Great Council of their privileges. In late May 1794, Trauttmansdorff called upon the provincial Estates and city Magistrates to conscript 5 % of all able-bodied men, or 1 % of the general population of the Austrian Netherlands, in order to fight against the French troops.[142] An earlier call for volunteers had been unsuccessful as not a single recruit had presented himself. Trauttmansdorff's threats were unmistakable: if the Belgian provinces were unable to assemble a satisfying number of their residents to join the army, the Austrians would abandon their attempts to defend these territories and concentrate on the protection of their own homelands.[143] Apart from recruits, additional donations to the army's treasuries were equally essential.

The Magistrate of Malines forwarded Trauttmansdorff's letters to the Great Council, with the cunning remark that there was a lot of willingness in the *Breede Raad* to support the government with troops and funds, but that the deans of the guilds did not want to consent unless the privileges and tax exemptions of the councilors of the Great Council were abolished. The aldermen added that they had already agreed to give up their own privileges and that there could be no doubt in their minds that the members of the Great Council would also willingly support the war effort.[144] The councilors had no other option than to oblige, which they did on June 5th. Exactly 3 weeks later, the French army inflicted a final blow to the Austrian defense forces at the Battle of Fleurus. For the third time in less than 5 years, the members of the government and all major institutions went into exile, this time for good.

5.2.4 The Curtain Falls: July 1794–February 1804

On June 29th, just 3 days after the defeat at Fleurus, the Great Council once again packed its most valuable items and records and prepared to retreat to Roermond. The actual exodus began on July 4th around 4.30 in the morning; some 10 days

[140] Brussels, ARA, GRMOF, BD 70, f.14–16, May 13, 1793; f. 28–30, May 23, 1793; f.251–260, November 14, 1793.

[141] Brussels, ARA, GRMOF, BD 70, f.262–272, December 7, 1793.

[142] Brussels, ARA, GRM 140, Correspondances du Grand Conseil, f.161, May 31, 1794.

[143] Brussels, ARA, GRM 140, Correspondances du Grand Conseil, f.162–164, May 31, 1794.

[144] Brussels, ARA, GRM 140, Correspondances du Grand Conseil, f.160, June 3, 1794.

later, the French entered the city of Malines.[145] Contrary to what had happened in 1792, not all members of the Great Council followed the tribunal into exile. In his letter of June 30, Metternich mentioned the possibility the members of the Great Council would have to request the president for permission to remain in Malines, if they had any health or other particular reasons.[146] Councilors Ghison, de Villers, de Waepenaert, Douglas, Van Cutsem, Reniers and de Guchtenaere, together with secretaries Crabeels, Pansius and Wirix, registrar Richterich and collector Rijckaert eagerly made use of this opportunity.[147]

It is remarkable how most of the councilors and other members of the Great Council hid behind their wives and families when requesting the president for permission to stay in Malines. While they mentioned their own infirmities, they claimed that it was especially the health of their spouses which did not allow for travel, while leaving them behind was not an option either.[148] Clerical councilor Van Cutsem of course could not blame his wife, but he instead asserted that he could not abandon his 78-year-old mother, who had already been 'crying for over 10 days'. Douglas, Reniers and Wirix were the only members who outwardly admitted that they could not go into exile out of financial concerns: the former because he had no means to bring his spouse and children with him, the latter two because their adult family members did not have the necessary funds to take care of themselves.

Had these councilors decided that they would sit out a second French storm in their home country in the firm conviction that the Habsburg regime would return? Or had there, on the contrary, already been an indication that the Austrians had no intention of regaining possession of the Netherlands a third time and that the inhabitants of the Belgian Provinces would have to resign to French dominance for years to come? The fact that de Waepenaert requested his resignation, hoping that he could thereby thwart any problems the French might cause him as member of the Great Council, certainly suggests the latter hypothesis may be closer to the truth.

Either way, the Austrians very quickly took away all doubts regarding their plans for the Belgian provinces. While Trauttmansdorff, president of the newly established Chancellery of the Netherlands, was still thinking about ways to regain the lost possessions, Emperor Francis II understood that the entire machinery of gov-

[145] Stroobant, Louis. 1901. Ce que devinrent les archives et la bibliothèque du Grand Conseil. *Bulletin du cercle archéologique, littéraire et artistique de Malines* 11: 293–302.

[146] Vienna, HHStA, Belgien DDB rot 80 (alt 53), letter from minister plenipotentiary Metternich to the Great Council. Brussels, June 30, 1794.

[147] Vienna, HHStA, Belgien DDB rot 80 (alt 53). Requests from de Waepenaert, Villers, Ghison, Douglas, Reniers, de Guchtenaere, Van Cutsem, Crabeels, Pansius, Richterich, Wirix and Rijckaert. All these requests are dated either July 2nd or 3rd, except de Waepenaert's, which is dated November 28, 1794. This does not make sense, as by then the Great Council had already moved to Würzburg, while de Waepenaert's letter was written in Malines. He actually never left the city in 1794, which is confirmed by his correspondence with the new French government: Brussels, ARA, Papiers des commissaires du gouvernement dits Papiers Bouteville 439, f.3. We can only assume that his request was misdated.

[148] This is the case for de Waepenaert, Villers, Ghison, de Guchtenaere, Pansius, Richterich and Rijckaert.

ernment could not be maintained much longer. On August 2, 1794, he took the first step towards renouncing all Austrian claims on the Belgian provinces by *de facto* dissolving their government. At the end of that same month, Metternich informed Trauttmansdorff that the emperor had ordered the complete liquidation of what was left of the Belgian institutions.[149] By then, popular feeling in the Austrian Succession States was firmly against a new attempt to take possession of the Netherlands; these 'rebellious provinces' were even blamed for all the troubles the Austrians found themselves in.[150] The French as well left little doubt as to their policy towards the Belgian provinces: this time they did not even claim to liberate them. The Belgian provinces were to be treated as conquered territory; on 9 Vendemaire of the year IV (October 1, 1795), they were officially annexed to the French Republic.

5.2.4.1 The Fate of the Stay-Behind Councilors

As far as the members of the Great Council who stayed behind in Malines are concerned, they seemed to have deliberately opted to keep a low profile as much as possible. While there are no accounts of the wrath of the French being directed specifically at former employees of the Austrian government, we do know that the remaining members of the tribunals were harassed into retaking their positions as judges. However, the former councilors of the Great Council were not very eager to work for the new government.[151] In response to the decision of the temporary French authorities of 27 Thermidor III (August 24, 1794) which stipulated that 'the criminal and civil tribunals will be provisionally maintained under the protection of the French Republic in order to continue their activities in their respective jurisdictions', the members of the Great Council wrote a letter to explain why they believed they should not and could not be integrated into the new structure.[152]

First, they claimed that while the other tribunals of the Netherlands had been fully incorporated into their respective provinces and could therefore remain func-

[149] Zedinger, Renate. 2004. *Migration und Karriere: Habsburgische Beamte in Brüssel und Wien im 18. Jahrhundert* (Schriftenreihe der Österreichischen Gesellschaft zur Erforschung des 18. Jahrhunderts 9). Vienna: Böhlau, 45: "er [Franz II] verkündete mit Daum von 2 August 1794: ‚Mon intention est que le gouvernement des Pays-Bas soit dissous sans plus de délai, avec cessation entière des appointements des employés, et avec défense d'exercer leurs fonctions et de vouloir continuer à représenter un similaire de gouvernement. Le seul secrétaire d'Etat Müller sera conservé avec un nombre de personnes le plus restreint que possible…".

[150] Zedinger, Renate. 2004. *Migration und Karriere: Habsburgische Beamte in Brüssel und Wien im 18. Jahrhundert* (Schriftenreihe der Österreichischen Gesellschaft zur Erforschung des 18. Jahrhunderts 9). Vienna: Böhlau, 46.

[151] Rousseaux also mentioned that the French had a hard time finding qualified people to staff the tribunals, even when the new judicial organization had been set up. Rousseaux, Xavier. 1993. *Le personnel judiciaire en Belgique à travers les révolutions (1780–1832)*. In *Het politiek personeel tijdens de overgang van het Ancien Régime naar het nieuwe regiem in België (1780–1830)*, eds. Piet Lenders e.a. Heule: UGA, 29.

[152] Brussels, ARA, PapBout 439, f.3: letter from the remaining members of the Great Council of 26 Brumaire III (November 16, 1794).

tional, the Great Council was only answerable to the emperor himself and would not attach itself to one single locality. Following an express order by Francis II, the Great Council as a corpus had left the Southern Netherlands before the arrival of the republican armies. Therefore, the remaining councilors argued, they had no jurisdiction at all to revive the Great Council; consequently, they must be considered as private citizens. Moreover, they asserted that there was nothing left to work with, given that the *émigrés* had taken along the most essential records and that the Magistrate had sealed the premises of the Great Council. For all these reasons, councilors Ghison, de Villers, de Waepenaert, Douglas, Van Cutsem and Renlers considered themselves to be excluded from the decision of 27 Thermidor.[153]

Apparently, de Waepenaert was not entirely convinced that the French would drop the matter so easily. The next day, he sent a personal letter to the provisional government, putting forward the reasons why he, in particular, should not be forced to again take up the position of judge:[154] being over the age of 75, with more than 50 years of service to the Great Council, and suffering from several conditions—including cataracts in both eyes, for which he had surgery—he was no longer capable of the strenuous work of a judge. Moreover, he informed the provisional government that he had resigned from the Great Council before its departure from Malines.

The arguments of the councilors did not convince the members of the provisional *Comité de surveillance* (Surveillance Committee) of Malines. Following the complaint of a litigant who demanded the settlement of his case before the Great Council, they brought official charges to the Central Administration of Belgium. In response, the councilors of the Great Council submitted another written defense on 16 Nivôse III (January 5, 1795), repeating their previous arguments. In the end, the Central Administration decided not to act upon the complaint of the *Comité de surveillance*.[155] From then on, we lose all trace of the councilors who stayed behind in Malines until the establishment of the United Kingdom of the Netherlands in 1814.[156]

5.2.4.2 In the Footsteps of the *Emigrés*

The councilors who went into exile fared no better than those who remained in Malines. Ever since the French Revolution, throngs of emigrants—first Frenchmen, who were later joined by 'Belgians', 'Germans', etc.—fled to the lands under

[153] De Guchtenaere did not emigrate either, but apparently was absent from Malines at the moment the letter was written.

[154] Brussels, ARA, PapBout 439, f.1: letter from de Waepenaert, 27 Brumaire III (November 17, 1794).

[155] Verhaegen, Paul. 1894. Le Grand Conseil de Malines en 1795. *Handelingen van de Koninklijke Kring voor Oudheidkunde, Letteren en Kunst in Mechelen* 5: 209–217. Verhaegen included a transcription of the letter of protest the members of the Great Council wrote, but he did not mention a reference to his source. However, as the content is very much similar to the letter preserved in the *papiers de Bouteville*, we have no reason to doubt its authenticity.

[156] Cf. infra, 4.3 Epilogue.

Habsburg control. Consequently, conditions were extremely difficult: many had left behind their assets and effects, they had to rely on a very small income and were forced to live in places where all the basic necessities had become increasingly expensive due to both the requirements of the army and the masses of *émigrés* who were fleeing in front of the advancing republican armies.[157] It did not take long for the Austrian authorities to understand that this situation might stir up ill-feelings among their own population, especially in Vienna which most *émigrés* tried to reach, hoping that they could find another position in the central administration corresponding to their talents and experience. Many saw these hopes crushed in November 1794 when Count de Pergen, minister of police, convinced the emperor to close off the capital to the majority of the emigrants, arguing that the city was already overcrowded and that the shortage of food would further disgruntle the population and cause 'unpleasant consequences'.[158]

The Belgian émigrés felt harshly treated by the Austrian government, especially because they considered themselves—contrary to the French emigrants—citizens of the Habsburg Empire, whose long-lasting loyalty to the Austrian Crown had brought them in their difficult situation in the first place. Even de Stassart—former procurator-general of the Great Council, president of the Council of Namur and unwavering supporter of the Austrian authorities—complained about the treatment the emigrants received at the hands of the government: "*Il n'est point du tout consolant de voir que le gouvernement porte si peu son attention sur les besoins des bons et fidèles sujets qui ont été contraints de quitter leur pays pour traîner leur famille dans des pays étrangers, où il se trouvent sans ressources et sans crédit [...]*".[159] Moreover, the French government in Belgium made it almost impossible for the *émigrés* to return to their home country: on December 14, 1794 all emigrants were declared to be banished for eternity and in February 1795 the sale of their goods was decreed.[160]

The Austrian government did foresee the possibility of a pension, a (limited) amount of money for which the former functionaries of the Austrian Netherlands could apply. In November 1794, the emperor decreed that all employees were entitled to half their normal salary for the period between August 20, 1794 and August 20, 1795. After that date, they might be eligible for a pension, for which they should

[157] Zedinger, Renate. 2004. *Migration und Karriere: Habsburgische Beamte in Brüssel und Wien im 18. Jahrhundert* (Schriftenreihe der Österreichischen Gesellschaft zur Erforschung des 18. Jahrhunderts 9). Vienna: Böhlau, 62.

[158] Zedinger, Renate. 1998. Un fonds à découvrir pour l'histoire des Pays-Bas autrichiens: les requêtes des fonctionnaires et pensionnés émigrés conservées au 'Finanz- und Hofkammerarchiv Wien'. *Bulletin de la commission royale d'histoire* 164: 178. "Il [de Pergen] mentionnait que '...in der ohnedies schon zu bevölkerten Residentzstadt [könne] der Mangel an Lebensdürfnissen sofort Missvergnügen im Volke und unangenehme Folge [hervorrufen]'."

[159] Citation in Bernard, Bruno. 1998. Les hauts fonctionnaires des Pays-Bas autrichiens en emigration (1789–1803). In *Camporformio 1797: la Belgique change de maitres*. Brussels: Legermuseum, 107. De Stassart was one of the few higher functionaries who in the end was allowed to join Vienna. By then, he had already sent his family back to the Netherlands.

[160] Bernard, Bruno. 1998. Les hauts fonctionnaires des Pays-Bas autrichiens en emigration (1789–1803). In *Camporformio 1797: la Belgique change de maitres*. Brussels: Legermuseum, 107.

submit an application before March 1, 1795. All those who could prove that they had more than 40 years of seniority were qualified for up to two thirds of their normal salary; those with more than 25 years of service would retain half their wages; all others would continue to receive a third. Those whose yearly income did not exceed 300 German florins (the equivalent of 420 Brabant florins[161]) retained the entirety of that sum; 300 German florins was also the lower limit for those whose salaries were reduced.

Certain conditions were attached to these measures: first, the functionaries had to prove that they had emigrated before the Belgian provinces were occupied by the French armies, and secondly, they had to demonstrate by official certificate where they had lived since their emigration. Only those who had stayed in the lands under Habsburg control during their travels and who were planning on remaining there were entitled to a pension.[162] These requests for pensions confirm that president Le Clerc together with councilors Baujoz, Goubeau, d'Hoop, Van Volxem, de Laing, de Steenhault, Diu and several other lower employees of the Council—one registrar, one secretary, the deputy procurator-general, two proctors, a bailiff, etc.—went into exile and filed for a pension, although at different times and in different places.[163]

'Adventures' The scarce literature that is available on the history of the Great Council after 1794 mentions that a few of its members continued its sessions in Regensburg and Augsburg, before the tribunal was finally abolished by the Treaty of Campo Formio of 1797.[164] Although none of the authors refer to a source, we may assume that the story goes back to the account of the first registrar of the High Court of Justice in Brussels Audoor, who in 1827 sent a report on and a preliminary

[161] In what follows, we use the term florins in general, simply because the sources do not specify if we are dealing with German or Brabant florins.

[162] Zedinger, Renate. 1998. Un fonds à découvrir pour l'histoire des Pays-Bas autrichiens: les requêtes des fonctionnaires et pensionnés émigrés conservées au 'Finanz- und Hofkammerarchiv Wien'. *Bulletin de la commission royale d'histoire* 164: 175–176.

[163] Goubau sent his request from Düsseldorf on September 4, 1794, d'Hoop from Elberfeld on August 27, 1794, de Laing from Würzburg on January 9, 1795, and Le Clerc from Elberfeld on August 15, 1794. Diu, de Steenhault and Baujouz apparently never sent a request for financial support, yet they did receive a pension because president Le Clerc mentioned them—and many other members of the Council—in his own request. Vienna, FHKA, Österreichische Kamerale 2309. Also, Zedinger, Renate. 1998. Un fonds à découvrir pour l'histoire des Pays-Bas autrichiens: les requêtes des fonctionnaires et pensionnés émigrés conservées au 'Finanz- und Hofkammerarchiv Wien'. *Bulletin de la commission royale d'histoire* 164: 181–196.

[164] Cf. Leyder, Dirk. 2010. *Les archives du Grand Conseil des Pays-Bas à Malines (vers 1445–1797)*. Brussels: Algemeen Rijksarchief, 22; Maes, Louis Th. 2009. *Het Parlement en de Grote Raad van Mechelen: 1473–1797.* Antwerp: De Vries-Brouwers, 158; Gilissen, John. 1980. De Grote Raad van Mechelen. Historisch overzicht. In *Miscelannea Consilii Magni. Ter gelegenheid van twintig jaar Werkgroep Grote Raad van Mechelen.* Amsterdam: Universiteit van Amsterdam. Faculteit der rechtsgeleerdheid, 41–42; Wijffels, Alain. 1994. Grote Raad voor de Nederlanden te Mechelen (ca.1445–1797). In *De centrale overheidsinstellingen van de Habsburgse Nederlanden*, ed. Erik Aerts e.a. Brussels: Algemeen Rijksarchief, 449. These and other works on the Great Council dedicate at most a few lines to the later years of its existence.

inventory of (a part of) the archives of the Great Council to the government.[165] Herein, Audoor recalled how several members of the Great Council—after they had gone into exile in 1794—continued to discuss ongoing cases and prepare dicta, first in Regensburg and later in Augsburg, in order to be able to resume their activities as quickly as possible after their longed-for return to Malines. Only when the Treaty of Campo Formio took away their hopes of a reestablishment of the Great Council, did they send the remaining consigned cash reserves, as well as their records, to Vienna.

Yet, already in 1830, in the margin of a struggle over the responsibility for the preservation of the Great Council's records,[166] P.J. L'Ortye—former secretary of the Privy Council and the first archivist of the United Kingdom of the Netherlands[167]—contested several elements in Audoor's version of the facts.[168] According to him, the majority of the councilors indeed went into exile, taking with them the consigned cash reserves and a considerable part of the archives. Their journey initially brought them to Roermond, but they soon had to flee again, first to Würzburg and then to Regensburg. L'Ortye did not believe that the councilors of the Great Council ever set foot in Augsburg.

Yet, he confirmed Audoor's assertion that the councilors in exile rallied around their archives and consigned cash reserves and continued their activities, despite the order from the Austrian Emperor that all institutions of the Netherlands should be dissolved. In 1796 in Regensburg, they even appeared to be handling a rather high-profile lawsuit—with a claim amounting up to 100,000 pounds sterling—between the brother of Lord Popham, member of the English Parliament, and a certain Vercoustre.[169] L'Ortye claimed that the Austrian government put an end to it, declaring once again that the Great Council had been abolished and that the councilors should make their way to the Austrian Succession States as private citizens if they wanted to further enjoy their pensions. Secretary Van Grootven became solely responsible

---

165 Brussels, ARA, INV 16, f.1–7.

166 For more information on the history of the records of the eighteenth century Great Council, including their travels together with the councilors of the Great Council, their confiscation by the French revolutionary government and their return to Brussels in 1815 has been published in Verscuren, An. 2014. Archieven in oorlog, speelbal van politiek. Het archief van de Grote Raad van Mechelen (1746–1869)'. In *Macht en Onmacht. De rol van archieven in oorlog en bij rechtsherstel,* eds. Ron Blom e.a., 49–59. 's-Gravenhage: Stichting Archiefpublicaties.

167 For more information on L'Ortye: Bruneel, Claude and Hoyois, Jean-Paul. 2001. *Les grands commis des Pays-Bas autrichiens: dictionnaire biographique du personnel des institutions centrales*. Brussels: Algemeen Rijksarchief, 391–393. Schoups, Inge. 1987. P.J.M. L'Ortye, Rijksarchivaris te Brussel, 1814–1831. Een vergeten figuur. In *Album Carlos Wyffels: aangeboden door zijn wetenschappelijke medewerkers*, eds. Herman Coppejans and Georges Hansotte, 403–412. Brussels: Algemeen Rijksarchief.

168 Brussels, ARA, GRM 175/10 (19A), Archives du Grand Conseil de Malines, 1794–1830. Rapport hollandais.

169 In theory, this is certainly possible. The distribution books mention a lawsuit between Popham and Vercoustre which, after the promotion of councilor Pouppez to the Privy Council, was redistributed to councilor de Steenhault on May 26, 1794. Cf. Excel database: distribution records of the eighteenth century Great Council.

for the consigned cash reserves and the records, which shortly after 1796 he had to hand over to the imperial government in Vienna.

Given that L'Ortye was a former member of the Privy Council and therefore undoubtedly well-connected and probably well-informed, it may be assumed that his version of the facts was more or less trustworthy, especially as he had been an *émigré* himself. However, several details in his account are inconsistent with what can be found in both the Viennese and Brussels archives.

The Great Council certainly first moved to Roermond, but its stay there was very short. Already on July 18th, a mere 14 days after their departure from Mallnes, president Le Clerc and his seven councilors received an order to move to the city of Elberfeld,[170] some 100 kilometers east of Roermond, while one part of the government moved to Düsseldorf with Metternich[171] and the other to Kaiserswerth.[172] Le Clerc reported that the chancellor de Juliers et de Berg, Count of Nesselrode, had allowed the Great Council to continue its sessions at the president's residence in Elberfeld, provided that its meetings were not public and that the work done was only preparatory to getting cases ready for judgment.[173]

On August 20th, the Great Council was notified in a letter from Governor Charles Louis d'Autriche that the emperor had resolved to dissolve the entire government of the Netherlands. Despite the emperor's decision, the Great Council continued its activities, convinced that it was not included in this general dissolution of all governmental institutions. In fact, the governor's letter had been somewhat ambiguous in that regard: he had not explicitly stated that the councilors should cease their sessions, and had even specifically asked that they should send all their reports, requests and information directly to him. Therefore, the councilors—probably genuinely—believed that the emperor allowed their court to continue its work.[174]

Nevertheless, similarly to their exile 2 years earlier in Düsseldorf, the councilors were not at all satisfied with their banishment to isolated Elberfeld. In a letter from early September 1794,[175] Goubau mentioned that, while spending some time with the Great Council in Elberfeld in order to catch up on some of his work as councilor

---

170 The Great Council's move to Elberfeld is confirmed by an entry in the distribution books. The lawsuit between Joseph Bernard de Saeger, appealing against a sentence of the Council of Flanders, and widow Piers, distributed on March 26, 1794 was apparently '*baillé à Mr. Van Volxem à Elberfeld le 29 aout 1794*'. Cf. Excel database: distribution records of the eighteenth century Great Council.

171 This is somewhat ironic, as the Great Council was forced to remain in Düsseldorf during the first emigration while the rest of the government stayed in Roermond. This time, the government moved to Düsseldorf but the Great Council was ordered to move even further east to Elberfeld.

172 Vienna, FHKA, Österreichische Kamerale 2309. Letter from Metternich. Roermond, July 17, 1794.

173 Vienna, FHKA, Österreichische Kamerale 2309. Letter from president Le Clerc. Würzburg, January 9, 1795.

174 Vienna, FHKA, Österreichische Kamerale 2309. Letter from Charles Louis d'Autriche to the Great Council in Elberfeld. 's Gravenvoeren, August 20, 1794.

175 Vienna, FHKA, Österreichische Kamerale 2309. Letter from Goubau to—presumably—Trauttmansdorff; the addressee is not specifically mentioned, but Goubau calls him '*Son Excellence*'. (cf. Gaillard, Arthur. 1898–1902. *Le Conseil de Brabant: histoire, organisation, procédure*. Brus-

(he usually stayed in Düsseldorf as member of the *Jointe d'Etat*[176]) he had noticed distress and dejection among the members of the Great Council. Being exiled to a place which was surrounded by high mountains and therefore almost inaccessible, the councilors had the impression that the government had completely forgotten and abandoned them. Moreover, Goubau claimed that despite all their requests to be treated like they had been in 1793—meaning with full salary and additional support—the councilors had to be satisfied with a mere 183 florins.[177]

The advocate-fiscal was convinced that a one-time gift of 4000 to 5000 florins would suffice to mitigate the members' financial difficulties. He wondered if maybe the governor could even send a letter to the Great Council in Elberfeld with some 'gracious remarks' from the emperor to boost the morale of the councilors? If only the Great Council was reminded of how grateful the government was for its loyalty and attachment to the Austrian Emperor—even if for now the treasury was too burdened to express this gratitude financially—Goubau believed that there could be no doubt that such a letter would instill the members with renewed courage and zeal. As if he additionally wanted to underline the loyalty of the Great Council, Goubau added to his letter an assessment of how the government should deal with the unmanageable Council of Brabant after the French had been driven from the Netherlands.[178]

One month earlier, Le Clerc had complained about the meager finances the members of the Great Council had at their disposal.[179] When abandoning their homes to follow the tribunal, they had not expected to be treated any differently than during the last two emigration episodes. Le Clerc claimed that both in 1790 and 1792, the government had awarded them an additional assistance of 600 florins per trimester, to compensate for the loss of *sportules*. According to the president, this time the extra support would be even less of a burden for the Royal Treasury as it was merely an advance. Given that the Great Council was still fully functioning, Le Clerc believed that the money could easily be recovered from the litigants once the French had been driven from the Netherlands. As far as he personally was concerned, the president asserted that he was entitled to at least the 6000 florins he had received since 1786, including the 1000 florins Joseph II had awarded him as an *ad personam*. Yet, he had noticed that his salary for the last trimester had been reduced

sels: Lebègue t.2, 159—governors usually enjoyed the privilege of being called *Altesse,* contrary to ministers). Düsseldorf, September 4, 1794.

176 The *Jointe d'Etat* was an *ad hoc* commission, established in June 1794, intended to discuss the major affairs of the Netherlands in the presence of Governor Charles d'Autriche. Cf. Van Honacker, Karin. 1994. Jointe van State (1794). In *De centrale overheidsinstellingen van de Habsburgse Nederlanden*, ed. Erik Aerts e.a., 356–359. Brussels: Algemeen Rijksarchief.

177 Goubau does not specify if this is their salary for a month or for a trimester, presumably the latter. In fact, the councilors had a fixed income of approximately 1200 florins a year. This, however, was reduced both by the *arrha* and the annual patriotic gift of 400 florins to fund the war.

178 Vienna, FHKA, Österreichische Kamerale 2309. Letter from Goubau, Düsseldorf, September 4, 1794.

179 Vienna, FHKA, Österreichische Kamerale 2309. Letter from Le Clerc to Trauttmansdorff, August 15, 1794.

to that of an ordinary councilor of State under the pretext that his promotion to the presidency of the Great Council had terminated this *ad personam* of 1000 florins.

Goubau's request—certainly much more so than Le Clerc's complaint—might have had a positive effect. On September 22, 1794 Trauttmansdorff informed the Great Council that the emperor had decided, at least temporarily, to award all the Council's members—including the lower employees—the same salary and additional assistance they had received in 1792–1793.[180] Not much later, the Great Council's exile in Elberfeld also ended, however not by a decision of the emperor but by the sheer necessity to emigrate further east due to the threat of the advancing French armies. Sometime in early October, the Great Council moved to Würzburg, where the prince-bishop allowed the members to continue their sessions and store their archives in the city's citadel.[181] The rest of the government moved to Dillenburg.

The situation did not exactly become any easier for the members of the Great Council. Even though the decision of September 22nd seemingly did not leave much room for doubt, the councilors' wages continued to be a subject of much discussion. They still had not received their salary in December for the months August through October and the Council of Finance had no intention to pay them their full wages or the additional supplement. Le Clerc complained about this course of events to Trauttmansdorff, explaining that the Council of Finance apparently wrongfully assumed that the Great Council was included in the latest regulations of November 11 concerning the *membres et suppôts des tribunaux de justice*.[182]

These new measures foresaw in the reduction of the salary of all members of the Belgian tribunals to half of what they had received before, starting August 20 1794 and ending exactly 1 year later. However, Le Clerc argued, since this settlement was only relevant for those officials who had been put out of work, and since the Great Council was still fully functioning, it was obvious that the councilors were still entitled to what had been promised in September 1794. In the same breath, Le Clerc once again reminded Trauttmansdorff of his personal situation and especially of his *ad personam*.

The debate continued throughout the rest of 1794 and the beginning of early 1795. By then, Trauttmansdorff had explicitly made known to the councilors that their salary—just like that of all other former members of the government—was reduced to one half of what they had received originally and this up to August 20, 1795. Afterwards, they would be eligible for a pension, the amount of which depended on their seniority.[183] In response, Le Clerc asked Trauttmansdorff if the

[180] Vienna, HHStA, Belgien DDB rot 80 (alt C53). Letter from Trauttmansdorff to Count de Clerfayt. September 22, 1794.

[181] Vienna, FHKA, Österreichische Kamerale 2309, note, dated on October 24, attached to a letter from Le Clerc to Trauttmansdorff of January 5, 1795.

[182] Vienna, FHKA, Österreichische Kamerale 2309, letter from Le Clerc to Trauttmansdorff, December 16, 1794.

[183] Vienna, FHKA, Österreichische Kamerale 2309, letter from Le Clerc to Trauttmansdorff complaining about the new regulations. Würzburg, December 28, 1794.

Great Council should cease its activities as all other governmental councils had done, or if the members should continue to prepare their sentences so that the delay the litigants had to suffer due the absence of the Council could be reduced to a minimum.[184] As far as we know, Trauttmansdorff never bothered to answer this question.

Nevertheless, less than 5 years later, on December 18, 1799, when the Committee for the Liquidation of the Belgian Financial Affairs discussed the Great Council's accounts, the expenses made to keep the tribunal operational during 1794 and 1795 were considered especially problematic.[185] As an interested party, Goubau withdrew from the assembly; Pouppez—himself also a former councilor of the Great Council—acted as reporter.

The first item of discussion were the 20 *louis* paid for by the *caisse des exploits* to president Le Clerc for the rent of chambers in Elberfeld, used by the Great Council to hold its sessions between mid-July and the end of September 1794. Although Pouppez agreed that these expenses were somewhat debatable, he advised the Committee to have them passed without further questions. However, the Committee refused to pay the bill of 182 florins for the rent and heating of the chambers of president Le Clerc in Würzburg, where the councilors had assembled during the seven winter months between October 1794 and April 1795. The Committee deemed this expenditure entirely unacceptable, given that not only the decree of August 20, 1794 but also a specific order of Trauttmansdorff of December 28 had stipulated that the Great Council should immediately suspend its activities.

The additional request of the councilors—which had already been discussed a first time in the Committee on August 20, 1798[186] and a second time on February 27, 1799[187]—to be fully paid for the period between August 20, 1794 and December 28 of that same year was also rejected. The Committee asserted that there was no merit to the councilors' arguments that they had continued to perform their duties during that timeframe and that they had not been notified of the reduction of their salary until December 28th; indeed, the decree of August 20, 1794 had left no doubt that the Great Council had been dissolved together with all other governmental institutions. The Committee judged that only their travel expenses could be reimbursed, even though the members of the Great Council had been sloppy in providing the necessary details and supporting documents for their expenses while they, as judges of a superior court, should especially set the example.

There can be no doubt that the councilors were baffled by this decision. In several requests to the government throughout 1794, they had explicitly mentioned that they were still working their cases, while in early January 1795 their president had unequivocally asked Trauttmansdorff if the Great Council was allowed to continue its activities, never to receive an answer. Not only did the Committee decline their rightful claims, but they were also blamed for their diligence. And to add insult

[184] Vienna, FHKA, Österreichische Kamerale 2309, letter from Le Clerc to Trauttmansdorff. Würzburg, January 9, 1795.

[185] Brussels, ARA, DeptNed 955, N°51, December 18, 1799.

[186] Brussels, ARA, DeptNed 953, N°509, August 10, 1798.

[187] Brussels, ARA, DeptNed 954, N°885, February 27, 1799.

to injury, this was done by a former councilor of the Great Council, who was a member of a Committee in which former advocate-fiscal of the Great Council Goubau—who had always supported the Council's decision to carry on with its sessions in Elberfeld and Würzburg—also occupied a seat. Indirectly, in fact, Goubau was condemned for his actions in 1794–1795.

Was it because Trauttmansdorff had finally ordered the Great Council to cease its sessions or because the councilors had to acknowledge that they would not receive their full salary anymore, either way, the Great Council probably did not extend its activities beyond April, 1795. Although there is no direct proof of this end date, there are two indications that they did indeed close their books sometime in the spring of 1795. First, there are no financial accounts regarding the period after April, 1795. While this is of course only indirect and negative evidence, it stands to reason that the councilors would have asked for their salary and for the rent for their chambers for the entire period they had been working, instead of merely until April, 1795. Moreover, Van Volxem died in July 1795[188] and d'Hoop left for the Netherlands sometime during that same year,[189] reducing the Great Council to a mere six members, which was certainly no longer enough to take any major decisions.

Moreover, it is certain that sometime in late September or early October 1795, the councilors were forced to flee once again, this time to Regensburg.[190] Finally, following an order of the emperor to all émigrés who wished to continue to receive their pension to establish themselves somewhere in the Austrian Succession States, the remaining members moved to Linz, together with their archives.[191] After 1796, we lose track of most of the Council's members, except for advocate-fiscal Goubau and president Le Clerc who were allowed to live in Vienna and councilor Diu and registrar Van Grootven who remained in Linz with the Council's records. Nevertheless, it is certain that the Great Council never went to Augsburg, at least not as a corpus, as Audoor claimed and as has been repeated ever since by several authors.

Living Conditions No matter where the Council was established, life in exile was hard for the *émigrés*, being far away from home, cut off from their regular income and forced to live in cities where all essentials had become increasingly expensive with the masses of emigrants that were on the roads by then. In addition, many of them had to fight the bureaucracy of the Austrian government in order to receive what they deserved and, at least for some, to exonerate themselves from the financial claims the government made. This becomes especially clear in the—sometimes multiple—requests the councilors and other members of the Great Council sent,

188 Vienna, FHKA, Österreichische Kamerale 2309, N°24: he is reported to have died on July 23, 1795.

189 Vienna, FHKA, Österreichische Kamerale 2309, N°15, file of de Vivario. In his request of December 12, de Vivario mentioned that d'Hoop had left Regensburg to go back to Malines.

190 Brussels, ARA, DeptNed 952/1, N°9, f.19, February 10, 1797: report of the Committee on the need to pay banker Dibold of Regensburg for the storage of the archives of the Great Council from October 6, 1795 on and for their transport to Linz.

191 Vienna, FHKA, Österreichische Kamerale 2310. Letter from Goubau and Diu concerning the Great Council's archives. Regensburg, March 2, 1796.

first to Trauttmansdorff in the period between 1794 and 1796 and later to the Committee for the Liquidation of Belgian Financial Affairs from 1797 on.

We have already referred to the many requests Le Clerc sent to receive his full salary as councilor of the Council of State and even more importantly his *ad personam* of 1000 florins that Joseph II had awarded him in 1786. Moreover, he claimed that his residence in Malines should also be considered a part of his income and be valued at another 1000 florins at least. Despite all his pleas and demands, the decision was made on December 11, 1794, that his *ad personam* could no longer be awarded and that the president would, until August 20, 1795, just as all other Belgian officials, receive half of the salary he was entitled to as councilor of State.[192] After that date, his pension amounted to 3347 florins.[193] While this must have been a serious letdown in and of itself, Le Clerc also became entangled, from 1798 on, in long negotiations with the Committee over accounts relating to advances he had received for travels and assignments he had done for the government between the years 1786 and 1794.

The president of the Great Council had been a notorious debtor for a long time[194] and his finances had undoubtedly not become any healthier with his exile. While he might have escaped his creditors at least for some time—being far away from most of them probably helped—the Committee started to harass him about expenses he had made and advances he had secured while on several missions for the government, among them Vienna and Liège, and about the excessive remuneration he allegedly had received for his work as president of the *Jointe* for Valenciennes.[195]

Le Clerc put up a fight against the Committee's claims, asserting that not only he did not have to return any of the advances he had secured, but that instead he was entitled to a considerable additional sum of money: firstly, because he had not been paid enough for his mission to Liège, and secondly, because he had not been compensated for the loss of income he had suffered during his assignment in Valenciennes when he had missed out on his salary as president of the Great Council. While the majority of the Committee's members did not buy his arguments—especially

---

[192] Vienna, HHStA, Belgien DDB rot 80 (alt C 53), decision of December 11, 1794. Le Clerc sent an entire array of other requests after that date—especially to complain about the loss of his *ad personam* and the reduction of his salary—but to no avail.

[193] Vienna, FHKA, Österreichische Kamerale 2309, list of the pensions awarded to the members of the Great Council.

[194] Cf. supra, Chap. 2. He even consigned his personal library to the registry of the Great Council as collateral for his debts. Antwerp, RA Antwerpen, PRAFT liasse 69, N°365: "Tableau des absents non rentrés dans la commune de Malines depuis l'expiration du délai de quinzaine porté par l'arrêté des représentants du peuple en date du 27 thermidor de l'an 2 républicaine."

[195] Brussels, ARA, DeptNed 953, N°740, f.1212, July 20, 1798; DeptNed 953, N°831, f.1340, August 10, 1798; DeptNed 953, N°s 364 and 842, f.1381, August 21, 1798; DeptNed 953, N°951, September 28, 1798; DeptNed 953, N°971, f.1630, October 9, 1798; DeptNed 953, N°516, f.1677–1678, October 26, 1798; DeptNed 953, N°971, f.1686, October 26, 1798; DeptNed 953, N°7, f.11, November 3, 1798; DeptNed 953, N°s 1 and 12, f.52, November 16, 1798; DeptNed 953, N°28, f.72–74, November 23, 1798; DeptNed 953, N°44, f.158–162, December 14, 1798; DeptNed 954, N°985, f.617, April 12, 1799.

since he could not prove anything, supposedly because all his personal archives had been destroyed during the first French invasion—and took the view that he should repay his debts to the government, Le Clerc found a supporter in his former colleague Goubau. Finally, the Committee decided that at least for now, Le Clerc did not have to reimburse anything, and that his case would be settled at the time the emperor would make his decision on how to compensate his loyal Belgian subjects for the losses they had suffered at the hands of the French.

Similar complaints and requests from the members of the Council abound in both the documents preserved at the *Finanz-und Hofkammerarchiv* and in the Committee's reports. Somewhat surprising are the many letters advocate-fiscal Goubau sent from late 1795 onwards, even to Archduke Charles Louis d'Autriche, to raise the matter of his 'meager income'.[196] While Charles d'Autriche demonstrated sympathy for this request and even asked for an exception, given that the Great Council's advocate-fiscal had been a very loyal and useful subject,[197] Goubau's pension remained limited to 1395 florins, or one third of his previous salary. However, in late 1800 the former advocate-fiscal addressed the Committee for the Liquidation of the Belgian Financial Affairs to raise once again the matter of his earnings. For both parties, this must have felt somewhat awkward because Goubau had been a member of the Committee himself, until in October 1800 he as well as Pouppez were dismissed.[198] This time, Goubau proved successful: while his complicated calculations, intended to demonstrate that he was still entitled to 6138 florins in overdue payments for his work for the *Jointe d'Etat* and his many travels, did not entirely convince the Committee, the members agreed on granting it, considering his only modest income and his many services to the state.[199]

If the councilors of the Great Council might not have been able to live as sumptuously as they wanted, their circumstances were nothing compared to the hardships many of the lower employees of the Council had to endure. Their wages were only a fraction of what the councilors received. Given that they were employed as guards of the archives and therefore obligated to follow the Council wherever it went, they also had to live with their families in very expensive cities.[200] Moreover, being

[196] Vienna, FHKA, Österreichische Kamerale 2209, N°12: requests of Goubau on October 20, 1795, December 28, 1795 and January 9, 1796.

[197] Vienna, FHKA, Österreichische Kamerale 2209. Former Governor Charles d'Autriche forwarded Goubau's request on January 23, 1796 to an unknown recipient. Potentially, this was Trauttmansdorff, as we know that other requests were often addressed to him.

[198] From that time on, the Committee would mainly deal with strictly financial matters and their background in the Great and Privy Council made them less suitable for those discussions. Goubau did stay on as the primary prosecutor in the lawsuit of the government against de Reul, a former employee of the national lottery who was accused of embezzling state funds, but his dismissal from the Committee apparently signaled for him the opportunity to pursue his own financial claims. Brussels, ARA, DeptNed 957, N°512, f.1302, October 15, 1800.

[199] Brussels, ARA, DeptNed 957, N°294, f.764–767, August 28, 1801.

[200] Vienna, FHKA, Österreichische Kamerale 2309, N°s 18, 19, 20, 21, 22 and 23: requests from G. Picard, P.F. Picard, J.J. Leleux, N.F. Picard, P. Picard, P.M. Mentz, A. Verbruggen and E. Benckendorff.

much less well-connected, they were also less likely to receive a positive response to their requests to the Committee.[201]

5.3 Epilogue

By early 1800, the days were numbered for the Great Council as an institution. As the Austrian government was constantly being pushed for money, the Committee for the Liquidation of the Belgian Financial Affairs decided to auction off several effects—though not documents—that had made the journey from the Netherlands to Austria. Numerous goods, often in gold, belonging to the Chapter of Saint Gudule in Brussels had already been sold before 1800. It was precisely because these items were not government property—and without a doubt because there was not much chance the owners would reclaim them any time soon—that they were put up for sale to pay for the 'costs of transportation and preservation'.[202] However, once these stocks were exhausted, the government turned to other marketable items, among others from the Great Council.[203] Without much ceremony, the Committee decided to sell the large and small silver seals of the court in February 1801: the message that the Great Council was dead and buried could not have been any clearer.[204]

Also in February 1801, the Austrian Empire and the French Republic signed the Treaty of Lunéville. One of the articles foresaw a general amnesty for the *émigrés*, giving them the opportunity to return to their home country on the express condition that they would take the oath of allegiance to the French Republic. Around

---

[201] Former proctor of the Great Council and one of the persons in charge of its records Picard was a case in point. In the summer of 1800, he addressed two requests to the Committee for additional support: his very modest pension—which stood at 250 florins a year—did not cover the high medical costs he had had for his sick daughter who had emigrated with him. Goubau—regardless of him being a former colleague at the Great Council—advised against any additional financial aid for Picard. Brussels, ARA, DeptNed 957, N°385, f.1004, July 9, 1800; DeptNed 957, N°430, f.1142, August 6, 1800. Picard was certainly not the only one: the archives contain several requests from notaries and lower functionaries of the Great Council, such as bailiffs. Cf. Brussels, ARA, DeptNed 957, N°477, f.1240, September 10, 1800; DeptNed 958, N°s 76, 103, 104 and 130, f.277, March 30, 1801; DeptNed 958, N°155, f.335, April 8, 1801. Although a limited number of these requests were successful, they all demonstrate the strenuous conditions in which many of the *émigrés* lived.

[202] Brussels, ARA, DeptNed 958, N°82, f.198–205, February 18, 1801. Only items that were not related to worship were auctioned off.

[203] Others included the papers of the heraldic chamber of the Netherlands. Cf. Laloire, Emile. 1914. Comité de liquidation des affaires belgiques de 1797 à 1804. In *Mélanges d'histoire offerts à Charles Moeller à l'occasion de son jubilé de 50 années de professorat à l'Université de Louvain*. Leuven: Bureaux de Recueil, 525.

[204] Brussels, ARA, DeptNed 958, N°85, f.212–214, February 25, 1801.

the same time, the Austrian authorities decided to reduce the *émigrés*' pensions.[205] Several former functionaries, quite a few of whom used to be at the pinnacle of the judicial hierarchy, such as de Fierlant and Crumpipen, decided to settle back into the Netherlands under French control. The fate of the emigrated councilors of the Great Council is less well-known. As mentioned before, Van Volxem had already passed away in the summer of 1795. President Le Clerc died in Vienna around 1812[206] whereas d'Hoop preferred to go back to the Netherlands in an early phase.[207] De Laing, Diu, Baujoz, Goubau and de Steenhault were listed as *absents non rentrés dans la commune de Malines.*[208] Baujouz and Diu died in 1799 and 1800, respectively, most likely someplace in the Habsburg lands; Goubau eventually returned to the Netherlands in 1814 and took up a new position under the Dutch rule.[209]

While the scattering of its members and its archives, its official abolishment and the sale of its silver seals seemingly left no room for doubt that the more than 300-year-old Great Council was never to rise again, some of the surviving members did make an attempt at revival in 1814. In a petition addressed to King William I of the United Kingdom of the Netherlands, de Villers, Ghison, de Guchtenaere, Richterich and Wirix—referring to themselves as respectively vice-president, councilors, registrar and secretary of the Great Council—pleaded to have the tribunal reestablished once again.[210] Recounting the long history of the Great Council, its importance as 'first tribunal' of the Netherlands[211] and its reputation as a 'loyal supporter' of the Crown—had the Austrian Emperor not recognized this quality by awarding the position of councilor of State to its senior member?—the councilors tried to convince King William to restore the Great Council to its former glory.[212] Needless to say, the Dutch King was not persuaded: there could be no question of reviving an institution so closely linked to the Ancien Régime as the Great Council.

A definitive settlement of the Great Council's consigned cash reserves and undecided lawsuits was not arranged until almost 50 years after its abolishment by

---

[205] Zedinger, Renate. 2004. *Migration und Karriere: Habsburgische Beamte in Brüssel und Wien im 18. Jahrhundert* (Schriftenreihe der Österreichischen Gesellschaft zur Erforschung des 18. Jahrhunderts 9). Vienna: Böhlau, 77.

[206] Brussels, ARA, Manuscrits divers 860A, p. 25.

[207] Antwerp, RA Antwerpen, PRAFT liasse 69, N°365. The document mentions that d'Hoop was a '*royaliste acharné, grand partisan de la maison d'Autriche*'; Vienna, FHKA, Österreichische Kamerale 2309: d'Hoop: '*Nach Niederland zurück*'

[208] Antwerp, RA Antwerpen, PRAFT liasse 69, N°365: "Tableau des absents non rentrés dans la commune de Malines depuis l'expiration du délai de quinzaine porté par l'arrêté des représentants du peuple en date du 27 thermidor de l'an 2 républicaine."

[209] Bruneel, Claude and Hoyois, Jean-Paul. 2001. *Les grands commis des Pays-Bas autrichiens: dictionnaire biographique du personnel des institutions centrales*. Brussels: Algemeen Rijksarchief, 293–294.

[210] Brussels, ARA, Staatssecretarie voor België, 6798, file 4516–556798, August 1814. We are grateful to our colleague Geert Leloup who referred us to this document.

[211] They listed the Great Council's jurisdiction as consisting, apart from its authority in first instance cases, of dealing with appeals from the Councils of Luxemburg, Flanders, Namur, Tournai and the Magistrate of Malines.

[212] The need to bring back life to the city of Malines was another argument.

King Leopold I of Belgium in December 1845.[213] Contrary to some of the undecided cases of the Council of Brabant which had been taken over by the new court of justice in Brussels,[214] the lawsuits of the Great Council were not reopened. The scattering of its archives was certainly one of the reasons.

The cash deposited by the litigants at the Great Council's registry continued to be a matter of concern. After the invasion of the French, the consigned cash reserves had been transported together with the archives to Austria. While the treaties of Campo Formio, Lunéville and Presbourg did not contain any stipulations concerning these sums, a convention concluded in 1828 between the United Kingdom of the Netherlands and Vienna provided for the return of the money as well as for the settlement of all 'pending' cases by the Superior Court of Justice in Brussels. However, the events of 1830 made it impossible for the Brussels tribunal to further deal with the matter. Firstly, in March 1839 and again in November 1842, the agreement was renegotiated, this time between Belgium and the Netherlands. Eventually, it was decided that the Dutch treasury would return the money to the Belgian treasury, which effectively happened on July 19, 1843. The decree of December 5, 1845 finally arranged the details of the restitution of the consigned cash reserves to the parties (art.1–6; 8) and provided for the possibility to resume the undecided lawsuits of the Great Council at the then competent tribunals (art.7). In 1845, the curtain had finally fallen for good.

Concluding Remarks

Looking back on the events of the late 1780s and early 1790s, it might seem that, already in 1787, it was obvious that the Great Council was bound to disappear. Nevertheless, the councilors, and without a doubt other contemporaries, were blissfully unaware that the curtain was falling over their court. Apart from the external events, the 7 years between 1787 and 1794 must have seemed from the Great Council's perspective rather similar to the rest of the eighteenth century. And even the French invasion was not so out of the ordinary: the French had occupied parts of the Southern Netherlands twice before in the eighteenth century, once during the War of the Spanish Succession and once during the War of the Austrian Succession.

Several characteristic traits of the Great Council that we have already distinguished in the previous chapters continue to pop up in the final decade of its history. The self-consciousness of the Council and the status anxiety of the councilors, for example, are omnipresent in their constant reminders to the sovereign of their unwavering loyalty and of the special position of the council as the 'Emperor's Court'

[213] *Le moniteur belge*, December 11, 1845.

[214] Cf. Depoortere, Rolande. 1999. *Les cours d'appel en Belgique et leurs prédécesseurs en droit 1795–1799: compétences et organisation, production et conservation des archives*. Brussels: Algemeen Rijksarchief.

par excellence. Yet, the perpetual fear of the Council's members to be ignored and undervalued becomes especially obvious during their exile in 1792. Unmistakably, the councilors were banned from the center of activity—first located in Roermond, later in Wesel—where all other governmental councils were allowed to continue their work; instead, they were singled out to remain in Düsseldorf as private citizens. And while the Great Council's members did not actually go so far as to complain about their situation, de Fierlant's letters and their refusal to move to a city other than Roermond or Wesel indicate that they were well aware that their exile in Düsseldorf was indicative of the Great Council's position in the hierarchy.

The rivalry with the other provincial councils and their attempts to undermine the Great Council's authority continued throughout the late 1780s and early 1790s. The Council of Flanders and the Magistrate of Malines in particular persisted in trouble-making. While the Privy Council often ruled these conflicts of jurisdiction to the advantage of the Great Council, the court was sometimes harshly rebuffed. The refusal of the Council of Finance to refund the expenses made for the jurisdictional infighting with the Council of Flanders, not only jeopardized the Great Council's future efforts to keep it in line, but also sent the signal that maintaining Malines' authority against its subordinate tribunals was no longer deemed important. The culmination of this lack of governmental support for the Great Council's claims certainly was the Valenciennes case, when the Council of Hainaut—which only a few years earlier had opposed the Habsburg rule—was awarded jurisdiction over this newly conquered territory at the expense of the 'Emperor's Court'.

In general, the central government adopted an ambivalent attitude towards the Great Council. In times of crisis, which the late eighteenth century certainly was for the Habsburg dynasty, the Great Council thrived. When the instigators of the various revolts needed to be punished, the government explicitly fell back on the Great Council and the loyalty of its members. Likewise, when the position of the Council of Brabant had become untenable in the eyes of the government, the Great Council was awarded the—admittedly somewhat dubious—honor of taking over the jurisdiction of the Council of Brabant through the establishment of a satellite in Brussels. Nevertheless, once the immediate crisis had passed and the outlook was somewhat better, the government degraded the Great Council again to a mere secondary role, up to the point that it even turned down the Great Council's request to regain its jurisdiction over Luxemburg and Tournai.

In the end, the Great Council demonstrated a remarkable resistance against actually disappearing. Even though the tribunal had to go into exile in 1794, was officially abolished in 1797 and its silver seals were sold in 1801, some of its remaining members attempted to revive the Great Council in 1814 and disputes over its records were still fought out in 1830. It was not until approximately 1845, or more than half a century after its official abolishment, that the books on the Great Council eventually could be closed for good.

References

Archival Sources

Antwerp, State Archives

Provinciaal Archief Frans Tijdvak
69

Beveren, State Archives

R 53, Rechtbank van Eerste Aanleg, EA Mechelen
48

Brussels, General State Archives

Algemene Regeringsraad
857, 858, 974
Departement voor de Nederlanden van de Hof- en Staatskanselarij
952/1, 953–959, 960/1, 960/2
Geheime Raad, Oostenrijkse Periode. Registers
482, 484
Grote Raad van Mechelen. Registers

3 *Preliminary documents*

GRM 3 includes a small register as well as a limited number of separate documents concerning the archives of the Great Council during and after the Brabant Revolution and the first and second French invasion (1789–1894). It contains detailed descriptions of the inspection and confiscation of certain archives of the Great Council during the Brabant Revolution including their retrieval by a specifically for that purpose designated councilor and secretary in late 1790. In addition, it includes an account of the examination of the Great Council's chambers and their sealing by the French revolutionaries in 1792. The set of separate documents holds the order of June 1794 to provide the Great Council with carriages to transport its most important archives to Roermond and a short account by the warden of the Great Council of the events in Malines right after the evacuation of the Great Council from the city. The documents also give a privileged insight into the preservation of the records of the Great Council, their arrangement and even to a certain extent into the use of the premises of the Council (e.g.: it is described which archives are preserved in what rooms and specifies the employees that hold the keys to certain chambers).

4–5 *Patent letters*

GRM 4–5 mainly contains the lettres patentes or open letters by which the employees of the Great Council—both the president, councilors and the lower personnel—were appointed into their position. Appointment letters were always standardized texts, describing the 'rights' and 'duties' of the appointee in question in which only the names and dates were changed. To a smaller extent, the patent letters also include letters of naturalization and habilitation which foreign-born candidates for a councillorship in the Great Council needed to be considered. Patent letters for the Great Council have been preserved for the period between 1686 and 1794. The appointment files, which do give ample information about a prospective candidate, can be found in the Privy Council, which was responsible for the nomination of councilors and other personnel at the royal courts.

97–98; 133; 135–140 Correspondence

The "recueils de la correspondance du Grand Conseil" have been preserved for the entire history of the Council, covering the period between 1464 and 1794. The correspondence of the Great Council consists of a diverse array of letters and requests sent to or by the Great Council. The central government, usually through the Privy Council, is the main correspondent, but other institutions, such as provincial councils, and even individuals figure in these registers. The subject matter ranges from orders to organize a Te Deum, requests of all sort of dispensations, conflicts of jurisdiction with especially the Council of Flanders or the Magistrate of Malines, to instructions of the governor on how to respond to a potential invasion by the French. The only structure in this mishmash of documents is the date on which they were composed or received, but even this chronological criterion was not always rigorously followed. The registers provide a privileged insight into the judicial but even more into the non-judicial aspects of the Great Council's workings. However, the enormous volume of the series (consisting of 129 registers over a period of 330 years) and the lack of organization make research into the correspondence very time-consuming. The correspondence of the Great Council has its counterpart in the archives of the office-fiscal (GRMOF, Banden en Delen) which, however, suffers from the same problems.

175/10 *Decrees* and *Ordonnances*

Number GRM 175/10 is ranged under the heading *Edits, Placards et Ordonnances* (comprising GRM 169 to 175/11). This series contains, at least in theory, a list of all ordinances and decrees that the Great Council had to publish—or at least give the order to have them published—in its jurisdiction, predominantly for the second half of the eighteenth century, although some earlier periods are also included. However, the title is somewhat misleading; in fact the inventory specifies for this specific number that it deals with the judicial administration for the period 1789 to 1794 in addition to information about residences of the Great Council outside of Malines, ceremonial issues, relations with other institutions and procedure for the period between 1466 and 1794. In practice, number 175/10 is not a register but a 'file' filled with a mishmash of documents with little or no internal connection. Documents concerning the period between 1789 and 1795—the official act that abolished the Great Council in 1789 can be found here—are included, as well as descriptions of the paintings that are hanging in the premises of the Great Council. In addition, the move of the Great Council to Namur in 1746 is extensively described. Moreover, the file also contains several documents about the archives of the Great Council that were not necessarily written during the Ancien Régime: e.g. the letter of P.J. L'Orye from 1830, criticizing Audoor's report on the archives of the Great Council, an overview of the documents of the Great Council that were eventually returned by the French in 1770 and several accounts of the chaotic situation the archives of the office-fiscal were in. Finally, the file contains a separate subfile that deals with the problems concerning the jurisdiction of the Council of Luxemburg. It is obvious that a wealth of information is hidden behind an inadequate description.

231–232 Miscellaneous

The "miscellaneous" category in Van den Bussche's inventory (consisting of the numbers 231 to 261/3) is indeed a collection of unrelated documents that do not really fit anywhere else. It consists mostly of marriage contracts, last wills and 'letters written by famous people that have been extracted from their case files'. The numbers 231 and 232, however, are even in this "miscellaneous" category somewhat "outsiders". Van den Bussche describes GRM 231 as cahier portant des annotations au sujet de certains faits auxquels le grand conseil s'est trouvé mêlé ou qui l'ont mis dans le cas de devoir prendre une délibération ou une consulte officieuse (1701–1800). In practice, the first part of this register is indeed an overview of unofficial decisions taken by the Great Council, mostly with regards to their ceremonial duties (such as congratulating a newly appointed governor or organizing a holy mess for the sovereign's health). The second part, however, mostly deals with the first invasion of the French in 1792 and describes in great detail the decisions regarding the stay of the Council in Düsseldorf and the councilors' dissatisfaction with this 'exile'. Finally, the register also includes the documents regarding the awarding of the title of 'Councilor of State' to the senior councilor of the Great Council in 1794. If the description of GRM 231 does not entirely cover its content and is probably an artificially put together collection, this is equally true for GRM 232. While the register is described in the inventory as Recueil des documents concernant le personnel du Grand Conseil, particulièrement les secrétaires, et diverses pièces touchant le rétablissement du siège en 1791, not many documents about any of those two subjects are included. Even though there is a long complaint by the secretaries denouncing the fact that, in violation of all ordinances, councilors 'steal' their work (and thereby their income) by awarding copying jobs to their personal assistants and a document describing the re-erection of the Great Council after the Brabant Revolution, the main part of the register is filled with a long letter of the councilors of the Great Council, dated in 1771, denouncing the ever growing jurisdiction of the Council of Luxemburg. As a rule, a wealth of information is often hidden behind inadequate descriptions, in the archives of the Great Council.

Grote Raad van Mechelen. Officie-fiscaal. Banden en Delen.
32–34, 42, 43, 61, 65–70, 96–99
Grote Raad van Mechelen. Officie-fiscaal. Procesdossiers.
717–751
Inventarissen van de Derde Afdeling
13, 14, 16, 48, 102
Manuscrits Divers
860/A
Papiers des commissaires du gouvernement dits Papiers Bouteville
439
Staatssecretarie voor België
6798

Malines, City Archives

Archives de la ville de Malines: affaires civiles et ecclésiastiques
23, 129/5, 138

Vienna, Haus-, Hof-Und Staatsarchiv

Belgien DD-B rot
80 (alt C53)

Vienna, Finanz-Und Hofkammerarchiv

Österreichisches Kamerale
2308, 2309, 2310

Published and Printed Sources

Le moniteur belge, 15e Jaargang, N°345, 11 December 1845

Literature

Beales, Derek. 2009. *Joseph II. Vol II: Against the World*. Cambridge: Cambridge University Press.

Bérenger, Jean. 2007. *Joseph II d'Autriche: serviteur de l'Etat*. Paris: Fayard.

Bernard, Bruno. 1998. Les hauts fonctionnaires des Pays-Bas autrichiens en emigration (1789–1803). In *Camporformio 1797: la Belgique change de maîtres*, 105–110. Brussels: Legermuseum.

Blanning, Timothy. 1994. *Joseph II*. London: Longman.

Blitz, Rudolph. 1989. The religious reforms of Joseph II (1780–1790) and their economic significance. *Journal of European Economic History* 18 3: 583–595.

Bosch, J.W. 1965. Keizer Joseph II en de president Goswin de Fierlant. *Tijdschrift voor Rechtsgeschiedenis* 33.2: 283–289.

Bruneel, Claude. 2001. Le personnel de la chambre des comptes des Pays-Bas face à la Révolution Belgique (1787–1792). *Handelingen van de Koninklijke Commissie voor Geschiedenis* 156: 1–252.

Bruneel, Claude, and Hoyois, Jean-Paul. 2001. *Les grands commis des Pays-Bas autrichiens: dictionnaire biographique du personnel des institutions centrales*. Brussels: Algemeen Rijksarchief.

Cauchies, Jean Marie, Desmaele, Bernard, and Mariage, Florian. 2009. *Les institutions publiques régionales et locales en Hainaut et Tournais-Tournaisis sous l'Ancien Régime*. Brussels: Algemeen Rijksarchief.

Cosemans, A. 1955. De Brabantse Omwenteling en de vestiging van een nieuw bewind in de Zuidelijke Nederlanden. In *Algemene Geschiedenis der Nederlanden*, eds. Jacob Presser e.a., t. 8, 170–194. Zeist: De Haan.

Craeybeckx, Jan. 1967. De Brabantse Omwenteling: een conservatieve opstand in een achterlijk land? *Tijdschrift voor geschiedenis* 80: 303–330.

De Gryse, Piet, Lefèvre, Patrick, and Lorette, Jean eds. 1984. *Handelingen van het colloquium over de Brabantse Omwenteling, 13–14 Oktober 1983*. Brussels: Koninklijk Legermuseum.

Depoortere, Rolande. 1999. *Les cours d'appel en Belgique et leurs prédécesseurs en droit 1795–1799: compétences et organisation, production et conservation des archives*. Brussels: Algemeen Rijksarchief.

Dhondt, Luc. 1989. De conservatieve Brabantse omwenteling van 1789 en het proces van revolutie en contrarevolutie in de Zuidelijke Nederlanden tussen 1780 en 1830. *Tijdschrift voor Geschiedenis* 92: 422–450.

Dhondt, Luc. 1993. *Verlichte monarchie, Ancien Regime en revolutie*. 7t. Ghent: RUG.

Gaillard, Arthur. 1898–1902. *Le Conseil de Brabant: histoire, organisation, procédure*. Brussels: Lebègue.

Gilissen, John. 1980. De Grote Raad van Mechelen. Historisch overzicht. In *Miscelannea Consilii Magni. Ter gelegenheid van twintig jaar Werkgroep Grote Raad van Mechelen*, 13–43. Amsterdam: Universiteit van Amsterdam. Faculteit der rechtsgeleerdheid.

Hasquin, Hervé. 1987. Slotbeschouwingen. Jozef II en de Franse Revolutie: punten van overeenkomst en breuk. In *Oostenrijks België 1713–1794: de Zuidelijke Nederlanden onder de Oostenrijkse Habsburgers*, ed. Hervé Hasquin, 533–534. Brussels: Gemeentekrediet van België.

Hasquin, Hervé. 2007. *Joseph II: catholique antéclerical et réformateur impatient 1741–1790*. Brussels: Racine.

Hermans, Victor and Van Doren, Pierre.-Joseph. 1859–1896. *Inventaire des archives de la ville de Malines*. Malines: Van Velsen.

Hubert, Eugène. 1900. *Le voyage de l'empereur Joseph II dans les Pays-Bas (31 mai 1781–27 juillet 1781): etude d'histoire politique et diplomatique*. Brussels: Lebègue.

Jacob, Steve. 1999. Jacques-Antoine Le Clerc (1731-après 1797). Un fonctionnaire au service d'une politique réformatrice. In *La haute administration dans les Pays-Bas autrichiens (Ambroise-Joseph de Herzelles, Denis-Benoît de Cazier, Jacques-Antoine Le Clerc)* (Etudes sur le XVIIIe siècle 27), eds. Hervé Hasquin and Roland Mortier, 243–354. Brussels: Université de Bruxelles

Janssens, Paul, Roegiers, Jan, and Vanhemelryck, Fernand. 1990. *Revolutie in Brabant 1787–1793*. Brussels: UFSAL.

Kisters, Frédéric. 1996. Les intendances instituées par Joseph II en 1787. *Revue belge de philologie et d'histoire* 74.3–4: 761–803.

Laenen, Joseph. 1905. *Etude sur la suppression des couvents par l'empereur Joseph II dans les Pays-Bas autrichiens et plus spécialement dans le Brabant (1783–1794)*. Antwerp: Van Hille-De Backer.

Laloire, Emile. 1914. Comité de liquidation des affaires belgiques de 1797 à 1804. In *Mélanges d'histoire offerts à Charles Moeller à l'occasion de son jubilé de 50 années de professorat à l'Université de Louvain*, 521–526. Leuven: Bureaux de Recueil.

Lefevre, Joseph. 1928. *Le conseil du gouvernement général*. Brussels: Lamertin.

Leyder, Dirk. 2010. *Les archives du Grand Conseil des Pays-Bas à Malines (vers 1445–1797)*. Brussels: Algemeen Rijksarchief.

Maes, Louis Th. 2009. *Het Parlement en de Grote Raad van Mechelen: 1473–1797*. Antwerp: De Vries-Brouwers.

Monballyu, Jos. 2000. L'idée d'un code criminel chez Goswin de Fierlant. *Tijdschrift voor Rechtsgeschiedenis* 68: 281–300.

Petit, Jean-Luc. 1986. Joseph de Crumpipen (1737–1789), les idées d'un haut fonctionnaire et magistrate des Pays-Bas autrichiens sur la justice de son temps. *Tijdschrift voor Rechtsgeschiedenis* 54: 127–148.

Polasky, Janet. 1985. *Revolution in Brussels 1787–1793*. Gembloux: Duculot.

Put, Eddy. 2002. Gedeelde soevereiniteit? De dubbelrol van de Raad van Brabant. In *Politieke representatie*, eds. Henk de Smaele and Johan Tollebeek, 221–229. Leuven: Universitaire Pers Leuven.

Roegiers, Jan. 1980. *Kerk en Staat in de Oostenrijkse Nederlanden*. In In *Algemene Geschiedenis der Nederlanden*, eds. Walter Prevenier e.a, t. 9, 361–375. Haarlem: Fibula-Van Dishoeck.

Rousseaux, Xavier. 1993. *Le personnel judiciaire en Belgique à travers les révolutions (1780–1832)*. In *Het politiek personeel tijdens de overgang van het Ancien Régime naar het nieuwe regiem in België (1780–1830)*, eds. Piet Lenders e.a., 18–40. Heule: UGA.

Schoups, Inge. 1987. P.J.M. L'Ortye, Rijksarchivaris te Brussel, 1814–1831. Een vergeten figuur. In *Album Carlos Wyffels: aangeboden door zijn wetenschappelijke medewerkers*, eds. Herman Coppejans and Georges Hansotte, 403–412. Brussels: Algemeen Rijksarchief.

Stevens, Fred. 2000. Goswinus Anna Maria Felix de Fierlant (1735–1804): Een Turnhoutse bevoorrechte getuige van het einde van een tijdperk. *Taxandria: jaarboek van de Koninklijke geschied-en oudheidkundige kring van de Antwerpse Kempen* 71: 7–21.

Stroobant, Louis. 1901. Ce que devinrent les archives et la bibliothèque du Grand Conseil. *Bulletin du cercle archéologique, littéraire et artistique de Malines* 11: 293–302.

Szantay, Antal. 2005. *Regionalpolitik im Alten Europa: die Verwaltungsreformen Josephs II in Ungarn, in der Lombardei und in den Österreichischen Niederlanden 1785–1790*. Budapest: Akadémiai Kiadó.

Tassier, Suzanne. 1989. *Les démocrates belges de 1789*. Brussels: Hayez.

Tesch, Marie-Eve. 2004. La réforme de la justice de l'empereur Joseph II dans les Pays-Bas autrichiens. Le séjour à Bruxelles du baron Karl Anton von Martini. 29 novembre 1786–31 mai 1787. In *Bruxellois à Vienne, Viennois à Bruxelles*, ed. Bruno Bernard, 113–161. Brussels: Université de Bruxelles.

Vandermeersch, Bernard. 2010. *Comme il importe au bien de l'Eglise et de l'Etat...: l'opposition de l'épiscopat 'Belgique' aux réformes ecclésiastiques de Joseph II (1780–1790)*. Louvain-la-Neuve: Collège Erasme.

Van Hille, Philippe. 1973. *De gerechtelijke hervorming van Keizer Jozef II*. Tielt: Veys.

Van Honacker, Karin. 1994. Jointe van State (1794). In *De centrale overheidsinstellingen van de Habsburgse Nederlanden*, ed. Erik Aerts e.a., 356–359. Brussels: Algemeen Rijksarchief.

Van Honacker, Karin. 1994. Jointe voor het voorlopig bestuur van het op Frankrijk veroverde land (Jointe te Valencijn) (1793–1794). In *De centrale overheidsinstellingen van de Habsburgse Nederlanden*, ed. Erik Aerts e.a., 360–366. Brussels: Algemeen Rijksarchief.

Van Honacker, Karin. 1994. Tijdelijk comité voor de vereffening van de Nederlandse financiële kwesties te Wenen (1797–1804). In *De centrale overheidsinstellingen van de Habsburgse Nederlanden*, ed. Erik Aerts e.a., 144–148. Brussels: Algemeen Rijksarchief.

Verscuren, An. 2014. Archieven in oorlog, speelbal van politiek. Het archief van de Grote Raad van Mechelen (1746–1869)'. In *Macht en Onmacht. De rol van archieven in oorlog en bij rechtsherstel*, eds. Ron Blom e.a., 49–59. 's-Gravenhage: Stichting Archiefpublicaties

Vervondel, Eva. 2004. *De Grote Raad van Mechelen van 1780 tot 1797. De laatste jaren en de verdwijning*. Leuven, Unpublished Master's Thesis. Katholieke Universiteit Leuven.

Wijffels, Alain. 1994. Grote Raad voor de Nederlanden te Mechelen (ca.1445–1797). In *De centrale overheidsinstellingen van de Habsburgse Nederlanden*, ed. Erik Aerts e.a., 448–461. Brussels: Algemeen Rijksarchief.

Zedinger, Renate. 1998. Un fonds à découvrir pour l'histoire des Pays-Bas autrichiens: les requêtes des fonctionnaires et pensionnés émigrés conservées au 'Finanz- und Hofkammerarchiv Wien'. *Bulletin de la commission royale d'histoire* 164: 173–256.

Zedinger, Renate. 2004. *Migration und Karriere: Habsburgische Beamte in Brüssel und Wien im 18. Jahrhundert* (Schriftenreihe der Österreichischen Gesellschaft zur Erforschung des 18. Jahrhunderts 9). Vienna: Böhlau.

Chapter 6
Conclusion

In 1772—as a result of the decision to limit the Great Council's jurisdiction over Luxemburg—the councilors expressed their worries about a potential abolition of their tribunal.[1] In 1785, the members of the Council of Flanders casted doubt on the usefulness of the Great Council, given that it derived its sole reason for existence from its competence as appeal court for the province of Flanders.[2] While these remarks must be understood in context, they do suggest that already in the late eighteenth century, doubts were cast over the position of the Great Council, both by critics of the tribunal—the councilors of Flanders—and by its most staunch defenders—its own members.

The questions raised by these two comments are at the base of this dissertation: did the Great Council outlive its usefulness? Was the tribunal indeed characterized by decline, as eighteenth century institutions are generally assumed to be? And what does this mean for the position of the Great Council as instrument of state formation?

In order to answer these questions, we predominantly made use of archival materials, keeping in mind throughout our research that archives are 'ruins,' incomplete and disparate remainders of the past, which allow us to reconstruct, at best, a partial picture of the subject. At the same time, the surviving records of the Great Council are incredibly rich and diverse and provide a privileged insight into the eighteenth century court. It also means that the history of the records of the eighteenth century Great Council as well as of its record-keeping were crucial in our understanding of the history of the court itself.

A firm quantitative approach towards the sources, supplemented with qualitative methods, proved to be the only way to arrive at an answer to the previously formulated questions. Statistical processing of *Ancien Régime* archival materials is always a precarious enterprise. Nevertheless, we believe that a quantitative analysis was imperative to properly measure the changes in case-load at the Great Council over time and, consequently, to evaluate the impact of the tribunal in the eighteenth century. The use of quantitative methods not only made it possible to

[1] ARA, GR Register 466, f.89–96, March 14, 1772. Cf. supra, Chap. 2.

[2] ARA, GR Registers 481, f.197–203, August 1785. Cf. supra, Chap. 2.

A. Verscuren, *The Great Council of Malines in the 18th century*,
Studies in the History of Law and Justice 3, DOI 10.1007/978-3-319-09638-4_6

uncover specific patterns and pose some uncommon questions to the source material, but it also enabled us to map the reach of the administration of justice at the Great Council, and, as a corollary, of the tribunal itself, both as an institution and as an instrument of state-building.

6.1 An Instrument of State Formation?

In the approximately 300 years between the establishment of the Great Council and its eventual demise, society in the Netherlands had changed in multiple perspectives. Apart from the repercussions the 80 Years' War had on the Southern Netherlands in the late sixteenth and early seventeenth centuries, the eighteenth century in itself was a century in transformation.

During the 1700s, the ideas of Enlightenment started to trickle down into several aspects of life. The first cracks in the authority of the Church appeared, in particular in its relationship with the State. Especially from the 1750s on, the central government, imbued with regalist ideas, was no longer reluctant to oppose the ultramontane Church.

Furthermore, the Austrian Habsburgs increased state intervention in the economic domain. In the course of the eighteenth century, taxation became more rationalized, the power of the guilds was curtailed and a certain proto-industrialization stimulated. At the same time, Maria Theresa managed to extract the Southern Netherlands from the nefarious commercial stranglehold of, in particular, the United Provinces and Great-Britain.[3] The result of these economic policies was the emergence of a new class of wealthy people, who could not be fitted into the traditional Ancien Régime society dominated by the three Estates.

Interventions in internal policy-making were limited, given that the constraints of the composite state did not allow for much change in that regard. Yet, certain subtle changes, aimed at more centralization, were made. For example, the authority of the governor was eroded in favor of the Minister Plenipotentiary, who, much more than the former, was an agent of the Viennese government.

Despite the changing society and the influence of the Age of Enlightenment, the administration of justice in the eighteenth century was still very similar to what it had been in the late sixteenth century. Until Joseph II, the Austrian Habsburgs had not put much effort into fundamentally reforming the judicial system or the law, except for some small attempts at humanizing the criminal law under Maria

[3] Aerts, Erik. 2013. Economische interventie van de centrale staat in de Spaanse en Oostenrijkse Nederlanden (1555–1795). In *Gouvernance et administration dans les provinces belges (XVIe-XVIIIe siècles)* (Archives et Bibliothèques de Belgique 99), Eds. Claude De Morbeau de Gerbehaye e.a., 399–452. Brussels: Archives et Bibliothèques de Belgique; Lenders, Piet. 1995. Ontstaan en ontwikkeling van de moderne staat in de Nederlanden. In *Symposium over de centrale instellingen van de Habsburgse Nederlanden, Brussel 3 December 1994. Tien Bijdragen over de staat, de regering en de ambtenaren van de 16de tot de 18de eeuw* (Standen en Landen Bijzondere Reeks nr. 2), eds. Herman Coppens en Karin Van Honacker. Brussels: Algemeen Rijksarchief, 20–21; 39.

Theresa. Justice in the eighteenth century was still class bound, with the Great Council as the tribunal *par excellence* for the privileged. In addition, the administration of justice continued to be a slow process, due to the complicated and time-consuming procedure and the fact that the councilors had a financial incentive to let cases drag on.

The central government was apparently unwilling to implement the reforms necessary to adapt the court to the changed circumstances of the eighteenth century. Moreover, the ambiguous attitude of the Austrian Habsburgs towards the Great Council also suggests that they no longer considered the tribunal as the prime instrument it had once been to provide a check on the Provincial Councils or the local authorities. In addition, it can be assumed that the decline in litigation at the Council diminished its ability to work as a tool of centralization and unification.

An active policy was certainly never reserved for the eighteenth century Great Council. Somewhat ironically, the fact that it had to stand by and watch the events unfold from the sideline was the direct result of its special position as the Sovereign's Court. Having no Estates to rely on for support to defend its rights and privileges—as was the case for the provincial councils—the Great Council was entirely dependent on the government's whim. While the Great Council might have been an excellent tool of centralization in the fifteenth and sixteenth centuries, it was no longer actively promoted by the monarchs of the eighteenth century to play that role.

Failing to reinforce the Great Council to serve once again as an instrument of state-building might have been a deliberate strategy as part of the Austrian Habsburgs' attempts—at least until Maria Theresa—not to upset the delicate balance of the composite state. A strong Great Council was bound to hurt the particularistic feelings of the provinces at some point, something which was especially avoided in the period of the Theresian Compromise.

Brabant, in particular, had to be treated with care. From all components of the composite state, Brabant was the most influential, not only because it was wealthy, but also because the Charter of the *Blijde Inkomst* gave it a privileged status not shared by any other province. Accordingly, its provincial council was powerful, much more so than the Great Council.[4] Not only was it sovereign, but—contrary to the Great Council—it also had a right of remonstration, which it could use to block reforms that were considered to be a contravention against the *Blijde Inkomst*. Indeed, more than any other judicial institution in the Netherlands, the Council of Brabant was a political actor the government could not lightly pass over.

In addition, the position of the Council of Brabant was highly ambiguous. While administering justice in the name of the sovereign, it also represented the inhabitants of Brabant due to its oath to the *Blijde Inkomst*. Consequently, it was

[4] Wijffels, Alain. 1997. Grand Conseil de Malines: la rédaction des sentences étendues et le recueil de jurisprudence de Guillaume de Grysperre. In *Case law in the making: the techniques and methods of judicial records and law reports (Comparative studies in continental and Anglo-American Legal History* 17) v.1, ed. Alain Wijffels. Berlin: Duncker und Humblot, 312.

frequently torn between its allegiance to the sovereign and its loyalty to the Brabant Estates, which inevitably caused problems and provided the Council of Brabant with a reputation of unruliness.[5] This is no surprise given that there was much more at stake for the Council of Brabant than for the Great Council. While the latter merely attempted to preserve its position and justify its existence towards the government, the former had an entire array of privileges and competences to safeguard. Therefore, the Austrian Habsburgs had every reason not to antagonize the Council or the Estates of Brabant. Indeed, the composite state and the peace it guaranteed benefited the central government, given that the Netherlands had become an important source of financial profit.[6]

As is well-known, Joseph II broke with this tradition, but he was equally unwilling to use the Great Council as an instrument of state-formation, albeit for different reasons. In the Emperor's worldview, the Great Council as court *par excellence* for the privileged must have been something of an anomaly, an outdated remainder of the old order. When he rearranged the entire judicial organization of the Netherlands, there could be no doubt in his mind that the court needed to be abolished. If possible, its members were to be integrated into the new structure, without however in any way giving them a preferential treatment. Indeed, the Sovereign Council of Justice counted as many members from the Council of Luxemburg as from the Great Council.

Apparently, the Great Council never really protested this course of events. If the councilors' attachment and even devotion to their own institution was indisputable, their loyalty to the emperor must have been even greater. Moreover, even if they had been willing to resist the new measures, they would not have been able to count on outside support: there was not much love lost between the Magistrate of Malines and the Great Council. As the Sovereign's Council by excellence, it could do nothing but obey the sovereign, even if it meant that the Great Council and its members would be demoted to a position of secondary importance. Only in times of crisis did the Austrian Habsburgs again rely on the tribunal. Yet, once peace had been more or less restored, they degraded it back to a second-rate role. As a result, the Great Council never held (or took) its fate in its own hands, and merely underwent the events of the eighteenth century.

---

[5] Put, Eddy. 2002. Gedeelde soevereiniteit? De dubbelrol van de Raad van Brabant. In *Politieke representatie*, eds. Henk de Smaele and Johan Tollebeek. Leuven: Universitaire Pers Leuven, 221–229.

[6] Coppens, Herman. 1992. De financiën van de centrale regering van de Zuidelijke Nederlanden aan het einde van het Spaanse en onder Oostenrijks bewind (ca. 1680–1788). Brussel: Koninklijke Academie voor wetenschappen, letteren en schone kunsten van België, 339–341.

6.2 Superior Courts: Agencies of Change or Preservation?

Unlike the Great Council, the eighteenth century *Parlement de Paris*—the superior court on which the Great Council was initially based—is often regarded as a powerful tribunal, especially considering its resistance against the policies of Louis XV.[7] Indeed, the *Parlement* of Paris was not only the superior court of justice in France, but also had an extensive authority in the political domain, boasting the right to remonstrate edicts and decrees of the government before registering and publishing them. In that regard, the *Parlement de Paris* had characteristics of both the Great Council and the Council of Brabant, combining the supra-territorial jurisdiction of the former with the political authority of the latter. Moreover, functioning in a highly centralized state, the *Parlement* of Paris was the first tribunal of France, a status the Great Council could hardly claim in the Austrian Netherlands.

Contrary to the Great Council, the *Parlement* was no docile instrument of royal power. Indeed, resistance against the policies of Louis XV—combined with an internal strife between high officials—even led to the abolishment and later reform of several *parlements*, including the Parisian. After their restoration under Louis XVI and especially from the early 1780s on, the French superior courts, with the *Parlement de Paris* at the forefront, played an important role in the resistance leading up to the French Revolution. The bankruptcy of the state and the attempt to remedy the problem by increasing taxes incited the *Parlement* of Paris to use its right of remonstration. Therefore, it can be argued that the *Parlement de Paris* used its powerful position to act as an agency of change.

Despite this image of strength, the *Parlement* suffered from a decline in litigation during the eighteenth century comparable to that of the Great Council. The resulting reduction in income for the councilors affected the socio-professional outlook of the judiciary and firmly pushed them into opposition. Consequently, C. Kaiser is convinced that this volume deflation traced "one of the routes which led France to revolution."[8] When resisting the government, the "tribunal fought not only on behalf of the king's subjects, but also for its very existence."[9] Even if starting from entirely different premises, D. Feutry agrees with Kaiser that the *Parlement* did not act from a position of strength in its resistance against the government. Indeed, he

[7] E.g., Doyle, William. 1970. The Parlements of France and the breakdown of the Old Régime 1771–1788. *French Historical Studies* 6: 415–458; Rogister, John. 1995. *Louis XV and the Parlement of Paris, 1737–1755*. Cambridge: Cambridge University Press; Swann, Julian. 1995. *Politics and the Parlement of Paris under Louis XV, 1754–1774*. Cambridge: Cambridge University Press.

[8] Kaiser, Colin. 1980. The deflation in the volume of litigation at Paris in the Eighteenth Century and the waning of the old judicial order. *European Studies Review* 10.3: 330.

[9] Kaiser, Colin. 1980. The deflation in the volume of litigation at Paris in the Eighteenth Century and the waning of the old judicial order. *European Studies Review* 10.3: 326.

believes that the *Parlement's* oppositional activities found their origins in internal unrest and strife.[10]

Therefore, the *Parlement de Paris* was not solely or even predominantly an agency of change. Similarly, the Great Council was not merely an agency of preservation. True, the Great Council never brewed rebellion or supported it. On the contrary, it was rather docile in following orders from the government and very active in rooting out any form of revolt or protest in the period leading up to the Brabant Revolution. And indeed, the members of the Great Council—unlike those of most other provincial councils—actively supported the reform policies of Joseph II. While these were policies instigated by the government—as opposed to coming from below—the Emperor's reforms were in several regards comparable to the accomplishments of the French Revolution. Even if it was not entirely wholeheartedly, the councilors of the Great Council did embrace change and supported Joseph II's plans.

Contrary to de *Parlement de Paris* and the Great Council, the *Reichskammergericht* as superior court of the German Empire, could hardly be called an agency of change in any way. Over the course of the eighteenth century, neither the Emperor nor the Estates had much incentive to improve the *Reichskammergericht*'s functioning and standing. In that regard, the *Reichskammergericht* was actually quite similar to the Great Council. Given that the Emperor had its own tribunal in the *Reichshofrat*, he had no desire to reinforce the *Reichskammergericht*, as this could only be to his own disadvantage. The Estates were equally recalcitrant to intervene, convinced as they were that their own local tribunals could only benefit from a malfunctioning central tribunal. In addition, at the end of the Ancien Régime, the *Reichskammergericht* was constantly underfinanced and severely weakened by internal strife. Consequently, the eighteenth century *Reichskammergericht* was a powerless institution, which, ignored by both the Emperor and the Estates, no longer had much significance in the German Empire.

Eventually, it might be argued that none of these three superior courts had much agency at all. Rather than actively steering policies in their countries, the *Parlement de Paris*, the Great Council and the *Reichskammergericht* to varying degrees passively underwent the changes. If superior courts might have played a major role as agencies of change in earlier times, they certainly no longer did so at the end of the eighteenth century.

6.3 Continuity?

In general, it can be said that the eighteenth century Great Council was characterized by continuity, or the appearance of it, at least in those areas on which the court itself or the central government could exert any influence. Indeed it seems that, ever since the sixteenth century, the Council had merely been going with the

[10] Feutry, David. 2012. The historian's mountain of paper. *French History* 26.3: 295.

flow, impervious to most of the change the world around it was experiencing. In a sense, this continuity also created stability, which was exactly what the Austrian Habsburgs, with the exception of Joseph II, were striving for in their Netherlands possessions. Lacking any incentive to brew rebellion and having every reason to maintain the status quo, the Great Council was an instrument the central government could rely on in times of crisis and which, unlike the Council of Brabant, could easily be kept in check at all times.

In the personnel policy of the Great Council, this continuity manifested itself in an intergenerational approach towards the selection of new councilors. Given the significance of family networks and relationships of affinity as sources of support for a strong, centralized state, it is no wonder that these two elements constituted the main recruitment criteria for personnel at the tribunal. As a result, candidates with kinship in the higher administration, especially if they were of noble blood, were preferred over less well-connected applicants. The *droit de terne* in particular was an ideal instrument to create continuity in the personnel policy of the Great Council, which not only served the sovereign well but undoubtedly also the incumbent members of the tribunal. The latter were assured that new members would belong to the same 'caste' of civil servants, and moreover, they could expect that their relatives had a good chance at acquiring an interesting position. In addition to nurturing the 'right' network, a prospective councilor needed to be born in the Austrian Netherlands, have a legal education and a certain level of experience. However, in practice, none of these conditions were rigorously followed.

The criteria used for recruitment evidently influenced the profile of the councilors. All had acquired a law degree while most of them had some years of experience before being awarded with a councillorship. More importantly, the majority of them had relations within the civil service, which was of course the direct result of the significance attached to family and networks. This also had repercussions for the origins of the councilors. Members of the Great Council had to be born within the Austrian Netherlands, but not necessarily within the jurisdiction of the court. Brabant-born councilors were therefore not excluded; yet, their preponderance is somewhat unexpected, given that the decisions of the Great Council had no repercussions for Brabant. Partially, this phenomenon was the result of historical circumstances—at its establishment the Great Council had been competent for the entirety of the 17 provinces—but mostly it was due to the fact that Brabant and especially Brussels constituted the center of the civil servant world. Family members of men working in the higher administration in Brussels formed an important recruiting pool for the Great Council. This also explains why a relatively small percentage of the councilors came from the outskirts of the Netherlands, such as Luxemburg or Namur.

In general, the profiles of the eighteenth century members of the Great Council were very similar to those of their predecessors in the fifteenth, early sixteenth and seventeenth centuries. However, there were two small but not insignificant differences. Firstly, over the course of the 1700s, ever more candidates for a councillorship came from the ranks of the tribunal's own advocates, while the number of external applicants diminished. Secondly, compared to previous centuries, far less members of the eighteenth century Great Council considered their councillorship as a springboard to another position in the higher administration; promotion to the court was apparently regarded as an award for civil servants who seemed to *mériter de jouir de repos*.[11] Other eighteenth century 'umbrella' tribunals—such as the High Council or the *Reichskammergericht*—displayed a similar pattern.[12]

Continuity also marked the internal organization and inner workings of the court. Indeed, the last all-encompassing Procedure Ordinance dated from 1559. While individual decrees were directed at remedying certain pressing problems and other issues were solved almost organically, the central government never made a profound attempt to adapt the court to the changed circumstances of the eighteenth century. Therefore, even though the Great Council still considered itself the most important tribunal of the Austrian Netherlands, the central government did not actively support its claims in that regard, as it might have done, for example, by issuing a new Procedure Ordinance or raising the councilors' salaries, despite their bitter complaints about the inadequacy of their incomes and the ensuing recruiting difficulties.

This ambivalent attitude of the central government was even more evident in the conflicts the Great Council had with other institutions in the Austrian Netherlands. With the Provincial Councils and the Magistrate of Malines in particular, the Great Council constantly clashed over jurisdiction and influence. In deciding on these conflicts, the central government was far from consistent: at times it supported the Great Council in its bid for power, at other times it firmly ruled against the Council's claims at superiority. This—probably semi-conscious—divide and rule strategy avoided that the Great Council—or any other tribunal—was able to accrue too much power.

At the same time, the government's janus-faced attitude towards the Great Council caused the councilors to suffer from some sort of inferiority complex and collective status anxiety that manifested itself in particular in its relations with the Privy Council. Indeed, the latter—which benefited from its direct line of communication with the governor and/or minister plenipotentiary—constantly attempted to interfere in the Great Council's inner workings and grasped every opportunity to assert its superiority. Even though the central government used the same divide and rule strategy when deciding the conflicts between the Great and the Privy Councils—playing both institutions off against each other—the members of the former often felt the need to underline that they were in no way subordinate to the latter, having the same origins and enjoying the same privileges. The councilors' self-consciousness and desire to vigorously defend their court against real or perceived attacks indicate that they were worried about the position and status the Great Council could still claim in the eighteenth century.

---

[11] Brussels, ARA, GRO 442A, 1761. Cf. supra, Chap. 2.

[12] Jahns, Sigrid. 1990. Die Personalverfassung des Reichskammergerichts unter Anpassungsdruck. Lösungen im Spannungsfeld zwischen Modernität und Überalterung. In *Das Reichskammergericht in der deutschen Geschichte: Stand der Forschung, Forschungsperspektiven* (Quellen und Forschungen zur höchsten Gerichtsbarkeit im alten Reich 21), ed. Bernhard Diestelkamp, 59–109. Cologne: Böhlau; Van Poelgeest, L. 1988. De raadsheren van de Hoge Raad van Holland, Zeeland en West-Friesland in de achttiende eeuw. *Bijdragen en mededelingen betreffende de geschiedenis der Nederlanden* 103.1: 20–51.

An important aspect of their fears must certainly have been the consistent decline in the number of lawsuits, not only because it affected their incomes, but also because it could raise questions about the court's overall purpose and relevance. Indeed, as far as litigation was concerned, there was certainly no continuity at the Great Council. Unsurprisingly, this was one of the few aspects that neither the Great Council itself nor the central government could really influence. Except for those lawsuits that were instigated by the office-fiscal, it was the parties who decided if they would take their disputes to court or rather find an alternative solution to their differences. Explaining the great litigation decline should therefore focus on the potential litigants and their socio-economic profile as well as on any external reasons that could have deterred them from litigating at the Great Council: the duration of the lawsuits, the perceived unreliability of the judges, the fact that legal precedents resulting from litigation in the sixteenth century often avoided the need to take a matter to court afterwards, or the obsoleteness of the tribunal, caused by a lack of interest from the government to implement necessary reforms.

Despite the fact that the decline in litigation was unmistakable, the councilors still attempted to create, consciously or not, the appearance of continuity. The accumulated caseload of the Great Council also inevitably dropped, but not as steeply as the number of distributed lawsuits. The councilors' attempts to draw out the duration of the lawsuits were undoubtedly associated with the effect this great litigation decline had on their income. While the central government seemed to have intervened around 1740 to force the councilors to deal with lawsuits more quickly, it apparently refrained from doing so in the late eighteenth century, when the average case-duration again started to lengthen. The only 'real' increase can be observed in the number of criminal trials, a phenomenon affected both by the more hands on prosecution style of the fiscals—especially after 1780—and by the turbulent times of the 1780s and 1790s.

Notwithstanding the decline in litigation, the late eighteenth century Great Council was still to a large extent characterized by continuity, regardless of the reforms introduced by Joseph II and the reaction against them. Certainly, the central government did make increased use of the tribunal in these times of crisis, especially to prosecute the perpetrators of the revolts but also to replace the Council of Brabant when it turned out to be a hotbed of opposition. However, it maintained its ambivalent attitude towards the Great Council. Once the immediate crisis had passed and the government adopted a policy of amnesty and reconciliation, it degraded the Great Council once again to a secondary role. The refusal to restore the tribunal's jurisdiction over Luxemburg and Tournai and the assignment of jurisdiction over Valenciennes to the Council of Hainaut must indeed have hit the members of the Great Council hard. This ambiguous attitude also continued to feed the councilors' self-consciousness and collective status anxiety, which became most apparent during their exile in Düsseldorf. Therefore, the position held by the eighteenth century Great Council was—despite the turbulent external circumstances—in many ways similar to what it had been in the earlier decades.

Eventually, continuity even typified the court's death-throes. While it might have seemed that the Great Council was already on its last legs in the latter part of the eighteenth century, the court demonstrated a remarkable resistance against actually disappearing. Notwithstanding the exile of its councilors, its official abolition in 1797 and the sale of its silver seals in 1801, it was not until the mid-nineteenth century that all matters regarding the Great Council were finally settled.

In summary, characterized as it was by continuity in its personnel policy and inner organization, lacking firm support from the government in its conflicts with other institutions, suffering from an enduring decline in litigation, having played out its role as instrument of state-formation and being, at best, an indirect and passive agency of change'—if at all—the eighteenth century Great Council was truly an 'aging court in a changing world'.

References

Aerts, Erik. 2013. Economische interventie van de centrale staat in de Spaanse en Oostenrijkse Nederlanden (1555–1795). In *Gouvernance et administration dans les provinces belges (XVIe-XVIIIe siècles)* (Archives et Bibliothèques de Belgique 99), Eds. Claude De Morbeau de Gerbehaye e.a., 399–452. Brussels: Archives et Bibliothèques de Belgique.

Coppens, Herman. 1992. *De financiën van de centrale regering van de Zuidelijke Nederlanden aan het einde van het Spaanse en onder Oostenrijks bewind (ca. 1680–1788)*. Brussel: Koninklijke Academie voor wetenschappen, letteren en schone kunsten van België.

Doyle, William. 1970. The Parlements of France and the breakdown of the Old Régime 1771–1788. *French Historical Studies* 6: 415–458.

Feutry, David. 2012. The historian's mountain of paper. *French History* 26.3: 277–297.

Jahns, Sigrid. 1990. Die Personalverfassung des Reichskammergerichts unter Anpassungsdruck. Lösungen im Spannungsfeld zwischen Modernität und Überalterung. In *Das Reichskammergericht in der deutschen Geschichte: Stand der Forschung, Forschungsperspektiven* (Quellen und Forschungen zur höchsten Gerichtsbarkeit im alten Reich 21), ed. Bernhard Diestelkamp, 59–109. Cologne: Böhlau.

Kaiser, Colin. 1980. The deflation in the volume of litigation at Paris in the Eighteenth Century and the waning of the old judicial order. *European Studies Review* 10.3: 309–336.

Lenders, Piet. 1995. Ontstaan en ontwikkeling van de moderne staat in de Nederlanden. In *Symposium over de centrale instellingen van de Habsburgse Nederlanden, Brussel 3 December 1994. Tien Bijdragen over de staat, de regering en de ambtenaren van de 16de tot de 18de eeuw* (Standen en Landen Bijzondere Reeks nr. 2), eds. Herman Coppens en Karin Van Honacker, 1–42. Brussels: Algemeen Rijksarchief.

Put, Eddy. 2002. Gedeelde soevereiniteit? De dubbelrol van de Raad van Brabant. In *Politieke representatie*, eds. Henk de Smaele and Johan Tollebeek, 221–229. Leuven: Universitaire Pers Leuven.

Rogister, John. 1995. *Louis XV and the Parlement of Paris, 1737–1755*. Cambridge: Cambridge University Press.

Swann, Julian. 1995. *Politics and the Parlement of Paris under Louis XV, 1754–1774*. Cambridge: Cambridge University Press.

Van Poelgeest, L. 1988. De raadsheren van de Hoge Raad van Holland, Zeeland en West-Friesland in de achttiende eeuw. *Bijdragen en mededelingen betreffende de geschiedenis der Nederlanden* 103.1: 20–51.

Wijffels, Alain. 1997. Grand Conseil de Malines: la rédaction des sentences étendues et le recueil de jurisprudence de Guillaume de Grysperre. In *Case law in the making: the techniques and methods of judicial records and law reports (Comparative studies in continental and Anglo-American Legal History* 17) v.1, ed. Alain Wijffels, 299–316. Berlin: Duncker und Humblot.